·Bartholomew·
COMPACT WORLD ATLAS

· Bartholomew ·

COMPACT WORLD ATLAS

Bartholomew

A Division of HarperCollins*Publishers*

Bartholomew
A Division of HarperCollins Publishers
Duncan Street, Edinburgh EH9 1TA

First published by Bartholomew 1991

©Bartholomew 1991

ISBN 0 7028 1700 7

Printed in Great Britain by HarperCollins Manufacturing, Glasgow

Details included in this atlas are subject to change without notice. Whilst
every effort is made to keep information up to date Bartholomew will not be
responsible for any loss, damage or inconvenience caused by inaccuracies in
this atlas. The publishers are always pleased to acknowledge any corrections
brought to their notice, and record their appreciation of the valuable services
rendered in the past by map users in assisting to maintain the accuracy of
their publications.

D/B4858

CONTENTS

viii-ix   World Physical
x-xi   World Political
xii-xiii World Time Zones
xiv-xv   World Environment
xvi   Key to Symbols

1	Arctic Ocean 1:40M
2-3	North America – Political 1:35M
4-5	Canada, West 1:15M
6-7	Canada, East 1:15M
8-9	USA, West 1:12·5M
10-11	USA, East 1:12·5M
12	USA, Alaska 1:10M
13	Canada Pacific 1:7·5M
14-15	Lower Canada, USA North-East 1:5M
16	Washington – New York – Boston 1:2·5M
17	USA, South-East 1:5M
18-19	USA, South-Central 1:5M
20	USA, Pacific NW 1:5M
21	USA, Pacific S 1:5M
22	San Francisco & Los Angeles 1:2·5M
23	Central Mexico 1:5M
24-25	Mexico & Central America 1:15M
26-27	Caribbean 1:10M
28	South America - Political 1:40M
29	South America, South 1:15M
30	South America, Central 1:15M
31	South America, NE 1:15M
32-33	South America, North 1:15M
34	Central Argentina 1:7·5M
35	South-East Brazil 1:7·5M

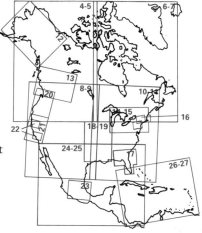

36–37	Europe – Political 1:16M
38–39	Scandinavia 1:7·5M
40–41	British Isles 1:5M
42–43	England & Wales 1:2·5M
44	Scotland, North 1:2·5M
45	Ireland 1:2·5M
46	Paris - Brussels – Ruhr 1:2·5M
47	Alps 1:2·5M
48–49	France 1:5M
50–51	Spain 1:5M
52–53	Italy 1:5M
54–55	The Balkans 1:5M
56–57	Germany & Austria 1:5M
58–59	East-Central Europe 1:5M
60–61	Central European Russia 1:10M
62	USSR – Political 1:45M

63	USSR, East 1:20M
64–65	USSR, West 1:20M
66–67	South Asia – Political 1:40M
68–69	East Asia 1:20M
70–71	South-East Asia 1:20M
72–73	Central China 1:10M
74	Japan & Korea 1:10M
75	Central Japan 1:5M
76–77	Indo-China & Singapore 1:10M
78	Indonesia, Central 1:10M
79	Philippines 1:10M
80–81	Middle East 1:20M
82–83	India & West China 1:20M
84–85	India, NW & Pakistan 1:7·5M

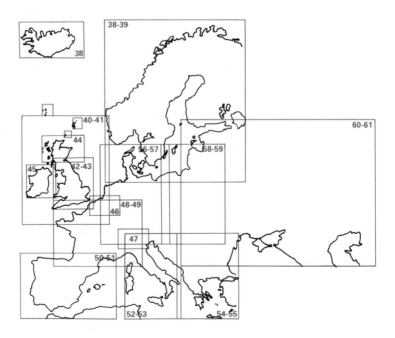

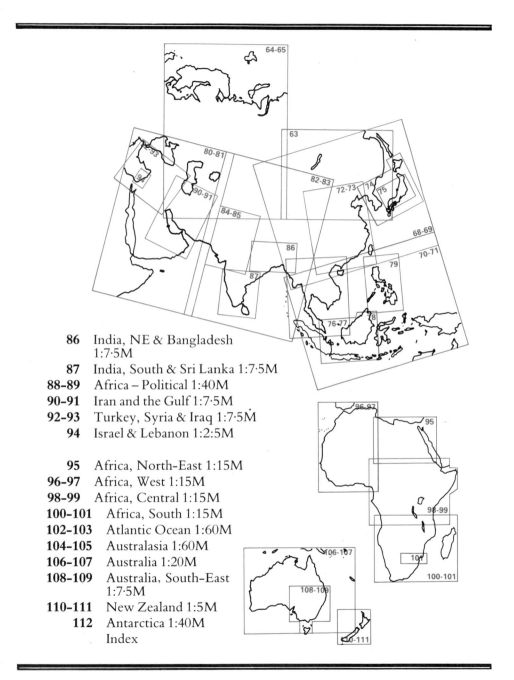

86	India, NE & Bangladesh 1:7·5M
87	India, South & Sri Lanka 1:7·5M
88–89	Africa – Political 1:40M
90–91	Iran and the Gulf 1:7·5M
92–93	Turkey, Syria & Iraq 1:7·5M
94	Israel & Lebanon 1:2:5M
95	Africa, North-East 1:15M
96–97	Africa, West 1:15M
98–99	Africa, Central 1:15M
100–101	Africa, South 1:15M
102–103	Atlantic Ocean 1:60M
104–105	Australasia 1:60M
106–107	Australia 1:20M
108–109	Australia, South-East 1:7·5M
110–111	New Zealand 1:5M
112	Antarctica 1:40M
	Index

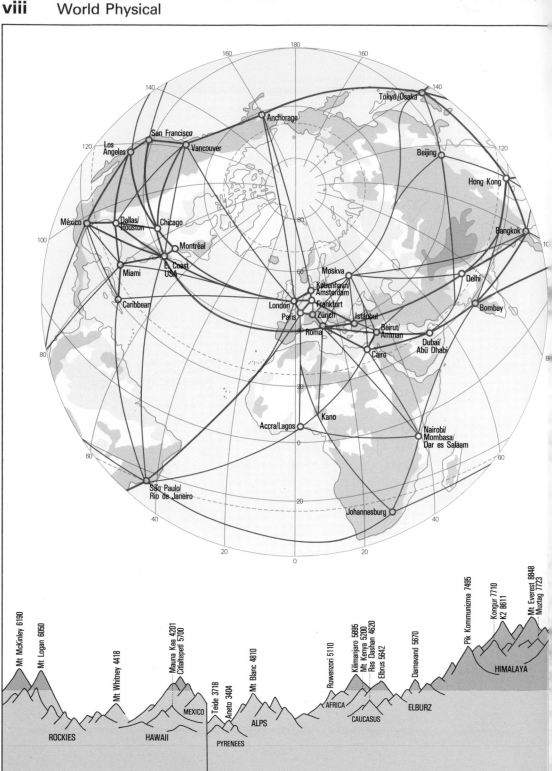

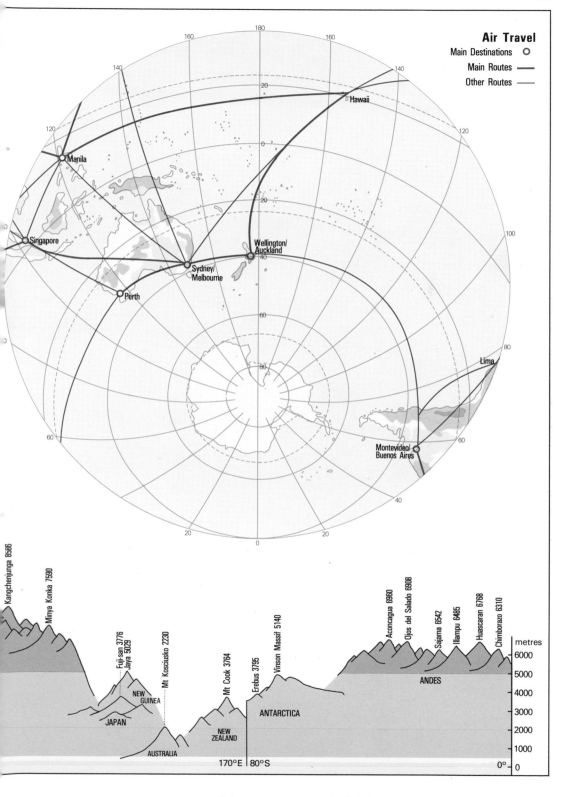

Air Travel

Main Destinations	O
Main Routes	▬
Other Routes	▬

Hawaii

Manila

Singapore

Sydney/
Melbourne

Wellington/
Auckland

Perth

Lima

Montevideo/
Buenos Aires

Kangchenjunga 8586

Minya Konka 7590

Fuji-san 3776
Jaya 5029

Mt Kosciusko 2230

Mt Cook 3764

Erebus 3795

Vinson Massif 5140

Aconcagua 6960

Ojos del Salado 6908

Sajama 6542

Illampu 6485

Huascaran 6768

Chimborazo 6310

NEW
GUINEA

JAPAN

AUSTRALIA

NEW
ZEALAND

ANTARCTICA

ANDES

170°E 80°S

0°

	metres
	6000
	5000
	4000
	3000
	2000
	1000
	0

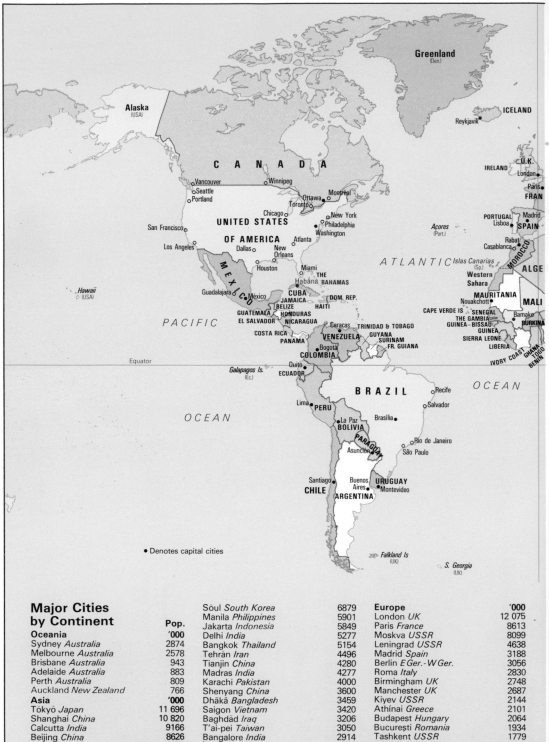

Greenland
(Den.)

ICELAND

Reykjavik

Alaska
(USA)

C A N A D A

Vancouver
Seattle
Portland
Winnipeg
Montréal
Ottawa
Toronto

IRELAND

U.K.
London
Paris
FRAN

Chicago
New York
Philadelphia
Washington

PORTUGAL
Lisboa
Madrid
SPAIN

UNITED STATES

San Francisco

OF AMERICA
Atlanta
Dallas
New
Orleans

Açores
(Port.)

Rabat
Casablanca
MOROCCO

ATLANTIC
Islas Canarias
(Sp.)

ALGE

Los Angeles

Houston

Hawaii
(USA)

Miami

THE
Habána BAHAMAS

Western
Sahara

MAURITANIA
Nouakchott

MALI

Guadalajara
México

CUBA
JAMAICA
BELIZE
HAITI
DOM. REP.

CAPE VERDE IS
SENEGAL
THE GAMBIA
GUINEA-BISSAU
Bamako
BURKINA

PACIFIC

GUATEMALA HONDURAS
EL SALVADOR NICARAGUA
COSTA RICA
PANAMA
Caracas
VENEZUELA
TRINIDAD & TOBAGO
GUYANA
SURINAM
FR. GUIANA

GUINEA
SIERRA LEONE
LIBERIA

Bogotá
COLOMBIA

IVORY COAST
GHANA
TOGO
BENIN

Equator

Galapagos Is.
(Ec.)

Quito
ECUADOR

BRAZIL

Recife

OCEAN

Lima
PERU

Salvador

OCEAN

La Paz
BOLIVIA

Brasília

PARAGUAY
Asunción

Río de Janeiro
São Paulo

Santiago
CHILE

Buenos
Aires
ARGENTINA

URUGUAY
Montevideo

• Denotes capital cities

Falkland Is
(UK)

S. Georgia
(UK)

Major Cities
by Continent

	Pop.
Oceania	**'000**
Sydney *Australia*	2874
Melbourne *Australia*	2578
Brisbane *Australia*	943
Adelaide *Australia*	883
Perth *Australia*	809
Auckland *New Zealand*	766
Asia	**'000**
Tōkyō *Japan*	11 696
Shanghai *China*	10 820
Calcutta *India*	9166
Beijing *China*	8626
Bombay *India*	8203

Sŏul *South Korea*	6879
Manila *Philippines*	5901
Jakarta *Indonesia*	5849
Delhi *India*	5277
Bangkok *Thailand*	5154
Tehrān *Iran*	4496
Tianjin *China*	4280
Madras *India*	4277
Karachi *Pakistan*	4000
Shenyang *China*	3600
Dhākā *Bangladesh*	3459
Saigon *Vietnam*	3420
Baghdād *Iraq*	3206
T'ai-pei *Taiwan*	3050
Bangalore *India*	2914
İstanbul *Turkey*	2773

Europe	**'000**
London *UK*	12 075
Paris *France*	8613
Moskva *USSR*	8099
Leningrad *USSR*	4638
Madrid *Spain*	3188
Berlin *E Ger.-W Ger.*	3056
Roma *Italy*	2830
Birmingham *UK*	2748
Manchester *UK*	2687
Kiyev *USSR*	2144
Athínai *Greece*	2101
Budapest *Hungary*	2064
Bucureşti *Romania*	1934
Tashkent *USSR*	1779
Barcelona *Spain*	1755

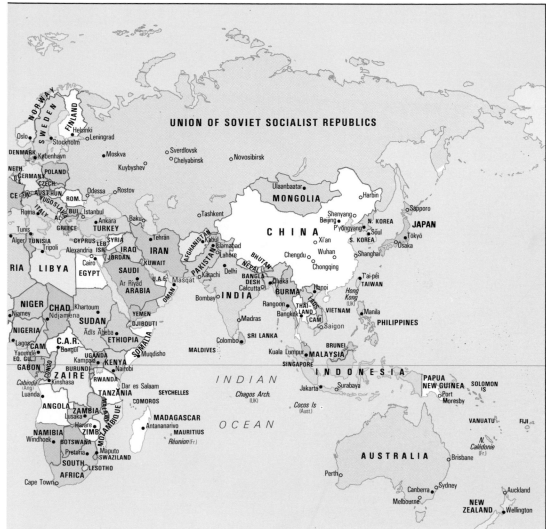

NORWAY SWEDEN FINLAND
Oslo Stockholm Helsinki Leningrad
DENMARK København Moskva
NETH. GERMANY POLAND Sverdlovsk Chelyabinsk Novosibirsk
CZECH. Kuybyshev
CE SW AUST HUN Odessa Rostov
ROM. Ulaanbaatar Harbin Sapporo
Roma ITALY YUGOSLAV BUL. Istanbul MONGOLIA
GREECE TURKEY Ankara Baku Tashkent Shenyang N. KOREA JAPAN
Tunis ALB. Tehrān Beijing Pyŏngyang Sŏul Tōkyō
Alger TUNISIA CYPRUS LEB SYRIA CHINA Xi'an S. KOREA Ōsaka
Tripoli ISR IRAQ AFGHANISTAN Kabul Xi'an Wuhan Shanghai
JORDAN Alexandria Cairo Islamabad Chengdu Chongqing
RIA LIBYA EGYPT SAUDI KUWAIT PAKISTAN Lahore BHUTAN T'ai-pei
Ar Riyāḍ U.A.E Masqat Delhi NEPAL BANGLA TAIWAN
ARABIA OMAN Karachi DESH Dhāka Hong Kong (UK)
NIGER CHAD Khartoum YEMEN Bombay INDIA Calcutta BURMA Hanoi
Niamey Ndjamena DJIBOUTI Rangoon THAI- LAOS VIETNAM Manila
NIGERIA SUDAN Ādīs Ābeba Madras LAND Bangkok CAM PHILIPPINES
Lagos CAM C.A.R. ETHIOPIA Colombo Saigon
Yaoundé Bangui SRI LANKA BRUNEI
EQ. GU. UGANDA SOMALIA MALDIVES Kuala Lumpur MALAYSIA
GABON CONGO KENYA Kampala Muqdisho SINGAPORE
ZAIRE BURUNDI Nairobi INDONESIA PAPUA SOLOMON
Cabinda RWANDA NEW GUINEA IS
(Ang) Kinshasa Dar es Salaam SEYCHELLES Jakarta Surabaya Port
Luanda TANZANIA COMOROS Chagos Arch. Moresby
ANGOLA ZAMBIA MADAGASCAR (UK) VANUATU FIJI
Lusaka Cocos Is
Harare (Aust.) N.
NAMIBIA ZIMB. MAURITIUS Calédonie
Windhoek BOTSWANA Antananarivo Réunion (Fr.) (Fr.)
Pretoria Maputo OCEAN Brisbane
SOUTH SWAZILAND AUSTRALIA
AFRICA LESOTHO Perth Sydney
Cape Town Canberra Auckland
Melbourne NEW
ZEALAND Wellington

North and Central America	'000	South America	'000	Africa	'000
New York *USA*	16 120	Buenos Aires *Argentina*	9910	Cairo *Egypt*	6588
México *Mexico*	14 750	São Paulo *Brazil*	8584	Alexandria *Egypt*	2320
Los Angeles *USA*	11 496	Rio de Janeiro *Brazil*	5184	Kinshasa *Zaire*	2008
Chicago *USA*	7868	Santiago *Chile*	4039	Casablanca *Morocco*	1753
Philadelphia *USA*	5549	Lima *Peru*	3969	Johannesburg *South Africa*	1536
San Francisco *USA*	5182	Bogotá *Colombia*	3831	Alger *Algeria*	1503
Detroit *USA*	4618	Caracas *Venezuela*	2576	Lagos *Nigeria*	1477
Boston *USA*	3448	Belo Horizonte *Brazil*	1815	El Gîza *Egypt*	1247
Houston *USA*	3102	Salvador *Brazil*	1526	Addis Ababa *Ethiopia*	1133
Washington *USA*	3060	Medellín *Colombia*	1442	Cape Town *South Africa*	1108
Toronto *Canada*	2999	Fortaleza *Brazil*	1339	Dar es Salaam *Tanzania*	870
Dallas *USA*	2975	Montevideo *Uruguay*	1314	Durban *South Africa*	851
Cleveland *USA*	2834	Recife *Brazil*	1241	Abidjan *Ivory Coast*	850
Montréal *Canada*	2828	Brasília *Brazil*	1203	Ibadan *Nigeria*	847
Miami *USA*	2640	Pôrto Alegre *Brazil*	1159	Nairobi *Kenya*	835

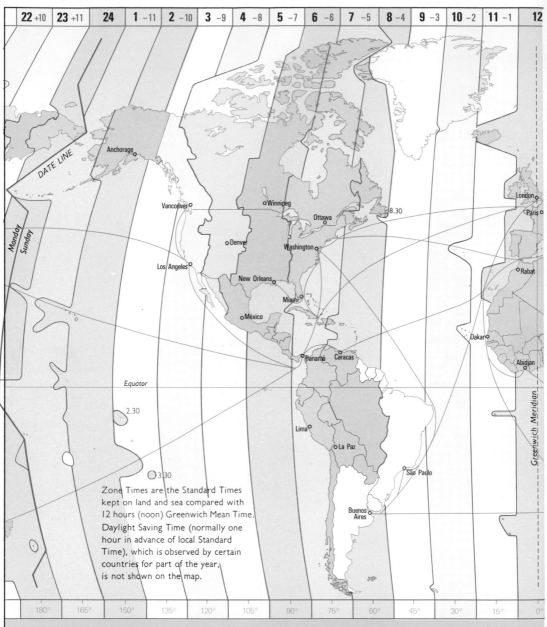

| 22 +10 | 23 +11 | 24 | 1 −11 | 2 −10 | 3 −9 | 4 −8 | 5 −7 | 6 −6 | 7 −5 | 8 −4 | 9 −3 | 10 −2 | 11 −1 | 12 |

DATE LINE

Monday / Sunday

Anchorage
Vancouver
Winnipeg
Ottawa
8.30
London
Paris
Denver
Washington
Los Angeles
New Orleans
Rabat
Miami
México
Dakar
Equator
Panamá Caracas
Abidjan
2.30
Lima
3.30
La Paz
São Paulo
Buenos Aires

Greenwich Meridian

Zone Times are the Standard Times
kept on land and sea compared with
12 hours (noon) Greenwich Mean Time.
Daylight Saving Time (normally one
hour in advance of local Standard
Time), which is observed by certain
countries for part of the year,
is not shown on the map.

| 180° | 165° | 150° | 135° | 120° | 105° | 90° | 75° | 60° | 45° | 30° | 15° | 0° |

Journey Times

Sail (via Cape)
164 days

Steam (via Cape)
43 days

Steam (via Suez)
30 days

Supertanker
(via Cape)
28 days

Singapore ←

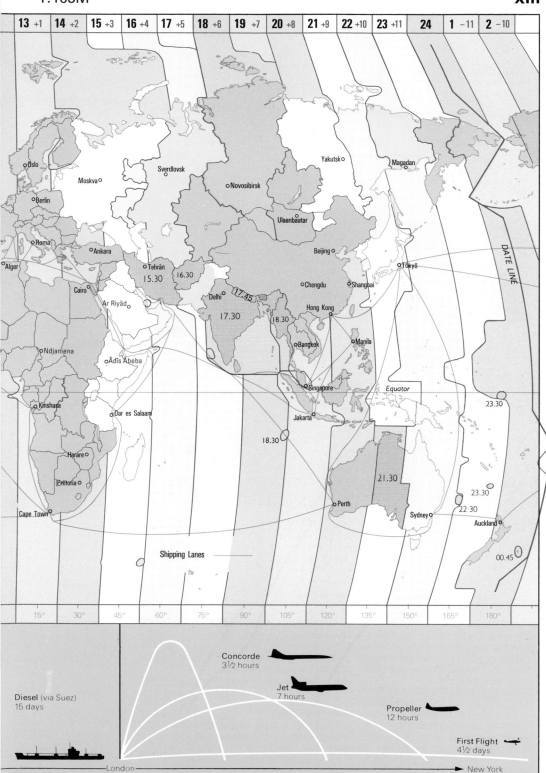

| 13 +1 | 14 +2 | 15 +3 | 16 +4 | 17 +5 | 18 +6 | 19 +7 | 20 +8 | 21 +9 | 22 +10 | 23 +11 | 24 | 1 −11 | 2 −10 |

Oslo

Moskva

Sverdlovsk

Yakutsk

Magadan

Berlin

Novosibirsk

Roma

Ankara

Ulaanbaatar

Tehrān 15.30 16.30

Beijing

DATE LINE

Alger

Tōkyō

Cairo

Chengdu

Shanghai

Delhi 17.45

Ar Riyād

17.30

Hong Kong

18.30

Ndjamena

Ādīs Ābeba

Bangkok

Manila

Kinshasa

Singapore

Equator

Dar es Salaam

23.30

Jakarta

18.30

Harāre

21.30

Pretoria

23.30

Cape Town

Perth

Sydney 22·30

Auckland

Shipping Lanes

00.45

15° 30° 45° 60° 75° 90° 105° 120° 135° 150° 165° 180°

Concorde
3½ hours

Jet
7 hours

Diesel (via Suez)
15 days

Propeller
12 hours

First Flight
4½ days

London → New York

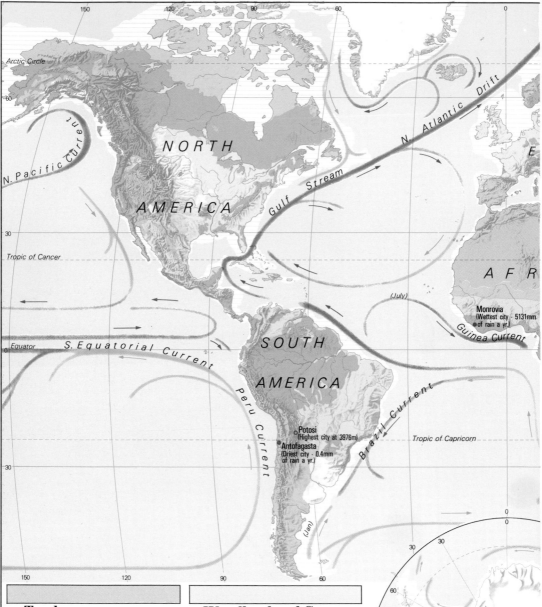

Tundra

Flat areas frozen over except during brief summers when flooding occurs. Habitat of compact, wind resistant plants; lichens and mosses: animals ; lemmings and reindeer.

Northern Forest

Extensive coniferous forest area where winters are severe, summers brief. Conifers include spruce, fir, giant redwoods. Habitat of beavers, squirrels and red deer.

Woodland and Grass

Temperate areas of richer soils, its forest characterised by deciduous trees - oak, beech, maple. Region most exploited by man for intensive farming, settlements and industry.

Grassland

Hot summers, cold winters, moderate rainfall. Vast area of grassland and 'black' soils. Ideal for growing grain crops, grazing beef cattle. Also called steppe, veld, pampas, prairie.

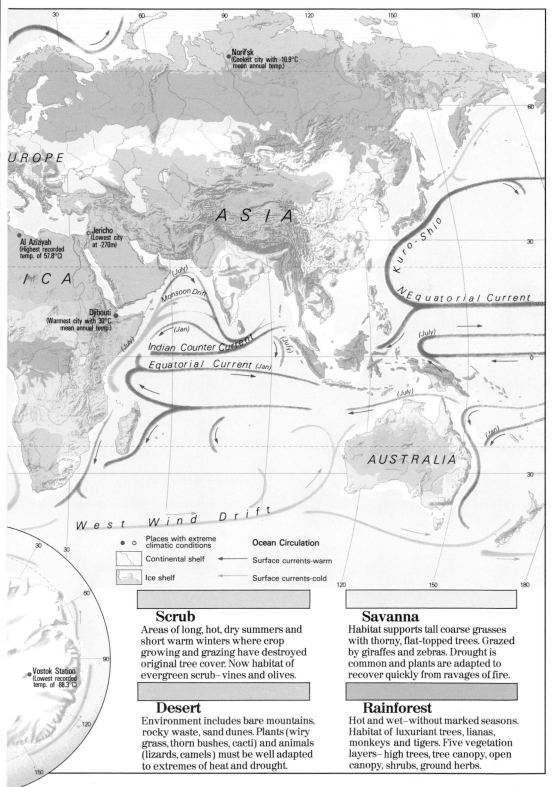

Noril'sk
(Coolest city with -10.9°C
mean annual temp.)

EUROPE

ASIA

Al Aziziyah
(Highest recorded
temp. of 57.8°C)

Jericho
(Lowest city
at -270m)

AFRICA

Djibouti
(Warmest city with 30°C
mean annual temp.)

Kuro-Shio

N Equatorial Current

(July)

Monsoon Drift

(Jan)

(July)

(July)

Indian Counter Current

Equatorial Current (Jan)

(July)

(July)

AUSTRALIA

(Jan)

West Wind Drift

Vostok Station
(Lowest recorded
temp. of -88.3°C)

Ocean Circulation

- ● ○ Places with extreme climatic conditions
- Continental shelf
- Ice shelf

◄── Surface currents-warm

◄── Surface currents-cold

Scrub
Areas of long, hot, dry summers and short warm winters where crop growing and grazing have destroyed original tree cover. Now habitat of evergreen scrub–vines and olives.

Savanna
Habitat supports tall coarse grasses with thorny, flat-topped trees. Grazed by giraffes and zebras. Drought is common and plants are adapted to recover quickly from ravages of fire.

Desert
Environment includes bare mountains, rocky waste, sand dunes. Plants (wiry grass, thorn bushes, cacti) and animals (lizards, camels) must be well adapted to extremes of heat and drought.

Rainforest
Hot and wet–without marked seasons. Habitat of luxuriant trees, lianas, monkeys and tigers. Five vegetation layers– high trees, tree canopy, open canopy, shrubs, ground herbs.

BOUNDARIES

————————	International
— — — —	International under Dispute
· · · · · · · ·	Cease Fire Line
————————	Autonomous or State/ Administrative
— — — —	Maritime (National)
— — — — —	International Date Line

COMMUNICATIONS

══════ ════	Motorway / Under Construction
————————	Major / Other Road
— — — —	Under Construction
· · · · · · · ·	Track
⇒===⇐	Road Tunnel
— — — —	Car Ferry
————————	Main / Other Railway
— — — —	Under Construction
· · · · · · · ·	Rail Ferry
→----←	Rail Tunnel
┴┴┴┴┴┴┴	Canal
⊕ ✈	International / Other Airport

LANDSCAPE FEATURES

	Glacier, Ice Cap
	Marsh, Swamp
	Sand Desert, Dunes
	Freshwater
	Saltwater
	Seasonal
	Salt Pan

OTHER FEATURES

∿∿∿⌐ᵥ→	River / Seasonal
≍	Pass, Gorge
	Dam, Barrage
∿∿∿	Waterfall, Rapid
————————	Aqueduct
∿∿∿∿∿	Reef
·217 ▲4231	Spot Height, Depth/ Summit, Peak
⌄	Well
Δ ▲	Oil / Gas Field
Gas / Oil	Oil / Natural Gas Pipeline
Gemsbok Nat. Pk	National Park
∴ᵁᴿ	Historic Site

LETTERING STYLES

CANADA	Independent Nation
FLORIDA	State, Province or Autonomous Region
Gibraltar (U.K.)	Sovereignty of Dependent Territory
Lothian	Administrative Area
LANGUEDOC	Historic Region
Loire ***Vosges***	Physical Feature or Physical Region

TOWNS AND CITIES

Square symbols denote capital cities   *Population*

■	●	**New York**	over 5 000 000
■	●	**Montréal**	over 1 000 000
□	○	Ottawa	over 500 000
▪	●	**Québec**	over 100 000
▫	○	St John's	over 50 000
▫	○	Yorkton	over 10 000
▫	○	Jasper	under 10 000
			Built-up-area

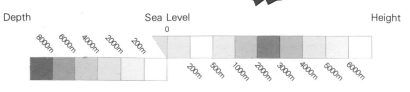

Depth   Sea Level   Height
                   0

8000m 6000m 4000m 2000m 200m

200m 500m 1000m 2000m 3000m 4000m 5000m 6000m

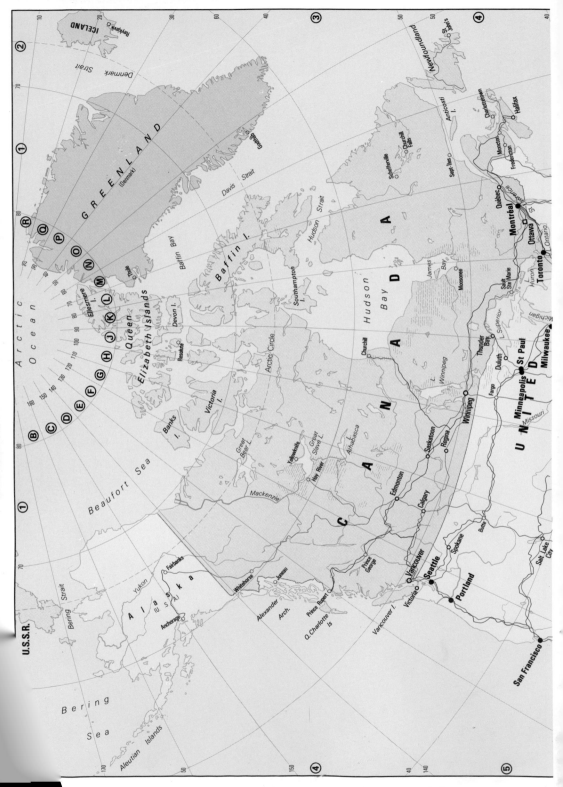

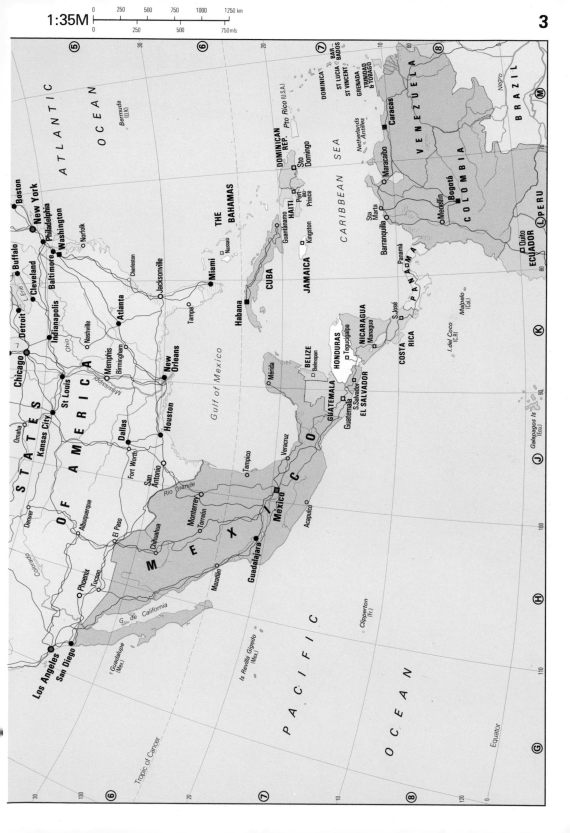

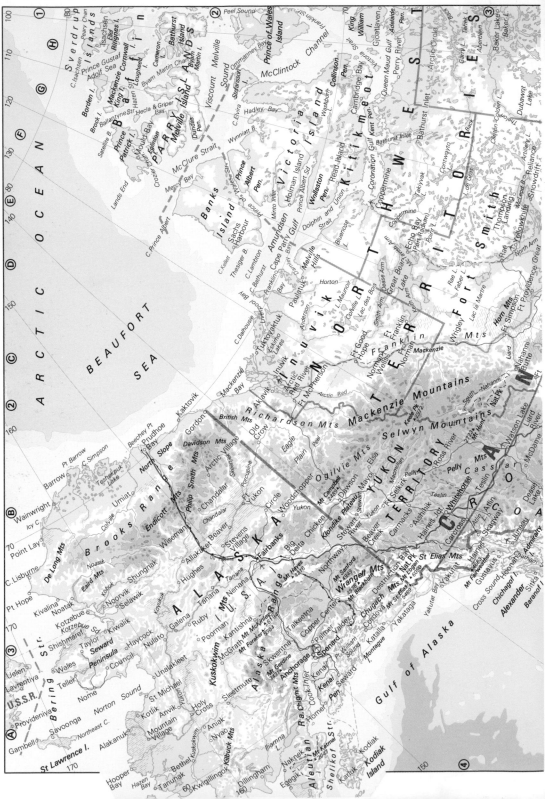

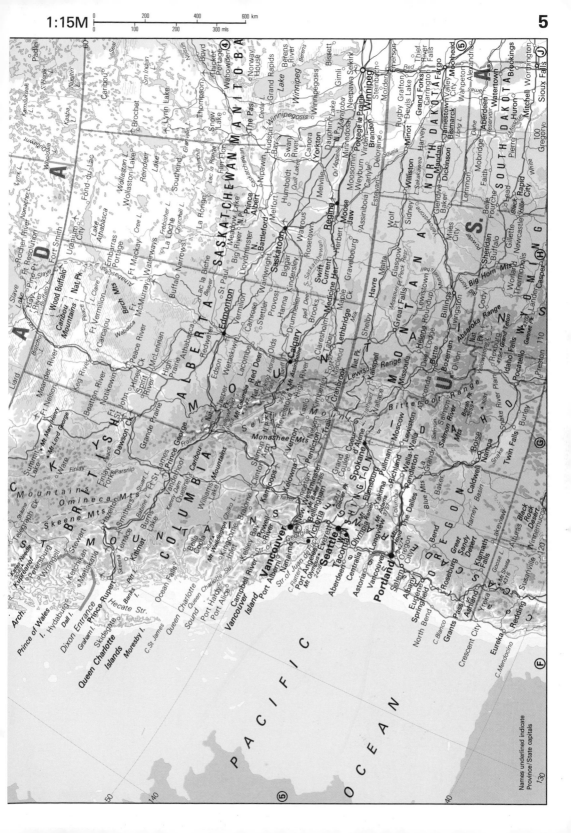

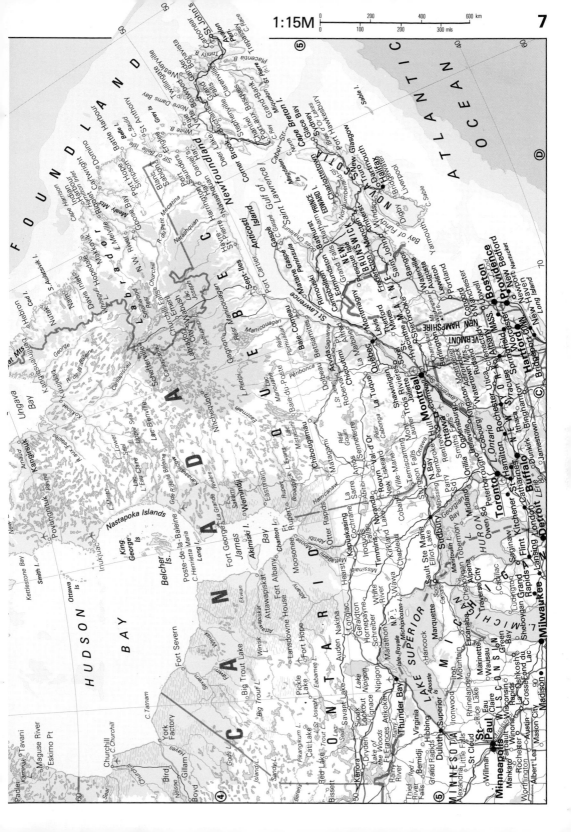

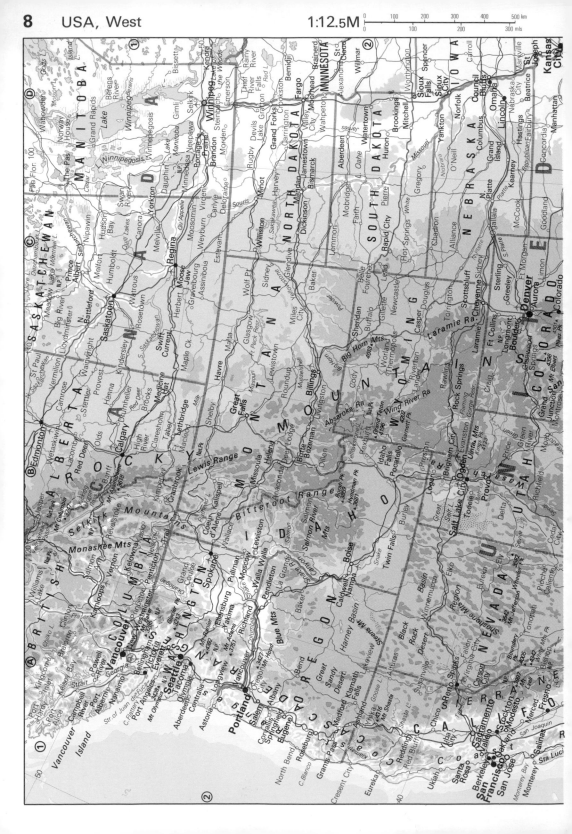

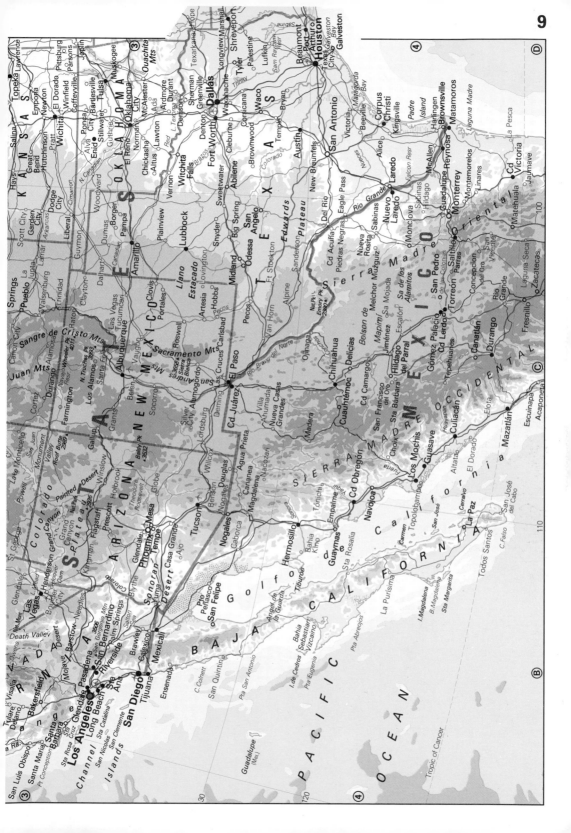

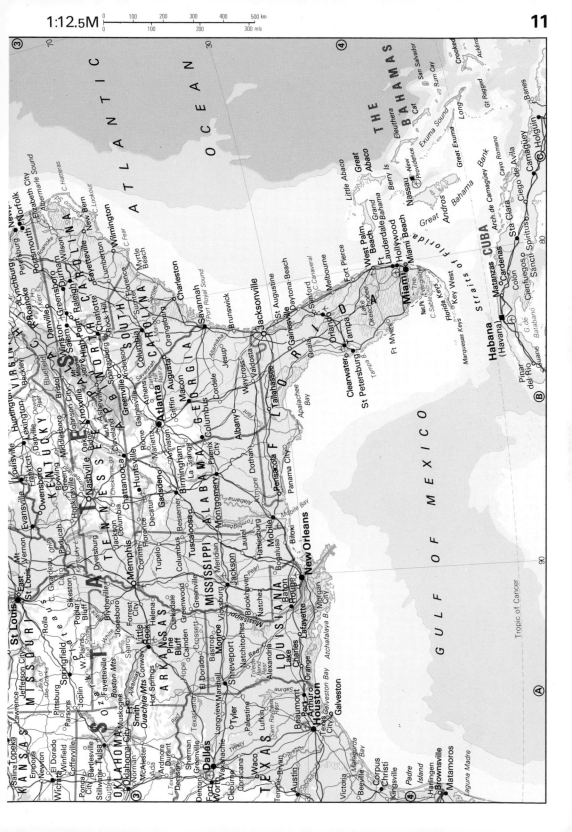

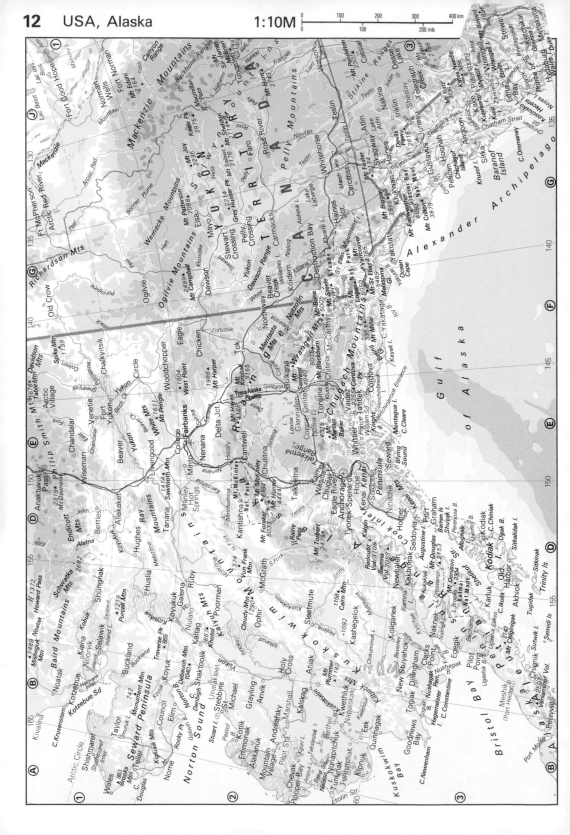

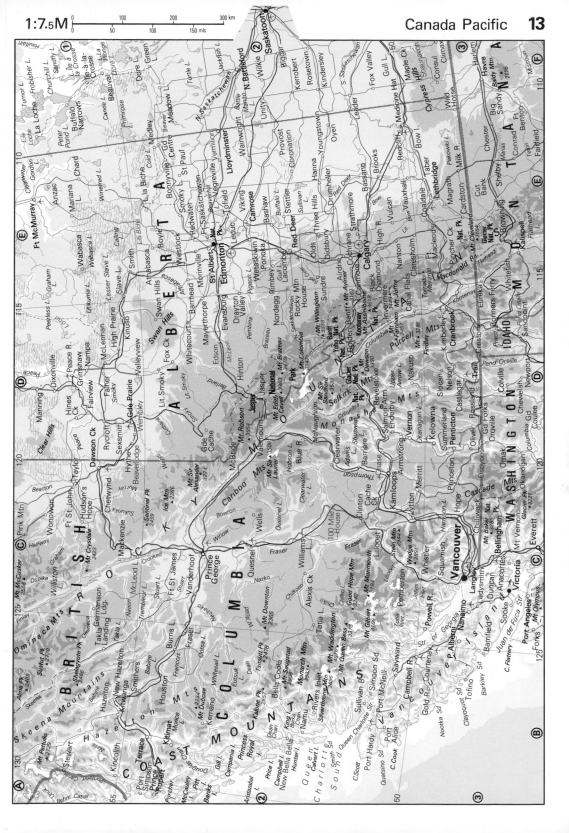

1:7.5M

100 200 300 km
50 100 150 mls

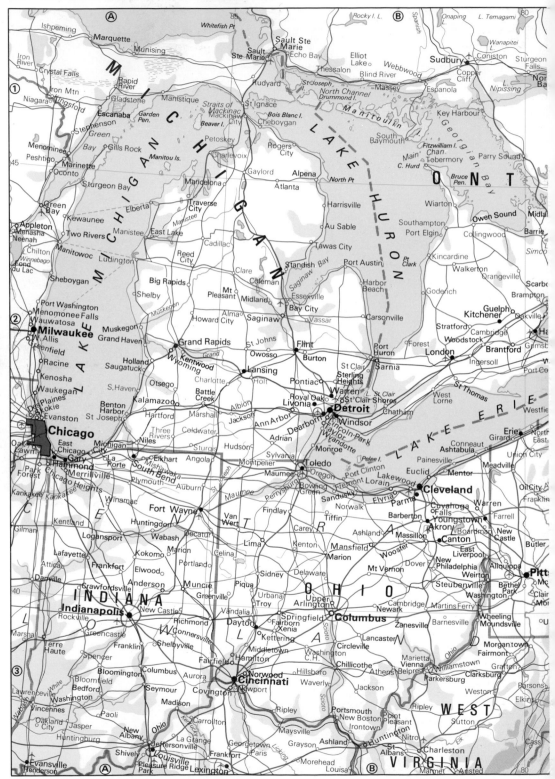

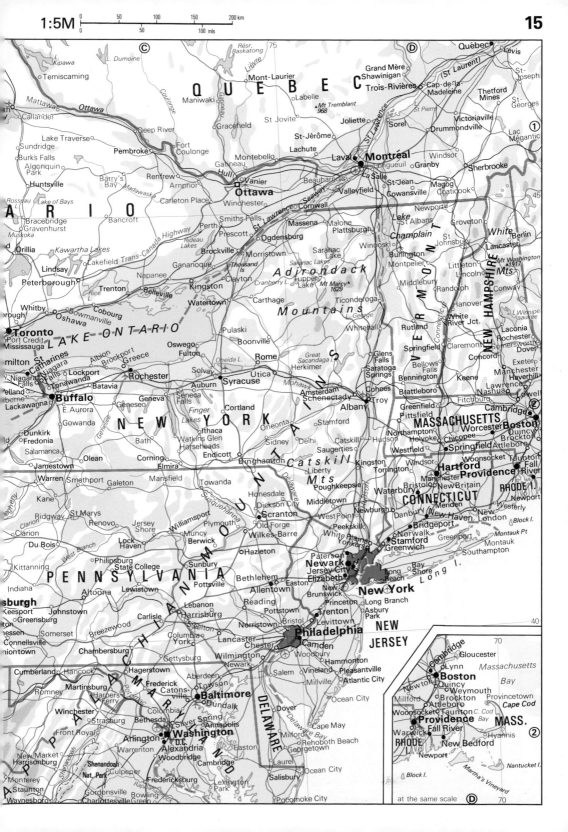

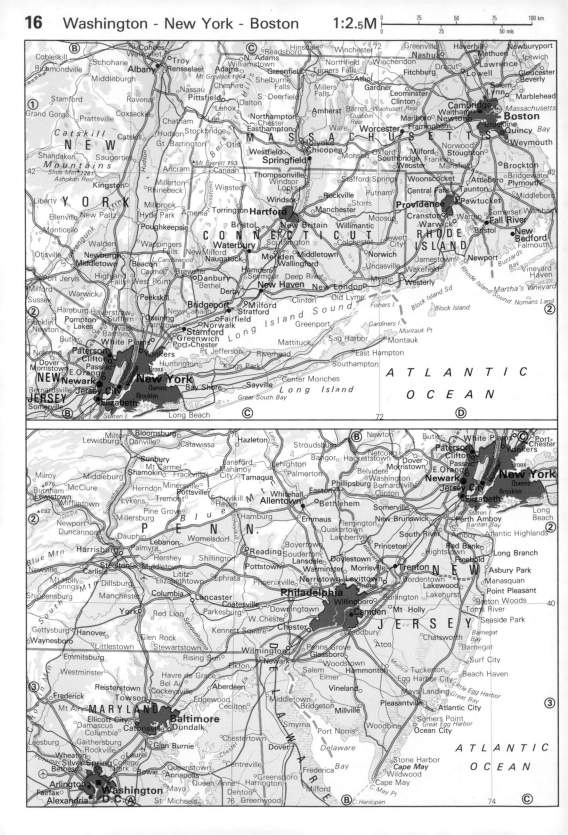

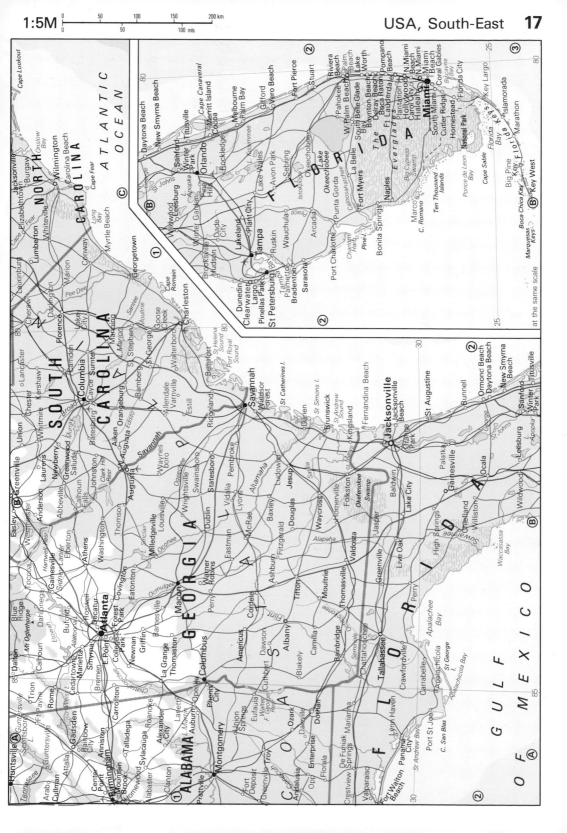

A T L A N T I C   O C E A N

N O R T H   C A R O L I N A

S O U T H   C A R O L I N A

G E O R G I A

A L A B A M A

F L O R I D A

G U L F   O F   M E X I C O

Atlanta

Miami

Tampa

Jacksonville

Savannah

Charleston

Columbia

Montgomery

Birmingham

Tallahassee

Key West

The Everglades

Lake Okeechobee

at the same scale

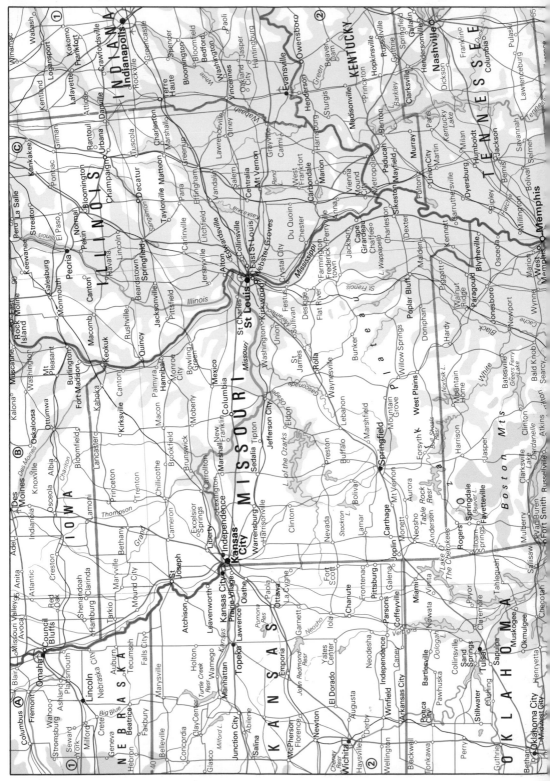

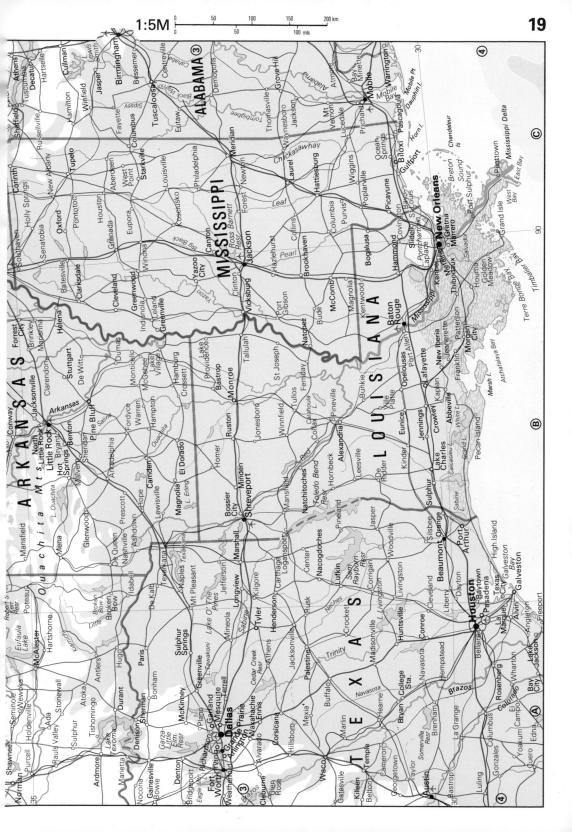

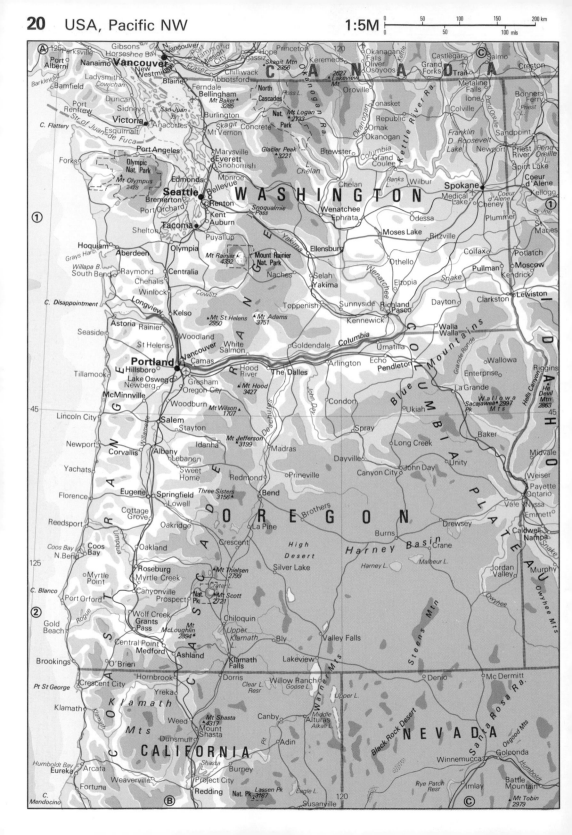

1:5M

50 100 150 200 km
50 100 mls

PACIFIC OCEAN

NEVADA

CALIFORNIA

Humboldt Bay
Arcata
Eureka
Fortuna
Weaverville
Garberville
Cummings
Fort Bragg
Ukiah
Lakeport
Healdsburg
Pt Arena
Santa Rosa
Bodega Head
Petaluma
San Rafael
Berkeley
San Francisco
Daly City
San Mateo
Redwood City
Sunnyvale
Santa Clara
Los Gatos
Santa Cruz
Watsonville
Monterey Bay
Pt Pinos
Monterey
Salinas
Gonzales
King City
Coalinga
Paso Robles
Morro Bay
Grover City
San Luis Obispo
Santa Maria
Lompoc
Pt Conception

Dunsmuir
Shasta
Project City
Redding
Nat. Pk. Lassen Pk 3187
Chester
Red Bluff
L. Almanor
Paradise
Chico
Oroville
Grass Valley
Marysville
Yuba City
Colfax
Auburn
Roseville
Woodland
Davis
Carmichael
Sacramento
Vacaville
Fairfield
Vallejo
Antioch
Concord
Oakland
Alameda
Hayward
Livermore
Pleasanton
San Jose
Gilroy
Gustine
Los Banos
Madera
Pinedale
Fresno
Hanford
Lemoore
Visalia
Tulare
Porterville
Earlimart
Delano
Wasco
Oildale
Bakersfield
Arvin
Tehachapi Pass
Lancaster

Adin
Burney
Eagle L.
Susanville
Honey L.
Quincy
Feather Mid. Fork
Reno
Sparks
Donner Pass
Tahoe City
Lake Tahoe
S. Lake Tahoe
Placerville
Sutter Creek
Galt
Lodi
Stockton
Oakdale
Modesto
Turlock
Sonora
El Portal
Merced
Mariposa
Yosemite Nat. Park
Sutter Creek
San Andreas
Bridgeport
Mono L.
Bishop
Big Pine
Kings Canyon Nat. Park
Independence
Lone Pine
Sequoia Nat. Park
Mt Whitney 4418
Exeter
Keeler
Inyokern
Johannesburg
Mojave
Barstow
Yermo

Pt
Adin
120
Winnemucca
Golconda
Emigrant Pass
Rye Patch Resr
Imlay
Battle Mountain
Lovelock
Mt Tobin 2979
Pyramid
Humboldt L.
Fernley
Fallon
Eastgate
Austin
Summit Mtn 3188
Virginia City
Silver City
Carson City
Stewart
Yerington
Schurz
Gabbs
Mt Jefferson 3642
Walker L.
Hawthorne
Coaldale
Warm Springs
Tonopah
Boundary Peak 4005
Piper Pk
Goldfield
White Mtn Peak 4342
Beatty
Owens L.
Telescope Peak 3368
Death Valley
Panamint Range
Mojave Desert
Victorville
Mt San Antonio 3068
San Bernardino
Redlands
Beaumont
Pomona
Riverside
Anaheim
Santa Ana
San Jacinto Peak 3301
Palm Springs
Palomar Mtn 1871
Vista
Escondido
Ramona
Mesa
El Cajon
National City
Chula Vista
Tijuana
Tecate
Descanso

Santa Barbara
Santa Paula
Fillmore
Ventura
Oxnard
Beverly
Santa Monica
Burbank
Glendale
Pasadena
Los Angeles
Torrance
Long Beach
Huntington Beach
Laguna Beach
San Clemente
Oceanside
Carlsbad
San Diego
Santa Catalina
Gulf of Santa Catalina
San Clemente

Channel Islands
San Miguel
Santa Rosa
Santa Cruz
Santa Barbara Chan.

Sacramento Valley
COAST RANGES
SIERRA NEVADA
SAN JOAQUIN VALLEY
Diablo Range
Santa Lucia Range
Gabilan Range
Tehachapi Mts
Stillwater Ra.
Shoshone Mts
Monitor Ra.

40
35
① ② ③

USA, Hawaii

100 200 km
50 100 mls

PACIFIC OCEAN

160
Kauai
Hanalei
Lihue
1548
Mana
Niihau
Kaulakahiki Channel
Kauai Channel
Oahu
Wahiawa
Kaena Pt
Kaiwi Chan.
Pearl City
Kailua
Pearl Harbor
Honolulu
Kahuku Pt
1227
Molokai
Kaunakakai
Pailolo Chan.
Lanai
Lanai City
Kalaeakahiki Chan.
Kahoolawe
Alenuihaha Channel
Nailuku
Hana
Nat. Pk
3058
Maui
Kapaau
Upolu Point
Waimea
Kealaikahiki Chan.
Hakalou
Mauna Kea 4201
Hilo
Kailua
Kilauea Crater
Mauna Loa 4169
1243
Hawaii
Hawaii Volcanoes Nat. Park
Pahoa
Milolii
Naalehu
Ka Lae (South Cape)

20N
160
155
120
Ⓐ Ⓑ Ⓒ
④

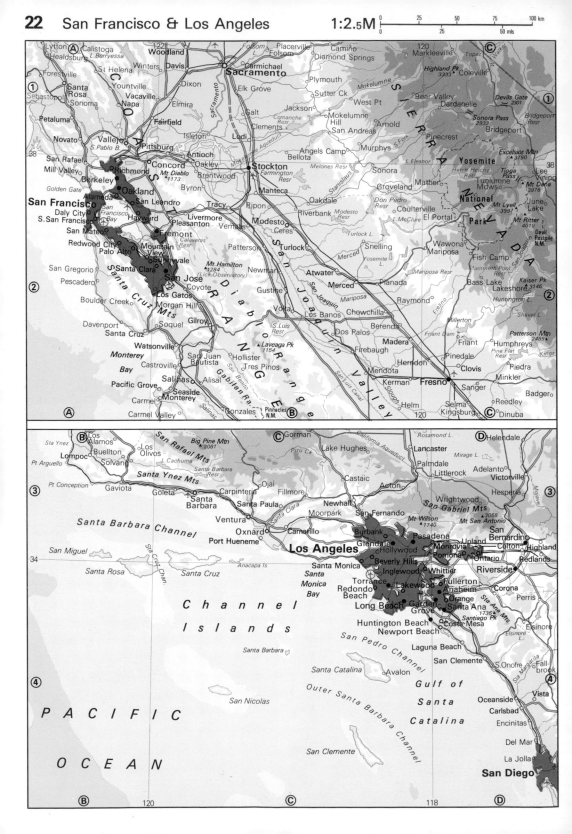

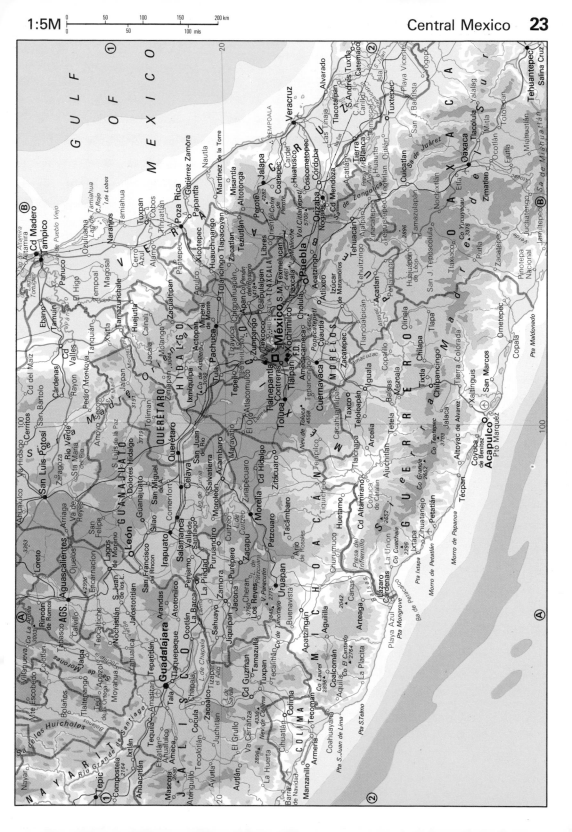

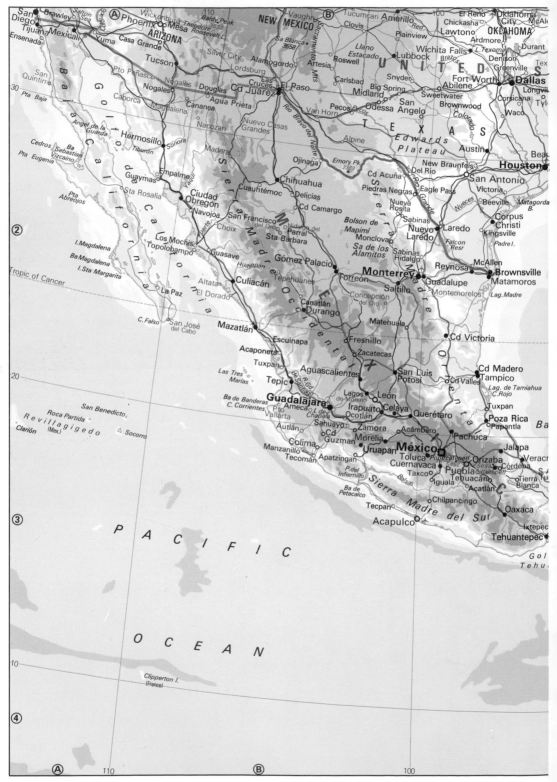

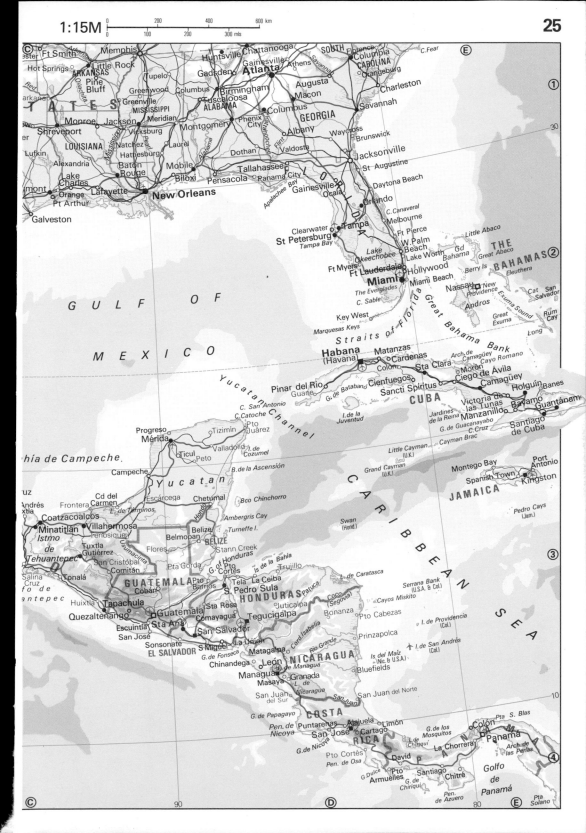

Map labels

Scale: 1:15M
0 — 200 — 400 — 600 km
0 — 100 — 200 — 300 mils

United States region
C'ester, Ft Smith, Memphis, Huntsville, Chattanooga, SOUTH, Florence, Columbia, C.Fear, E
Hot Springs, ARKANSAS, Little Rock, Gainesville, Athens, CAROLINA, Orangeburg, ①
Red, Pine Bluff, Tupelo, Gadsden, Atlanta, Savannah, Augusta, Charleston
arkana, STATES, Greenwood, Columbus, Birmingham, Macon, Savannah
Monroe, Jackson, MISSISSIPPI, ALABAMA, Tuscaloosa, GEORGIA
Shreveport, Vicksburg, Meridian, Montgomery, Phenix City, Columbus, Waycross, Brunswick, 30
LOUISIANA, Natchez, Hattiesburg, Laurel, Albany, Jacksonville
Lufkin, Alexandria, Baton Rouge, Dothan, Valdosta, St Augustine
Lake Charles, Mobile, Tallahassee, FLORIDA, Daytona Beach
Orange, Lafayette, New Orleans, Biloxi, Pensacola, Panama City, Gainesville, Ocala, Orlando
Pt Arthur, Apalachee Bay, C.Canaveral
Galveston, Melbourne
Clearwater, Tampa, Ft Pierce, Little Abaco
St Petersburg, Tampa Bay, W.Palm Beach, Gd Bahama, THE, ②
Ft Myers, Lake Okeechobee, Lake Worth, Berry Is, Great Abaco, BAHAMAS
Ft Lauderdale, Hollywood, Eleuthera
Miami, Miami Beach, Nassau, New Providence
The Everglades, Andros, Great Exuma, Cat, San Salvador
C. Sable, Exuma Sound
Key West, Rum Cay
Marquesas Keys, Long

Gulf and Caribbean
GULF OF MEXICO
Straits of Florida
Great Bahama Bank
Habana (Havana), Matanzas, Arch.de Camagüey, Cayo Romano
Pinar del Rio, Colón, Morón, Sta Clara, Ciego de Ávila, Camagüey
Guane, G.de Batabanó, Cienfuegos, Sancti Spiritus, Holguín, Banes
Yucatan Channel, CUBA, Victoria de las Tunas, Bayamo, Guantánamo
C. San Antonio, I.de la Juventud, Manzanillo, Santiago de Cuba
C.Catoche, Jardines de la Reina, G.de Guacanayabo, C.Cruz
Pto Juárez, Little Cayman, Cayman Brac
Tizimin, Valladolid, I. de Cozumel, Grand Cayman (U.K.), Port Antonio
Progreso, Mérida, Montego Bay, Spanish Town, Kingston
Ticul, Peto, B.de la Ascensión, JAMAICA, Pedro Cays (Jam.)
Campeche, Yucatan, Escárcega, Chetumal, Bco Chinchorro
Bahía de Campeche
Cd del Carmen, Frontera, Ambergris Cay, CARIBBEAN SEA
Coatzacoalcos, L. de Términos, Turneffe I., Swan (Hond.)
Minatitlán, Villahermosa, Tenosique, Belize, Serrana Bank (U.S.A. & Col.)
Istmo de Tehuantepec, Flores, Belmopan, BELIZE, Stann Creek
Tuxtla Gutiérrez, San Cristóbal, Pta Gorda, G.of Honduras, Trujillo, L. de Caratasca
Comitán, Pto Cortés, Is de la Bahía, Cayos Miskito
Salina Cruz, GUATEMALA, Pto Barrios, Tela, La Ceiba, Serrana, Pto Providencia (Col.)
Tonalá, Cobán, S. Pedro Sula, HONDURAS, Coco, Segovia, I. de Providencia (Col.)
Huixtla, Tapachula, Sta Rosa, Comayagua, Patuca, Bonanza, Pto Cabezas
Quezaltenango, Guatemala, Tegucigalpa, Juticalpa, I. de San Andrés (Col.)
Escuintla, STA ANA, San Salvador, Cord.Isabelía, Prinzapolca
San José, S.Miguel, La Unión, Rio Grande, NICARAGUA, Bluefields
Sonsonate, EL SALVADOR, G.de Fonseca, Matagalpa, Is del Maíz (Nic. & U.S.A.)
Chinandega, León, Managua, L. de Managua, San Juan del Norte
Masaya, Granada, L. de Nicaragua, San Juan
San Juan del Sur, San Juan, 10
COSTA, Pen. de Nicoya, Puntarenas, Alajuela, Limón, G.de los Mosquitos, Colón, Pta S. Blas
San José, Cartago, RICA, L. de Chiriquí, La Chorrera, PANAMA, Arch.de las Perlas, ④
G.de Nicoya, Pto Cortés, David, Santiago, Chitré, Golfo de Panamá
Pen. de Osa, G.Dulce, Pto Armuelles, G. de Chiriquí, Pen. de Azuero, Pta Solano

90, D, 80, E

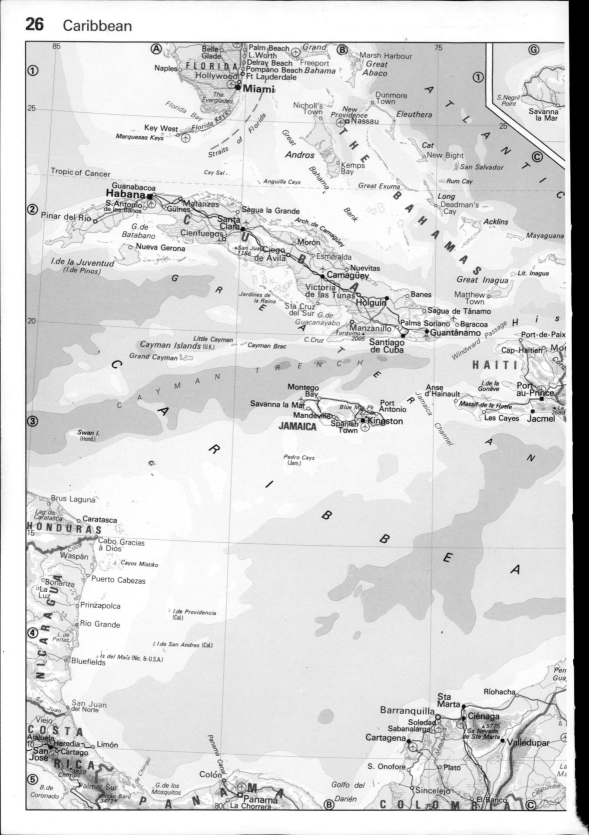

Florida Bay

Naples

FLORIDA

Belle Glade
Palm Beach
L. Worth
Delray Beach
Pompano Beach
Ft Lauderdale
Hollywood
Miami
The Everglades

Grand Bahama
Freeport
Marsh Harbour
Great Abaco

Key West
Marquesas Keys
Florida Keys
Straits of Florida

Nicholl's Town
New Providence
Nassau
Dunmore Town
Eleuthera

Cay Sal
Anguilla Cays
Andros
Kemps Bay
Bahama Bank
Great Bank

Tropic of Cancer

Cat
New Bight
San Salvador
Rum Cay

Guanabacoa
Habana
S. Antonio de los Baños
Güines
Matanzas
Sagua la Grande
Arch. de Camagüey

Pinar del Rio
G. de Batabano
Santa Clara
Cienfuegos

Great Exuma

Long
Deadman's Cay

THE BAHAMAS

Acklins
Mayaguana

Nueva Gerona
I. de la Juventud
(I. de Pinos)

San Juan 1156
Ciego de Avila
Morón
Esmeralda
Nuevitas
Camagüey
Victoria de las Tunas

GREE

Great Inagua
Lit. Inagua
Matthew Town

Jardines de la Reina
Sta Cruz del Sur
G. de Guacanayabo
Turquino 2005
Manzanillo
Holguín
Banes
Sagua de Tánamo
Palma Soriano
Baracoa
Guantánamo
C. Cruz
Santiago de Cuba

Windward Passage
Port-de-Paix
Cap-Haïtien
HAITI

His

Cayman Islands (U.K.)
Little Cayman
Cayman Brac
Grand Cayman

CAYMAN TRENCH

Montego Bay
Savanna la Mar
Mandeville
JAMAICA
Blue Mn Pk 2256
Spanish Town
Port Antonio
Kingston

Jamaica Channel

Anse d'Hainault
I. de la Gonâve
Massif de la Hotte
Les Cayes
Jacmel
Port-au-Prince
La 2680

Swan I.
(Hond.)

CARIBBE

Pedro Cays
(Jam.)

Brus Laguna
Lag. de Caratasca
Caratasca
HONDURAS
Cabo Gracias à Dios
Waspán
Cayos Mistiko
Coco

Puerto Cabezas
Bonanza
La Luz
Prinzapolca
Rio Grande
I. de Providencia
(Col.)

NICARAGUA
L. de Perlas
Is del Maíz (Nic. & U.S.A.)
Bluefields

I. de San Andres (Col.)

Río
Sta Marta
Ríohacha
Barranquilla
Ciénaga
Soledad
Sabanalarga
Sa Nevada de Sta Marta 5775
Valledupar

COSTA
Alajuela
Heredia
Limón
San José
Cártago
RICA
Chirripó

Panama Canal
Colón
Panama
La Chorrera
PANAMA

G. de los Mosquitos
Volcán Barú 3477

Cartagena
S. Onofore
Plato
El Banco
Sincelejo
Golfo del Darién
COLOMBIA

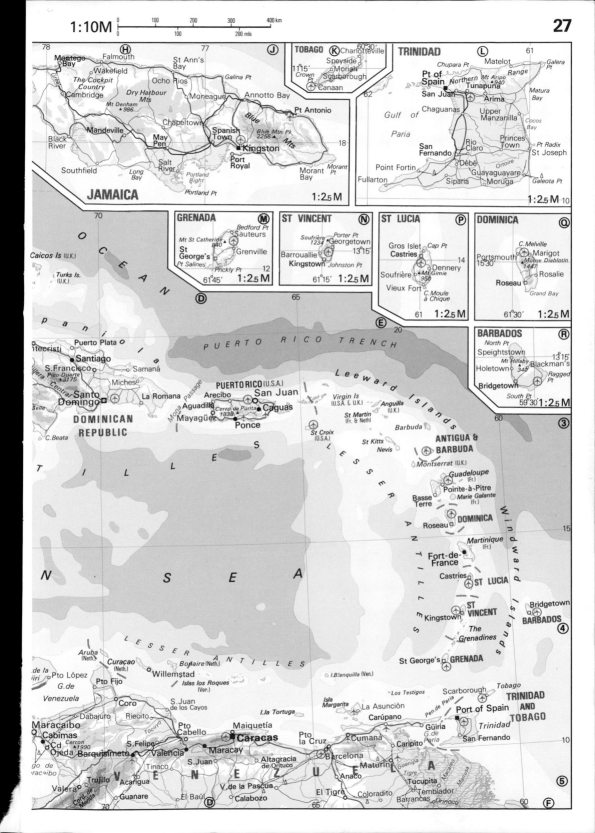

1:10M

0 100 200 300 400 km
0 100 200 mls

JAMAICA

78 H
Montego Bay
Falmouth
Wakefield
St Ann's Bay
St Ann's Bay
77 J
Ocho Rios
Galina Pt
The Cockpit Country
Cambridge
Dry Harbour Mts
Moneague
Annotto Bay
Mandeville
Mt Denham 986
Chapeltown
Pt Antonio
Blue Mtn Pk 2256
May Pen
Spanish Town
Blue Mts
Black River
Kingston
18
Southfield
Salt River
Port Royal
Long Bay
Portland Bight
Morant Bay
Morant Pt
Portland Pt
1:2.5M

TOBAGO K
Charlotteville
Speyside
Moriah
Scarborough
Crown
Canaan
1°15'
60°30'

TRINIDAD L
Chupara Pt
Matelot
Range
Galera Pt
61
Pt of Spain
Northern
Mt Aripo 940
San Juan
Tunapuna
Arima
Matura Bay
Gulf of Paria
Chaguanas
Upper Manzanilla
Cocos Bay
San Fernando
Rio Claro
Princes Town
Pt Radix
St Joseph
62
Point Fortin
Débé
Guayaguayare
Fullarton
Siparia
Moruga
Galeota Pt
1:2.5M 10

O C E A N

70

GRENADA M
Bedford Pt
Sauteurs
Mt St Catherine 840
St George's
Grenville
Pt Salines
Prickly Pt
12
61°45'
1:2.5M

ST VINCENT N
Soufrière 1234
Porter Pt
Georgetown
Barrouallie
13°15'
Kingstown
Johnston Pt
61°15'
1:2.5M

ST LUCIA P
Gros Islet
Cap Pt
Castries
14
Dennery
Soufrière
Mt Gimie 950
Vieux Fort
C.Moule à Chique
61
1:2.5M

DOMINICA Q
C.Melville
Portsmouth
Marigot
15°30'
Morne Diablotin 1447
Rosalie
Roseau
Grand Bay
61°30'
1:2.5M

Caicos Is (U.K.)

Turks Is. (U.K.)

P a n i o l a

65

D

E
20

BARBADOS R
North Pt
Speightstown
13°15'
Mt Hillaby 340
Holetown
Blackman's
Ragged Pt
Bridgetown
South Pt
59°30'
1:2.5M

P U E R T O R I C O T R E N C H

ntecristi
Puerto Plata
Santiago
S.Francisco
Pico Duarte 3175
Samaná
Miches
Cordillera Central
Santo Domingo
La Romana

DOMINICAN REPUBLIC

Selle
C.Beata

PUERTO RICO (U.S.A.)
Arecibo
San Juan
Aguadilla
Caguas
Mayagüez
Cerro de Punta 1338
Ponce
Mona Passage

L e e w a r d I s l a n d s

Virgin Is (U.S.A. & U.K.)
Anguilla (U.K.)
St Croix (U.S.A.)
St Martin (Fr. & Neth)
Barbuda
St Kitts
Nevis
ANTIGUA & BARBUDA
Montserrat (U.K.)
Guadeloupe (Fr.)
Pointe-à-Pitre
Basse Terre
Marie Galante (Fr.)
Roseau
DOMINICA
15
Martinique (Fr.)
Fort-de-France
Castries
ST LUCIA
Kingstown
ST VINCENT
Bridgetown
BARBADOS
The Grenadines
St George's
GRENADA

60
3

G R E A T E R
A N T I L L E S

L E S S E R

A N T I L L E S

W i n d w a r d
I s l a n d s

C A R I B B E A N S E A

4

N

L E S S E R A N T I L L E S

Aruba (Neth.)
Curaçao (Neth.)
Bonaire (Neth.)
Willemstad
Islas los Roques (Ven.)
I.Blanquilla (Ven.)
Los Testigos
Tobago
Scarborough
TRINIDAD AND TOBAGO

de la Güiri
Pto López
G.de Venezuela
Coro
Pto Fijo
S.Juan de los Cayos
I.la Tortuga
Isla Margarita
La Asunción
Carúpano
Pen de Paria
Port of Spain
Trinidad
San Fernando

Maracaibo
Cabimas
Cerrón 1990
Cd Ojeda
Barquisimeto
S.Felipe
Pto Cabello
Maiquetía
Caracas
Pto la Cruz
Cumaná
Güiria
G.de Paria
Caripito
10

go de aracaibo
Valera
Trujillo
Acarigua
Valencia
Maracay
S.Juan
Altagracia de Orituco
Barcelona
Maturín
Guanipa
Tigre
Tucupita

Cord. de Mérida
Guanare
El Bául
V.de la Pascua
Calabozo
El Tigre
Coloradito
Temblador
Barrancas
Orinoco

V E N E Z U E L A

70
D
65
60
F
5

1:40M

0	400	800	1200	1600 km
0	400	800	800 mls	

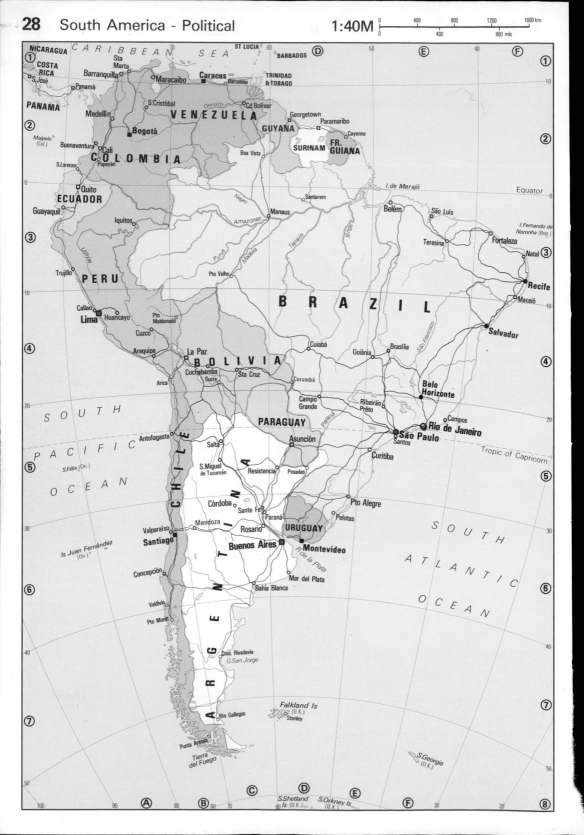

NICARAGUA

COSTA RICA
S.José
Panamá

PANAMA

Malpelo (Col.)

CARIBBEAN SEA

ST LUCIA

BARBADOS

TRINIDAD & TOBAGO

Sta Marta
Barranquilla
Maracaibo
Caracas
Barcelona
S.Cristóbal
VENEZUELA
Medellín
Bogotá
Buenaventura
Cali
Popayán
COLOMBIA
S.Lorenzo
Quito
ECUADOR
Guayaquil
Iquitos

Orinoco
Cd Bolivar
Georgetown
Paramaribo
GUYANA
Cayenne
SURINAM
FR. GUIANA
Boa Vista

Negro

Equator

I.de Marajó

Santarem

Belém
São Luís

I.Fernando de Noronha (Braz.)

PERU
Trujillo
Callao
Lima
Huancayo
Cuzco
Arequipa
La Paz
BOLIVIA
Cochabamba
Sucre
Sta Cruz
Arica

Amazonas
Purús
Madeira
Tapajós
Xingu
Manaus
Pto Velho

Teresina
Fortaleza
Natal
Recife
Maceió

Pto Maldonado

Cuiabá
Goiânia
Brasília
Salvador

São Francisco

BRAZIL

Corumbá
Campo Grande

Belo Horizonte

Ribeirão Prêto
Campos
Rio de Janeiro
São Paulo
Santos

SOUTH

PACIFIC

OCEAN

S.Félix (Chi.)

Antofagasta

CHILE

Salta
S.Miguel de Tucumán
Córdoba
Sante Fe
Mendoza
Rosario
Valparaíso
Santiago
Is Juan Fernández (Chi.)
Concepción
Valdivia
Pto Montt

PARAGUAY
Asunción
Resistencia
Posadas

Paraná

ARGENTINA

Buenos Aires

Bahía Blanca

Cmd. Rivadavia
G.San Jorge

Río Gallegos

Punta Arenas

Tierra del Fuego

Curitiba
Pto Alegre
Pelotas

URUGUAY
Montevideo
R.de la Plata
Mar del Plata

Tropic of Capricorn

SOUTH

ATLANTIC

OCEAN

Falkland Is (U.K.)
Stanley

S.Georgia (U.K.)

S.Shetland Is (U.K.)
S.Orkney Is (U.K.)

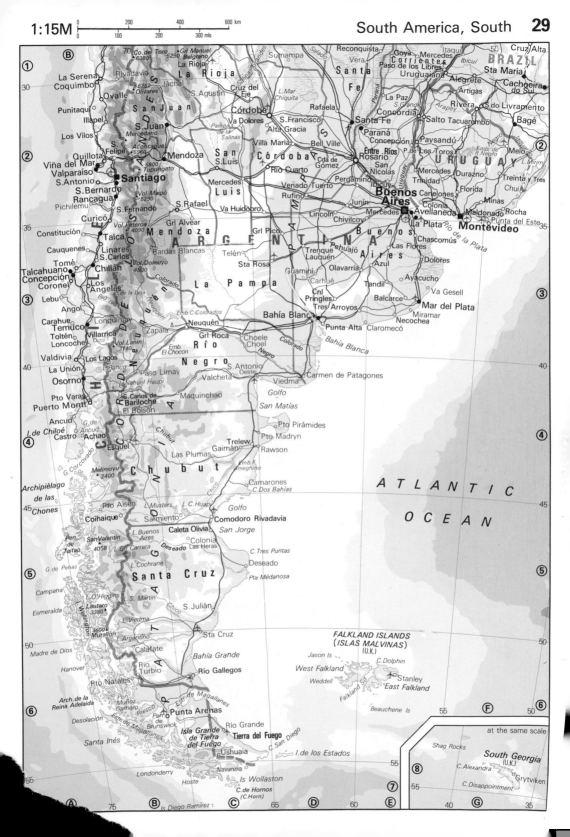

0   200   400   600 km
0   100   200   300 mls

B ① Co.del Toro 6380 Grl Manuel Belgrano 5250 La Rioja
70
La Serena Rivadavia Jáchal
Coquimbo 6282 Olivares La Rioja
30 Ovalle Olivares Cruz del Eje S.Agustin
Punitaqui San Juan Mercedario L.Mar Chiquita Sumampa Salado
Illapel S.Juan Va Dolores Córdoba
Los Vilos Mercedario Pampa Alta Gracia S.Francisco Rafaela Santa
S. 6960 de la Salinas Villa María Fe
② Quillota Felipe Aconcagua Bell Ville Paraná La Paz
Viña del Mar Mendoza San Córdoba Santa Fe Concordia Rivera
Valparaíso 6800 S.Luis Cda de Rosario Entre Ríos P.de Los Toros
S.Antonio Tupungato Gómez San Durazno
Santiago Mendoza Río Cuarto Pergamino Nicolas Trinidad
S.Bernardo Mercedes Venado Tuerto **Buenos** Colonia URUGUAY
Rancagua 5290 Luis Rufino Junín **Aires** Canelones Florida
Pichilemu S.Rafael Va Huidobro Lincoln Mercedes La Plata Minas
35 Curicó Grl Alvear Chivilcoy Avellaneda **Montevideo**
Constitución Mendoza Grl Pico **Buenos** Chascomús Punta del Este
Talca 4090 Bardas Blancas Telén Pehuajó Las Flores Dolores
Cauquenes Linares Sta Rosa Trenque Lauquén Azul
Tomé S.Carlos Vol.Domuyo Guamini Olavarría
Talcahuano Chillán 4800 La Pampa Carhué Tandil
Concepción Los Colorado Cnl Ayacucho
Coronel Ángeles Pringles Balcarce Va Gesell
③ Lebu Bío Bío Emb.C.Colorados Tres Arroyos **Mar del Plata**
Angol Lonquimay Neuquén Bahía Blanca Miramar
Carahue Zapala Grl Roca Choele Necochea
Temuco Villarrica Vol.Lanin Choel Colorado Bahía Blanca Claromecó
Toltén 3740 Río Negro Punta Alta
Loncoche Emb. El Chocón Negro
Valdivia Los Lagos Paso Limay S.Antonio Oeste
La Unión L.Ranco Valcheta Viedma
Osorno L.Nahuel Haupi Maquinchao Carmen de Patagones 40
Pto Varas S.Carlos de Golfo
Puerto Montt Bariloche San Matías
Ancud El Bolsón Pto Pirámides
G.de Chubut Pto Madryn
I.de Chiloé Ancud Trelew
Castro Achao Gaimán Rawson
Las Plumas
Melimoyu Emb.F. Ameghino
G.Corcovado 2400 Chubut
Archipiélago Camarones
de las C.Dos Bahías
Chones Pto Aisén L.Musters L.C.Huapi Golfo ATLANTIC
45 Coihaique Sarmiento San Jorge OCEAN
L.Buenos Caleta Olivia
Pen San Valentín Aires Colonia
de 4058 L.Grl Carrera Deseado Las Heras
Taitao C.Tres Puntas
G.de Penas L.Cochrane Deseado
Campana Pta Médanosa
L.O'Higgins Santa Cruz
Esmeralda Lautaro L.S.Martin
3380 Chico S.Julián
Wellington L.Viedma **FALKLAND ISLANDS**
50 Madre de Dios 3600 L.Argentino Sta Cruz **(ISLAS MALVINAS)** 50
Murallón **(U.K.)**
Hanover Bahía Grande Jason Is C.Dolphin
Río West Falkland Stanley
Turbio Río Gallegos Weddell East Falkland
Pto Natales Falkland Sd
Arch.de la Pen Beauchene Is 55
Reina Adelaida Muñoz **F**
Gamero Riesco Estrde Magallanes
Desolación Pta Punta Arenas Río Grande at the same scale
Santa Inés de Isla Grande Shag Rocks
Brunswick de Tierra del Fuego **Tierra del Fuego** ⑧ **South Georgia**
C.San Diego **(U.K.)**
Ushuaia I.de los Estados C.Alexandra
55 Londonderry Navarino Grytviken
Hoste Is Wollaston C.Disappointment
55 **A** C.de Hornos ⑦
75 **B** Is Diego Ramírez (C.Horn) **D** 60 **E** 55 **G** 40 35
C 65 50

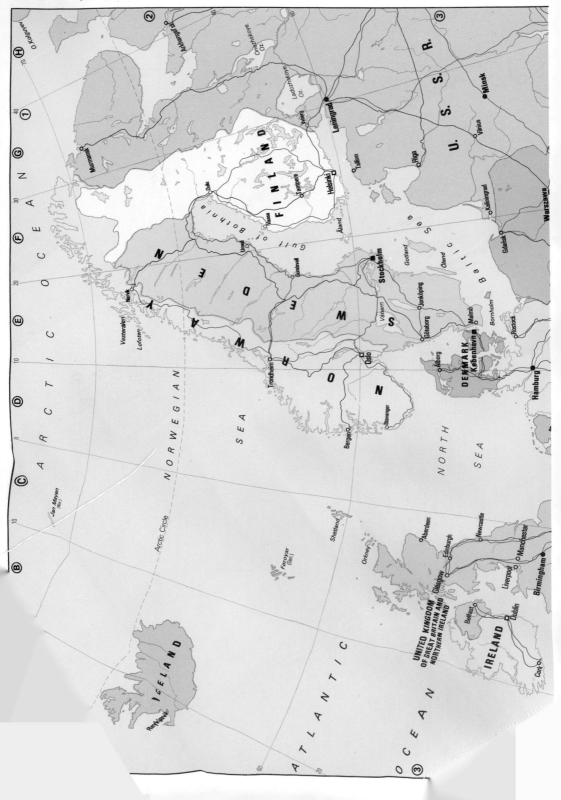

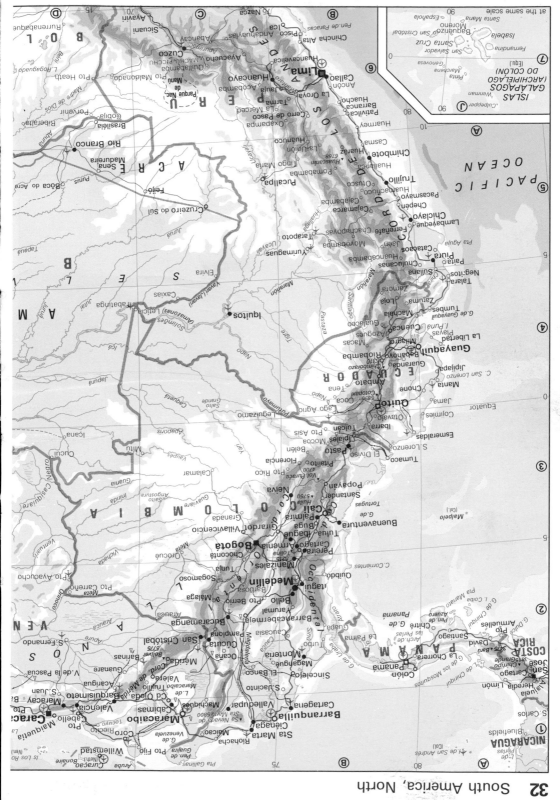

PACIFIC OCEAN

ISLAS GALAPAGOS (ARCHIPIELAGO DO COLON) (Equ.)

at the same scale

NICARAGUA

COSTA RICA

PANAMA

COLOMBIA

ECUADOR

PERU

BRAZIL

ACRE

BOLIVIA

VENEZUELA

ANDES

LOS ANDES

CORDILLERA

Caracas

Maracaibo

Barranquilla

Bogotá

Medellín

Cali

Quito

Guayaquil

Lima

Callao

Cuzco

Iquitos

Rio Branco

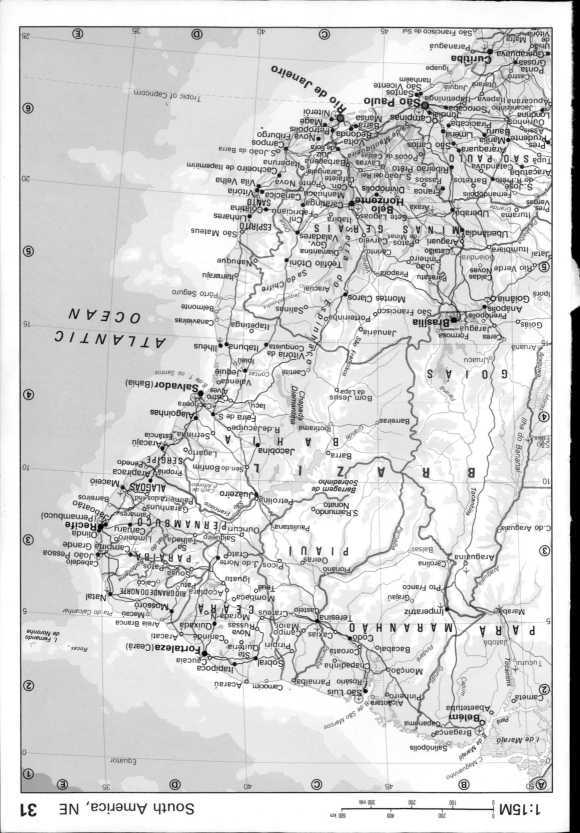

1:15M

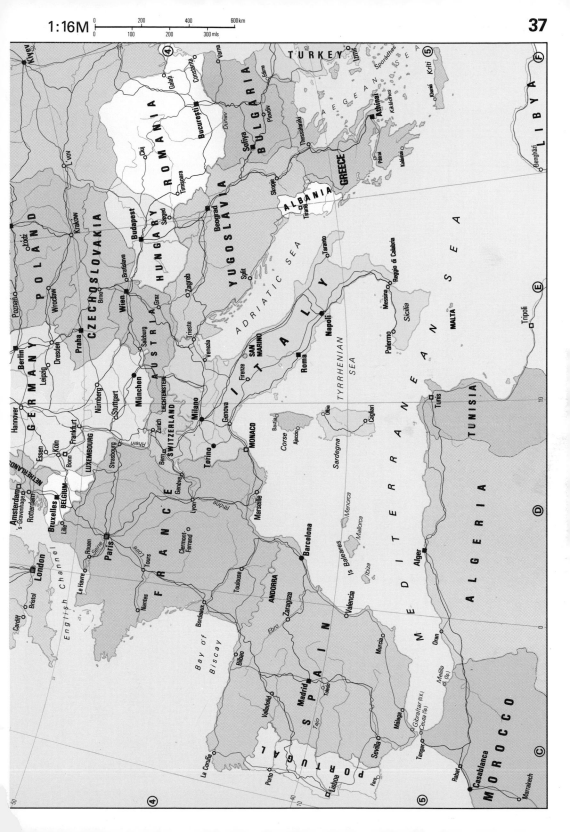

1:16M

0   200   400   600km
0 100 200 300 mls

④   ⑤   ⑥   Ⓕ

Kyev

TURKEY

İzmir   Sporadhes   SEA   Kriti

Varna   BULGARIA   Khaniá

Lvov   ROMANIA   Galati   Constanta   Edirne

Bucuresti   AEGEAN   Athínai

Cluj   Dunav   Plovdiv   Kikládhes

Timisoara   Sofiya   BULGARIA   Pátrai   LIBYA

Kalamái

POLAND   Skopje   GREECE   Benghàzi

Poznań   HUNGARY   Szeged   Beograd   ALBANIA

CZECHOSLOVAKIA   Budapest   Tiranë

Wrocław   Bratislava   Zagreb   YUGOSLAVIA

Kraków   Wien   Graz   Split   Taranto

Berlin   Brno   AUSTRIA   Trieste   Reggio di Calabria

Leipzig   Dresden   Praha   Salzburg   Venezia   ADRIATIC SEA

GERMANY   Nürnberg   München   LIECHTENSTEIN   SAN MARINO   Messina

Hannover   Stuttgart   Milano   Firenze   Napoli   Sicilia   MALTA   Tripoli

Essen   Frankfurt   Zürich   Genova   ITALY   Palermo   TYRRHENIAN SEA

NETHERLANDS   Köln   Bonn   SWITZERLAND   Bern   MONACO   Roma

Amsterdam   LUXEMBOURG   Strasbourg   Torino   Bastia   TUNISIA   Tunis

's-Gravenhage   Rotterdam   BELGIUM   Geneva   Corse   Cagliari

Bruxelles   Lille   Lyon   Marseille   Sardegna

London   Rouen   Paris   Clermont   Ferrand   Menorca   MEDITERRANEAN SEA   ALGERIA

Bristol   Le Havre   Seine   Toulouse   FRANCE   Barcelona   Baleares Is   Alger

Cardiff   Nantes   Loire   Bordeaux   ANDORRA   Zaragoza   Ibiza   Valencia   Oran

English Channel   Bay of Biscay   Bilbao   Ebro   Murcia   Melilla (Sp.)   TUNISIA

La Coruña   Valladolid   Madrid   SPAIN   Tajo   Málaga   Gibraltar (U.K.)   Ceuta (Sp.)

Porto   PORTUGAL   Lisboa   Faro   Sevilla   Tanger   MOROCCO

Rabat   Casablanca   Marrakech

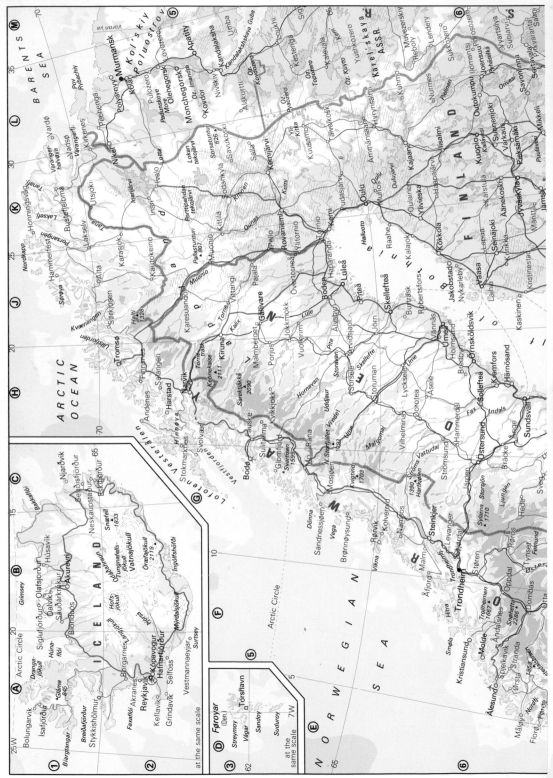

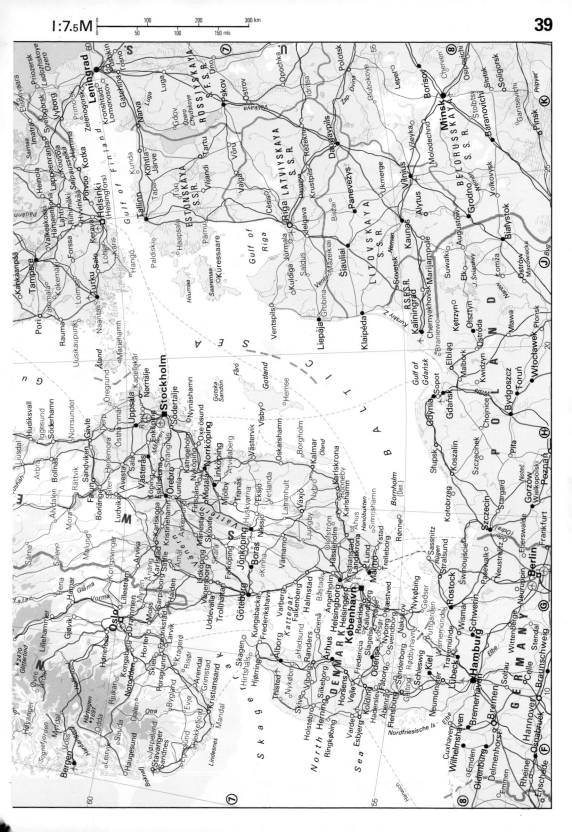

100   200   300 km
50   100   150 mls

1:5M

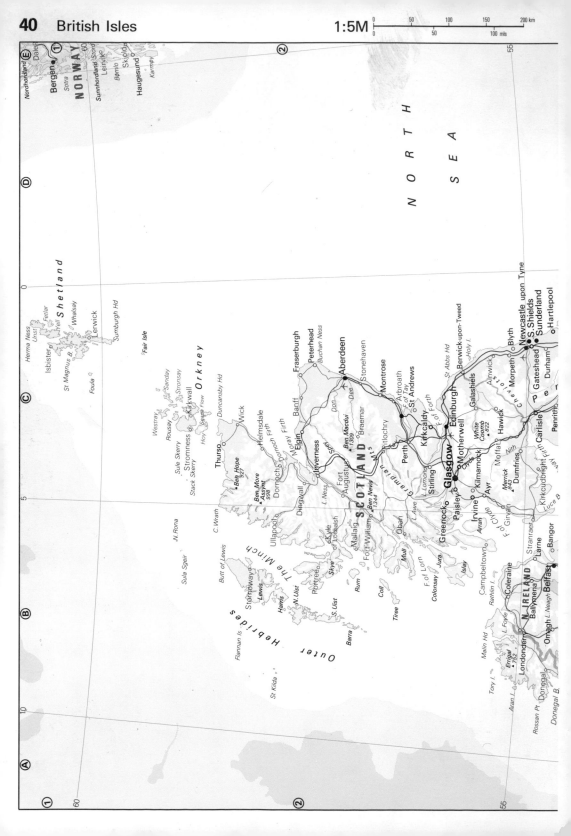

NORWAY

Nordhordland
Dale
Bergen
Sotra
Sunnhordland
Stord
Leirvik
Bømlo
Skjold
Haugesund
Karmøy

NORTH SEA

Shetland
Herma Ness
Unst
Yell
Fetlar
Isbister
St Magnus B.
Whalsay
Foula
Lerwick
Sumburgh Hd
Fair Isle

Orkney
Westray
Rousay
Sanday
Stronsay
Stromness
Kirkwall
Hoy
Scapa Flow
Duncansby Hd

Sule Skerry
Stack Skerry
Thurso
Wick
Helmsdale
Dornoch Firth
Moray Firth
C. Wrath
Ben Hope 927
Ben More Assynt 998
Dingwall
Elgin
Banff
Fraserburgh
Peterhead
Buchan Ness
Aberdeen
Stonehaven
Montrose
Arbroath
St Andrews
N. Rona
Ullapool
L.Ness
Fort Augustus
Ben Macdui 1309
Braemar
Dee
Don
Spey
Inverness
Pitlochry
Perth
F. of Tay
Kirkcaldy
Edinburgh
St Abbs Hd
Holy I.
Berwick-upon-Tweed
Sula Sgeir
Butt of Lewis
Kyle of Lochalsh
Mallaig
Ben Nevis 1344
Fort William
Oban
L.Awe
Stirling
Glasgow
Motherwell
Galashiels
Hawick
White Coomb 822
Alnwick
Morpeth
Blyth
Newcastle upon Tyne
Gateshead
S. Shields
Sunderland
Durham
Hartlepool
Tyne
Cheviot Hills
Flannan Is
Lewis
Harris
N. Uist
Stornoway
The Minch
Outer Hebrides
Portree
Skye
Rum
Coll
Tiree
Mull
Colonsay
Jura
Islay
F. of Lorn
L.Lomond
Paisley
Greenock
Kilmarnock
Irvine
Ayr
Arran
Girvan
Merrick 843
Dumfries
Moffat
Nith
Carlisle
Penrith
St Kilda
S. Uist
Barra
Campbeltown
Stranraer
Larne
Bangor
Belfast
Coleraine
Ballymena
N. IRELAND
Omagh
L. Neagh
Londonderry
Errigal 752
Tory I.
Malin Hd
L. Foyle
Rathlin I.
F. of Clyde
Kintyre
Kirkcudbright
Luce B.
Aran I.
Rossan Pt
Donegal
Donegal B.

SCOTLAND
Grampian Mts
Moray Firth
Dornoch Firth

0
50
100
150
200 km
0
50
100 mls

60
55
0
5
10
55
60

E
D
C
B
A
1
2

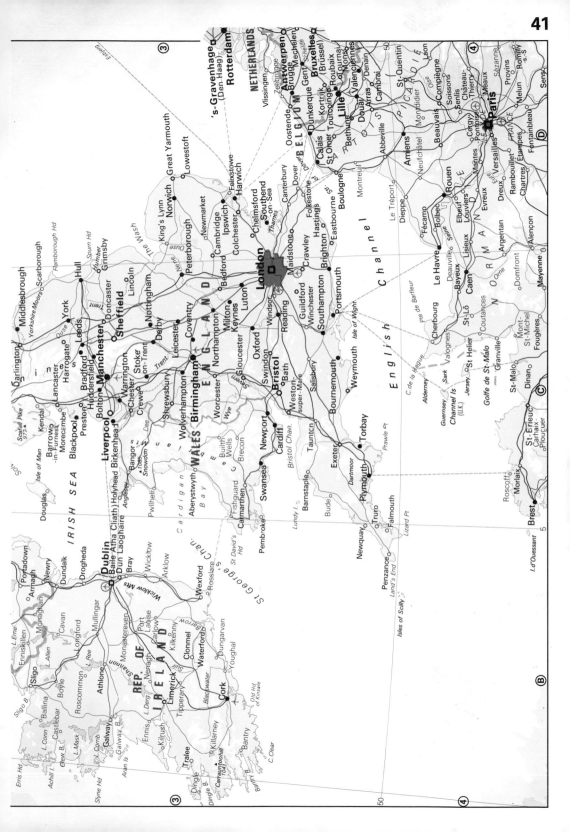

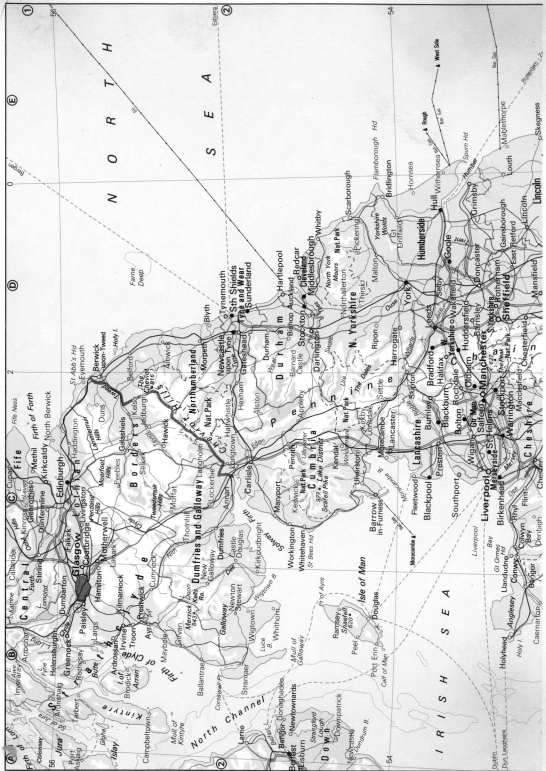

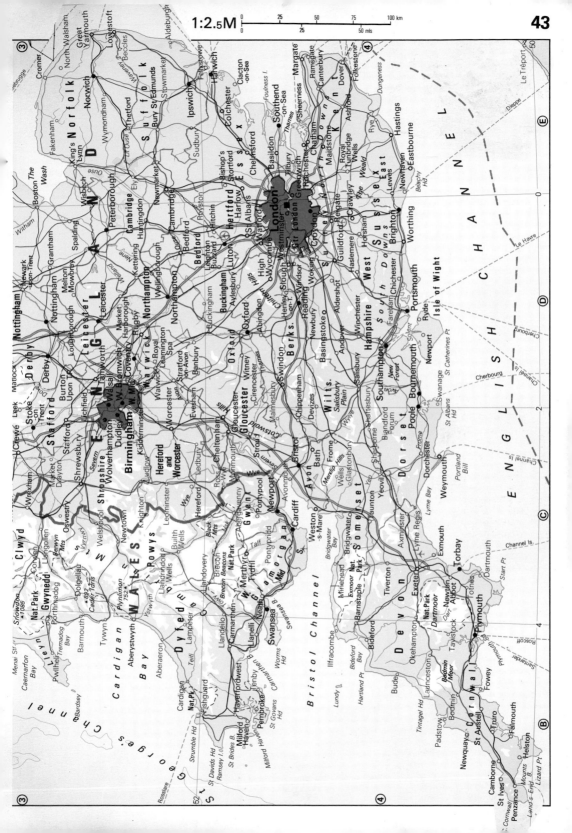

1:2.5M

25 50 75 100 km
25 50 mls

1:2.5M

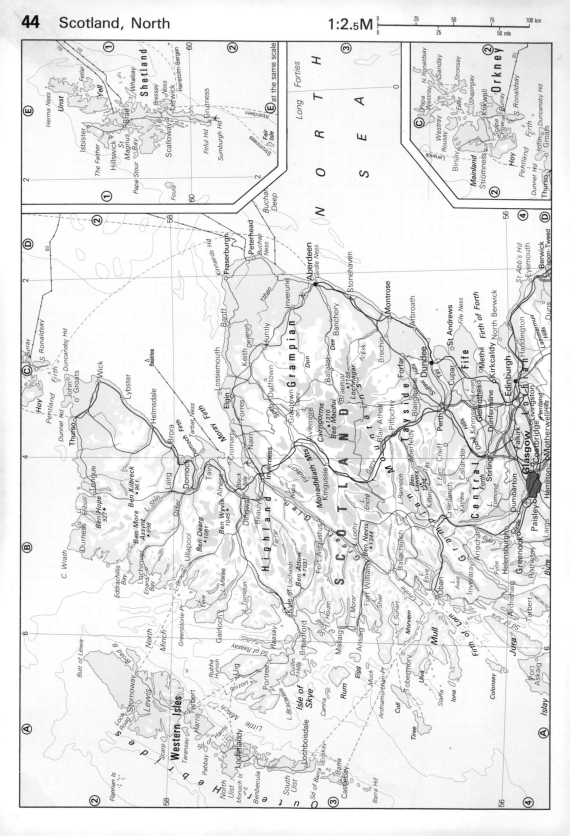

Shetland

Herma Ness, Unst, Fetlar, Yell, Whalsay, Bressay, Out Skerries, Muckle Flugga, Hanstolm-Bergen, Isbister, The Father, Papa Stour, Foula, Hillswick, St Magnus Bay, Scalloway, Lerwick, Grutness, Fitful Hd, Sumburgh Hd, Fair Isle

Orkney

Papa Westray, N. Ronaldsay, Sanday, Stronsay, Shapinsay, Eday, Rousay, Burray, Westray, Kirkwall, Birsay, Mainland, Stromness, Hoy, Scapa Flow, S. Ronaldsay, Duncansby, Groats, Pentland Firth, Dunnet Hd, Thurso

N O R T H   S E A

Long Forties, Buchan Deep

SCOTLAND

Highland

Grampian

Tayside

Central

Fife

Western Isles

C. Wrath, Durness, Loch Inver, Eddrachillis Bay, Enard Bay, Lochinver, Ben More Assynt ▲998, Ben Hope ▲927, Ben Kilbreck ▲961, Loch Shin, Tongue, Hope, Kinlochbervie, Dunnet Hd, John o' Groats, Duncansby Hd, Pentland Firth, Hoy, Thurso, Wick, Lybster, Helmsdale, Brora, Laing, Dornoch, Tain, Dornoch Firth, Tarbat Ness, Beatrice, Ben Wyvis ▲1045, Dingwall, Beauly, Inverness, Moray Firth, Cromarty, Black Isle, Nairn, Forres, Elgin, Lossiemouth, Buckie, Keith, Dufftown, Huntly, Banff, Kinnairds Hd, Fraserburgh, Buchan Ness, Peterhead, Ythan, Inverurie, Aberdeen, Girdle Ness, Stonehaven, Montrose, Arbroath, St Andrews, North Berwick, Fife Ness, Dundee, Carnoustie, Arbroath, Brechin, Forfar, Kirriemuir, Blairgowrie, Perth, Cupar, Kinross, Glenrothes, Kirkcaldy, Methil, Leven, Dunfermline, Firth of Forth, Edinburgh, Haddington, Dunbar, St Abb's Hd, Eyemouth, Berwick-upon-Tweed, Duns, Lammermuir Hills, Pentland Hills, Livingston, Falkirk, Glasgow, Motherwell, Hamilton, Paisley, Dumbarton, Stirling, Callander, Crieff, L. Earn, Killin, Crianlarich, L. Lomond, Helensburgh, Greenock, Gourock, Largs, Rothesay, Bute, Ardrishaig, Tarbert, Inveraray, Arrochar, L. Fyne, Oban, Firth of Lorn, Mull, Tobermory, Iona, Staffa, Ulva, Coll, Tiree, Colonsay, Islay, Jura, Sd of Jura, Port Askaig, Port Ellen, Ardnamurchan Pt, Morvern, L. Sunart, Fort William, Ben Nevis ▲1344, Ballachulish, L. Linnhe, L. Etive, L. Awe, Ben Cruachan, Loch Leven, L. Eil, Mallaig, L. Morar, Arisaig, Eigg, Muck, Rum, Canna, Isle of Skye, Cuillin Hills, Broadford, Portree, Raasay, Sd of Raasay, Uig, Loch Snizort, Rubha Hunish, Dunvegan, L. Bracadale, L. Maree, L. Torridon, Gairloch, Greenstone Pt, Ullapool, Loch Broom, Eye, Loch Carron, Kyle of Lochalsh, Ben Attow ▲1031, L. Hourn, L. Nevis, L. Shiel, L. Morar, Glen Garry, Loch Ness, Fort Augustus, Glen More, Loch Lochy, Loch Oich, Spean Bridge, Monadhliath Mts, Kingussie, Newtonmore, Aviemore, Cairngorms ▲1310, Grantown-on-Spey, Ben Macdui ▲1310, Lochnagar ▲1155, Braemar, Ballater, Banchory, Dee, Don, Deeside, Blair Atholl, Pitlochry, Aberfeldy, L. Tay, L. Tummel, L. Rannoch, L. Ericht, Ben Lawers ▲1214, L. Lyon, L. Katrine, Grampian Mountains

Monach Is, Flannan Is, N. Uist, North Uist, Benbecula, South Uist, Lochmaddy, Lochboisdale, Castlebay, Barra, Barra Hd, Eriskay, Sd of Barra, Harris, Sd of Harris, Taransay, Pabbay, Scarp, Sea of the Hebrides, Little Minch, The Minch, Lewis, Stornoway, Tarbert, Loch Roag, Butt of Lewis, Broad B, Butt of Lewis Hd

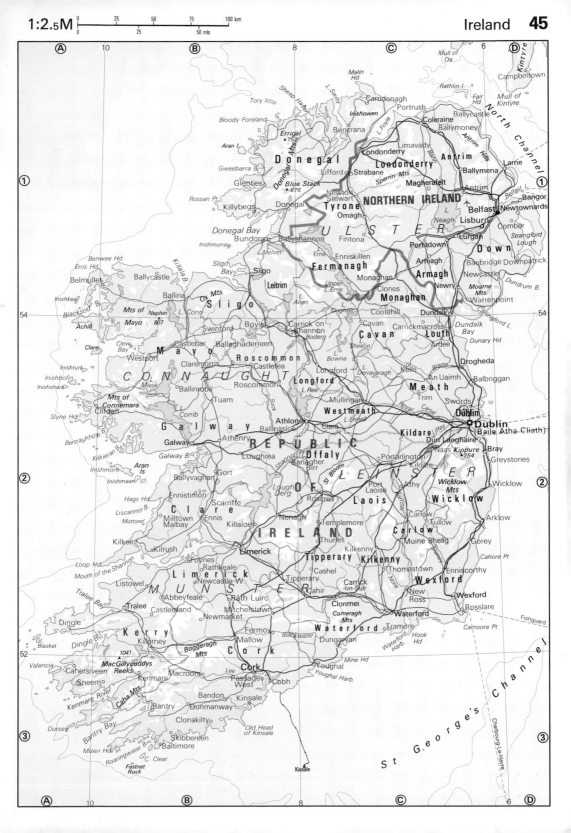

North Channel

St George's Channel

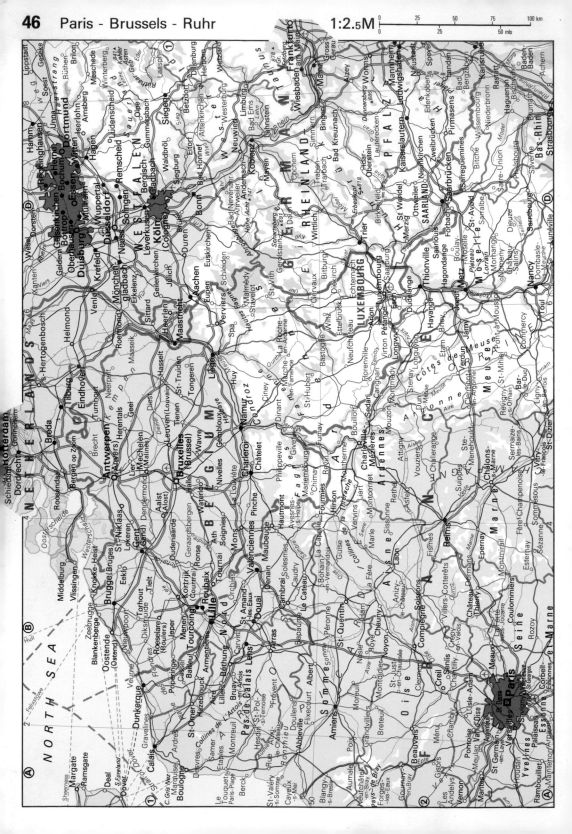

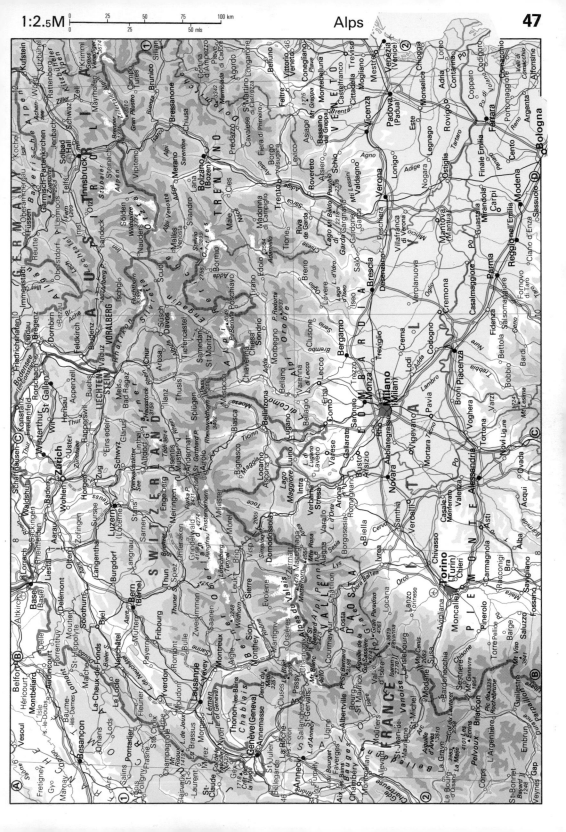

1:2.5M

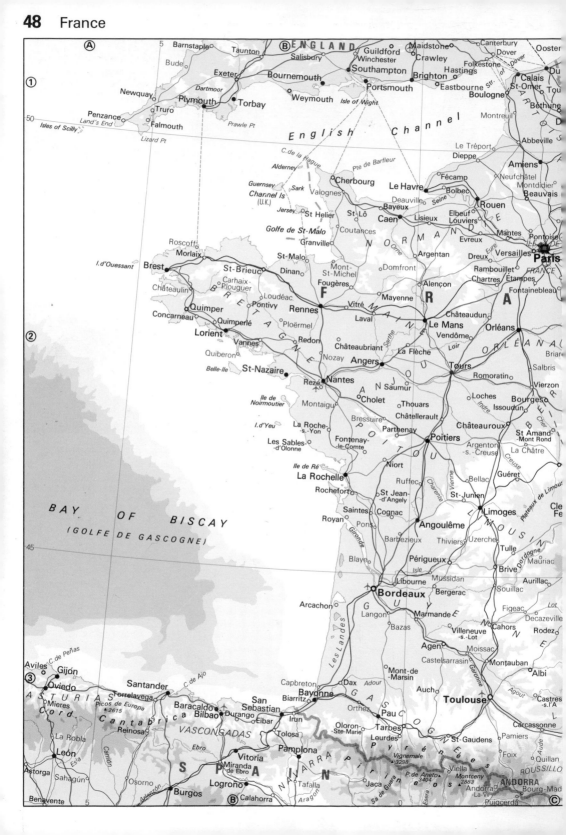

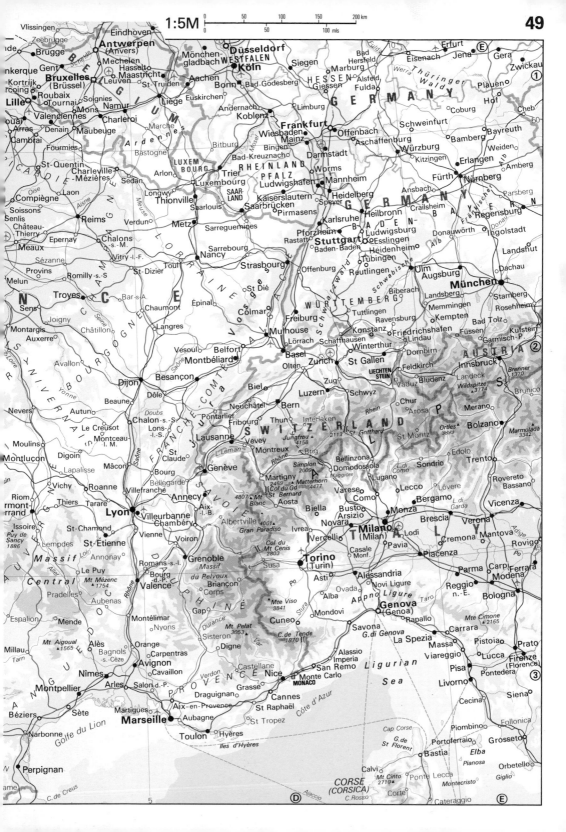

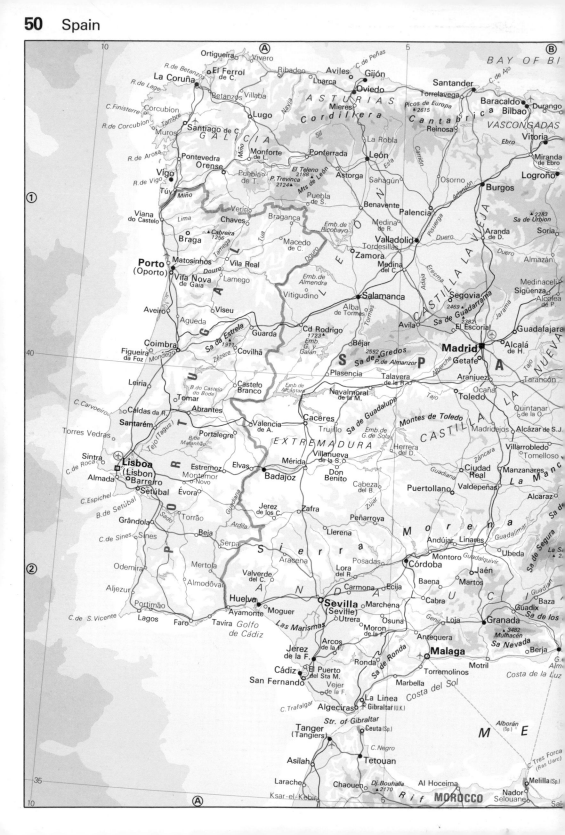

A

B

BAY OF BI

Ortigueira
Vivero
Ribadeo
C. de Peñas
Aviles
Gijón
Santander
C. de Ajo
R. de Betanzos
El Ferrol
de C.
Luarca
Oviedo
Torrelavega
Baracaldo
Bilbao
Durango
La Coruña
Betanzos
Villaba
Mieres
A S T U R I A S
Picos de Europa
2615
Reinosa
VASCONGADAS
R. de Lage
C. Finisterre
Corcubion
Lugo
C o r d i l l e r a
C a n t a b r i c a
Vitoria
Muros
R. de Corcubion
Tambre
Santiago de C.
G A L I C I A
Sil
La Robla
Ebro
Miranda
de Ebro
Logroño
R. de Arosa
Pontevedra
Monforte
de L.
Ponferrada
León
Osorno
Burgos
Vigo
Orense
Puebla
de T.
El Teleno
2188
Astorga
Sahagún
Sa de Urbion
2283
R. de Vigo
Túy
Miño
P. Trevinca
2124
Mts de León
Benavente
Palencia
Pisuerga
Aranda
de D.
Soria
Viana
do Castelo
Verin
Bragança
Emb. de
Ricobayo
Medina
de R.
Valladolid
Tordesillas
Duero
Almazán
Lima
Cabreira
1256
Macedo
de C.
Duero
Zamora
Medina
del C.
Medinaceli
Braga
Chaves
Tua
Emb. de
Almendra
Segovia
2469
Sigüenza
Alcofea
de P.
Porto
(Oporto)
Matosinhos
Vila Real
Lamego
Vitigudino
Salamanca
Sa de Guadarrama
2382
El Escorial
Guadalajara
Vila Nova
de Gaia
Douro
Viseu
Alba
de Tormes
Avila
Madrid
Alcalá
de H.
Aveiro
Agueda
Guarda
Cd Rodrigo
1723
Tormes
Getafe
Figueira
da Foz
Coimbra
Sa da Estrela
1991
Emb.
G. y
Galán
Béjar
Sa de Gredos
2592
P. de Almanzor
Alberche
Aranjuez
Tarancón
Leiria
Tomar
Castelo
Branco
Emb. de
Alcántara
Navalmoral
de la M.
Plasencia
Talavera
de la R.
Ocaña
Toledo
Quintanar
de la O.
C. Carvoeiro
Caldas da R.
Abrantes
Valencia
de A.
Cáceres
Sa de Guadalupe
Tajo
Madridejos
Alcázar de S.J.
Torres Vedras
Santarém
Portalegre
E X T R E M A D U R A
Trujillo
Emb. de
G. de Sola
Montes de Toledo
C A S T I L L A
Villarrobledo
Tomelloso
Sintra
Lisboa
(Lisbon)
Estremoz
Mérida
Villanueva
de la S.
Herrera
del D.
Ciudad
Real
Manzanares
Almada
Barreiro
Montemor
o-Novo
Évora
Badajoz
Don
Benito
Guadiana
Valdepeñas
Alcaraz
C. Espichel
Setúbal
Cabeza
del B.
Puertollano
B. de Setúbal
Torrão
Jerez
de los C.
Zafra
Zújar
C. de Sines
Grândola
Sines
Beja
Serpa
Peñarroya
M o r e n a
Andújar
Linares
Ubeda
Odemira
Mertola
Valverde
del C.
Almodôvar
Lora
del R.
Posadas
Montoro
Córdoba
Jaén
Martos
Aljezur
Huelva
Carmona
Ecija
Baena
Cabra
Portimão
Moguer
Sevilla
(Seville)
Marchena
Osuna
Loja
Granada
Lagos
Faro
Tavira
Ayamonte
Utrera
Morón
de la F.
Antequera
Guadix
C. de S. Vicente
Golfo
de Cádiz
Las Marismas
Mulhacén
3482
Sa Nevada
Berja
Jerez
de la F.
Arcos
de la F.
Sa de Ronda
Ronda
Malaga
Motril
Cádiz
El Puerto
del Sta M.
Torremolinos
Costa de la Luz
San Fernando
Vejer
de la F.
Marbella
Costa del Sol
C. Trafalgar
Algeciras
La Linea
Gibraltar (U.K.)
Str. of Gibraltar
Alborán
(Sp.)
Tanger
(Tangiers)
Ceuta (Sp.)
C. Negro
Asilah
Tetouan
Melilla (Sp.)
Larache
Chaouen
Dj. Bouhalla
2170
Al Hoceima
Nador
Ksar-el-Kebir
Rif
MOROCCO

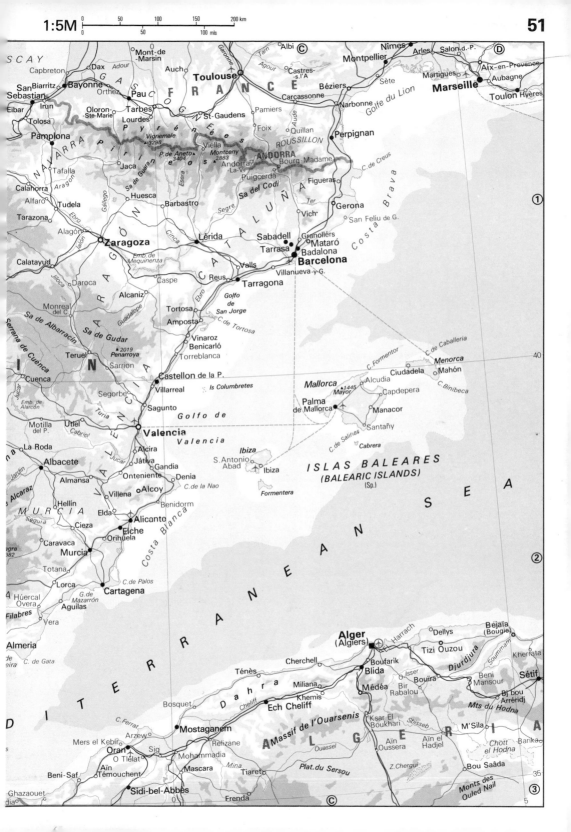

50 100 150 200 km
50 100 mls

SCAY
Capbreton
San Sebastian
Eibar
Tolosa
Biarritz
Bayonne
Irun
Pamplona
NAVARRA
Tafalla
Calahorra
Alfaro
Tarazona
Alagón
Tudela
Mont-de-Marsin
Dax
Orthez
Pau
Oloron-Ste-Marie
Lourdes
Tarbes
Jaca
Sa de Guara
Huesca
Barbastro
Auch
St-Gaudens
Pamiers
Foix
P. de Aneto 3404
Vignemale 3298
Viella
Montceny 2883
Andorra-La-Vª
Puigcerdá
Sa del Codi
Toulouse
FRANCE
Albi
Castres-s.l'A
Carcassonne
Narbonne
Béziers
Quillan
ROUSSILLON
ANDORRA
Bourg-Madame
Figueras
Gerona
C. de Creus
San Feliu de G.
Costa Brava
Montpellier
Sète
Golfe du Lion
Perpignan
Nîmes
Arles
Salon-d.-P.
Martigues
Aix-en-Provence
Aubagne
Marseille
Toulon
Hyères
D

Calatayud
Zaragoza
Emb. de Mequinenza
Daroca
Monreal del C.
Sa de Albarracin
Serrana de Cuenca
Teruel
2019 Penarroya
Sarrion
Cuenca
ARAGÓN
Caspe
Alcaniz
Lérida
Sabadell
Tarrasa
Granollérs
Mataró
Badalona
Barcelona
Reus
Valls
Tarragona
Villanueva-y-G.
CATALUÑA
Vich
Ter
Segre
Cinca
Gállego
Ebro
Jiloca
Jalón
Guadalope

Sa de Gudar
Motilla del P.
Utiel
Cabriel
La Roda
Albacete
Almansa
Villena
Elda
Hellín
Cieza
Caravaca
Murcia
Totana
Lorca
Cartagena
Almeria
Segorbe
Villarreal
Sagunto
Valencia
Alcira
Játiva
Gandia
Ontiniente
Denia
Alcoy
Benidorm
Alicante
Elche
Orihuela
VALENCIA
MURCIA
Castellon de la P.
Is Columbretes
C. de la Nao
Golfo de Valencia
Ibiza
S. Antonio Abad
Ibiza
Formentera
Mallorca
Mayor 1445
Palma de Mallorca
Manacor
Santañy
Cabrera
C. de Salinas
C. de Caballeria
Menorca
Ciudadela
Mahón
C. Binibeca
C. Formentor
Alcudia
Capdepera
ISLAS BALEARES
(BALEARIC ISLANDS)
(Sp.)

Tortosa
Amposta
Vinaroz
Benicarló
Torreblanca
Golfo de San Jorge
C. de Tortosa

MEDITERRANEAN SEA

40
1
2
3
35
5

Almeria
C. de Gata
Aguilas
Vera
Huercal Overa
Filabres

Alger (Algiers)
Cherchell
Ténès
Bosquet
Mostaganem
Arzew
Mers el Kebir
Oran
O Tlelat
Sig
Mohammadia
Mascara
Beni-Saf
Aïn Témouchent
Ghazaouet
Sidi-bel-Abbès
Frenda
Relizane
Mina
Tiaret
Boufarik
Blida
Médéa
Miliana
Khemis
Ech Cheliff
Cheliff
Dahra
Massif de l'Ouarsenis
Ksar El Boukhari
Spisseb
Ouassel
Plat. du Sersou
Z. Chergui
Dellys
Tizi Ouzou
Bouira
Isser
Bir Rabalou
Aïn Oussera
Aïn el Hadjel
Harrach
Djurdjura
Beni Mansour
Mts du Hodna
Bj bou Arréridj
M'Sila
Chott el Hodna
Bou Saâda
Monts des Ouled Nail
Béjaïa (Bougie)
Kherrata
Sétif
Soummam
Barika
ALGERIA
C. Ferrat

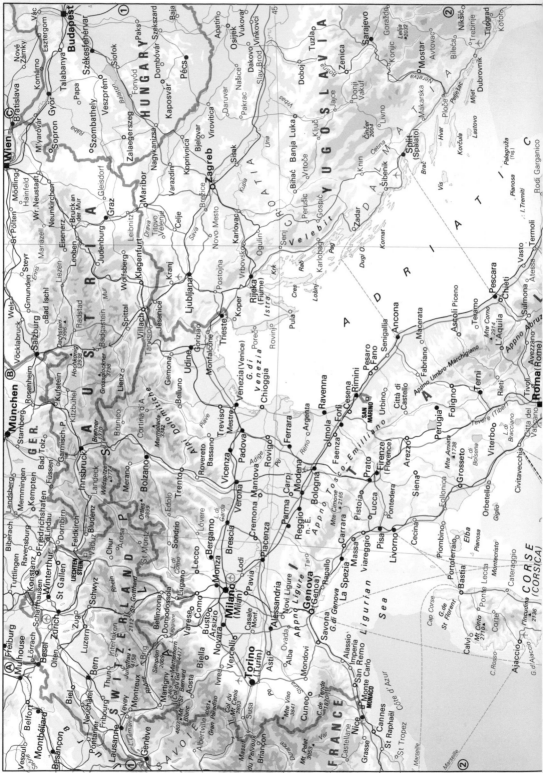

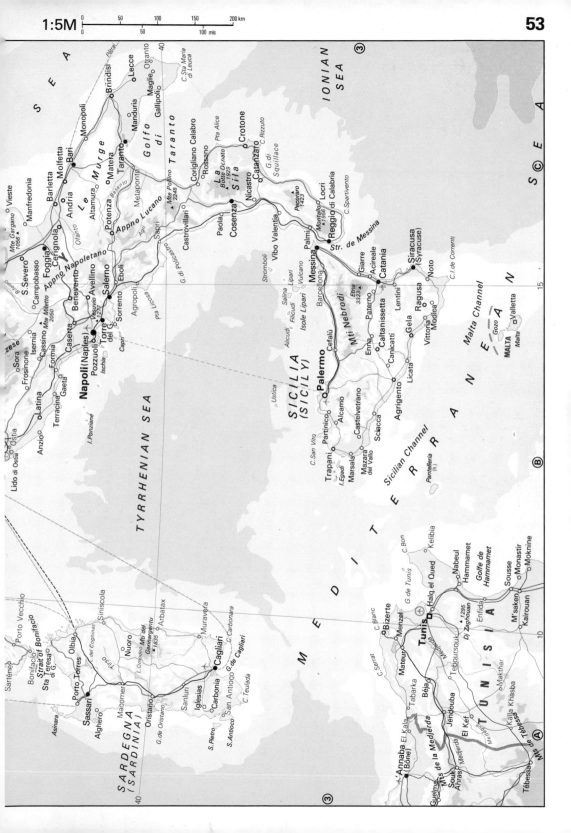

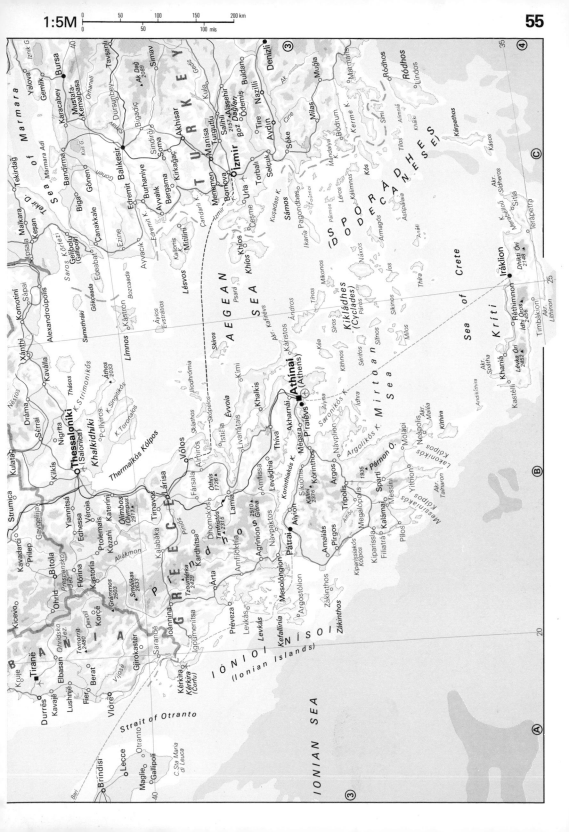

1:5M

0 50 100 150 200 km
0 50 100 mls

Sea of Marmara

İznik G.
Bursa
Yalova
Gemlik
İzmit
Karacabey
Mustafa-Kemalpaşa
Orhaneli
Ak Dağ 2089
Simav
Denizli ③
Tavşanlı
Bigadiç
Buldano
③
Tekirdağ
Marmara Adi
Dursunbey
Balat G.
Gediz
Bandırma
Gönen
Sındırğı
Soma
Kula
Alaşehir 2157
Nazilli
Buyurbaşa
Akhisar
Ödemiş
Manisa
Turgutlu
Bos Dağları
Tire
Aydın
Çine
Muğla
Marmaris
Ródhos
Lindos
İzmir
Menemen
Bornova
Urla
Çeşme
Torbalı
Selçuk
Söke
Milas
Bodrum
Kerme K.
Sími
Alimniá
Khálki
Ródhos
Kárpathos
Kásos
Édremit
Çanakkale
Ezine
Ayvacık
Bergama
Burhaniye
Ayvalık
Çandarlı K.
İzmir K.
Kuşadası K.
Sámos
Pagondhas
Léros
Kálimnos
Kos
Astipálaia
Kárpathos
Tekir D.
Keşan
Malkara
Gelibolu (Gallipoli)
Eceabat
Bozcaada
Mitilíni
Kallonís
Lésvos
Khíos
Khíos
Psará
Ikaría
Pátmos
Fourni
Dhktí Óri 2148
Iráklion
İpsala
Sáros Körfezi
Gökçeada
Áyios Evstrátios
Límnos
Kástron
Samothráki
Áthos 2033
Náxos
Thíra
Íos
Sérifos
Síkinos
Réthimnon
Idhi Óros 2456
Akr. Sídheros
Terápetra
Alexandroúpolis
Sapai
Komotiní
Xánthi
Kavála
Thásos
K. Strimonikós
Skíros
Iliodhrómia
Skópelos
Ándros
Tínos
Míkonos
Síros
Páros
Síros
Kíklâdhes (Cyclades)
Mílos
Sea of Crete
Khaniá
Lévka Óri 2452
Akr. Spátha
Kastélli
Andikíthira
Kríti
Akr. Líthinon
Drāma
Sérrai
Nigríta
Strumica
Kilkís
Kulata
Kíevo
Strumica
Prilep
Kavadarci
Bitola
Ohrid
Ohridsko Jez.
Kičevo
Tomorrica 2480
Devoll
Korçë
Grammos 2503
Smólikas 2637
Prespansko Jez.
Flórina
Kastoriá
Kozáni
Ptolemaís
Kalabáka
Olimbos (Olympus) 2917
Katerini
Tírnavos
Lárisa
Pindos
Thessaloníki (Saloníki)
Khalkidhikí
K. Singitikós
K. Toronéos
Thermaïkós Kólpos
Vólos
Skíathos
Istiéa
Évvoia
Livanátais
Kími
Khalkís
Thíva
Aíyina
Akhamaí
Athínai (Athens)
Piraiévs
Mégara
Korinthós
Korinthiakós K.
Kiáton
Sikióna
Árgos
Tripolis
Argolikós K.
Návplion
Ídhra
Spétsai
Mirtóon Sea
Saronikós K.
Kéa
Kíthnos
Káristos
Akr. Kafirévs
Tínos
Saronikós K.
Pátrai
Aíyion
Amaliás
Pírgos
Megalópolis
Spárti
Párnon Ó. 1935
Sikía
Kíparissía
Filiatrá
Kalámai
Messíni
Yíthion
Akr. Maléa
Kíthira
Moláoi
Neápolis
Lakonikós Kólpos
Akr. Taínaron
Messiniakós Kólpos
Kiparissiakós Kólpos
Pílos
Ídha
Yerákini
Olimbos (Olympus)
Yiannitsá
Edhessa
Véroia
Aliákmon
Smólikas
Kardhítsa
Othris 1726
Dhomokós
Lamía
Levádhia
Anfíssa
Amfíklia
Gíona 2510
Návpaktos
Mesolóngion
Agrínion
Amfilokhía
Arta
Préveza
Tríkkala
Tzoumérka 2429
Ágrafa
Tímfi 2225
Ioánnina
Igoumenítsa
Sarandë
Kérkira (Corfu)
Levkás
Levkás
Kefallinía
Zákinthos
Zákinthos
Katákolon
Argostólion
IÓNIOI NÍSOI (Ionian Islands)
Tiranë
Kruje
Elbasan
Berat
Fier
Vlorë
Vijosë
Gjirokastër
Durrës
Kavajë
Lushnjë
Shkumbin
Sarandë
Strait of Otranto
Otranto
C. Sta Maria di Leuca
Lecce
Maglie
Gallipoli
Brindisi
Bari

IONIAN SEA

TURKEY

AEGEAN SEA

GREECE

SPORÁDHES (DODECANESE)

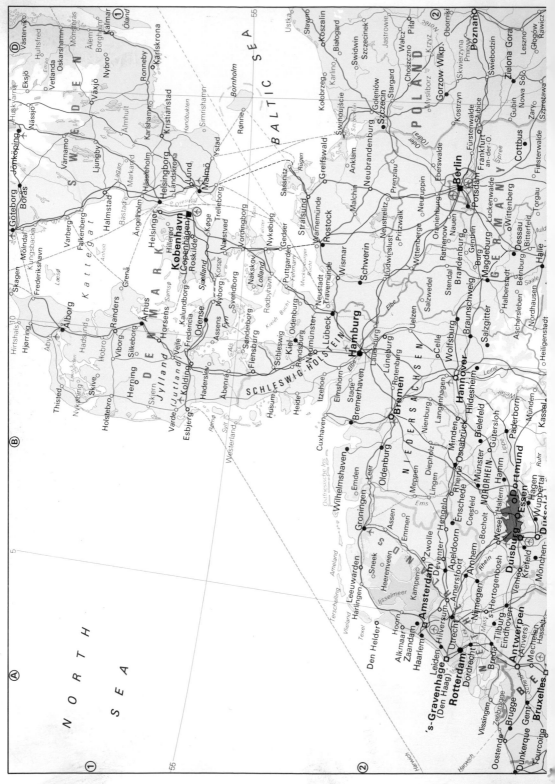

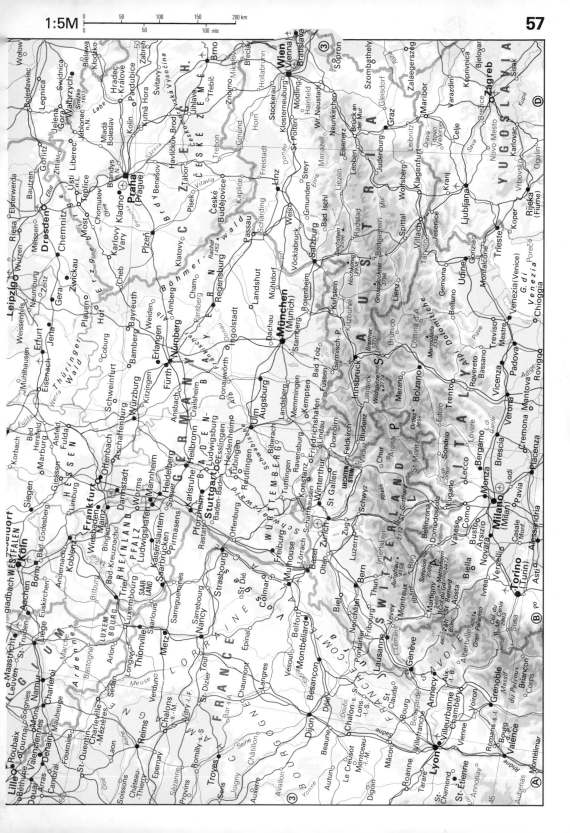

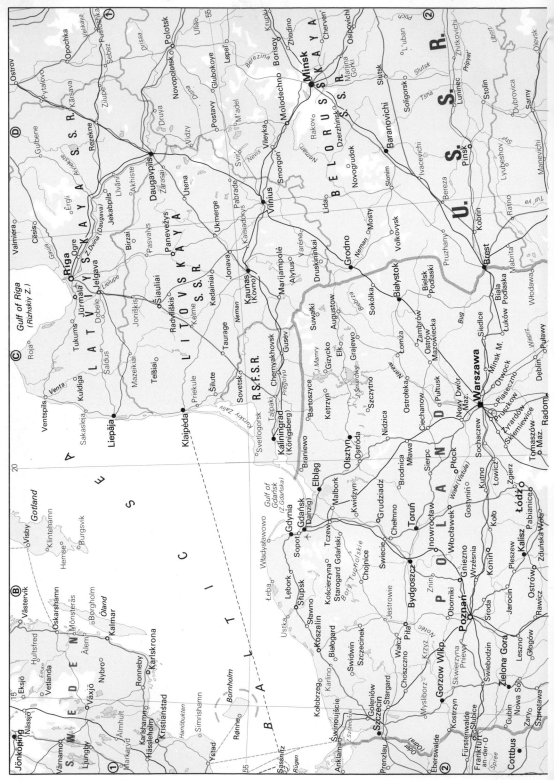

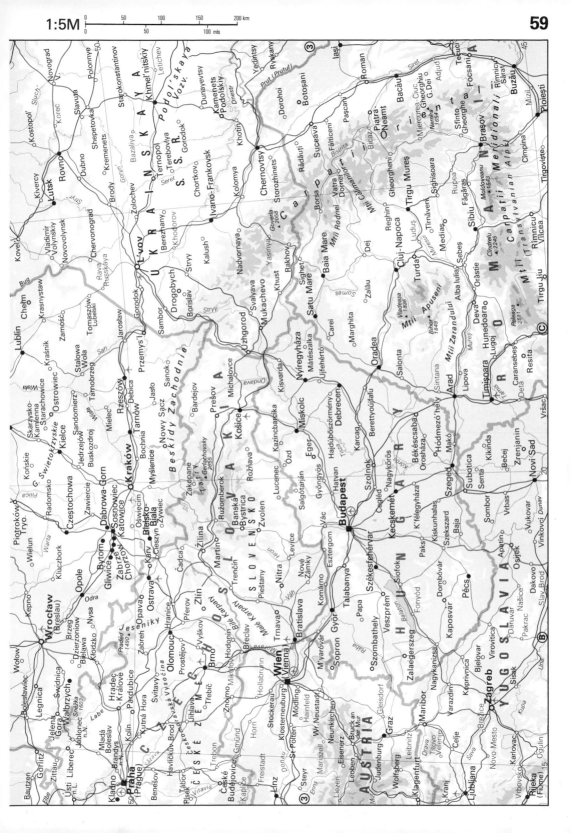

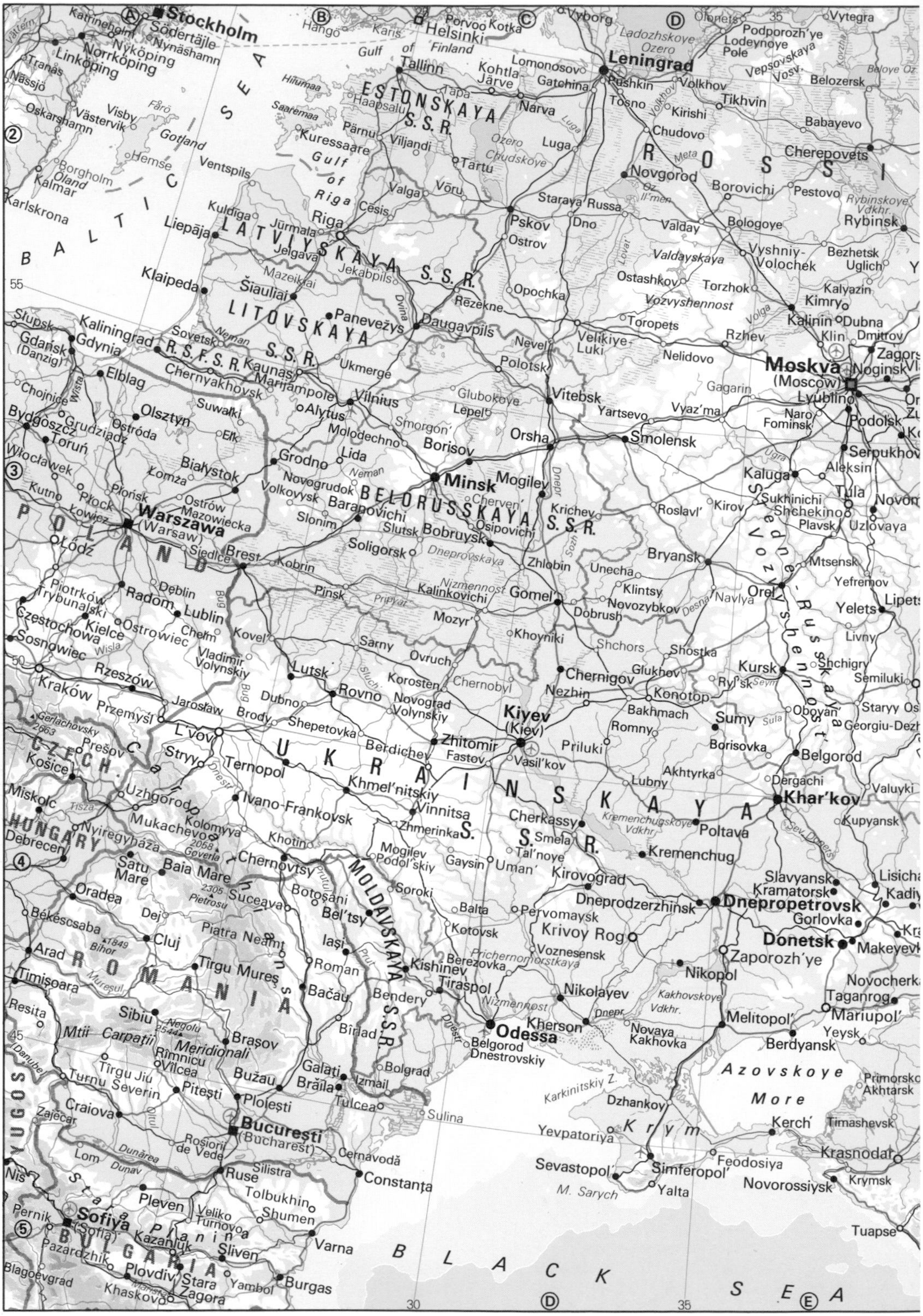

Katrineholm
Södertälje **Stockholm**
Nyköping Nynäshamn
Norrköping
Linköping
Tranås
Nässjö

Hangö Karis Porvoo Kotka
Helsinki
Gulf of Finland
Tallinn Kohtla-Järve
Narva

Visby
Gotland

Oskarshamn
Västervik

Borgholm
Öland Kalmar

Karlskrona

ESTONSKAYA S.S.R.
Haapsalu Rapla
Saaremaa Pärnu Viljandi
Kuressaare Tartu
Valga Võru

Gulf of Riga
Riga Cēsis
Jūrmala
Jelgava Jēkabpils

Klaipėda Šiauliai

LATVIYSKAYA S.S.R.

LITOVSKAYA S.S.R.

Kaliningrad
Sovetsk R.S.F.S.R.
Neman Kaunas
Chernyakhovsk Marijampole
Alytus
Molodechno
Vilnius
Smorgon'

BELORUSSKAYA S.S.R.
Minsk Mogilev
Cherven' Krichev
Osipovichi
Slutsk Bobruysk

Leningrad
Lomonosov Volkhov Tikhvin
Pushkin Tosno
Gatchina Kirishi
Luga Chudovo
Novgorod Borovichi Pestovo
Staraya Russa
Il'men
Pskov Dno Valday Bologoye
Ostrov Valdayskaya

Cherepovets
Rybinskoye Vdkhr.
Rybinsk

Vyshniy-Volochek Uglich
Torzhok
Kalyazin
Rzhev Kalinin Dubna
Klin Dmitrov
Vyaz'ma **Moskva (Moscow)** Noginsk
Yartsevo Lyublino
Smolensk Naro-Fominsk Podolsk

Kaluga Serpukhov
Aleksin
Sukhinichi Tula
Shchekino
Plavsk Uzlovaya

Bryansk
Orel
Kursk

U K R A I N S K A Y A   S.S.R.

POLAND
Warszawa (Warsaw)
Łódź
Kraków

CZECH

HUNGARY

ROMANIA
București (Bucharest)

BULGARIA
Sofiya (Sofia)

Kiyev (Kiev)
Zhitomir Fastov
Vinnitsa
Cherkassy
Poltava **Khar'kov**
Kremenchug
Dnepropetrovsk
Dneprodzerzhinsk **Donetsk**
Krivoy Rog
Nikopol Zaporozh'ye

Odessa
Kherson
Nikolayev
Melitopol'
Berdyansk

AZOVSKOYE MORE

Sevastopol' Simferopol' Yalta
Feodosiya Kerch'

Novorossiysk Krasnodar

B L A C K   S E A

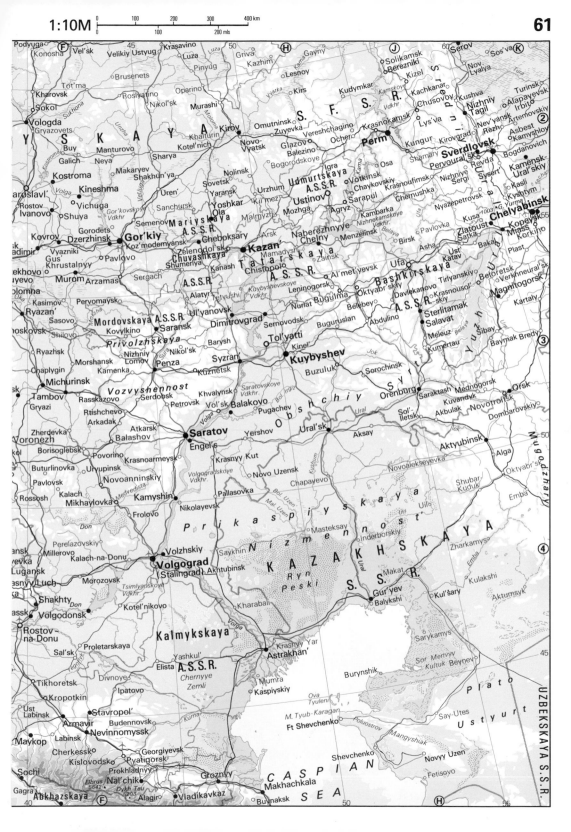

1:45M

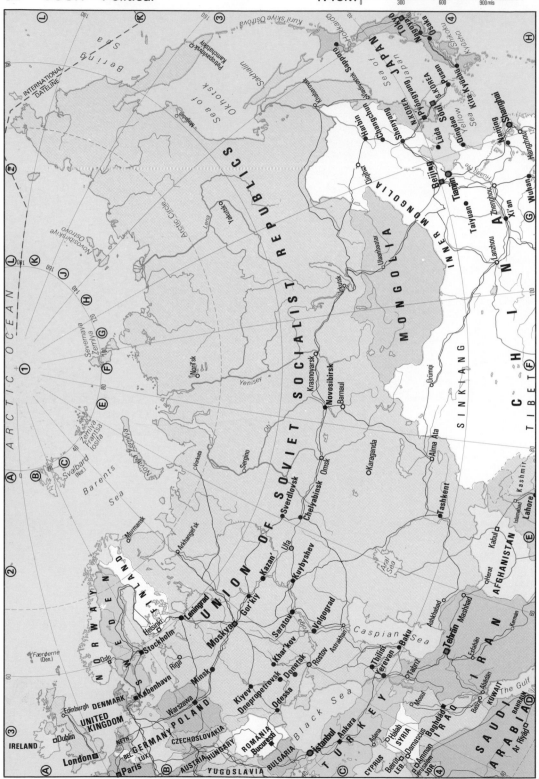

600   1200   1800 km
300   600   900mls

USSR - Political

ARCTIC OCEAN

INTERNATIONAL DATELINE

Bering Sea

Kuril'skiye Ostrova

Petropavlovsk-Kamchatskiy

Sakhalin

Sea of Okhotsk

JAPAN

Sapporo
Hokkaido
TOKYO
Nagoya
Osaka
Shikoku
Kyushu
Kita Kyushu

Yokohama

Sea of Japan

Vladivostok
Khabarovsk

N.KOREA
Pyongyang
Harbin
Changchun
Shenyang
S.KOREA
Soul
Busan
Qingdao
Yellow Sea
Nanjing
Shanghai
Wuhan
Hangzhou

Beijing
Tianjin
Taiyuan
Xi'an
Zhengzhou
Lanzhou

MONGOLIA
Ulaanbaatar

INNER MONGOLIA

Ürümqi

SINKIANG

C H I N A

TIBET

Kashmir
Islamabad
Lahore
Kabul
AFGHANISTAN
Herat

U N I O N   O F   S O V I E T   S O C I A L I S T   R E P U B L I C S

Novosibirskiye Ostrova

Severnaya Zemlya

Zemlya Frantsa Iosifa

Norit'sk

Yenisey

Krasnoyarsk
Novosibirsk
Barnaul

Vakutsk

Ob

Sverdlovsk
Chelyabinsk
Omsk
Karaganda

Alma Ata
Tashkent

Aral Sea

Svalbard (Nor.)

Barents Sea

Murmansk
Arkhangel'sk
Vorkuta
Sergino

NORWAY
SWEDEN
FINLAND
Helsinki
Oslo
Stockholm
Riga
Leningrad
Moskva
Gor'kiy
Kazan
Ufa
Kuybyshev
Saratov
Volgograd
Astrakhan'
Rostov
Caspian Sea
Baku
Tbilisi
Yerevan
Tabriz
Mashhad
Ashkhabad
Tehran
Esfahan
Kerman
I R A N

Faeroerne (Den.)

Kobenhavn
Minsk
Warszawa
POLAND
GERMANY
CZECHOSLOVAKIA
Kiyev
Dnepropetrovsk
Odessa
Khar'kov
Donetsk
Black Sea
Istanbul
Ankara
T U R K E Y
CYPRUS
SYRIA
Adana
Halab
Damascus
Beirut
LEB.
Amman
JOR.
Jerusalem

IRELAND
Dublin
UNITED KINGDOM
Edinburgh
London
Paris
NETH.
BEL.
LUX.
DENMARK
AUSTRIA HUNGARY
ROMANIA
Bucuresti
BULGARIA
YUGOSLAVIA

Mosul
Baghdad
IRAQ
KUWAIT
The Gulf
BAHRAIN
Ar Riyad
S A U D I   A R A B I A
Basra
Abadan

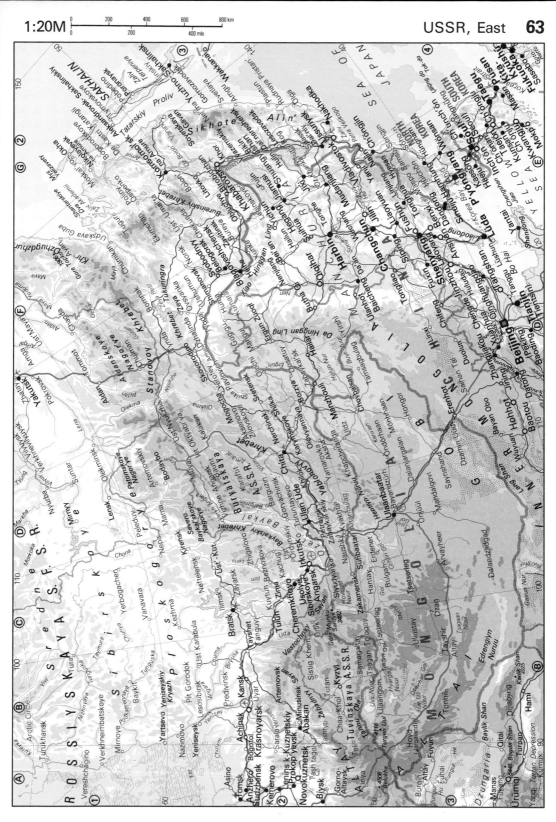

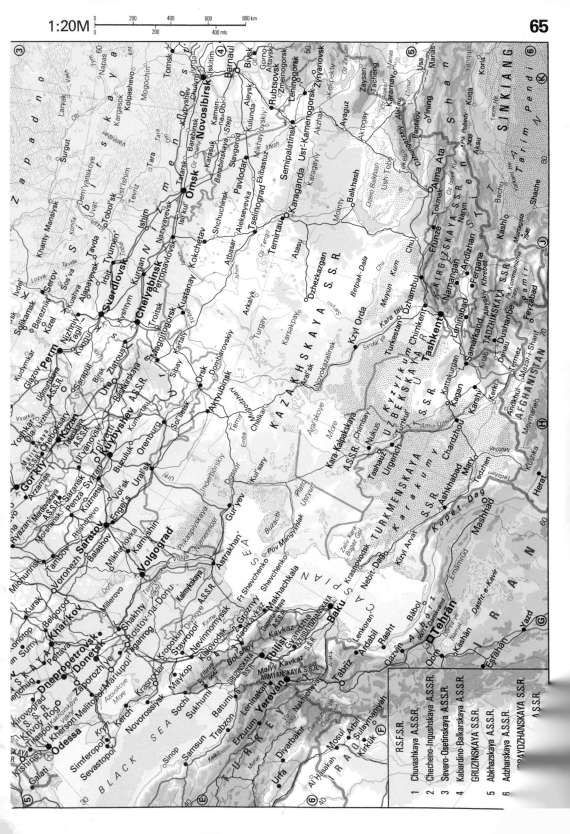

1:20M

200 400 600 800 km
200 400 mls

Legend:

R.S.F.S.R.
1 Chuvashkaya A.S.S.R.
2 Checheno-Ingushskaya A.S.S.R.
3 Severo-Osetinskaya A.S.S.R.
4 Kabardino-Balkarskaya A.S.S.R.
GRUZINSKAYA S.S.R.
5 Abkhazskaya A.S.S.R.
6 Adzharskaya A.S.S.R.
AYDZHANSKAYA S.S.R.
A.S.S.R.

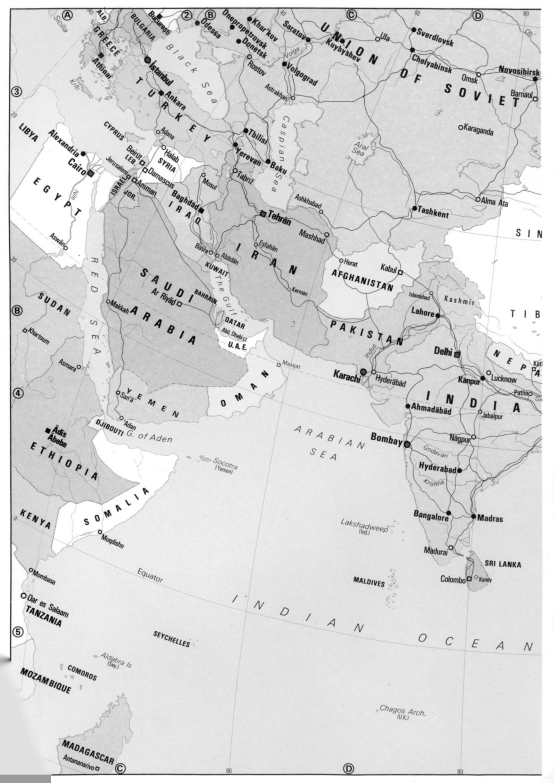

Ⓐ ② Ⓑ Ⓒ Ⓓ

Sicilia
GREECE
BULGARIA
Alb.
Bucureşti
Odessa
Dnepropetrovsk
Kharkov
Saratov
UNION
OF
SOVIET
Ufa
Sverdlovsk
Chelyabinsk
Omsk
Novosibirsk
Barnaul
Kríti
Athínai
İstanbul
Ankara
TURKEY
Donetsk
Rostov
Black Sea
Volgograd
Volga
Kuybyshev
Astrakhan
Karaganda

③ 20

LIBYA
Alexandria
Cairo
EGYPT
Nile
Aswân

CYPRUS
Adana
Beirut
L.E.B.
Halab
SYRIA
Damascus
Jerusalem
ISRAEL
Amman
JOR.
IRAQ
Baghdād
Mosul
Tbilisi
Yerevan
Tabrīz
Baku
Caspian Sea
Aral Sea
Ashkhabad
Alma Ata
Tashkent
SIN

④ 20

RED SEA
SUDAN
Khartoum
Asmara
Adis Abeba
ETHIOPIA
KENYA
Mombasa
0

SAUDI
ARABIA
Makkah
Ar Riyāḍ
KUWAIT
BAHRAIN
QATAR
Abū Dhabi
U.A.E.
The Gulf
Başra
Abādān
IRAN
Tehrān
Eşfahān
Mashhad
Herat
Kabul
AFGHANISTAN
Kermān
Masqat
OMAN
YEMEN
San'ā
Aden
DJIBOUTI
G. of Aden
Socotra (Yemen)
SOMALIA
Muqdisho

Islamabad
Kashmir
PAKISTAN
Indus
Lahore
Delhi
Kānpur
Lucknow
Patna
Islamabad
TIB
NEPA
Kāt
Karachi
Hyderābād
Ahmadābād
Jabalpur
Nāgpur
INDIA
Bombay
Godavari
Hyderabad
Krishna
Bangalore
Madras
Madurai
SRI LANKA
Colombo
Kandy

ARABIAN
SEA
Lakshadweep (Ind.)
MALDIVES

Dar es Salaam
TANZANIA
Equator
INDIAN OCEAN

⑤

SEYCHELLES
Aldabra Is (Sey.)
COMOROS
MOZAMBIQUE
MADAGASCAR
Antananarivo

Chagos Arch. (U.K.)

Ⓐ Ⓒ 60 Ⓓ 80

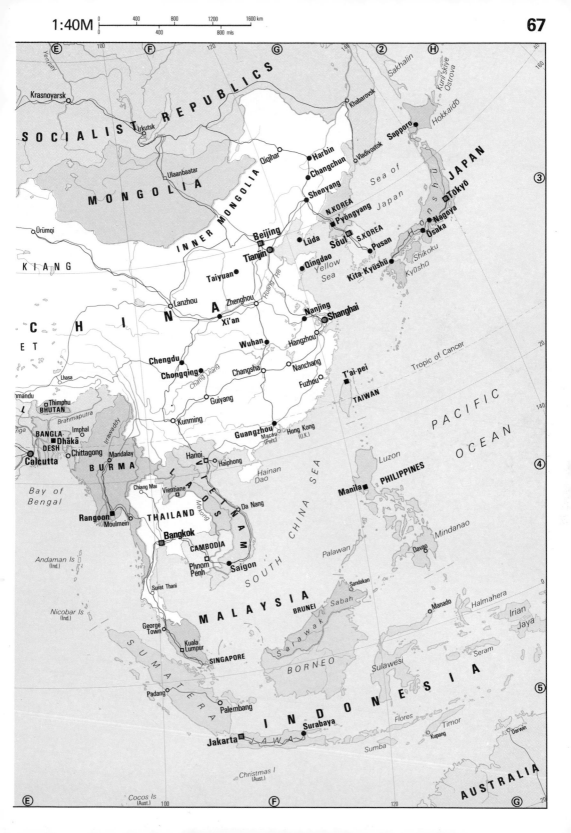

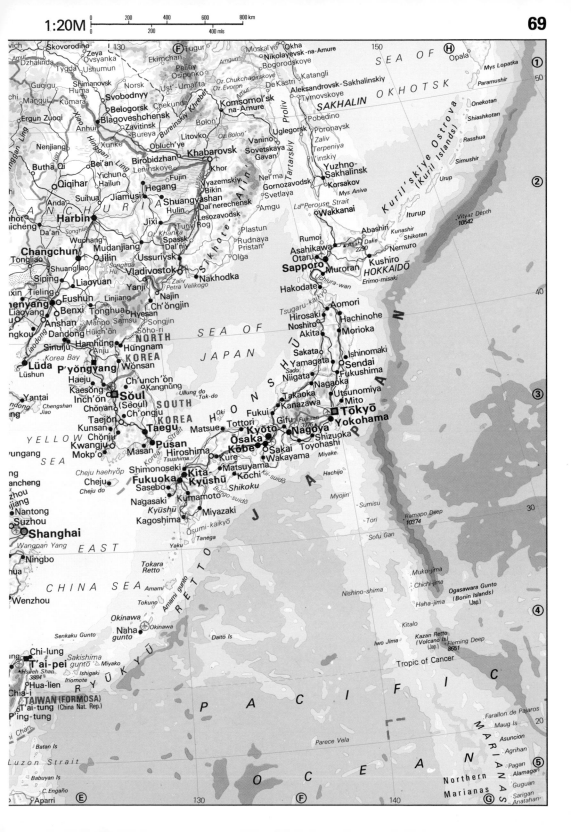

200   400   600   800 km

200   400 mls

SEA OF OKHOTSK

Skovorodino   Zeya   Tugur   Moskal'vo   Okha   Opala

Dzhalinda   Ovsyanka   Ekimchan   PelIny   Nikolayevsk-na-Amure   Mys Lopatka

Tygda   Ushumun   Amgun   Bogorodskoye   Paramushir

Gugigu   Shimanovsk   Norsk   Ust'-Umal'ta   De Kastri   Katangli

Huma   Svobodnyy   Oz.Chukchagirskoye

Kumara   Belogorsk   Chekunda   Oz. Evoron   Aleksandrovsk-Sakhalinskiy   Onekotan

Mangui   Blagoveshchensk   Komsomol'sk   Tymovskoye   Shiashkotan

Ergun Zuoqi   Anhui   Zavitinsk   na-Amure   Pobedino

Nenjiang   Bureya   Litovko   Uglegorsk   Poronaysk   Rasshua

Butha Qi   Bei'an Ling   Obluch'ye   Vanino   Zaliv   Simushir

Qiqihar   Yichun   Birobidzhan   Khabarovsk   Terpeniya

Suihua   Hailun   Iskorskoye   Khor   Il'inskiy   Vityaz Depth 10542

Anda   Jiamusi   Vyazemskiy   Gornozavodsk   Yuzhno-Sakhalinsk

Harbin   Jixi   Bikin   Svetlaya   Korsakov

Da'an   Songhua   Hulin   Dal'nerechensk   Lesozavodsk   Amgu   Mys Aniva

Changchun   Wuchang   Spassk   Rudnaya   La Perouse Strait   **Wakkanai**

Tongliao   Jilin   Mudanjiang   Dal'niy   Pristan'   Abashiri   Kunashir

Shuanglao   Ussuriysk   Oz. Khanka   Olga   Rumoi   **Asahikawa**   Asahi Dake 2290   Nemuro

Siping   Liaoyuan   Yanji   Plastun   Otaru   **Sapporo**   Kushiro

Tieling   **Vladivostok**   Zaliv   Muroran   **HOKKAIDŌ**

Shenyang   Fushun   Linjiang   Petra Velikogo   Najin   Hakodate   Erimo-misaki

Anshan   Benxi   Tonghua   Ch'ŏngjin   Uchiura-wan

Dandong   Manpo   Semsu   Hyesan   Songjin   Aomori

Sinŭiju   Hŭich'ŏn   Sŏho-ri   **NORTH**   Hirosaki   Hachinohe

Lüda   Hamhŭng   **KOREA**   Noshiro   Morioka

Lüshun   Anju   Hŭngnam   Akita

Korea Bay   **P'yŏngyang**   Wŏnsan   Sakata   Ishinomaki

Yantai   Haeju   Kaesŏng   Ch'unch'ŏn   Yamagata   **Sendai**

Chengshan Jiao   Inch'ŏn   **Sŏul** (Seoul)   Kangnŭng   Niigata   Fukushima

Ch'ŏngju   Ullung do   Nagaoka   Utsunomiya

Chŏnan   Tok-to   Takaoka   Mito

SOUTH   Taejŏn   Kanazawa   **Tōkyō**

KOREA   Kunsan   Matsue   Fukui   Gifu   **Yokohama**

Chŏnju   **Taegu**   Tottori   Fuji-san 3776   **Nagoya**   Shizuoka

Kwangju   Masan   **Pusan**   **Kyōto**   **Ōsaka**   Toyohashi

Mokp'o   Hiroshima   Sakai   **Kōbe**   Wakayama   Miyake

YELLOW SEA   Tsushima   Kure   Matsuyama   Hachijo

Cheju haehyŏp   Shimonoseki   **Kita-**   Kōchi   Myojin

Cheju   Cheju do   **Fukuoka**   **Kyūshū**   Shikoku   Sumisu

Sasebo   Kumamoto   Tori

Nagasaki   Kyūshū   Miyazaki   Sofu Gan

Shanghai   Kagoshima   Ōsumi-kaikyō   Tanega   Ramapo Deep 10374

Ningbo   Yaku   Muko-jima   Chichi-jima

CHINA SEA   Tokara Retto   Amami   Nishino-shima   Haha-jima   Ogasawara Gunto (Bonin Islands) (Jap.)

Wenzhou   Tokuno   Kitalo

EAST   Senkaku Gunto   Okinawa   Iwo Jima   Kazan Retto (Volcano Is.) (Jap.)   Fleming Deep 8651

Chi-lung   **Naha** gunto   Daitō Is   Tropic of Cancer

Sakishima gunto   Miyako   Farallon de Pajaros

T'ai-pei   Hsieh Shan 3884   Ishigaki   Maug Is

Hua-lien   Iriomote   Parece Vela   Asuncion

Chia-i   **TAIWAN (FORMOSA)** (China Nat. Rep.)   Pagan

T'ai-tung   Alamagan

P'ing-tung   **PACIFIC**   Guguan

Batan Is   Sarigan

Babuyan Is   Pagan

C. Engaño   **Northern**   Anatahan

Aparri   Luzon Strait   **Marianas**   **OCEAN**

SEA OF JAPAN

HONSHŪ

MANCHURIA

SIKHOTE ALIN'

TARTARSKIY

SAKHALIN

Kuril'skiye Ostrova (Kuril Islands)

RYŪKYŪ RETTO

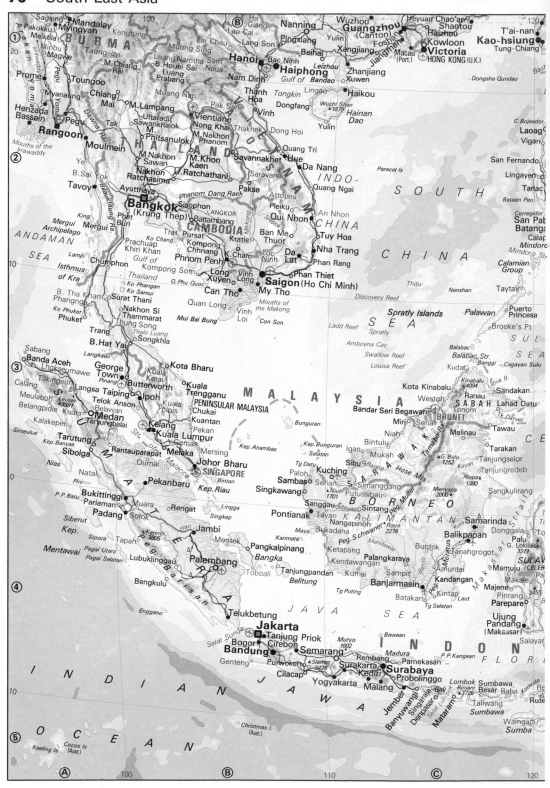

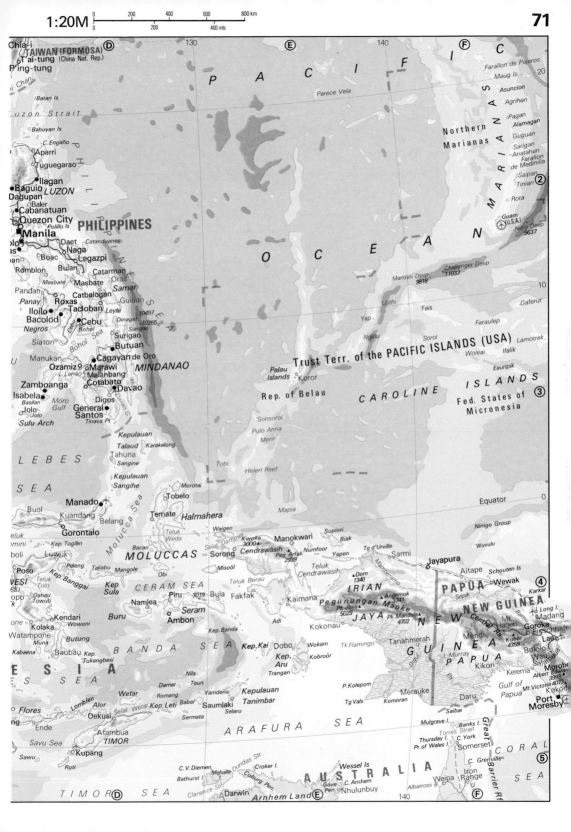

PACIFIC

OCEAN

Chia-i
TAIWAN (FORMOSA) D
(China Nat. Rep.)
T'ai-tung
P'ing-tung

Luzon Strait
Batan Is
Babuyan Is
Aparri
C.Engaño
Tuguegarao
Ilagan
Baguio **LUZON**
Dagupan
Baler
Cabanatuan
Quezon City
Manila
PHILIPPINES
Daet
Boac Naga Catanduanes
Bulan Legazpi
Romblon
Masbate Catarman
Pandan Masbate **Samar**
Panay Catbalogan
Roxas Calbayog
Iloilo Tacloban **Leyte**
Bacolod Guiuan
Negros Cebu Dinagat
Bohol Siargao
Siaton **Bohol Sea** Surigao
Manukan Butuan
Cagayan de Oro
Ozamiz Marawi
Zamboanga Malanbang **MINDANAO**
Isabela Cotabato
Jolo Davao
Moro Digos
Gulf General
Santos Tinaca Pt

Farallon de Pajaros
Maug Is 20
Asuncion
Agrihan
Pagan **Northern**
Alamagan **Marianas**
Guguan
Sarigan
Anatahan
Farallon
de Medinilla
Saipan ②
Tinian
Rota

Parece Vela

Mansyu Deep 9818
Challenger Deep 11033
10
Ulithi
Yap Fais Gaferut
Ngulu Faraulep
Trust Terr. of the PACIFIC ISLANDS (USA)
Sorol Woleai Lamotrek
Palau Koror Ifalik
Islands Eauripik
Rep. of Belau **CAROLINE** **ISLANDS** ③
Fed. States of
Micronesia
Sonsorol
Pulo Anna
Merir

Naro Deep 9637
Guam U.S.A.

Equator 0

LEBES
SEA
Kepulauan
Talaud Karakelong
Tahuna
Sangine
Kepulauan
Sangihe
Tobi
Helen Reef
Mapia

MOLUCCAS

Morotai
Manado Tobelo
Buol
Kuandang Belang
Gorontalo Ternate **Halmahera**
Teluk
Weda
Waigeo

Ninigo Group
Wuvulu

Teluk Tomini
Kep. Togian
Luwuk
Bacan Dampir
Selat Sorong Manokwari
Misoöl Supiori
Kwoka 3000 Biak
Peg. Arfak Numfoor Tg d'Urville
Poso Peleng Taliabu 2930 Yapen Sarmi
Danau Mangole Obi **IRIAN** Mamberamo Jayapura
Towuti Kep. Teluk Aitape Schouten Is
Sula Berau Dom Angemuk Wewak
Namlea Piru 3019 Bula Fakfak 1340 3741 Sepik
Kendari Buru Seram Kaimana Pegunungan Maoke **PAPUA**
Wowoni Ambon Adi Pk Jaya 5029 Pk Mandala **NEW GUINEA**
Kolaka Kep. Banda **JAYA** 4702 Mendi Mt
Watampone Butung Kokonau Tanahmerah **GUINEA** Hagen Goroka
Muna Dobo Wokam Tk Flamingo L. Murray Kubor
Baubau Kep. Kobroör Kikori 4359
Kabaena Tukangbesi Kep. Tanahmerah Kerema
Nila **Aru** **PAPUA**
Damar Teun Trangan Merauke
Romang Yamdena P.Kolepom
Wetar Babar Kepulauan Daru
Lomblen Alor Selat Wetar Kep. Leti Saumlaki **Tanimbar** Mulgrave I.

Supiori
Biak
Long I.
Madang
Finschhafen
Lae
Bulolo
Wau Morobe
Albert Edward 3993
Mt Victoria 4073
Gulf Port
of Moresby
Papua

BANDA
SEA
CERAM SEA
SEA

Flores Ende Oekusi Selaru Tg Vals Saibai Banks I.
Atambua Sermata Komoran Torres Strait Great
Kupang **TIMOR** Thursday I. C. York
Roti Mulgrave I. Pr.of Wales I. Somerset **CORAL** ⑤
Savu Sea Somerset
Sawu C. Grenville

ARAFURA **SEA**

Iron
Range Barrier Rf
SEA

TIMOR **SEA**
Darwin
C.V. Diemen Melville I. Croker I. Wessel Is
Bathurst I. Coburg Pen. C. Arnhem
Clarence Str. Dundas Str. Gove Weipa
Arnhem Land Nhulunbuy Albatross B.
Coburg Pen. **AUSTRALIA**
ESIA

130 140 140
D E F

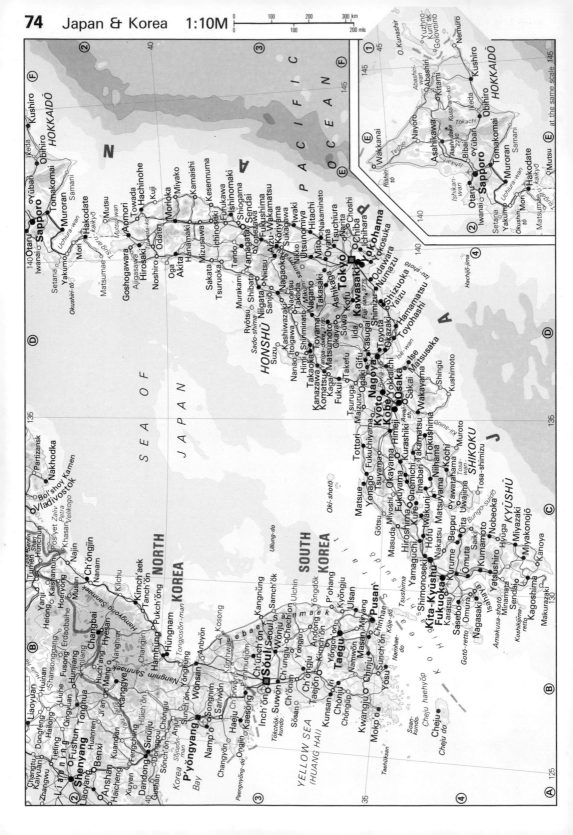

1:5M

0   50   100   150   200 km
0   50   100 mls

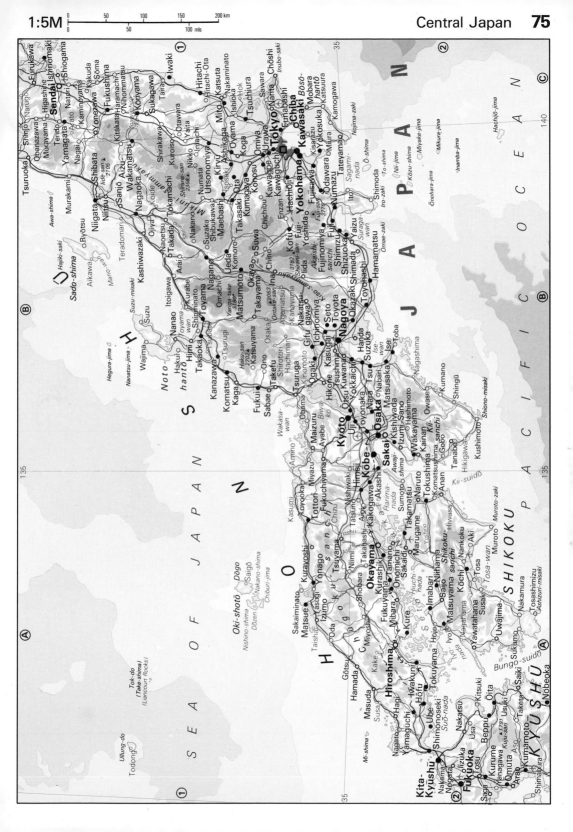

SEA OF JAPAN

PACIFIC OCEAN

JAPAN

SHIKOKU

KYŪSHŪ

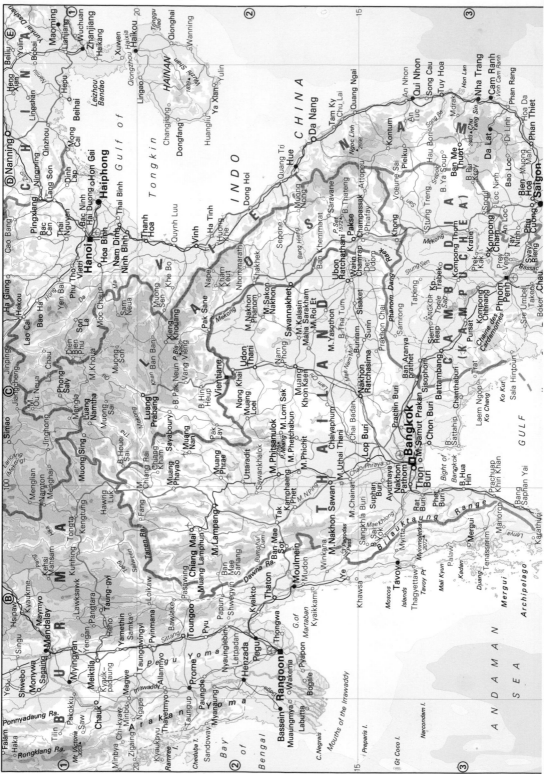

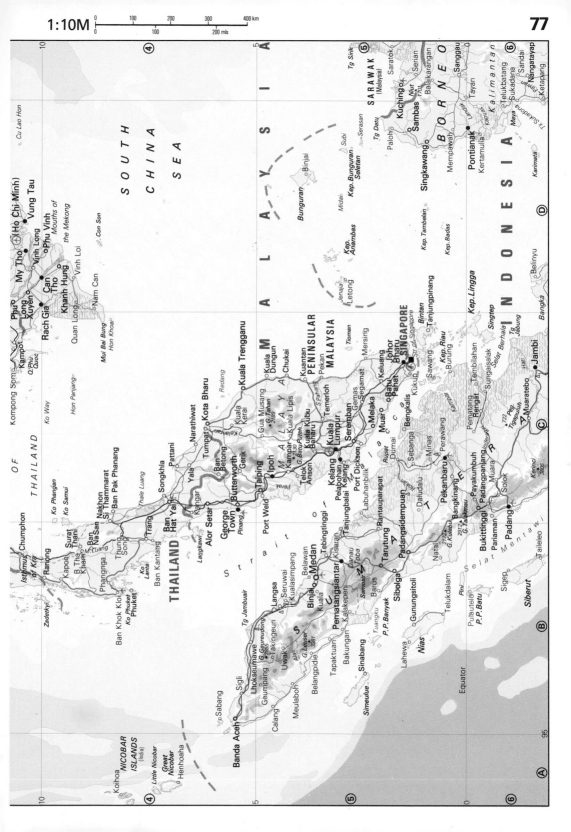

1:10M

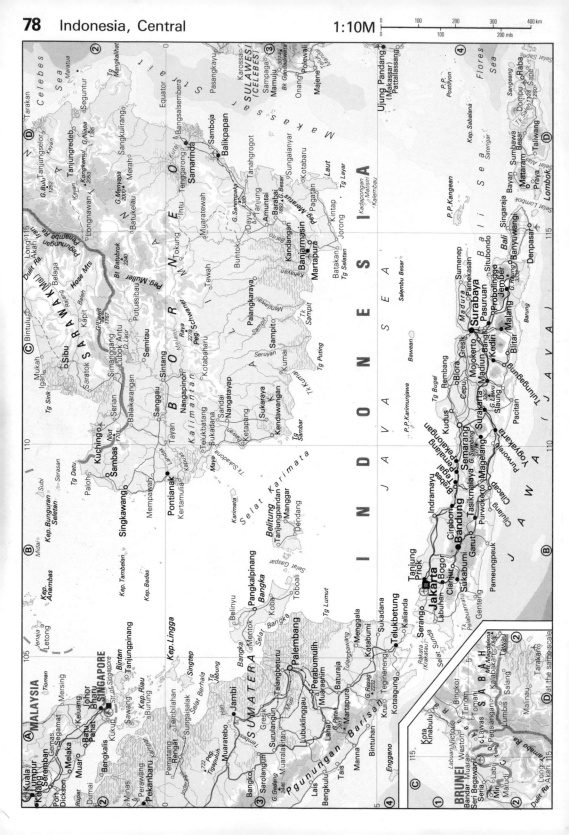

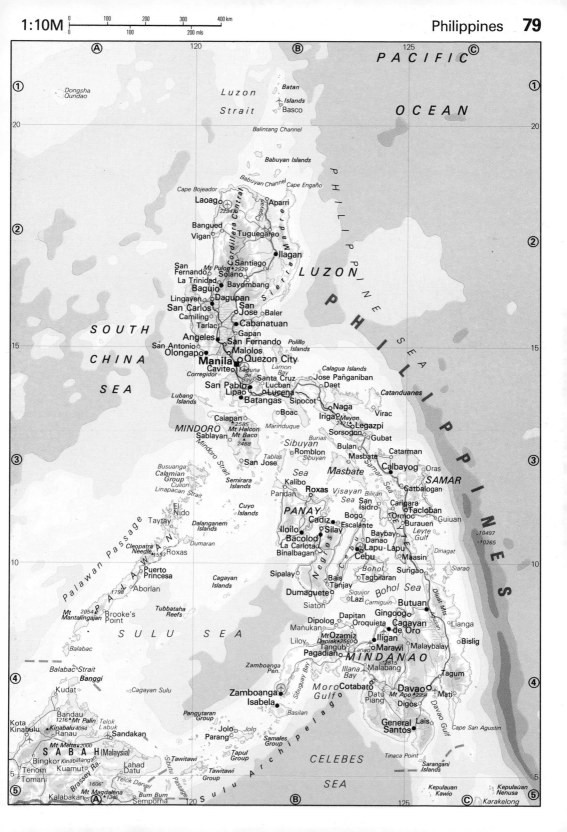

100   200   300   400 km

100   200 mls

PACIFIC

OCEAN

Dongsha
Qundao

Luzon
Strait

Batan
Islands
Basco

Balintang Channel

Babuyan Islands

Babuyan Channel   Cape Engaño

Cape Bojeador

Laoag
2234

Aparri

Banguel

Vigan   Tuguegarao

Ilagan

San
Fernando   Santiago
Solano

Mt Pulog 2929

La Trinidad   Bayombang

Baguio   Dagupan
Lingayen

San Carlos   San
Jose   Baler

Camiling

Tarlac

Angeles   Gapan

San Antonio   San Fernando
Olongapo   Malolos

Manila   Quezon City

Cavite

Corregidor

San Pablo   Santa Cruz
Lipao   Lucban

Batangas   Sipocot

Boac

Calapan   2585
Mt Halcon   Mt Baco
Sablayan   2488

MINDORO

Marinduque

LUZON

Polillo
Islands

Lamon
Bay

Calagua Islands

Jose Pañganiban
Daet

Naga
Iriga   Mayon
2421   Legazpi

Sorsogon

Gubat

Bulan

Catanduanes

Virac

SOUTH

CHINA

SEA

Lubang
Islands

Busuanga
Calamian
Group
Culion

Linapacan Strait

Mindoro Strait

Semirara
Islands

Cuyo
Islands

El
Nido

Taytay

Dalanganem
Islands

Dumaran

Cleopatra
Needle 1593
Roxas

Puerto
Princesa

1798

Aborlan

Mt   2054
Mantalingajan

Brooke's
Point

Balabac

Balabac Strait

Banggi

Kudat

Bandau
1216 Mt Palin
Ranau

Kota
Kinabalu   Mt Melfa 2000
Kinabalu 4094

SABAH (Malaysia)

Bingkor Kinabatangan

Tenom   Kuamut

Tomani   1606
Mt Magdalena 1346

Kalabakan   Ⓐ   120

Semporna

Sablayan

San Jose

Romblon
Sibuyan

Sibuyan

Sea

Tablas

Masbate

Kalibo

Pandan

Roxas

PANAY

Iloilo   Cadiz
Bacolod   Silay
La Carlota

Binalbagan

Sipalay

Dumaguete

Siaton

Masbate

Catarman

Calbayog   Oras

SAMAR

Catbalogan

San
Isidro   Carigara
Tacloban
Bogo   Ormoc
Escalante   Burauen

Baybay

Danao   *Leyte*
Lapu-Lapu   *Gulf*

Cebu   Maasin

Bais

Tanjay   Tagbilaran

Siquijor

Lazi

Bohol

Carniguin

10497
10265

Dinagat

Surigao

Siarao

Guiuan

Bohol Sea

Butuan   Lianga

Gingoog

Dapitan   Oroquieta   Cagayan
de Oro

Dipolog

Manukan   Dapiak 2560
Liloy   Tangub
Pagadian

MINDANAO

Bislig

Malaybalay

Iligan   2815
Marawi   Lanao

Malabang

Ozamiz

Zamboanga
Pen.

Zamboanga
Isabela

Moro

Cotabato   Datu
Gulf   Piang   Mt Apo 2954

Illana
Bay

Digos

Tagum

Davao

Mati

SULU   SEA

Cagayan
Islands

Tubbataha
Reefs

Cagayan Sulu

Pangutaran
Group

Jolo   Jolo
Parang

Samales
Group

Tapul
Group

Basilan

General
Santos   Lais

Cape San Agustin

Davao Gulf

Sarangani
Islands

Tinaca Point

CELEBES

SEA

Kepulauan
Kawio

Kepulauan
Nenusa

Karakelong

Bandau

Sandakan

Lahad
Datu

Tawitawi
Group

Tawitawi

Bum Bum

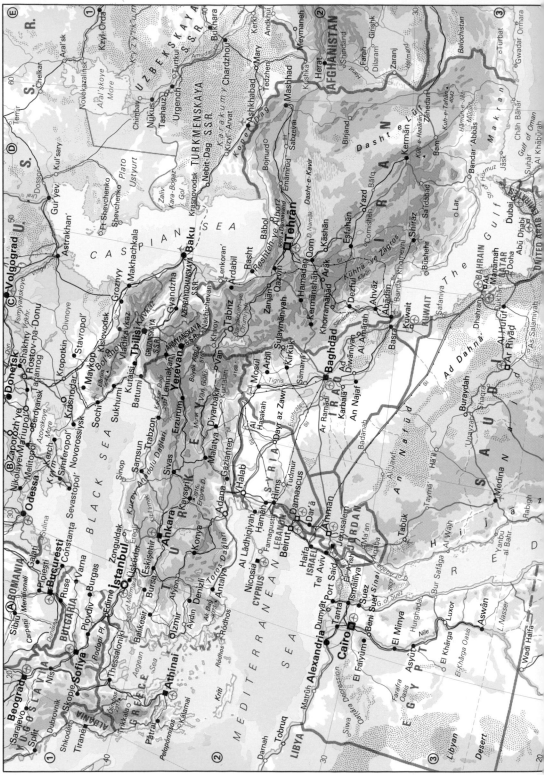

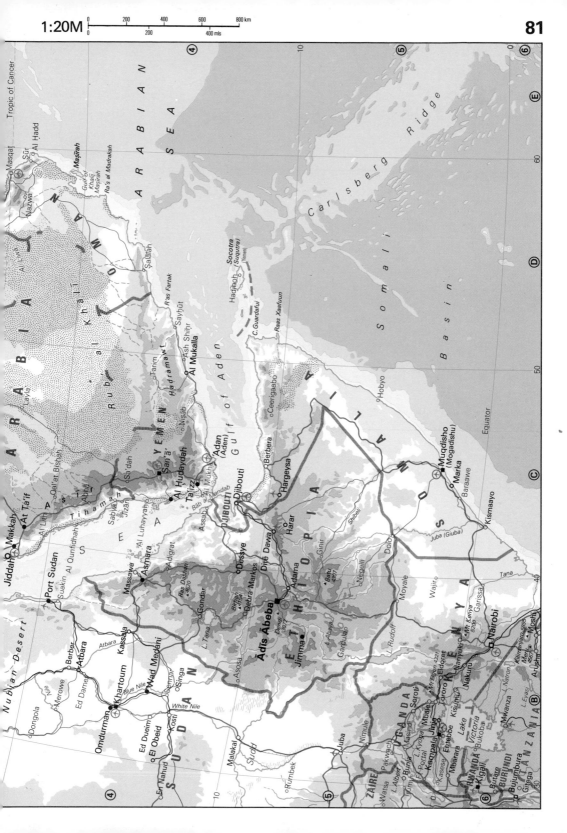

200   400   600   800 km
200   400 mls

Tropic of Cancer

A R A B I A N   S E A

Carlsberg Ridge

Somali Basin

Masqat
Sūr
Al Hadd
Nazwā
O M A N
Gulf of Masīrah
Masīrah
Ra's al Madrakah

R u b '   a l   K h a l i

Şalālah
Ras Fartak
Sayhūt
Ash Shiḥr
Al Mukalla
Ḥaḍramawt
Tarīm
Nişāb
Bīshah
Saywūn

Socotra
(Suqutra) (Yemen)
Hadīboh
C. Guardafui
Raas Xaafuun

A R A B I A
At Tā'if
Al Lith
Qal'at Bīshah
'Asīr
Abhā
Lawlā
Jīzān
Sa'dah
Y E M E N
San'ā'
Al Hudaydah
Ta'izz
Al Mukhā
Tihāmah
Al Luhayyah
Sabyā

Makkah
Jiddah
Port Sudan
Suakin
Al Qunfidhah
S E A

Gulf of Aden
'Adan
(Aden)
Bāb al Mandab
Assab
Djibouti
Berbera
Ceerigaabo
Hargeysa

Hobyo

Muqdisho
(Mogadishu)
Marka
Baraawe
Equator

Massawa
Asmara
Adigrat
Gonda
Ras Dashan
4620
Birhan
4154
Debra Markos

Dire Dawa
Harar
Jijiga
Giinir
Shibeli

S O M A L I A

Dolo
Negelli

Kismaayo

Juba (Giuba)

Tana

Nubian Desert
Dongola
Merowe
Ed Damer
Berber
Atbara
Atbara
Kassala
Kosti
Ed Dueim
En Nahud
El Obeid
S U D A N
Khartoum
Omdurman
Wad Medani
Blue Nile
White Nile
Singa
Sennar
Nile
Ed Dueim

Dese
Desye
Adama
Ādīs Ābeba
Dendi
8012
E T H I O P I A
Jimma
Asosa
L. Tana
L. Abaya
Batu
4307
Gardulla
Movale
Wajir
L. Rudolf
Garissa

K E N Y A
Nairobi
Garsen
Nakuru
Eldoret
Mt Elgon
4321
Kisumu
Tororo
Mt Kenya
5200
Kilimanjaro
5895
Arusha
Moshi
Meru
4565

Malakal
Sobat
Rumbek
Juba
Nimule
Z A I R E
Pakwach
Lira
L. Albert
Butiaba
Masindi
Portal
Kasese
L. Kyoga
Jinja
Kampala
Soroti
Mbale
U G A N D A
L. Edward
Mbarara
R W A N D A
Kigali
Butare
B U R U N D I
Bujumbura
Gitega
Kigoma
L. Natron
Mwanza
Bukoba
Musoma
Lake Victoria
Mara
T A N Z A N I A

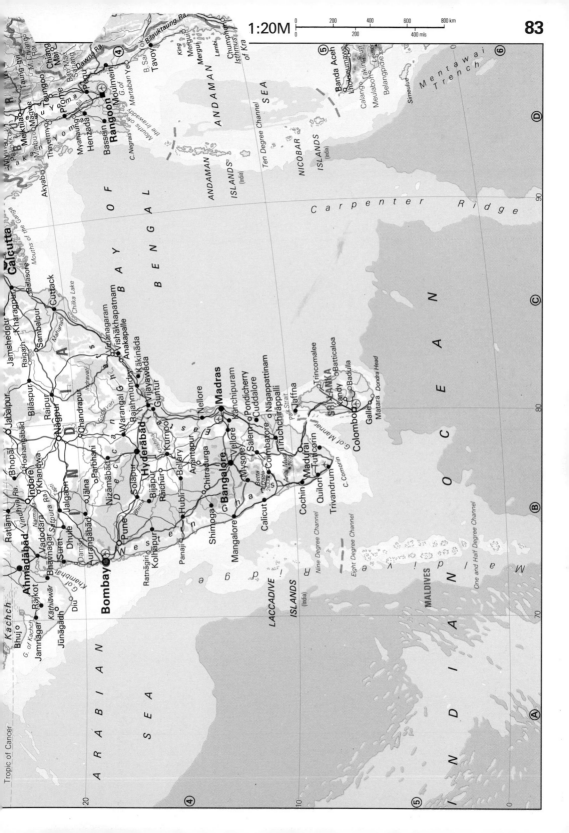

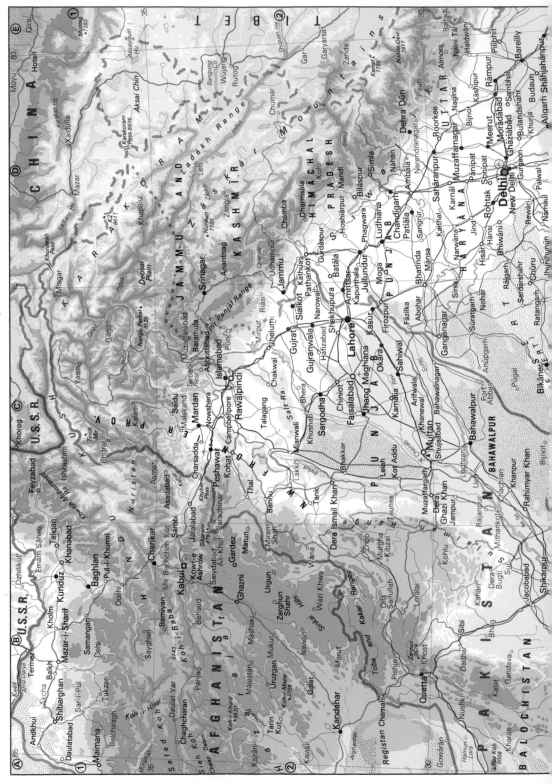

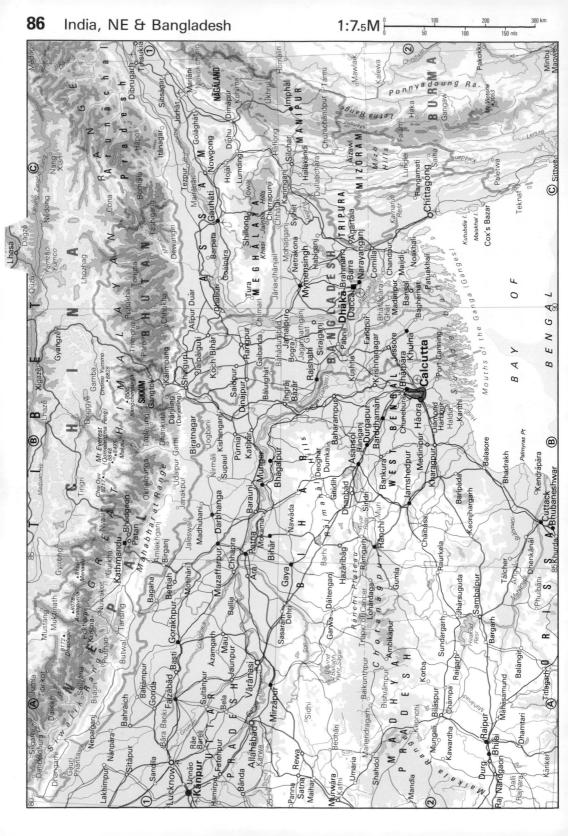

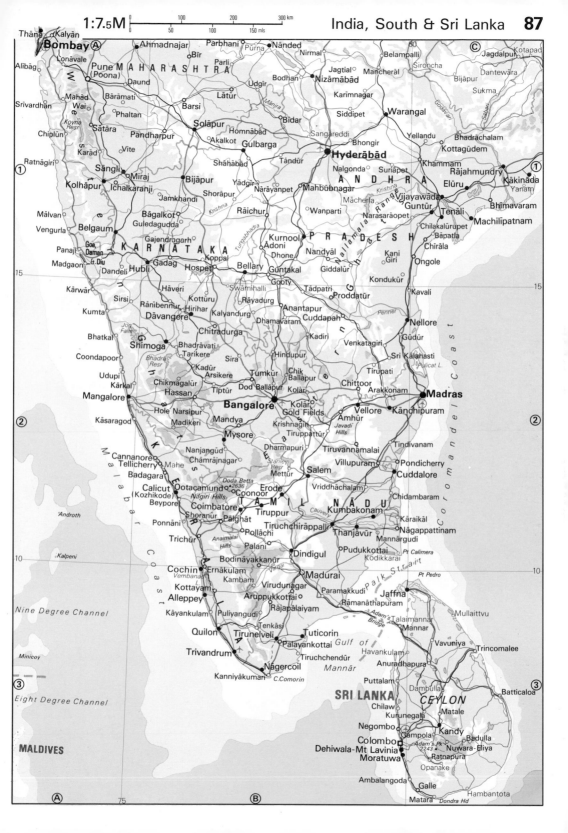

1:7.5M

100   200   300 km
50   100   150 mls

Thāne Kalyān
Bombay Ⓐ   Parbhani   Purna Nānded   Ⓒ Jagdalpur Kotapad
Alībāg Lonāvale   Ahmadnajar Bīr   Nirmal   Belampalli   Sironcha
         Pune MAHARASHTRA   Parli   Jagtial Mancherāl   Dantewāra
         (Poona) Daund   Bodhan Nizāmābad   Bījāpur
Srivardhan Mahād Bārāmati Udgīr   Karimnagar   Sukma
       Wai Phaltan Lātūr   Siddipet   Yellandu
Chiplūn Sātāra   Barsi Homnābad Bīdar Warangal   Bhadrāchalam
       Pandharpur Solāpur Akalkot   Sangareddi Bhongir   Kottagūdem
Karād Vite   Gulbarga   Hyderābād   Khammam
Sāngli Miraj   Shāhābād   Nalgonda Suriāpet Rājahmundry
Kolhāpur Ichalkaranji Bijāpur Yādgir Nārāyanpet A N D H R A   Elūru Kākināda
       Jamkhandi Shorāpur Mahbūbnagar Māchērla Vijayawāda Yanam
Mālvan Bāgalkot Rāichur   Wanparti Narasārāopet Guntūr Bhimavaram
Vengurla Guledagudda   Krishna   Chilakalūrupet Tenāli Machilīpatnam
       Gajendragarh P R A D E S H   Bāpatla
Goa, KARNATAKA Koppal Kurnool Nandyāl Kani Chirāla
Panaji Daman   Ādoni Dhone   Giri Ongole
Madgaon Diu Gadag Hospet Bellary Giddalūr Kondukūr
       Dandeli Hubli   Gooty   Kavali
Kārwār   Swāmihalli Tādpatri Proddatūr
Sirsi Hāveri Rāyadurg   Pennar Nellore
Kumta Rānibennur Hirihar Anantapur   Gūdūr
       Dāvangere Kalyandurg Cuddapah Sri Kālahasti
Bhatkal Chitradurga Dhamavaram Kadiri   Pulicat L.
Shimoga Bhadrāvati Sira   Tirupati
Coondapoor Tarikere   Hindupur Chik Chittoor Arakkonam Madras
Udupi Chikmagalūr Tumkūr Ballāpur   Kolār Vellore Kānchipuram
Kārkal Hassan Tiptūr Dod Ballāpur Kolar Gold Fields Āmhūr
Mangalore Hole Narsipur Mandya Bangalore Krishnagiri Javadi
Kāsaragod Madikeri Mysore Dharmapuri Tiruppattūr Tindivanam
Cannanore Nanjangūd Chāmrājnagar Tiruvannāmalai Pondicherry
Tellicherry Mahe   Mettur Salem Villupuram Cuddalore
Badagara Ootacamund Erode Vriddhāchalam Chidambaram
Calicut Coonoor Tiruppur Kumbakonam Nāgappattinam
(Kozhikode) Coimbatore TAMIL NĀDU Kāraikāl
Beypore Shoranur Palghāt Tiruchchirāppalli Mannārgudi
Ponnāni Pollāchi Palani Thanjavūr Pudukkottai Pt Calimera
Trichūr Dindigul Kodikkarai
Cochin Bodināyakkanūr Madurai Pt Pedro
Ernākulam Kambam Virudunagar Paramakkudi Jaffna
Kottayam Aruppukkottai Rāmanāthapuram Mullaittvu
Alleppey Rājapālaiyam Talaimannar
Kāyankulam Puliyangudi Tenkāsi Mannar Vavuniya
Quilon Tirunelveli Tuticorin Trincomalee
Trivandrum Palayankottai Gulf of Havankulam
Nāgercoil Tiruchchendūr Mannār Anurādhapura
Kanniyākumari C.Comorin Puttalam Dambulla Batticaloa
SRI LANKA CEYLON
Chilaw Matale
Negombo Kurunegala Kandy
Colombo Gampola Badulla
Dehiwala-Mt Lavinia Nuwara-Eliya
Moratuwa Ratnapura
MALDIVES Opanake
Ambalangoda Galle
Matara Dondra Hd Hambantota

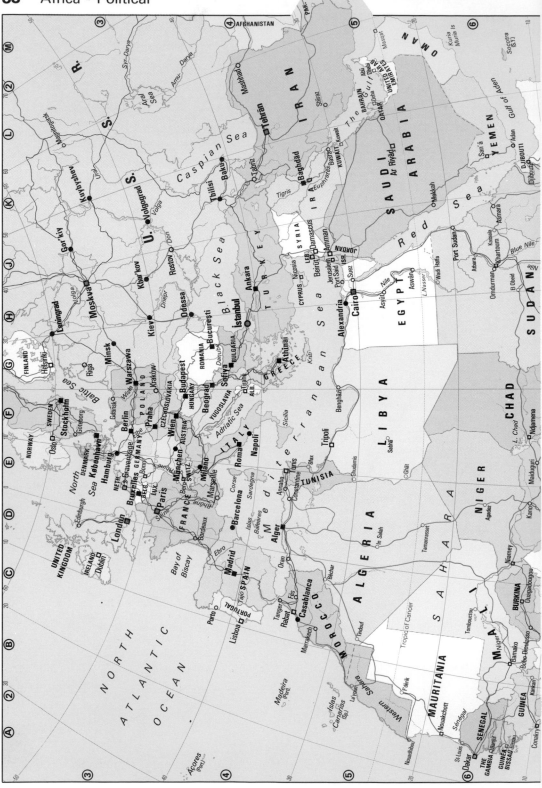

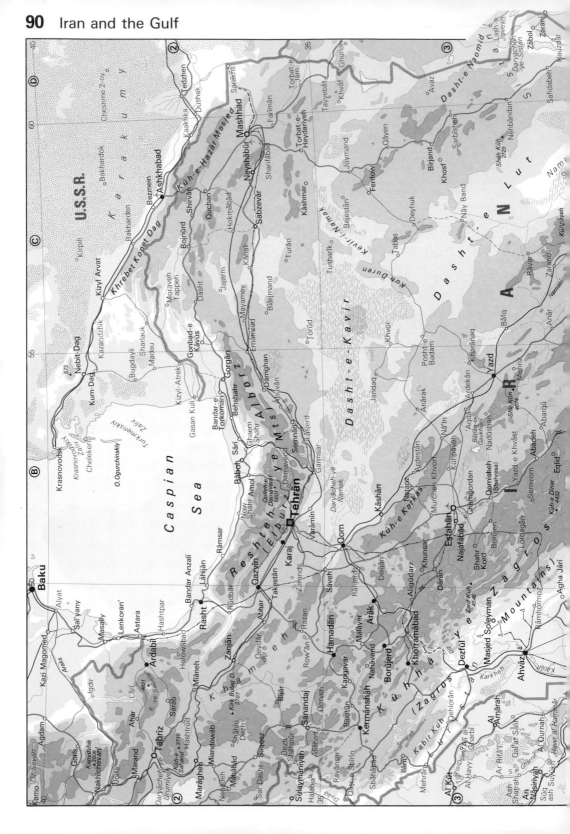

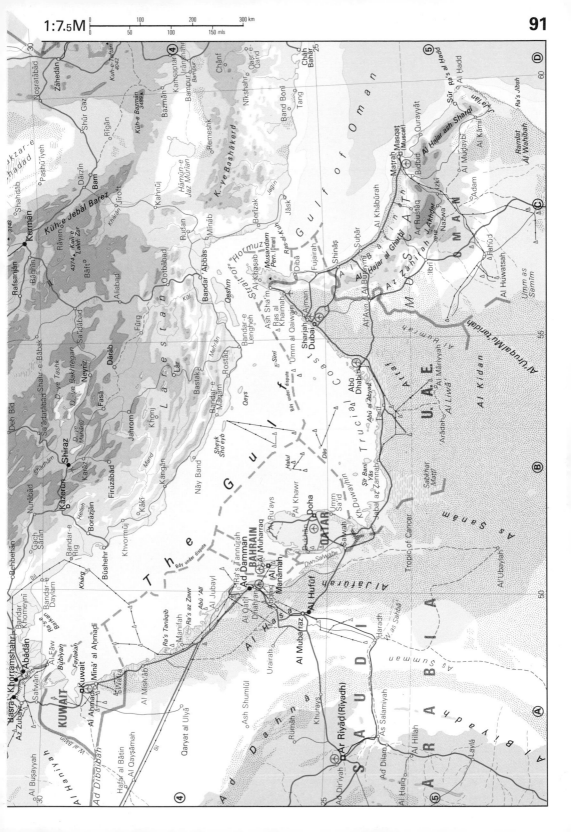

Nosratābād
Zāhedān
30

Shūr Gaz
Rīgān
Pashū'iyeh
Kūh-e Taftān
4042

Bazmān
Kamsaptān
Bampūr Irānshahr
Chānf

Kūh-e Baznān
3498

Bāmp
Nīkshahr
Chāh Bahār
25

Kermān
3143
Shahdād

Kūh-e Jebāl Barez
Rāvene
Kūh-e Lalel Zar
4374
4642
Bāft

Dārzīn
Bam
Kahnūj
Remeshk
Band Boni
Tang
Ra's al Hadd
Sūr
Ra's al Hadd

Rafsanjān
Bāghīn

Sa'ādatābād Shahr-e Bābak
Jīroft
Rudān
Hāmūn-e Jaz Mūriān
Mīnāb
Berīzak
Jāsk
Jagin
Ra's al-Kūh
Matrah
Maskat (Muscat)
Al Ḥajar ash Sharqi
Bidbid
Quraiyāt
Al Kāmil
Ramlat Al Wahibah
Ra's Jibsh

Sirjān
Ney rīz
Qotbābād
Allābād
Kūl
Bandar Abbās
Qeshm
Strait of Hormuz
Ash Sha'm
Al Khasab
Musandam Pen. (Omān)
Dibā
Shinās
Suḥār
Al Khābūrah
Izki
Nazwā
J. Akhdar
3018
Adam
Ra's al Hadd
O M A N

Deh Bīd
Dārāb
Fürg
Bastak
Rostāq
Bandar-e Lengheh
Ra's al Khaimah
Umm al Qaiwain
Al Buraymī
Al Ayn
Ibrī
Fahūd
Al Huwatsah
Umm as Samīm

Shīrāz
Jahrom
Khonj
Lār
Mehrān
Bandar-e Maqām
Qeys
Sirrī
Shārjah
Dubai
Abu Dhabi
U.A.E.
Al Manvīyah
Arāḍah
Al Liwā'
Al Kidan

Kāzerūn
Kafāt
Fasā
Firūzābād
Kākī
Kāngān
Nāy Band
Sheyk Sho'eyb
Qeys
Halūl
Das
Sh. Bani Yās
Jabal az Zannah
Sabkhat Matti
As Sanam

Nūrābād
Borāzjān
Khormūj
Bushehr
Bandar-e Rīg
Bandar-e Daylam
Khārg
Ra's Tanāqib
Ra's az Zawr
Al Khawr
Doha
Umm Sa'īd
Salwah
Tropic of Cancer
Al Ubaylah

Behbehān
Bandar-e Khomeyni
Bandar Māʿshahr
Faylakah
Būbiyan
Ra's Tanāqib
Manīfah
Al Jubayl
Al Qatīf
Dhahrān
Ad Dammān
BAHRAIN
Al Muharraq
Al Manāmah
Al Hufūf
Al Mubarraz
Al Jatūn

Basra
Khorramshahr
Az Zubayr
Ābādān
Al-Fāw
Al Aḥmadī
Minā' al Aḥmadī
KUWAIT
Al Mishāb
Abū 'Alī
Ash Shumlūl
Urairah
Haradh
W as Sahbā
As Sahbā
As Sulaiyil

KUWAIT
Al Aḥmadī
Qaryat al Ulyā
Ad Dahnā
Khurays
Rūmāh
Ar Riyāḍ (Riyadh)
Ad Dilam
Al Ḥillah
Laylā
S A U D I
A R A B I A
Al Biyādh

Ḥafar al Bāṭin
Al Qayṣāmah
Ad Dirīyah
Ad Dilam
As Salamīyah
Al Harīq

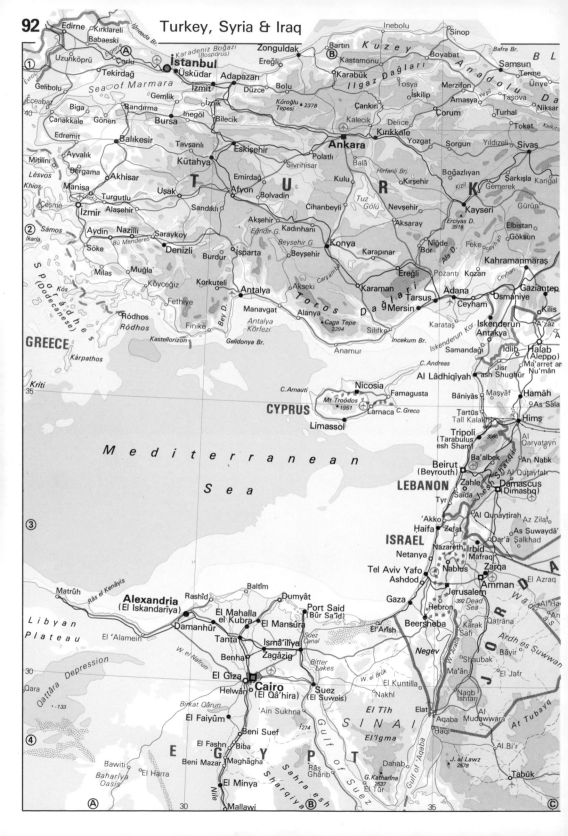

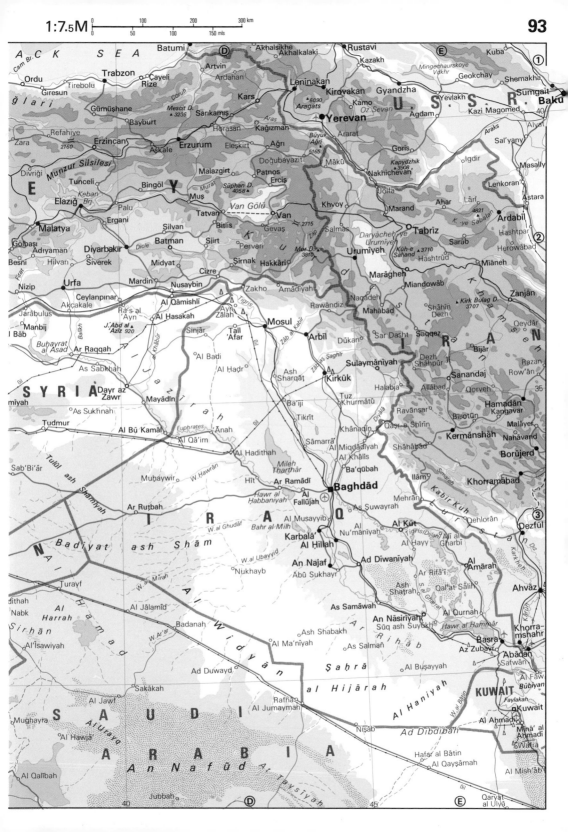

1:2.5M

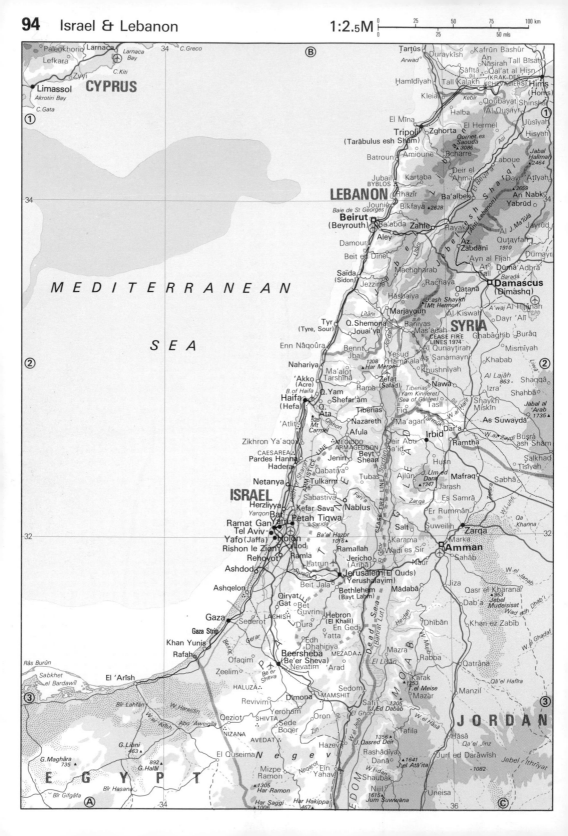

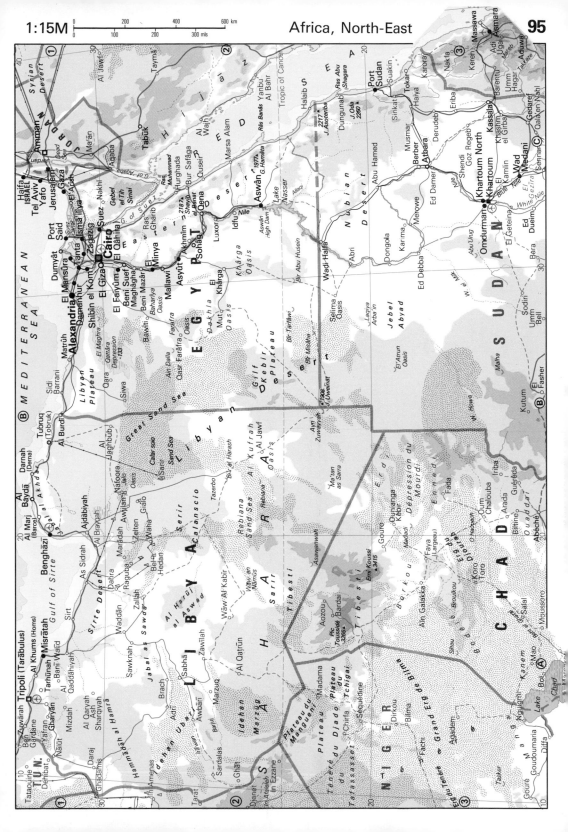

200 400 600 km
100 200 300 mls

Africa, North-East

MEDITERRANEAN SEA

Syrian Desert

Nefud

Hijaz

E G Y P T

L I B Y A

Libyan Desert

Nubian Desert

S U D A N

C H A D

N I G E R

T U N.

Jerusalem
Tel Aviv
Yafo
Amman
Haifa
Gaza
El 'Arish
Suez
Cairo
El Qâhira
Port Said
Alexandria
El Giza
El Faiyûm
Beni Suef
El Minya
Asyût
Sohâg
Luxor
Aswân
Qena
Wâdi Halfa

Khartoum
Omdurman
Wad Medani
Kassala
Port Sudan
Massawa
Asmara

Benghâzi
Tripoli (Tarâbulus)
Misrâtah

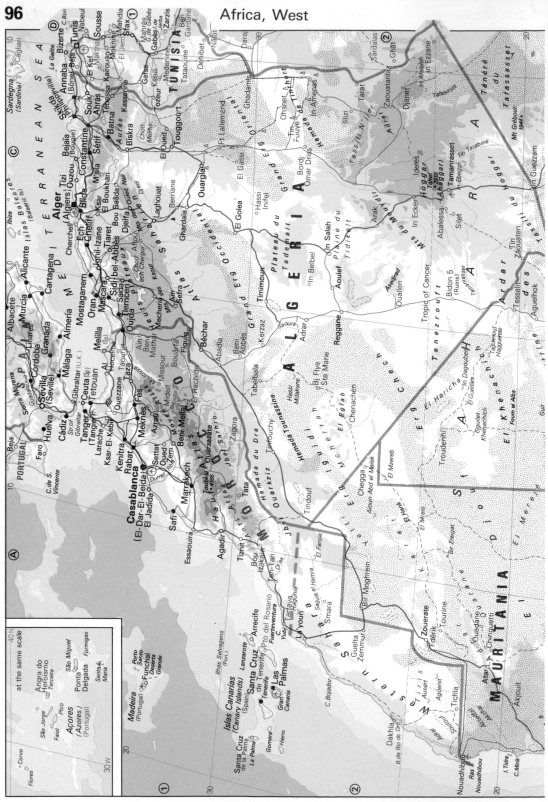

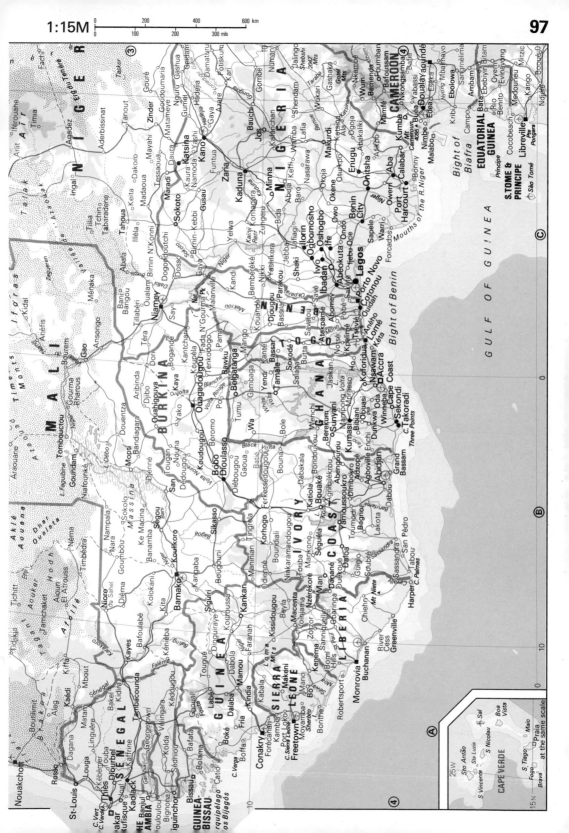

200   400   600 km
100   200   300 mils

③

N I G E R

CAMEROON ④

Aïr

Arlit
Iférouane
Timïa
Agadez
Aderbissinat
Tanout

Bilma
Dirkou

Agadem

du Ténéré

Gouré
Goudoumaria
Nguru
Damatturu
Maiduguri
Dikwa
Bama
Gashua
Geidam
Nguru
Hadejia
Kari
Gumel
Potiskum
Mubi
Yola
Numan
Garoua
Jalingo
Mbé
Mayo
Ngaoundéré

Ingal
Tchin-
Tabaradène
Keita
Tanout
Madaoua
Tessaoua
Dakoro
Mayahi
Matameye
Zinder
Magaria
Daura
Katsina
Kaura Namoda

Kano
Funtua
Zaria
Bauchi
Jos
Gombe
Biu
Shendam
Wamba
Wukari
Gashaka
Gotel
Mts
Banyo
Foumban
Bafoussam
Bamenda
Wum

Kumba
Buéa
Douala ④
Edéa

S. TOME &
PRINCIPE

M A L I

Anéfis
Kidal
Ménaka
Téggéren
Anderamboukane
Andéramboukane
Gao
Ansongo
Bourem
Gourma
Rharous
Gossi
Hombori
Douentza
Bandiagara
Mopti
Djenné
Oualam
Téra
Tillabéri
Niamey
Say
Gaya
Birnin
Kebbi
Dosso
Dogondoutchi
Birnin N'Konni
Illéla
Sokoto
Gusau
Minna
Kaduna
Abuja
Baro
Lafia
Keffi
Nasarawa
Makurdi
Abakaliki
Enugu
Onitsha
Aba
Owerri
Calabar

B U R K I N A

Tombouctou
Goundam
Niafunké
L. Faguibine
L'Débo
Niono
Ke Macina
Ségou
San
Djenné
Tougan
Nouna
Dédougou
Bobo
Dioulasso
Ouagadougou
Koudougou
Kaya
Kantchari
Fada N'Gourma
Bogandé
Kupéla
Tenkodogo
Pama
Kandi
Malanville
Djougou
Nikki
Parakou
Bassila
Savé
Abeokuta
Ibadan
Oshogbo
Ife
Ilorin
Ogbomosho
Oyo
Iwo
Ilesha
Benin
City
Warri
Sapele
Port
Harcourt
Bonny

I V O R Y   C O A S T

Odienné
Boundiali
Korhogo
Ferkéssédougou
Katiola
Bouaké
Bouaflé
Daloa
Gagnoa
Divo
Abengourou
Agboville
Abidjan
Grand
Bassam

G H A N A

Wa
Bole
Tumu
Bolgatanga
Bawku
Navrongo
Yendi
Tamale
Salaga
Wenchi
Sunyani
Berekum
Kumasi
Obuasi
Bibiani
Dunkwa
Oda
Koforidua
Nsawam
Accra
Winneba
Cape
Coast
Sekondi
Takoradi
C. Three Points

T O G O

Mango
Sokodé
Bassar
Kandé
Atakpamé
Notsé
Kpalimé
Palimé
Lomé

BENIN

Kandi
Djougou
Parakou
Savalou
Abomey
Bohicon
Savé
Porto Novo
Cotonou
Ouidah

Lagos
Ijebu-Ode
Bight of Benin
Keta
Anécho
Tsévié

C A M E R O O N

Mamfé
Kumba
Buéa
Douala ④
Edéa
Nkongsamba ④
Bafang
Nkambé
Bafoussam
Bamenda
Foumban
Banyo

**EQUATORIAL
GUINEA**
Bata
Rio
Benito
Mbini
Ebebiyin
Evinayong
Mongomo
Oyem
Mitzic

GABON
Libreville
Kango
Médouneu
Ndjolé
Oyem

Principe
São Tomé

Bight of
Biafra

G U L F   O F   G U I N E A

ⓒ

0

10

ⓑ

L I B E R I A

Monrovia
Buchanan
River
Cess
Greenville
Harper
C. Palmas
Robertsport
Kakata
Zwedru
Tapeta
Ganta
Saniquellie
Voinjama
Gbarnga

**S I E R R A
L E O N E**
Kabala
Makeni
Magburaka
Freetown
Waterloo
Bo
Kenema
Kailahun
Moyamba
Mano
Pujehun

G U I N E A
Kindia
Mamou
Dalaba
Labé
Tougué
Dabola
Faranah
Kissidougou
Guéckédou
Macenta
Nzérékoré
Beyla
Kankan
Kouroussa
Siguiri
Dinguiraye
Dabola

SENEGAL
St-Louis
Louga
Thiès
Dakar
Rufisque
Mbour
Kaolack
Diourbel
Touba
Linguère
Matam
Bakel
Tambacounda
Kédougou
Kolda
Ziguinchor
Sédhiou

**THE
GAMBIA**
Banjul

**GUINEA-
BISSAU**
Bissau
Bolama
Catió
Cacheu
Bafatá
Bissorã
Gabú

Nouakchott
Rosso

MALI
Kayes
Kita
Kati
Bamako
Koulikoro
Kangaba
Bougouni
Sikasso
Koutiala
Ségou
Nara
Nioro
Diéma
Nampala

CAPE VERDE
Sto. Antão
S. Vicente
S. Nicolau
Sal
Boa Vista
Maio
S. Tiago
Praia
Fogo
Brava
ⓐ
25W
15N

at the same scale

④

0

③

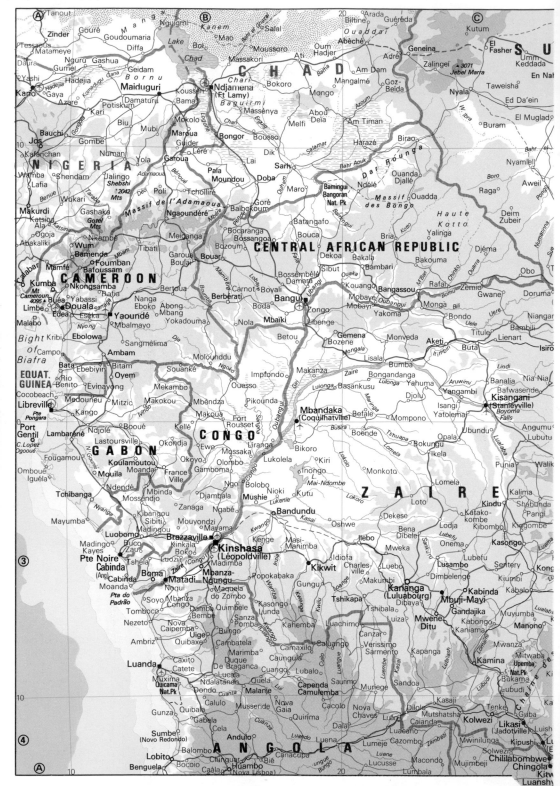

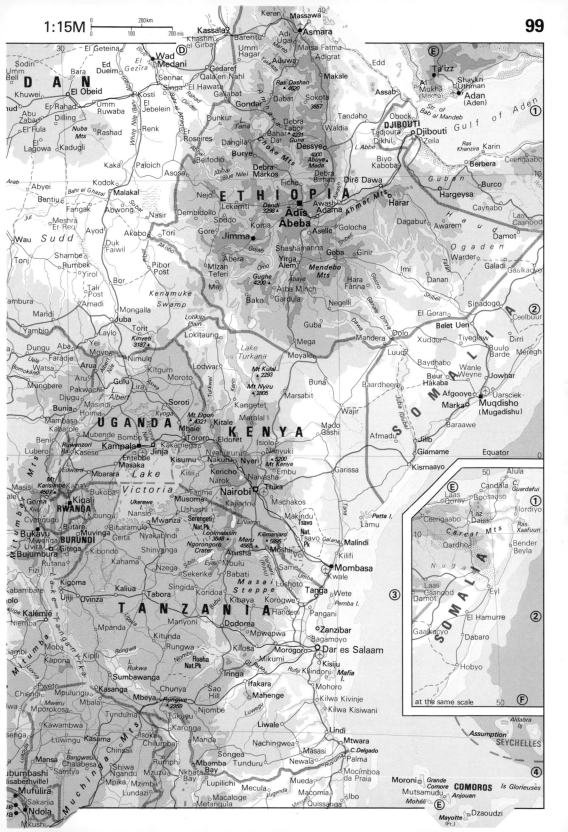

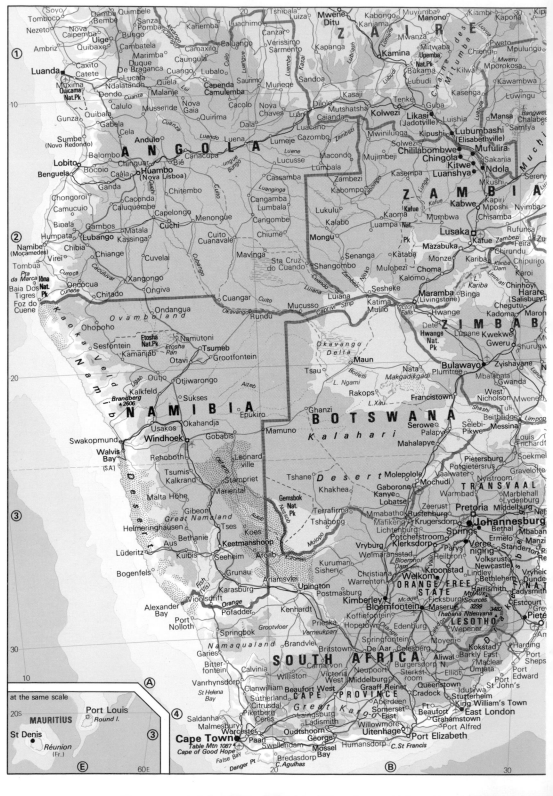

Soyo
Tomboco
Nezeto
Damba Quimbele
Bembe
Sanza Pomba
Quimbele
Luachimo
Tshibala
Luiza
Mwene
Ditu
Kabongo
Muyumba
Manono
Kiambi
Kapona
Kipi
Ambriz
Nova
Caipemba
Uige
Quibaxe
Bungo
Cambatela
Marimba
Camaxilo
Caungula
Verissimo
Sarmento
Kahemba
Canzar
Z A I R E
Mwanza
Kamina
Upemba
Nat.Pk.
Bukama
Lubudi
Chiengi
Pweto
Kilwa
Mweru
Mporokoso
Mpulungu

Luanda
Muxima
Quiçama
Nat.Pk.
Caxito
Catete
Lucala
Dondo
Ndalatando
Duque
De Bragança
Malanje
Cuango
Lubalo
Quela
Saurimo
Capenda
Camulemba
Sandoa
Dilolo
Kolwezi
Mutshatsha
Likasi
(Jadotville)
Kipushi
Lubumbashi
(Elisabethville)
Kasenga
Luishia
Luwingu
Bangwe
Chalabes
Samfya

Gunza
Quibale
Calulu
Mussende
Nova
Gaia
Cacolo
Nova
Chaves
Luau
Luacano
Caianda
Guba
Chililabombwe
Chingola
Kitwe
Luanshya
Mufulira
Sakania
Ndola
Mkushi
Serenj
Muchi

Sumbe
(Novo Redondo)
Andulo
Balombo
Bié
Canacupa
Lumeje
Cazombo
Zambezi
Macondo
Lumbala
Mujimbeji
Solwezi
Kasempa
Kabompo
Lunga
Kabwe
Kapiri
Mposhi
Nyimba

Lobito
Benguela
Bocoio
Caála
Huambo
(Nova Lisboa)
Chinguar
Ganda
Chitembo
Cangamba
Lumbala
Cassamba
Zambezi
Lukulu
Kaoma
Mumbwa
Chisamba
Lusaka
Rufunsa

Chongoroi
Camucuio
Bipala
Caconda
Caluquembe
Capelongo
Menongue
Cuito
Cangombe
Chiume
Kalabo
Mongu
Luampa Nat.
Pk
Mazabuka
Monze
Kafue
Zambezi
Zu

Namibe
(Moçâmedes)
Humpata
Gambos
Matala
Lubango
Kassinga
Chiange
Cuvelai
Mavinga
Sta Cruz
do Cuando
Shangombo
Senanga
Kataba
Kariba
Chirundu
Chipuriro

Tombua
Pta
da Marca
Iôna
Nat.
Pk.
Baia Dos
Tigres
Foz do
Cuene
Virei
Chibia
Curoca
Caculuvar
Xangongo
Cuangar
Cuito
Mucusso
Luiana
Katima
Mulilo
Sesheke
Kalomo
Choma
Maramba
(Livingstone)
Binga
Kariba
Dam
Chinhoyi
Harare
(Salisbury)

Ona
Oncocua
Cunene
Chitado
Ongiva
Ondangua
Rundu
Okavango Strip
Caprivi
Victoria
Falls
Hwange
Dete
Chegutu
Maron

Kaokoveld
Ohopoho
Sesfontein
Etosha
Nat.Pk
Namutoni
Erosha
Pan
Tsumeb
Grootfontein
Okavango
Delta
Maun
Nata
Bulawayo
Hwange
Nat.
Pk
Lupane
Z I M B A B
Kwekwe
Gweru
Shurugw

Ovamboland
Kamanjab
Otavi
Otjiwarongo
Tsau
Botletti
Makgadikgadi
L. Ngami
Plumtree
Zyishavane
Mbalabala
Gwanda

Kalkfeld
Brandberg
2606
Sukses
Epukiro
L. Xau
Rakops
Francistown
West
Nicholson
Mweneze
Tuli
Beitbridge
Limpop

N A M I B I A
Okahandja
Ghanzi
B O T S W A N A
Serowe
Palapye
Selebi-
Pikwe
Messina
Louis
Trichardt

Swakopmund
Walvis
Bay
(S.A.)
Windhoek
Rehoboth
Gobabis
Mamuno
K a l a h a r i
Mahalapye
Pietersburg
Potgietersrus
Gravelotte

Tsumis
Kalkrand
Leonard-
ville
Tshane
D e s e r t
Molepolole
Mochudi
Vaalwater
Nylstroom
Soekme

Malta Hohe
Mariental
Gemsbok
Nat.
Pk
Khakhea
Gaborone
Kanye
Lobatse
Zeerust
Warmbad
T R A N S V A A L
Marblehall
Lydenburg
Nel

Gibeon
Helmeringhausen
Tses
Terrafirma
Tshabong
Mmabatho
Mafikeng
Rustenburg
Krugersdorp
Lichtenburg
Pretoria
Middelburg
Johannesburg
Mbaban

Bethanie
Koes
Molopo
Kuruman
Sishen
Vryburg
Potchefstroom
Klerksdorp
Parys
Springs
Bethal
Ermelo
Manzi

Lüderitz
Aus
Keetmanshoop
Seeheim
Christiana
Wolmaransstad
Bloem-
hof
Heilbron
Vereeniging
Volksrust
Standerton

Bogenfels
Kuibis
Grunau
Ariamsvlei
Warrenton
Kimberley
Kroonstad
Lindley
Newcastle
Vryheid
Dunde

Fish
(Visl)
Karasburg
Vioolsdrift
Orange
Upington
Postmasburg
Welkom
O R A N G E F R E E
S T A T E
Bethlehem
Harrismith
Ladysmith
Estcourt

Alexander
Bay
Port
Nolloth
Pofadder
Kenhardt
Prieska
Hopetown
Koffiefontein
Bloemfontein
Maseru
Ficksburg
Sources
3299
Thabana Ntlenyana
3482
L E S O T H O
Wepener
Piete

Springbok
Grootvloer
Verneukpan
Springfontein
De Aar
Colesberg
Moyeni
Kokstad
Harding
Port
Sheps

Garies
Brandvlei
Britstown
Aliwal
North
Burgersdorp
Barkly East
Maclear
Port
Edward

N a m a q u a l a n d
Bitter-
fontein
Calvinia
Williston
Carnarvon
Victoria
West
Middelburg
Sterk-
stroom
Elliot
Umtata
St John's

Vanrhynsdorp
Clanwilliam
Beaufort West
Graaff Reinet
Aberdeen
Queenstown
Idutwa
King William's Town

St Helena
Bay
Sutherland
Citrusdal
Piketberg
Ceres
C A P E   P R O V I N C E
G r e a t   K a r o o
Somerset
East
Cradock
Fort
Beaufort
East London

Saldanha
Malmesbury
Worcester
Paarl
Laingsburg
Ladismith
Oudtshoorn
George
Willowmore
Uitenhage
Grahamstown
Port Alfred

Cape Town
Table Mtn 1087
Cape of Good Hope
False Bay
Swellendam
Mossel
Bay
Humansdorp
Port Elizabeth

Bredasdorp
Danger Pt
C. Agulhas
C. St Francis

A N G O L A

Z A M B I A

N A M I B I A

S O U T H   A F R I C A

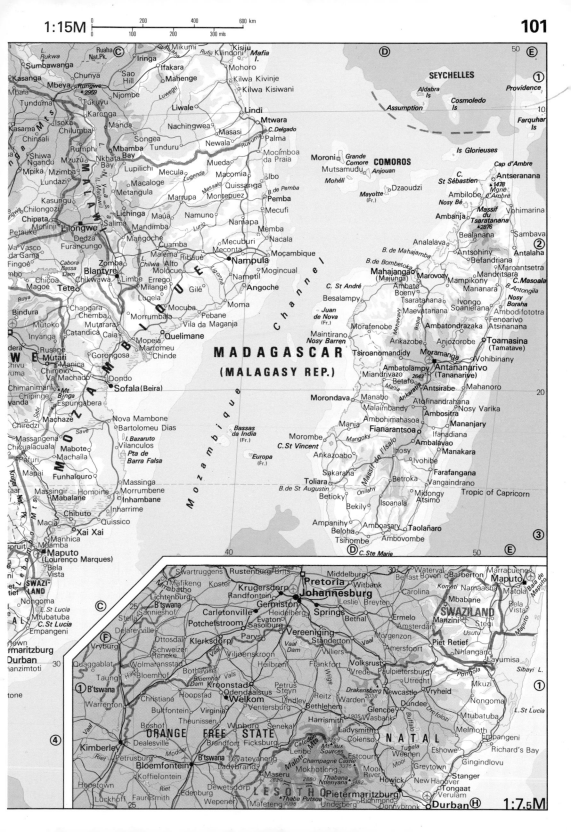

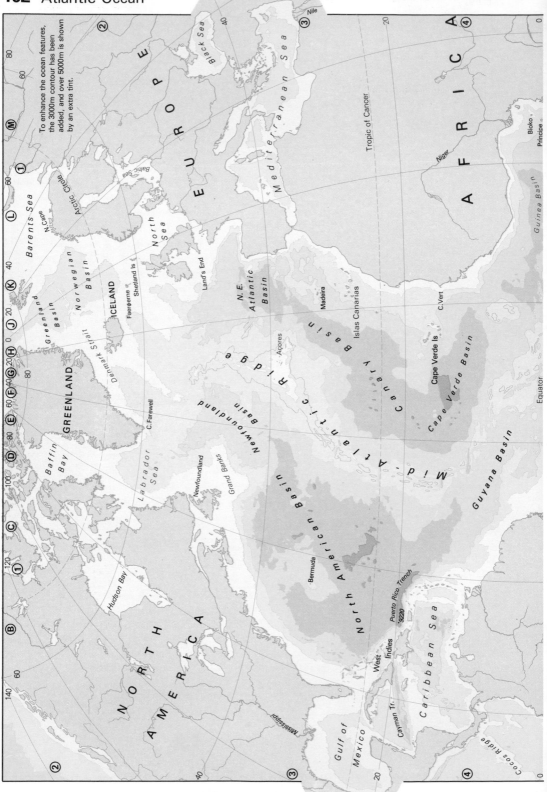

To enhance the ocean features, the 3000m contour has been added, and over 5000m is shown by an extra tint.

EUROPE

AFRICA

NORTH AMERICA

GREENLAND

ICELAND

Barents Sea

Black Sea

Mediterranean Sea

Nile

Tropic of Cancer

Niger

Guinea Basin

Bioko

Príncipe

Baltic Sea

North Sea

Norwegian Basin

Greenland Basin

Denmark Strait

Arctic Circle

N.Cape

Land's End

Faerøerne

Shetland Is

N.E. Atlantic Basin

Madeira

Islas Canarias

C.Vert

Cape Verde Is

Canary Basin

Cape Verde Basin

Açores

Mid-Atlantic Ridge

Newfoundland Basin

Baffin Bay

Labrador Sea

C.Farewell

Newfoundland

Grand Banks

North American Basin

Bermuda

Guyana Basin

Equator

Puerto Rico Trench

9220

West Indies

Caribbean Sea

Cayman Tr.

Hudson Bay

Gulf of Mexico

Mississippi

Cocos Ridge

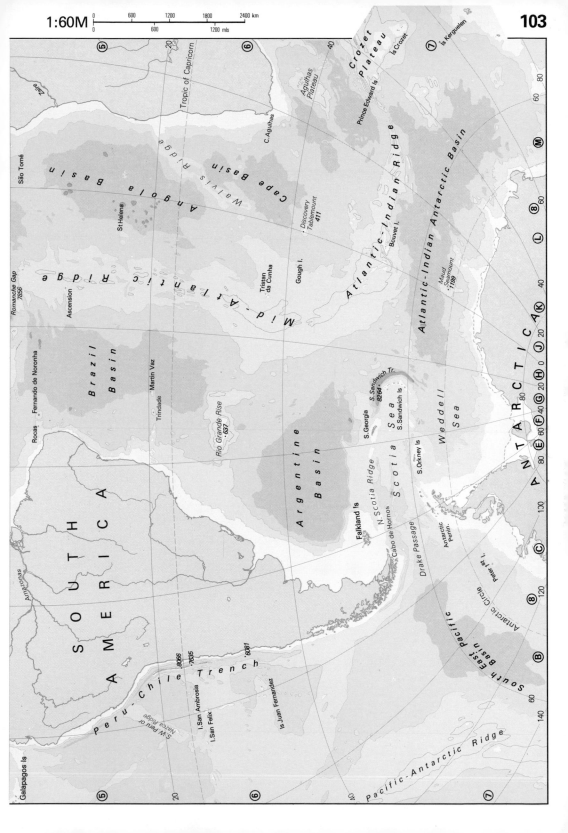

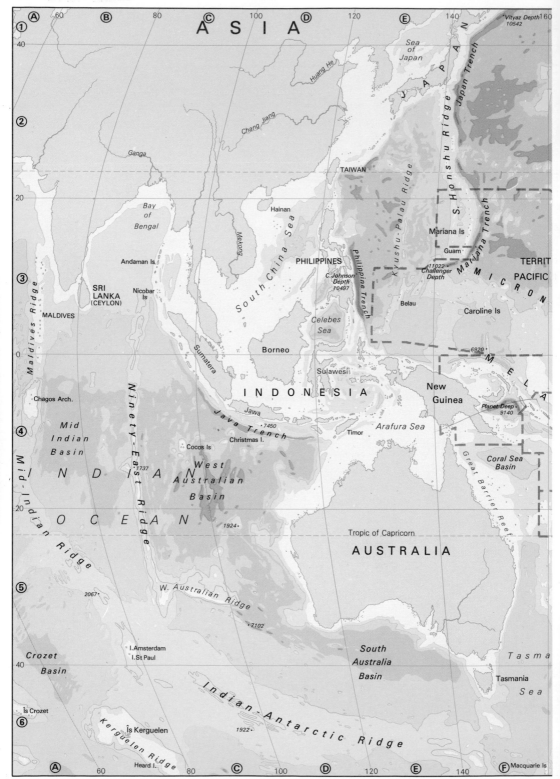

*Vityaz Depth 160
10542

A S I A

Sea
of
Japan

Huang He

Chang Jiang

Ganga

TAIWAN

Bay
of
Bengal

Hainan

Andaman Is.

SRI
LANKA
(CEYLON)

Nicobar
Is

MALDIVES

Maldives Ridge

Chagos Arch.

Mekong

South China Sea

PHILIPPINES

C.Johnson
Depth
10497

Celebes
Sea

Borneo

Sulawesi

I N D O N E S I A

Sumatera

Java Trench

•7450

Jawa

Cocos Is

Christmas I.

•1737

West
Australian
Basin

•1924

Mid
Indian
Basin

I N D I A N

Ninety-East Ridge

O C E A N

Mid-Indian Ridge

2067•

W. Australian Ridge

•7102

Crozet
Basin

40

I.Amsterdam
I.St Paul

Îs Crozet

Kerguelen Ridge

Îs Kerguelen

•1922

Heard I.

Indian-Antarctic Ridge

Timor

Arafura Sea

Tropic of Capricorn

A U S T R A L I A

South
Australia
Basin

Kyushu-Palau Ridge

Philippine Trench

S. Honshu Ridge

Japan Trench

Mariana Trench

Mariana Is

Guam

11022
Challenger
Depth

Belau

Caroline Is

M I C R O N

TERRIT
PACIFIC

6920•

M E L A

New
Guinea

Planet Deep
9140

Great Barrier Reef

Coral Sea
Basin

T a s m a

Tasmania

Sea

Macquarie Is

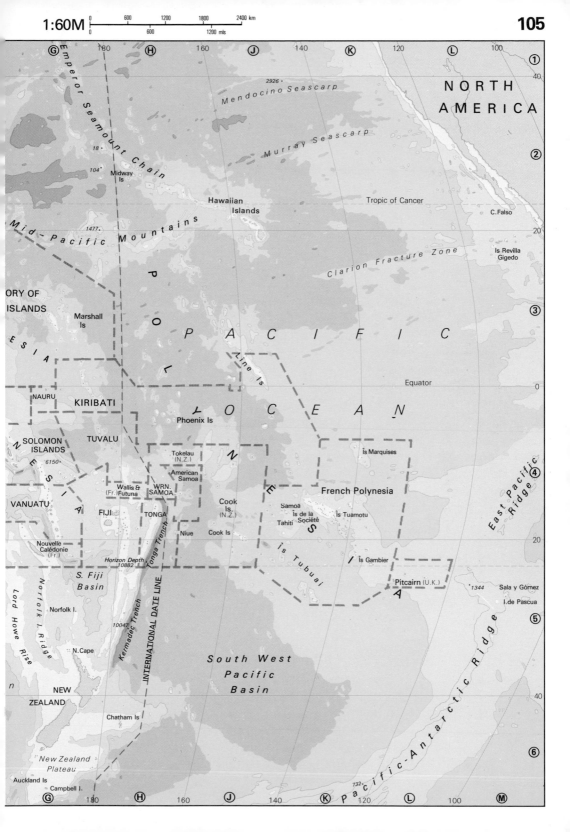

1:60M

600   1200   1800   2400 km

600   1200 mls

G   180   H   160   J   140   K   120   L   100

① 40

N O R T H
A M E R I C A

2926·
Mendocino Seascarp

②

Murray Seascarp

18·

104· Midway
        Is

Hawaiian
Islands   Tropic of Cancer

C.Falso   20

Mid - Pacific Mountains   1477·

Clarion Fracture Zone   Is Revilla
Gigedo

P
O
L   ORY OF
ISLANDS

Marshall
Is   ③

E
S   *Line Is*
I
A   Equator   0

NAURU

KIRIBATI   P   A   C   I   F   I   C

Phoenix Is   Y   O   C   E   A   N

TUVALU

SOLOMON
ISLANDS   6150·   Tokelau
                          (N.Z.)   Îs Marquises   ④

Wallis &   American
M   (Fr.)Futuna   Samoa
E   WRN.
L   VANUATU   SAMOA
A   FIJI   Cook   French Polynesia
N   TONGA   Is.
E   (N.Z.)   Samoa   Îs de la   Îs Tuamotu
S   Niue   Cook Is   Tahiti   Société
I   Nouvelle   A   Îs Tubuai   Îs Gambier   20
A   Calédonie
    (Fr.)   Horizon Depth
              10882

S. Fiji   Pitcairn (U.K.)   1344·   Sala y Gómez
Basin   I.de Pascua

Norfolk I.   10042   ⑤

N.Cape   *South West*
              Pacific
              Basin

NEW   40
ZEALAND

Chatham Is

New Zealand
Plateau   ⑥

Auckland Is   Campbell I.

G   180   H   160   J   140   K   120   L   100   M

732·

East Pacific Ridge

Pacific-Antarctic Ridge

Lord Howe Rise

Norfolk I. Ridge

INTERNATIONAL DATE LINE

Kermadec Trench

Tonga Trench

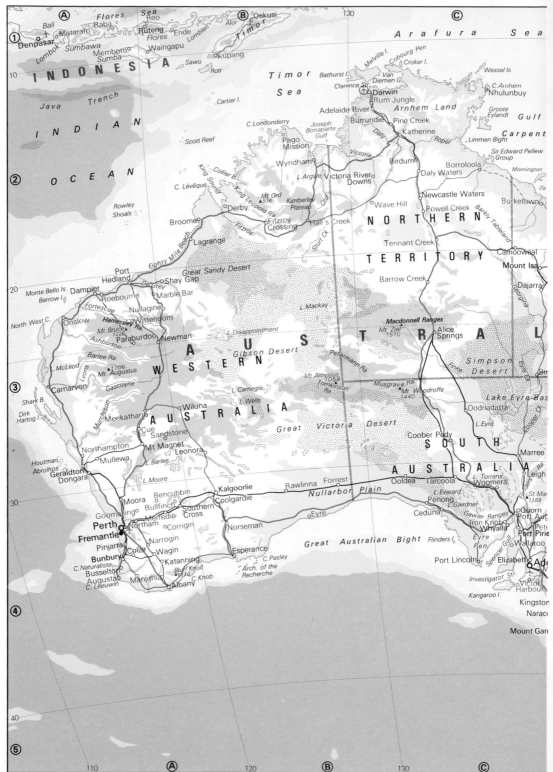

Ⓐ   Ⓑ   130   Ⓒ

① Denpasar
Bali
Mataram
Lombok Sumbawa
Sumba Memboro
Flores Sea
Reo Ruteng
Raba Ende
Lomblen Flores
Waingapu
Alor Oekusi Ⓑ
Timor
Kupang
Sawu
Roti

Arafura Sea

Melville I. Cobourg Pen
Van Croker I.
Bathurst I. Diemen G.
Clarence Str. Darwin
Rum Jungle
Burrundie Pine Creek
Katherine
Roper
Wessel Is
C. Arnhem Nhulunbuy
Groote Eylandt
Gulf
Carpent

10

INDONESIA

INDIAN

OCEAN

Java Trench

Rowley Shoals

C. Londonderry
Scott Reef
Cartier I.
Pago Mission
Joseph Bonaparte Gulf
Wyndham
L. Argyle Victoria River Downs
Victoria
Birdum
Daly Waters
Limmen Bight
Sir Edward Pellew Group
Mornington

② C. Léveque
King Sound
Collier B.
C. Lévéque
King Leopold Ra.
Mt Ord 936
Kimberley Plateau
Ord
Wave Hill
Newcastle Waters
Burketown
Derby
Fitzroy Crossing
Fitzroy
Hall's Creek
Sturt Ck
NORTHERN
Powell Creek
Barkly Tableland
Broome
Lagrange
Tennant Creek
TERRITORY
Camooweal
Mount Isa

20

North West C.
Port Hedland
De Grey
Shay Gap
Great Sandy Desert
Barrow Creek
Dajarra
Monte Bello Is
Barrow I.
Dampier
Roebourne
Marble Bar
Georgina

Onslow
Fortescue
Nullagine
Wittenoom
Hamersley Ra.
Mt Bruce 1226
Paraburdoo
Newman
L. Mackay
L. Disappointment
Macdonnell Ranges
Mt Ziel 1510
Alice Springs
Simpson
Eyre

Ashburton
Barlee Ra.
Gibson Desert
Petermann Ra.
Finke
Desert

L. McLeod
1106
Lyons
Mt. Augustus
Gascoyne
WESTERN
Mt Aloysius 1058
Tomkinson Ra.
Musgrave Ra.
Mt Woodroffe 1440
Lake Eyre Bas

Carnarvon
Shark B.
Dirk Hartog I.
Murchison
Meekatharra
AUSTRALIA
L. Carnegie
L. Wells
Great Victoria Desert
Oodnadatta
L.Eyre
Cooper

③
Wiluna
Cue
Sandstone
Coober Pedy
SOUTH
Marree

Northampton
Mullewa
Mt Magnet
Leonora
Leigh
L. Barlee
L. Eyre
AUSTRALIA
L. Everard
L.Gairdner
Woomera
St Mar 1189

Houtman Abrolhos
Geraldton
Dongara
L. Moore
Kalgoorlie
Rawlinna Forrest
Ooldea
Tarcoola
L. Torrens
Flinders Ra.
Quorn
Port Aug

30
Moora
Bencubbin
Bullfinch
Coolgardie
Nullarbor Plain
Eyre
Ceduna
Penong
Gawler Ranges
Iron Knob
Whyalla
Port Pirie
Goomalling
Merredin
Southern Cross
Spencer Gulf
Wallaroo
Perth
Northam
Corrigin
Norseman
Eyre Pen.
Adel
Fremantle
Narrogin
Pinjarra
Colie
Wagin
Esperance
Great Australian Bight
Flinders I.
Port Lincoln
Elizabeth
Bunbury
Katanning
C. Pasley
Kangaroo I.
Victor Harbour
Busselton
C. Naturaliste
Bluff Knoll M10
C. Knob
Arch. of the Recherche
Investigator Str.
Kingston
Augusta
Manjimup
Albany
C. Leeuwin
Narac
Mount Gan

④

40

⑤

110   Ⓐ   120   Ⓑ   130   Ⓒ

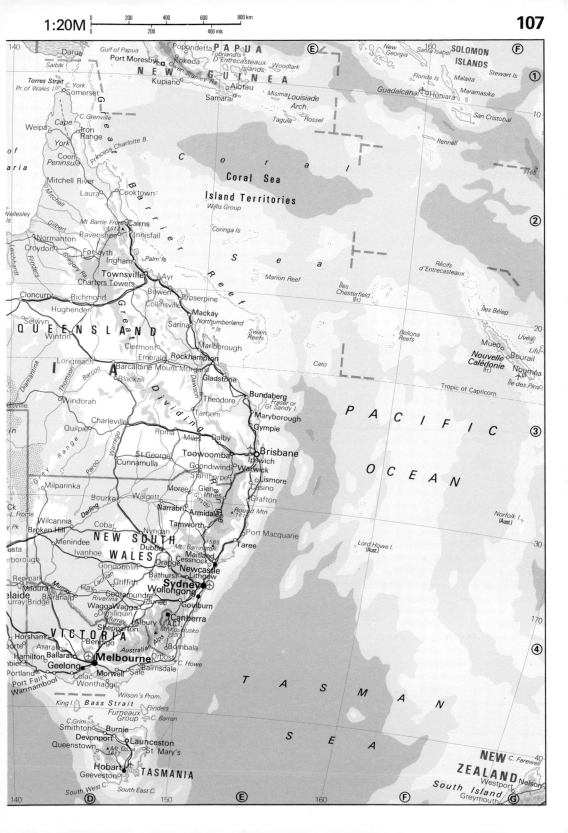

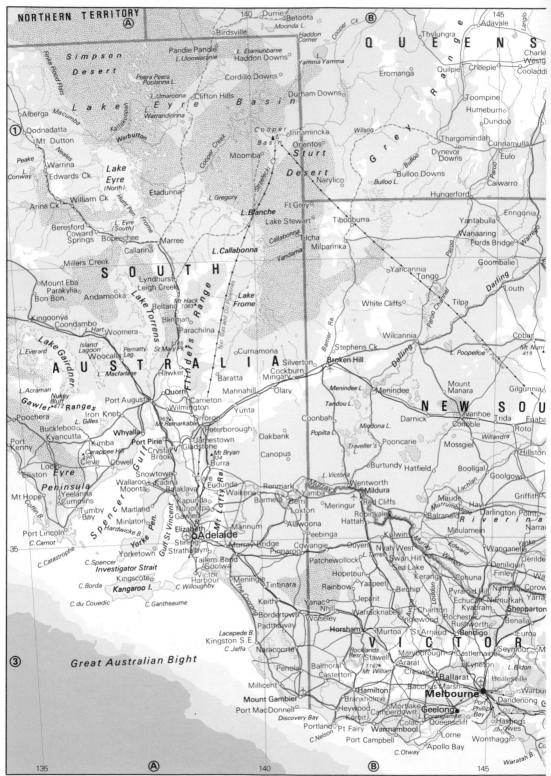

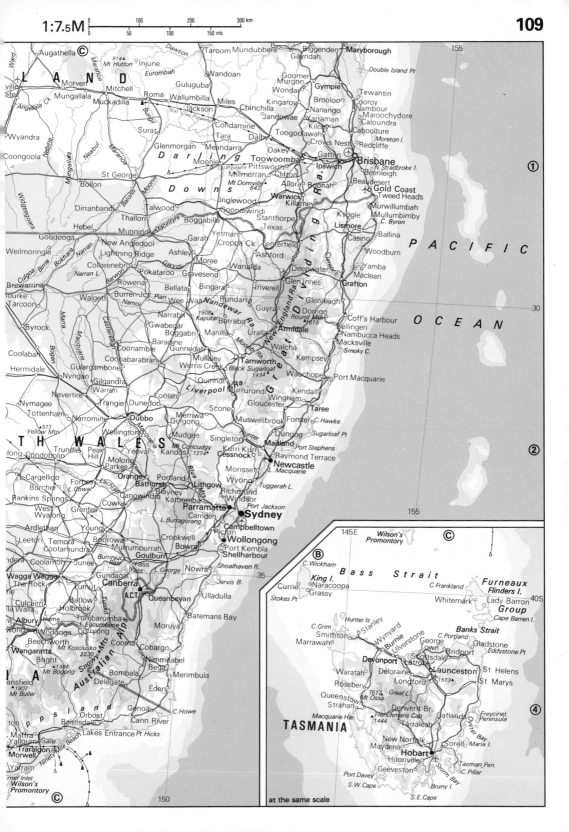

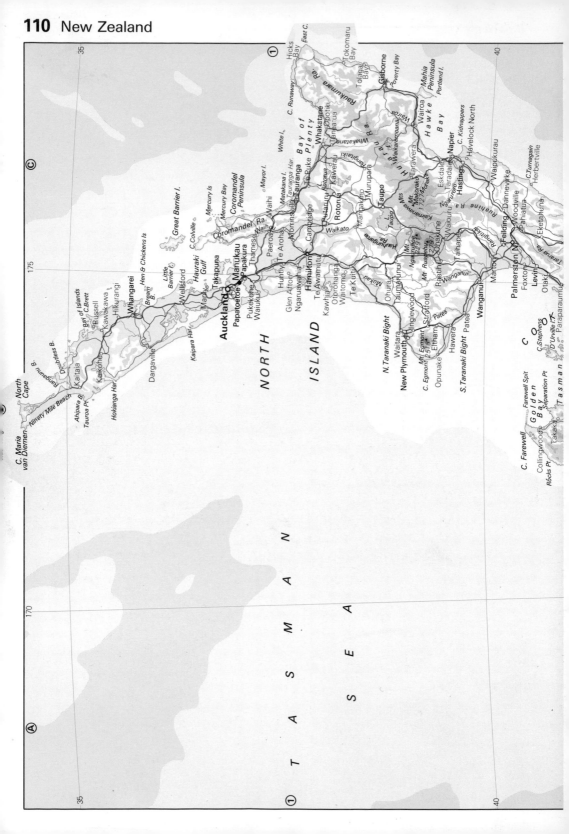

NORTH ISLAND

T A S M A N

S E A

C O O K

Auckland

North Cape
C. Maria van Diemen
Ninety Mile Beach
Ahipara B.
Tauroa Pt.
Reinga B.
Doubtless B.
Kaitaia
Kaikohe
Kawakawa
Russell
Bay of Islands
C. Brett
Hokianga Har.
Hikurangi
Whangarei
Bream B.
Bream Hd.
Hen & Chickens Is
Dargaville
Kaipara Har.
Wellsford
Maple
Little Barrier I.
Great Barrier I.
Hauraki Gulf
Takapuna
Manukau
Papatoetoe
Papakura
Pukekohe
Waiuku
Thames
C. Colville
Coromandel Pen.
Coromandel Peninsula
Mercury Is
Mercury Bay
Mayor I.
White I.
Matakana I.
Waihi
Waihou
Paeroa
Te Aroha
Huntly
Ngaruawahia
Hamilton
Cambridge
Waikato
Glen Afton
Te Awamutu
Kawhia
Otorohanga
Waitomo
Te Kuiti
Mokau
Ohura
Raglan
Morrinsville
Tauranga
Tauranga Har.
Puke
Bay of Plenty
Rotorua
L. Rotorua
Te Puke
Kawerau
Whakatane
Opotiki
Tarawera
L. Tarawera
Murupara
Taupo
L. Taupo
Hawera
N. Taranaki Bight
Waitara
New Plymouth
Mt. Egmont 2518
Inglewood
Stratford
Eltham
Opunake
Patea
S. Taranaki Bight
Wanganui
Taumarunui
Raetihi
Ohakune
Mt. Ruapehu 2797
Mt. Ngauruhoe 2291
Mt. Tongariro
Waiouru
Taihape
Mangaweka
Rangitikei R.
Marton
Feilding
Palmerston N.
Foxton
Levin
Otaki
Paraparaumu
Waikanae
East C.
Hicks Bay
Tokomaru Bay
Gisborne
Poverty Bay
Mahia Peninsula
Portland I.
Raukumara Ra.
C. Runaway
Wairoa
Hawke Bay
Napier
Hastings
Havelock North
C. Kidnappers
Eskdale
Taradale
Waipukurau
Waipawa
Danevirke
Woodville
Pahiatua
Eketahuna
Herbertville
C. Turnagain
Ruahine Ra.
Kaimanawa Mts
Kaweka Ra.
Makorako 1727
Waikaremoana
Waikari R.
Ruatahuna
Urewera
Rangitaiki R.
Whakatane R.
Mohaka R.

Golden B.
Farewell Spit
C. Farewell
Collingwood
Rocks Pt.
Takaka
Separation Pt.
D'Urville I.
C. Stephens

35
175
170
35
40
40

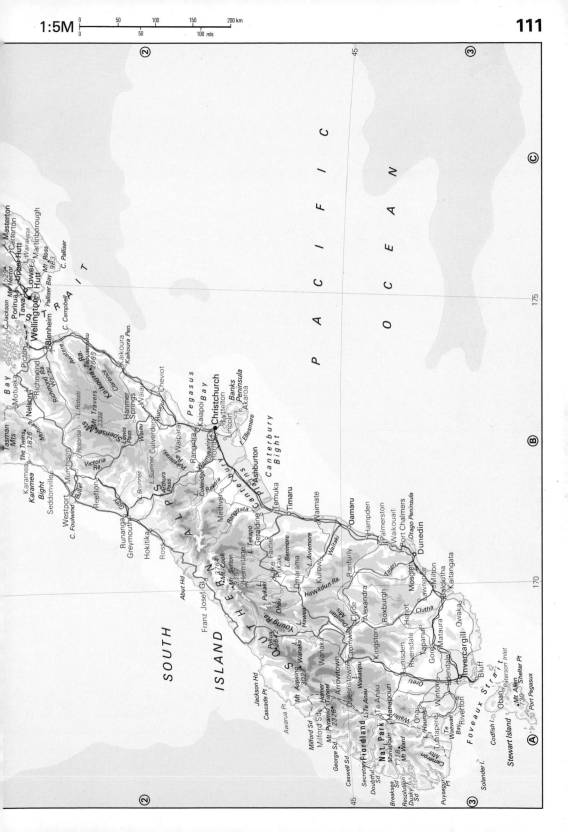

1:40M

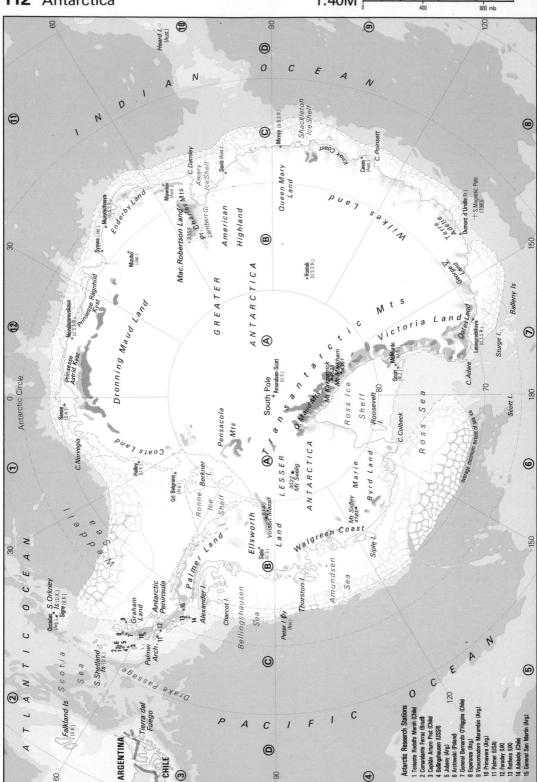

Antarctic Research Stations
1 Teniente Rodolfo Marsh (Chile)
2 Comandante Ferraz (Brazil)
3 Capitán Arturo Prat (Chile)
4 Bellingshausen (USSR)
5 Jubany (Arg.)
6 Arctowski (Poland)
7 General Bernardo O'Higgins (Chile)
8 Esperanza (Arg.)
9 Vicecomodoro Marambio (Chile)
10 Primavera (Arg.)
11 Palmer (USA)
12 Faraday (UK)
13 Rothera (UK)
14 Adelaide (Chile)
15 General San Martín (Arg.)

Index

In the index, the first number refers to the page, and the following letter
and number to the section of the map in which the index entry
can be found. For example, 48C2 **Paris** means that Paris can
be found on page 48 where column C and row 2 meet.

Abbreviations used in the index

Afghan	Afghanistan	Germ	Germany	Phil	Philippines	Arch	Archipelago
Alb	Albania	Hung	Hungary	Pol	Poland	B	Bay
Alg	Algeria	Ind	Indonesia	Port	Portugal	C	Cape
Ant	Antarctica	Irish Rep	Ireland	Rom	Romania	Chan	Channel
Arg	Argentina	Leb	Lebanon	S Arabia	Saudi Arabia	Gl	Glacier
Aust	Australia	Lib	Liberia	Scot	Scotland	I(s)	Island(s)
Bang	Bangladesh	Liech	Liechtenstein	Sen	Senegal	Lg	Lagoon
Belg	Belgium	Lux	Luxembourg	S Africa	South Africa	L	Lake
Bol	Bolivia	Madag	Madagascar	Switz	Switzerland	Mt(s)	Mountain(s)
Bulg	Bulgaria	Malay	Malaysia	Tanz	Tanzania	O	Ocean
Burk	Burkina	Maur	Mauritania	Thai	Thailand	P	Pass
Camb	Cambodia	Mor	Morocco	Turk	Turkey	Pen	Peninsula
Can	Canada	Mozam	Mozambique		Union of	Plat	Plateau
CAR	Central African Republic	Neth	Netherlands		Soviet Socialist	Pt	Point
Czech	Czechoslovakia	NZ	New Zealand	USSR	Republics	Res	Reservoir
Den	Denmark	Nic	Nicaragaua		United States	R	River
Dom Rep	Dominican Republic	N Ire	Northern Ireland	USA	of America	S	Sea
El Sal	El Salvador	Nig	Nigeria	Urug	Uruguay	Sd	Sound
Eng	England	Nor	Norway	Ven	Venezuela	Str	Strait
Eq Guinea	Equatorial Guinea	Pak	Pakistan	Viet	Vietnam	V	Valley
Eth	Ethiopia	PNG	Papua New Guinea	Yugos	Yugoslavia		
Fin	Finland	Par	Paraguay	Zim	Zimbabwe		

A

57B2 **Aachen** Germany
46C1 **Aalst** Belg
38K6 **Äänekoski** Fin
47C1 **Aarau** Switz
47B1 **Aare** R Switz
72A3 **Aba** China
97C4 **Aba** Nig
99D2 **Aba** Zaïre
91A3 **Ābādān** Iran
90B3 **Ābādeh** Iran
96B1 **Abadla** Alg
35B1 **Abaeté** Brazil
35B1 **Abaeté** R Brazil
31B2 **Abaetetuba** Brazil
72D1 **Abagnar Qi** China
97C4 **Abakaliki** Nig
63B2 **Abakan** USSR
97C3 **Abala** Niger
96C2 **Abalessa** Alg
32C6 **Abancay** Peru
90B3 **Abarqū** Iran
74E2 **Abashiri** Japan
74E2 **Abashiri-wan** B Japan
71F4 **Abau** PNG
99D2 **Abaya** L Eth
99D1 **Abbai** R Eth
99E1 **Abbe** L Eth
48C1 **Abbeville** France
19B4 **Abbeville** Louisiana, USA
17B1 **Abbeville** S Carolina, USA
45B2 **Abbeyfeale** Irish Rep
47C2 **Abbiategrasso** Italy
20B1 **Abbotsford** Can
84C2 **Abbottabad** Pak
61H3 **Abdulino** USSR
98C1 **Abéché** Chad
39F7 **Åbenrå** Den
97C4 **Abeokuta** Nig
99D2 **Abera** Eth
43B3 **Aberaeron** Wales

15C3 **Aberdeen** Maryland, USA
100B4 **Aberdeen** S Africa
44C3 **Aberdeen** Scot
8D2 **Aberdeen** S Dakota, USA
8A2 **Aberdeen** Washington, USA
4J3 **Aberdeen L** Can
44C3 **Aberfeldy** Scot
43C4 **Abergavenny** Wales
43B3 **Aberystwyth** Wales
81C4 **Abhā** S Arabia
90A2 **Abhar** Iran
97B4 **Abidjan** Ivory Coast
18A2 **Abilene** Kansas, USA
9D3 **Abilene** Texas, USA
43D4 **Abingdon** Eng
7B4 **Abitibi** R Can
7C5 **Abitibi,L** Can
61F5 **Abkhazskaya** Republic, USSR
84C2 **Abohar** India
97C4 **Abomey** Benin
98B2 **Abong Mbang** Cam
79A4 **Aborlan** Phil
98B1 **Abou Deïa** Chad
91A4 **Abqaiq** S Arabia
50A2 **Abrantes** Port
95C2 **Abri** Sudan
106A3 **Abrolhos** Is Aust
8B2 **Absaroka Range** Mts USA
91B5 **Abū al Abyad** I UAE
91A4 **Abū 'Ali** I S Arabia
91B5 **Abū Dhabi** UAE
95C3 **Abu Hamed** Sudan
97C4 **Abuja** Nig
33D5 **Abunã** Brazil
32D6 **Abunã** R Bol
93D3 **Abū Sukhayr** Iraq
111B2 **Abut Head** C NZ
95C3 **Abu 'Urug** Well Sudan
99D1 **Abuye Meda** Mt Eth

99C1 **Abu Zabad** Sudan
99D2 **Abwong** Sudan
56B1 **Åby** Den
94B3 **Aby 'Aweigila** Well Egypt
99C2 **Abyei** Sudan
24B2 **Acambaro** Mexico
24B2 **Acaponeta** Mexico
24B3 **Acapulco** Mexico
31D2 **Acaraú** Brazil
32D2 **Acarigua** Ven
24C3 **Acatlán** Mexico
23B2 **Acatzingo** Mexico
97B4 **Accra** Ghana
85D4 **Achalpur** India
29B4 **Achao** Chile
47D1 **Achensee** L Austria
46E2 **Achern** Germany
41A3 **Achill** I Irish Rep
63B2 **Achinsk** USSR
53C3 **Acireale** Italy
26C2 **Acklins** I Caribbean S
32C6 **Acobamba** Peru
29B2 **Aconcagua** Mt Chile
31D3 **Acopiara** Brazil
88B4 **Açores** Is Atlantic O
47C2 **Acqui** Italy
108A2 **Acraman,L** Aust
Acre = 'Akko
32C5 **Acre** State, Brazil
22C3 **Acton** USA
23B2 **Actopan** Mexico
19A3 **Ada** USA
50B1 **Adaja** R Spain
91C5 **Adam** Oman
99D2 **Adama** Eth
35A2 **Adamantina** Brazil
98B2 **Adamaoua** Region, Nig/Cam
47D1 **Adamello** Mt Italy
16C1 **Adams** USA
87B3 **Adam's Bridge** India/Sri Lanka
13D2 **Adams L** Can
8A2 **Adams,Mt** USA

87C3 **Adam's Peak** Mt Sri Lanka
81C4 **'Adan** Yemen
92C2 **Adana** Turk
60D5 **Adapazari** Turk
112B7 **Adare,C** Ant
108B1 **Adavale** Aust
47C2 **Adda** R Italy
91A4 **Ad Dahna'** Region, S Arabia
96A2 **Ad Dakhla** Mor
91B4 **Ad Damman** S Arabia
91A4 **Ad Dibdibah** Region, S Arabia
91A5 **Ad Dilam** S Arabia
91A5 **Ad Dir'iyah** S Arabia
93D3 **Ad Diwanīyah** Iraq
81C4 **Ad Dīī'** Yemen
93D3 **Ad Duwayd** S Arabia
106C4 **Adelaide** Aust
4J3 **Adelaide Pen** Can
22D3 **Adelanto** USA
Aden = 'Adan
81C4 **Aden,G of** Yemen/Somalia
97C3 **Aderbissinat** Niger
94C2 **Adhra** Syria
71E4 **Adi** I Indon
52B1 **Adige** R Italy
99D1 **Adigrat** Eth
85D5 **Adīlābād** India
20B2 **Adin** USA
15D2 **Adirondack Mts** USA
99D2 **Ādīs Ābeba** Eth
95C3 **Adi Ugai** Eth
93C2 **Adiyaman** Turk
54C1 **Adjud** Rom
4E4 **Admiralty I** USA
6B2 **Admiralty Inlet** B Can
87B1 **Ādoni** India
48B3 **Adour** R France
96A2 **Adrar** Region, Maur

96C2 **Adrar** *Mts* Alg
96A2 **Adrar Soutouf** Region, Mor
98C1 **Adré** Chad
95A2 **Adri** Libya
47E2 **Adria** Italy
14B2 **Adrian** Michigan, USA
52B2 **Adriatic S** Italy/Yugos
99D1 **Aduwa** Eth
97B4 **Adzopé** Ivory Coast
55B3 **Aegean** *S* Greece
80E2 **Afghanistan** Republic, Asia
99E2 **Afgooye** Somalia
97C4 **Afikpo** Nig
38G6 **Åfjord** Nor
96C1 **Aflou** Alg
99E2 **Afmadu** Somalia
97A3 **Afollé** Region, Maur
94B2 **Afula** Israel
92B2 **Afyon** Turk
95A3 **Agadem** Niger
97C3 **Agadez** Niger
96B1 **Agadir** Mor
85D4 **Agar** India
86C2 **Agartala** India
20B1 **Agassiz** Can
97B4 **Agboville** Ivory Coast
93E1 **Agdam** USSR
75B1 **Agematsu** Japan
48C3 **Agen** France
90A3 **Agha Jārī** Iran
96A2 **Aghwinit** *Well* Mor
47D2 **Agno** *R* Italy
47E1 **Agordo** Italy
48C3 **Agout** *R* France
85D3 **Āgra** India
93D2 **Ağri** Turk
53C2 **Agri** *R* Italy
53B3 **Agrigento** Italy
55B3 **Agrínion** Greece
34A3 **Agrio** *R* Chile
53B2 **Agropoli** Italy
61H2 **Agryz** USSR
6E3 **Agto** Greenland
27D3 **Aguadilla** Puerto Rico
24B1 **Agua Prieta** Mexico
24B2 **Aguascalientes** Mexico
23A1 **Aguascalientes** State, Mexico
35C1 **Aguas Formosas** Brazil
50A1 **Agueda** Port
96C3 **Aguelhok** Mali
50B2 **Aguilas** Spain
23A2 **Aguililla** Mexico
100B4 **Agulhas,C** S Africa
79C4 **Agusan** *R* Phil
Ahaggar = Hoggar
93E2 **Ahar** Iran
110B1 **Ahipara B** NZ
85C4 **Ahmadābād** India
87A1 **Ahmadnagar** India
99E2 **Ahmar** *Mts* Eth
46D1 **Ahr** *R* Germany
46D1 **Ahrgebirge** Region, Germany
23A1 **Ahuacatlán** Mexico
23A1 **Ahualulco** Mexico
39G7 **Åhus** Sweden
90B2 **Ahvān** Iran
90A3 **Ahvāz** Iran
26A4 **Aiajuela** Costa Rica
47B1 **Aigle** Switz
47B2 **Aiguille d'Arves** *Mt* France
47B2 **Aiguille de la Grand Sassière** *Mt* France
75B1 **Aikawa** Japan
17B1 **Aiken** USA
73A5 **Ailao Shan** *Upland* China
35C1 **Aimorés** Brazil
96B1 **Ain Beni Mathar** Mor
95B2 **Ain Dalla** *Well* Egypt
51C2 **Aïn el Hadjel** Alg
95A3 **Aïn Galakka** Chad
96B1 **Aïn Sefra** Alg

92B4 **'Ain Sukhna** Egypt
75A2 **Aioi** Japan
96B2 **Aioun Abd el Malek** *Well* Maur
97B3 **Aïoun El Atrouss** Maur
30C2 **Aiquile** Bol
97C3 **Aïr** *Desert Region* Niger
13E2 **Airdrie** Can
46B1 **Aire** France
42D3 **Aire** *R* Eng
46C2 **Aire** *R* France
6C3 **Airforce I** Can
47C1 **Airolo** Switz
4E3 **Aishihik** Can
12G2 **Aishihik L** Can
46B2 **Aisne** Department, France
49C2 **Aisne** *R* France
71F4 **Aitape** PNG
58D1 **Aiviekste** *R* USSR
72B2 **Aixa Zuogi** China
49D3 **Aix-en-Provence** France
47A2 **Aix-les-Bains** France
86B2 **Aiyar Res** India
55B3 **Aíyion** Greece
55B3 **Aíyna** *I* Greece
86C2 **Āizawl** India
100A3 **Aizeb** *R* Namibia
74E3 **Aizu-Wakamatsu** Japan
52A2 **Ajaccio** Corse
23B2 **Ajalpan** Mexico
95B1 **Ajdabiyah** Libya
74E2 **Ajigasawa** Japan
94B2 **Ajlūn** Jordan
91C4 **Ajman** UAE
85C3 **Ajmer** India
9B3 **Ajo** USA
23A2 **Ajuchitan** Mexico
55C3 **Ak** *R* Turk
75B1 **Akaishi-sanchi** *Mts* Japan
87B1 **Akalkot** India
111B2 **Akaroa** NZ
75A2 **Akashi** Japan
61J3 **Akbulak** USSR
93C2 **Akçakale** Turk
96A2 **Akchar** *Watercourse* Maur
55C3 **Akdağ** *Mt* Turk
98C2 **Aketi** Zaïre
93D1 **Akhalkalaki** USSR
93D1 **Akhalsikhe** USSR
55B3 **Akharnái** Greece
12D3 **Akhiok** USA
92A2 **Akhisar** Turk
58D1 **Akhiste** USSR
95C2 **Akhmîm** Egypt
61G4 **Akhtubinsk** USSR
60D4 **Akhtyrka** USSR
75A2 **Aki** Japan
7B4 **Akimiski I** Can
74E3 **Akita** Japan
96A3 **Akjoujt** Maur
94B2 **'Akko** Israel
4E3 **Aklavik** USA
97B3 **Aklé Aouana** *Desert Region* Maur
99D2 **Akobo** Sudan
99D2 **Akobo** *R* Sudan
84B1 **Akoha** Afghan
85D4 **Akola** India
85D4 **Akot** India
6D3 **Akpatok I** Can
55B3 **Ákra Kafirévs** *C* Greece
55B3 **Ákra Maléa** *C* Greece
38A2 **Akranes** Iceland
55C3 **Ákra Sídheros** *C* Greece
55B3 **Ákra Spátha** *C* Greece
55B3 **Ákra Taínaron** *C* Greece
10B2 **Akron** USA
94A1 **Akrotiri B** Cyprus

84D1 **Aksai Chin** *Mts* China
92B2 **Aksaray** Turk
61H3 **Aksay** USSR
84D1 **Aksayquin Hu** *L* China
92B2 **Akşehir** Turk
92B2 **Akseki** Turk
63D2 **Aksenovo Zilovskoye** USSR
68D1 **Aksha** USSR
82C1 **Aksu** China
65J5 **Aktogay** USSR
61J4 **Aktumsyk** USSR
65G4 **Aktyubinsk** USSR
38B1 **Akureyri** Iceland
65K5 **Akzhal** USSR
11B3 **Alabama** State, USA
11B3 **Alabama** *R* USA
17A1 **Alabaster** USA
92C2 **Ala Dağlari** *Mts* Tur
61F5 **Alagir** USSR
47B2 **Alagna** Italy
31D3 **Alagoas** State, Brazil
31D4 **Alagoinhas** Brazil
51B1 **Alagón** Spain
93E4 **Al Ahmadi** Kuwait
25D3 **Alajuela** Costa Rica
12B2 **Alakanuk** USA
38L5 **Alakurtti** USSR
93E3 **Al Amārah** Iraq
21A2 **Alameda** USA
23B1 **Alamo** Mexico
9C3 **Alamogordo** USA
9C3 **Alamosa** USA
39H6 **Åland** *I* Fin
92B2 **Alanya** Turk
17B1 **Alapaha** *R* USA
65H4 **Alapayevsk** USSR
92A2 **Alaşehir** Turk
68C3 **Ala Shan** *Mts*'China
4C3 **Alaska** State, USA
4D4 **Alaska,G of** USA
12C3 **Alaska Pen** USA
4C3 **Alaska Range** *Mts* USA
52A2 **Alassio** Italy
12D1 **Alatna** *R* USA
61G3 **Alatyr** USSR
108B2 **Alawoona** Aust
91C5 **Al'Ayn** UAE
82B2 **Alayskiy Khrebet** *Mts* USSR
49D3 **Alba** Italy
92C2 **Al Bāb** Syria
51B2 **Albacete** Spain
50A1 **Alba de Tormes** Spain
93D2 **Al Badi** Iraq
54B1 **Alba Iulia** Rom
54A2 **Albania** Republic, Europe
106A4 **Albany** Aust
17B1 **Albany** Georgia, USA
15D2 **Albany** New York, USA
8A2 **Albany** Oregon, USA
7B4 **Albany** *R* Can
34B2 **Albardón** Arg
91C5 **Al Batinah** Region, Oman
71F5 **Albatross B** Aust
95B1 **Al Baydā** Libya
11C3 **Albemarle Sd** USA
50B1 **Alberche** *R* Spain
108A1 **Alberga** Aust
46B1 **Albert** France
5G4 **Alberta** Province, Can
99D2 **Albert,L** Uganda/Zaïre
10A2 **Albert Lea** USA
99D2 **Albert Nile** *R* Uganda
49D2 **Albertville** France
48C3 **Albi** France
18B1 **Albia** USA
33G2 **Albina** Suriname
14B2 **Albion** Michigan, USA
15C2 **Albion** New York, USA
92C4 **Al Bi'r** S Arabia
91A5 **Al Biyadh** Region, S Arabia
50B2 **Alborán** *I* Spain

39G7 **Ålborg** Den
95A1 **Al Brayqah** Libya
93D3 **Al Bū Kamāl** Syria
47C1 **Albula** *R* Switz
9C3 **Albuquerque** USA
91C5 **Al Buraymi** Oman
95B1 **Al Burdī** Libya
107D4 **Albury** Aust
93E3 **Al Buşayyah** Iraq
50B1 **Alcalá de Henares** Spain
53B3 **Alcamo** Italy
51B1 **Alcaniz** Spain
31C2 **Alcântara** Brazil
50B2 **Alcaraz** Spain
50B2 **Alcázar de San Juan** Spain
51B2 **Alcira** Spain
35D1 **Alcobaça** Brazil
50B1 **Alcolea de Pinar** Spain
51B2 **Alcoy** Spain
51C2 **Alcudia** Spain
89J8 **Aldabra** *Is* Indian O
63E2 **Aldan** USSR
63E2 **Aldanskoye Nagor'ye** *Upland* USSR
43E3 **Aldeburgh** Eng
48B2 **Alderney** *I* UK
43D4 **Aldershot** Eng
97A3 **Aleg** Maur
30E4 **Alegrete** Brazil
34C2 **Alejandro Roca** Arg
30H6 **Alejandro Selkirk** *I* Chile
63G2 **Aleksandrovsk Sakhalinskiy** USSR
65J4 **Alekseyevka** USSR
60E3 **Aleksin** USSR
58B1 **Älem** Sweden
35C2 **Além Paraíba** Brazil
49C2 **Alençon** France
21C4 **Alenuihaha Chan** Hawaiian Is
Aleppo = Ḥalab
6D1 **Alert** Can
49C3 **Alès** France
52A2 **Alessandria** Italy
64B3 **Ålesund** Nor
12C3 **Aleutian Range** *Mts* USA
4E4 **Alexander Arch** USA
100A3 **Alexander Bay** S Africa
17A1 **Alexander City** USA
112C3 **Alexander I** Ant
111A3 **Alexandra** NZ
29G8 **Alexandra,C** South Georgia
6C2 **Alexander Fjord** Can
95B1 **Alexandria** Egypt
11A3 **Alexandria** Louisiana, USA
10A2 **Alexandria** Minnesota, USA
10C3 **Alexandria** Virginia, USA
55C2 **Alexandroúpolis** Greece
13C2 **Alexis Creek** Can
94B2 **Aley** Leb
65K4 **Aleysk** USSR
93D3 **Al Fallūjah** Iraq
51B1 **Alfaro** Spain
54C2 **Alfatar** Bulg
93E3 **Al Fāw** Iraq
35B2 **Alfenas** Brazil
55B3 **Alfiós** *R* Greece
47D2 **Alfonsine** Italy
35C2 **Alfonzo Cláudio** Brazil
35C2 **Alfredo Chaves** Brazil
61J4 **Alga** USSR
34B3 **Algarrobo del Águila** Arg
50A2 **Algeciras** Spain
96C1 **Alger** Alg
96B2 **Algeria** Republic, Africa
53A2 **Alghero** Sardegna

Algiers = Alger
15C1 Algonquin Park Can
91C5 Al Hadd Oman
93D3 Al Hadīthah Iraq
92C3 Al Hadīthah S Arabia
93D2 Al Haḍr Iraq
91C5 Al Hajar al Gharbī Mts Oman
91C5 Al Hajar ash Sharqī Mts Oman
93C3 Al Hamad Desert Region Jordan/ S Arabia
93E4 Al Haniyah Desert Region Iraq
91A5 Al Harīq S Arabia
93C3 Al Harrah Desert Region S Arabia
95A2 Al Harūj al Aswad Upland Libya
91A4 Al Hasa Region, S Arabia
93D2 Al Hasakah Syria
93C4 Al Hawjā' S Arabia
93E3 Al Hayy Iraq
94C2 Al Hījānah Syria
93D3 Al Hillah Iraq
91A5 Al Hillah S Arabia
96B1 Al Hoceima Mor
91A4 Al Hufūf S Arabia
91B5 Al Humrah Region, UAE
91C5 Al Huwatsah Oman
90A2 Alīābad Iran
91C4 Aliabad Iran
55B2 Aliákmon R Greece
93E3 Al ī al Gharbī Iraq
87A1 Alībāg India
51B2 Alicante Spain
9D4 Alice USA
106C3 Alice Springs Aust
53B3 Alicudi I Italy
84D3 Aligarh India
90A3 Aligūdarz Iran
84B2 Ali-Khel Afghan
55C2 Alimniá I Greece
86B1 Alīpur Duār India
14B2 Aliquippa USA
22B2 Alisal USA
93C3 Al' Īsawīyah S Arabia
100B4 Aliwal North S Africa
95B2 Al Jaghbūb Libya
93D3 Al Jālamīd S Arabia
95B2 Al Jawf Libya
93C4 Al Jawf S Arabia
93D2 Al Jazīrah Desert Region Syria/Iraq
50A2 Aljezur Port
91A4 Al Jubayl S Arabia
91C5 Al Kāmil Oman
93D2 Al Khābūr R Syria
91C5 Al Khābūrah Oman
93D3 Al Khālis Iraq
91C4 Al Khasab Oman
91B4 Al Khawr Qatar
95A1 Al Khums Libya
91B5 Al Kidan Region, S Arabia
94C2 Al Kiswah Syria
56A2 Alkmaar Neth
95B2 Al Kufrah Oasis Libya
93E3 Al Kūt Iraq
92C2 Al Lādhiqīyah Syria
86A1 Allahābād India
94C2 Al Lajāh Mt Syria
12D1 Allakaket USA
76B2 Allanmyo Burma
95C2 'Allaqi Watercourse Egypt
17B1 Allatoona L USA
15C2 Allegheny R USA
10C3 Allegheny Mts USA
17B1 Allendale USA
111A3 Allen,Mt NZ
15C2 Allentown USA
87B3 Alleppey India
49C2 Aller R France
47D1 Allgäu Mts Germany

8C2 Alliance USA
81C3 Al Līth S Arabia
91B5 Al Liwā Region, UAE
109D1 Allora Aust
14B2 Alma Michigan, USA
82B1 Alma Ata USSR
50A2 Almada Port
Al Madīnah = Medina
71F2 Almagan I Pacific O
91B4 Al Manāmah Bahrain
93D3 Al Ma'nīyah Iraq
21A1 Almanor,L USA
51B2 Almansa Spain
13B1 Alma Peak Mt Can
91B5 Al Māriyyah UAE
95B1 Al Marj Libya
50B1 Almazán Spain
35C1 Almenara Brazil
50B2 Almeria Spain
61H3 Al'met'yevsk USSR
56C1 Älmhult Sweden
93E3 Al Miqdādīyah Iraq
112C3 Almirante Brown Base Ant
34A1 Almirante Latorre Chile
55B3 Almirós Greece
91A4 Al Mish'āb S Arabia
50A2 Almodôvar Port
84D3 Almora India
91A4 Al Mubarraz S Arabia
92C4 Al Mudawwara Jordan
91C5 Al Mudaybi Oman
91B4 Al Muharraq Bahrain
81C4 Al Mukallā Yemen
81C4 Al Mukhā Yemen
93D3 Al Musayyib Iraq
44B3 Alness Scot
93E3 Al Nu'mānīyah Iraq
42D2 Alnwick Eng
71D4 Alor I Indon
77C4 Alor Setar Malay
Alost = Aalst
107E2 Alotau PNG
106B3 Aloysius,Mt Aust
34C3 Alpachiri Arg
14B1 Alpena USA
47B2 Alpes du Valais Mts Switz
52B1 Alpi Dolomitiche Mts Italy
47B2 Alpi Graie Mts Italy
9C3 Alpine Texas, USA
47C1 Alpi Orobie Mts Italy
47B2 Alpi Pennine Mts Italy
47C1 Alpi Retiche Mts Switz
47D1 Alpi Venoste Mts Italy
52A1 Alps Mts Europe
95A1 Al Qaddāhiyah Libya
94C1 Al Qadmūs Syria
93D3 Al Qā'im Iraq
93C4 Al Qalībah S Arabia
93D2 Al Qāmishlī Syria
95A1 Al Qaryah Ash Sharqiyah Libya
92C3 Al Qaryatayn Syria
91A4 Al Qātif S Arabia
95A2 Al Qatrūn Libya
91A4 Al Qayşāmah S Arabia
94C2 Al Quatayfah Syria
92C3 Al Qunayţirah Syria
81C4 Al Qunfidhah S Arabia
93E3 Al Qurnah Iraq
94C1 Al Quşayr Syria
92C3 Al Qutayfah Syria
56B1 Als I Den
49D2 Alsace Region, France
57B2 Alsfeld Germany
42C2 Alston Eng
38J5 Alta Nor
29D2 Alta Gracia Arg
27D5 Altagracia de Orituco Ven
68A2 Altai Mts Mongolia
17B1 Altamaha R USA

33G4 Altamira Brazil
23B1 Altamira Mexico
53C2 Altamura Italy
68C1 Altanbulag Mongolia
71F4 Altape PNG
24B2 Altata Mexico
63A3 Altay China
63B3 Altay Mongolia
63A2 Altay Mts USSR
47C1 Altdorf Switz
46D1 Altenkirchen Germany
34B3 Altiplanicie del Payún Plat Arg
47B1 Altkirch France
101C2 Alto Molócue Mozam
10A3 Alton USA
15C2 Altoona USA
34B2 Alto Pencoso Mts Arg
35A1 Alto Sucuriú Brazil
23B2 Altotonga Mexico
23A2 Altoyac de Alvarez Mexico
82C2 Altun Shan Mts China
20B2 Alturas USA
9D3 Altus USA
91B5 Al'Ubaylh S Arabia
99F1 Alula Somalia
93C4 Al Urayq Desert Region S Arabia
91B5 Al'Uruq al Mu'taridah Region, S Arabia
9D2 Alva USA
23B2 Alvarado Mexico
19A3 Alvarado USA
39G6 Älvdalen Sweden
19A4 Alvin USA
38J5 Alvsbyn Sweden
80B3 Al Wajh S Arabia
85D3 Alwar India
93D3 Al Widyān Desert Region Iraq/ S Arabia
72A2 Alxa Yougi China
93E2 Alyat USSR
39J8 Alytus USSR
46E2 Alzey Germany
23B2 Amacuzac R Mexico
99D2 Amadi Sudan
93D2 Am ādīyah Iraq
6C3 Amadjuak L Can
74B4 Amakusa-shotō I Japan
39G7 Åmål Sweden
63D2 Amalat R USSR
55B3 Amaliás Greece
85D4 Amalner India
69E4 Amami I Japan
69E4 Amami gunto Arch Japan
100C4 Amanzimtoti S Africa
33G3 Amapá Brazil
33G3 Amapá State, Brazil
9C3 Amarillo USA
60E5 Amasya Turk
23A1 Amatitan Mexico
Amazonas = Solimões
32D4 Amazonas State, Brazil
28C3 Amazonas R Brazil
84D2 Ambāla India
87C3 Ambalangoda Sri Lanka
101D3 Ambalavao Madag
98B2 Ambam Cam
101D2 Ambanja Madag
1C7 Ambarchik USSR
32B4 Ambato Ecuador
101D2 Ambato-Boeny Madag
101D2 Ambatolampy Madag
101D2 Ambatondrazaka Madag
57C3 Amberg Germany
25D3 Ambergris Cay I Belize
86A2 Ambikāpur India
101D2 Ambilobe Madag
101D3 Amboasary Madag
101D2 Ambodifototra Madag

101D3 Ambohimahasoa Madag
71D4 Ambon Indon
101D3 Ambositra Madag
101D3 Ambovombe Madag
98B3 Ambriz Angola
98C1 Am Dam Chad
64H3 Amderma USSR
24B2 Ameca Mexico
23B2 Amecacameca Mexico
34C2 Ameghino Arg
56B2 Ameland I Neth
16C2 Amenia USA
112B10 American Highland Upland Ant
105H4 American Samoa Is Pacific O
17B1 Americus USA
101G1 Amersfoort S Africa
112C10 Amery Ice Shelf Ant
55B3 Amfilokhía Greece
55B3 Amfissa Greece
63F1 Amga USSR
63F1 Amgal R USSR
69F2 Amgu USSR
69F1 Amgun' R USSR
99D1 Amhara Region Eth
7D5 Amherst Can
16C1 Amherst Massachusetts, USA
87B2 Amhūr India
48C2 Amiens France
75B1 Amino Japan
94B1 Amioune Leb
89K8 Amirante Is Indian O
86B1 Amlekhgan Nepal
92C3 Amman Jordan
38K6 Ämmänsaario Fin
56B2 Ammersfoort Neth
80E1 Amoda'ya R USSR
90B2 Amol Iran
55C3 Amorgós I Greece
7C5 Amos Can
Amoy = Xiamen
101D3 Ampanihy Madag
35B2 Amparo Brazil
51C1 Amposta Spain
85D4 Amrāvati India
85C4 Amreli India
84C2 Amritsar India
56A2 Amsterdam Neth
101H1 Amsterdam S Africa
15D2 Amsterdam USA
98C1 Am Timan Chad
88L3 Amu Darya R USSR
6A2 Amund Ringes I Can
4F2 Amundsen G Can
112B4 Amundsen S Ant
112A Amundsen-Scott Base Ant
78D3 Amuntai Indon
63E2 Amur R USSR
33E2 Anaco Ven
8B2 Anaconda USA
20B1 Anacortes USA
55C3 Anáfi I Greece
93D3 'Ānah Iraq
21B3 Anaheim USA
87B2 Anaimalai Hills India
83C4 Anakapalle India
12E1 Anaktuvuk P USA
101D2 Analalava Madag
92B2 Anamur Turk
75A2 Anan Japan
87B2 Anantapur India
84D2 Anantnag India
31B5 Anápolis Brazil
90C3 Anār Iran
90B3 Anārak Iran
71F2 Anatahan I Pacific O
30D4 Añatuya Arg
74B3 Anbyŏn N Korea
22C4 Ancapa Is USA
4D3 Anchorage USA
30C2 Ancohuma Mt Bol
32B6 Ancón Peru
52B2 Ancona Italy
16C1 Ancram

29B4 **Ancud** Chile
69E2 **Anda** China
34A3 **Andacollo** Arg
108A1 **Andado** Aust
32C6 **Andahuaylas** Peru
38F6 **Andalsnes** Nor
50A2 **Andalucia** Region, Spain
17A1 **Andalusia** USA
83D4 **Andaman Is** Burma
83D4 **Andaman S** Burma
108A2 **Andamooka** Aust
38H5 **Andenes** Nor
47C1 **Andermatt** Switz
57B2 **Andernach** Germany
14A2 **Anderson** Indiana, USA
18B2 **Anderson** Missouri, USA
17B1 **Anderson** S Carolina, USA
4F3 **Anderson** *R* Can
87B1 **Andhra Pradesh** State, India
55B3 **Andikithira** *I* Greece
65J5 **Andizhan** USSR
65H6 **Andkhui** Afghan
74B3 **Andong** S Korea
51C1 **Andorra** Principality, SW Europe
51C1 **Andorra-La-Vella** Andorra
43D4 **Andover** Eng
35A2 **Andradina** Brazil
12B2 **Andreafsky** USA
92B2 **Andreas,C** Cyprus
53C2 **Andria** Italy
11C4 **Andros** *I* The Bahamas
55B3 **Ándros** *I* Greece
87A2 **Androth** *I* India
50B2 **Andújar** Spain
100A2 **Andulo** Angola
97C4 **Anécho** Togo
97C3 **Anéfis** Mali
34B3 **Añelo** Arg
63C2 **Angarsk** USSR
38H6 **Ånge** Sweden
24A2 **Angel de la Guarda** *I* Mexico
79B2 **Angeles** Phil
39G7 **Angelholm** Sweden
109C1 **Angellala Creek** *R* Aust
22B1 **Angels Camp** USA
71E4 **Angemuk** *Mt* Indon
48B2 **Angers** France
76C3 **Angkor** *Hist Site* Camb
41C3 **Anglesey** *I* Wales
19A4 **Angleton** USA
6G3 **Angmagssalik** Greenland
101D2 **Angoche** Mozam
29B3 **Angol** Chile
14B2 **Angola** Indiana, USA
100A2 **Angola** Republic, Africa
103H6 **Angola Basin** Atlantic O
12H3 **Angoon** USA
48C2 **Angoulême** France
96A1 **Angra do Heroismo** Açores
35C2 **Angra dos Reis** Brazil
34C3 **Anguil** Arg
27E3 **Anguilla** *I* Caribbean S
26B2 **Anguilla Cays** *Is* Caribbean S
86B2 **Angul** India
99C3 **Angumu** Zaïre
56C1 **Anholt** *I* Den
73C4 **Anhua** China
72D3 **Anhui** Province, China
12C2 **Aniak** USA
35B1 **Anicuns** Brazil

46B2 **Anizy-le-Château** France
4C3 **Anjak** USA
48B2 **Anjou** Republic, France
101D2 **Anjouan** *I* Comoros
101D2 **Anjozorobe** Madag
74B3 **Anju** N Korea
72B3 **Ankang** China
92B2 **Ankara** Turk
101D2 **Ankaratra** *Mt* Madag
101D3 **Ankazoabo** Madag
101D2 **Ankazobe** Madag
56C2 **Anklam** Germany
76D3 **An Loc** Viet
73B4 **Anlong** China
73C3 **Anlu** China
18C2 **Anna** USA
96C1 **'Annaba** Alg
92C3 **An Nabk** S Arabia
92C3 **An Nabk** Syria
108A1 **Anna Creek** Aust
80C3 **An Nafūd** *Desert* S Arabia
93D3 **An Najaf** Iraq
42C2 **Annan** Scot
15C3 **Annapolis** USA
86A1 **Annapurna** *Mt* Nepal
14B2 **Ann Arbor** USA
94C1 **An Nāsirah** Syria
93E3 **An Nāsirīyah** Iraq
47B2 **Annecy** France
47B1 **Annemasse** France
76D3 **An Nhon** Viet
73A5 **Anning** China
17A1 **Anniston** USA
89E8 **Annobon** *I* Eq Guinea
49C2 **Annonay** France
27J1 **Annotto Bay** Jamaica
73D3 **Anqing** China
72B2 **Ansai** China
57C3 **Ansbach** Germany
26C3 **Anse d'Hainault** Haiti
72E1 **Anshan** China
73B4 **Anshun** China
97C3 **Ansongo** Mali
14B3 **Ansted** USA
92C2 **Antakya** Turk
101E2 **Antalaha** Madag
92B2 **Antalya** Turk
92B2 **Antalya Körfezi** *B* Turk
101D2 **Antananarivo** Madag
112C1 **Antarctic Circle** Ant
112C3 **Antarctic Pen** Ant
50B2 **Antequera** Spain
96B2 **Anti-Atlas** *Mts* Mor
7D5 **Anticosti I** Can
27E3 **Antigua** *I* Caribbean S
Anti Lebanon = Jebel esh Sharqi
21A2 **Antioch** USA
19A3 **Antlers** USA
30B3 **Antofagasta** Chile
45C1 **Antrim** County, N Ire
45C1 **Antrim** N Ire
45C1 **Antrim Hills** N Ire
101D2 **Antseranana** Madag
101D2 **Antsirabe** Madag
101D2 **Antsohiny** Madag
76D3 **An Tuc** Viet
46C1 **Antwerpen** Belg
45C2 **An Uaimh** Irish Rep
84C3 **Anupgarh** India
87C3 **Anuradhapura** Sri Lanka
Anvers = Antwerpen
4B3 **Anvik** USA
63B3 **Anxi** China
72C2 **Anyang** China
72A3 **A'nyêmaqên Shan** *Upland* China
47C2 **Anza** *R* Italy
13E1 **Anzac** Can
65K4 **Anzhero-Sudzhensk** USSR
53B2 **Anzio** Italy
74E2 **Aomori** Japan

52A1 **Aosta** Italy
97B3 **Aoukar** *Desert Region* Maur
96C2 **Aoulef** Alg
95A2 **Aozou** Chad
30E3 **Apa** *R* Brazil/Par
11B4 **Apalachee B** USA
17B2 **Apalachicola** USA
17A2 **Apalachicola B** USA
23B2 **Apan** Mexico
64E3 **Apatity** USSR
32C3 **Apaporis** *R* Colombia
35A2 **Aparecida do Taboado** Brazil
79B2 **Aparri** Phil
54A1 **Apatin** Yugos
64E3 **Apatity** USSR
24B3 **Apatzingan** Mexico
56B2 **Apeldoorn** Neth
35B2 **Apiai** Brazil
33F2 **Apoera** Surinam
108B3 **Apollo Bay** Aust
79C4 **Apo,Mt** *Mt* Phil
17B2 **Apopka,L** USA
30F2 **Aporé** *R* Brazil
10A2 **Apostle Is** USA
10A2 **Apostle L** USA
23A1 **Apozol** Mexico
11B3 **Appalachian Mts** USA
52B2 **Appennino Abruzzese** *Mts* Italy
52A2 **Appennino Ligure** *Mts* Italy
53C2 **Appennino Lucano** *Mts* Italy
53B2 **Appennino Napoletano** *Mts* Italy
52B2 **Appennino Tosco-Emilliano** *Mts* Italy
52B2 **Appennino Umbro-Marchigiano** *Mts* Italy
47C1 **Appenzell** Switz
42C2 **Appleby** Eng
14A2 **Appleton** Wisconsin, USA
30F3 **Apucarana** Brazil
23B1 **Apulco** Mexico
32D2 **Apure** *R* Ven
32C6 **Apurimac** *R* Peru
92C4 **'Aqaba** Jordan
92B4 **'Aqaba,G of** Egypt/S Arabia
90B3 **'Aqdā** Iran
30E3 **Aquidauana** Brazil
23A2 **Aquila** Mexico
86A1 **Ara** India
17A1 **Arab** USA
81D4 **Arabian** *S* Asia/Arabian Pen
31D4 **Aracajú** Brazil
31D2 **Aracati** Brazil
30F3 **Araçatuba** Brazil
50A2 **Aracena** Spain
31C5 **Araçuai** Brazil
94B3 **Arad** Israel
60B4 **Arad** Rom
98C1 **Arada** Chad
91B5 **'Arādah** UAE
106C1 **Arafura S** Indon/Aust
30F2 **Aragarças** Brazil
51B1 **Aragón** Region, Spain
50B1 **Aragon** *R* Spain
33G6 **Araguaia** *R* Brazil
31B3 **Araguaína** Brazil
31B5 **Araguari** Brazil
35B1 **Araguari** *R* Brazil
75B1 **Arai** Japan
96C2 **Arak** Alg
90A3 **Arāk** Iran
76A2 **Arakan Yoma** *Mts* Burma
87B2 **Arakkonam** India
93E2 **Araks** *R* USSR
Aral S = Aral'skoye More
80E1 **Aral'sk** USSR

65G5 **Aral'skoye More** *S* USSR
40B2 **Aran** *I* Irish Rep
41B3 **Aran** *Is* Irish Rep
50B1 **Aranda de Duero** Spain
23A1 **Arandas** Mexico
50B1 **Aranjuez** Spain
75A2 **Arao** Japan
97B3 **Araouane** Mali
29E2 **Arapey** *R* Urug
31D4 **Arapiraca** Brazil
35A2 **Araporgas** Brazil
30G4 **Ararangua** Brazil
31B6 **Araraquara** Brazil
35B2 **Araras** Brazil
107D4 **Ararat** Aust
93D2 **Ararat** USSR
93D1 **Aras** *R* Turk
75C1 **Arato** Japan
32D2 **Arauca** *R* Ven
34A3 **Arauco** Chile
32C2 **Arauea** Colombia
85C4 **Arāvalli Range** *Mts* India
31B5 **Araxá** Brazil
99D2 **Arba Minch** Eth
53A3 **Arbatax** Sardegna
93D2 **Arbīl** Iraq
47A1 **Arbois** France
39H6 **Arbrå** Sweden
44C3 **Arbroath** Scot
47A1 **Arc** France
47B2 **Arc** *R* France
48B3 **Arcachon** France
17B2 **Arcadia** USA
20B2 **Arcata** USA
23A2 **Arcelia** Mexico
26B2 **Archipiélago de Camaguey** *Arch* Cuba
29B6 **Archipiélago de la Reina Adelaida** *Arch* Chile
29B4 **Archipiélago de las Chones** *Arch* Chile
32B2 **Archipiélago de las Perlas** *Arch* Panama
35B2 **Arcos** Brazil
50A2 **Arcos de la Frontera** Spain
1C1 **Arctic Circle**
4E3 **Arctic Red** Can
4E3 **Arctic Red R** Can
4D3 **Arctic Village** USA
112C2 **Arctowski** *Base* Ant
54C2 **Arda** *R* Bulg
65F6 **Ardabīl** Iran
93D1 **Ardahan** Turk
39F6 **Ardal** Nor
96C2 **Ardar des Iforas** *Upland* Alg/Mali
45C2 **Ardee** Irish Rep
90B3 **Ardekān** Iran
46C2 **Ardennes** Department, France
57A2 **Ardennes** Region, Belg
90B3 **Ardestan** Iran
92C3 **Ardh es Suwwan** *Desert Region* Jordan
50A2 **Ardila** *R* Port
109C2 **Ardlethan** Aust
9D3 **Ardmore** USA
44A3 **Ardnamurchan** *Pt* Scot
46A1 **Ardres** France
44B3 **Ardrishaig** Scot
42B2 **Ardrossan** Scot
27D3 **Arecibo** Puerto Rico
31D2 **Areia Branca** Brazil
21A2 **Arena,Pt** USA
39F7 **Arendal** Nor
30B2 **Arequipa** Peru
52B2 **Arezzo** Italy
52B2 **Argenta** Italy
49C2 **Argentan** France

46B2 **Argenteuil** France
28C7 **Argentina** Republic, S America
103F7 **Argentine Basin** Atlantic O
48C2 **Argenton-sur-Creuse** France
54C2 **Argeş** R Rom
84B2 **Arghardab** R Afghan
55B3 **Argolikós Kólpos** G Greece
46C2 **Argonne** Region, France
55B3 **Árgos** Greece
55B3 **Argostólion** Greece
22B3 **Arguello,Pt** USA
106B2 **Argyle,L** Aust
56C1 **Århus** Den
100A3 **Ariamsvlei** Namibia
34C2 **Arias** Arg
97B3 **Aribinda** Burkina
30B2 **Arica** Chile
84C2 **Arifwala** Pak
Arihā = Jericho
27L1 **Arima** Trinidad
35B1 **Arinos** Brazil
33F6 **Arinos** R Brazil
23A2 **Ario de Rosales** Mexico
27L1 **Aripo,Mt** Trinidad
33E5 **Aripuana** Brazil
33E5 **Aripuaná** R Brazil
44B3 **Arisaig** Scot
87B2 **Ariskere** India
13B2 **Aristazabal I** Can
34B3 **Arizona** Arg
9B3 **Arizona** State, USA
39G7 **Årjäng** Sweden
61F3 **Arkadak** USSR
19B3 **Arkadelphia** USA
65H4 **Arkalya** USSR
11A3 **Arkansas** State, USA
11A3 **Arkansas** R USA
18A2 **Arkansas City** USA
64F3 **Arkhangel'sk** USSR
41B3 **Arklow** Irish Rep
50B1 **Arlanzón** R Spain
47D1 **Arlberg P** Austria
49C3 **Arles** France
19A3 **Arlington** Texas, USA
15C3 **Arlington** Virginia, USA
20B1 **Arlington** Washington, USA
97C3 **Arlit** Niger
57B3 **Arlon** Belg
Armageddon= Megiddo
45C1 **Armagh** County, N Ire
45C1 **Armagh** N Ire
61F5 **Armavir** USSR
23A2 **Armena** Mexico
32B3 **Armenia** Colombia
107E4 **Armidale** Aust
13D2 **Armstrong** Can
65F5 **Armyanskaya SSR** Republic, USSR
7C3 **Arnaud** R Can
92B2 **Arnauti** C Cyprus
56B2 **Arnhem** Neth
106C2 **Arnhem,C** Aust
106C2 **Arnhem Land** Aust
22B1 **Arnold** USA
15C1 **Arnprior** Can
46E1 **Arnsberg** Germany
100A3 **Aroab** Namibia
47C2 **Arona** Italy
12B2 **Aropuk L** USA
52A1 **Arosa** Switz
97A3 **Arquipélago dos Bijagós** Arch Guinea-Bissau
93D3 **Ar Ramādī** Iraq
42B2 **Arran** I Scot
93C2 **Ar Raqqah** Syria
49C1 **Arras** France
96A2 **Arrecife** Canary Is
34C2 **Arrecifes** Arg

23A1 **Arriaga** Mexico
93E3 **Ar Rifa't** Iraq
93E3 **Ar Rihāb** Desert Region Iraq
91A5 **Ar Riyāḍ** S Arabia
44B3 **Arrochar** Scot
111A2 **Arrowtown** NZ
23B1 **Arroyo Seco** Mexico
91B4 **Ar Ru'ays** Qatar
91C5 **Ar Rustaq** Oman
93D3 **Ar Rutbah** Iraq
47D2 **Arsiero** Italy
49D2 **Arsizio** Italy
61G2 **Arsk** USSR
55B3 **Árta** Greece
23A2 **Arteaga** Mexico
63B2 **Artemovsk** USSR
63D2 **Artemovskiy** USSR
9C3 **Artesia** USA
111B2 **Arthurs P** NZ
6B2 **Artic Bay** Can
29E2 **Artigas** Urug
4H3 **Artillery L** Can
48C1 **Artois** Region, France
112C2 **Arturo Prat** Base Ant
93D1 **Artvin** Turk
99D2 **Aru** Zaïre
33G6 **Aruanã** Brazil
27C4 **Aruba** I Caribbean S
86B1 **Arun** R Nepal
86C1 **Arunāchal Pradesh** Union Territory, India
87B3 **Aruppukkottai** India
99D3 **Arusha** Tanz
98C2 **Aruwimi** R Zaïre
68C2 **Arvayheer** Mongolia
47B2 **Arve** R France
7C5 **Arvida** Can
38H5 **Arvidsjaur** Sweden
39G7 **Arvika** Sweden
21B2 **Arvin** USA
94B1 **Arwad** I Syria
61F2 **Arzamas** USSR
84C2 **Asadabad** Afghan
75A2 **Asahi** R Japan
74E2 **Asahi dake** Mt Japan
74E2 **Asahikawa** Japan
86B2 **Asansol** India
95A2 **Asawanwah** Well Libya
61K2 **Asbest** USSR
15D2 **Asbury Park** USA
103H5 **Ascension** I Atlantic O
57B3 **Aschaffenburg** Germany
56C2 **Aschersleben** Germany
52B2 **Ascoli Piceno** Italy
47C1 **Ascona** Switz
96C2 **Asedjirad** Upland Alg
38H6 **Åsele** Sweden
99D2 **Aselle** Eth
54B2 **Asenovgrad** Bulg
46C2 **Asfeld** France
61J2 **Asha** USSR
17B1 **Ashburn** USA
111B2 **Ashburton** NZ
106A3 **Ashburton** R Aust
92B3 **Ashdod** Israel
19B3 **Ashdown** USA
11B3 **Asheville** USA
109D1 **Ashford** Aust
43E4 **Ashford** Eng
74D3 **Ashikaga** Japan
75A2 **Ashizuri-misaki** Pt Japan
65G6 **Ashkhabad** USSR
10B3 **Ashland** Kentucky, USA
18A1 **Ashland** Nebraska, USA
14B2 **Ashland** Ohio, USA
8A2 **Ashland** Oregon, USA
109C1 **Ashley** Aust
16B2 **Ashokan Res** USA
94B3 **Ashqelon** Israel
93D3 **Ash Shabakh** Iraq

91C4 **Ash Sha'm** UAE
93D2 **Ash Sharqāt** Iraq
93E3 **Ash Shatrah** Iraq
81C4 **Ash Shihr** Yemen
91A4 **Ash Shumlul** S Arabia
14B2 **Ashtabula** USA
7D4 **Ashuanipi L** Can
92C3 **'Aşī** R Syria
47D2 **Asiago** Italy
53A2 **Asinara** I Medit S
65K4 **Asino** USSR
93D2 **Aşkale** Turk
39G7 **Askersund** Sweden
84C1 **Asmar** Afghan
95C3 **Asmara** Eth
75A2 **Aso** Japan
99D1 **Asosa** Eth
111A2 **Aspiring,Mt** NZ
99E1 **Assab** Eth
93C2 **As Sabkhah** Syria
91A5 **As Salamiyah** S Arabia
92C2 **As Salamīyah** Syria
93D3 **As Salmañ** Iraq
86C1 **Assam** State, India
93E3 **As Samāwah** Iraq
91B5 **As Şanām** Region, S Arabia
94C2 **As Sanamayn** Syria
56B2 **Assen** Neth
56B1 **Assens** Den
95A1 **As Sidrah** Libya
5H5 **Assiniboia** Can
5G4 **Assiniboine,Mt** Can
30F3 **Assis** Brazil
93C3 **As Sukhnah** Syria
91A5 **As Summan** Region, S Arabia
99E3 **Assumption** I Seychelles
92C3 **As Suwaydā'** Syria
93D3 **As Suwayrah** Iraq
93E2 **Astara** USSR
52A2 **Asti** Italy
55C3 **Astipálaia** I Greece
50A1 **Astorga** Spain
8A2 **Astoria** USA
61G4 **Astrakhan'** USSR
50A1 **Asturias** Region, Spain
30E4 **Asunción** Par
99D2 **Aswa** R Uganda
80B3 **Aswân** Egypt
95C2 **Aswân High Dam** Egypt
95C2 **Asyût** Egypt
92C3 **As Zilaf** Syria
97C4 **Atakpamé** Togo
71D4 **Atambua** Indon
6E3 **Atangmik** Greenland
96A2 **Atar** Maur
65J5 **Atasu** USSR
95C3 **Atbara** Sudan
65H4 **Atbasar** USSR
11A4 **Atchafalaya B** USA
10A3 **Atchison** USA
16B3 **Atco** USA
23A1 **Atenguillo** Mexico
52B2 **Atessa** Italy
46B1 **Ath** Belg
13E2 **Athabasca** Can
5G4 **Athabasca** R Can
5H4 **Athabasca L** Can
45B2 **Athenry** Irish Rep
Athens = Athínai
11B3 **Athens** Georgia, USA
14B3 **Athens** Ohio, USA
19A3 **Athens** Texas, USA
55B3 **Athínai** Greece
41B3 **Athlone** Irish Rep
16C1 **Athol** USA
55B2 **Áthos** Mt Greece
45C2 **Athy** Irish Rep
98B1 **Ati** Chad
7A5 **Atikoken** Can
61F3 **Atkarsk** USSR
18B2 **Atkins** USA
23B2 **Atlacomulco** Mexico

11B3 **Atlanta** Georgia, USA
14B2 **Atlanta** Michigan, USA
18A1 **Atlantic** USA
10C3 **Atlantic City** USA
16B2 **Atlantic Highlands** USA
103H8 **Atlantic Indian Basin** Atlantic O
103H7 **Atlantic Indian Ridge** Atlantic O
96C1 **Atlas Saharien** Mts Alg
4E4 **Atlin** Can
4E4 **Atlin L** Can
94B2 **'Atlit** Israel
23B2 **Atlixco** Mexico
11B3 **Atmore** USA
101D3 **Atofinandrahana** Madag
12D3 **Atognak I** USA
19A3 **Atoka** USA
23A1 **Atotonilco** Mexico
23B2 **Atoyac** R Mexico
32B2 **Atrato** R Colombia
91B5 **Attaf** Region, UAE
81C3 **At Tā'if** S Arabia
94C2 **At Tall** Syria
17A1 **Attalla** USA
7B4 **Attauapiskat** Can
7B4 **Attauapiskat** R Can
93D3 **At Taysiyah** Desert Region S Arabia
14A2 **Attica** Indiana, USA
46C2 **Attigny** France
15D2 **Attleboro** Massachusetts, USA
76D3 **Attopeu** Laos
92C4 **At Tubayq** Upland S Arabia
34B3 **Atuel** R Arg
39H7 **Atvidaberg** Sweden
22B2 **Atwater** USA
49D3 **Aubagne** France
46C2 **Aube** Department, France
49C3 **Aubenas** France
17A1 **Auburn** Alabama, USA
21A2 **Auburn** California, USA
14A2 **Auburn** Indiana, USA
18A1 **Auburn** Nebraska, USA
15C2 **Auburn** New York, USA
20B1 **Auburn** Washington, USA
48C3 **Auch** France
110B1 **Auckland** NZ
105G6 **Auckland Is** NZ
48C3 **Aude** R France
7B4 **Auden** Can
47B1 **Audincourt** France
109C1 **Augathella** Aust
57C3 **Augsburg** Germany
106A4 **Augusta** Aust
11B3 **Augusta** Georgia, USA
18A2 **Augusta** Kansas, USA
10D2 **Augusta** Maine, USA
12D3 **Augustine I** USA
58C2 **Augustow** Pol
106A3 **Augustus,Mt** Aust
46A2 **Aumale** France
85D3 **Auraiya** India
85D5 **Aurangābād** India
96C1 **Aurès** Mts Alg
48C3 **Aurillac** France
8C3 **Aurora** Colorado, USA
10B2 **Aurora** Illinois, USA
14B3 **Aurora** Indiana, USA
18B2 **Aurora** Mississippi, USA
100A3 **Aus** Namibia
14B2 **Au Sable** USA
10A2 **Austin** Minnesota, USA

Austin

21B2 **Austin** Nevada, USA
9D3 **Austin** Texas, USA
107D4 **Australian Alps** *Mts*
Aust
37E4 **Austria** Federal
Republic, Europe
46A1 **Authie** *R* France
24B3 **Autlán** Mexico
49C2 **Autun** France
49C2 **Auvergne** Region,
France
49C2 **Auxerre** France
46B1 **Auxi-le-Châteaux** France
49C2 **Avallon** France
22C4 **Avalon** USA
7E5 **Avalon Pen** Can
35B2 **Avaré** Brazil
90D3 **Avaz** Iran
94B3 **Avedat** *Hist Site* Israel
33F4 **Aveiro** Brazil
50A1 **Aveiro** Port
29E2 **Avellaneda** Arg
53B2 **Avellino** Italy
46B1 **Avesnes-sur-Helpe**
France
39H6 **Avesta** Sweden
52B2 **Avezzano** Italy
44C3 **Aviemore** Scot
111B2 **Aviemore,L** NZ
47B2 **Avigliana** Italy
49C3 **Avignon** France
50B1 **Avila** Spain
50A1 **Aviles** Spain
47D1 **Avisio** *R* Italy
108B3 **Avoca** *R* Aust
43C4 **Avon** County, Eng
43D4 **Avon** *R* Dorset, Eng
43D3 **Avon** *R* Warwick, Eng
43C4 **Avonmouth** Wales
17B2 **Avon Park** USA
46B2 **Avre** *R* France
54A2 **Avtovac** Yugos
94C2 **A'waj** *R* Syria
74D4 **Awaji-shima** *B* Japan
99E2 **Awarem** Eth
111A2 **Awarua Pt** NZ
99E2 **Awash** Eth
99E2 **Awash** *R* Eth
75B1 **Awa-shima** *I* Japan
111B2 **Awatere** *R* NZ
95A2 **Awbārī** Libya
98C2 **Aweil** Sudan
95B2 **Awjilan** Libya
96A2 **Awserd** *Well* Mor
6A2 **Axel Heiburg I** Can
43C4 **Axminster** Eng
75B1 **Ayabe** Japan
29E3 **Ayacucho** Arg
32C6 **Ayacucho** Peru
65K5 **Ayaguz** USSR
82C2 **Ayakkum Hu** *L* China
50A2 **Ayamonte** Spain
63F2 **Ayan** USSR
32C6 **Ayauiri** Peru
92A2 **Aydin** Turk
55C3 **Áyios Evstrátios** *I*
Greece
43D4 **Aylesbury** Eng
13D2 **Aylmer,Mt** Can
94C2 **'Ayn al Fijah** Syria
93D2 **Ayn Zālah** Iraq
95B2 **Ayn Zuwayyah** *Well*
Libya
99D2 **Ayod** Sudan
107D2 **Ayr** Aust
42B2 **Ayr** Scot
42B2 **Ayr** *R* Scot
42B2 **Ayre,Pt of** Eng
54C2 **Aytos** Bulg
76C3 **Aytthaya** Thai
23A1 **Ayutla** Mexico
55C3 **Ayvacik** Turk
55C3 **Ayvalik** Turk
86A1 **Āzamgarh** India
97B3 **Azaouad** *Desert Region*
Mali
97D3 **Azare** Nig
92C2 **A'Zāz** Syria

Azbine = Aïr
96A2 **Azzeffal** *R* Maur
65F5 **Azerbaydzhanskaya**
SSR Republic, USSR
32B4 **Azogues** Ecuador
Azores = Açores
98C1 **Azoum** *R* Chad
60E4 **Azovskoye More** *S*
USSR
96B1 **Azrou** Mor
34D3 **Azucena** Arg
32A2 **Azuero,Pen de** Panama
29E3 **Azúl** Arg
94C2 **Az-Zabdānī** Syria
91C5 **Az Zāhirah** *Mts* Oman
93E3 **Az Zubayr** Iraq

B

94B2 **Ba'abda** Leb
92C3 **Ba'albek** Leb
94B3 **Ba'al Hazor** *Mt* Israel
99E2 **Baardheere** Somalia
54C2 **Babadag** Rom
92A1 **Babaeski** Turk
32B4 **Babahoyo** Ecuador
81C4 **Bāb al Mandab** *Str*
Djibouti/Yemen
71D4 **Babar** *I* Indon
99D3 **Babati** Tanz
60E2 **Babayevo** USSR
14B2 **Baberton** USA
13B1 **Babine** *R* Can
5F4 **Babine L** Can
90B2 **Bābol** Iran
79B2 **Babuyan Chan** Phil
79B2 **Babuyan Is** Phil
31C2 **Bacabal** Brazil
71D4 **Bacan** *I* Indon
60C4 **Bačau** Rom
76D1 **Bac Can** Viet
108B3 **Bacchus Marsh** Aust
82B2 **Bachu** China
4J3 **Back** *R* Can
12J2 **Backbone Ranges** *Mts*
Can
76D1 **Bac Ninh** Viet
79B3 **Bacolod** Phil
79B3 **Baco,Mt** Phil
87B2 **Badagara** India
72A1 **Badain Jaran Shamo**
Desert China
50A2 **Badajoz** Spain
51C1 **Badalona** Spain
93D3 **Badanah** S Arabia
46D2 **Bad Bergzabern**
Germany
46D1 **Bad Ems** Germany
47C1 **Baden** Switz
57B3 **Baden-Baden** Germany
57B3 **Baden-Württemberg**
State, Germany
57C3 **Badgastein** Austria
22C2 **Badger** USA
57B2 **Bad-Godesberg**
Germany
57B2 **Bad Hersfeld** Germany
46D1 **Bad Honnef** Germany
85B4 **Badin** Pak
52B1 **Bad Ischl** Austria
93C3 **Badiyat ash Sham**
Desert Region
Jordan/Iraq
57B3 **Bad-Kreuznach**
Germany
46D1 **Bad Nevenahr-**
Ahrweiler Germany
47C1 **Bad Ragaz** Switz
57C3 **Bad Tolz** Germany
87C3 **Badulla** Sri Lanka
50B2 **Baena** Spain
97A3 **Bafatá** Guinea-Bissau
4H2 **Baffin** *Region* Can
6C2 **Baffin B** Greenland/Can
6C2 **Baffin I** Can
98B2 **Bafia** Cam
97A3 **Bafing** *R* Mali

97A3 **Bafoulabé** Mali
98B2 **Bafoussam** Cam
90C3 **Bāfq** Iran
60E5 **Bafra Burun** *Pt* Turk
91C4 **Bāft** Iran
98C2 **Bafwasende** Zaïre
86A1 **Bagaha** India
87B1 **Bāgalkot** India
99D3 **Bagamoyo** Tanz
29F2 **Bagé** Brazil
93D3 **Baghdād** Iraq
86B2 **Bagherhat** Bang
91C3 **Bāghīn** Iran
84B1 **Baghlan** Afghan
49C3 **Bagnols-sur-Cèze**
France
97B3 **Bagoé** *R* Mali
79B2 **Baguio** Phil
86B1 **Bāhādurābād** India
11C4 **Bahamas,The** *Is*
Caribbean S
86B2 **Baharampur** India
99D1 **Bahar Dar** Eth
92A4 **Baharîya Oasis** Egypt
84C3 **Bahawalpur** Pak
84C3 **Bahawalpur** Province,
Pak
85C3 **Bahawathagar** Pak
Bahia = Salvador
31C4 **Bahia** State, Brazil
29D3 **Bahia Blanca** Arg
29D3 **Bahia Blanca** *B* Arg
34A3 **Bahia Concepción** *B*
Chile
35C2 **Bahia da Ilha Grande** *B*
Brazil
24B2 **Bahia de Banderas** *B*
Mexico
24C2 **Bahia de Campeche** *B*
Mexico
25D3 **Bahia de la Ascension**
B Mexico
24B3 **Bahia de Petacalco** *B*
Mexico
96A2 **Bahia de Rio de Oro** *B*
Mor
35C2 **Bahia de Sepetiba** *B*
Brazil
29C6 **Bahía Grande** *B* Arg
9B4 **Bahia Kino** Mexico
24A2 **Bahia Magdalena** *B*
Mexico
24A2 **Bahia Sebastia**
Vizcaino *B* Mexico
86A1 **Bahraich** India
80D3 **Bahrain** Sheikdom,
Arabian Pen
93D3 **Bahr al Milh** *L* Iraq
98C2 **Bahr Aouk** *R* Chad/CAR
Bahrat Lut = Dead S
98C2 **Bahr el Arab**
Watercourse Sudan
99D2 **Bahr el Ghazal** *R*
Sudan
98B1 **Bahr el Ghazal**
Watercourse Chad
101H1 **Baia de Maputo** *B*
Mozam
31B2 **Baia de Marajó** *B*
Brazil
101D2 **Baiá de Pemba** *B*
Mozam
31C2 **Baia de São Marcos** *B*
Brazil
50A2 **Baia de Setúbal** *B* Port
31D4 **Baia de Todos os**
Santos *B* Brazil
100A2 **Baia dos Tigres** Angola
60B4 **Baia Mare** Rom
98B2 **Baïbokoum** Chad
69E2 **Baicheng** China
101E2 **Baie Antongila** *B*
Madag
7D5 **Baie-Comeau** Can
101D2 **Baie de Bombetoka** *B*
Madag
101D2 **Baie de Mahajamba** *B*
Madag

101D3 **Baie de St Augustin** *B*
Madag
94B2 **Baie de St Georges** *B*
Leb
10D2 **Baie des Chaleurs** *B*
Can
7C4 **Baie-du-Poste** Can
72B3 **Baihe** China
72C3 **Bai He** *R* China
93D3 **Ba'ījī** Iraq
86A2 **Baikunthpur** India
Baile Atha Cliath =
Dublin
54B2 **Băilesti** Rom
46B1 **Bailleul** France
72A3 **Baima** China
17B1 **Bainbridge** USA
12B2 **Baird Inlet** USA
4B3 **Baird Mts** USA
72D1 **Bairin Youqi** China
72D1 **Bairin Zuoqi** China
107D4 **Bairnsdale** Aust
79B4 **Bais** Phil
54A1 **Baja** Hung
9B3 **Baja California** State,
Mexico
24A1 **Baja California** *Pen*
Mexico
61J2 **Bakal** USSR
98C2 **Bakala** CAR
97A3 **Bakel** Sen
8C2 **Baker** Montana, USA
8B2 **Baker** Oregon, USA
6A3 **Baker Foreland** *Pt*
Can
4J3 **Baker L** Can
4J3 **Baker Lake** Can
8A2 **Baker,Mt** USA
9B3 **Bakersfield** USA
90C2 **Bakharden** USSR
90C2 **Bakhardok** USSR
60D3 **Bakhmach** USSR
38C1 **Bakkaflói** *B* Iceland
99D2 **Bako** Eth
98C2 **Bakouma** CAR
65F5 **Baku** USSR
92B2 **Balâ** Turk
79A4 **Balabac** *I* Phil
70C3 **Balabac** *Str* Malay
78C2 **Balaikarangan** Indon
108A2 **Balaklava** Aust
61G3 **Balakovo** USSR
86A2 **Balāngir** India
61F3 **Balashov** USSR
86B2 **Balasore** India
80A3 **Balât** Egypt
52C1 **Balaton** *L* Hung
45C2 **Balbriggan** Irish Rep
29E3 **Balcarce** Arg
54C2 **Balchik** Bulg
111B3 **Balclutha** NZ
18B2 **Bald Knob** USA
17B1 **Baldwin** USA
9C3 **Baldy Peak** *Mt* USA
Balearic Is = Islas
Baleares
78C2 **Baleh** *R* Malay
79B2 **Baler** Phil
61H2 **Balezino** USSR
106A1 **Bali** *I* Indon
92A2 **Balıkesir** Turk
93C2 **Balīkh** *R* Syria
78D3 **Balikpapan** Indon
79B2 **Balintang Chan** Phil
78C4 **Bali** *S* Indon
35A1 **Baliza** Brazil
84B1 **Balkh** Afghan
65J5 **Balkhash** USSR
44B3 **Ballachulish** Scot
45B2 **Ballaghaderreen**
Irish Rep
42B2 **Ballantrae** Scot
4G2 **Ballantyne Str** Can
87B2 **Ballapur** India
107D4 **Ballarat** Aust
44C3 **Ballater** Scot
112C7 **Balleny Is** Ant
86A1 **Ballia** India

109D1 **Ballina** Aust
41B3 **Ballina** Irish Rep
45B2 **Ballinasloe** Irish Rep
45B2 **Ballinrobe** Irish Rep
45B1 **Ballycastle** Irish Rep
45C1 **Ballycastle** N Ire
45C1 **Ballymena** N Ire
45C1 **Ballymoney** N Ire
45B1 **Ballyshannon**
    Irish Rep
45B2 **Ballyvaghan** Irish Rep
108B3 **Balmoral** Aust
34C2 **Balnearia** Arg
84B3 **Balochistan** Region,
    Pak
100A2 **Balombo** Angola
109C1 **Balonn** R Aust
85C3 **Balotra** India
86A1 **Balrāmpur** India
107D4 **Balranald** Aust
31B3 **Balsas** Brazil
23B2 **Balsas** Mexico
24B3 **Balsas** R Mexico
60C4 **Balta** USSR
39H7 **Baltic S** N Europe
92B3 **Baltim** Egypt
45B3 **Baltimore** Irish Rep
10C3 **Baltimore** USA
86B1 **Balurghāt** India
61H4 **Balykshi** USSR
91C4 **Bam** Iran
98B1 **Bama** Nig
97B3 **Bamako** Mali
98C2 **Bambari** CAR
17B1 **Bamberg** USA
57C3 **Bamberg** Germany
98C2 **Bambili** Zaïre
35B2 **Bambui** Brazil
98B2 **Bamenda** Cam
13C3 **Bamfield** Can
98B2 **Bamingui** R CAR
98B2 **Bamingui Bangoran**
    National Park CAR
84B2 **Bamiyan** Afghan
91D4 **Bampur** Iran
91D4 **Bampur** R Iran
98C2 **Banalia** Zaïre
97B3 **Banamba** Mali
76C3 **Ban Aranyaprathet**
    Thai
76C2 **Ban Ban** Laos
77C4 **Ban Betong** Thai
45C1 **Banbridge** N Ire
43D3 **Banbury** Eng
44C3 **Banchory** Scot
25D3 **Banco Chinchorro** *Is*
    Mexico
15C1 **Bancroft** Can
86A1 **Bānda** India
70A3 **Banda Aceh** Indon
97B4 **Bandama** R Ivory
    Coast
91C4 **Bandar Abbās** Iran
90A2 **Bandar Anzalī** Iran
91B4 **Bandar-e Daylam** Iran
91B4 **Bandar-e Lengheh**
    Iran
91B4 **Bandar-e Māqām** Iran
91B4 **Bandar-e Rig** Iran
90B2 **Bandar-e Torkoman**
    Iran
91A3 **Bandar Khomeynī** Iran
78C2 **Bandar Seri Begawan**
    Brunei
71D4 **Banda S** Indon
91C4 **Band Bonī** Iran
35C2 **Bandeira** *Mt* Brazil
97B3 **Bandiagara** Mali
60C5 **Bandirma** Turk
45B3 **Bandon** Irish Rep
98B3 **Bandundu** Zaïre
78B4 **Bandung** Indon
25E2 **Banes** Cuba
13D2 **Banff** Can
44C3 **Banff** Scot
5G4 **Banff** R Can
13D2 **Banff Nat Pk** Can
87B2 **Bangalore** India

98C2 **Bangassou** CAR
70C3 **Banggi** I Malay
76D2 **Bang Hieng** R Laos
78B3 **Bangka** I Indon
78A3 **Bangko** Indon
76C3 **Bangkok** Thai
82C3 **Bangladesh** Republic,
    Asia
84D2 **Bangong Co** L China
10D2 **Bangor** Maine, USA
45D1 **Bangor** N Ire
16B2 **Bangor** Pennsylvania,
    USA
42B3 **Bangor** Wales
78D3 **Bangsalsembera**
    Indon
76B3 **Bang Saphan Yai** Thai
79B2 **Bangued** Phil
98B2 **Bangui** CAR
100C2 **Bangweulu** L Zambia
77C4 **Ban Hat Yai** Thai
76C2 **Ban Hin Heup** Laos
76C1 **Ban Houei Sai** Laos
76B3 **Ban Hua Hin** Thai
97B3 **Bani** R Mali
97C3 **Bani Bangou** Niger
95A1 **Banī Walīd** Libya
92C2 **Bāniyās** Syria
94B2 **Baniyas** Syria
52C2 **Banja Luka** Yugos
78C3 **Banjarmasin** Indon
97A3 **Banjul** The Gambia
77B4 **Ban Kantang** Thai
76D2 **Ban Khemmarat** Laos
77B4 **Ban Khok Kloi** Thai
71F5 **Banks I** Aust
5E4 **Banks I** British
    Columbia, Can
4F2 **Banks I** Northwest
    Territories, Can
20C1 **Banks L** USA
111B2 **Banks Pen** NZ
109C4 **Banks Str** Aust
86B2 **Bankura** India
76B2 **Ban Mae Sariang** Thai
76B2 **Ban Mae Sot** Thai
76D3 **Ban Me Thuot** Viet
45C1 **Bann** R N Ire
77B4 **Ban Na San** Thai
84C2 **Bannu** Pak
34A3 **Baños Maule** Chile
76C2 **Ban Pak Neun** Laos
77C4 **Ban Pak Phanang** Thai
76D3 **Ban Ru Kroy** Camb
76B3 **Ban Sai Yok** Thai
76C3 **Ban Sattahip** Thai
59B3 **Banská Bystrica** Czech
85C4 **Bānswāra** India
77B4 **Ban Tha Kham** Thai
76D2 **Ban Thateng** Laos
76C2 **Ban Tha Tum** Thai
41B3 **Bantry** Irish Rep
41A3 **Bantry** B Irish Rep
76D3 **Ban Ya Soup** Viet
78C4 **Banyuwangi** Indon
72C3 **Baofeng** China
76C1 **Bao Ha** Viet
72B3 **Baoji** China
76D3 **Bao Loc** Viet
68B4 **Baoshan** China
72C1 **Baotou** China
87C1 **Bāpatla** India
46B1 **Bapaume** France
93D3 **Ba'Qūbah** Iraq
32J7 **Baquerizo Morena**
    Ecuador
54A2 **Bar** Yugos
99D1 **Bara** Sudan
99E2 **Baraawe** Somalia
78D3 **Barabai** Indon
86A1 **Bāra Banki** India
65J4 **Barabinsk** USSR
65J4 **Barabinskaya Step**
    Steppe USSR
50B1 **Baracaldo** Spain
26C2 **Baracoa** Cuba
94C2 **Baradá** R Syria
109C2 **Baradine** Aust

87A1 **Bārāmati** India
84C2 **Baramula** Pak
85D3 **Bārān** India
79B3 **Barangas** Phil
4E4 **Baranof I** USA
60C3 **Baranovichi** USSR
108A2 **Baratta** Aust
86B1 **Barauni** India
31C6 **Barbacena** Brazil
27F4 **Barbados** I
    Caribbean S
51C1 **Barbastro** Spain
101H1 **Barberton** S Africa
48B2 **Barbezieux** France
32C2 **Barbòsa** Colombia
27E3 **Barbuda** I
    Caribbean S
107D3 **Barcaldine** Aust
    Barce = Al Marj
53C3 **Barcellona** Italy
51C1 **Barcelona** Spain
33E1 **Barcelona** Ven
107D3 **Barcoo** R Aust
34B3 **Barda del Medio** Arg
95A2 **Bardai** Chad
29C3 **Bardas Blancas** Arg
86B2 **Barddhamān** India
59C3 **Bardejov** Czech
47C2 **Bardi** Italy
47B2 **Bardonecchia** Italy
43B3 **Bardsey** I Wales
84D3 **Bareilly** India
64D2 **Barentsøya** I
    Barents S
64E2 **Barents S** USSR
95C3 **Barentu** Eth
86A2 **Bargarh** India
47B2 **Barge** Italy
63D2 **Barguzin** USSR
63D2 **Barguzin** R USSR
86B2 **Barhi** India
53C2 **Bari** Italy
51D2 **Barika** Alg
32C2 **Barinas** Ven
86B2 **Baripāda** India
85C4 **Bari Sādri** India
86C2 **Barisal** Bang
78C3 **Barito** R Indon
95A2 **Barjuj** *Watercourse*
    Libya
73A3 **Barkam** China
18C2 **Barkley,L** USA
13B3 **Barkley Sd** Can
100B4 **Barkly East** S Africa
106C2 **Barkly Tableland** *Mts*
    Aust
46C2 **Bar-le-Duc** France
106A3 **Barlee,L** Aust
106A3 **Barlee Range** *Mts*
    Aust
53C2 **Barletta** Italy
85C3 **Barmer** India
108B2 **Barmera** Aust
43B3 **Barmouth** Wales
42D2 **Barnard Castle** Eng
65K4 **Barnaul** USSR
16B3 **Barnegat** USA
16B3 **Barnegat B** USA
6C2 **Barnes Icecap** Can
17B1 **Barnesville** Georgia,
    USA
14B3 **Barnesville** Ohio, USA
42D3 **Barnsley** Eng
43B4 **Barnstaple** Eng
97C4 **Baro** Nig
86C1 **Barpeta** India
32D1 **Barquisimeto** Ven
31C4 **Barra** Brazil
44A3 **Barra** I Scot
109D2 **Barraba** Aust
23A2 **Barra de Navidad**
    Mexico
35C2 **Barra de Piraí** Brazil
35A1 **Barra do Garças** Brazil
50A2 **Barragem do Castelo**
    do Bode *Res* Port
50A2 **Barragem do**
    Maranhão Port

44A3 **Barra Head** *Pt* Scot
31C6 **Barra Mansa** Brazil
32B6 **Barranca** Peru
32C2 **Barrancabermeja**
    Colombia
33E2 **Barrancas** Ven
30E4 **Barranqueras** Arg
32C1 **Barranquilla** Colombia
44A3 **Barra,Sound of** Chan
    Scot
16C1 **Barre** USA
34B2 **Barreal** Arg
31C4 **Barreiras** Brazil
50A2 **Barreiro** Port
31D3 **Barreiros** Brazil
107D5 **Barren,C** Aust
12D3 **Barren Is** USA
31B6 **Barretos** Brazil
13E2 **Barrhead** Can
14C2 **Barrie** Can
13C2 **Barrière** Can
108B2 **Barrier Range** *Mts*
    Aust
107E4 **Barrington,Mt** Aust
27N2 **Barrouaillie** St Vincent
4C2 **Barrow** USA
45C2 **Barrow** R Irish Rep
106C3 **Barrow Creek** Aust
106A3 **Barrow I** Aust
42C2 **Barrow-in-Furness**
    Eng
4C2 **Barrow,Pt** USA
6A2 **Barrow Str** Can
15C1 **Barry's Bay** Can
87B1 **Barsi** India
9B3 **Barstow** USA
49C2 **Bar-sur-Aube** France
33F2 **Bartica** Guyana
92B1 **Bartın** Turk
107D2 **Bartle Frere,Mt** Aust
9D3 **Bartlesville** USA
101C3 **Bartolomeu Dias**
    Mozam
58C2 **Bartoszyce** Pol
78C4 **Barung** I Indon
85D4 **Barwāh** India
85C4 **Barwāni** India
109C1 **Barwon** R Aust
61G3 **Barysh** USSR
98B2 **Basankusu** Zaïre
34D2 **Basavilbas** Arg
79B1 **Basco** Phil
52A1 **Basel** Switz
53C2 **Basento** R Italy
13E2 **Bashaw** Can
79B1 **Bashi Chan** Phil
61H3 **Bashkirskaya ASSR**
    Republic, USSR
79B4 **Basilan** I Phil
43E4 **Basildon** Eng
43D4 **Basingstoke** Eng
8B2 **Basin Region** USA
93E3 **Basra** Iraq
46D2 **Bas-Rhin** Department,
    France
76D3 **Bassac** R Camb
13E2 **Bassano** Can
52B1 **Bassano** Italy
47D2 **Bassano del Grappa**
    Italy
97C4 **Bassari** Togo
101C3 **Bassas da India** I
    Mozam Chan
76A2 **Bassein** Burma
27E3 **Basse Terre**
    Guadeloupe
97C4 **Bassila** Benin
22C2 **Bass Lake** USA
107D4 **Bass Str** Aust
39G7 **Båstad** Sweden
91B4 **Bastak** Iran
86A1 **Basti** India
52A2 **Bastia** Corse
57B3 **Bastogne** Belg
19B3 **Bastrop** Louisiana,
    USA
19A3 **Bastrop** Texas, USA
98A2 **Bata** Eq Guinea

78C3 **Batakan** Indon
84D2 **Batala** India
68B3 **Batang** China
98B2 **Batangafo** CAR
79B1 **Batan Is** Phil
35B2 **Batatais** Brazil
15C2 **Batavia** USA
109D3 **Batemans Bay** Aust
17B1 **Batesburg** USA
18B2 **Batesville** Arkansas, USA
19C3 **Batesville** Mississippi, USA
43C4 **Bath** Eng
15C2 **Bath** New York, USA
98B1 **Batha** R Chad
107D4 **Bathurst** Aust
7D5 **Bathurst** Can
4F2 **Bathurst,C** Can
106C2 **Bathurst I** Aust
4H2 **Bathurst I** Can
4H3 **Bathurst Inlet** B Can
97B3 **Batié** Burkina
90B3 **Bātlāq-e-Gavkhūnī** Salt Flat Iran
109C3 **Batlow** Aust
93D2 **Batman** Turk
96C1 **Batna** Alg
11A3 **Baton Rouge** USA
94B1 **Batroun** Leb
76C3 **Battambang** Camb
87C3 **Batticaloa** Sri Lanka
13F2 **Battle** R Can
10B2 **Battle Creek** USA
7E4 **Battle Harbour** Can
20C2 **Battle Mountain** USA
78D2 **Batukelau** Indon
65F5 **Batumi** USSR
77C5 **Batu Pahat** Malay
78A3 **Baturaja** Indon
94B2 **Bat Yam** Israel
71D4 **Baubau** Indon
97C3 **Bauchi** Nig
47B2 **Bauges** Mts France
7E4 **Bauld,C** Can
47B1 **Baumes-les-Dames** France
63D2 **Baunt** USSR
31B6 **Bauru** Brazil
35A1 **Baus** Brazil
57C2 **Bautzen** Germany
78C4 **Baween** I Indon
95B2 **Bawîti** Egypt
97B3 **Bawku** Ghana
76B2 **Bawlake** Burma
108A2 **Bawlen** Aust
17B1 **Baxley** USA
25E2 **Bayamo** Cuba
78D4 **Bayan** Indon
72A1 **Bayandalay** Mongolia
68C2 **Bayandzürh** Mongolia
68B3 **Bayan Har Shan** Mts China
72A1 **Bayan Mod** China
72B1 **Bayan Obo** China
47A2 **Bayard** P France
12J3 **Bayard,Mt** Can
79B3 **Baybay** Phil
93D1 **Bayburt** Turk
10B2 **Bay City** Michigan, USA
19A4 **Bay City** Texas, USA
92B2 **Bay Dağlari** Turk
64H3 **Baydaratskaya Guba** B USSR
99E2 **Baydhabo** Somalia
48B2 **Bayeux** France
47D1 **Bayerische Alpen** Mts Germany
57C3 **Bayern** State, Germany
92C3 **Bāyir** Jordan
68C1 **Baykalskiy Khrebet** Mts USSR
63B1 **Baykit** USSR
63B3 **Baylik Shan** Mts China/Mongolia
61J3 **Baymak** USSR

79B2 **Bayombong** Phil
48B3 **Bayonne** France
57C3 **Bayreuth** Germany
19C3 **Bay St Louis** USA
15D2 **Bay Shore** USA
15C1 **Bays,L of** Can
68A2 **Baytik Shan** Mts China
Bayt Lahm=Bethlehem
19B4 **Baytown** USA
50B2 **Baza** Spain
59D3 **Bazaliya** USSR
48B3 **Bazas** France
73B3 **Bazhong** China
91D4 **Bazmān** Iran
94C1 **Bcharre** Leb
16B3 **Beach Haven** USA
43E4 **Beachy Head** Eng
16C2 **Beacon** USA
101D2 **Bealanana** Madag
18B1 **Beardstown** USA
Bear I = Bjørnøya
22B1 **Bear Valley** USA
8D2 **Beatrice** USA
44C2 **Beatrice** Oilfield N Sea
13C1 **Beatton** R Can
5F4 **Beatton River** Can
29E6 **Beauchene Is** Falkland Is
109D1 **Beaudesert** Aust
1B5 **Beaufort S** Can
100B4 **Beaufort West** S Africa
15D1 **Beauharnois** Can
44B3 **Beauly** Scot
21B3 **Beaumont** California, USA
11A3 **Beaumont** Texas, USA
49C2 **Beaune** France
48C2 **Beauvais** France
13F1 **Beauval** Can
12E1 **Beaver** Alaska, USA
13F2 **Beaver** R Saskatchewan, Can
4D3 **Beaver Creek** Can
12E1 **Beaver Creek** USA
18C2 **Beaver Dam** Kentucky, USA
13E2 **Beaverhill L** Can
14A1 **Beaver I** USA
18B2 **Beaver L** USA
13D1 **Beaverlodge** Can
85C3 **Beawar** India
34B2 **Beazley** Arg
35B2 **Bebedouro** Brazil
43E3 **Beccles** Eng
54B1 **Bečej** Yugos
96B1 **Béchar** Alg
12C3 **Becharof L** USA
11B3 **Beckley** USA
43D3 **Bedford County,** Eng
43D3 **Bedford** Eng
14A3 **Bedford** Indiana, USA
27M2 **Bedford Pt** Grenada
4D2 **Beechey** Pt USA
109C3 **Beechworth** Aust
109D1 **Beenleigh** Aust
92B3 **Beersheba** Israel
Beèr Sheva = Beersheba
94B3 **Beér Sheva** R Israel
9D4 **Beeville** USA
98C2 **Befale** Zaïre
101D2 **Befandriana** Madag
109C3 **Bega** Aust
91B3 **Behbehān** Iran
12H3 **Behm Canal** Sd USA
90B2 **Behshahr** Iran
84B2 **Behsud** Afghan
69E2 **Bei'an** China
73B5 **Beihai** China
72D2 **Beijing** China
76E1 **Beiliu** China
73B4 **Beipan Jiang** R China
72E1 **Beipiao** China
Beira = Sofala
92C3 **Beirut** Leb

68B2 **Bei Shan** Mts China
94B2 **Beit ed Dîne** Leb
94B3 **Beit Jala** Israel
50A2 **Beja** Port
96C1 **Beja** Tunisia
96C1 **Bejaïa** Alg
50A1 **Béjar** Spain
90C3 **Bejestān** Iran
59C3 **Békéscsaba** Hung
101D3 **Bekily** Madag
86A1 **Bela** India
85B3 **Bela** Pak
78C2 **Belaga** Malay
16A3 **Bel Air** USA
87B1 **Belamoalli** India
71D3 **Belang** Indon
70A3 **Belangpidie** Indon
71E3 **Belau** Republic, Pacific O
104E3 **Belau** I Pacific O
101C3 **Bela Vista** Mozam
70A3 **Belawan** Indon
61J2 **Belaya** R USSR
6A2 **Belcher Chan** Can
7C4 **Belcher Is** Can
84B1 **Belchiragh** Afghan
61H3 **Belebey** USSR
31B2 **Belém** Brazil
32B3 **Belén** Colombia
34D2 **Belén** Urug
9C3 **Belen** USA
99E2 **Belet Uen** Somalia
45D1 **Belfast** N Ire
101H1 **Belfast** S Africa
45D1 **Belfast Lough** Estuary N Ire
99D1 **Belfodio** Eth
42D2 **Belford** Eng
49D2 **Belfort** France
87A1 **Belgaum** India
56A2 **Belgium** Kingdom, N W Europe
60E3 **Belgorod** USSR
60D4 **Belgorod Dnestrovskiy** USSR
Belgrade = Beograd
95A2 **Bel Hedan** Libya
78B3 **Belinyu** Indon
78B3 **Belitung** I Indon
25D3 **Belize** Belize
25D3 **Belize** Republic, Cent America
48C2 **Bellac** France
5F4 **Bella Coola** Can
47C2 **Bellagio** Italy
19A4 **Bellaire** USA
47C1 **Bellano** Italy
87B1 **Bellary** India
109C1 **Bellata** Aust
47B2 **Belledonne** Mts France
8C2 **Belle Fourche** USA
49D2 **Bellegarde** France
17B2 **Belle Glade** USA
7E4 **Belle I** Can
48B2 **Belle-Ile** I France
7E4 **Belle Isle,Str of** Can
7C5 **Belleville** Can
18A2 **Belleville** Kansas, USA
20B1 **Bellevue** Washington, USA
109D2 **Bellingen** Aust
8A2 **Bellingham** USA
112C2 **Bellingshausen** Base Ant
112C3 **Bellingshausen S** Ant
52A1 **Bellinzona** Switz
32B2 **Bello** Colombia
107E3 **Bellona Reefs** Nouvelle Calédonie
22B1 **Bellota** USA
15D2 **Bellows Falls** USA
6B3 **Bell Pen** Can
52B1 **Belluno** Italy
29D2 **Bell Ville** Arg
31D5 **Belmonte** Brazil
25D3 **Belmopan** Belize
45B1 **Belmullet** Irish Rep

69E1 **Belogorsk** USSR
101D3 **Beloha** Madag
31C5 **Belo Horizonte** Brazil
10B2 **Beloit** Wisconsin, USA
64E3 **Belomorsk** USSR
61J3 **Beloretsk** USSR
60C3 **Belorusskaya SSR** Republic, USSR
101D2 **Belo-Tsiribihina** Madag
64E3 **Beloye More** S USSR
60E1 **Beloye Ozero** L USSR
60E1 **Belozersk** USSR
14B3 **Belpre** USA
108A2 **Beltana** Aust
19A3 **Belton** USA
59D3 **Bel'tsy** USSR
16B2 **Belvidere** New Jersey, USA
98B3 **Bembe** Angola
97C3 **Bembéréke** Benin
10A2 **Bemidji** USA
39G6 **Bena** Nor
98C3 **Bena Dibele** Zaïre
108C3 **Benalla** Aust
44B3 **Ben Attow** Mt Scot
50A1 **Benavente** Spain
44A3 **Benbecula** I Scot
106A4 **Bencubbin** Aust
8A2 **Bend** USA
44B3 **Ben Dearg** Mt Scot
99F2 **Bender Beyla** Somalia
60C4 **Bendery** USSR
107D4 **Bendigo** Aust
57C3 **Benešov** Czech
53B2 **Benevento** Italy
83C4 **Bengal,B of** Asia
96D1 **Ben Gardane** Tunisia
72D3 **Bengbu** China
95B1 **Benghāzī** Libya
78A2 **Bengkalis** Indon
78A3 **Bengkulu** Indon
100A2 **Benguela** Angola
92B3 **Benha** Egypt
44B2 **Ben Hope** Mt Scot
99C2 **Beni** Zaïre
32D6 **Béni** R Bol
96B1 **Beni Abbes** Alg
51C1 **Benicarló** Spain
7A5 **Benidji** USA
51B2 **Benidorm** Spain
51C2 **Beni Mansour** Alg
95C2 **Beni Mazar** Egypt
96B1 **Beni Mellal** Mor
97C4 **Benin** Republic, Africa
97C4 **Benin City** Nig
95C2 **Beni Suef** Egypt
44B2 **Ben Kilbreck** Mt Scot
44B3 **Ben Lawers** Mt UK
109C4 **Ben Lomond** Mt Aust
44C3 **Ben Macdui** Mt Scot
44B2 **Ben More Assynt** Mt Scot
111B2 **Benmore,L** NZ
44B3 **Ben Nevis** Mt Scot
15D2 **Bennington** USA
94B2 **Bennt Jbail** Leb
98B2 **Bénoué** R Cam
9B3 **Benson** Arizona, USA
99C2 **Bentiu** Sudan
19B3 **Benton** Arkansas, USA
18C2 **Benton** Kentucky, USA
14A2 **Benton Harbor** USA
97C4 **Benue** R Nig
45B1 **Benwee Hd** C Irish Rep
44B3 **Ben Wyvis** Mt Scot
72E1 **Benxi** China
54B2 **Beograd** Yugos
86A2 **Beohāri** India
74C4 **Beppu** Japan
55A2 **Berat** Alb
95C3 **Berber** Sudan
99E1 **Berbera** Somalia
98B2 **Berbérati** CAR
46A1 **Berck** France

60C4	Berdichev USSR
60E4	Berdyansk USSR
97B4	Berekum Ghana
22B2	Berenda USA
5J4	Berens *R* Can
5J4	Berens River Can
108A1	Beresford Aust
59C3	Berettyoújfalu Hung
58D2	Bereza USSR
59C3	Berezhany USSR
65G4	Berezniki USSR
60D4	Berezovka USSR
64H3	Berezovo USSR
92A2	Bergama Turk
52A1	Bergamo Italy
39F6	Bergen Nor
46C1	Bergen op Zoom Neth
48C3	Bergerac France
46D1	Bergisch-Gladbach Germany
12F2	Bering GI USA
1C6	Bering Str USA/USSR
91C4	Berïzak Iran
50B2	Berja Spain
8A3	Berkeley USA
112B2	Berkner I Ant
54B2	Berkovitsa Bulg
43D4	Berkshire County, Eng
16C1	Berkshire Hills USA
13D2	Berland *R* Can
56C2	Berlin Germany
56C2	Berlin State, Germany
15D2	Berlin New Hampshire, USA
30D3	Bermejo Bol
30D4	Bermejo *R* Arg
3M5	Bermuda *I* Atlantic O
52A1	Bern Switz
16B2	Bernardsville USA
34C3	Bernasconi Arg
56C2	Bernburg Germany
47B1	Berner Oberland *Mts* Switz
6B2	Bernier B Can
57C3	Berounka *R* Czech
108B2	Berri Aust
96C1	Berriane Alg
48C2	Berry Region, France
22A1	Berryessa,L USA
11C4	Berry Is The Bahamas
98B2	Bertoua Cam
45B2	Bertraghboy B Irish Rep
15C2	Berwick USA
42C2	Berwick-upon-Tweed Eng
43C3	Berwyn *Mts* Wales
101D2	Besalampy Madag
49D2	Besançon France
59C3	Beskidy Zachodnie *Mts* Pol
93C2	Besni Turk
94B3	Besor *R* Israel
11B3	Bessemer USA
101D2	Betafo Madag
50A1	Betanzos Spain
94B3	Bet Guvrin Israel
101G1	Bethal S Africa
100A3	Bethanie Namibia
18B1	Bethany Missouri, USA
18A2	Bethany Oklahoma, USA
4B3	Bethel Alaska, USA
16C2	Bethel Connecticut, USA
14B2	Bethel Park USA
15C3	Bethesda USA
94B3	Bethlehem Israel
101G1	Bethlehem S Africa
15C2	Bethlehem USA
48C1	Bethune France
101D3	Betioky Madag
108B1	Betoota Aust
98B2	Betou Congo
82A1	Betpak Dala *Steppe* USSR
101D3	Betroka Madag

7D5	Betsiamites Can
86A1	Bettiah India
12D1	Bettles USA
47C2	Béttola Italy
85D4	Bétul India
85D3	Betwa *R* India
46D1	Betzdorf Germany
12C3	Beverley,L USA
16D1	Beverly USA
21B3	Beverly Hills USA
97B4	Beyla Guinea
87B2	Beypore India
	Beyrouth = Beirut
92B2	Beyşehir Turk
92B2	Beyşehir Gölü *L* Turk
94B2	Beyt Shean Israel
47C1	Bezau Austria
60E2	Bezhetsk USSR
49C3	Béziers France
90C2	Bezmein USSR
63C2	Beznosova USSR
86B1	Bhadgaon Nepal
87C1	Bhadrāchalam India
86B2	Bhadrakh India
87B2	Bhadra Res India
87B2	Bhadrāvati India
84B3	Bhag Pak
86B1	Bhāgalpur India
84C2	Bhakkar Pak
82D3	Bhamo Burma
85D4	Bhandāra India
85D3	Bharatpur India
85C4	Bharūch India
86B2	Bhātiāpāra Ghat Bang
84C2	Bhatinda India
87A2	Bhatkal India
86B2	Bhātpāra India
85C4	Bhāvnagar India
84C2	Bhera Pak
86A1	Bheri *R* Nepal
86A2	Bhilai India
85C3	Bhilwāra India
87C1	Bhīmavaram India
85D3	Bhind India
84D3	Bhiwāni India
87B1	Bhongir India
85D4	Bhopāl India
86B2	Bhubaneshwar India
85B4	Bhuj India
85D4	Bhusāwal India
82C3	Bhutan Kingdom, Asia
71E4	Biak *I* Indon
58C2	Biala Podlaska Pol
58B2	Bialograd Pol
58C2	Bialystok Pol
38A1	Biargtangar *C* Iceland
90C2	Biarjmand Iran
48B3	Biarritz France
47C1	Biasca Switz
92B4	Biba Egypt
74E2	Bibai Japan
100A2	Bibala Angola
57B3	Biberach Germany
97B4	Bibiani Ghana
54C1	Bicaz Rom
97C4	Bida Nig
87B1	Bīdar India
91C5	Bidbid Oman
43B4	Bideford Eng
43B4	Bideford B Eng
96C2	Bidon 5 Alg
100A2	Bié Angola
58C2	Biebrza Pol
52A1	Biel Switz
59B2	Bielawa Pol
56B2	Bielefeld Germany
47B1	Bieler See *L* Switz
52A1	Biella Italy
58C2	Bielsk Podlaski Pol
76D3	Bien Hoa Viet
53B2	Biferno *R* Italy
92A1	Biga Turk
55C3	Bigadiç Turk
19C3	Big Black *R* USA
18A1	Big Blue *R* USA
17B2	Big Cypress Swamp USA

4D3	Big Delta USA
49D2	Bigent Germany
13F2	Biggar Can
5H4	Biggar Kindersley Can
109D1	Biggenden Aust
12G3	Bigger,Mt Can
8C2	Bighorn *R* USA
76C3	Bight of Bangkok *B* Thai
97C4	Bight of Benin *B* W Africa
97C4	Bight of Biafra *B* Cam
6C3	Big I Can
47C1	Bignasco Switz
97A3	Bignona Sen
21B2	Big Pine USA
17B2	Big Pine Key USA
22C3	Big Pine Mt USA
14A2	Big Rapids USA
5H4	Big River Can
9C3	Big Spring USA
7A4	Big Trout L Can
7B4	Big Trout Lake Can
52C2	Bihać Yugos
86B1	Bihār India
86B2	Bihar State, India
99D3	Biharamulo Tanz
60B4	Bihor *Mt* Rom
87B1	Bijāpur India
87C1	Bijapur India
90A2	Bījar Iran
86A1	Bijauri Nepal
54A2	Bijeljina Yugos
73B4	Bijie China
84D3	Bijnor India
84C3	Bijnot Pak
84C3	Bikāner India
94B2	Bikfaya Leb
69F2	Bikin USSR
98B3	Bikoro Zaïre
85C3	Bilara India
84D2	Bilaspur India
86A2	Bilāspur India
76B3	Bilauktaung Range *Mts* Thai
50B1	Bilbao Spain
59B3	Bilé *R* Czech
54A2	Bileća Yugos
92B1	Bilecik Turk
98C2	Bili *R* Zaïre
79B3	Biliran *I* Phil
8C2	Billings USA
95A3	Bilma Niger
11B3	Biloxi USA
98C1	Biltine Chad
85D4	Bina-Etawa India
79B3	Binalbagan Phil
101C2	Bindura Zim
100B2	Binga Zim
101C2	Binga *Mt* Zim
109D1	Bingara Aust
57B3	Bingen Germany
10C2	Binghamton USA
78D1	Bingkor Malay
93D2	Bingöl Turk
72D3	Binhai China
78A2	Bintan *I* Indon
78A3	Bintuhan Indon
78C2	Bintulu Malay
29B3	Bió Bió *R* Chile
102J4	Bioko *I* Atlantic O
87B1	Bir India
95B2	Bîr Abu Husein *Well* Egypt
95B2	Bi'r al Harash *Well* Libya
98C1	Birao CAR
86B1	Biratnagar Nepal
12E1	Birch Creek USA
108B3	Birchip Aust
5G4	Birch Mts Can
7A4	Bird Can
106C3	Birdsville Aust
106C2	Birdum Aust
86A1	Birganj Nepal
94A3	Bîr Gifgâfa *Well* Egypt
94A3	Bîr Hasana *Well* Egypt

35A2	Birigui Brazil
90C3	Birjand Iran
92B4	Birkat Qarun *L* Egypt
46D2	Birkenfeld Germany
42C3	Birkenhead Eng
60C4	Bîrlad Rom
94A3	Bir Lahfân *Well* Egypt
43C3	Birmingham Eng
11B3	Birmingham USA
95B2	Bîr Misâha *Well* Egypt
96A2	Bir Moghrein Maur
97C3	Birnin Kebbi Nig
97C3	Birni N'Konni Nig
69F2	Birobidzhan USSR
45C2	Birr Irish Rep
51C2	Bir Rabalou Alg
109C1	Birrie *R* Aust
44C2	Birsay Scot
61J2	Birsk USSR
95B2	Bîr Tarfâwi *Well* Egypt
63B2	Biryusa USSR
39J7	Birzai USSR
96B2	Bir Zreigat *Well* Maur
48A2	Biscay,B of France/Spain
17B2	Biscayne B USA
46D2	Bischwiller France
73B4	Bishan China
8B3	Bishop USA
42D2	Bishop Auckland Eng
43E4	Bishop's Stortford Eng
86A2	Bishrāmpur India
96C1	Biskra Alg
79C4	Bislig Phil
8C2	Bismarck USA
90A3	Bîsotūn Iran
97A3	Bissau Guinea-Bissau
10A1	Bissett Can
5G4	Bistcho L Can
54C1	Bistrita *R* Rom
98B2	Bitam Gabon
57B3	Bitburg Germany
46D2	Bitche France
93D2	Bitlis Turk
55B2	Bitola Yugos
56C2	Bitterfeld Germany
100A4	Bitterfontein S Africa
92B3	Bitter Lakes Egypt
8B2	Bitteroot Range *Mts* USA
74D3	Biwa-ko *L* Japan
99E1	Biyo Kaboba Eth
65K4	Biysk USSR
96C1	Bizerte Tunisia
51C2	Bj bou Arréridj Alg
52C1	Bjelovar Yugos
96B2	Bj Flye Ste Marie Alg
64C2	Bjørnøya *I* Barents S
12F1	Black *R* USA
18B2	Black *R* USA
107D3	Blackall Aust
42C3	Blackburn Eng
4D3	Blackburn,Mt USA
13E2	Black Diamond Can
5H5	Black Hills USA
44B3	Black Isle *Pen* Scot
27R3	Blackman's Barbados
43C4	Black Mts Wales
43C3	Blackpool Eng
27H1	Black River Jamaica
8B2	Black Rock Desert USA
65E5	Black S USSR/Europe
45A1	Blacksod B Irish Rep
109D2	Black Sugarloaf *Mt* Aust
97B3	Black Volta *R* Ghana
41B3	Blackwater *R* Irish Rep
18A2	Blackwell USA
54B2	Blagoevgrad Bulg
63E2	Blagoveshchensk USSR
20B1	Blaine USA
44C3	Blair Atholl Scot
44C3	Blairgowrie Scot

Blakely

17B1 **Blakely** USA
108A1 **Blanche,L** Aust
34A2 **Blanco** *R* Arg
34B1 **Blanco** *R* Arg
8A2 **Blanco,C** USA
7E4 **Blanc Sablon** Can
43C4 **Blandford Forum** Eng
46A2 **Blangy-sur-Bresle**
France
46B1 **Blankenberge** Belg
101C2 **Blantyre** Malawi
48B2 **Blaye** France
109C2 **Blayney** Aust
111B2 **Blenheim** NZ
96C1 **Blida** Alg
14B1 **Blind River** Can
108A2 **Blinman** Aust
78C4 **Blitar** Indon
15D2 **Block I** USA
16D2 **Block Island Sd** USA
101G1 **Bloemfontein** S Africa
101G1 **Bloemhof** S Africa
101G1 **Bloemhof Dam** *Res*
S Africa
33F3 **Blommesteinmeer** *L*
Surinam
38A1 **Blonduós** Iceland
45B1 **Bloody Foreland** *C*
Irish Rep
14A3 **Bloomfield** Indiana,
USA
18B1 **Bloomfield** Iowa, USA
10B2 **Bloomington** Illinois,
USA
14A3 **Bloomington** Indiana,
USA
16A2 **Bloomsburg** USA
78C4 **Blora** Indon
6H3 **Blosseville Kyst** *Mts*
Greenland
57B3 **Bludenz** Austria
11B3 **Bluefield** USA
32A1 **Bluefields** Nic
26B3 **Blue Mountain Peak**
Mt Jamaica
16A2 **Blue Mt** USA
109D2 **Blue Mts** Aust
27J1 **Blue Mts** Jamaica
8A2 **Blue Mts** USA
**Blue Nile = Bahr el
Azraq**
99D1 **Blue Nile** *R* Sudan
4G3 **Bluenose L** Can
11B3 **Blue Ridge Mts** USA
13D2 **Blue River** Can
45B1 **Blue Stack** *Mt*
Irish Rep
111A3 **Bluff** NZ
106A4 **Bluff Knoll** *Mt* Aust
30G4 **Blumenau** Brazil
49D2 **Blundez** Austria
20B2 **Bly** USA
12E3 **Blying Sd** USA
42D2 **Blyth** Eng
9B3 **Blythe** USA
11B3 **Blytheville** USA
97A4 **Bo** Sierra Leone
79B3 **Boac** Phil
72D2 **Boading** China
14B2 **Boardman** USA
63C3 **Boatou** China
33E3 **Boa Vista** Brazil
97A4 **Boa Vista** *I* Cape
Verde
76E1 **Bobai** China
47C2 **Bóbbio** Italy
97B3 **Bobo Dioulasso**
Burkina
60C3 **Bobruysk** USSR
17B2 **Boca Chica Key** *I* USA
32D5 **Bôca do Acre** Brazil
35C1 **Bocaiúva** Brazil
98B2 **Bocaranga** CAR
17B2 **Boca Raton** USA
59C3 **Bochnia** Pol
56B2 **Bocholt** Germany
46D1 **Bochum** Germany
100A2 **Bocoio** Angola

98B2 **Boda** CAR
63D2 **Bodaybo** USSR
21A2 **Bodega Head** *Pt* USA
95A3 **Bodélé** *Region* Chad
38J5 **Boden** Sweden
47C1 **Bodensee** *L* Switz/
Germany
87B1 **Bodhan** India
87B2 **Bodinàyakkanūr** India
43B4 **Bodmin** Eng
43B4 **Bodmin Moor** *Upland*
Eng
38G5 **Bodø** Nor
63G2 **Bodorodskoye** USSR
55C3 **Bodrum** Turk
98C3 **Boende** Zaïre
97A3 **Boffa** Guinea
76B2 **Bogale** Burma
19C3 **Bogalusa** USA
109C2 **Bogan** *R* Aust
97B3 **Bogandé** Burkina
6H3 **Bogarnes** Iceland
92C2 **Boğazlıyan** Turk
61K2 **Bogdanovich** USSR
68A2 **Bogda Shan** *Mt* China
100A3 **Bogenfels** Namibia
109D1 **Boggabilla** Aust
109C2 **Boggabri** Aust
45B2 **Boggeragh Mts**
Irish Rep
79B3 **Bogo** Phil
109C3 **Bogong,Mt** Aust
78B4 **Bogor** Indon
61H2 **Bogorodskoye** USSR
32C3 **Bogotá** Colombia
63A2 **Bogotol** USSR
86B2 **Bogra** Bang
72D2 **Bo Hai** *B* China
46B2 **Bohain-en-Vermandois**
France
72B2 **Bohai Wan** *B* China
57C3 **Böhmer-Wald** *Upland*
Germany
79B4 **Bohol** *I* Phil
79B4 **Bohol S** Phil
35A1 **Bois** *R* Brazil
14B1 **Bois Blanc I** USA
8B2 **Boise** USA
96A2 **Bojador,C** Mor
79B2 **Bojeador,C** Phil
90C2 **Bojnūrd** Iran
97A3 **Boké** Guinea
109C1 **Bokhara** *R* Aust
39F7 **Boknafjord** *Inlet* Nor
98B3 **Boko** Congo
76C3 **Bokor** Camb
98C3 **Bokungu** Zaïre
98B1 **Bol** Chad
97A3 **Bolama** Guinea-Bissau
23A1 **Bolaños** Mexico
23A1 **Bolanos** *R* Mexico
48C2 **Bolbec** France
97B4 **Bole** Ghana
59B2 **Boleslawiec** Pol
97B3 **Bolgatanga** Ghana
60C4 **Bolgrad** USSR
34C3 **Bolívar** Arg
18B2 **Bolivar** Missouri, USA
18C2 **Bolivar** Tennessee,
USA
30C2 **Bolivia** Republic,
S America
38H6 **Bollnas** Sweden
109C1 **Bollon** Aust
32C2 **Bollvar** *Mt* Ven
52B2 **Bologna** Italy
60D2 **Bologoye** USSR
69F2 **Bolon** USSR
61G3 **Bol'shoy Irgiz** *R* USSR
74C2 **Bol'shoy Kamen**
USSR
65F5 **Bol'shoy Kavkaz** *Mts*
USSR
61G4 **Bol'shoy Uzen** *R*
USSR
9C4 **Bolson de Mapimi**
Desert Mexico
43C3 **Bolton** Eng

92B1 **Bolu** Turk
38A1 **Bolungarvik** Iceland
92B2 **Bolvadin** Turk
52B1 **Bolzano** Italy
98B3 **Boma** Zaïre
107D4 **Bombala** Aust
87A1 **Bombay** India
99D2 **Bombo** Uganda
35B1 **Bom Despacho** Brazil
86C1 **Bomdila** India
97A4 **Bomi Hills** Lib
31C4 **Bom Jesus da Lapa**
Brazil
63E2 **Bomnak** USSR
99C2 **Bomokandi** *R* Zaïre
98C2 **Bomu** *R* CAR/Zaïre
27D4 **Bonaire** *I* Caribbean S
12F2 **Bona,Mt** USA
25D3 **Bonanza** Nic
7E5 **Bonavista** Can
108A2 **Bon Bon** Aust
98C2 **Bondo** Zaïre
97B4 **Bondoukou** Ivory Coast
Bône = 'Annaba
33E3 **Bonfim** Guyana
98C2 **Bongandanga** Zaïre
98B1 **Bongor** Chad
19A3 **Bonham** USA
53A2 **Bonifacio** Corse
52A2 **Bonifacio,Str of** *Chan*
Medit S
**Bonin Is = Ogasawara
Gunto**
17B2 **Bonita Springs** USA
57B2 **Bonn** Germany
20C1 **Bonners Ferry** USA
12H1 **Bonnet Plume** *R* Can
13E2 **Bonnyville** Can
97A4 **Bonthe** Sierra Leone
99E1 **Booaaso** Somalia
108B2 **Booligal** Aust
109D1 **Boonah** Aust
15C2 **Boonville** USA
109C2 **Boorowa** Aust
6A2 **Boothia,G of** Can
6A2 **Boothia Pen** Can
98B3 **Booué** Gabon
108A1 **Bopeechee** Aust
99D2 **Bor** Sudan
92B2 **Bor** Turk
54B2 **Bor** Yugos
8B2 **Borah Peak** *Mt* USA
39G7 **Borås** Sweden
91B4 **Borāzjan** Iran
108A3 **Borda,C** Aust
48B3 **Bordeaux** France
4G2 **Borden I** Can
6B2 **Borden Pen** Can
16B2 **Bordentown** USA
42C2 **Borders** Region, Scot
108B3 **Bordertown** Aust
96C2 **Bordi Omar Dris** Alg
8D1 **Borens River** Can
38A2 **Borgarnes** Iceland
9C3 **Borger** USA
39H7 **Borgholm** Sweden
47C2 **Borgosia** Italy
47D1 **Borgo Valsugana** Italy
59C3 **Borislav** USSR
61F3 **Borisoglebsk** USSR
60C3 **Borisov** USSR
60E3 **Borisovka** USSR
95A3 **Borkou** *Region* Chad
39H6 **Borlänge** Sweden
47C2 **Bormida** Italy
47D1 **Bormio** Italy
67F5 **Borneo** *I* Malay/Indon
39H7 **Bornholm** *I* Den
55C3 **Bornova** Turk
98C2 **Boro** *R* Sudan
97B3 **Boromo** Burkina
60D2 **Borovichi** USSR
106C2 **Borroloola** Aust
54B1 **Borsa** Rom
90A3 **Borūjed** Iran
90B3 **Borūjerd** Iran
58B2 **Bory Tucholskie**
Region, Pol

63D2 **Borzya** USSR
54A1 **Bosanki Brod** Yugos
73B5 **Bose** China
101G1 **Boshof** S Africa
54A2 **Bosna** *R* Yugos
75C1 **Bösö-hantö** *B* Japan
**Bosporus = Karadeniz
Boğazi**
51C2 **Bosquet** Alg
98B2 **Bossangoa** CAR
98B2 **Bossèmbélé** CAR
19B3 **Bossier City** USA
65K5 **Bosten Hu** *L* China
43D3 **Boston** Eng
10C2 **Boston** USA
11A3 **Boston Mts** USA
85C4 **Botād** India
54B2 **Botevgrad** Bulg
101G1 **Bothaville** S Africa
64C3 **Bothnia,G of** Sweden/
Fin
100B3 **Botletli** *R* Botswana
60C4 **Botosani** Rom
100B3 **Botswana** Republic,
Africa
53C3 **Botte Donato** *Mt* Italy
46D1 **Bottrop** Germany
35B2 **Botucatu** Brazil
7E5 **Botwood** Can
89D7 **Bouaké** Ivory Coast
98B2 **Bouar** CAR
96B1 **Bouârfa** Mor
98B2 **Bouca** CAR
51C2 **Boufarik** Alg
Bougie = Bejaïa
97B3 **Bougouni** Mali
46C2 **Bouillon** France
96B2 **Bou Izakarn** Mor
46D2 **Boulay-Moselle**
France
8C2 **Boulder** Colorado,
USA
9B3 **Boulder City** USA
22A2 **Boulder Creek** USA
48C1 **Boulogne** France
98B2 **Boumba** *R* CAR
97B4 **Bouna** Ivory Coast
8B3 **Boundary Peak** *Mt*
USA
97B4 **Boundiali** Ivory Coast
107F3 **Bourail** Nouvelle
Calédonie
97B3 **Bourem** Mali
49D2 **Bourg** France
49D2 **Bourg de Péage**
France
48C2 **Bourges** France
48C3 **Bourg-Madame**
France
49C2 **Bourgogne** Region,
France
47B2 **Bourg-St-Maurice**
France
108C2 **Bourke** Aust
43D4 **Bournemouth** Eng
96C1 **Bou Saâda** Alg
98B1 **Bousso** Chad
97A3 **Boutilmit** Maur
103J7 **Bouvet I** Atlantic O
34D2 **Bovril** Arg
13E2 **Bow** *R* Can
107D2 **Bowen** Aust
19A3 **Bowie** Texas, USA
13E2 **Bow Island** Can
11B3 **Bowling Green**
Kentucky, USA
18B2 **Bowling Green**
Missouri, USA
14B2 **Bowling Green** Ohio,
USA
15C3 **Bowling Green**
Virginia, USA
15C2 **Bowmanville** Can
109D2 **Bowral** Aust
13C2 **Bowron** *R* Can
72D3 **Bo Xian** China
72D2 **Boxing** China
92B1 **Boyabat** Turk

98B2 **Boyali** CAR
5J4 **Boyd** Can
16B2 **Boyertown** USA
13E2 **Boyle** Can
41B3 **Boyle** Irish Rep
45C2 **Boyne** R Irish Rep
17B2 **Boynoton Beach** USA
98C2 **Boyoma Falls** Zaïre
55C3 **Bozca Ada** I Turk
55C3 **Boz Dağlari** Mts Turk
8B2 **Bozeman** USA
Bozen = Bolzano
98B2 **Bozene** Zaïre
98B2 **Bozoum** CAR
47B2 **Bra** Italy
52C2 **Brač** I Yugos
15C1 **Bracebridge** Can
95A2 **Brach** Libya
38H6 **Bräcke** Sweden
17B2 **Bradenton** USA
42D3 **Bradford** Eng
44E1 **Brae** Scot
44C3 **Braemar** Scot
50A1 **Braga** Port
34C3 **Bragado** Arg
50A1 **Bragana** Port
31B2 **Bragança** Brazil
35B2 **Bragança Paulista** Brazil
86C2 **Brahman-Baria** Bang
86B2 **Brāhmani** R India
86C1 **Brahmaputra** R India
7E5 **Braie Verte** Can
60C4 **Brăila** Rom
10A2 **Brainerd** USA
97A3 **Brakna** Region, Maur
5F4 **Bralorne** Can
14C2 **Brampton** Can
33E3 **Branco** R Brazil
100A3 **Brandberg** Mt Namibia
56C2 **Brandenburg** Germany
56C2 **Brandenburg** State, Germany
101G1 **Brandfort** S Africa
8D2 **Brandon** Can
100B4 **Brandvlei** S Africa
57C2 **Brandys nad Lebem** Czech
58B2 **Braniewo** Pol
10B2 **Brantford** Can
108B3 **Branxholme** Aust
7D5 **Bras d'Or L** Can
35C1 **Brasila de Minas** Brazil
32D6 **Brasiléia** Brazil
31B5 **Brasilia** Brazil
54C1 **Brasov** Rom
78D1 **Brassay Range** Mts Malay
59B3 **Bratislava** Czech
63C2 **Bratsk** USSR
15D2 **Brattleboro** USA
56C2 **Braunschweig** Germany
97A4 **Brava** I Cape Verde
9B3 **Brawley** USA
45C2 **Bray** Irish Rep
6C3 **Bray I** Can
13D2 **Brazeau** R Can
13D2 **Brazeau,Mt** Can
28D4 **Brazil** Republic, S America
103G5 **Brazil Basin** Atlantic O
9D3 **Brazos** R USA
98B3 **Brazzaville** Congo
57C3 **Brdy** Upland Czech
111A3 **Breaksea Sd** NZ
110B1 **Bream B** NZ
78B4 **Brebes** Indon
44C3 **Brechin** Scot
46C1 **Brecht** Belg
59B3 **Břeclav** Czech
43C4 **Brecon** Wales
43C4 **Brecon Beacons** Mts Wales
43B3 **Brecon Beacons Nat Pk** Wales

56A2 **Breda** Neth
100B4 **Bredasdorp** S Africa
38H6 **Bredbyn** Sweden
61J3 **Bredy** USSR
15C2 **Breezewood** USA
47C1 **Bregenz** Austria
47C1 **Bregenzer Ache** R Austria
38A1 **Breiðafjörður** B Iceland
47C2 **Brembo** R Italy
17A1 **Bremen** USA
56B2 **Bremen** Germany
56B2 **Bremerhaven** Germany
20B1 **Bremerton** USA
19A3 **Brenham** USA
57C3 **Brenner** P Austria/Italy
47D2 **Breno** Italy
47D2 **Brenta** R Italy
22B2 **Brentwood** USA
52B1 **Brescia** Italy
Breslau = Wrocław
47D1 **Bressanone** Italy
44E1 **Bressay** I Scot
48B2 **Bressuire** France
48B2 **Brest** France
58C2 **Brest** USSR
48B2 **Bretagne** Region, France
46B2 **Breteuil** France
16B2 **Breton Woods** USA
110B1 **Brett,C** NZ
109C1 **Brewarrina** Aust
16C2 **Brewster** New York, USA
20C1 **Brewster** Washington, USA
101G1 **Breyten** S Africa
52C1 **Brežice** Yugos
98C2 **Bria** CAR
49D3 **Briancon** France
49C2 **Briare** France
21B2 **Bridgeport** California, USA
15D2 **Bridgeport** Connecticut, USA
19A3 **Bridgeport** Texas, USA
22C1 **Bridgeport Res** USA
16B3 **Bridgeton** USA
27F4 **Bridgetown** Barbados
7D5 **Bridgewater** Can
16D2 **Bridgewater** USA
43C4 **Bridgwater** Eng
43C4 **Bridgwater B** Eng
42D2 **Bridlington** Eng
109C4 **Bridport** Aust
47B1 **Brienzer See** L Switz
46C2 **Briey** France
52A1 **Brig** Switz
8B2 **Brigham City** USA
109C3 **Bright** Aust
43D4 **Brighton** Eng
46E1 **Brilon** Germany
55A2 **Brindisi** Italy
19B3 **Brinkley** USA
107E3 **Brisbane** Aust
15D2 **Bristol** Connecticut, USA
43C4 **Bristol** Eng
15D2 **Bristol** Pennsylvania, USA
16D2 **Bristol** Rhode Island, USA
11B3 **Bristol** Tennessee, USA
12B3 **Bristol B** USA
43B4 **Bristol Chan** Eng/Wales
4D3 **British** Mts USA
5F4 **British Columbia** Province, Can
6B1 **British Empire Range** Mts Can
101G1 **Brits** S Africa
100B4 **Britstown** S Africa

48C2 **Brive** France
59B3 **Brno** Czech
17B1 **Broad** R USA
7C4 **Broadback** R Can
44A2 **Broad Bay** Inlet Scot
44B3 **Broadford** Scot
5H4 **Brochet** Can
4G2 **Brock I** Can
15C2 **Brockport** USA
16D1 **Brockton** USA
15C2 **Brockville** Can
6B2 **Brodeur Pen** Can
42B2 **Brodick** Scot
58B2 **Brodnica** Pol
60C3 **Brody** USSR
19B3 **Broken Bow** Oklahoma, USA
19B3 **Broken Bow L** USA
107D4 **Broken Hill** Aust
47C2 **Broni** Italy
38G5 **Brønnøysund** Nor
16C2 **Bronx** Borough, New York, USA
79A4 **Brooke's Point** Phil
18B2 **Brookfield** Missouri, USA
11A3 **Brookhaven** USA
20B2 **Brookings** Oregon, USA
8D2 **Brookings** South Dakota, USA
16D1 **Brookline** USA
16C2 **Brooklyn** Borough, New York, USA
5G4 **Brooks** Can
12C3 **Brooks,L** USA
12A1 **Brooks Mt** USA
4C3 **Brooks Range** Mts USA
17B2 **Brooksville** USA
109D1 **Brooloo** Aust
106B2 **Broome** Aust
44C2 **Brora** Scot
20B2 **Brothers** USA
95A3 **Broulkou** Chad
13E3 **Browning** USA
9D4 **Brownsville** USA
9D3 **Brownwood** USA
46B1 **Bruay-en-Artois** France
106A3 **Bruce,Mt** Aust
14B1 **Bruce Pen** Can
59B3 **Brück an der Mur** Austria
Bruges = Brugge
46B1 **Brugge** Belg
46D1 **Brühl** Germany
78C2 **Brunei** Sultanate, S E Asia
52B1 **Brunico** Italy
111B2 **Brunner,L** NZ
11B3 **Brunswick** Georgia, USA
18B2 **Brunswick** Mississippi, USA
29B6 **Brunswick,Pen de** Chile
109C4 **Bruny I** Aust
61F1 **Brusenets** USSR
26A3 **Brus Laguna** Honduras
Brüssel = Bruxelles
56A2 **Bruxelles** Belg
9D3 **Bryan** USA
108A2 **Bryan,Mt** Aust
60D3 **Bryansk** USSR
19B3 **Bryant** USA
59B2 **Brzeg** Pol
93E4 **Būbiyan** I Kuwait/Iraq
99D3 **Bubu** R Tanz
32C2 **Bucaramanga** Colombia
44D3 **Buchan** Oilfield N Sea
97A4 **Buchanan** Lib
44D3 **Buchan Deep** N Sea
6C2 **Buchan G** Can
40C2 **Buchan Ness** Pen Scot

7E5 **Buchans** Can
34C2 **Buchardo** Arg
Bucharest = Bucureşti
47C1 **Buchs** Switz
43D3 **Buckingham** Eng
12B1 **Buckland** USA
12B1 **Buckland** R USA
108A2 **Buckleboo** Aust
98B3 **Buco Zau** Congo
54C2 **Bucureşti** Rom
59B3 **Budapest** Hung
84D3 **Budaun** India
43B4 **Bude** Eng
19B3 **Bude** USA
61F5 **Budennovsk** USSR
54A2 **Budva** Yugos
98A2 **Buéa** Cam
22B3 **Buellton** USA
34B2 **Buena Esperanza** Arg
32B3 **Buenaventura** Colombia
23A2 **Buenavista** Mexico
29E2 **Buenos Aires** Arg
29D3 **Buenos Aires** State, Arg
18B2 **Buffalo** Mississipi, USA
10C2 **Buffalo** New York, USA
8C2 **Buffalo** South Dakota, USA
19A3 **Buffalo** Texas, USA
8C2 **Buffalo** Wyoming, USA
101H1 **Buffalo** R S Africa
13E2 **Buffalo L** Alberta, Can
5G3 **Buffalo L** Northwest Territories, Can
5H4 **Buffalo Narrows** Can
17B1 **Buford** USA
54C2 **Buftea** Rom
59C2 **Bug** R Pol/USSR
32B3 **Buga** Colombia
90B2 **Bugdayli** USSR
61H3 **Bugulma** USSR
61H3 **Buguruslan** USSR
93C2 **Buhayrat al Asad** Res Syria
41C3 **Builth Wells** Wales
34A2 **Buin** Chile
99C3 **Bujumbura** Burundi
98C3 **Bukama** Zaïre
99C3 **Bukavu** Zaïre
80E2 **Bukhara** USSR
78C2 **Bukit Batubrok** Mt Indon
70B4 **Bukittinggi** Indon
99D3 **Bukoba** Tanz
78D3 **Buku Gandadiwata** Mt Indon
71E4 **Bula** Indon
79B3 **Bulan** Phil
84D3 **Bulandshahr** India
100B3 **Bulawayo** Zim
55C3 **Buldan** Turk
85D4 **Buldāna** India
68C2 **Bulgan** Mongolia
54B2 **Bulgaria** Republic, Europe
47B1 **Bulle** Switz
111B2 **Buller** R NZ
109C3 **Buller,Mt** Aust
106A4 **Bullfinch** Aust
108B1 **Bulloo** R Aust
108B1 **Bulloo Downs** Aust
108B1 **Bulloo L** Aust
18B2 **Bull Shoals Res** USA
34A3 **Bulnes** Chile
71F4 **Bulolo** PNG
101G1 **Bultfontein** S Africa
98C2 **Bumba** Zaïre
76B2 **Bumphal Dam** Thai
99D2 **Buna** Kenya
106A4 **Bunbury** Aust
45C1 **Buncrana** Irish Rep
107E3 **Bundaberg** Aust
109D2 **Bundarra** Aust
85D3 **Būndi** India

45B1 **Bundoran** Irish Rep
109C1 **Bungil** R Aust
98B3 **Bungo** Angola
75A2 **Bungo-suidō** Str Japan
70B3 **Bunguran** I Ind
99D2 **Bunia** Zaïre
18B2 **Bunker** USA
19B3 **Bunkie** USA
17R2 **Bunnell** USA
78C3 **Buntok** Indon
71D3 **Buol** Indon
94C2 **Burāg** Syria
98C1 **Buram** Sudan
79B3 **Burauen** Phil
80C3 **Buraydah** S Arabia
21B3 **Burbank** USA
109C2 **Burcher** Aust
99E2 **Burco** Somalia
92B2 **Burdur** Turk
63F3 **Bureinskiy Khrebet** Mts USSR
56C2 **Burg** Germany
54C2 **Burgas** Bulg
17C1 **Burgaw** USA
47B1 **Burgdorf** Switz
100B4 **Burgersdorp** S Africa
65K5 **Burgin** USSR
50B1 **Burgos** Spain
58B1 **Burgsvik** Sweden
55C3 **Burhaniye** Turk
85D4 **Burhānpur** India
79B3 **Burias** I Phil
76C2 **Buriram** Thai
35B1 **Buritis** Brazil
13B2 **Burke Chan** Can
106C2 **Burketown** Aust
97B3 **Burkina** Republic, Africa
15C1 **Burks Falls** Can
8B2 **Burley** USA
10A2 **Burlington** Iowa, USA
16B2 **Burlington** New Jersey, USA
10C2 **Burlington** Vermont, USA
20B1 **Burlington** Washington, USA
83D3 **Burma** Republic, Asia
20B2 **Burney** USA
16A2 **Burnham** USA
107D5 **Burnie** Aust
42C3 **Burnley** Eng
20C2 **Burns** USA
5F4 **Burns Lake** Can
82C1 **Burqin** China
108A2 **Burra** Aust
109D2 **Burragorang,L** Aust
44C2 **Burray** I Scot
109C2 **Burren Junction** Aust
109C2 **Burrinjuck Res** Aust
60C5 **Bursa** Turk
80B3 **Bur Safâga** Egypt
Bûr Sa'îd = Port Said
14B2 **Burton** USA
43D3 **Burton upon Trent** Eng
38J6 **Burtrask** Sweden
108B2 **Burtundy** Aust
71D4 **Buru** Indon
99C3 **Burundi** Republic, Africa
78A2 **Burung** Indon
63D2 **Buryatskaya ASSR** Republic, USSR
99D1 **Burye** Eth
61H4 **Burynshik** USSR
43E3 **Bury St Edmunds** Eng
91B4 **Būshehr** Iran
98B3 **Busira** R Zaïre
58C2 **Buskozdroj** Pol
94C2 **Busrā ash Shām** Syria
106A4 **Busselton** Aust
49D2 **Busto** Italy
52A1 **Busto Arsizio** Italy
79A3 **Busuanga** I Phil
98C2 **Buta** Zaïre
34B3 **Buta Ranquil** Arg

99C3 **Butare** Rwanda
42B2 **Bute** I Scot
69E2 **Butha Qi** China
14C2 **Butler** USA
8B2 **Butte** USA
77C4 **Butterworth** Malay
40B2 **Butt of Lewis** C Scot
6D3 **Button Is** Can
79C4 **Butuan** Phil
71D4 **Butung** I Indon
61F3 **Buturlinovka** USSR
86A1 **Butwal** Nepal
99E2 **Buulo Barde** Somalia
99E2 **Buur Hakaba** Somalia
61F2 **Buy** USSR
72B1 **Buyant Ovvo** Mongolia
61G5 **Buynaksk** USSR
63D3 **Buyr Nuur** L Mongolia
93D2 **Büyük Ağri** Mt Turk
92A2 **Büyük Menderes** R Turk
54C1 **Buzău** Rom
54C1 **Buzau** R Rom
61H3 **Buzuluk** USSR
16D2 **Buzzards B** USA
54C2 **Byala** Bulg
54B2 **Byala Slatina** Bulg
4H2 **Byam Martin** Chan Can
4H2 **Byam Martin I** Can
Byblos = Jubail
94B1 **Byblos** Hist Site, Leb
58B2 **Bydgoszcz** Pol
39F7 **Bygland** Nor
6C2 **Bylot I** Can
109C2 **Byrock** Aust
22B2 **Byron** USA
109D1 **Byron,C** Aust
59B2 **Bytom** Pol

C

30E4 **Caacupé** Par
100A2 **Caála** Angola
13B2 **Caamano Sd** Can
30E4 **Caazapá** Par
79B2 **Cabanatuan** Phil
31E3 **Cabedelo** Brazil
50A2 **Cabeza del Buey** Spain
34C3 **Cabildo** Arg
34A2 **Cabildo** Chile
32C1 **Cabimas** Ven
98B3 **Cabinda** Angola
98B3 **Cabinda** Province, Angola
27C3 **Cabo Beata** Dom Rep
51C2 **Cabo Binibeca** C Spain
53A3 **Cabo Carbonara** C Sardegna
34A3 **Cabo Carranza** C Chile
50A2 **Cabo Carvoeiro** C Port
9B3 **Cabo Colnett** C Mexico
32B2 **Cabo Corrientes** C Colombia
24B2 **Cabo Corrientes** C Mexico
26B3 **Cabo Cruz** C Cuba
50B1 **Cabo de Ajo** C Spain
51C1 **Cabo de Caballeria** C Spain
51C1 **Cabo de Creus** C Spain
50B2 **Cabo de Gata** C Spain
29C7 **Cabo de Hornos** C Chile
51C2 **Cabo de la Nao** C Spain
50A1 **Cabo de Peñas** C Spain

50A2 **Cabo de Roca** C Port
51C2 **Cabo de Salinas** C Spain
35C2 **Cabo de São Tomé** C Brazil
50A2 **Cabo de São Vicente** C Port
50A2 **Cabo de Sines** C Port
51C1 **Cabo de Tortosa** C Spain
29C4 **Cabo Dos Bahias** C Arg
50A2 **Cabo Espichel** C Port
9B4 **Cabo Falso** C Mexico
51B2 **Cabo Ferrat** C Alg
50A1 **Cabo Finisterre** C Spain
51C1 **Cabo Formentor** C Spain
35C2 **Cabo Frio** Brazil
35C2 **Cabo Frio** C Brazil
26A4 **Cabo Gracias à Dios** Honduras
31B2 **Cabo Maguarinho** C Brazil
50A2 **Cabo Negro** C Mor
10C2 **Cabonga,Résr** Can
109D1 **Caboolture** Aust
33G3 **Cabo Orange** C Brazil
21B3 **Cabo Punta Banda** C Mexico
101C2 **Cabora Bassa Dam** Mozam
24A1 **Caborca** Mexico
24C2 **Cabo Rojo** C Mexico
23B1 **Cabos** Mexico
29C6 **Cabo San Diego** C Arg
32A4 **Cabo San Lorenzo** C Ecuador
53A3 **Cabo Teulada** C Sardegna
50A2 **Cabo Trafalgar** C Spain
50B2 **Cabo Tres Forcas** C Mor
29C5 **Cabo Tres Puntas** C Arg
7D5 **Cabot Str** Can
50B2 **Cabra** Spain
50A1 **Cabreira** Mt Port
51C2 **Cabrera** I Spain
34A3 **Cabrero** Chile
51B2 **Cabriel** R Spain
23B2 **Cacahuamilpa** Mexico
54C2 **Čačak** Yugos
23B2 **C A Carillo** Mexico
30E2 **Cáceres** Brazil
50A2 **Caceres** Spain
18B2 **Cache** R USA
13C2 **Cache Creek** Can
30C4 **Cachi** Arg
33G5 **Cachimbo** Brazil
31D4 **Cachoeira** Brazil
35A1 **Cachoeira Alta** Brazil
31D3 **Cachoeira de Paulo Alfonso** Waterfall Brazil
29F2 **Cachoeira do Sul** Brazil
31C6 **Cachoeiro de Itapemirim** Brazil
22C3 **Cachuma,L** USA
100A2 **Cacolo** Angola
100A2 **Caconda** Angola
35A1 **Caçu** Brazil
100A2 **Caculuvar** R Angola
59B3 **Čadca** Czech
43C3 **Cader Idris** Mts Wales
10B2 **Cadillac** USA
79B3 **Cadiz** Phil
50A2 **Cadiz** Spain
48B2 **Caen** France
42B3 **Caernarfon** Wales
43B3 **Caernarfon B** Wales
94B2 **Caesarea** Hist Site Israel
31C4 **Caetité** Brazil

30C4 **Cafayate** Arg
92B2 **Caga Tepe** Turk
79B2 **Cagayan** R Phil
79B4 **Cagayan de Oro** Phil
79B4 **Cagayan Is** Phil
79A4 **Cagayan Sulu** I Phil
53A3 **Cagliari** Sardegna
27D3 **Caguas** Puerto Rico
45B3 **Caha Mts** Irish Rep
45A3 **Cahersiveen** Irish Rep
45C2 **Cahir** Irish Rep
45C2 **Cahone Pt** Irish Rep
48C3 **Cahors** France
101C2 **Caia** Mozam
100B2 **Caianda** Angola
35A1 **Caiapó** R Brazil
35A1 **Caiapônia** Brazil
31D3 **Caicó** Brazil
26C2 **Caicos Is** Caribbean S
11C4 **Caicos Pass** The Bahamas
12C2 **Cairn Mt** USA
44C3 **Cairngorms** Mts Scot
107D2 **Cairns** Aust
92B3 **Cairo** Egypt
11B3 **Cairo** USA
108B1 **Caiwarro** Aust
32B5 **Cajabamba** Peru
32B5 **Cajamarca** Peru
27D5 **Calabozo** Ven
54B2 **Calafat** Rom
29B6 **Calafate** Arg
79B3 **Calagua Is** Phil
51B1 **Calahorra** Spain
48C1 **Calais** France
30C3 **Calama** Chile
32C3 **Calamar** Colombia
79A3 **Calamian Group** Is Phil
70A3 **Calang** Indon
95B2 **Calanscio Sand Sea** Libya
79B3 **Calapan** Phil
54C2 **Calarasi** Rom
51B1 **Calatayud** Spain
22B2 **Calaveras Res** USA
79B3 **Calbayog** Phil
19B4 **Calcasieu L** USA
86B2 **Calcutta** India
50A2 **Caldas da Rainha** Port
31B5 **Caldas Novas** Brazil
30B4 **Caldera** Chile
8B2 **Caldwell** USA
29C5 **Caleta Olivia** Arg
9B3 **Calexico** USA
5G4 **Calgary** Can
17B1 **Calhoun** USA
17B1 **Calhoun Falls** USA
32B3 **Cali** Colombia
87B2 **Calicut** India
8B3 **Caliente** Nevada, USA
8A3 **California** State, USA
22C3 **California Aqueduct** USA
87B2 **Calimera,Pt** India
34B2 **Calingasta** Arg
22A1 **Calistoga** USA
108B1 **Callabonna** R Aust
108A1 **Callabonna,L** Aust
15C1 **Callander** Can
44B3 **Callander** Scot
108A1 **Callanna** Aust
32B6 **Callao** Peru
13E1 **Calling L** Can
23B1 **Calnali** Mexico
17B2 **Caloosahatchee** R USA
109D1 **Caloundra** Aust
23B2 **Calpulalpan** Mexico
53B3 **Caltanissetta** Italy
98B3 **Caluango** Angola
100A2 **Calulo** Angola
100A2 **Caluquembe** Angola
13B2 **Calvert I** Can
52A2 **Calvi** Corse
23A1 **Calvillo** Mexico
100A4 **Calvinia** S Africa
25E2 **Camagüey** Cuba

25E2 Camagüey,Arch de *Is* Cuba	9C3 Canadian *R* USA	100A2 Capelongo Angola	35C1 Carlos Chagas Brazil
30B2 Camaná Peru	60C5 Canakkale Turk	15D3 Cape May USA	45C2 Carlow County, Irish Rep
30C3 Camargo Bol	34B3 Canalejas Arg	5F5 Cape Mendocino USA	45C2 Carlow Irish Rep
22C3 Camarillo USA	13D2 Canal Flats Can	98B3 Capenda Camulemba Angola	21B3 Carlsbad California, USA
29C4 Camarones Arg	24A1 Cananea Mexico	4F2 Cape Perry Can	9C3 Carlsbad New Mexico, USA
20B1 Camas USA	102G3 Canary Basin Atlantic O	100B4 Cape Province S Africa	
98B3 Camaxilo Angola	Canary Is = Islas Canarias	7A4 Cape Tatnam Can	5H5 Carlyle Can
98B3 Cambatela Angola	23A2 Canas Mexico	100A4 Cape Town S Africa	12G2 Carmacks Can
76C3 Cambodia Republic, S E Asia	24B2 Canatlán Mexico	102G4 Cape Verde *Is* Atlantic O	47B2 Carmagnola Italy
43B4 Camborne Eng	11B4 Canaveral,C USA		43B4 Carmarthen Wales
49C1 Cambrai France	31D5 Canavieiras Brazil	102G4 Cape Verde Basin Atlantic O	43B4 Carmarthen B Wales
43C3 Cambrian Mts Wales	107D4 Canberra Aust	12F3 Cape Yakataga USA	22B2 Carmel California, USA
14B2 Cambridge Can	20B2 Canby California, USA	107D2 Cape York Pen Aust	16C2 Carmel New York, USA
43D3 Cambridge County, Eng	99F1 Candala Somalia	46A1 Cap Gris Nez *C* France	94B2 Carmel,Mt Israel
43E3 Cambridge Eng	55C3 Çandarli Körfezi *B* Turk	26C3 Cap-Haitien Haiti	34D2 Carmelo Urug
27H1 Cambridge Jamaica	16C2 Candlewood,L USA	31B2 Capim *R* Brazil	22B2 Carmel Valley USA
15C3 Cambridge Maryland, USA	29E2 Canelones Urug	27P2 Cap Moule à Chique *C* St Lucia	9B4 Carmen *I* Mexico
15D2 Cambridge Massachussets, USA	18A2 Caney USA	53C3 Capo Isola de Correnti *C* Italy	29D4 Carmen de Patagones Arg
110C1 Cambridge NZ	100A2 Cangamba Angola		18C2 Carmi USA
14B2 Cambridge Ohio, USA	100B2 Cangombe Angola	53C3 Capo Rizzuto *C* Italy	21A2 Carmichael USA
4H3 Cambridge Bay Can	72D2 Cangzhou China	55A3 Capo Santa Maria di Leuca *C* Italy	35B1 Carmo do Paranaiba Brazil
60E5 Cam Burun *Pt* Turk	7D4 Caniapiscau *R* Can	53B3 Capo San Vito Italy	50A2 Carmona Spain
11A3 Camden Arkansas, USA	7D4 Caniapiscau,L Can	53C3 Capo Spartivento *C* Italy	106A3 Carnarvon Aust
109D2 Camden Aust	53B3 Canicatti Italy	27P2 Cap Pt St Lucia	100B4 Carnarvon S Africa
15D3 Camden New Jersey, USA	31D2 Canindé Brazil	53B2 Capri *I* Italy	35D1 Carncacá Brazil
17B1 Camden South Carolina, USA	92B1 Çankırı Turk	100B2 Caprivi Strip Region, Namibia	45C1 Carndonagh Irish Rep
18B2 Cameron Missouri, USA	13D2 Canmore Can	52A2 Cap Rosso *C* Corse	106B3 Carnegi,L Aust
19A3 Cameron Texas, USA	44A3 Canna *I* Scot	102H4 Cap Vert *C* Sen	98B2 Carnot CAR
4H2 Cameron *I* Can	87B2 Cannanore India	32C4 Caquetá *R* Colombia	108A2 Carnot,C Aust
111A3 Cameron Mts NZ	49D3 Cannes France	54B2 Caracal Rom	17B2 Carol City USA
98A2 Cameroon Federal Republic, Africa	109C3 Cann River Aust	33E3 Caracaraí Brazil	31B3 Carolina Brazil
98A2 Cameroun *Mt* Cam	30F4 Canôas Brazil	32D1 Caracas Ven	101H1 Carolina S Africa
31B2 Cametá Brazil	13F1 Canoe L Can	35B2 Caraguatatuba Brazil	17C1 Carolina Beach USA
79B4 Camiguin *I* Phil	9C3 Canon City USA	29B3 Carahue Chile	104F3 Caroline Is Pacific O
79B2 Camiling Phil	108B2 Canopus Aust	35C1 Caraí Brazil	60B4 Carpathians *Mts* E Europe
17B1 Camilla USA	5H4 Canora Can	35C2 Carandaí Brazil	
22B1 Camino USA	109C2 Canowindra Aust	31C6 Carangola Brazil	59D3 Carpatii Orientali *Mts* Rom
30D3 Camiri Bol	45C2 Cansore Pt Irish Rep	54B1 Caransebeş Rom	106C2 Carpentaria,G of Aust
31C2 Camocim Brazil	43E4 Canterbury Eng	108A2 Carappee Hill *Mt* Aust	83C5 Carpenter Ridge Indian O
106C2 Camooweal Aust	111B2 Canterbury Bight *B* NZ	26A3 Caratasca Honduras	49D3 Carpentras France
34D2 Campana Arg	111B2 Canterbury Plains NZ	35C1 Caratinga Brazil	52B2 Carpi Italy
29A5 Campana *I* Chile	77D4 Can Tho Viet	51B2 Caravaca Spain	22C3 Carpinteria USA
13B2 Campania *I* Can	Canton = Guangzhou	35D1 Caravelas Brazil	17B2 Carrabelle USA
111B2 Campbell,C NZ	19C3 Canton Mississippi, USA	18C2 Carbondale Illinois, USA	52B2 Carrara Italy
13B2 Campbell I Can	18B1 Canton Missouri, USA	53A3 Carbonia Sardegna	41B3 Carrauntoohill *Mt* Irish Rep
105G6 Campbell I NZ	10B2 Canton Ohio, USA	7E5 Carborear Can	45C2 Carrickmacross Irish Rep
4E3 Campbell,Mt Can	12E2 Cantwell USA	5G4 Carcaion Can	45B2 Carrick on Shannon Irish Rep
84C2 Campbellpore Pak	20C2 Canyon City USA	99E1 Carcar Mts Somalia	
5F5 Campbell River Can	12J2 Canyon Range *Mts* Can	48C3 Carcassonne France	45C2 Carrick-on-Suir Irish Rep
7D5 Campbellton Can		4E3 Carcross Can	
109D2 Campbellton Aust	20B2 Canyonville USA	23B2 Cardel Mexico	108A2 Carrieton Aust
42B2 Campbeltown Scot	98C3 Canzar Angola	25D2 Cárdenas Cuba	8D2 Carrington USA
25C3 Campeche Mexico	76D1 Cao Bang Viet	23B1 Cárdenas Mexico	50B1 Carrión *R* Spain
108B3 Camperdown Aust	31B2 Capanema Brazil	43C4 Cardiff Wales	10A2 Carroll USA
31D3 Campina Grande Brazil	35B2 Capão Bonito Brazil	43B3 Cardigan Wales	17A1 Carrollton Georgia, USA
	48B3 Capbreton France	43B3 Cardigan B Wales	
31B6 Campinas Brazil	24B2 Cap Corrientes *C* Mexico	13E2 Cardston Can	14A3 Carrollton Kentucky, USA
35B1 Campina Verde Brazil		54B1 Carei Rom	
98A2 Campo Cam	52A2 Cap Corse *C* Corse	33F4 Careiro Brazil	18B2 Carrollton Missouri, USA
53B2 Campobasso Italy	101D2 Cap d'Ambre *C* Madag	34A2 Carén Chile	
35B2 Campo Belo Brazil	48B2 Cap de la Hague *C* France	14B2 Carey USA	18C2 Carruthersville USA
35B1 Campo Florido Brazil	15D1 Cap-de-la-Madeleine Can	48B2 Carhaix-Plouguer France	60E5 Carsamba Turk
30D4 Campo Gallo Arg		29D3 Carhué Arg	92B2 Carsamba *R* Turk
30F3 Campo Grande Brazil	6C3 Cap de Nouvelle-France *C* Can	31C6 Cariacica Brazil	8B3 Carson City USA
31C2 Campo Maior Brazil	51C2 Capdepera Spain	5J4 Caribou Can	14B2 Carsonville USA
30F3 Campo Mourão Brazil	23A2 Cap de Tancitiario *C* Mexico	5G4 Caribou Mts Alberta, Can	26B4 Cartagena Colombia
35C2 Campos Brazil			51B2 Cartagena Spain
35B1 Campos Altos Brazil	109C4 Cape Barren I Aust	5F4 Caribou Mts British Columbia, Can	32B3 Cartago Colombia
47D1 Campo Tures Italy	103J6 Cape Basin Atlantic O		25D4 Cartago Costa Rica
76D3 Cam Ranh Viet	7E5 Cape Breton *I* Can	79B3 Carigara Phil	111C2 Carterton NZ
5G4 Camrose Can	97B4 Cape Coast Ghana	46C2 Carignan France	18B2 Carthage Missouri, USA
100A2 Camucuio Angola	15D2 Cape Cod B USA	33E1 Caripito Ven	
27K1 Canaan Tobago	6C3 Cape Dorset Can	15C1 Carleton Place Can	15C2 Carthage New York, USA
16C1 Canaan USA	17C1 Cape Fear *R* USA	101G1 Carletonville S Africa	
100A2 Canacupa Angola	18C2 Cape Girardeau USA	18C2 Carlinville USA	19B3 Carthage Texas, USA
2F3 Canada Dominion, N America	6B3 Cape Henrietta Maria Can	42C2 Carlisle Eng	106B2 Cartier I Timor S
	Cape Horn = Cabo de Hornos	15C2 Carlisle USA	7E4 Cartwright Can
29D2 Cañada de Gomez Arg	104E3 Cape Johnston Depth Pacific O	34C3 Carlos Arg	31D3 Caruaru Brazil
	35C1 Capelinha Brazil		
	4B3 Cape Lisburne USA		

33E1 **Carúpano** Ven
46B1 **Carvin** France
34A2 **Casablanca** Chile
96B1 **Casablanca** Mor
35B2 **Casa Branca** Brazil
9B3 **Casa Grande** USA
52A1 **Casale Monferrato** Italy
47D2 **Casalmaggiore** Italy
34C3 **Casares** Arg
13C3 **Cascade Mts** Can/USA
111A2 **Cascade Pt** NZ
8A2 **Cascade Range** Mts
USA
30F3 **Cascavel** Brazil
53B2 **Caserta** Italy
112C9 **Casey** Base Ant
45C2 **Cashel** Irish Rep
34C2 **Casilda** Arg
107E3 **Casino** Aust
32B5 **Casma** Peru
51B1 **Caspe** Spain
8C2 **Casper** USA
65G6 **Caspian S** USSR
14C3 **Cass** USA
100B2 **Cassamba** Angola
46B1 **Cassel** France
12J3 **Cassiar** Can
4E3 **Cassiar Mts** Can
35A1 **Cassilândia** Brazil
53B2 **Cassino** Italy
22C3 **Castaic** USA
34B2 **Castaño** R Arg
47D2 **Castelfranco** Italy
49D3 **Castellane** France
34D3 **Castelli** Arg
51B2 **Castellon de la Plana**
Spain
31C3 **Castelo** Brazil
50A2 **Castelo Branco** Port
48C3 **Castelsarrasin** France
53B3 **Castelvetrano** Italy
108B3 **Casterton** Aust
50B2 **Castilla La Nueva**
Region, Spain
50B1 **Castilla La Vieja**
Region, Spain
41B3 **Castlebar** Irish Rep
44A3 **Castlebay** Scot
42C2 **Castle Douglas** Scot
20C1 **Castlegar** Can
45B2 **Castleisland** Irish Rep
108B3 **Castlemain** Aust
45B2 **Castlerea** Irish Rep
109C2 **Castlereagh** Aust
48C3 **Castres-sur-l'Agout**
France
27E4 **Castries** St Lucia
29B4 **Castro** Arg
30F3 **Castro** Brazil
31D4 **Castro Alves** Brazil
53C3 **Castrovillari** Italy
22B2 **Castroville** USA
111A2 **Caswell Sd** NZ
25E2 **Cat** / The Bahamas
79B3 **Catabalogan** Phil
32A5 **Catacaos** Peru
35C2 **Cataguases** Brazil
19B3 **Catahoula L** USA
35B1 **Catalão** Brazil
51C1 **Cataluña** Region, Spain
30C4 **Catamarca** Arg
30C4 **Catamarca** State, Arg
101C2 **Catandica** Mozam
79B3 **Catanduanes** / Phil
31B6 **Catanduva** Brazil
53C3 **Catania** Italy
53C3 **Catanzaro** Italy
79B3 **Catarman** Phil
108A2 **Catastrophe,C** Aust
26C5 **Catatumbo** R Ven
16A2 **Catawissa** USA
23B2 **Catemaco** Mexico
49D3 **Cater** Corse
52A2 **Cateraggio** Corse
98B3 **Catete** Angola
97A3 **Catio** Guinea-Bissau
7A4 **Cat Lake** Can
13D3 **Catlegar** Can

107E3 **Cato** / Aust
25D2 **Catoche,C** Mexico
16A3 **Catoctin Mt** USA
15C3 **Catonsville** USA
34C3 **Catrilo** Arg
15D2 **Catskill** USA
15D2 **Catskill Mts** USA
32C2 **Cauca** R Colombia
31D2 **Caucaia** Brazil
32B2 **Caucasia** Colombia
Caucasus = Bol'shoy
Kavkaz
46B1 **Caudry** France
98B3 **Caungula** Angola
29B3 **Cauquenes** Chile
87B2 **Cauvery** R India
49D3 **Cavaillon** France
47D1 **Cavalese** italy
97B4 **Cavally** R Lib
45C2 **Cavan** County,
Irish Rep
45C2 **Cavan** Irish Rep
79B3 **Cavite** Phil
31C2 **Caxias** Brazil
32C4 **Caxias** Brazil
30F4 **Caxias do Sul** Brazil
98B3 **Caxito** Angola
17B1 **Cayce** USA
93D1 **Çayeli** Turk
33G3 **Cayenne** French
Guiana
46A1 **Cayeux-sur-Mer**
France
25E3 **Cayman Brac** /
Caribbean S
26A3 **Cayman Is**
Caribbean S
26A3 **Cayman Trench**
Caribbean S
99E2 **Caynabo** Somalia
25E2 **Cayo Romana** / Cuba
25D3 **Cayos Miskitos** Is Nic
26A2 **Cay Sal** / Caribbean S
100B2 **Cazombo** Angola
Ceará = Fortaleza
31C3 **Ceara** State, Brazil
79B3 **Cebu** Phil
79B3 **Cebu** / Phil
16B3 **Cecilton** USA
52B2 **Cecina** Italy
8B3 **Cedar City** USA
19A3 **Cedar Creek Res** USA
5J4 **Cedar L** Can
10A2 **Cedar Rapids** USA
17A1 **Cedartown** USA
24A2 **Cedros** / Mexico
106C4 **Ceduna** Aust
99E2 **Ceelbuur** Somalia
99E1 **Ceerigaabo** Somalia
53B3 **Cefalù** Italy
59B3 **Cegléd** Hung
100A2 **Cela** Angola
24B2 **Celaya** Mexico
Celebes = Sulawesi
70C3 **Celebes S** S E Asia
14B2 **Celina** USA
52C1 **Celje** Yugos
56C2 **Celle** Germany
71E4 **Cendrawasih** Pen
Indon
47C2 **Ceno** R Italy
19B3 **Center** USA
16C2 **Center Moriches** USA
17A1 **Center Point** USA
47D2 **Cento** Italy
44B3 **Central** Region, Scot
98B2 **Central African**
Republic Africa
16D2 **Central Falls** USA
18C2 **Centralia** Illinois, USA
8A2 **Centralia** Washington,
USA
20B2 **Central Point** USA
71F4 **Central Range** Mts
PNG
16A3 **Centreville** Maryland,
USA
78C4 **Cepu** Indon

Ceram = Seram
71D4 **Ceram Sea** Indon
34C3 **Cereales** Arg
31B5 **Ceres** Brazil
100A4 **Ceres** S Africa
22B2 **Ceres** USA
48C2 **Cergy-Pontoise** France
53C2 **Cerignola** Italy
60C5 **Cernavodă** Rom
9C4 **Cerralvo** / Mexico
23A1 **Cerritos** Mexico
34B2 **Cerro Aconcagua** Mt
Arg
23B1 **Cerro Azul** Mexico
34A3 **Cerro Campanario** Mt
Chile
34C2 **Cerro Champaqui** Mt
Arg
23A2 **Cerro Cuachaia** Mt
Mexico
23B1 **Cerro de Astillero**
Mexico
34B2 **Cerro de Olivares** Mt
Arg
32B6 **Cerro de Pasco** Peru
27D3 **Cerro de Punta** Mt
Puerto Rico
23A2 **Cerro El Cantado** Mt
Mexico
34B3 **Cerro El Nevado** Mt
Arg
23A2 **Cerro Grande** Mts
Mexico
34A2 **Cerro Juncal** Mt Arg/
Chile
23A1 **Cerro la Ardilla** Mts
Mexico
34B1 **Cerro las Tortolas** Mt
Chile
23A2 **Cerro Laurel** Mt Mexico
34A2 **Cerro Mercedario** Mt
Arg
34A3 **Cerro Mora** Mt Chile
27C4 **Cerron** Mt Ven
34B3 **Cerro Payún** Mt Arg
23B2 **Cerro Penón del Rosario**
Mt Mexico
34B2 **Cerro Sosneado** Mt
Arg
23A2 **Cerro Teotepec** Mt
Mexico
34B2 **Cerro Tupungato** Mt
Arg
23B2 **Cerro Yucuyacau** Mt
Mexico
47C2 **Cervo** R Italy
52B2 **Cesena** Italy
60B2 **Cēsis** USSR
57C3 **České Budějovice**
Czech
57C3 **České Zemé** Region,
Czech
59B3 **Českomoravská**
Vysočina U Czech
55C3 **Çeşme** Turk
107E4 **Cessnock** Aust
52C2 **Cetina** R Yugos
96B1 **Ceuta** N W Africa
92C2 **Ceyham** Turk
92C2 **Ceyhan** R Turk
93C2 **Ceylanpınar** Turk
Ceylon = Sri Lanka
63B2 **Chaa-Khol** USSR
48C2 **Chaâteaudun** France
47B1 **Chablais** Region,
France
34C2 **Chacabuco** Arg
32B5 **Chachapoyas** Peru
34B3 **Chacharramendi** Arg
84C3 **Chachran** Pak
30D4 **Chaco** State, Arg
98B1 **Chad** Republic, Africa
98B1 **Chad** L C Africa
34B3 **Chadileuvu** R Arg
8C2 **Chadron** USA
18C2 **Chaffee** USA
85A3 **Chagai** Pak
63F2 **Chagda** USSR

84B2 **Chaghcharan** Afghan
104B4 **Chagos Arch** Indian O
27L1 **Chaguanas** Trinidad
91D4 **Chāh Bahār** Iran
76C2 **Chai Badan** Thai
86B2 **Chāībāsa** India
76C3 **Chaine des**
Cardamomes Mts
Camb
98C4 **Chaine des Mitumba**
Mts Zaïre
76C2 **Chaiyaphum** Thai
34D2 **Chajari** Arg
84C2 **Chakwal** Pak
30B2 **Chala** Peru
100C2 **Chalabesa** Zambia
84A2 **Chalap Dalam** Mts
Afghan
73C4 **Chaling** China
85C4 **Chālisgaon** India
12F1 **Chalkyitsik** USA
46C2 **Challerange** France
46C2 **Châlons sur Marne**
France
49C2 **Chalon sur Saône**
France
57C3 **Cham** Germany
84B2 **Chaman** Pak
84D2 **Chamba** India
85D3 **Chambal** R India
15C3 **Chambersburg** USA
49D2 **Chambéry** France
46B2 **Chambly** France
85A3 **Chambor Kalat** Pak
90B3 **Chamgordan** Iran
34B2 **Chamical** Arg
47B2 **Chamonix** France
86A2 **Champa** India
49C2 **Champagne** Region,
France
101G1 **Champagne Castle** Mt
Lesotho
47A1 **Champagnole** France
10B2 **Champaign** USA
76D3 **Champassak** Laos
10C2 **Champlain,L** USA
87B2 **Chāmrājnagar** India
30B4 **Chañaral** Chile
34A3 **Chanco** Chile
4D3 **Chandalar** USA
4D3 **Chandalar** R USA
84D2 **Chandīgarh** India
86C2 **Chandpur** Bang
85D5 **Chandrapur** India
91D4 **Chānf** Iran
101C2 **Changara** Mozam
74B2 **Changbai** China
69E2 **Changchun** China
73C4 **Changde** China
68E4 **Chang-hua** Taiwan
76D2 **Changjiang** China
73D3 **Chang Jiang** R China
74B2 **Changjin** N Korea
73C4 **Changsha** China
72E3 **Changshu** China
74A2 **Changtu** China
72B2 **Changwu** China
74B3 **Changyǒn** N Korea
72C2 **Changzhi** China
73E3 **Changzhou** China
48B2 **Channel Is** UK
9B3 **Channel Is** USA
7E5 **Channel Port-aux-**
Basques Can
76C3 **Chanthaburi** Thai
46B2 **Chantilly** France
18A2 **Chanute** USA
73D5 **Chaoàn** China
73D5 **Chao'an** China
73D3 **Chao Hu** L China
76C3 **Chao Phraya** R Thai
72E1 **Chaoyang** China
31C4 **Chapada Diamantina**
Mts Brazil
31C2 **Chapadinha** Brazil
23A1 **Chapala** Mexico
23A1 **Chapala,Lac de** L
Mexico

61H3 **Chapayevo** USSR
30F4 **Chapecó** Brazil
27H1 **Chapeltown** Jamaica
7B5 **Chapleau** Can
61E3 **Chaplygin** USSR
112C3 **Charcot I** Ant
80E2 **Chardzhou** USSR
48C2 **Charente** R France
98B1 **Chari** R Chad
98B1 **Chari Baguirmi**
    Region, Chad
84B1 **Charikar** Afghan
18B1 **Chariton** R USA
33F2 **Charity** Guyana
85D3 **Charkhāri** India
46C1 **Charleroi** Belg
18C2 **Charleston** Illinois,
    USA
18C2 **Charleston** Missouri,
    USA
11C3 **Charleston** S Carolina,
    USA
10B3 **Charleston** W Virginia,
    USA
98C3 **Charlesville** Zaïre
107D3 **Charleville** Aust
49C2 **Charleville-Mézières**
    France
14A1 **Charlevoix** USA
14B2 **Charlotte** Michigan,
    USA
11B3 **Charlotte** N Carolina,
    USA
17B2 **Charlotte Harbor** B
    USA
10C3 **Charlottesville** USA
7D5 **Charlottetown** Can
27K1 **Charlotteville** Tobago
108B3 **Charlton** Aust
10C1 **Charlton I** Can
84C2 **Charsadda** Pak
107D3 **Charters Towers** Aust
48C2 **Chartres** France
29E3 **Chascomús** Arg
13D2 **Chase** Can
48B2 **Châteaubriant** France
48C2 **Châteaudun** France
48B2 **Châteaulin** France
48C2 **Châteauroux** France
46D2 **Château-Salins** France
49C2 **Château-Thierry**
    France
46C1 **Châtelet** Belg
48C2 **Châtellerault** France
43E4 **Chatham** Eng
7D5 **Chatham** New
    Brunswick, Can
16C1 **Chatham** New York,
    USA
14B2 **Chatham** Ontario, Can
13A2 **Chatham Sd** Can
12H3 **Chatham Str** USA
49C2 **Châtillon** France
47B2 **Châtillon** Italy
16B3 **Chatsworth** USA
17B1 **Chattahoochee** USA
17A1 **Chattahoochee** R
    USA
11B3 **Chattanooga** USA
76A1 **Chauk** Burma
49D2 **Chaumont** France
46B2 **Chauny** France
77D3 **Chau Phu** Viet
50A1 **Chaves** Port
50B2 **Chazaouet** Alg
34C2 **Chazón** Arg
32C2 **Chcontá** Colombia
57C2 **Cheb** Czech
65F4 **Cheboksary** USSR
10B2 **Cheboygan** USA
74B3 **Chech'on** S Korea
85C3 **Chechro** Pak
18A2 **Checotah** USA
76A2 **Cheduba** I Burma
108B1 **Cheepie** Aust
96B2 **Chegga** Maur
100C2 **Chegutu** Zim
20B1 **Chehalis** USA

74B4 **Cheju** S Korea
74B4 **Cheju do** I S Korea
74B4 **Cheju-haehyŏp** Str
    S Korea
63F2 **Chekunda** USSR
20B1 **Chelan,L** USA
90B2 **Cheleken** USSR
34B3 **Chelforo** Arg
80D1 **Chelkar** USSR
59C2 **Chelm** Pol
58B2 **Chelmno** Pol
43E4 **Chelmsford** Eng
43C4 **Cheltenham** Eng
65H4 **Chelyabinsk** USSR
101C2 **Chemba** Mozam
57C2 **Chemnitz** Germany
84D2 **Chenab** R India/Pak
96B2 **Chenachane** Alg
20C1 **Cheney** USA
18A2 **Cheney Res** USA
72D1 **Chengda** China
73A3 **Chengdu** China
72E2 **Chengshan Jiao** Pt
    China
73C4 **Chenxi** China
73C4 **Chen Xian** China
73D3 **Cheo Xian** China
32B5 **Chepén** Peru
34B2 **Chepes** Arg
48C2 **Cher** R France
23A2 **Cheran** Mexico
17C1 **Cheraw** USA
48B2 **Cherbourg** France
96C1 **Cherchell** Alg
63C2 **Cheremkhovo** USSR
60E2 **Cherepovets** USSR
60D4 **Cherkassy** USSR
61F5 **Cherkessk** USSR
60D3 **Chernigov** USSR
60D2 **Chernobyl** USSR
60C4 **Chernovtsy** USSR
61J2 **Chernushka** USSR
60B3 **Chernyakhovsk** USSR
61G4 **Chernyye Zemli**
    Region, USSR
18A2 **Cherokees,L o'the**
    USA
34A3 **Cherquenco** Chile
86C1 **Cherrapunji** India
60C3 **Cherven' USSR
59C2 **Chervonograd** USSR
10C3 **Chesapeake** B USA
42C3 **Cheshire** County, Eng
16C1 **Cheshire** USA
64F3 **Chëshskaya Guba** B
    USSR
21A1 **Chester** California,
    USA
42C3 **Chester** Eng
18C2 **Chester** Illinois, USA
16C1 **Chester**
    Massachusets, USA
15C3 **Chester** Pennsylvania,
    USA
17B1 **Chester** S Carolina,
    USA
16A3 **Chester** R USA
42D3 **Chesterfield** Eng
6A3 **Chesterfield Inlet** Can
16A3 **Chestertown** USA
25D3 **Chetumal** Mexico
13C1 **Chetwynd** Can
12A2 **Chevak** USA
111B2 **Cheviot** NZ
40C2 **Cheviots** Hills Eng/
    Scot
13D3 **Chewelah** USA
8C2 **Cheyenne** USA
86A1 **Chhapra** India
86C1 **Chhatak** Bang
85D4 **Chhatarpur** India
85D4 **Chhindwāra** India
86B1 **Chhuka** Bhutan
73E5 **Chia'i** Taiwan
100A2 **Chiange** Angola
76C2 **Chiang Kham** Thai
76B2 **Chiang Mai** Thai
47C1 **Chiavenna** Italy

74E3 **Chiba** Japan
100A2 **Chibia** Angola
7C4 **Chibougamou** Can
75A1 **Chiburi-jima** I Japan
101C3 **Chibuto** Mozam
10B2 **Chicago** USA
14A2 **Chicago Heights** USA
12G3 **Chichagof I** USA
43D4 **Chichester** Eng
75B1 **Chichibu** Japan
69G4 **Chichi-jima** I Japan
11B3 **Chickamauga L** USA
19C3 **Chickasawhay** R USA
9D3 **Chickasha** USA
12F2 **Chicken** USA
32A5 **Chiclayo** Peru
8A3 **Chico** USA
29C4 **Chico** R Arg
101C2 **Chicoa** Mozam
15D2 **Chicopee** USA
7C5 **Chicoutimi** Can
101C3 **Chicualacuala** Mozam
87B2 **Chidambaram** India
6D3 **Chidley,C** Can
17B2 **Chiefland** USA
99C3 **Chiengi** Zambia
47B2 **Chieri** Italy
46C2 **Chiers** R France
47C1 **Chiesa** Italy
47D2 **Chiese** R Italy
52B2 **Chieti** Italy
72D1 **Chifeng** China
12C3 **Chiginigak,Mt** USA
4C3 **Chigmit Mts** USA
23B2 **Chignahuapán** Mexico
12C3 **Chignik** USA
24B2 **Chihuahua** Mexico
87B2 **Chik Ballāpur** India
87B2 **Chikmagalūr** India
12C2 **Chikuminuk L** USA
101C2 **Chikwawa** Malawi
76A1 **Chi-kyaw** Burma
87C1 **Chilakalūrupet** India
23B2 **Chilapa** Mexico
87B3 **Chilaw** Sri Lanka
28B6 **Chile** Republic
34B2 **Chilecito** Mendoza,
    Arg
100B2 **Chililabombwe**
    Zambia
86B2 **Chilka** L India
13C2 **Chilko** R Can
5F4 **Chilko L** Can
13C2 **Chilkotin** R Can
34A3 **Chillán** Chile
34D3 **Chillar** Arg
18B2 **Chillicothe** Missouri,
    USA
14B3 **Chillicothe** Ohio, USA
13C3 **Chilliwack** Can
86B1 **Chilmari** India
101C2 **Chilongozi** Zambia
20B2 **Chiloquin** USA
24C3 **Chilpancingo** Mexico
43D4 **Chiltern Hills** Upland
    Eng
14A2 **Chilton** USA
101C2 **Chilumba** Malawi
69E4 **Chi-lung** Taiwan
101C2 **Chilwa** L Malawi
100C2 **Chimanimani** Zim
46C1 **Chimay** Belg
65G5 **Chimbay** USSR
32B4 **Chimborazo** Mt
    Ecuador
32B5 **Chimbote** Peru
65H5 **Chimkent** USSR
101C2 **Chimoio** Mozam
67E3 **China** Republic, Asia
    China National
    Republic = Taiwan
25D3 **Chinandega** Nic
32B6 **Chincha Alta** Peru
109D1 **Chinchilla** Aust
101C2 **Chinde** Mozam
86C2 **Chindwin** R Burma
100B2 **Chingola** Zambia
100A2 **Chinguar** Angola

96A2 **Chinguetti** Maur
74B3 **Chinhae** S Korea
100C2 **Chinhoyi** Zim
12D3 **Chiniak,C** USA
84C2 **Chiniot** Pak
74B3 **Chinju** S Korea
98C2 **Chinko** R CAR
75B1 **Chino** Japan
101C2 **Chinsali** Zambia
52B1 **Chioggia** Italy
101C2 **Chipata** Zambia
101C3 **Chipinge** Zim
87A1 **Chiplūn** India
43C4 **Chippenham** Eng
10A2 **Chippewa Falls** USA
32A4 **Chira** R Peru
87C1 **Chīrāla** India
101C3 **Chiredzi** Zim
95A2 **Chirfa** Niger
32A2 **Chiriqui** Mt Panama
54C2 **Chirpan** Bulg
32A2 **Chirripo Grande** Mt
    Costa Rica
100B2 **Chirundu** Zim
100B2 **Chisamba** Zambia
73B4 **Chishui He** R China
47B2 **Chisone** R Italy
68D1 **Chita** USSR
100A2 **Chitado** Angola
100A2 **Chitembo** Angola
12F2 **Chitina** USA
12F2 **Chitina** R USA
87B2 **Chitradurga** India
84C1 **Chitral** Pak
32A2 **Chitré** Panama
86C2 **Chittagong** Bang
85C4 **Chittaurgarh** India
87B2 **Chittoor** India
100B2 **Chiume** Angola
47D1 **Chiusa** Italy
47B2 **Chivasso** Italy
29D2 **Chivilcoy** Arg
100C2 **Chivu** Zim
75A1 **Chizu** Japan
29C3 **Choele Choel** Arg
34C3 **Choique** Arg
24B2 **Choix** Mexico
58B2 **Chojnice** Pol
99D1 **Choke** Mts Eth
48B2 **Cholet** France
23B2 **Cholula** Mexico
100B2 **Choma** Zambia
86B1 **Chomo Yummo** Mt
    China/India
57C2 **Chomutov** Czech
63C1 **Chona** R USSR
74B3 **Ch'ŏnan** S Korea
76C3 **Chon Buri** Thai
32A4 **Chone** Ecuador
74B2 **Ch'ŏngjin** N Korea
74B3 **Chongju** N Korea
74B3 **Ch'ŏngju** S Korea
100A2 **Chongoroi** Angola
73B4 **Chongqing** China
74B3 **Chŏngŭp** S Korea
74B3 **Chŏnju** S Korea
86B1 **Chooyu** Mt China/
    Nepal
59D3 **Chortkov** USSR
74B3 **Ch'ŏrwŏn** N Korea
59B2 **Chorzow** Pol
74E3 **Choshi** Japan
34A3 **Chos-Malal** Arg
58B2 **Choszczno** Pol
86A2 **Chotanāgpur** Region,
    India
96C1 **Chott Melrhir** Alg
22B2 **Chowchilla** USA
63D3 **Choybalsan** Mongolia
6A3 **Chrantrey Inlet** B Can
61H2 **Chraykovskiy** USSR
111B2 **Christchurch** NZ
101G1 **Christiana** S Africa
6D2 **Christian,C** Can
12H3 **Christian Sd** USA
6E3 **Christianshab**
    Greenland
104D4 **Christmas I** Indian O

61G2	**Christopol** USSR
65J5	**Chu** USSR
65J5	**Chu** *R* USSR
29C4	**Chubut** State, Arg
29C4	**Chubut** *R* Arg
60D2	**Chudovo** USSR
64D4	**Chudskoye Ozer** *L* USSR
4D3	**Chugach Mts** USA
12E2	**Chugiak** USA
75A1	**Chūgoku-sanchi** *Mts* Japan
29F2	**Chuí** Brazil
29B3	**Chuillán** Chile
77C5	**Chukai** Malay
76D2	**Chu Lai** Viet
21B3	**Chula Vista** USA
12E2	**Chulitna** USA
63E2	**Chulman** USSR
32A5	**Chulucanas** Peru
30C2	**Chulumani** Bol
65K4	**Chulym** USSR
63A2	**Chulym** *R* USSR
63B2	**Chuma** *R* USSR
84D2	**Chumar** India
63F2	**Chumikan** USSR
77B3	**Chumphon** Thai
74B3	**Ch'unch'ŏn** S Korea
86B2	**Chunchura** India
74B3	**Ch'ungju** S Korea
	Chungking=Chongqing
99D3	**Chunya** Tanz
63C1	**Chunya** *R* USSR
27L1	**Chupara Pt** Trinidad
30C3	**Chuquicamata** Chile
52A1	**Chur** Switz
86C2	**Churāchāndpur** India
7A4	**Churchill** Can
7D4	**Churchill** *R* Labrador, Can
7A4	**Churchill** *R* Manitoba, Can
7A4	**Churchill,C** Can
7D4	**Churchill Falls** Can
5H4	**Churchill L** Can
84C3	**Chūru** India
23A2	**Churumuco** Mexico
61J2	**Chusovoy** USSR
61G2	**Chuvashkaya ASSR** Republic, USSR
68B4	**Chuxiong** China
76D3	**Chu Yang Sin** *Mt* Viet
78B4	**Cianjur** Indon
47D2	**Ciano d'Enza** Italy
35A2	**Cianorte** Brazil
58C2	**Ciechanow** Pol
25E2	**Ciego de Avila** Cuba
32C1	**Ciénaga** Colombia
25D2	**Cienfuegos** Cuba
59B3	**Cieszyn** Pol
51B2	**Cieza** Spain
92B2	**Cihanbeyli** Turk
23A2	**Cihuatlán** Mexico
78B4	**Cijulang** Indon
78B4	**Cilacap** Indon
54C1	**Cîmpina** Rom
51C1	**Cinca** *R* Spain
52C2	**Činčer** *Mt* Yugos
10B3	**Cincinnati** USA
54B1	**Cindrelu** *Mt* Rom
55C3	**Cine** *R* Turk
46C1	**Ciney** Belg
34B3	**Cipolletti** Arg
4D3	**Circle** Alaska, USA
14B3	**Circleville** USA
78B4	**Cirebon** Indon
43D4	**Cirencester** Eng
47D2	**Citadella** Italy
24C3	**Citlaltepetl** *Mt* Mexico
100A4	**Citrusdal** S Africa
52B2	**Citta del Vaticano** Italy
52B2	**Città di Castello** Italy
24B2	**Ciudad Acuña** Mexico
23A2	**Ciudad Altamirano** Mexico
33E2	**Ciudad Bolivar** Ven
24B2	**Ciudad Camargo** Mexico

25C3	**Ciudad del Carmen** Mexico
23B1	**Ciudad del Maiz** Mexico
51C1	**Ciudadela** Spain
33E2	**Ciudad Guayana** Ven
24B3	**Ciudad Guzman** Mexico
23A2	**Ciudad Hidalgo** Mexico
24B1	**Ciudad Juárez** Mexico
9C4	**Ciudad Lerdo** Mexico
24C2	**Ciudad Madero** Mexico
23B2	**Ciudad Mendoza** Mexico
24B2	**Ciudad Obregon** Mexico
27C4	**Ciudad Ojeda** Ven
33E2	**Ciudad Piar** Ven
50B2	**Ciudad Real** Spain
50A1	**Ciudad Rodrigo** Spain
24C2	**Ciudad Valles** Mexico
24C2	**Ciudad Victoria** Mexico
52B2	**Civitavecchia** Italy
93D2	**Cizre** Turk
43E4	**Clacton-on-Sea** Eng
5G4	**Claire,L** Can
14C2	**Clairton** USA
47A1	**Clairvaux** France
17A1	**Clanton** USA
100A4	**Clanwilliam** S Africa
45C2	**Clara** Irish Rep
34D3	**Claraz** Arg
45B2	**Clare** County, Irish Rep
14B2	**Clare** USA
45A2	**Clare** *I* Irish Rep
15D2	**Claremont** USA
18A2	**Claremore** USA
45B2	**Claremorris** Irish Rep
109D1	**Clarence** *R* Aust
111B2	**Clarence** *R* NZ
106C2	**Clarence Str** Aust
12H3	**Clarence Str** USA
19B3	**Clarendon** USA
7E5	**Clarenville** Can
5G4	**Claresholm** Can
18A1	**Clarinda** USA
15C2	**Clarion** Pennsylvania, USA
24A3	**Clarión** *I* Mexico
15C2	**Clarion** *R* USA
105J3	**Clarion Fracture Zone** Pacific O
11B3	**Clark Hill Res** USA
14B2	**Clark,Pt** Can
14B3	**Clarksburg** USA
11A3	**Clarksdale** USA
12C3	**Clarks Point** USA
20C1	**Clarkston** USA
18B2	**Clarksville** Arkansas, USA
35A1	**Claro** *R* Brazil
29D3	**Claromecó** Arg
18A2	**Clay Center** USA
44D2	**Claymore** *Oilfield* N Sea
13B3	**Clayoquot Sd** Can
9C3	**Clayton** New Mexico, USA
15C2	**Clayton** New York, USA
41B3	**Clear** *C* Irish Rep
12E3	**Cleare,C** USA
13D1	**Clear Hills** *Mts* Can
21A2	**Clear L** USA
20B2	**Clear Lake Res** USA
13D2	**Clearwater** Can
11B4	**Clearwater** USA
13E1	**Clearwater** *R* Can
13C2	**Clearwater L** Can
9D3	**Cleburne** USA
22B1	**Clements** USA
79A3	**Cleopatra Needle** *Mt* Phil
107D3	**Clermont** Aust

46B2	**Clermont** France
46C2	**Clermont-en-Argonne** France
49C2	**Clermont-Ferrand** France
46D1	**Clervaux** Germany
47D1	**Cles** Italy
108A2	**Cleve** Aust
42D2	**Cleveland** County, Eng
19B3	**Cleveland** Mississippi, USA
10B2	**Cleveland** Ohio, USA
11B3	**Cleveland** Tennessee, USA
19A3	**Cleveland** Texas, USA
41B3	**Clew** *B* Irish Rep
45A2	**Clifden** Irish Rep
109D1	**Clifton** Aust
16B2	**Clifton** New Jersey, USA
108A1	**Clifton Hills** Aust
13F3	**Climax** Can
18B2	**Clinton** Arkansas, USA
5F4	**Clinton** Can
16C2	**Clinton** Connecticut, USA
16D1	**Clinton** Massachusetts, USA
19B3	**Clinton** Mississippi, USA
18B2	**Clinton** Missouri, USA
16B2	**Clinton** New Jersey, USA
4H3	**Clinton-Colden L** Can
24B3	**Clipperton I** Pacific O
30C2	**Cliza** Bol
45B3	**Clonakilty** Irish Rep
107D3	**Cloncurry** Aust
45C1	**Clones** Irish Rep
45C2	**Clonmel** Irish Rep
10A2	**Cloquet** USA
12C2	**Cloudy Mt** USA
22C2	**Clovis** California, USA
9C3	**Clovis** New Mexico, USA
60B4	**Cluj** Rom
54B1	**Cluj-Napoca** Rom
47B1	**Cluses** France
47C2	**Clusone** Italy
111A3	**Clutha** *R* NZ
43C3	**Clwyd** County, Wales
6D2	**Clyde** Can
111A3	**Clyde** NZ
42B2	**Clyde** *R* Scot
23A2	**Coahuayana** Mexico
23A2	**Coalcomán** Mexico
13E2	**Coaldale** Can
21B2	**Coaldale** USA
21A2	**Coalinga** USA
33E5	**Coari** *R* Brazil
17A1	**Coastal Plain** USA
4E4	**Coast Mts** Can
8A2	**Coast Ranges** *Mts* USA
42B2	**Coatbridge** Scot
23B2	**Coatepec** Mexico
16B3	**Coatesville** USA
15D1	**Coaticook** Can
6B3	**Coats I** Can
112B1	**Coats Land** Region, Ant
25C3	**Coatzacoalcos** Mexico
7C5	**Coaticook** Can
25C3	**Cobán** Guatemala
107D4	**Cobar** Aust
109C3	**Cobargo** Aust
45B3	**Cobh** Irish Rep
32D6	**Cobija** Bol
16B1	**Cobleskill** USA
51B2	**Cobo de Palos** *C* Spain
7C5	**Cobourg** Can
106C2	**Cobourg Pen** Aust
57C2	**Coburg** Germany
32B4	**Coca** Ecuador
17B2	**Coca** USA
30C2	**Cochabamba** Bol

46D1	**Cochem** Germany
87B3	**Cochin** India
13E2	**Cochrane** Alberta, Can
7B5	**Cochrane** Ontario, Can
108B2	**Cockburn** Aust
16A3	**Cockeysville** USA
27H1	**Cockpit Country,The** Jamaica
25D3	**Coco** *R* Honduras/Nic
98A2	**Cocobeach** Gabon
27L1	**Cocos B** Trinidad
104C4	**Cocos Is** Indian O
23A1	**Cocula** Mexico
10C2	**Cod,C** USA
111A3	**Codfish I** NZ
7D4	**Cod I** Can
47E2	**Codigoro** Italy
31C2	**Codó** Brazil
47C2	**Codogno** Italy
8C2	**Cody** USA
56B2	**Coesfeld** Germany
8B2	**Coeur d'Alene** USA
9D3	**Coffeyville** USA
108A2	**Coffin B** Aust
109D2	**Coff's Harbour** Aust
23B2	**Cofre de Perote** *Mt* Mexico
48B2	**Cognac** France
15D2	**Cohoes** USA
108B3	**Cohuna** Aust
29B5	**Coihaique** Chile
87B2	**Coimbatore** India
50A1	**Coimbra** Port
32A3	**Cojimies** Ecuador
107D4	**Colac** Aust
31C5	**Colatina** Brazil
112B6	**Colbeck,C** Ant
43E4	**Colchester** Eng
16C2	**Colchester** USA
47B1	**Col de la Faucille** France
13E2	**Cold L** Can
52A1	**Col du Grand St Bernard** *P* Italy/Switz
47B2	**Col du Lautaret** *P* France
52A1	**Col du Mont Cenis** *P* France/Italy
14B2	**Coldwater** USA
12F1	**Coleen** *R* USA
14B2	**Coleman** Michigan, USA
101G1	**Colenso** S Africa
45C1	**Coleraine** N Ire
111B2	**Coleridge,L** NZ
100B4	**Colesberg** S Africa
22C1	**Coleville** USA
21A2	**Colfax** California, USA
19B3	**Colfax** Louisiana, USA
20C1	**Colfax** Washington, USA
24B3	**Colima** Mexico
23A2	**Colima** State, Mexico
34A2	**Colina** Chile
44A3	**Coll** *I* Scot
109C1	**Collarenebri** Aust
52A2	**Colle de Tende** *P* France/Italy
12E2	**College** USA
17B1	**College Park** Georgia, USA
16A3	**College Park** Washington, USA
19A3	**College Station** USA
106A4	**Collie** Aust
106B2	**Collier B** Aust
46A1	**Collines de L'Artois** *Mts* France
46B2	**Collines De Thiérache** France
14B2	**Collingwood** Can
110B2	**Collingwood** NZ
19C3	**Collins** Mississippi, USA
4H2	**Collinson Pen** Can
107D3	**Collinsville** Aust
18C2	**Collinsville** Illinois, USA

18A2 **Collinsville** Oklahoma, USA
34A3 **Collipulli** Chile
49D2 **Colmar** France
Cologne = Köln
35B2 **Colômbia** Brazil
32B3 **Colombia** Republic, S America
15C3 **Colombia** USA
87B3 **Colombo** Sri Lanka
25D2 **Colon** Cuba
32B2 **Colón** Panama
29E2 **Colonia** Urug
34D2 **Colonia del Sacramento** Urug
34B3 **Colonia 25 de Mayo** Arg
29C5 **Colonia Las Heras** Arg
44A3 **Colonsay** I Scot
23A1 **Colontlán** Mexico
27E5 **Coloradito** Ven
8C3 **Colorado** State, USA
9B3 **Colorado** R Arizona, USA
29D3 **Colorado** R Buenos Aires, Arg
9D3 **Colorado** R Texas, USA
9B3 **Colorado Plat** USA
8C3 **Colorado Springs** USA
22D3 **Colton** USA
16A3 **Columbia** Maryland, USA
19C3 **Columbia** Mississippi, USA
10A3 **Columbia** Missouri, USA
15C2 **Columbia** Pennsylvania, USA
11B3 **Columbia** S Carolina, USA
11B3 **Columbia** Tennessee, USA
13D2 **Columbia** R Can
8A2 **Columbia** R USA
5G4 **Columbia,Mt** Can
20C1 **Columbia Plat** USA
11B3 **Columbus** Georgia, USA
14A3 **Columbus** Indiana, USA
11B3 **Columbus** Mississippi, USA
8D2 **Columbus** Nebraska, USA
10B2 **Columbus** Ohio, USA
19A4 **Columbus** Texas, USA
20C1 **Colville** USA
4C3 **Colville** R USA
110C1 **Colville,C** NZ
4F3 **Colville L** Can
42C3 **Colwyn Bay** Wales
47E2 **Comacchio** Italy
22B1 **Comanche Res** USA
25D3 **Comayagua** Honduras
34A2 **Combarbalá** Chile
45C2 **Comeragh** Mts Irish Rep
86C2 **Comilla** Bang
25C3 **Comitán** Mexico
46C2 **Commercy** France
6B3 **Committees B** Can
52A1 **Como** Italy
29C5 **Comodoro Rivadavia** Arg
23A1 **Comonfort** Mexico
87B3 **Comorin,C** India
101D2 **Comoros** Is Indian O
49C2 **Compiègne** France
23A1 **Compostela** Mexico
34B2 **Comte Salas** Arg
86C1 **Cona** China
97A4 **Conakry** Guinea
34B2 **Concarán** Arg
48B2 **Concarneau** France
35D1 **Conceiçao da Barra** Brazil
31B3 **Conceição do Araguaia** Brazil
35C1 **Conceiçao do Mato Dentro** Brazil
29B3 **Concepción** Chile

30E3 **Concepción** Par
29E2 **Concepción** R Arg
24B2 **Concepcion del Oro** Mexico
34D2 **Concepcion del Uruguay** Arg
9A3 **Conception,Pt** USA
35B2 **Conchas** Brazil
9C4 **Conchos** R Mexico
21A2 **Concord** California, USA
10C2 **Concord** New Hampshire, USA
29E2 **Concordia** Arg
8D3 **Concordia** USA
20B1 **Concrete** USA
109D1 **Condamine** Aust
107D4 **Condobolin** Aust
20B1 **Condon** USA
46C1 **Condroz** Mts Belg
17A1 **Conecuh** R USA
47E2 **Conegliano** Italy
89F8 **Congo** Republic, Africa
89F8 **Congo** R Congo
Congo,R = Zaïre
14B1 **Coniston** Can
45B2 **Connaught** Region, Irish Rep
14B2 **Conneaut** USA
10C2 **Connecticut** State, USA
15D2 **Connecticut** R USA
15C2 **Connellsville** USA
45B2 **Connemara,Mts of** Irish Rep
14A3 **Connersville** USA
108B2 **Conoble** Aust
19A3 **Conroe** USA
35C2 **Conselheiro Lafaiete** Brazil
77D4 **Con Son** Is Viet
Constance,L=Bodensee
60C5 **Constanta** Rom
96C1 **Constantine** Alg
12C3 **Constantine,C** USA
29B3 **Constitución** Chile
13F3 **Consul** Can
47E2 **Contarina** Italy
31C4 **Contas** R Brazil
23B2 **Contreras** Mexico
4H3 **Contuoyto L** Can
11A3 **Conway** Arkansas, USA
15D2 **Conway** New Hampshire, USA
17C1 **Conway** South Carolina, USA
108A1 **Conway,L** Aust
42C3 **Conwy** Wales
106C3 **Cooder Pedy** Aust
110B2 **Cook** Str NZ
13B2 **Cook,C** Can
4C3 **Cook Inlet** B USA
105H4 **Cook Is** Pacific O
111B2 **Cook,Mt** NZ
107D2 **Cooktown** Aust
109C2 **Coolabah** Aust
108C1 **Cooladdi** Aust
109C2 **Coolah** Aust
109C2 **Coolamon** Aust
106B4 **Coolgardie** Aust
109C3 **Cooma** Aust
109C2 **Coonabarraban** Aust
109C2 **Coonambie** Aust
108B2 **Coonbah** Aust
108A2 **Coondambo** Aust
87A2 **Coondapoor** India
108C1 **Coongoola** Aust
87B2 **Coonoor** India
108B1 **Cooper Basin** Aust
106C3 **Cooper Creek** Aust
108B1 **Cooper Creek** R Aust
108A3 **Coorong,The** Aust
109D1 **Cooroy** Aust
20B2 **Coos B** USA
20B2 **Coos Bay** USA
107D4 **Cootamundra** Aust
45C1 **Cootehill** Irish Rep

23B2 **Copala** Mexico
23B2 **Copalillo** Mexico
Copenhagen= København
30B4 **Copiapó** Chile
47D2 **Copparo** Italy
12F2 **Copper** R USA
4D3 **Copper Centre** USA
14B1 **Copper Cliff** Can
4G3 **Coppermine** Can
4G3 **Coppermine** R Can
Coquilhatville = Mbandaka
30B4 **Coquimbo** Chile
54B2 **Corabia** Rom
17B2 **Coral Gables** USA
6B3 **Coral Harbour** Can
107D2 **Coral S** Aust/PNG
104F4 **Coral Sea Basin** Pacific O
107E2 **Coral Sea Island Territories** Aust
108B3 **Corangamite,L** Aust
33F3 **Corantijn** R Surinam/ Guyana
46B2 **Corbeil-Essonnes** France
50A1 **Corcubíon** Spain
11B3 **Cordele** USA
50A1 **Cordillera Cantabrica** Mts Spain
26C3 **Cordillera Central** Mts Dom Rep
79B2 **Cordillera Central** Mts Phil
34B2 **Cordillera de Ansita** Mts Arg
32B5 **Cordillera de los Andes** Mts Peru
30C4 **Cordillera del Toro** Mt Arg
32C2 **Cordillera de Mérida** Ven
34A3 **Cordillera de Viento** Mts Arg
25D3 **Cordillera Isabelia** Mts Nic
32B3 **Cordillera Occidental** Mts Colombia
32B3 **Cordillera Oriental** Mts Colombia
108B1 **Cordillo Downs** Aust
29D2 **Córdoba** Arg
24C3 **Córdoba** Mexico
50B2 **Córdoba** Spain
29D2 **Córdoba** State, Arg
4D3 **Cordova** USA
Corfu = Kérkira
109D2 **Coricudgy,Mt** Aust
53C3 **Corigliano Calabro** Italy
11B3 **Corinth** Mississippi, USA
31C5 **Corinto** Brazil
45B2 **Cork** County, Irish Rep
41B3 **Cork** Irish Rep
92A1 **Çorlu** Turk
31C5 **Cornel Fabriciano** Brazil
35A2 **Cornelio Procópio** Brazil
7E5 **Corner Brook** Can
109C3 **Corner Inlet** B Aust
15C2 **Corning** USA
7C5 **Cornwall** Can
43B4 **Cornwall** County, Eng
43B4 **Cornwall,C** Eng
4H2 **Cornwall I** Can
6A2 **Cornwallis I** Can
32D1 **Coro** Ven
31C2 **Coroatá** Brazil
30C2 **Coroico** Bol
35B1 **Coromandel** Brazil
87C2 **Coromandel Coast** India
110C1 **Coromandel Pen** NZ
110C1 **Coromandel Range** Mts NZ
22D4 **Corona** California, USA

13E2 **Coronation** Can
4G3 **Coronation G** Can
34C2 **Coronda** Arg
29B3 **Coronel** Chile
34D3 **Coronel Brandsen** Arg
34C3 **Coronel Dorrego** Arg
35C1 **Coronel Fabriciano** Brazil
30E4 **Coronel Oviedo** Par
29D3 **Coronel Pringles** Arg
34C3 **Coronel Suárez** Arg
34D3 **Coronel Vidal** Arg
30B2 **Coropuna** Mt Peru
109C3 **Corowa** Aust
49D3 **Corps** France
9D4 **Corpus Christi** USA
9D4 **Corpus Christi,L** USA
79B3 **Corregidor** I Phil
35A1 **Corrente** R Mato Grosso, Brazil
30E4 **Corrientes** Arg
30E4 **Corrientes** State, Arg
19B3 **Corrigan** USA
106A4 **Corrigin** Aust
107E2 **Corringe Is** Aust
109C3 **Corryong** Aust
52A2 **Corse** I Medit S
42B2 **Corsewall** Pt Scot
Corsica = Corse
9D3 **Corsicana** USA
52A2 **Corte** Corse
9C3 **Cortez** USA
52B1 **Cortina d'Ampezzo** Italy
15C2 **Cortland** USA
23A2 **Coruca de Catalan** Mexico
93D1 **Çoruh** R Turk
60E5 **Corum** Turk
30E2 **Corumbá** Brazil
35B1 **Corumba** R Brazil
35B1 **Corumbaiba** Brazil
20B2 **Corvallis** USA
96A1 **Corvo** I Açores
43C3 **Corwen** Wales
23B2 **Coscomatopec** Mexico
53C3 **Cosenza** Italy
101D1 **Cosmoledo** Is Seychelles
34C2 **Cosquín** Arg
51B2 **Costa Blanca** Region, Spain
51C1 **Costa Brava** Region, Spain
50B2 **Costa de la Luz** Region, Spain
50B2 **Costa del Sol** Region, Spain
22D4 **Costa Mesa** USA
25D3 **Costa Rica** Republic, Cent America
79B4 **Cotabato** Phil
30C3 **Cotagaita** Bol
49D3 **Côte d'Azur** Region, France
46C2 **Côtes de Meuse** Mts France
97C4 **Cotonou** Benin
32B4 **Cotopaxi** Mt Ecuador
43C4 **Cotswold Hills** Upland Eng
20B2 **Cottage Grove** USA
56C2 **Cottbus** Germany
108A3 **Couedic,C du** Aust
20C1 **Couer d'Alene L** USA
46B2 **Coulommiers** France
15C1 **Coulonge** R Can
22B2 **Coulterville** USA
4B3 **Council** USA
8D2 **Council Bluffs** USA
47B2 **Courmayeur** Italy
13B3 **Courtenay** Can
Courtrai = Kortrijk
48B2 **Coutances** France
43D3 **Coventry** Eng
50A1 **Covilhã** Spain
17B1 **Covington** Georgia, USA

19B3 **Covington** Louisiana, USA
109C2 **Cowal,L** Aust
108B3 **Cowangie** Aust
15D1 **Cowansville** Can
108A1 **Coward Springs** Aust
108A2 **Cowell** Aust
108C3 **Cowes** Aust
20B1 **Cowichan L** Can
20B1 **Cowiltz** R USA
109C2 **Cowra** Aust
30F2 **Coxim** Brazil
16C1 **Coxsackie** USA
86C2 **Cox's Bazar** Bang
22B2 **Coyote** USA
23A2 **Coyuca de Benitez** Mexico
100B4 **Cradock** S Africa
8C2 **Craig** USA
57C3 **Crailsheim** Germany
54B2 **Craiova** Rom
15D2 **Cranberry L** USA
5G5 **Cranbrook** Can
20C2 **Crane** Oregon, USA
16D2 **Cranston** USA
20B2 **Crater L** USA
20B2 **Crater Lake Nat Pk** USA
31C3 **Crateus** Brazil
31D3 **Crato** Brazil
14A2 **Crawfordsville** USA
17B1 **Crawfordville** USA
43D4 **Crawley** Eng
5H4 **Cree L** Can
46B2 **Creil** France
47C2 **Crema** Italy
52B1 **Cremona** Italy
46B2 **Crépy-en-Valois** France
52B2 **Cres** I Yugos
20B2 **Crescent City** USA
34C2 **Creston** Arg
13D3 **Creston** Can
18B1 **Creston** USA
17A1 **Crestview** USA
108B3 **Creswick** Aust
47A1 **Crêt de la Neige** Mt France
Crete = Kríti
18A1 **Crete** USA
55B3 **Crete,S of** Greece
48C2 **Creuse** R France
43C3 **Crewe** Eng
44B3 **Crianlarich** Scot
30G4 **Criciuma** Brazil
44C3 **Crieff** Scot
12G3 **Crillon,Mt** USA
35B1 **Cristalina** Brazil
52C1 **Croatia** Region, Yugos
78D1 **Crocker Range** Mts Malay
19A3 **Crockett** USA
106C2 **Croker I** Aust
44C3 **Cromarty** Scot
43E3 **Cromer** Eng
111A3 **Cromwell** NZ
11C4 **Crooked** I The Bahamas
13C2 **Crooked** R Can
8D2 **Crookston** USA
109C2 **Crookwell** Aust
109D1 **Croppa Creek** Aust
11A3 **Crossett** USA
12G3 **Cross Sd** USA
53C3 **Crotone** Italy
19B3 **Crowley** USA
27K1 **Crown Pt** Tobago
109D1 **Crows Nest** Aust
107D2 **Croydon** Aust
43D4 **Croydon** Eng
104B5 **Crozet Basin** Indian O
4F2 **Crozier Chan** Can
30F4 **Cruz Alta** Brazil
25E3 **Cruz,C** Cuba
29D2 **Cruz del Eje** Arg
35C2 **Cruzeiro** Brazil
32C5 **Cruzeiro do Sul** Brazil
13C1 **Crysdale,Mt** Can

108A2 **Crystal Brook** Aust
18B2 **Crystal City** Missouri, USA
14A1 **Crystal Falls** USA
101C2 **Cuamba** Mozam
100B2 **Cuando** R Angola
100A2 **Cuangar** Angola
Cuango,R = Kwango,R
34C2 **Cuarto** R Arg
24B2 **Cuauhtémoc** Mexico
23B2 **Cuautla** Mexico
25D2 **Cuba** Republic, Caribbean S
100A2 **Cubango** R Angola
100A2 **Cuchi** Angola
100A2 **Cuchi** R Angola
34C3 **Cuchillo Có** Arg
32D3 **Cucui** Brazil
32C2 **Cúcuta** Colombia
87B2 **Cuddalore** India
87B2 **Cuddapah** India
106A3 **Cue** Aust
32B4 **Cuenca** Ecuʊador
51B1 **Cuenca** Spain
24C3 **Cuernavaca** Mexico
19A4 **Cuero** USA
30E2 **Cuiabá** Brazil
30E2 **Cuiabá** R Brazil
23B2 **Cuicatlan** Mexico
35C1 **Cuieté** R Brazil
44A3 **Cuillin Hills** Mts Scot
98B3 **Cuilo** R Angola
100A2 **Cuito** R Angola
100A2 **Cuito Cunavale** Angola
23A2 **Cuitzeo** Mexico
77D3 **Cu Lao Hon** I Viet
109C3 **Culcairn** Aust
109C1 **Culgoa** R Aust
24B2 **Culiacán** Mexico
79A3 **Culion** I Phil
17A1 **Cullman** USA
47A2 **Culoz** France
15C3 **Culpeper** USA
32J7 **Culpepper** I Ecuador
17B2 **Culter Ridge** USA
111B2 **Culverden** NZ
33E1 **Cumaná** Ven
10C3 **Cumberland** Maryland, USA
11B3 **Cumberland** R USA
6D3 **Cumberland Pen** Can
6D3 **Cumbernauld Sd** Can
42C2 **Cumbria** Eng
21A2 **Cummings** USA
108A2 **Cummins** Aust
42B2 **Cumnock** Scot
34A3 **Cunco** Chile
100A2 **Cunene** R Angola/ Namibia
52A2 **Cuneo** Italy
107D3 **Cunnamulla** Aust
44C3 **Cupar** Scot
54B2 **Čuprija** Yugos
27D4 **Curaçao** I Caribbean S
34A3 **Curacautin** Chile
34B3 **Curaco** R Arg
34A3 **Curanilahue** Chile
34A3 **Curepto** Chile
29B2 **Curicó** Chile
30G4 **Curitiba** Brazil
108A2 **Curnamona** Aust
100A2 **Curoca** R Angola
31C5 **Curvelo** Brazil
18A2 **Cushing** USA
13D2 **Cutbank** R Can
17B1 **Cuthbert** USA
34B3 **Cutral-Có** Arg
86B2 **Cuttack** India
100A2 **Cuvelai** Angola
56B2 **Cuxhaven** Germany
14B2 **Cuyahoga Falls** USA
79B3 **Cuyo Is** Phil
32C6 **Cuzco** Peru
99C3 **Cyangugu** Zaïre
Cyclades = Kikládhes
13F3 **Cypress Hills** Mts Can
92B3 **Cyprus** Republic, Medit S

6D3 **Cyrus Field B** Can
59B3 **Czechoslovakia** Republic, Europe
59B2 **Częstochowa** Pol

D

76C1 **Da** R Viet
69E2 **Da'an** China
94C3 **Dab'a** Jordan
27C4 **Dabajuro** Ven
99E2 **Dabaro** Somalia
73B3 **Daba Shan** Mts China
99D1 **Dabat** Eth
85C4 **Dabhoi** India
73C3 **Dabie Shan** U China
97A3 **Dabola** Guinea
97B4 **Dabou** Ivory Coast
59B2 **Dabrowa Gorn** Pol
57C3 **Dachau** Germany
52B1 **Dachstein** Mt Austria
73A3 **Dada He** R China
17B2 **Dade City** USA
84B3 **Dadhar** Pak
85B3 **Dadu** Pak
68C3 **Dadu He** R China
79B3 **Daet** Phil
73B4 **Dafang** China
76B2 **Daga** R Burma
99E2 **Dagabur** Eth
97A3 **Dagana** Sen
65F5 **Dagestanskaya ASSR** Republic, USSR
79B2 **Dagupan** Phil
92B4 **Dahab** Egypt
63E3 **Da Hinggan Ling** Mts China
17B1 **Dahlonega** USA
85C4 **Dāhod** India
95A2 **Dahra** Libya
51C2 **Dahra** Region, Alg
86A1 **Dailekh** Nepal
34C3 **Daireaux** Arg
Dairen = Lüda
69F4 **Daitō** Is Pacific O
106C3 **Dajarra** Aust
97A3 **Dakar** Sen
95B2 **Dakhla Oasis** Egypt
97C3 **Dakoro** Niger
54B2 **Dakovica** Yugos
54A1 **Dakovo** Yugos
100B2 **Dala** Angola
97A3 **Dalaba** Guinea
72D1 **Dalai Nur** L China
68C2 **Dalandzadgad** Mongolia
79B3 **Dalanganem Is** Phil
68C2 **Dalanjargalan** Mongolia
76D3 **Da Lat** Viet
107E3 **Dalby** Aust
39F7 **Dalen** Nor
42C2 **Dales,The** Upland Eng
17A1 **Daleville** USA
9C3 **Dalhart** USA
4E2 **Dalhousie,C** Can
9D3 **Dallas** USA
20B1 **Dalles,The** USA
5E4 **Dall I** USA
86A2 **Dalli Rajhara** India
97C3 **Dallol** R Niger
97C3 **Dallol Bosso** R Niger
52C2 **Dalmatia** Region Yugos
69F2 **Dal'nerechensk** USSR
97B4 **Daloa** Ivory Coast
73B4 **Dalou Shan** Mts China
86A2 **Dāltenganj** India
17B1 **Dalton** Georgia, USA
16C1 **Dalton** Massachusetts, USA
106C2 **Daly** R Aust
21A2 **Daly City** USA
106C2 **Daly Waters** Aust
79B4 **Damaguete** Phil
85C4 **Damān** India
92B3 **Damanhûr** Egypt

71D4 **Damar** I Indon
98B2 **Damara** CAR
92C3 **Damascus** Syria
16A3 **Damascus** USA
97D3 **Damaturu** Nig
90B2 **Damavand** Iran
98B3 **Damba** Angola
87C3 **Dambulla** Sri Lanka
90B2 **Damghan** Iran
85D4 **Damoh** India
99E2 **Damot** Eth
94B2 **Damour** Leb
106A3 **Dampier** Aust
94B3 **Danā** Jordan
22C2 **Dana,Mt** USA
97B4 **Danané** Lib
76D2 **Da Nang** Viet
79B3 **Danao** Phil
70A3 **Danau Tobu** L Indon
71D4 **Danau Tuwuti** L Indon
73A3 **Danbu** China
15D2 **Danbury** USA
86A1 **Dandeldhura** Nepal
87A1 **Dandeli** India
108C3 **Dandenong** Aust
74A2 **Dandong** China
100A4 **Danger Pt** S Africa
99D1 **Dangila** Eth
6D1 **Danguard Jenson Land** Region Can
7E4 **Daniels Harbour** Can
6G3 **Dannebrogs Øy** I Greenland
110C2 **Dannevirke** NZ
87C1 **Dantewāra** India
Danube = Donau
10B2 **Danville** Illinois, USA
11B3 **Danville** Kentucky, USA
16A2 **Danville** Pennsylvania, USA
11C3 **Danville** Virginia, USA
Danzig = Gdańsk
73C4 **Dao Xian** China
73B4 **Daozhen** China
79B4 **Dapiak,Mt** Phil
79B4 **Dapitan** Phil
68B3 **Da Qaidam** China
94C2 **Dar'a** Syria
91B4 **Dārāb** Iran
95A1 **Daraj** Libya
90B3 **Dārān** Iran
92C3 **Dar'ā Salkhad** Syria
86B1 **Darbhanga** India
22C1 **Dardanelle** USA
18B2 **Dardanelle,L** USA
99D3 **Dar es Salaam** Tanz
110B1 **Dargaville** NZ
17B1 **Darien** USA
Darjeeling = Dārjiling
86B1 **Dārjiling** India
107D4 **Darling** R Aust
109C1 **Darling Downs** Aust
6C1 **Darling Pen** Can
108B2 **Darlington** Aust
42D2 **Darlington** Eng
17C1 **Darlington** USA
57B3 **Darmstadt** Germany
95B1 **Darnah** Libya
108B2 **Darnick** Aust
4F3 **Darnley B** Can
112C10 **Darnley,C** Ant
51B1 **Daroca** Spain
98C2 **Dar Rounga** Region, CAR
43C4 **Dart** R Eng
41C3 **Dartmoor** Moorland Eng
43C4 **Dartmoor Nat Pk** Eng
7D5 **Dartmouth** Can
43C4 **Dartmouth** Eng
107D1 **Daru** PNG
52C1 **Daruvar** Yugos
106C2 **Darwin** Aust
91B4 **Daryacheh-ye Bakhtegan** L Iran
91B4 **Daryacheh-ye Mahārlū** L Iran

90B3 **Daryācheh-ye Namak** *Salt Flat* Iran
90D3 **Daryacheh-ye-Sistan** *Salt L* Iran/Afghan
91B4 **Daryācheh-ye Tashk** *L* Iran
80C2 **Daryācheh-ye Orūmīyeh** *L* Iran
91C4 **Dārzīn** Iran
91B4 **Das** *I* UAE
73C3 **Dashennonglia** *Mt* China
90C2 **Dasht** Iran
90B3 **Dasht-e-Kavir** *Salt Desert* Iran
90C3 **Dasht-e Lut** *Salt Desert* Iran
90D3 **Dasht-e Naomid** *Desert Region* Iran
85D3 **Datia** India
72A2 **Datong** China
72C1 **Datong** China
72A2 **Datong He** *R* China
79B4 **Datu Piang** Phil
39K7 **Daugava** *R* USSR
60C2 **Daugavpils** USSR
6D1 **Dauguard Jensen Land** Greenland
84A1 **Daulatabad** Afghan
85D3 **Daulpur** India
46D1 **Daun** Germany
87A1 **Daund** India
5H4 **Dauphin** Can
16A2 **Dauphin** USA
49D2 **Dauphiné** *Region,* France
97C3 **Daura** Nig
85D3 **Dausa** India
87B2 **Dāvangere** India
79C4 **Davao** Phil
79C4 **Davao G** Phil
22A2 **Davenport** California, USA
10A2 **Davenport** Iowa, USA
32A2 **David** Panama
4D3 **Davidson Mts** USA
21A2 **Davis** USA
112C10 **Davis** *Base* Ant
7D4 **Davis Inlet** Can
6E3 **Davis Str** Greenland/ Can
61J3 **Davlekanovo** USSR
47C1 **Davos** Switz
99E2 **Dawa** *R* Eth
73A4 **Dawan** China
84B2 **Dawat Yar** Afghan
91B4 **Dawḥat Salwah** *B* Qatar/S Arabia
76B2 **Dawna Range** *Mts* Burma
4E3 **Dawson** Can
17B1 **Dawson** Georgia, USA
107D3 **Dawson** *R* Aust
5F4 **Dawson Creek** Can
13D2 **Dawson,Mt** Can
12G2 **Dawson Range** *Mts* Can
73A3 **Dawu** China
73C3 **Dawu** China
48B3 **Dax** France
73B3 **Daxian** China
73B5 **Daxin** China
73A3 **Daxue Shan** *Mts* China
73C4 **Dayong** China
94C2 **Dayr'Ali** Syria
94C1 **Dayr'Atīyah** Syria
93D2 **Dayr az Zawr** Syria
10B3 **Dayton** Ohio, USA
19B4 **Dayton** Texas, USA
20C1 **Dayton** Washington, USA
11B4 **Daytona Beach** USA
73C4 **Dayu** China
78D3 **Dayu** Indon
72D2 **Da Yunhe** *R* China
20C2 **Dayville** USA
73B3 **Dazhu** China

100B4 **De Aar** S Africa
26C2 **Deadman's Cay** The Bahamas
92C3 **Dead S** Israel/Jordan
46A1 **Deal** Eng
101G1 **Dealesville** S Africa
13B2 **Dean** *R* Can
13B2 **Dean Chan** Can
34C2 **Deán Funes** Arg
14B2 **Dearborn** USA
4F3 **Dease Arm** *B* Can
4E4 **Dease Lake** Can
9B3 **Death V** USA
48C2 **Deauville** France
97B4 **Debakala** Ivory Coast
12B2 **Debauch Mt** USA
27L1 **Débé** Trinidad
59C2 **Debica** Pol
58C2 **Deblin** Pol
97B3 **Débo,L** Mali
99D2 **Debra Birhan** Eth
99D1 **Debra Markos** Eth
99D1 **Debra Tabor** Eth
59C3 **Debrecen** Hung
11B3 **Decatur** Alabama, USA
17B1 **Decatur** Georgia, USA
10B3 **Decatur** Illinois, USA
14B2 **Decatur** Indiana, USA
48C3 **Decazeville** France
73A4 **Dechang** China
97B3 **Dédougou** Burkina
101C2 **Dedza** Malawi
42B2 **Dee** *R* Dumfries and Galloway, Scot
42C3 **Dee** *R* Eng/Wales
44C3 **Dee** *R* Grampian, Scot
15C1 **Deep River** Can
16C2 **Deep River** USA
109D1 **Deepwater** Aust
7E5 **Deer Lake** Can
8B2 **Deer Lodge** USA
34D3 **Defferrari** Arg
17A1 **De Funiak Springs** USA
68B3 **Dêgê** China
106A3 **De Grey** *R* Aust
91B3 **Deh Bīd** Iran
84B1 **Dehi** Afghan
96D1 **Dehibat** Tunisia
87B3 **Dehiwala-Mt Lavinia** Sri Lanka
90A3 **Dehlorān** Iran
84D2 **Dehra Dūn** India
86A2 **Dehri** India
98C2 **Deim Zubeir** Sudan
94B2 **Deir Abu Sa'id** Jordan
94C1 **Deir el Ahmar** Leb
60B4 **Dej** Rom
19B3 **De Kalb** Texas, USA
63G2 **De Kastri** USSR
98C3 **Dekese** Zaïre
98B2 **Dekoa** CAR
106B1 **Dekusi** Indon
9B3 **Delano** USA
10C3 **Delaware** State, USA
14B2 **Delaware** USA
15C2 **Delaware** *R* USA
10C3 **Delaware B** USA
109C3 **Delegate** Aust
47B1 **Delemont** Switz
101D2 **Delgado** *C* Mozam
84D3 **Delhi** India
15D2 **Delhi** New York, USA
92B1 **Delice** Turk
24B2 **Delicias** Mexico
90B3 **Delijān** Iran
47B1 **Delle** France
22D4 **Del Mar** USA
39F8 **Delmenhorst** Germany
4B3 **De Long Mts** USA
109C4 **Deloraine** Aust
5H5 **Deloraine** Can
17B2 **Delray Beach** USA
9C4 **Del Rio** USA
8B3 **Delta** USA
12E2 **Delta** *R* USA
12E2 **Delta Junction** USA

99D2 **Dembidollo** Eth
46C1 **Demer** *R* Belg
9C3 **Deming** USA
54C2 **Demirköy** Turk
49C1 **Denain** France
82A2 **Denau** USSR
42C3 **Denbigh** Wales
12B2 **Denbigh,C** USA
78B3 **Dendang** Indon
46C1 **Dendermond** Belg
99D2 **Dendi** *Mt* Eth
46B1 **Dèndre** *R* Belg
72B1 **Dengkou** China
72C3 **Deng Xian** China
Den Haag =
** 's-Gravenhage**
27H1 **Denham,Mt** Jamaica
56A2 **Den Helder** Neth
51C2 **Denia** Spain
107D4 **Deniliquin** Aust
20C2 **Denio** USA
9D3 **Denison** Texas, USA
12D3 **Denison,Mt** USA
92A2 **Denizli** Turk
39F7 **Denmark** Kingdom, Europe
1C1 **Denmark Str** Greenland/Iceland
27P2 **Dennery** St Lucia
78D4 **Denpasar** Indon
16B3 **Denton** Maryland, USA
9D3 **Denton** Texas, USA
107E1 **D'Entrecasteaux Is** PNG
47B1 **Dents du Midi** *Mt* Switz
8C3 **Denver** USA
98B2 **Déo** *R* Cam
86B2 **Deoghar** India
85C5 **Deolāli** India
84D1 **Deosai Plain** India
95B3 **Dépression du Mourdi** Chad
19B3 **De Queen** USA
84C3 **Dera** Pak
84B3 **Dera Bugti** Pak
84C2 **Dera Ismail Khan** Pak
106B2 **Derby** Aust
16C2 **Derby** Connecticut, USA
43D3 **Derby** County, Eng
43D3 **Derby** Eng
18A2 **Derby** Kansas, USA
60E3 **Dergachi** USSR
19B3 **De Ridder** USA
Derna = Darnah
95C3 **Derudeb** Sudan
109C4 **Derwent Bridge** Aust
34B2 **Desaguadero** Arg
34B2 **Desaguadero** *R* Arg
30C2 **Désaguadero** *R* Bol
21B3 **Descanso** Mexico
20B2 **Deschutes** *R* USA
29C5 **Deseado** Arg
29C5 **Deseado** *R* Arg
47D2 **Desenzano** Italy
96A1 **Deserta Grande** *I* Medeira
30C4 **Desierto de Atacama** *Desert* Chile
18B2 **Desloge** USA
10A2 **Des Moines** Iowa, USA
60D3 **Desna** *R* USSR
29B6 **Desolación** *I* Chile
14A2 **Des Plaines** USA
56C2 **Dessau** Germany
99D1 **Dessye** Eth
12G2 **Destruction Bay** Can
46A1 **Desvres** France
54B1 **Deta** Rom
100B2 **Dete** Zim
10B2 **Detroit** USA
76D3 **Det Udom** Thai
54B1 **Deva** Rom
56B2 **Deventer** Neth
44C3 **Deveron** *R* Scot
85C3 **Devikot** India

22C2 **Devil Postpile Nat Mon** USA
22C1 **Devils Gate** *P* USA
Devil's Island = Isla du Diable
8D2 **Devils Lake** USA
12H3 **Devils Paw** *Mt* Can
43D4 **Devizes** Eng
85D3 **Devli** India
55B2 **Devoll** *R* Alb
43B4 **Devon** County, Eng
6A2 **Devon I** Can
107D5 **Devonport** Aust
86C1 **Dewangiri** Bhutan
85D4 **Dewās** India
101G1 **Dewetsdorp** S Africa
11B3 **Dewey Res** USA
19B3 **De Witt** USA
18C2 **Dexter** Missouri, USA
73A3 **Deyang** China
90C3 **Deyhuk** Iran
90A3 **Dezfūl** Iran
72D2 **Dezhou** China
90A2 **Dezh Shāhpūr** Iran
91B4 **Dhahran** S Arabia
86C2 **Dhākā** Bang
87B2 **Dhamavaram** India
86A2 **Dhamtari** India
86B2 **Dhanbād** India
86A1 **Dhangarhi** Nepal
86B1 **Dhankuta** Nepal
85D4 **Dhār** India
87B2 **Dharmapuri** India
84D2 **Dharmsāla** India
97B3 **Dhar Oualata** *Desert Region* Maur
86A1 **Dhaulagiri** *Mt* Nepal
86B2 **Dhenkānai** India
94B3 **Dhibah** Jordan
55C3 **Dhíkti Óri** *Mt* Greece
55C3 **Dhodhekánisos** *Is* Greece
55B3 **Dhomokós** Greece
87B1 **Dhone** India
85C4 **Dhoraji** India
85C4 **Dhrāngadhra** India
86B1 **Dhuburi** India
85C4 **Dhule** India
22B2 **Diablo,Mt** USA
21A2 **Diablo Range** *Mts* USA
34C2 **Diamante** Arg
34B2 **Diamante** *R* Arg
31C5 **Diamantina** Brazil
107D3 **Diamantina** *R* Aust
86B2 **Diamond Harbours** India
22B1 **Diamond Springs** USA
91C4 **Dibā** UAE
98C3 **Dibaya** Zaïre
86C1 **Dibrugarh** India
8C2 **Dickinson** USA
1B10 **Dickson** USSR
15C2 **Dickson City** USA
93D2 **Dicle** *R* Turk
13E2 **Didsbury** Can
85C3 **Didwāna** India
97B3 **Diebougou** Burkina
46D2 **Diekirch** Lux
97B3 **Diéma** Mali
76C1 **Dien Bien Phu** Viet
56B2 **Diepholz** Germany
48C2 **Dieppe** France
46C1 **Diest** Belg
46D2 **Dieuze** France
7D5 **Digby** Can
49D3 **Digne** France
49C2 **Digoin** France
79C4 **Digos** Phil
71E4 **Digul** *R* Indon
86C1 **Dihang** *R* India
Dijlah = Tigris
49C2 **Dijon** France
98B2 **Dik** Chad
99E1 **Dikhil** Djibouti
46B1 **Diksmuide** Belg
82A2 **Dilaram** Afghan
76D3 **Di Linh** Viet

46E1 **Dillenburg** Germany
99C1 **Dilling** Sudan
12C3 **Dillingham** USA
8B2 **Dillon** USA
16A2 **Dillsburg** USA
100B2 **Dilolo** Zaïre
Dimashq = Damascus
98C3 **Dimbelenge** Zaïre
97B4 **Dimbokro** Ivory Coast
54C2 **Dimitrovgrad** Bulg
61G3 **Dimitrovgrad** USSR
94B3 **Dimona** Israel
86C1 **Dimpāpur** India
79C3 **Dinagat** I Phil
86B1 **Dinajpur** India
48B2 **Dinan** France
46C1 **Dinant** Belg
92B2 **Dinar** Turk
99D1 **Dinder** R Sudan
87B2 **Dindigul** India
72B2 **Dingbian** China
86B1 **Dinggyê** China
41A3 **Dingle** Irish Rep
41A3 **Dingle** B Irish Rep
97A3 **Dinguiraye** Guinea
44B3 **Dingwall** Scot
72A2 **Dingxi** China
72D2 **Ding Xian** China
76D1 **Dinh Lap** Viet
22C2 **Dinuba** USA
97A3 **Diouloulou** Sen
86C1 **Diphu** India
99E2 **Dirè Dawa** Eth
106A3 **Dirk Hartog** I Aust
95A3 **Dirkou** Niger
109C1 **Dirranbandi** Aust
99E2 **Dirri** Somalia
29G8 **Disappointment,C**
South Georgia
20B1 **Disappointment,C** USA
106B3 **Disappointment,L** Aust
108B3 **Discovery B** Aust
103J7 **Discovery Tablemount**
Atlantic O
47C1 **Disentis Muster** Switz
6E3 **Disko** Greenland
6E3 **Disko Bugt** B Greenland
6E3 **Diskorjord** Greenland
58D1 **Disna** R USSR
35B1 **Distrito Federal** Federal
District, Brazil
85C4 **Diu** India
79C4 **Diuat Mts** Phil
31C6 **Divinópolis** Brazil
61F4 **Divnoye** USSR
93C2 **Divriği** Turk
22B1 **Dixon** California, USA
5E4 **Dixon Entrance** Sd Can/
USA
13D1 **Dixonville** Can
93E3 **Diyālā** R Iraq
65F6 **Diyarbakir** Turk
90A3 **Diz** R Iran
98B2 **Dja** R Cam
96C1 **Djadi** R Alg
95A2 **Djado,Plat du** Niger
98B3 **Djambala** Congo
96C2 **Djanet** Alg
50A2 **Djebel Bouhalla** Mt Mor
96C1 **Djelfa** Alg
98C2 **Djéma** CAR
97B3 **Djenné** Mali
97B3 **Djibo** Burkina
99E1 **Djibouti** Djibouti
99E1 **Djibouti** Republic, E
Africa
98C2 **Djolu** Zaïre
97C4 **Djougou** Benin
99D2 **Djugu** Zaïre
38C2 **Djúpivogur** Iceland
51C2 **Djurdjura** Mts Alg
60E2 **Dmitrov** USSR
60D4 **Dnepr** R USSR
60D4 **Dneprodzerzhinsk** USSR
60E4 **Dnepropetrovsk** USSR
60C3 **Dneprovskaya**
Nizmennost' Region,
USSR

60B4 **Dnestr** R USSR
60D2 **Dno** USSR
98B2 **Doba** Chad
58C1 **Dobele** USSR
34C3 **Doblas** Arg
71E4 **Dobo** Indon
54A2 **Doboj** Yugos
54B2 **Dobreta-Turnu-Severin**
Rom
60D3 **Dobrush** USSR
31C5 **Doce** R Brazil
30D3 **Doctor R P Peña** Arg
87B2 **Dod** India
87B2 **Doda Betta** Mt India
Dodecanese =
Sporádhes
9C3 **Dodge City** USA
99D3 **Dodoma** Tanz
75A1 **Dōgo** I Japan
97C3 **Dogondoutchi** Niger
93D2 **Doğubayazit** Turk
91B4 **Doha** Qatar
7C5 **Dolbeau** Can
49D2 **Dôle** France
43C3 **Dolgellau** Wales
99E2 **Dolo** Eth
47D1 **Dolomitche** Mts Italy
29E3 **Dolores** Arg
34D2 **Dolores** Urug
23A1 **Dolores Hidalgo**
Mexico
4G3 **Dolphin and Union Str**
Can
29E6 **Dolphin,C** Falkland Is
71E4 **Dom** Mt Indon
65G4 **Dombarovskiy** USSR
38F6 **Dombas** Nor
46D2 **Dombasle-sur-Meurthe**
France
54A1 **Dombóvár** Hung
48B2 **Domfront** France
27E3 **Dominica** I
Caribbean S
27C3 **Dominican Republic**
Caribbean S
6C3 **Dominion,C** Can
7E4 **Domino** Can
68D1 **Domna** USSR
52A1 **Domodossola** Italy
78D4 **Dompu** Indon
29B3 **Domuyo** Mt Arg
109D1 **Domville,Mt** Aust
65H4 **Dom-yanskoya** USSR
44C3 **Don** R Scot
61F4 **Don** R USSR
45C1 **Donaghadee** N Ire
57C3 **Donau** R Germany
57C3 **Donauwörth** Germany
50A2 **Don Benito** Spain
42D3 **Doncaster** Eng
98B3 **Dondo** Angola
101C2 **Dondo** Mozam
87C3 **Dondra Head** C
Sri Lanka
45B1 **Donegal** County,
Irish Rep
40B3 **Donegal** Irish Rep
40B3 **Donegal B** Irish Rep
45B1 **Donegal Mts** Irish Rep
60E4 **Donetsk** USSR
73C4 **Dong'an** China
106A3 **Dongara** Aust
73A4 **Dongchuan** China
76D2 **Dongfang** China
74B2 **Dongfeng** China
70C4 **Donggala** Indon
68B3 **Donggi Cona** L China
74A3 **Donggou** China
73C5 **Donghai Dao** I China
72A1 **Dong He** R China
76D2 **Dong Hoi** Viet
73C5 **Dong Jiang** R China
95C3 **Dongola** Sudan
73D5 **Dongshan** China
68D4 **Dongsha Qundao** I
China
72C2 **Dongsheng** China
72E3 **Dongtai** China

73C4 **Dongting Hu** L China
73B5 **Dongxing** China
73D3 **Dongzhi** China
18B2 **Doniphan** USA
52C2 **Donji Vakuf** Yugos
38G5 **Dönna** I Nor
21A2 **Donner** P USA
46D2 **Donnersberg** Mt
Germany
101G1 **Donnybrook** S Africa
22B2 **Don Pedro Res** USA
12D1 **Doonerak,Mt** USA
79B4 **Dopolong** Phil
73A3 **Do Qu** R China
47B2 **Dora Baltea** R Italy
49D2 **Dorbirn** Austria
43C4 **Dorchester** Eng
6C3 **Dorchester,C** Can
48C2 **Dordogne** R France
56A2 **Dordrecht** Neth
13F2 **Doré** L Can
13F2 **Doré Lake** Can
97B3 **Dori** Burkina
46B2 **Dormans** France
57B3 **Dornbirn** Austria
44B3 **Dornoch** Scot
44B3 **Dornoch Firth** Estuary
Scot
38H6 **Dorotea** Sweden
109D2 **Dorrigo** Aust
20B2 **Dorris** USA
43C4 **Dorset** County, Eng
46D1 **Dorsten** Germany
56B2 **Dortmund** Germany
98C2 **Doruma** Zaïre
63D2 **Dosatuy** USSR
84B1 **Doshi** Afghan
22B2 **Dos Palos** USA
97C3 **Dosso** Niger
65G5 **Dossor** USSR
11B3 **Dothan** USA
49C1 **Douai** France
98A2 **Douala** Cam
109D1 **Double Island Pt** Aust
49D2 **Doubs** R France
111A3 **Doubtful Sd** NZ
97B3 **Douentza** Mali
9C3 **Douglas** Arizona, USA
42B2 **Douglas** Eng
17B1 **Douglas** Georgia, USA
8C2 **Douglas** Wyoming,
USA
12A1 **Douglas,C** USA
13B2 **Douglas Chan** Can
12D3 **Douglas,Mt** USA
46B1 **Doullens** France
45C1 **Doun** County, N Ire
30F3 **Dourados** Brazil
50A1 **Douro** R Port
15C3 **Dover** Delaware, USA
43E4 **Dover** Eng
15D2 **Dover** New
Hampshire, USA
16B2 **Dover** New Jersey,
USA
14B2 **Dover** Ohio, USA
43D3 **Dover** R Eng
41D3 **Dover,Str of** UK/
France
16B3 **Downington** USA
42B2 **Downpatrick** N Ire
13C2 **Downton,Mt** Can
16B2 **Doylestown** USA
75A1 **Dōzen** I Japan
96A2 **Dr'aa** R Mor
35A2 **Dracena** Brazil
16D1 **Dracut** USA
49D3 **Draguignan** France
101C3 **Drakensberg** Mts
S Africa
101G1 **Drakensberg** Mt
S Africa
103E7 **Drake Pass** Pacific/
Atlantic O
55B2 **Dráma** Greece
39G7 **Drammen** Nor
38A1 **Drangajökull** Iceland
52C1 **Drava** R Yugos

13D2 **Drayton Valley** Can
49C2 **Dreaux** France
57C2 **Dresden** Germany
48C2 **Dreux** France
20C2 **Drewsey** USA
54B2 **Drin** R Alb
54A2 **Drina** R Yugos
58D1 **Drissa** R USSR
45C2 **Drogheda** Irish Rep
59C3 **Drogobych** USSR
112B12 **Dronning Maud Land**
Region, Ant
30D3 **Dr P.P. Pená** Par
5G4 **Drumheller** Can
14B1 **Drummond I** USA
15D1 **Drummondville** Can
58C2 **Druskininksi** USSR
12G3 **Dry B** USA
7A5 **Dryden** Can
27H1 **Dry Harbour Mts**
Jamaica
76B3 **Duang** I Burma
91C4 **Dubai** UAE
5H3 **Dubawnt** R Can
4H3 **Dubawnt L** Can
107D4 **Dubbo** Aust
45C2 **Dublin** County,
Irish Rep
45C2 **Dublin** Irish Rep
17B1 **Dublin** USA
60E2 **Dubna** USSR
60C3 **Dubno** USSR
15C2 **Du Bois** USA
13B2 **Dubose,Mt** Can
58D2 **Dubrovica** USSR
54A2 **Dubrovnik** Yugos
10A2 **Dubuque** USA
46D2 **Dudelange** Lux
1C10 **Dudinka** USSR
43C3 **Dudley** Eng
97B4 **Duekoué** Ivory Coast
50B1 **Duero** R Spain
44C3 **Dufftown** Scot
52B2 **Dugi Otok** I Yugos
56B2 **Duisburg** Germany
93E3 **Dūkan** Iraq
99D2 **Duk Faiwil** Sudan
91B4 **Dukhān** Qatar
73A4 **Dukou** China
68B3 **Dulan** China
34C2 **Dulce** R Arg
78C2 **Dulit Range** Mts
Malay
86C2 **Dullabchara** India
10A2 **Duluth** USA
94C2 **Dūmā** Syria
78A2 **Dumai** Indon
79A3 **Dumaran** I Phil
9C3 **Dumas** USA
94C2 **Dumayr** Syria
42B2 **Dumbarton** Scot
42C2 **Dumfries** Scot
42B2 **Dumfries and**
Galloway Region,
Scot
86B2 **Dumka** India
15C1 **Dumoine,L** Can
112C8 **Dumont d'Urville** Base
Ant
95C1 **Dumyat** Egypt
54C2 **Dunărea** R Rom
45C2 **Dunary Head** Pt
Irish Rep
54B2 **Dunav** R Bulg
59D3 **Dunayevtsy** USSR
13C3 **Duncan** Can
16A2 **Duncannon** USA
44C2 **Duncansby Head** Pt
Scot
45C1 **Dundalk** Irish Rep
16A3 **Dundalk** USA
45C2 **Dundalk B** Irish Rep
6D2 **Dundas** Greenland
4G2 **Dundas Pen** Can
71E5 **Dundas Str** Aust
101H1 **Dundee** S Africa
44C3 **Dundee** Scot
108B1 **Dundoo** Aust

42B2 **Dundrum** *B* N Ire
111B3 **Dunedin** NZ
17B2 **Dunedin** USA
109C2 **Dunedoo** Aust
44C3 **Dunfermline** Scot
85C4 **Dungarpur** India
45C2 **Dungarvan** Irish Rep
43E4 **Dungeness** Eng
109D2 **Dungog** Aust
99C2 **Dungu** Zaïre
95C2 **Dungunab** Sudan
68B2 **Dunhuang** China
46B1 **Dunkerque** France
10C2 **Dunkirk** USA
99D1 **Dunkur** Eth
97B4 **Dunkwa** Ghana
41B3 **Dun Laoghaire** Irish Rep
45B3 **Dunmanway** Irish Rep
26B1 **Dunmore Town** The Bahamas
44C2 **Dunnet Head** *Pt* Scot
42C2 **Duns** Scot
20B2 **Dunsmuir** USA
111A2 **Dunstan Mts** NZ
46C2 **Dun-sur-Meuse** France
72D1 **Duolun** China
98B3 **Duque de Braganca** Angola
18C2 **Du Quoin** USA
94B3 **Dura** Israel
49D3 **Durance** *R* France
24B2 **Durango** Mexico
50B1 **Durango** Spain
9C3 **Durango** USA
29E2 **Durano** Urug
9D3 **Durant** USA
94C1 **Duraykish** Syria
101H1 **Durban** S Africa
46D1 **Duren** Germany
86A2 **Durg** India
86B2 **Durgapur** India
42D2 **Durham** County, Eng
42D2 **Durham** Eng
11C3 **Durham** N Carolina, USA
16D1 **Durham** New Hampshire, USA
108B1 **Durham Downs** Aust
54A2 **Durmitor** *Mt* Yugos
44B2 **Durness** Scot
55A2 **Durrës** Alb
108B1 **Durrie** Aust
45A3 **Dursey** *I* Irish Rep
55C3 **Dursunbey** Turk
110B2 **D'Urville I** NZ
90D2 **Dushak** USSR
73B4 **Dushan** China
82A2 **Dushanbe** USSR
111A3 **Dusky Sd** NZ
56B2 **Düsseldorf** Germany
73B4 **Duyun** China
92B1 **Düzce** Turk
60C2 **Dvina** *R* USSR
85B4 **Dwārka** India
6D3 **Dyer,C** Can
11B3 **Dyersburg** USA
43B3 **Dyfed** County, Wales
61F5 **Dykh Tau Dağlari** *Mt* USSR
108B1 **Dynevor Downs** Aust
68B2 **Dzag** Mongolia
63C3 **Dzamin Uüd** USSR
101D2 **Dzaoudzi** Mayotte
68C2 **Dzarnïn Uüd** Mongolia
68B2 **Dzavhan Gol** *R* Mongolia
80E1 **Dzhezkazgan** USSR
61F2 **Dzerzhinsk** USSR
63E2 **Dzhalinda** USSR
65J5 **Dzhambul** USSR
60D4 **Dzhankoy** USSR
65H4 **Dzhezkazgan** USSR
84B1 **Dzhilikul'** USSR
65J5 **Dzhungarskiy Alatau** *Mts* USSR
59B2 **Dzierzoniow** Pol
82C1 **Dzungaria** Basin, China

E

7B4 **Eabamet L** Can
12F2 **Eagle** Alaska, USA
20B2 **Eagle L** California, USA
19A3 **Eagle Mountain L** USA
9C4 **Eagle Pass** USA
4E3 **Eagle Plain** Can
12E2 **Eagle River** USA
21B2 **Earlimart** USA
17B1 **Easley** USA
15C2 **East Aurora** USA
43E4 **Eastbourne** Eng
14A2 **East Chicago** USA
69E3 **East China Sea** China/Japan
83B4 **Eastern Ghats** *Mts* India
29E6 **East Falkland** *I* Falkland Is
12E1 **East Fork** *R* USA
21B2 **Eastgate** USA
16C1 **Easthampton** USA
16C2 **East Hampton** USA
14A2 **East Lake** USA
14B2 **East Liverpool** USA
100B4 **East London** S Africa
7C4 **Eastmain** Can
7C4 **Eastmain** *R* Can
17B1 **Eastman** USA
15C3 **Easton** Maryland, USA
15C2 **Easton** Pennsylvania, USA
16B2 **East Orange** USA
105L4 **East Pacific Ridge** Pacific O
17B1 **East Point** USA
42D3 **East Retford** Eng
11A3 **East St Louis** USA
1B7 **East Siberian S** USSR
43E4 **East Sussex** County, Eng
17B1 **Eatonton** USA
10A2 **Eau Claire** USA
71F3 **Eauripik** *I* Pacific O
23B1 **Ebano** Mexico
98B2 **Ebebiyin** Eq Guinea
56C2 **Eberswalde** Germany
73A4 **Ebian** China
65K5 **Ebinur** *L* China
53C2 **Eboli** Italy
98B2 **Ebolowa** Cam
51B1 **Ebro** *R* Spain
92A1 **Eceabat** Turk
96C1 **Ech Cheliff** Alg
72D2 **Eching** China
20C1 **Echo** USA
4G3 **Echo Bay** Can
46D2 **Echternach** Lux
108B3 **Echuca** Aust
50A2 **Ecija** Spain
6B2 **Eclipse Sd** Can
32B4 **Ecuador** Republic, S America
44C2 **Eday** *I* Scot
99E1 **Edd** Eth
98C1 **Ed Da'ein** Sudan
95C3 **Ed Damer** Sudan
95C3 **Ed Debba** Sudan
44B2 **Eddrachillis** *B* Scot
99D1 **Ed Dueim** Sudan
109C4 **Eddystone Pt** Aust
98A2 **Edea** Cam
109C3 **Eden** Aust
42C2 **Eden** *R* Eng
101G1 **Edenburg** S Africa
111A3 **Edendale** NZ
46E2 **Edenkoben** Germany
46E1 **Eder** *R* Germany
6D3 **Edgell I** Can
64D2 **Edgeøya** *I* Barents S
16A3 **Edgewood** USA
94B3 **Edh Dhahiriya** Israel
55B2 **Edhessa** Greece
44C3 **Edinburgh** Scot
60C5 **Edirne** Turk

17B1 **Edisto** *R* USA
13D2 **Edith Cavell,Mt** Can
20B1 **Edmonds** USA
5G4 **Edmonton** Can
7D5 **Edmundston** Can
19A4 **Edna** USA
12H3 **Edna Bay** USA
52B1 **Edolo** Italy
94B3 **Edom** Region, Jordan
92A2 **Edremit** Turk
55C3 **Edremit Körfezi** *B* Turk
68B2 **Edrengiyn Nuruu** *Mts* Mongolia
5G4 **Edson** Can
34C3 **Eduardo Castex** Arg
12J2 **Eduni,Mt** Can
108B3 **Edward** *R* Aust
99C3 **Edward,L** Uganda\Zaïre
108A1 **Edwards Creek** Aust
9C3 **Edwards Plat** USA
18C2 **Edwardsville** USA
12H3 **Edziza,Mt** Can
12B2 **Eek** USA
46B1 **Eeklo** Belg
10B3 **Effingham** USA
6E3 **Egedesminde** Greenland
12C3 **Egegik** USA
59C3 **Eger** Hung
39F7 **Egersund** Nor
16B3 **Egg Harbor City** USA
4G2 **Eglinton I** Can
110B1 **Egmont,C** NZ
110B1 **Egmont,Mt** NZ
92B2 **Eğridir Gölü** *L* Turk
95B2 **Egypt** Republic, Africa
50B1 **Eibar** Spain
49C2 **Eibeuf** France
46D1 **Eifel** Region, Germany
44A3 **Eigg** *I* Scot
83B5 **Eight Degree Chan** Indian O
106B2 **Eighty Mile Beach** Aust
108C3 **Eildon,L** Aust
56B2 **Eindhoven** Neth
47C1 **Einsiedeln** Switz
94B3 **Ein Yahav** Israel
57C2 **Eisenach** Germany
57C3 **Eisenerz** Austria
46D1 **Eitorf** Germany
72A1 **Ejin qi** China
23B2 **Ejutla** Mexico
110C2 **Eketahuna** NZ
65J4 **Ekibastuz** USSR
63F2 **Ekimchan** USSR
92B3 **Ek Mahalla el Kubra** Egypt
39H7 **Eksjo** Sweden
10B1 **Ekwen** *R* Can
92A3 **El'Alamein** Egypt
92B3 **El'Arish** Egypt
92B4 **Elat** Israel
95B3 **El'Atrun Oasis** Sudan
93C2 **Elazig** Turk
92C3 **El Azraq** Jordan
52B2 **Elba** *I* Italy
95C2 **El Balyana** Egypt
32C2 **El Banco** Colombia
55B2 **Elbasan** Alb
27D5 **Elbaul** Ven
57C2 **Elbe** *R* Germany
94C1 **El Bega'a** *R* Leb
14A2 **Elberta** USA
8C3 **Elbert,Mt** USA
17B1 **Elberton** USA
92C2 **Elbistan** Turk
58B2 **Elblag** Pol
29B4 **El Bolson** Arg
61F5 **Elbrus** *Mt* USSR
Elburz Mts =
Reshteh-ye Alborz
21B3 **El Cajon** USA
19A4 **El Campo** USA
51B2 **Elche** Spain
51B2 **Elda** Spain

32B3 **El Diviso** Colombia
96B2 **El Djouf** *Desert Region* Maur
18B2 **Eldon** USA
11A3 **El Dorado** Arkansas, USA
35B2 **Eldorado** Brazil
9D3 **El Dorado** Kansas, USA
24B2 **El Dorado** Mexico
33E2 **El Dorado** Ven
99D2 **Eldoret** Kenya
22C1 **Eleanor,L** USA
96B2 **El Eglab** Region, Alg
50B1 **El Escorial** Spain
93D2 **Eleşkirt** Turk
11C4 **Eleuthera** *I* The Bahamas
92B4 **El Faiyûm** Egypt
96B2 **El Farsia** *Well* Mor
98C1 **El Fasher** Sudan
92B4 **El Fashn** Egypt
50A1 **El Ferrol del Caudillo** Spain
99C1 **El Fula** Sudan
96C1 **El Gassi** Alg
99D1 **El Geteina** Sudan
99D1 **El Gezira** Region, Sudan
94B3 **El Ghor** *V* Israel/Jordan
10B2 **Elgin** Illinois, USA
44C3 **Elgin** Scot
92B3 **El Gîza** Egypt
96C1 **El Golea** Alg
99D2 **Elgon,Mt** Uganda/Kenya
99E2 **El Goran** Eth
23A2 **El Grullo** Mexico
96B2 **El Guettara** *Well* Mali
99E2 **El Hamurre** Somalia
96B2 **El Haricha** *Desert Region* Mali
92A4 **El Harra** Egypt
51C2 **El Harrach** Alg
99D1 **El Hawata** Sudan
23B1 **El Higo** Mexico
34A3 **El Huecu** Arg
92B4 **El'Igma** *Desert Region* Egypt
12B2 **Elim** USA
4H2 **Elira,C** Can
Elisabethville =
Lubumbashi
39K6 **Elisenvaara** Fin
El Iskandarîya =
Alexandria
61F4 **Elista** USSR
106C4 **Elizabeth** Aust
15D2 **Elizabeth** USA
11C3 **Elizabeth City** USA
17C1 **Elizabethtown** N Carolina, USA
16A2 **Elizabethtown** Pennsylvania, USA
96B1 **El Jadida** Mor
92C3 **El Jafr** Jordan
99D1 **El Jebelein** Sudan
96D1 **El Jem** Tunisia
58C2 **Elk** Pol
16B3 **Elk** *R* Maryland, USA
14B3 **Elk** *R* W Virginia, USA
95C3 **El Kamlin** Sudan
22B1 **Elk Grove** USA
El Khalil = Hebron
80B3 **El Khârga** Egypt
80B3 **El-Khârga Oasis** Egypt
14A2 **Elkhart** USA
96B2 **El Khenachich** *Desert Region* Mali
54C2 **Elkhovo** Bulg
14C3 **Elkins** USA
8B2 **Elko** USA
16B3 **Elkton** USA
92B3 **El Kuntilla** Egypt
99C1 **El Lagowa** Sudan
4H2 **Ellef Ringnes I** Can
8A2 **Ellensburg** USA

16B2 **Ellenville** USA
6B2 **Ellesmere I** Can
111B2 **Ellesmere,L** NZ
16A3 **Ellicott City** USA
100B4 **Elliot** S Africa
7B5 **Elliot Lake** Can
94B3 **El Lisan** *Pen* Jordan
112B3 **Ellsworth Land** *Region*
Ant
95B1 **El Maghra** *L* Egypt
92B3 **El Mansûra** Egypt
16B3 **Elmer** USA
96B3 **El Merelé** *Desert Region*
Maur
34B2 **El Milagro** Arg
94B1 **El Mina** Leb
92B4 **El Minya** Egypt
22B1 **Elmira** California, USA
10C2 **Elmira** New York, USA
96B2 **El Mreitl** *Well* Maur
56B2 **Elmshorn** Germany
98C1 **El Muglad** Sudan
96B2 **El Mzereb** *Well* Mali
79A3 **El Nido** Phil
99D1 **El Obeid** Sudan
23A2 **El Oro** Mexico
96C1 **El Oued** Alg
9C3 **El Paso** USA
21A2 **El Porta** USA
22C2 **El Portal** USA
50A2 **El Puerto del Sta Maria**
Spain
El Qâhira = Cairo
El Quds = Jerusalem
94B3 **El Quseima** Egypt
9D3 **El Reno** USA
4E3 **Elsa** Can
25D3 **El Salvador** Republic,
Cent America
22D4 **Elsinore L** USA
34B3 **El Sosneade** Arg
57C2 **Elsterwerde** Germany
El Suweis = Suez
50A1 **El Teleno** *Mt* Spain
110B1 **Eltham** NZ
33E2 **El Tigre** Ven
92B4 **El Tîh** *Desert Region*
Egypt
34C2 **El Tio** Arg
20C1 **Eltopia** USA
92B4 **El Tûr** Egypt
87C1 **Elûru** India
50A2 **Elvas** Port
32C5 **Elvira** Brazil
34A2 **El Volcán** Chile
14A2 **Elwood** USA
43E3 **Ely** Eng
10A2 **Ely** Minnesota, USA
8B3 **Ely** Nevada, USA
14B2 **Elyria** USA
90B2 **Emämrüd** Iran
84B1 **Emäm Säheb** Afghan
58B1 **Eman** *R* Sweden
61J4 **Emba** USSR
61J4 **Emba** *R* USSR
29C3 **Embalse Cerros**
Colorados *L* Arg
51B2 **Embalse de Alarcón**
Res Spain
50A2 **Embalse de Alcántarà**
Res Spain
50A1 **Embalse de Almendra**
Res Spain
50A2 **Embalse de Garcia de**
Sola *Res* Spain
33E2 **Embalse de Guri** *L* Ven
51B1 **Embalse de Mequinenza**
Res Spain
50A1 **Embalse de Ricobayo**
Res Spain
29E2 **Embalse de Rio Negro**
Res Urug
29C3 **Embalse El Chocón** *L*
Arg
29C4 **Embalse Florentine**
Ameghino *L* Arg
50A1 **Embalse Gabriel y Galan**
Res Spain

30D3 **Embarcación** Arg
5G4 **Embarras Portage** Can
47B2 **Embrun** France
99D3 **Embu** Kenya
56B2 **Emden** Germany
73A4 **Emei** China
107D3 **Emerald** Aust
7D4 **Emeri** Can
5J5 **Emerson** Can
21B1 **Emigrant P** USA
95A3 **Emi Koussi** *Mt* Chad
34B3 **Emilo Mitre** Arg
92B2 **Emirdağ** Turk
16B2 **Emmaus** USA
56B2 **Emmen** Neth
20C2 **Emmett** USA
16A3 **Emmitsburg** USA
12B2 **Emmonak** USA
9C4 **Emory Peak** *Mt* USA
24A2 **Empalme** Mexico
101H1 **Empangeni** S Africa
30E4 **Empedrado** Arg
105G1 **Emperor Seamount**
Chain Pacific O
18A2 **Emporia** Kansas, USA
56B2 **Ems** *R* Germany
44B2 **Enard** *B* Scot
23A1 **Encarnacion** Mexico
30E4 **Encarnación** Par
97B4 **Enchi** Ghana
22D4 **Encinitas** USA
35C1 **Encruzilhada** Brazil
106B1 **Ende** Indon
13D2 **Enderby** USA
112C11 **Enderby Land** Region,
Ant
15C2 **Endicott** USA
12D1 **Endicott Mts** USA
47D1 **Engadin** *Mts* Switz
79B2 **Engaño,C** Phil
94B3 **En Gedi** Israel
47C1 **Engelberg** Switz
61G3 **Engel's** USSR
78A4 **Enggano** *I* Indon
41C3 **England** Country, UK
7E4 **Englee** Can
41C3 **English Channel** Eng/
France
97B3 **Enji** *Well* Maur
39H7 **Enkoping** Sweden
53B3 **Enna** Italy
99C1 **En Nahud** Sudan
95B3 **Ennedi** *Region* Chad
109C1 **Enngonia** Aust
41B3 **Ennis** Irish Rep
19A3 **Ennis** Texas, USA
45C2 **Enniscorthy** Irish Rep
45C1 **Enniskillen** N Ire
45B2 **Ennistimon** Irish Rep
94B2 **Enn Naqoûra** Leb
57C3 **Enns** *R* Austria
39F8 **Enschede** Neth
24A1 **Ensenada** Mexico
73B3 **Enshi** China
99D2 **Entebbe** Uganda
17A1 **Enterprise** Alabama,
USA
20C1 **Enterprise** Oregon,
USA
97C4 **Enugu** Nig
75B1 **Enzan** Japan
49C2 **Epernay** France
16A2 **Ephrata** Pennsylvania,
USA
20C1 **Ephrata** Washington,
USA
49D2 **Épinal** France
46A2 **Epte** *R* France
100A3 **Epukiro** Namibia
34C3 **Epu pel** Arg
90B3 **Eqlid** Iran
89D7 **Equator**
98A2 **Equatorial Guinea**
Republic, Africa
47C2 **Erba** Italy
46D2 **Erbeskopf** *Mt*
Germany
34A3 **Ercilla** Chile

93D2 **Erciş** Turk
92C2 **Erciyas Daglari** *Mt*
Turk
74B2 **Erdaobaihe** China
72C1 **Erdene** Mongolia
68C2 **Erdenet** Mongolia
95B3 **Erdi** *Region* Chad
30F4 **Erechim** Brazil
92B1 **Ereğli** Turk
92B2 **Eregli** Turk
68D2 **Erenhot** China
50B1 **Eresma** *R* Spain
46D1 **Erft** *R* Germany
57C2 **Erfurt** Germany
93C2 **Ergani** Turk
96B2 **Erg Chech** *Desert*
Region Alg
95A3 **Erg du Djourab** *Desert*
Chad
97D3 **Erg Du Ténéré** *Desert*
Region Niger
92A1 **Ergene** *R* Turk
96B2 **Erg Iguidi** *Region* Alg
58D1 **Ergli** USSR
98B1 **Erguig** *R* Chad
63D2 **Ergun'** USSR
68D1 **Ergun** *R* USSR
63E2 **Ergun Zuoqi** China
95C3 **Eriba** Sudan
10C2 **Erie** USA
10B2 **Erie,L** Can/USA
42B2 **Erin Port** Eng
44A3 **Eriskay** *I* Scot
46D1 **Erkelenz** Germany
57C3 **Erlangen** Germany
19B3 **Erling,L** USA
101G1 **Ermelo** S Africa
87B3 **Ernäkulam** India
87B2 **Erode** India
108B1 **Eromanga** Aust
96B1 **Er Rachidia** Mor
99D1 **Er Rahad** Sudan
101C2 **Errego** Mozam
40B2 **Errigal** *Mt* Irish Rep
41A3 **Erris Head** *Pt* Irish Rep
99D1 **Er Roseires** Sudan
94B2 **Er Rummân** Jordan
57C2 **Erzgebirge** *Upland*
Germany
93C2 **Erzincan** Turk
65F6 **Erzurum** Turk
48C3 **Esara** *R* Spain
56B1 **Esbjerg** Den
9C4 **Escalón** Mexico
10B2 **Escanaba** USA
25C3 **Escárcega** Mexico
46C2 **Esch** Lux
21B3 **Escondido** USA
24B2 **Escuinapa** Mexico
25C3 **Escuintla** Guatemala
98B2 **Eséka** Cam
51C1 **Esera** *R* Spain
90B3 **Eşfahân** Iran
101H1 **Eshowe** S Africa
110C1 **Eskdale** NZ
38C1 **Eskifjörður** Iceland
39H7 **Eskilstuna** Sweden
4E3 **Eskimo L** Can
7A3 **Eskimo Point** Can
92B2 **Eskisehir** Turk
50A1 **Esla** *R* Spain
29A5 **Esmeralda** *I* Chile
32B3 **Esmeraldas** Ecuador
26B2 **Esmerelda** Cuba
49C3 **Espalion** France
14B1 **Espanola** Can
32J7 **Española** *I* Ecuador
106B4 **Esperance** Aust
34C2 **Esperanza** Arg
112C2 **Esperanza** *Base* Ant
35C1 **Espírito Santo** State,
Brazil
101C3 **Espungabera** Mozam
29B4 **Esquel** Arg
20B1 **Esquimalt** Can
34D2 **Esquina** Arg
94C2 **Es Samra** Jordan
96B1 **Essaouira** Mor

96A2 **Es Semara** Mor
56B2 **Essen** Germany
33F3 **Essequibo** *R* Guyana
43E4 **Essex** County, Eng
14B2 **Essexville** USA
57B3 **Esslingen** Germany
46B2 **Essonne** France
31D4 **Estância** Brazil
101G1 **Estcourt** S Africa
47D2 **Este** Italy
46B2 **Esternay** France
30D3 **Esteros** Par
5H5 **Estevan** Can
17B1 **Estill** USA
60B2 **Estonskaya SSR**
Republic, USSR
29B6 **Estrecho de**
Magallanes *Str*
Chile
50A2 **Estremoz** Port
59B3 **Esztergom** Hung
108A1 **Etadunna** Aust
46C2 **Etam** France
48C2 **Etampes** France
108A1 **Etamunbanie,L** Aust
46A1 **Etaples** France
85D3 **Etäwah** India
99D2 **Ethiopia** Republic,
Africa
23B2 **Etla** Mexico
53B3 **Etna** *Mt* Italy
12H3 **Etolin I** USA
12A2 **Etolin Str** USA
6C2 **Eton** Can
100A2 **Etosha Nat Pk**
Namibia
100A2 **Etosha Pan** *Salt L*
Namibia
17B1 **Etowah** *R* USA
46D2 **Ettelbruck** Lux
109C2 **Euabalong** Aust
14B2 **Euclid** USA
109C3 **Eucumbene,L** Aust
108A2 **Eudunda** Aust
19A2 **Eufala L** USA
17A1 **Eufaula** USA
8A2 **Eugene** USA
108C1 **Eulo** Aust
19B3 **Eunice** Louisiana, USA
46D1 **Eupen** Germany
93D3 **Euphrates** *R* Iraq
19C3 **Eupora** USA
48C2 **Eure** *R* France
20B2 **Eureka** California, USA
6B1 **Eureka** Can
8B3 **Eureka** Nevada, USA
6B2 **Eureka** *Sd* Can
108C3 **Euroa** Aust
109C1 **Eurombah** *R* Aust
101D3 **Europa** */ Mozam Chan
57B2 **Euskirchen** Germany
13B2 **Eutşuk L** Can
13D2 **Evansburg** Can
6B1 **Evans,C** Can
7C4 **Evans,L** Can
6B3 **Evans Str** Can
14A2 **Evanston** Illinois, USA
8B2 **Evanston** Wyoming,
USA
11B3 **Evansville** Indiana,
USA
101G1 **Evaton** S Africa
106C4 **Everard,L** Aust
82C3 **Everest,Mt** China/
Nepal
8A2 **Everett** Washington,
USA
16C1 **Everett,Mt** USA
11B4 **Everglades,The**
Swamp USA
43D3 **Evesham** Eng
98B2 **Evinayong** Eq Guinea
39F7 **Evje** Nor
47B1 **Evolène** Switz
50A2 **Évora** Port
48C2 **Evreux** France
55B3 **Évvoia** *I* Greece
98B3 **Ewo** Congo

22C1 **Excelisor Mt** USA
18B2 **Excelsior Springs** USA
21B2 **Exeter** California, USA
43C4 **Exeter** Eng
15D2 **Exeter** New
Hampshire, USA
43C4 **Exmoor Nat Pk** Eng
43C4 **Exmouth** Eng
50A2 **Extremadura** Region,
Spain
25E2 **Exuma Sd**
The Bahamas
99D3 **Eyasi** L Tanz
42C2 **Eyemouth** Scot
99E2 **Eyl** Somalia
106B4 **Eyre** Aust
106C3 **Eyre Creek** R Aust
106C3 **Eyre,L** Aust
106C4 **Eyre Pen** Aust
79B3 **Eyte** I Phil
23A1 **Ezatlan** Mexico
55C3 **Ezine** Turk

F

4G3 **Faber L** Can
39G7 **Fåborg** Den
52B2 **Fabriano** Italy
95A3 **Fachi** Niger
95B3 **Fada** Chad
97C3 **Fada N'Gourma**
Burkina
52B2 **Faenza** Italy
6E3 **Faeringehavn**
Greenland
98B2 **Fafa** R CAR
99E2 **Fafan** R Eth
54B1 **Fägäras** Rom
46C1 **Fagnes** Region, Belg
97B3 **Faguibine,L** L Mali
91C5 **Fahud** Oman
96A1 **Faiol** I Açores
4D3 **Fairbanks** USA
7A5 **Fairbault** USA
14B3 **Fairborn** USA
8D2 **Fairbury** USA
16A3 **Fairfax** USA
21A2 **Fairfield** California,
USA
16C2 **Fairfield** Connecticut,
USA
14B3 **Fairfield** Ohio, USA
45C1 **Fair Head** Pt N Ire
40C2 **Fair Isle** I Scot
111B2 **Fairlie** NZ
14B3 **Fairmont** W Virginia,
USA
13D1 **Fairview** Can
4E4 **Fairweather,Mt** USA
71F3 **Fais** I Pacific O
84C2 **Faisalabad** Pak
8C2 **Faith** USA
44E1 **Faither,The** Pen Scot
86A1 **Faizäbäd** India
43E3 **Fakenham** Eng
39G7 **Faköping** Sweden
86C2 **Falam** Burma
24C2 **Falcon Res** Mexico/
USA
97A3 **Falémé** R Mali/Sen
39G7 **Falkenberg** Sweden
42C2 **Falkirk** Scot
29D6 **Falkland Is**
Dependency,
S Atlantic
29E6 **Falkland Sd** Falkland Is
22D4 **Fallbrook** USA
8B3 **Fallon** USA
15D2 **Fall River** USA
18A1 **Falls City** USA
43B4 **Falmouth** Eng
27H1 **Falmouth** Jamaica
16D2 **Falmouth**
Massachusetts, USA
100A4 **False B** S Africa
24A2 **Falso,C** Mexico
56C2 **Falster** I Den

54C1 **Fälticeni** Rom
39H6 **Falun** Sweden
92B2 **Famagusta** Cyprus
46C1 **Famenne** Region, Belg
76B2 **Fang** Thai
99D2 **Fangak** Sudan
73E5 **Fang liao** Taiwan
52B2 **Fano** Italy
112C3 **Faraday** Base Ant
99C2 **Faradje** Zaïre
101D3 **Farafangana** Madag
95B2 **Farafra Oasis** Egypt
80E2 **Farah** Afghan
71F2 **Farallon de Medinilla** I
Pacific O
97A3 **Faranah** Guinea
71F3 **Faraulep** I Pacific O
43D4 **Fareham** Eng
Farewell,C = Kap Farvel
107G5 **Farewell,C** NZ
110B2 **Farewell Spit** Pt NZ
8D2 **Fargo** USA
94B2 **Fari'a** R Israel
10A2 **Faribault** USA
86B2 **Faridpur** Bang
90C2 **Farïmän** Iran
18B2 **Farmington** Missouri,
USA
9C3 **Farmington** New
Mexico, USA
22B2 **Farmington Res** USA
42D2 **Farne Deep** N Sea
13D2 **Farnham,Mt** Can
12H2 **Faro** Can
50A2 **Faro** Port
39H7 **Fåro** I Sweden
89K9 **Farquhar** Is Indian O
44B3 **Farrar** R Scot
14B2 **Farrell** USA
55B3 **Fársala** Greece
91B4 **Fasä** Iran
45B3 **Fastnet Rock** Irish Rep
60C3 **Fastov** USSR
86A1 **Fatehpur** India
13D1 **Father** Can
30F2 **Fatima du Sul** Brazil
101G1 **Fauresmith** S Africa
47B2 **Faverges** France
7B4 **Fawn** R Can
38H6 **Fax** R Sweden
38A2 **Faxaflói** B Iceland
95A3 **Faya** Chad
11A3 **Fayetteville** Arkansas,
USA
11C3 **Fayetteville** N
Carolina, USA
93E4 **Faylakah** I Kuwait
84C2 **Fäzilka** India
96A2 **Fdérik** Maur
11C3 **Fear,C** USA
21A2 **Feather Middle Fork** R
USA
48C2 **Fécamp** France
34D2 **Federación** Arg
34D2 **Federal** Arg
71F3 **Federated States of**
Micronesia Is
Pacific O
56C2 **Fehmarn** I Germany
32C5 **Feijó** Brazil
73C5 **Feilai Xai Bei Jiang** R
China
110C2 **Feilding** NZ
100C2 **Feira** Zambia
31D4 **Feira de Santan** Brazil
92C2 **Feke** Turk
57B3 **Feldkirch** Austria
34D2 **Feliciano** R Arg
41D3 **Felixstowe** Eng
47D1 **Feltre** Italy
38G6 **Femund** L Nor
74A2 **Fengcheng** China
73B4 **Fengdu** China
72D1 **Fengjie** China
73B3 **Fengjie** China
72B3 **Feng Xian** China
72C1 **Fengzhen** China
72C2 **Fen He** R China

101D2 **Fenoarivo Atsinanana**
Madag
60E5 **Feodosiya** USSR
90C3 **Ferdow** Iran
46B2 **Fère-Champenoise**
France
82B2 **Fergana** USSR
45C1 **Fermanagh** County,
N Ire
45B2 **Fermoy** Irish Rep
47D1 **Fern** Mt Austria
32J7 **Fernandina** I Ecuador
17B1 **Fernandina Beach**
USA
103G5 **Fernando de Noronha**
I Atlantic O
35A2 **Fernandópolis** Brazil
20B1 **Ferndale** USA
21B2 **Fernley** USA
52B2 **Ferrara** Italy
32B5 **Ferreñafe** Peru
19B3 **Ferriday** USA
9GB1 **Fès** Mor
18B2 **Festus** USA
54C2 **Feteşti** Rom
92A2 **Fethiye** Turk
61H5 **Fetisovo** USSR
44E1 **Fetlar** I Scot
84C1 **Feyzabad** Afghan
101D3 **Fianarantsoa** Madag
99D2 **Fiche** Eth
101G1 **Ficksburg** S Africa
47D2 **Fidenza** Italy
55A2 **Fier** Alb
47D1 **Fiera Di Primeiro** Italy
44C3 **Fife** Region, Scot
44C3 **Fife Ness** Pen Scot
48C3 **Figeac** France
50A1 **Figueira da Foz** Port
51C1 **Figueras** Spain
96B1 **Figuig** Mor
105G4 **Fiji** Is Pacific O
30D3 **Filadelfia** Par
54B2 **Filiaşi** Rom
55B3 **Filiatrá** Greece
53B3 **Filicudi** I Italy
21B3 **Fillmore** California,
USA
44B3 **Findhorn** R Scot
10B2 **Findlay** USA
13D2 **Findlay,Mt** Can
15C2 **Finger Lakes** USA
101C2 **Fingoè** Mozam
92B2 **Finike** Turk
106C3 **Finke** R Aust
108A1 **Finke Flood Flats** Aust
64D3 **Finland** Republic,
N Europe
39J7 **Finland,G of** N Europe
5F4 **Finlay** R Can
5F4 **Finlay Forks** Can
108C3 **Finley** Aust
38H5 **Finnsnes** Nor
71F4 **Finschhafen** PNG
47C1 **Finsteraarhorn** Mt
Switz
56C2 **Finsterwalde** Germany
45C1 **Fintona** N Ire
111A3 **Fiordland Nat Pk** NZ
94B2 **Fiq** Syria
93C2 **Firat** R Turk
22B2 **Firebaugh** USA
52B2 **Firenze** Italy
34C2 **Firmat** Arg
85D3 **Firozäbäd** India
84C2 **Firozpur** India
39H7 **Firspång** Sweden
42B2 **Firth of Clyde** Estuary
Scot
44C3 **Firth of Forth** Estuary
Scot
44A3 **Firth of Lorn** Estuary
Scot
40C2 **Firth of Tay** Estuary
Scot
91B4 **Firüzäbäd** Iran
100A3 **Fish** R Namibia
22C2 **Fish Camp** USA

16C2 **Fishers I** USA
6B3 **Fisher Str** Can
43B4 **Fishguard** Wales
6E3 **Fiskenaesset**
Greenland
46B2 **Fismes** France
15D2 **Fitchburg** USA
44E2 **Fitful Head** Pt Scot
17B1 **Fitzgerald** USA
106B2 **Fitzroy** R Aust
106B2 **Fitzroy Crossing** Aust
14B1 **Fitzwilliam I** Can
Fiume = Rijeka
99C3 **Fizi** Zaïre
9B3 **Flagstaff** USA
42D2 **Flamborough Head** C
Eng
8C2 **Flaming Gorge Res**
USA
44A2 **Flannan Isles** Is Scot
12J2 **Flat** R Can
13E3 **Flathead** R USA
8B2 **Flathead L** USA
18B2 **Flat River** USA
8A2 **Flattery,C** USA
42C3 **Fleetwood** Eng
39F7 **Flekkefjord** Nor
69G4 **Fleming Deep**
Pacific O
16B2 **Flemington** USA
56B2 **Flensburg** Germany
47B1 **Fleurier** Switz
106C4 **Flinders** I Aust
107D4 **Flinders** I Aust
107D2 **Flinders** R Aust
106C4 **Flinders Range** Mts
Aust
5H4 **Flin Flon** Can
10B2 **Flint** USA
42C3 **Flint** Wales
11B3 **Flint** R USA
46B1 **Flixecourt** France
17A1 **Florala** USA
Florence = Firenze
11B3 **Florence** Alabama,
USA
18A2 **Florence** Kansas, USA
20B2 **Florence** Oregon, USA
11C3 **Florence** S Carolina,
USA
32B3 **Florencia** Colombia
46C2 **Florenville** Belg
25D3 **Flores** Guatemala
96A1 **Flores** I Açores
106B1 **Flores** I Indon
34D3 **Flores** R Arg
70C4 **Flores** S Indon
31C3 **Floriano** Brazil
30G4 **Florianópolis** Brazil
25D2 **Florida** State, USA
29E2 **Florida** Urug
17B2 **Florida B** USA
17B2 **Florida City** USA
107E1 **Florida Is** Solomon Is
11B4 **Florida Keys** Is USA
11B4 **Florida,Strs of** USA
55B2 **Flórina** Greece
38F6 **Florø** Nor
47D1 **Fluchthorn** Mt Austria
54C1 **Focsani** Rom
53C2 **Foggia** Italy
97A4 **Fogo** I Cape Verde
48C3 **Foix** France
6C3 **Foley I** Can
52B2 **Foligno** Italy
43E4 **Folkestone** Eng
17B1 **Folkston** USA
52B2 **Follonica** Italy
22B1 **Folsom** USA
22B1 **Folsom L** L USA
5H4 **Fond-du-Lac** Can
10B2 **Fond du Lac** USA
48C2 **Fontainebleau** France
18B2 **Fontenac** USA
48B2 **Fontenay-le-Comte**
France
52C1 **Fonyód** Hung
Foochow = Fuzhou

12D2 **Foraker,Mt** USA
46D2 **Forbach** France
109C2 **Forbes** Aust
97C4 **Forcados** Nig
38F6 **Forde** Nor
108C1 **Fords Bridge** Aust
19B3 **Fordyce** USA
97A4 **Forécariah** Guinea
6G3 **Forel,Mt** Greenland
14B2 **Forest** Can
17B1 **Forest Park** USA
22A1 **Forestville** USA
44C3 **Forfar** Scot
46A2 **Forges-les-Eaux**
France
20B1 **Forks** USA
52B2 **Forlì** Italy
51C2 **Formentera** *I* Spain
53B2 **Formia** Italy
96A1 **Formigas** *I* Açores
Formosa = Taiwan
30E4 **Formosa** Arg
31B5 **Formosa** Brazil
30D3 **Formosa** State, Arg
73D5 **Formosa Str** Taiwan/
China
47D2 **Fornovo di Taro** Italy
38D3 **Føroyar** *Is*
N Atlantic O
44C3 **Forres** Scot
106B4 **Forrest** Aust
11A3 **Forrest City** USA
107D2 **Forsayth** Aust
39J6 **Forssa** Fin
109D2 **Forster** Aust
18B2 **Forsyth** Missouri, USA
84C3 **Fort Abbas** Pak
7B4 **Fort Albany** Can
31D2 **Fortaleza** Brazil
44B3 **Fort Augustus** Scot
100B4 **Fort Beaufort** S Africa
21A2 **Fort Bragg** USA
8C2 **Fort Collins** USA
15C1 **Fort Coulogne** Can
27E4 **Fort de France**
Martinique
17A1 **Fort Deposit** USA
10A2 **Fort Dodge** USA
106A3 **Fortescue** *R* Aust
7A5 **Fort Frances** Can
4F3 **Fort Franklin** Can
7C4 **Fort George** Can
4F3 **Fort Good Hope** Can
108B1 **Fort Grey** Aust
44B3 **Forth** *R* Scot
7B4 **Fort Hope** Can
34B3 **Fortin Uno** Arg
4F3 **Fort Laird** Can
96C1 **Fort Lallemand** Alg
Fort Lamy = Ndjamena
11B4 **Fort Lauderdale** USA
4F3 **Fort Liard** Can
5G4 **Fort Mackay** Can
5G5 **Fort Macleod** Can
5G4 **Fort McMurray** Can
4E3 **Fort McPherson** Can
18B2 **Fort Madison** USA
8C2 **Fort Morgan** USA
11B4 **Fort Myers** USA
5F4 **Fort Nelson** Can
4F3 **Fort Norman** Can
17A1 **Fort Payne** USA
8C2 **Fort Peck Res** USA
11B4 **Fort Pierce** USA
4G3 **Fort Providence** Can
5G3 **Fort Resolution** Can
98B3 **Fort Rousset** Congo
7C4 **Fort Rupert** Can
5F4 **Fort St James** Can
13C1 **Fort St John** Can
13E2 **Fort Saskatchewan**
Can
18B2 **Fort Scott** USA
4E3 **Fort Selkirk** Can
7B4 **Fort Severn** Can
61H5 **Fort Shevchenko**
USSR
4F3 **Fort Simpson** Can

5G3 **Fort Smith** Can
4G3 **Fort Smith** Region,
Can
11A3 **Fort Smith** USA
9C3 **Fort Stockton** USA
20B2 **Fortuna** California,
USA
5G4 **Fort Vermillion** Can
17A1 **Fort Walton Beach**
USA
10B2 **Fort Wayne** USA
44B3 **Fort William** Scot
9D3 **Fort Worth** USA
12F2 **Fortymile** *R* USA
12E1 **Fort Yukon** USA
73C5 **Foshan** China
47B2 **Fossano** Italy
12G3 **Foster,Mt** USA
98B3 **Fougamou** Gabon
48B2 **Fougères** France
44D1 **Foula** *I* Scot
43E4 **Foulness I** Eng
111B2 **Foulwind,C** NZ
98B2 **Foumban** Cam
49C1 **Fourmies** France
55C3 **Foúrnoi** *I* Greece
97A3 **Fouta Djallon** *Mts*
Guinea
111B3 **Foveaux** *Str* NZ
43B4 **Fowey** Eng
13D2 **Fox Creek** Can
6B3 **Foxe Basin** *G* Can
6B3 **Foxe Chan** Can
6C3 **Foxe Pen** Can
110C2 **Foxton** NZ
42F3 **Fox Valley** Can
45B2 **Foynes** Irish Rep
100A2 **Foz do Cuene** Angola
30F4 **Foz do Iquaçu** Brazil
16A2 **Frackville** USA
34B2 **Fraga** Arg
16D1 **Framingham** USA
31B6 **Franca** Brazil
49C2 **France**
Republic, Europe
10A2 **Frances** Can
12J2 **Frances** *R* Can
98B3 **France Ville** Gabon
49D2 **Franche Comté**
Region, France
100B3 **Francistown** Botswana
13B2 **Francois L** Can
14A2 **Frankfort** Indiana, USA
11B3 **Frankfort** Kentucky,
USA
101G1 **Frankfort** S Africa
57B2 **Frankfurt** Germany
46E1 **Frankfurt am Main**
Germany
56C2 **Frankfurt-an-der-Oder**
Germany
57C3 **Fränkischer Alb**
Upland Germany
14A3 **Franklin** Indiana, USA
19B4 **Franklin** Louisiana,
USA
16D1 **Franklin**
Massachusetts, USA
16B2 **Franklin** New Jersey,
USA
14C2 **Franklin** Pennsylvania,
USA
4F2 **Franklin B** Can
20C1 **Franklin D Roosevelt** *L*
USA
4F3 **Franklin Mts** Can
4J2 **Franklin Str** Can
64D5 **Frankovsk** USSR
111B2 **Franz Josef Glacier** NZ
**Franz-Joseph-Land =
Zemlya Frantsa Iosifa**
5F5 **Fraser** *R* Can
44C3 **Fraserburgh** Scot
107E3 **Fraser I** Aust
13B2 **Fraser L** Can
47B1 **Frasne** France
47C1 **Frauenfeld** Switz
34D2 **Fray Bentos** Urug

40C2 **Frazerburgh** Scot
16B3 **Frederica** USA
56B1 **Fredericia** Den
15C3 **Frederick** Maryland,
USA
15C3 **Fredericksburg**
Virginia, USA
12H3 **Frederick Sd** USA
18B2 **Fredericktown** USA
7D5 **Fredericton** Can
6E3 **Frederikshab**
Greenland
39G7 **Frederikshavn** Den
15C2 **Fredonia** USA
39G7 **Fredrikstad** Nor
16B2 **Freehold** USA
26B1 **Freeport** The Bahamas
19A4 **Freeport** Texas, USA
97A4 **Freetown** Sierra Leone
57B3 **Freiburg** Germany
57C3 **Freistadt** Austria
106A4 **Fremantle** Aust
22B2 **Fremont** California,
USA
18A1 **Fremont** Nebraska,
USA
14B2 **Fremont** Ohio, USA
33G3 **French Guiana**
Dependency,
S America
109C4 **Frenchmans Cap** *Mt*
Aust
105J4 **French Polynesia** *Is*
Pacific O
24B2 **Fresnillo** Mexico
8B3 **Fresno** USA
22C2 **Fresno** *R* USA
47A1 **Fretigney** France
46B1 **Frévent** France
109C4 **Freycinet Pen** Aust
97A3 **Fria** Guinea
22C2 **Friant** USA
22C2 **Friant Dam** USA
52A1 **Fribourg** Switz
57B3 **Friedrichshafen**
Germany
6D3 **Frobisher B** Can
6D3 **Frobisher Bay** Can
5H4 **Frobisher L** Can
61F4 **Frolovo** USSR
43C4 **Frome** Eng
108A1 **Frome** *R* Aust
43C4 **Frome** *R* Eng
106C4 **Frome,L** Aust
25C3 **Frontera** Mexico
15C3 **Front Royal** USA
53B2 **Frosinone** Italy
82B1 **Frunze** USSR
73C5 **Fuchuan** China
73E4 **Fuding** China
24B2 **Fuerte** *R* Mexico
30E3 **Fuerte Olimpo** Par
96A2 **Fuerteventura** *I*
Canary Is
72C2 **Fugu** China
68A2 **Fuhai** China
91C4 **Fujairah** UAE
75B1 **Fuji** Japan
73D4 **Fujian** Province, China
69F2 **Fujin** China
75B1 **Fujinomiya** Japan
74D3 **Fuji-san** *Mt* Japan
75B1 **Fujisawa** Japan
75B1 **Fuji-Yoshida** Japan
63A3 **Fukang** China
74C3 **Fukuchiyima** Japan
74D3 **Fukui** Japan
74C4 **Fukuoka** Japan
74E3 **Fukushima** Japan
74C4 **Fukuyama** Japan
57B2 **Fulda** Germany
57B2 **Fulda** *R* Germany
73B4 **Fuling** China
27L1 **Fullarton** Trinidad
22D4 **Fullerton** USA
18C2 **Fulton** Kentucky, USA
15C2 **Fulton** New York, USA
46C1 **Fumay** France

75C1 **Funabashi** Japan
96A1 **Funchal** Medeira
35C1 **Fundão** Brazil
7D5 **Fundy,B of** Can
101C3 **Funhalouro** Mozam
72D3 **Funing** China
73B5 **Funing** China
97C3 **Funtua** Nig
73D4 **Fuqing** China
101C2 **Furancungo** Mozam
91C4 **Fürg** Iran
47C1 **Furka** *P* Switz
107D5 **Furneaux Group** *Is*
Aust
56C2 **Fürstenwalde**
Germany
57C3 **Fürth** Germany
74D3 **Furukawa** Japan
6B3 **Fury and Hecla St** Can
74A2 **Fushun** Liaoning,
China
73A4 **Fushun** Sichuan, China
74B2 **Fusong** China
57C3 **Füssen** Germany
72E2 **Fu Xian** China
72E1 **Fuxin** China
72D3 **Fuyang** China
72E1 **Fuyuan** Liaoning,
China
73A4 **Fuyuan** Yunnan, China
68A2 **Fuyun** China
73D4 **Fuzhou** China
56C1 **Fyn** *I* Den

G

99E2 **Gaalkacyo** Somalia
21B2 **Gabbs** USA
100A2 **Gabela** Angola
96D1 **Gabe's** Tunisia
22B2 **Gabilan Range** *Mts*
USA
98B3 **Gabon** Republic, Africa
100B3 **Gaborone** Botswana
54C2 **Gabrovo** Bulg
91B3 **Gach Sārān** Iran
17A1 **Gadsden** Alabama,
USA
10A1 **Gads L** Can
53B2 **Gaeta** Italy
71F3 **Gaferut** *I* / Pacific O
96C1 **Gafsa** Tunisia
60D2 **Gagarin** USSR
97B4 **Gagnoa** Ivory Coast
7D4 **Gagnon** Can
61F5 **Gagra** USSR
86B1 **Gaibanda** India
29C4 **Gaimán** Arg
17B2 **Gainesville** Florida,
USA
17B1 **Gainesville** Georgia,
USA
19A3 **Gainesville** Texas,
USA
42D3 **Gainsborough** Eng
108A2 **Gairdner,L** Aust
44B3 **Gairloch** Scot
16A3 **Gaithersburg** USA
87B1 **Gajendragarh** India
73D4 **Ga Jiang** *R* China
99E2 **Galadi** Eth
99D3 **Galana** *R* Kenya
103D5 **Galapagos Is** Pacific O
42C2 **Galashiels** Scot
54C1 **Galaţi** Rom
4C3 **Galena** Alaska, USA
18B2 **Galena** Kansas, USA
27L1 **Galeota Pt** Trinidad
27L1 **Galera Pt** Trinidad
10A2 **Galesburg** USA
15C2 **Galeton** USA
61F2 **Galich** USSR
50A1 **Galicia** Region, Spain
Galilee,S of = Tiberias,L
27J1 **Galina Pt** Jamaica
99D1 **Gallabat** Sudan
47C2 **Gallarate** Italy

87C3 **Galle** Sri Lanka
51B1 **Gállego** *R* Spain
Gallipoli = Gelibolu
55A2 **Gallipoli** Italy
38J5 **Gällivare** Sweden
42B2 **Galloway** District
42B2 **Galloway,Mull of** *C* Scot
8C3 **Gallup** USA
22B1 **Galt** USA
96A2 **Galtat Zemmour** Mor
25C2 **Galveston** USA
11A4 **Galveston B** USA
34C2 **Galvez** Arg
49D3 **Galvi** Corse
45B2 **Galway** County, Irish Rep
41B3 **Galway** Irish Rep
41B3 **Galway** *B* Irish Rep
86B1 **Gamba** China
97B3 **Gambaga** Ghana
4A3 **Gambell** USA
97A3 **Gambia** *R* The Gambia/ Sen
97A3 **Gambia,The** Republic, Africa
98B3 **Gamboma** Congo
100A2 **Gambos** Angola
87C3 **Gampola** Sri Lanka
99E2 **Ganale Dorya** *R* Eth
15C2 **Gananoque** Can
Gand = Gent
100A2 **Ganda** Angola
98C3 **Gandajika** Zaïre
84B3 **Gandava** Pak
7E5 **Gander** Can
85C4 **Gāndhīdhām** India
85C4 **Gāndhīnagar** India
85D4 **Gāndhi Sāgar** *L* India
51B2 **Gandia** Spain
86B2 **Ganga** *R* India
85C3 **Ganganar** India
86C2 **Gangaw** Burma
72A2 **Gangca** China
82C2 **Gangdise Shan** *Mts* China
Ganges = Ganga
86B1 **Gangtok** India
72B3 **Gangu** China
8C2 **Gannett Peak** *Mt* USA
72B2 **Ganquan** China
108A3 **Gantheaume** *C* Aust
39K8 **Gantseviohi** USSR
73D4 **Ganzhou** China
97C3 **Gao** Mali
72A2 **Gaolan** China
72C2 **Gaoping** China
97B3 **Gaoua** Burkina
97A3 **Gaoual** Guinea
72D3 **Gaoyou Hu** *L* China
73C5 **Gaozhou** China
49D3 **Gap** France
79B2 **Gapan** Phil
84D2 **Gar** China
109C1 **Garah** Aust
31D3 **Garanhuns** Brazil
21A1 **Garberville** USA
35B2 **Garça** Brazil
35A2 **Garcias** Brazil
47D2 **Garda** Italy
9C3 **Garden City** USA
14A1 **Garden Pen** USA
34D3 **Gardey** Arg
84B2 **Gardez** Afghan
16C2 **Gardiners I** USA
16D1 **Gardner** USA
47D2 **Gardone** Italy
99D2 **Gardula** Eth
47D2 **Gargano** Italy
85D4 **Garhākota** India
61K2 **Gari** USSR
100A4 **Garies** S Africa
99D3 **Garissa** Kenya
19A3 **Garland** USA
57C3 **Garmisch-Partenkirchen** Germany
90B2 **Garmsar** Iran
18A2 **Garnett** USA

8B2 **Garnett Peak** *Mt* USA
48C3 **Garonne** *R* France
44B3 **Garry** *R* Scot
78B4 **Garut** Indon
86A2 **Garwa** India
14A2 **Gary** USA
82C2 **Garyarsa** China
4H3 **Gary L** Can
19A3 **Garza-Little Elm** *Res* USA
90A2 **Gasan Kuli** USSR
48B3 **Gascogne** Region, France
18B2 **Gasconade** *R* USA
106A3 **Gascoyne** *R* Aust
98B2 **Gashaka** Nig
97D3 **Gashua** Nig
10D2 **Gaspé** Can
10D2 **Gaspé,C** Can
10D2 **Gaspé Pen** Can
94A1 **Gata,C** Cyprus
60C2 **Gatchina** USSR
42D2 **Gateshead** Eng
19A3 **Gatesville** USA
15C1 **Gatineau** Can
15C1 **Gatineau** *R* Can
109D1 **Gatton** Aust
86C1 **Gauháti** India
58C1 **Gauja** *R* USSR
86A1 **Gauri Phanta** India
22B3 **Gaviota** USA
39H6 **Gävle** Sweden
108A2 **Gawler Ranges** *Mts* Aust
72A1 **Gaxun Nur** *L* China
86A2 **Gaya** India
97C3 **Gaya** Niger
14B1 **Gaylord** USA
109D1 **Gayndah** Aust
61H1 **Gayny** USSR
60C4 **Gaysin** USSR
92B3 **Gaza** Israel
92C2 **Gaziantep** Turk
97B4 **Gbaringa** Lib
58B2 **Gdańsk** Pol
58B2 **Gdańsk,G of** Pol
39K7 **Gdov** USSR
58B2 **Gdynia** Pol
94A3 **Gebel Halâl** *Mt* Egypt
95C2 **Gebel Hamata** *Mt* Egypt
92B4 **Gebel Katherina** *Mt* Egypt
94A3 **Gebel Libni** *Mt* Egypt
94A3 **Gebel Maghâra** *Mt* Egypt
99D1 **Gedaref** Sudan
55C3 **Gediz** *R* Turk
56C2 **Gedser** Den
46C1 **Geel** Belg
108B3 **Geelong** Aust
109C4 **Geeveston** Aust
97D3 **Geidam** Nig
46D1 **Geilenkirchen** Germany
99D3 **Geita** Tanz
73A5 **Gejiu** China
53B3 **Gela** Italy
46D1 **Geldern** Germany
55C2 **Gelibolu** Turk
92B2 **Gelidonya Burun** Turk
46D1 **Gelsenkirchen** Germany
39F8 **Gelting** Germany
77C5 **Gemas** Malay
46C1 **Gembloux** Belg
98B2 **Gemena** Zaïre
92C2 **Gemerek** Turk
92A1 **Gemlik** Turk
52B1 **Gemona** Italy
100B3 **Gemsbok** *Nat Pk* Botswana
98C1 **Geneina** Sudan
34C3 **General Acha** Arg
34C3 **General Alvear** Buenos Aires, Arg
34B2 **General Alvear** Mendoza, Arg

34C2 **General Arenales** Arg
34D3 **General Belgrano** Arg
112B2 **General Belgrano** *Base* Ant
112C2 **General Bernardo O'Higgins** *Base* Ant
34D3 **General Conesa** Buenos Aires, Arg
30D3 **General Eugenio A Garay** Par
34D3 **General Guido** Arg
34C3 **General La Madrid** Arg
34C2 **General Levalle** Arg
30C4 **General Manuel Belgrano** *Mt* Arg
34D3 **General Paz** Buenos Aires, Arg
34C3 **General Pico** Arg
34C2 **General Pinto** Arg
34D3 **General Pirán** Arg
29C3 **General Roca** Arg
79C4 **General Santos** Phil
34C3 **General Viamonte** Arg
34C3 **General Villegas** Arg
15C2 **Genesee** *R* USA
15C2 **Geneseo** USA
Geneva = Genève
18A1 **Geneva** Nebraska, USA
15C2 **Geneva** New York, USA
Geneva,L of = Lac Léman
52A1 **Genève** Switz
50B2 **Genil** *R* Spain
Genoa = Genova
109C3 **Genoa** Aust
52A2 **Genova** Italy
32J7 **Genovesa** *I* Ecuador
46B1 **Gent** Belg
78B4 **Genteng** Indon
56C2 **Genthin** Germany
93E1 **Geokchay** USSR
100B4 **George** S Africa
7D4 **George** *R* Can
109C2 **George,L** Aust
17B2 **George,L** Florida, USA
15D2 **George,L** New York, USA
111A2 **George Sd** NZ
109C4 **George Town** Aust
15C3 **Georgetown** Delaware, USA
33F2 **Georgetown** Guyana
14B3 **Georgetown** Kentucky, USA
77C4 **George Town** Malay
27N2 **Georgetown** St Vincent
17C1 **Georgetown** S Carolina, USA
19A3 **Georgetown** Texas, USA
97A3 **Georgetown** The Gambia
112C8 **George V Land** Region, Ant
17B1 **Georgia** State, USA
14B1 **Georgian B** Can
13C3 **Georgia,Str of** Can
106C3 **Georgina** *R* Aust
60E3 **Georgiu-Dezh** USSR
61F5 **Georgiyevsk** USSR
57C2 **Gera** Germany
46B1 **Geraardsbergen** Belg
111B2 **Geraldine** NZ
106A3 **Geraldton** Aust
10B2 **Geraldton** Can
94B3 **Gerar** *R* Israel
4C3 **Gerdine,Mt** USA
12E2 **Gerdova Peak** *Mt* USA
77C4 **Gerik** Malay
60B4 **Gerlachovsky** *Mt* Pol
13C1 **Germanson Lodge** Can
56C2 **Germany** Republic, Europe
101G1 **Germiston** S Africa
46D1 **Gerolstein** Germany
51C1 **Gerona** Spain

46E1 **Geseke** Germany
99E2 **Gestro** *R* Eth
50B1 **Getafe** Spain
16A3 **Gettysburg** Pennsylvania, USA
93D2 **Gevaş** Turk
55B2 **Gevgeliija** Yugos
47B1 **Gex** France
94C2 **Ghabāghib** Syria
96C1 **Ghadamis** Libya
90B2 **Ghaem Shahr** Iran
86A1 **Ghāghara** *R* India
97B4 **Ghana** Republic, Africa
100B3 **Ghanzi** Botswana
96C1 **Ghardaïa** Alg
95A1 **Gharyan** Libya
95A2 **Ghāt** Libya
84D3 **Ghāziābād** India
84C3 **Ghazi Khan** Pak
84B2 **Ghazni** Afghan
54C1 **Gheorghe G-Dej** Rom
54C1 **Gheorgheni** Rom
88E4 **Ghudamis** Alg
90D3 **Ghurian** Afghan
95B2 **Gialo** Libya
99E2 **Giamame** Somalia
53C3 **Giarre** Italy
100A3 **Gibeon** Namibia
50A2 **Gibraltar** Colony, SW Europe
50A2 **Gibraltar,Str of** Spain/ Africa
106B3 **Gibson Desert** Aust
20B1 **Gibsons** Can
87B1 **Giddalūr** India
57B2 **Giessen** Germany
17B2 **Gifford** USA
74D3 **Gifu** Japan
42B2 **Gigha** *I* Scot
52B2 **Giglio** *I* Italy
50A1 **Gijón** Spain
107D2 **Gilbert** *R* Aust
13C2 **Gilbert,Mt** Can
101C2 **Gilé** Mozam
94B2 **Gilead** Region, Jordan
95B2 **Gilf Kebir Plat** Egypt
109C2 **Gilgandra** Aust
84C1 **Gilgit** Pak
84C1 **Gilgit** *R* Pak
108C2 **Gilgunnia** Aust
7A4 **Gillam** Can
108A2 **Gilles** *L* Aust
13B2 **Gill I** Can
14A1 **Gills Rock** USA
14A2 **Gilman** USA
22B2 **Gilroy** USA
8D1 **Gimli** Can
101H1 **Gingindlovu** S Africa
79C4 **Gingoog** Phil
99E2 **Ginir** Eth
55B3 **Gióna** *Mt* Greece
109C3 **Gippsland** *Mts* Aust
14B2 **Girard** USA
32C3 **Girardot** Colombia
44C3 **Girdle Ness** *Pen* Scot
93C1 **Giresun** Turk
85C4 **Gir Hills** India
98B2 **Giri** *R* Zaïre
86B2 **Girīdīh** India
48B2 **Gironde** *R* France
42B2 **Girvan** Scot
111C2 **Gisborne** NZ
46A2 **Gisors** France
99C3 **Gitega** Burundi
Giuba,R = Juba,R
54C2 **Giurgiu** Rom
46C1 **Givet** Belg
58C2 **Gizycko** Pol
55B2 **Gjirokastër** Alb
4J3 **Gjoatlaven** Can
39G6 **Gjøvik** Nor
7D5 **Glace Bay** Can
12G3 **Glacier Bay Nat Mon** USA
13E3 **Glacier Nat Pk** USA/ Can
20B1 **Glacier Peak** *Mt* USA

6B2	Glacier Str Can
107E3	Gladstone Queensland, Aust
108A2	Gladstone S Aust, Aust
109C4	Gladstone Tasmania, Aust
14A1	Gladstone USA
38A1	Glama *Mt* Iceland
39G6	Glåma *R* Nor
46D2	Glan *R* Germany
47C1	Glarner *Mts* Switz
47C1	Glarus Switz
18A2	Glasco USA
8C2	Glasgow Montana, USA
42B2	Glasgow Scot
16B3	Glassboro USA
43C4	Glastonbury Eng
61H2	Glazov USSR
59B3	Gleisdorf Austria
110C1	Glen Afton NZ
16A3	Glen Burnie USA
101H1	Glencoe S Africa
9B3	Glendale Arizona, USA
22C3	Glendale California, USA
12E2	Glenhallen USA
109D1	Glen Innes Aust
109C1	Glenmorgan Aust
109D2	Glenreagh Aust
16A3	Glen Rock USA
19A3	Glen Rose USA
44C3	Glenrothes UK
15D2	Glens Falls USA
45B1	Glenties Irish Rep
19B3	Glenwood Arkansas, USA
8C3	Glenwood Springs USA
39F6	Glittertind *Mt* Nor
59B2	Gliwice Pol
9B3	Globe USA
58B2	Głogów Pol
38G5	Glomfjord Nor
109D2	Gloucester Aust
43C4	Gloucester Eng
16D1	Gloucester USA
58D1	Glubokoye USSR
60D3	Glukhov USSR
59B3	Gmünd Austria
57C3	Gmunden Austria
58B2	Gniezno Pol
100A3	Goabeg Namibia
87A1	Goa, Daman and Diu Union Territory, India
86C1	Goālpāra India
99D2	Goba Eth
100A3	Gobabis Namibia
34C2	Gobernador Crespo Arg
34B3	Gobernador Duval Arg
72B1	Gobi *Desert* China/ Mongolia
75B2	Gobo Japan
87B1	Godag India
87C1	Godāvari *R* India
14B2	Goderich Can
6E3	Godhavn Greenland
85C4	Godhra India
34B2	Godoy Cruz Arg
7A4	Gods L Can
6E3	Godthab Greenland
	Godwin Austen = K2
35B1	Goiandira Brazil
35B1	Goianésia Brazil
35B1	Goiânia Brazil
35A1	Goiás Brazil
31B4	Goiás State, Brazil
35A2	Goio-Erê Brazil
99D2	Gojab *R* Eth
55C2	Gökçeada *I* Turk
55C3	Gökova Körfezi *B* Turk
92C2	Göksun Turk
63C3	Gol *R* USSR

86C1	Golāghāt India
93C2	Gölbaşi Turk
20C2	Golconda USA
20B2	Gold Beach USA
109D1	Gold Coast Aust
13D2	Golden Can
110B2	Golden B NZ
20B1	Goldendale USA
22A2	Golden Gate *Chan* USA
19B4	Golden Meadow USA
21B2	Goldfield USA
13B3	Gold River Can
56C2	Goleniów Pol
22C3	Goleta USA
52A2	Golfe d'Ajaccio *G* Corse
96D1	Golfe de Gabes *G* Tunisia
	Golfe de Gascogne = Biscay,Bay of
52A2	Golfe de St Florent *G* Corse
48B2	Golfe de St-Malo *B* France
49C3	Golfe du Lion *G* France
29B4	Golfo Corcovado *G* Chile
50B2	Golfo de Almeira *G* Spain
29B4	Golfo de Ancud *G* Chile
25D2	Golfo de Batabano *G* Cuba
50A2	Golfo de Cadiz *G* Spain
53A3	Golfo de Cagliari *G* Sardegna
24A1	Golfo de California *G* Mexico
25D4	Golfo de Chiriqui *G* Panama
25D3	Golfo de Fonseca *G* Honduras
26B2	Golfo de Guacanayabo *G* Cuba
32A4	Golfo de Guayaquil *G* Ecuador
26B5	Golfo del Darien *G* Colombia/Panama
32A2	Golfo de los Mosquitos *G* Panama
25D3	Golfo del Papagaya *G* Nic
51B2	Golfo de Mazarrón *G* Spain
25D4	Golfo de Nicoya *G* Costa Rica
53A3	Golfo de Oristano *G* Sardegna
25E4	Golfo de Panamá *G* Panama
25D3	Golfo de Papagayo *G* Costa Rica
27E4	Golfo de Paria *G* Ven
29B5	Golfo de Penas *G* Chile
49D3	Golfo de St Florent *G* Corse
51C1	Golfo de San Jorge *G* Spain
24C3	Golfo de Tehuantepec *G* Mexico
32B3	Golfo de Torugas *G* Colombia
32B2	Golfo de Uraba *G* Colombia
51C2	Golfo de Valencia *G* Spain
27C4	Golfo de Venezuela *G* Ven
52A2	Golfo di Genova *G* Italy
53C3	Golfo di Policastro *G* Italy
53C3	Golfo di Squillace *G* Italy

53C2	Golfo di Taranto *G* Italy
52B1	Golfo di Venezia *G* Italy
25D4	Golfo Dulce *G* Costa Rica
29C5	Golfo San Jorge *G* Arg
29D4	Golfo San Matías *G* Arg
68B3	Golmud China
99E2	Golocha Eth
12B2	Golovin B USA
74F2	Golovnino USSR
99C3	Goma Zaïre
97D3	Gombe Nig
60D3	Gomel USSR
96A2	Gomera *I* Canary Is
24B2	Gómez Palacio Mexico
63E2	Gonam *R* USSR
90C2	Gonbad-e Kāvūs Iran
86A1	Gonda India
85C4	Gondal India
99D1	Gondar Eth
92A1	Gönen Turk
55C3	Gonen *R* Turk
73A4	Gongga Shan *Mt* China
72A2	Gonghe China
97D3	Gongola *R* Nig
22B2	Gonzales California, USA
19A4	Gonzales Texas, USA
34C3	Gonzalez Chaves Arg
13C2	Good Hope Mt Can
8C2	Goodland USA
12B3	Goodnews Bay USA
109C1	Goodooga *R* Aust
42D3	Goole Eng
108C2	Goolgowi Aust
108A3	Goolwa Aust
106A4	Goomalling Aust
108C2	Goombalie Aust
109D1	Goomer Aust
109D1	Goomeri Aust
109D1	Goondiwindi Aust
7E4	Goose Bay Can
17C1	Goose Creek USA
20B2	Goose L USA
87B1	Gooty India
63C2	Gora Munku Sardyk *Mt* USSR
54A2	Goražde Yugos
4D3	Gordon USA
13E1	Gordon L Can
15C3	Gordonsville USA
98B2	Goré Chad
99D2	Gore Eth
111A3	Gore NZ
63F2	Gore Topko *Mt* USSR
45C2	Gorey Irish Rep
90B2	Gorgān Iran
93E2	Goris USSR
52B1	Gorizia Italy
65F4	Gor'kiy USSR
61F2	Gor'kovskoye Vodokhranilishche *Res* USSR
57C2	Gorlitz Germany
60E4	Gorlovka USSR
22C3	Gorman USA
54C2	Gorna Orjahovica Bulg
68A1	Gorno-Altaysk USSR
69G2	Gornozavodsk USSR
61F2	Gorodets USSR
59C3	Gorodok Ukrainskaya S.S.R., USSR
59D3	Gorodok Ukrainskaya S.S.R., USSR
71F4	Goroka PNG
86A1	Gorokhpur India
101C2	Gorongosa Mozam
71D3	Gorontalo Indon
61K2	Goro Yurma *Mt* USSR
45B2	Gort Irish Rep
63C2	Goryachinsk USSR
59D3	Goryn' *R* USSR
59C2	Góry Świetokrzyskie *Upland* Pol

64G3	Gory Tel'pos-iz' *Mt* USSR
39H8	Gorzow Wielkopolski Pol
74E2	Goshogawara Japan
52C2	Gospić Yugos
54B2	Gostivar Yugos
58B2	Gostynin Pol
39G7	Göteborg Sweden
98B2	Gotel *Mts* Nig
39H7	Gotland *I* Sweden
74B4	Gotō-retto *I* Japan
39H7	Gotska Sandön *I* Sweden
74C3	Gōtsu Japan
98B1	Goudoumaria Niger
103H7	Gough I Atlantic O
109C2	Goulburn Aust
97B3	Goumbou Mali
97B3	Goundam Mali
98B1	Gouré Niger
97B3	Gourma Rharous Mali
46A2	Gournay-en-Bray France
95A3	Gouro Chad
71E5	Gove Pen Aust
60B4	Goverla *Mt* USSR
35C1	Governador Valadares Brazil
86A2	Govind Ballabh Paht Sāgar *L* India
15C2	Gowanda USA
84B3	Gowārān Afghan
30E4	Goya Arg
98C1	Goz-Beïda Chad
53B3	Gozo *I* Medit S
95C3	Goz Regeb Sudan
100B4	Graaff-Reinet S Africa
15C1	Gracefield Can
109D1	Grafton Aust
8D2	Grafton N Dakota, USA
14B3	Grafton W Virginia, USA
5E4	Graham *I* Can
13C1	Graham *R* Can
13E1	Graham L Can
100B4	Grahamstown S Africa
31B3	Grajaú Brazil
58C2	Grajewo Pol
55B2	Grámmos *Mt* Greece/ Alb
44C3	Grampian Region, Scot
44B3	Grampian Mts Scot
32C3	Granada Colombia
25D3	Granada Nic
50B2	Granada Spain
15D1	Granby Can
96A2	Gran Canaria *I* Canary Is
30D4	Gran Chaco *Region* Arg
14A2	Grand *R* Michigan, USA
18B1	Grand *R* Missouri, USA
27Q2	Grand B Dominica
11C4	Grand Bahama *I* The Bahamas
7E5	Grand Bank Can
102F2	Grand Banks Atlantic O
97B4	Grand Bassam Ivory Coast
9B3	Grand Canyon USA
26A3	Grand Cayman *I* Caribbean S
13E2	Grand Centre Can
20C1	Grand Coulee USA
34B3	Grande *R* Arg
31C4	Grande *R* Bahia, Brazil
35B1	Grande *R* Minas Gerais/São Paulo, Brazil
13D2	Grande Cache Can
47A2	Grande Chartreuse Region, France
101D2	Grande Comore *I* Comoros
13D1	Grande Prairie Can

19A3 **Grande Prairie** USA
95A3 **Grand Erg de Bilma**
        Desert Niger
96B2 **Grand erg Occidental**
        Mts Alg
96C2 **Grand erg Oriental**
        Mts Alg
7C4 **Grande Rivière de la**
        Baleine *R* Can
20C1 **Grande Ronde** *R* USA
7D5 **Grand Falls** New
        Brunswick, Can
7E5 **Grand Falls**
        Newfoundland, Can
20C1 **Grand Forks** Can
8D2 **Grand Forks** USA
16B1 **Grand Gorge** USA
14A2 **Grand Haven** USA
19C3 **Grand Isle** USA
19B4 **Grand L** USA
15D1 **Grand Mère** Can
50A2 **Grândola** Port
5J4 **Grand Rapids** Can
14A2 **Grand Rapids**
        Michigan, USA
10A2 **Grand Rapids**
        Minnesota, USA
47B2 **Grand St Bernard** *P*
        Italy/Switz
8B2 **Grand Teton** *Mt* USA
8B2 **Grand Teton Nat Pk**
        USA
46A2 **Grandvilliers** France
25D1 **Grangeburg** USA
51C1 **Granollérs** Spain
52A1 **Gran Paradiso** *Mt* Italy
47D1 **Gran Pilastro** *Mt*
        Austria/Italy
43D3 **Grantham** Eng
21B2 **Grant,Mt** USA
44C3 **Grantown-on-Spey**
        Scot
9C3 **Grants** USA
20B2 **Grants Pass** USA
48B2 **Granville** France
5H4 **Granville L** Can
35C1 **Grão Mogol** Brazil
49D3 **Grasse** France
21A2 **Grass Valley** USA
5H5 **Gravelbourg** Can
46B1 **Gravelines** France
100C3 **Gravelotte** S Africa
15C2 **Gravenhurst** Can
109D1 **Gravesend** Aust
12H3 **Gravina I** USA
12B2 **Grayling** USA
20B1 **Grays Harbor** *B* USA
14B3 **Grayson** USA
18C2 **Grayville** USA
59B3 **Graz** Austria
27H1 **Great** *R* Jamaica
11C4 **Great Abaco** *I*
        The Bahamas
106B4 **Great Australian Bight**
        G Aust
16B3 **Great B** New Jersey,
        USA
25E2 **Great Bahama Bank**
        The Bahamas
110C1 **Great Barrier I** NZ
107D2 **Great Barrier Reef** *Is*
'   Aust
16C1 **Great Barrington** USA
4F3 **Great Bear L** Can
9D2 **Great Bend** USA
107D3 **Great Dividing Range**
        Mts Aust
42D2 **Great Driffield** Eng
16B3 **Great Egg Harbor** *B*
        USA
112B10 **Greater Antarctic**
        Region, Ant
26B2 **Greater Antilles** *Is*
        Caribbean S
43D4 **Greater London**
        County, Eng
43C3 **Greater Manchester**
        County, Eng

25E2 **Great Exuma** *I*
        The Bahamas
8B2 **Great Falls** USA
44B3 **Great Glen** *V* Scot
86B1 **Great Himalayan Range**
        Mts Asia
11C4 **Great Inagua** *I*
        The Bahamas
100B4 **Great Karroo** *Mts*
        S Africa
109C4 **Great L** Aust
100A3 **Great Namaland**
        Region, Namibia
42C3 **Great Ormes Head** *C*
        Wales
11C4 **Great Ragged** *I*
        The Bahamas
99D3 **Great Ruaha** *R* Tanz
15D2 **Great Sacandaga L**
        USA
8B2 **Great Salt L** USA
95B2 **Great Sand Sea** Libya/
        Egypt
106B3 **Great Sandy Desert**
        Aust
8A2 **Great Sandy Desert**
        USA
        Great Sandy I=Fraser I
4G3 **Great Slave L** Can
16C2 **Great South B** USA
106B3 **Great Victoria Desert**
        Aust
72B2 **Great Wall** China
43E3 **Great Yarmouth** Eng
94B1 **Greco,C** Cyprus
55B3 **Greece**
        Republic, Europe
15C2 **Greece** USA
8C2 **Greeley** USA
6B1 **Greely Fjord** Can
14A1 **Green B** USA
14A2 **Green Bay** USA
14A3 **Greencastle** Indiana,
        USA
16C1 **Greenfield**
        Massachusetts, USA
14A2 **Greenfield** Wisconsin,
        USA
13F2 **Green Lake** Can
6F2 **Greenland**
        Dependency,
        N Atlantic O
102H1 **Greenland Basin**
        Greenland S
1B1 **Greenland S** Greenland
42B2 **Greenock** Scot
16C2 **Greenport** USA
16B3 **Greensboro** Maryland,
        USA
11C3 **Greensboro** N Carolina,
        USA
15C2 **Greensburg**
        Pennsylvania, USA
44B3 **Greenstone** *Pt* Scot
18C2 **Greenup** USA
17A1 **Greenville** Alabama,
        USA
97B4 **Greenville** Lib
19B3 **Greenville** Mississippi,
        USA
16D1 **Greenville**
        N Hampshire, USA
14B2 **Greenville** Ohio, USA
17B1 **Greenville** S Carolina,
        USA
19A3 **Greenville** Texas, USA
43E4 **Greenwich** Eng
16C2 **Greenwich** USA
16B3 **Greenwood** Delaware,
        USA
19B3 **Greenwood**
        Mississippi, USA
17B1 **Greenwood** S Carolina,
        USA
18B2 **Greers Ferry L** USA
108A1 **Gregory,L** Aust
107D2 **Gregory Range** *Mts*
        Aust

56C2 **Greifswald** Germany
64F3 **Gremikha** USSR
56C1 **Grenå** Den
19C3 **Grenada** USA
27E4 **Grenada** *I* Caribbean S
27E4 **Grenadines,The** *Is*
        Caribbean S
109C2 **Grenfell** Aust
49D2 **Grenoble** France
27M2 **Grenville** Grenada
107D2 **Grenville,C** Aust
20B1 **Gresham** USA
78C4 **Gresik** Jawa, Indon
78A3 **Gresik** Sumatera,
        Indon
19B4 **Gretna** USA
111B2 **Grey** *R* NZ
12G2 **Grey Hunter Pk** *Mt*
        Can
7E4 **Grey Is** Can
16C1 **Greylock,Mt** USA
111B2 **Greymouth** NZ
107D3 **Grey Range** *Mts* Aust
45C2 **Greystones** Irish Rep
101H1 **Greytown** S Africa
101F1 **Griekwastad** S Africa
17B1 **Griffin** USA
108C2 **Griffith** Aust
107D5 **Grim,C** Aust
15C2 **Grimsby** Can
42D3 **Grimsby** Eng
38B1 **Grimsey** *I* Iceland
13D1 **Grimshaw** Can
39F7 **Grimstad** Nor
47C1 **Grindelwald** Switz
6A2 **Grinnell Pen** Can
6B2 **Grise Fjord** Can
61H1 **Griva** USSR
39J7 **Grobina** USSR
58C2 **Grodno** USSR
86A1 **Gromati** *R* India
56B2 **Groningen** Neth
106C2 **Groote Eylandt** *I* Aust
100A2 **Grootfontein** Namibia
100B3 **Grootvloer** *Salt L*
        S Africa
27P2 **Gros Islet** St Lucia
46E1 **Grosser Feldberg** *Mt*
        Germany
52B2 **Grosseto** Italy
46E2 **Gross-Gerau** Germany
57C3 **Grossglockner** *Mt*
        Austria
47E1 **Gross Venediger** *Mt*
        Austria
12C3 **Grosvenor,L** USA
22B2 **Groveland** USA
21A2 **Grover City** USA
15D2 **Groveton** USA
61G5 **Groznyy** USSR
58B2 **Grudziadz** Pol
100A3 **Grünau** Namibia
44E2 **Grutness** Scot
65F5 **Gruzinskaya SSR**
        Republic, USSR
61F3 **Gryazi** USSR
61E2 **Gryazovets** USSR
29G8 **Grytviken** South
        Georgia
45A2 **Gt Blasket** *I* Irish Rep
35C2 **Guaçuí** Brazil
23A1 **Guadalajara** Mexico
50B1 **Guadalajara** Spain
107E1 **Guadalcanal** *I*
        Solomon Is
50B2 **Guadalimar** *R* Spain
51B1 **Guadalope** *R* Spain
50B2 **Guadalqivir** *R* Spain
24B2 **Guadalupe** Mexico
3G6 **Guadalupe** *I* Mexico
27E3 **Guadeloupe** *I*
        Caribbean S
50B2 **Guadian** *R* Spain
50A2 **Guadiana** *R* Port
50B2 **Guadix** Spain
32D6 **Guajará Mirim** Brazil
32C1 **Guajira,Pen de**
        Colombia

32B4 **Gualaceo** Ecuador
34D2 **Gualeguay** Arg
34D2 **Gualeguaychú** Arg
71F2 **Guam** *I* Pacific O
34C3 **Guamini** Arg
77C5 **Gua Musang** Malay
23A1 **Guanajuato** Mexico
23A1 **Guanajuato** State,
        Mexico
32D2 **Guanare** Ven
25D2 **Guane** Cuba
73C5 **Guangdong** Province,
        China
73A3 **Guanghan** China
72C3 **Guanghua** China
73A4 **Guangmao Shan** *Mt*
        China
73B5 **Guangnan** China
72B3 **Guangyuan** China
73D4 **Guangze** China
67F3 **Guangzhou** China
35C1 **Guanhães** Brazil
32D3 **Guania** *R* Colombia
27E5 **Guanipa** *R* Ven
26B2 **Guantánamo** Cuba
72D1 **Guanting Shuiku** *Res*
        China
73B5 **Guanxi** Province,
        China
73A3 **Guan Xian** China
32B2 **Guapa** Colombia
33E6 **Guaporé** *R* Brazil/Bol
30C2 **Guaquí** Bol
32B4 **Guaranda** Ecuador
30F4 **Guarapuava** Brazil
35B2 **Guaratinguetá** Brazil
50A1 **Guarda** Port
99F1 **Guardafui,C** Somalia
35B1 **Guarda Mor** Brazil
9C4 **Guasave** Mexico
47D2 **Guastalla** Italy
25C3 **Guatemala** Guatemala
25C3 **Guatemala** Republic,
        Cent America
34C3 **Guatraché** Arg
32C3 **Guavrare** *R* Colombia
35B2 **Guaxupé** Brazil
27L1 **Guayaguayare**
        Trinidad
32A4 **Guayaquil** Ecuador
24A2 **Guaymas** Mexico
34D2 **Guayquiraro** *R* Arg
99D2 **Guba** Eth
100B2 **Guba** Zaïre
99E2 **Guban** *Region*
        Somalia
79B3 **Gubat** Phil
56C2 **Gubin** Pol
87B2 **Güdür** India
14B2 **Guelpho** Can
26A2 **Guenabacoa** Cuba
98C1 **Guéréda** Chad
48C2 **Guéret** France
48B2 **Guernsey** *I* UK
23A2 **Guerrero** State,
        Mexico
99D2 **Gughe** *Mt* Eth
63E2 **Gugigu** China
71F2 **Guguan** *I* Pacific O
109C2 **Guiargambone** Aust
73C4 **Guidong** China
97B4 **Guiglo** Ivory Coast
73C5 **Gui Jiang** *R* China
43D4 **Guildford** Eng
73C4 **Guilin** China
47B2 **Guillestre** France
72A2 **Guinan** China
97A3 **Guinea** Republic,
        Africa
102H4 **Guinea Basin** Atlantic
        O
97A3 **Guinea-Bissau**
        Republic, Africa
97C4 **Guinea,G of** W Africa
26A2 **Güines** Cuba
97B3 **Guir** *Well* Mali
84C2 **Guiranwala** Pak
33E1 **Güiria** Ven

46B2 **Guise** France	56B2 **Gütersloh** Germany	74A2 **Haicheng** China	14C2 **Hamilton** Can
79C3 **Guiuan** Phil	18C2 **Guthrie** Kentucky, USA	76D1 **Hai Duong** Viet	110C1 **Hamilton** NZ
73B5 **Gui Xian** China	18A2 **Guthrie** Oklahoma, USA	94B2 **Haifa** Israel	14B3 **Hamilton** Ohio, USA
73B4 **Guiyang** China		94B2 **Haifa,B of** Israel	42B2 **Hamilton** Scot
73B4 **Guizhou** Province, China	23B1 **Gutiérrez Zamora** Mexico	72D2 **Hai He** R China	7E4 **Hamilton Inlet** B Can
85C4 **Gujarāt** State, India	33F3 **Guyana** Republic, S America	73C5 **Haikang** China	22B2 **Hamilton,Mt** USA
84C2 **Gujrat** Pak		76E1 **Haikou** China	38K6 **Hamina** Fin
87B1 **Gulbarga** India	102F4 **Guyana Basin** Atlantic O	80C3 **Ha'il** S Arabia	86A1 **Hamirpur** India
58D1 **Gulbene** USSR		86C2 **Hailākāndi** India	56B2 **Hamm** Germany
87B1 **Guledagudda** India	72C1 **Guyang** China	63D3 **Hailar** China	95A2 **Hammādah al Hamra** Upland Libya
80D3 **Gulf,The** S W Asia	48B3 **Guyenne** Region, France	74B2 **Hailong** China	
109C2 **Gulgong** Aust		69E2 **Hailun** China	38H6 **Hammerdal** Sweden
73B4 **Gulin** China	9C3 **Guymon** USA	38J5 **Hailuoto** I Fin	38J4 **Hammerfest** Nor
12E2 **Gulkana** USA	109D2 **Guyra** Aust	76D2 **Hainan** I China	14A2 **Hammond** Illinois, USA
12E2 **Gulkana** R USA	72B2 **Guyuan** China	12G3 **Haines** USA	
13E2 **Gull L** Can	109C2 **Gwabegar** Aust	12G2 **Haines Junction** Can	19B3 **Hammond** Louisiana, USA
13F2 **Gull Lake** Can	85D3 **Gwalior** India	59B3 **Hainfeld** Austria	
55C3 **Güllük Körfezi** B Turk	100B3 **Gwanda** Zim	73B5 **Haiphong** Vietnam	16B3 **Hammonton** USA
99D2 **Gulu** Uganda	98C2 **Gwane** Zaïre	26C3 **Haiti** Republic, Caribbean S	111B3 **Hampden** NZ
109C1 **Guluguba** Aust	82A3 **Gwardar** Pak		43D4 **Hampshire** County, Eng
97C3 **Gumel** Nig	45B1 **Gweebarra B** Irish Rep	95C3 **Haiya** Sudan	
46D1 **Gummersbach** Germany	89G9 **Gwelo** Zim	72A2 **Haiyan** China	19B3 **Hampton** Arkansas, USA
	43C4 **Gwent** County, Wales	72B2 **Haiyuan** China	
86A2 **Gumpla** India	100B2 **Gweru** Zim	72D3 **Haizhou Wan** B China	91C4 **Hāmūn-e Jaz Mūrīan** L Iran
93C1 **Gümüşhane** Turk	109C1 **Gwydir** R Aust	59C3 **Hajdúböszörmény** Hung	
85D4 **Guna** India	43C3 **Gwynedd** Wales		84B3 **Hamun-i-Lora** Salt L Pak
99D1 **Guna** Mt Eth	65F5 **Gyandzha** USSR	75B1 **Hajiki-saki** Pt Japan	
109C3 **Gundagai** Aust	86B1 **Gyangzê** China	86C2 **Haka** Burma	21C4 **Hana** Hawaiian Is
98B3 **Gungu** Zaïre	68B3 **Gyaring Hu** L China	21C4 **Hakalau** Hawaiian Is	21C4 **Hanalei** Hawaiian Is
6H3 **Gunnbjørn Fjeld** Mt Greenland	64J2 **Gydanskiy Poluostrov** Pen USSR	93D2 **Hakkâri** Turk	74E3 **Hanamaki** Japan
		74E2 **Hakodate** Japan	72C2 **Hancheng** China
109D2 **Gunnedah** Aust	86B1 **Gyirong** China	75B1 **Hakui** Japan	73C3 **Hanchuan** China
87B1 **Guntakal** India	6F3 **Gyldenløves** Fjord Greenland	75B1 **Haku-san** Mt Japan	15C3 **Hancock** Maryland, USA
17A1 **Guntersville** USA		92C2 **Ḥalab** Syria	
17A1 **Guntersville L** USA	109D1 **Gympie** Aust	93E3 **Halabja** Iraq	10B2 **Hancock** Michigan, USA
87C1 **Guntūr** India	59B3 **Gyöngyös** Hung	95C2 **Halaib** Sudan	
77C5 **Gunung Batu Putch** Mt Malay	59B3 **Györ** Hung	94C1 **Halba** Leb	75B2 **Handa** Japan
		56C2 **Halberstadt** Germany	72C2 **Handan** China
78D3 **Gunung Besar** Mt Indon		79B3 **Halcon,Mt** Phil	99D3 **Handeni** Tanz
	## H	39G7 **Halden** Nor	72B2 **Hanggin Qi** China
78D2 **Gunung Bulu** Mt Indon		86B2 **Haldia** India	39J7 **Hangö** Fin
	38K6 **Haapajärvi** Fin	84D3 **Haldwāni** India	73E3 **Hangzhou** China
78A3 **Gunung Gedang** Mt Indon	60B2 **Haapsalu** USSR	13C1 **Halfway** R Can	73E3 **Hangzhou Wan** B China
	56A2 **Haarlem** Neth	7D5 **Halifax** Can	
78C2 **Gunung Lawit** Mt Malay	46D1 **Haarstrang** Region, Germany	42D3 **Halifax** Eng	111B2 **Hanmer Springs** NZ
		6D1 **Hall Basin** Sd Can	13E2 **Hanna** Can
78C4 **Gunung Lawu** Mt Indon	25D2 **Habana** Cuba	6B3 **Hall Beach** Can	18B2 **Hannibal** USA
	86C2 **Habiganj** Bang	46C1 **Halle** Belg	56B2 **Hannover** Germany
78D2 **Gunung Menyapa** Mt Indon	74D4 **Hachijō-jima** I Japan	56C2 **Halle** Germany	39G7 **Hanöbukten** B Sweden
	75B1 **Hachiman** Japan	112B1 **Halley** Base Ant	
78D2 **Gunung Niapa** Mt Indon	74E2 **Hachinohe** Japan	39F6 **Hallingdal** R Nor	76D1 **Hanoi** Viet
	75B1 **Hachioji** Japan	6D3 **Hall Pen** Can	16A3 **Hanover** USA
78A3 **Gunung Patah** Mt Indon	16B2 **Hackettstown** USA	106B2 **Hall's Creek** Aust	29B6 **Hanover** I Chile
	108A2 **Hack,Mt** Aust	71D3 **Halmahera** I Indon	72B3 **Han Shui** China
78C4 **Gunung Raung** Mt Indon	42C2 **Haddington** Scot	39G7 **Halmstad** Sweden	73C3 **Han Shui** R China
	108B1 **Haddon Corner** Aust	56B2 **Haltern** Germany	85D3 **Hānsi** India
78A3 **Gunung Resag** Mt Indon	108B1 **Haddon Downs** Aust	38J5 **Halti** Mt Nor	68C2 **Hantay** Mongolia
	97D3 **Hadejia** Nig	42C2 **Haltwhistle** Eng	72B3 **Hanzhong** China
78D3 **Gunung Sarempaka** Mt Indon	97C3 **Hadejia** R Nig	91B4 **Halul** I Qatar	86B2 **Haora** India
	94B2 **Hadera** Israel	94B3 **Haluza** Hist Site Israel	38J5 **Haparanda** Sweden
78C4 **Gunung Sumbing** Mt Indon	56B1 **Haderslev** Den	75A2 **Hamada** Japan	86C1 **Hāpoli** India
	81D4 **Hadiboh** Socotra	96C2 **Hamada de Tinrhert** Desert Region Alg	92C4 **Haql** S Arabia
77C5 **Gunung Tahan** Mt Malay	4H2 **Hadley B** Can		91A5 **Haradh** S Arabia
	73B5 **Hadong** Vietnam	96B2 **Hamada du Dra** Upland Alg	99E2 **Hara Fanna** Eth
78A2 **Gunung Talakmau** Mt Indon	81C4 **Hadramawt** Region, Yemen		75C1 **Haramachi** Japan
		90A3 **Hamadān** Iran	99E2 **Harar** Eth
100A2 **Gunza** Angola	56C1 **Hadsund** Den	96B2 **Hamada Tounassine** Region, Alg	101C2 **Harare** Zim
72D3 **Guoyang** China	74B3 **Haeju** N Korea		98C1 **Harazé** Chad
84D2 **Gurdāspur** India	91A4 **Hafar al Bātin** S Arabia	92C2 **Hamāh** Syria	14B2 **Harbor Beach** USA
84D3 **Gurgaon** India		75B2 **Hamamatsu** Japan	85D4 **Harda** India
86A1 **Gurkha** Nepal	6D2 **Haffners Bjerg** Mt Greenland	39G6 **Hamar** Nor	39F6 **Hardangerfjord** Inlet Nor
92C2 **Gürün** Turk		87C3 **Hambantota** Sri Lanka	
31B2 **Gurupi** R Brazil	84C2 **Hafizabad** Pak	19B3 **Hamburg** Arkansas, USA	46D2 **Hardt** Region, Germany
100C2 **Guruve** Zim	86C1 **Hāflong** India	18A1 **Hamburg** Iowa, USA	
72A1 **Gurvan Sayhan Uul** Upland Mongolia	38A2 **Hafnafjöður** Iceland	16B2 **Hamburg** Pennsylvania, USA	108A2 **Hardwicke B** Aust
	12B3 **Hagemeister** I USA		18B2 **Hardy** USA
61H4 **Gur'yev** USSR	56B2 **Hagen** Germany	56B2 **Hamburg** Germany	99E2 **Hargeysa** Somalia
65F5 **Gurzinskaya** Republic, USSR	15C3 **Hagerstown** USA	16C2 **Hamden** USA	94B3 **Har Hakippa** Mt Israel
	75A2 **Hagi** Japan	39J6 **Hämeenlinna** Fin	68B3 **Harhu** L China
97C3 **Gusau** Nig	73A5 **Ha Giang** Vietnam	106A3 **Hamersley Range** Mts Aust	78A3 **Hari** R Indon
58C2 **Gusev** USSR	46D2 **Haguenau** France		75A2 **Harima-nada** B Japan
74A3 **Gushan** China	45B2 **Hags Hd** C Irish Rep	74B2 **Hamgyong Sanmaek** Mts N Korea	56B2 **Harlingen** Neth
61F2 **Gus'khrustalnyy** USSR	46D2 **Haguenan** France		9D4 **Harlingen** USA
	96A2 **Hagunia** Well Mor	74B2 **Hamhŭng** N Korea	43E4 **Harlow** Eng
12G3 **Gustavus** USA	69G4 **Haha-jima** I Japan	68B2 **Hami** China	94B2 **Har Meron** Mt Israel
22B2 **Gustine** USA	68B3 **Hah Xil Hu** L China	94B1 **Hamīdīyah** Syria	20C2 **Harney Basin** USA
11B3 **Guston** USA		108B3 **Hamilton** Aust	20C2 **Harney L** USA
			38H6 **Härnösand** Sweden

63B3 **Har Nuur** *L* Mongolia
97B4 **Harper** Lib
12F2 **Harper,Mt** USA
15C3 **Harpers Ferry** USA
94B3 **Har Ramon** *Mt* Israel
7C4 **Harricanaw** *R* Can
16B3 **Harrington** USA
7E4 **Harrington Harbour** Can
44A3 **Harris** *District* Scot
18C2 **Harrisburg** Illinois, USA
16A2 **Harrisburg** Pennsylvania, USA
101G1 **Harrismith** S Africa
18B2 **Harrison** USA
15C3 **Harrisonburg** USA
7E4 **Harrison,C** Can
13C3 **Harrison L** Can
18B2 **Harrisonville** USA
44A3 **Harris,Sound of** *Chan* Scot
14B2 **Harrisville** USA
42D3 **Harrogate** Eng
94B3 **Har Saggi** *Mt* Israel
38H5 **Harstad** Nor
12G2 **Hart** *R* Can
39F6 **Hårteigen** *Mt* Nor
16C2 **Hartford** Connecticut, USA
14A2 **Hartford** Michigan, USA
38G6 **Hartkjølen** *Mt* Nor
108A2 **Hart,L** Aust
43B4 **Hartland Pt** Eng
42D2 **Hartlepool** Eng
19A3 **Hartshorne** USA
17B1 **Hartwell Res** USA
101F1 **Hartz** *R* S Africa
68B2 **Har Us Nuur** *L* Mongolia
43E4 **Harwich** Eng
84D3 **Haryāna** State, India
94B3 **Hāsā** Jordan
94B2 **Hāsbaiya** Leb
43D4 **Haselmere** Eng
75B2 **Hashimoto** Japan
90A2 **Hashtpar** Iran
90A2 **Hashtrūd** Iran
87B2 **Hassan** India
56B2 **Hasselt** Belg
96C2 **Hassi Inifel** Alg
96B2 **Hassi Mdakane** *Well* Alg
96C1 **Hassi Messaoud** Alg
108C3 **Hastings** Aust
43E4 **Hastings** Eng
8D2 **Hastings** Nebraska, USA
110C1 **Hastings** NZ
108B2 **Hatfield** Aust
12B1 **Hatham Inlet** USA
85D3 **Hāthras** India
76D2 **Ha Tinh** Viet
108B2 **Hattah** Aust
11C3 **Hatteras,C** USA
19C3 **Hattiesburg** USA
59B3 **Hatvan** Hung
76D3 **Hau Bon** Viet
99E2 **Haud** Region, Eth
39F7 **Haugesund** Nor
110C1 **Hauhungaroa Range** *Mts* NZ
13F1 **Haultain** *R* Can
110B1 **Hauraki G** NZ
111A3 **Hauroko,L** NZ
47C1 **Hausstock** *Mt* Switz
96B1 **Haut Atlas** *Mts* Mor
98C2 **Haute Kotto** Region, CAR
46C1 **Hautes Fagnes** *Mts* Belg
46B1 **Hautmont** Belg
96B1 **Hauts Plateaux** *Mts* Alg
90D3 **Hauzdar** Iran
18B1 **Havana** USA
Havana = Habana

87B3 **Havankulam** Sri Lanka
110C1 **Havelock North** NZ
43B4 **Haverfordwest** Wales
16D1 **Haverhill** USA
87B2 **Hāveri** India
16C2 **Haverstraw** USA
59B3 **Havlíčkův Brod** Czech
8C2 **Havre** USA
16A3 **Havre de Grace** USA
7D4 **Havre-St-Pierre** Can
54C2 **Havsa** Turk
21C4 **Hawaii** *I* Hawaiian Is
21C4 **Hawaii Volcanoes Nat Pk** Hawaiian Is
111A2 **Hawea,L** NZ
110B1 **Hawera** NZ
42C2 **Hawick** Scot
111A2 **Hawkdun Range** *Mts* NZ
110C1 **Hawke B** NZ
109D2 **Hawke,C** Aust
108A2 **Hawker** Aust
76B1 **Hawng Luk** Burma
93D3 **Hawr al Habbanlyah** *L* Iraq
93E3 **Hawr al Hammár** *L* Iraq
21B2 **Hawthorne** USA
108B2 **Hay** Aust
5G3 **Hay** *R* Can
46D2 **Hayange** France
4B3 **Haycock** USA
7A4 **Hayes** *R* Can
6D2 **Hayes Halvø** *Region* Greenland
12E2 **Hayes,Mt** USA
5G3 **Hay River** Can
18A2 **Haysville** USA
22A2 **Hayward** California, USA
86B2 **Hazārībāg** India
46B1 **Hazebrouck** France
19B3 **Hazelhurst** USA
4G2 **Hazel Str** Can
5F4 **Hazelton** Can
13B1 **Hazelton Mts** Can
6C1 **Hazen L** Can
94B3 **Hazeva** Israel
16B2 **Hazleton** USA
22A1 **Healdsburg** USA
108C3 **Healesville** Aust
12E2 **Healy** USA
104B6 **Heard I** Indian O
19A3 **Hearne** USA
10B2 **Hearst** Can
72D2 **Hebei** Province, China
109C1 **Hebel** Aust
72C2 **Hebi** China
72C2 **Hebian** China
7D4 **Hebron** Can
94B3 **Hebron** Israel
18A1 **Hebron** Nebraska, USA
5E4 **Hecate** *Str* Can
12H3 **Heceta I** USA
73B5 **Hechi** China
4G2 **Hecla and Griper B** Can
111C2 **Hector,Mt** NZ
38G6 **Hede** Sweden
39H6 **Hedemora** Sweden
20C1 **He Devil Mt** USA
56B2 **Heerenveen** Neth
46C1 **Heerlen** Neth
Hefa = Haifa
73D3 **Hefei** China
73B4 **Hefeng** China
69F2 **Hegang** China
75B1 **Hegura-jima** *I* Japan
94B3 **Heidan** *R* Jordan
56B2 **Heide** Germany
101G1 **Heidelberg** Transvaal, S Africa
57B3 **Heidelberg** Germany
63E2 **Heihe** China
101G1 **Heilbron** S Africa
57B3 **Heilbronn** Germany
56C2 **Heiligenstadt** Germany
38K6 **Heinola** Fin
73B4 **Hejiang** China

6J3 **Hekla** *Mt* Iceland
76C1 **Hekou** Viet
73A5 **Hekou Yaozou Zizhixian** China
72B2 **Helan** China
72B2 **Helan Shan** *Mt* China
19B3 **Helena** Arkansas, USA
8B2 **Helena** Montana, USA
22D3 **Helendale** USA
71E3 **Helen Reef** *I* Pacific O
44B3 **Helensburgh** Scot
91B4 **Helleh** *R* Iran
51B2 **Hellin** Spain
20C1 **Hells Canyon** *R* USA
46D1 **Hellweg** Region, Germany
22B2 **Helm** USA
80E2 **Helmand** *R* Afghan
100A3 **Helmeringhausen** Namibia
46C1 **Helmond** Neth
44C2 **Helmsdale** Scot
74B2 **Helong** China
39G/ **Helsingborg** Sweden
Helsingfors = Helsinki
56C1 **Helsingør** Den
38J6 **Helsinki** Fin
43B4 **Helston** Eng
92B4 **Helwân** Egypt
19A3 **Hempstead** USA
39H7 **Hemse** Sweden
72A3 **Henan** China
72C3 **Henan** Province, China
110B1 **Hen and Chicken Is** NZ
14A3 **Henderson** Kentucky, USA
9B3 **Henderson** Nevada, USA
19B3 **Henderson** Texas, USA
73E5 **Heng-ch'un** Taiwan
68B4 **Hengduan Shan** *Mts* China
56B2 **Hengelo** Neth
72B2 **Hengshan** China
72D2 **Hengshui** China
76D1 **Heng Xian** China
73C4 **Hengyang** China
77A4 **Henhoaha** Nicobar Is
43D4 **Henley-on-Thames** Eng
16B3 **Henlopen,C** USA
7B4 **Henrietta Maria,C** Can
18A2 **Henryetta** USA
6D3 **Henry Kater Pen** Can
68C2 **Hentiyn Nuruu** *Mts* Mongolia
76B2 **Henzada** Burma
73B5 **Hepu** China
80E2 **Herat** Afghan
5H4 **Herbert** Can
110C2 **Herbertville** NZ
46E1 **Herborn** Germany
26A4 **Heredia** Costa Rica
43C3 **Hereford** Eng
43C3 **Hereford & Worcester** County, Eng
46C1 **Herentals** Belg
47B1 **Héricourt** France
18A2 **Herington** USA
111A3 **Heriot** NZ
47C1 **Herisau** Switz
15D2 **Herkimer** USA
44E1 **Herma Ness** *Pen* Scot
109C2 **Hermidale** Aust
111B2 **Hermitage** NZ
Hermon,Mt = Jebel ash Shaykh
24A2 **Hermosillo** Mexico
16A2 **Herndon** Pennsylvania, USA
22C2 **Herndon** California, USA
46D1 **Herne** Germany
56B1 **Herning** Den
90A2 **Herowābad** Iran
50A2 **Herrera del Duque** Spain

16A2 **Hershey** USA
43D4 **Hertford** County, Eng
94B2 **Herzliyya** Israel
46C1 **Hesbaye** Region, Belg
46B1 **Hesdin** France
72B2 **Heshui** China
22D3 **Hesperia** USA
12H2 **Hess** *R* Can
57B2 **Hessen** State, Germany
22C2 **Hetch Hetchy Res** USA
42C2 **Hexham** Eng
73C5 **He Xian** China
73C5 **Heyuan** China
108B3 **Heywood** Aust
72D2 **Heze** China
17B2 **Hialeah** USA
10A2 **Hibbing** USA
110C1 **Hicks Bay** NZ
109C3 **Hicks,Pt** Aust
23B1 **Hidalgo** State, Mexico
24B2 **Hidalgo del Parral** Mexico
35B1 **Hidrolândia** Brazil
96A2 **Hierro** *I* Canary Is
75C1 **Higashine** Japan
74B4 **Higashi-suidō** *Str* Japan
20B2 **High Desert** USA
19B4 **High Island** USA
44B3 **Highland** Region, Scot
22D3 **Highland** USA
22C1 **Highland Peak** *Mt* USA
16B2 **Highlands Falls** USA
11B3 **High Point** USA
13D1 **High Prairie** Can
5G4 **High River** Can
17B2 **High Springs** USA
16B2 **Hightstown** USA
43D4 **High Wycombe** Eng
39J7 **Hiiumaa** *I* USSR
80B3 **Hijāz** Region, S Arabia
75B2 **Hikigawa** Japan
75B1 **Hikone** Japan
110B1 **Hikurangi** NZ
9C4 **Hildago** Mexico
9C4 **Hildago del Parral** Mexico
56B2 **Hildesheim** Germany
27R3 **Hillaby,Mt** Barbados
56C1 **Hillerød** Den
14B3 **Hillsbø** Ohio, USA
20B1 **Hillsboro** Oregon, USA
19A3 **Hillsboro** Texas, USA
108C2 **Hillston** Aust
44E1 **Hillswick** Scot
21C4 **Hilo** Hawaiian Is
93C2 **Hilvan** Turk
56B2 **Hilversum** Neth
84D2 **Himachal Pradesh** State, India
82B3 **Himalaya** *Mts* Asia
85C4 **Himatnagar** India
74C4 **Himeji** Japan
74D3 **Himi** Japan
92C3 **Hims** Syria
12E2 **Hinchinbrook Entrance** USA
12E2 **Hinchinbrook I** USA
85D3 **Hindaun** India
84B1 **Hindu Kush** *Mts* Afghan
87B2 **Hindupur** India
13D1 **Hines Creek** Can
85D4 **Hinganghāt** India
69E2 **Hinggan Ling** *Upland* China
85B3 **Hingol** *R* Pak
85D5 **Hingoli** India
38H5 **Hinnøya** *I* Nor
16C1 **Hinsdale** USA
13D2 **Hinton** Can
34B2 **Hipolito Itrogoyen** Arg
86A2 **Hirakud Res** India
92B2 **Hirfanli Baraji** *Res* Turk

87B2	**Hirihar** India
74E2	**Hirosaki** Japan
74C4	**Hiroshima** Japan
46C2	**Hirson** France
54C2	**Hirşova** Rom
56B1	**Hirtshals** Den
84D3	**Hisär** India
26C3	**Hispaniola** *I* Caribbean S
94C1	**Hisyah** Syria
93D3	**Hīt** Iraq
74E3	**Hitachi** Japan
75C1	**Hitachi-Ota** Japan
43D4	**Hitchin** Eng
38F6	**Hitra** *I* Nor
75A4	**Hiuchi-nada** *B* Japan
75A2	**Hiwasa** Japan
56B1	**Hjørring** Den
76B1	**Hka** *R* Burma
97C4	**Ho** Ghana
76D1	**Hoa Binh** Viet
76D3	**Hoa Da** Viet
109C4	**Hobart** Aust
9C3	**Hobbs** USA
56B1	**Hobro** Den
13C2	**Hobson L** Can
99E2	**Hobyo** Somalia
	Ho Chi Minh = Saigon
57C3	**Hochkonig** *Mt* Austria
54B1	**Hódmező'hely** Hung
59B3	**Hodonin** Czech
74B2	**Hoeryong** N Korea
57C2	**Hof** Germany
38B2	**Hofsjökull** *Mts* Iceland
74C4	**Hōfu** Japan
96C2	**Hoggar** *Upland* Alg
46D1	**Hohe Acht** *Mt* Germany
72C1	**Hohhot** China
6J3	**Höhn** Iceland
68B3	**Hoh Sai Hu** *L* China
82C2	**Hoh Xil Shan** *Mts* China
99D2	**Hoima** Uganda
86C1	**Hojāi** India
75A2	**Hojo** Japan
110B1	**Hokianga Harbour** *B* NZ
111B2	**Hokitika** NZ
74E2	**Hokkaidō** Japan
90C2	**Hokmābād** Iran
109C3	**Holbrook** Aust
9B3	**Holbrook** USA
19A2	**Holdenville** USA
87B2	**Hole Narsipur** India
27R3	**Holetown** Barbados
26B2	**Holguín** Cuba
111B2	**Holitika** NZ
12C2	**Holitna** *R* USA
59B3	**Hollabrunn** Austria
14A2	**Holland** USA
22B2	**Hollister** USA
19C3	**Holly Springs** USA
22C3	**Hollywood** California, USA
17B2	**Hollywood** Florida, USA
4G2	**Holman Island** Can
38J6	**Holmsund** Sweden
94B2	**Holon** Israel
56B1	**Holstebro** Den
6E3	**Holsteinborg** Greenland
14B2	**Holt** USA
18A2	**Holton** USA
12C2	**Holy Cross** USA
42B3	**Holyhead** Wales
42D2	**Holy I** Eng
43B3	**Holy I** Wales
16C1	**Holyoke** Massachusetts, USA
86C2	**Homalin** Burma
6D3	**Home B** Can
12D3	**Homer** Alaska, USA
19B3	**Homer** Louisiana, USA
111A2	**Homer Tunnel** NZ

17B1	**Homerville** USA
17B2	**Homestead** USA
17A1	**Homewood** USA
87B1	**Homnābād** India
101C3	**Homoine** Mozam
25D3	**Hondo** *R* Mexico
25D3	**Honduras** Republic, Cent America
25D3	**Honduras,G of** Honduras
39G6	**Hønefoss** Nor
15C2	**Honesdale** USA
21A1	**Honey L** USA
76C1	**Hong** *R* Viet
76D1	**Hon Gai** Viet
73A4	**Hongguo** China
73C4	**Hong Hu** *L* China
72B2	**Honghui** China
73C4	**Hongjiang** China
73C5	**Hong Kong** Colony, S E Asia
68D2	**Hongor** Mongolia
73B5	**Hongshui He** *R* China
72A3	**Hongyuan** China
72D3	**Hongze Hu** *L* China
107E1	**Honiara** Solomon Is
77C4	**Hon Khoai** *I* Camb
76D3	**Hon Lan** *I* Viet
38K4	**Honningsvåg** Nor
21C4	**Honolulu** Hawaiian Is
77C4	**Hon Panjang** *I* Viet
74D3	**Honshu** *I* Japan
20B1	**Hood,Mt** USA
20B1	**Hood River** USA
45C2	**Hook Head** *C* Irish Rep
12G3	**Hoonah** USA
12A2	**Hooper Bay** USA
101G1	**Hoopstad** S Africa
56A2	**Hoorn** Neth
9B3	**Hoover Dam** USA
12E2	**Hope** Alaska, USA
19B3	**Hope** Arkansas, USA
13C3	**Hope** Can
7D4	**Hopedale** Can
64D2	**Hopen** *I* Barents S
6D3	**Hopes Advance,C** Can
108B3	**Hopetoun** Aust
100B3	**Hopetown** S Africa
18C2	**Hopkinsville** USA
20B1	**Hoquiam** USA
93D1	**Horasan** Turk
99F1	**Hordiyo** Somalia
47C1	**Horgen** Switz
105H5	**Horizon Depth** Pacific O
91C4	**Hormuz,Str of** Oman/Iran
59B3	**Horn** Austria
6H3	**Horn** *C* Iceland
38H5	**Hornavan** *L* Sweden
19B3	**Hornbeck** USA
20B2	**Hornbrook** USA
111B2	**Hornby** NZ
7B5	**Hornepayne** Can
4F3	**Horn Mts** Can
42D3	**Hornsea** Eng
72B1	**Horn Uul** *Mt* Mongolia
30E3	**Horqueta** Par
15C2	**Horseheads** USA
56C1	**Horsens** Den
20B1	**Horseshoe Bay** Can
108B3	**Horsham** Aust
43D4	**Horsham** Eng
39G7	**Horten** Nor
4F3	**Horton** *R* Can
78C2	**Hose Mts** Malay
85D4	**Hoshangābād** India
84D2	**Hoshiārpur** India
87B1	**Hospet** India
29C7	**Hoste** *I* Chile
82B2	**Hotan** China
19B3	**Hot Springs** Arkansas, USA
8C2	**Hot Springs** S. Dakota, USA
4G3	**Hottah** Can

46A2	**Houdan** France
72C2	**Houma** China
19B4	**Houma** USA
16C2	**Housatonic** *R* USA
13B2	**Houston** Can
19C3	**Houston** Mississippi, USA
19A4	**Houston** Texas, USA
106A3	**Houtman** *Is* Aust
68B2	**Hovd** Mongolia
68C1	**Hövsgol Nuur** *L* Mongolia
14A2	**Howard City** USA
12C1	**Howard P** USA
109C3	**Howe,C** Aust
101H1	**Howick** S Africa
44C2	**Hoy** *I* Scot
39F6	**Høyanger** Nor
59B2	**Hradeç-Králové** Czech
59B3	**Hranice** Czech
59B3	**Hron** *R* Czech
73E5	**Hsin-chu** Taiwan
73E5	**Hsüeh Shan** *Mt* Taiwan
72B2	**Huachi** China
32B6	**Huacho** Peru
72C1	**Huade** China
72D3	**Huaibei** China
72D3	**Huaibin** China
72D3	**Huai He** *R* China
73C4	**Huaihua** China
73C5	**Huaiji** China
72D3	**Huainan** China
69E4	**Hua-lien** Taiwan
32B5	**Huallaga** *R* Peru
32B5	**Huallanca** Peru
32B5	**Huamachuco** Peru
100A2	**Huambo** Angola
30C2	**Huanay** Bol
32B5	**Huancabamba** Peru
32B6	**Huancavelica** Peru
32B6	**Huancayo** Peru
73D3	**Huangchuan** China
	Huang Hai = Yellow S
72D2	**Huang He** *R* China
72B2	**Huangling** China
76D2	**Huangliu** China
73C3	**Huangpi** China
73D3	**Huangshi** China
34C3	**Huanguelén** Arg
73E4	**Huangyan** China
74B2	**Huanren** China
32B5	**Huánuco** Peru
30C2	**Huanuni** Bol
72B2	**Huan Xian** China
32B5	**Huaráz** Peru
32B6	**Huarmey** Peru
32B5	**Huascarán** *Mt* Peru
30B4	**Huasco** Chile
23A2	**Huatusco** Mexico
23B1	**Huauchinango** Mexico
23B2	**Huautla** Mexico
72C2	**Hua Xian** China
24B2	**Huayapan** *R* Mexico
73C3	**Hubei** Province, China
87B1	**Hubli** India
34C3	**Hucal** Arg
74B2	**Huch'ang** N Korea
42D3	**Huddersfield** Eng
39H6	**Hudiksvall** Sweden
17B2	**Hudson** Florida, USA
14B2	**Hudson** Michigan, USA
16C1	**Hudson** New York, USA
16C1	**Hudson** *R* USA
7B4	**Hudson B** Can
5H4	**Hudson Bay** Can
13C1	**Hudson's Hope** Can
6C3	**Hudson Str** Can
76D2	**Hue** Viet
23B1	**Huejutla** Mexico
50A2	**Huelva** Spain
23A2	**Hueramo** Mexico
51B2	**Huércal Overa** Spain
51B1	**Huesca** Spain
23B2	**Huexotla** *Hist Site* Mexico

107D3	**Hughenden** Aust
12D1	**Hughes** USA
86B2	**Hugli** *R* India
19A3	**Hugo** USA
73D4	**Hui'an** China
110C1	**Huiarau Range** *Mts* NZ
74B2	**Huich'ŏn** N Korea
74B2	**Huifa He** *R* China
32B3	**Huila** *Mt* Colombia
73D5	**Huilai** China
73A4	**Huili** China
74B2	**Huinan** China
34C2	**Huinca Renancó** Arg
25C3	**Huixtla** Mexico
73A4	**Huize** China
73C5	**Huizhou** China
23B2	**Hujuápan de Léon** Mexico
69F2	**Hulin** China
15C1	**Hull** Can
42D3	**Hull** Eng
58B1	**Hultsfred** Sweden
63D3	**Hulun Nur** *L* China
69E1	**Huma** China
33E5	**Humaita** Brazil
100B4	**Humansdorp** S Africa
42D3	**Humber** *R* Eng
42D3	**Humberside** County, Eng
5H4	**Humboldt** Can
20C2	**Humboldt** *R* USA
20B2	**Humboldt B** USA
6D2	**Humboldt Gletscher** *Gl* Greenland
21B2	**Humboldt L** USA
108C1	**Humeburn** Aust
109C3	**Hume,L** Aust
100A2	**Humpata** Angola
22C2	**Humphreys** USA
38A1	**Húnaflóri** *B* Iceland
73C4	**Hunan** Province, China
74C2	**Hunchun** China
13C2	**Hundred Mile House** Can
54B1	**Hunedoara** Rom
59B3	**Hungary** Republic, Europe
108B1	**Hungerford** Aust
74B3	**Hüngnam** N Korea
74B2	**Hunjiang** China
46D2	**Hunsrück** Mts, Germany
109D2	**Hunter** *R* Aust
13B2	**Hunter I** Can
109C4	**Hunter Is** Aust
12D2	**Hunter,Mt** USA
14A3	**Huntingburg** USA
43D3	**Huntingdon** Eng
14A2	**Huntingdon** Indiana, USA
14B3	**Huntington** W Virginia, USA
22C4	**Huntington Beach** USA
22C2	**Huntington L** USA
110C1	**Huntly** NZ
44C3	**Huntly** Scot
12J2	**Hunt,Mt** Can
108A1	**Hunt Pen** Aust
17A1	**Huntsville** Alabama, USA
15C1	**Huntsville** Can
19A3	**Huntsville** Texas, USA
76D2	**Huong Khe** Viet
71F4	**Huon Peninsula** *Pen* PNG
109C4	**Huonville** Aust
14B1	**Hurd,C** Can
80B3	**Hurghada** Egypt
8D2	**Huron** S Dakota, USA
14B1	**Huron,L** Can/USA
34A2	**Hurtado** Chile
111B2	**Hurunui** *R* NZ
38B1	**Husavik** Iceland
54C1	**Huşi** Rom
39G7	**Huskvarna** Sweden

Iron River

12C1 **Huslia** USA
94B2 **Husn** Jordan
56B2 **Husum** Germany
109C1 **Hutton,Mt** Aust
72D2 **Hutuo He** R China
46C1 **Huy** Belg
72A2 **Huzhu** China
52C2 **Hvar** I Yugos
100B2 **Hwange** Zim
100B2 **Hwange Nat Pk** Zim
15D2 **Hyannis** USA
68B2 **Hyaryas Nuur** L
        Mongolia
5E4 **Hydaburg** Can
16C2 **Hyde Park** USA
87B1 **Hyderābād** India
85B3 **Hyderabad** Pak
49D3 **Hyères** France
12J2 **Hyland** R Can
8B2 **Hyndman Peak** Mt
        USA
38K6 **Hyrynsalmi** Fin
13D1 **Hythe** Can
74C4 **Hyūga** Japan
39J6 **Hyvikää** Fin

I

31C4 **Iaçu** Brazil
54C2 **Ialomiţa** R Rom
54C1 **Iaşi** Rom
97C4 **Ibadan** Nig
32B3 **Ibagué** Colombia
54B2 **Ibar** R Yugos
32B3 **Ibarra** Ecuador
35B1 **Ibiá** Brazil
30E4 **Ibicuí** R Brazil
34D2 **Ibicuy** Arg
51C2 **Ibiza** Spain
51C2 **Ibiza** I Spain
101D2 **Ibo** Mozam
31C4 **Ibotirama** Brazil
91C5 **'Ibrī** Oman
32B6 **Ica** Peru
32D4 **Icá** R Brazil
32D3 **Icana** Brazil
38A1 **Iceland** Republic,
        N Atlantic O
13C2 **Ice Mt** Can
87A1 **Ichalkaranji** India
74E3 **Ichihara** Japan
75B1 **Ichinomiya** Japan
74E3 **Ichinoseki** Japan
12F3 **Icy B** USA
4B2 **Icy C** USA
63B2 **Ida** R USSR
19B3 **Idabell** USA
8B2 **Idaho Falls** USA
20B2 **Idanha** USA
46D2 **Idar Oberstein**
        Germany
95A2 **Idehan Marzūg** Desert
        Libya
95A2 **Idehan Ubari** Desert
        Libya
96C2 **Idelés** Alg
68B2 **Iderlym Gol** R
        Mongolia
95C2 **Idfu** Egypt
55B3 **Ídhi Óros** Mt Greece
55B3 **Ídhra** I Greece
98B3 **Idiofa** Zaïre
12C2 **Iditarod** R USA
92C2 **Idlib** Syria
39K7 **Idritsa** USSR
100B4 **Idutywa** S Africa
55C3 **Ierápetra** Greece
46B1 **Ieper** Belg
99D3 **Ifakara** Tanz
71F3 **Ifalik** I Pacific O
101D3 **Ifanadiana** Madag
97C4 **Ife** Nig
97C3 **Iférouane** Niger
78C2 **Igan** Malay
35B2 **Igaranava** Brazil
93E2 **Igdir** Iran
39H6 **Iggesund** Sweden

34B2 **Iglesia** Arg
53A3 **Iglesias** Sardegna
6B3 **Igloolik** Can
10A2 **Ignace** Can
55B3 **Igoumenítsa** Greece
61H2 **Igra** USSR
23B2 **Iguala** Mexico
31B6 **Iguape** Brazil
35B2 **Iguape** Brazil
35B2 **Iguatama** Brazil
31D3 **Iguatu** Brazil
98A3 **Iguéla** Gabon
101D3 **Ihosy** Madag
74D3 **Iida** Japan
75B1 **Iide-san** Mt Japan
38K6 **Iisalmi** Fin
75A2 **Iizuka** Japan
97C4 **Ijebu Ode** Nig
56B2 **Ijsselmeer** S Neth
55C3 **Ikaría** I Greece
74E2 **Ikeda** Japan
98C3 **Ikela** Zaïre
54B2 **Ikhtiman** Bulg
12D3 **Ikolik,C** USA
101D2 **Ikopa** R Madag
79B2 **Ilagan** Phil
90A3 **Ilām** Iran
47C1 **Ilanz** Switz
13F1 **Île à la Crosse** Can
13F1 **Île à la Crosse,L** Can
89G8 **Ilebo** Zaïre
96D1 **Île de Jerba** I Tunisia
48B2 **Ile de Noirmoutier** I
        France
48B2 **Ile de Ré** I France
107F3 **Île des Pins** I Nouvelle
        Calédonie
48A2 **Ile d'Ouessant** I
        France
48B2 **Ile d'Yeu** I France
61J3 **Ilek** R USSR
107F2 **Îles Bélèp** Nouvelle
        Calédonie
107E2 **Îs Chesterfield**
        Nouvelle Calédonie
49D3 **Iles d'Hyères** Is
        France
43B4 **Ilfracombe** Eng
92B1 **Ilgaz Dağlari** Mts Turk
101C3 **Ilha Bazaruto** I
        Mozam
33G3 **Ilha De Maracá** I Brazil
33G4 **Ilha de Marajó** I Brazil
35B2 **Ilha de São Sebastião**
        I Brazil
33G6 **Ilha do Bananal**
        Region Brazil
35C2 **Ilha Grande** I Brazil
35B2 **Ilha Santo Amaro** I
        Brazil
96A1 **Ilhas Selvegens** I
        Atlantic O
31D4 **Ilhéus** Brazil
12C3 **Iliamna L** USA
12D2 **Iliamna V** USA
79B4 **Iligan** Phil
63G3 **Il'inskiy** USSR
55B3 **Iliodhrómia** I Greece
79B4 **Illana B** Phil
34A2 **Illapel** Chile
34A2 **Illapel** R Chile
97C3 **Illéla** Niger
47D1 **Iller** R Germany
4C4 **Illiamna L** USA
10A2 **Illinois** State, USA
18B2 **Illinois** R USA
96C2 **Illizi** Alg
30B2 **Ilo** Peru
79B3 **Iloilo** Phil
38L6 **Ilomantsi** Fin
97C4 **Ilorin** Nig
75A2 **Imabari** Japan
75B1 **Imalchi** Japan
60C1 **Imatra** Fin
30G4 **Imbituba** Brazil
99E2 **Imi** Eth
20C2 **Imlay** USA
47D1 **Immenstadt** Germany

52B2 **Imola** Italy
31B3 **Imperatriz** Brazil
52A2 **Imperia** Italy
98B2 **Impfondo** Congo
86C2 **Imphāl** India
47D1 **Imst** Austria
12B1 **Imuruk L** USA
75B1 **Ina** Japan
96C2 **In Afahleleh** Well Alg
75B2 **Inamba-jima** I Japan
96C2 **In Amenas** Alg
38K5 **Inari** Fin
38K5 **Inarijärvi** L Fin
75C1 **Inawashiro-ko** L
        Japan
96C2 **In Belbel** Alg
60E5 **Ince Burun** Pt Turk
92B2 **Incekum Burun** Pt
        Turk
74B3 **Inch'ŏn** S Korea
96B2 **In Dagouber** Well
        Mali
35B1 **Indaia** R Brazil
38H6 **Indals** R Sweden
21B2 **Independence**
        California, USA
18A2 **Independence** Kansas,
        USA
18B2 **Independence**
        Missouri, USA
78A3 **Inderagiri** R Indon
61H4 **Inderborskly** USSR
83B3 **India** Federal
        Republic, Asia
14A2 **Indiana** State, USA
15C2 **Indiana** USA
104C6 **Indian-Antarctic Ridge**
        Indian O
14A3 **Indianapolis** USA
        Indian Desert = Thar
        Desert
7E4 **Indian Harbour** Can
104B4 **Indian O**
18B1 **Indianola** Iowa, USA
19B3 **Indianola** Mississippi,
        USA
35B1 **Indianópolis** Brazil
76D2 **Indo China** Region,
        S E Asia
70C4 **Indonesia** Republic,
        S E Asia
85D4 **Indore** India
78B4 **Indramayu** Indon
48C2 **Indre** R France
85B3 **Indus** R Pak
60D5 **Inebolu** Turk
96C2 **In Ebeggi** Well Alg
96C2 **In Ecker** Alg
92A1 **Inegöl** Turk
96D2 **In Ezzane** Alg
97C3 **Ingal** Niger
14B2 **Ingersoll** Can
107D2 **Ingham** Aust
6D2 **Inglefield Land** Region
        Can
110B1 **Inglewood** NZ
109D1 **Inglewood**
        Queensland, Aust
22C4 **Inglewood** USA
108B3 **Inglewood** Victoria,
        Aust
38B2 **Ingólfshöfòi** I Iceland
57C3 **Ingolstadt** Germany
86B2 **Ingrāj Bāzār** India
96C3 **In-Guezzam** Well Alg
101C3 **Inhambane** Mozam
101C3 **Inharrime** Mozam
35B1 **Inhumas** Brazil
32D3 **Inirida** R Colombia
45A2 **Inishbofin** I Irish Rep
45A1 **Inishkea** I Irish Rep
45B2 **Inishmaan** I Irish Rep
45B2 **Inishmore** I Irish Rep
45B1 **Inishmurray** I
        Irish Rep
45C1 **Inishowen** District,
        Irish Rep
45A2 **Inishshark** I Irish Rep

45A2 **Inishturk** I Irish Rep
109C1 **Injune** Aust
12H3 **Inklin** Can
12H3 **Inklin** R Can
12C1 **Inland L** USA
47D1 **Inn** R Austria
108B1 **Innamincka** Aust
68C2 **Inner Mongolia**
        Autonomous Region,
        China
107D2 **Innisfail** Aust
12C2 **Innoko** R USA
57C3 **Innsbruck** Austria
98B3 **Inongo** Zaïre
58B2 **Inowrocław** Pol
96C2 **In Salah** Alg
47B1 **Interlaken** Switz
24C3 **Intexpec** Mexico
47C2 **Intra** Italy
78D3 **Intu** Indon
75C1 **Inubo-saki** C Japan
7C4 **Inukjuac** Can
4E3 **Inuvik** Can
4F3 **Inuvik** Region Can
44B3 **Inveraray** Scot
111A3 **Invercargill** NZ
109D1 **Inverell** Aust
13D2 **Invermere** Can
44B3 **Inverness** Scot
44C3 **Inverurie** Scot
108A3 **Investigator Str** Aust
68A1 **Inya** USSR
101C2 **Inyanga** Zim
21B2 **Inyokern** USA
98B3 **Inzia** R Zaïre
55B3 **Ioánnina** Greece
18A2 **Iola** USA
44A3 **Iona** I Scot
100A2 **Iôna Nat Pk** Angola
20C1 **Ione** USA
        Ionian Is = Ioníoi Nísoi
55A3 **Ionian S** Italy/Greece
55B3 **Ioníoi Nísoi** Is Greece
55C3 **íos** I Greece
10A2 **Iowa** R USA
10A2 **Iowa City** USA
35B1 **Ipameri** Brazil
35C1 **Ipanema** Brazil
61F4 **Ipatovo** USSR
32B3 **Ipiales** Colombia
77C5 **Ipoh** Malay
30F2 **Iporá** Brazil
55C2 **Ipsala** Turk
109D1 **Ipswich** Aust
43E3 **Ipswich** Eng
16D1 **Ipswich** USA
30B3 **Iquique** Chile
32C4 **Iquitos** Peru
55C3 **Iráklion** Greece
80D2 **Iran** Republic, S W
        Asia
91D4 **Irānshahr** Iran
23A1 **Irapuato** Mexico
93D3 **Iraq** Republic, S W
        Asia
95A2 **Irā Wan** Watercourse
        Libya
94B2 **Irbid** Jordan
61K2 **Irbit** USSR
36C3 **Ireland** Republic,
        NW Europe
33F3 **Ireng** R Guyana
74B3 **Iri** S Korea
71E4 **Irian Jaya** Province,
        Indon
95B3 **Iriba** Chad
79B3 **Iriga** Phil
99D3 **Iringa** Tanz
69E4 **Iriomote** I Japan
33G5 **Iriri** R Brazil
42B3 **Irish S** Eng/Irish Rep
12D1 **Irklilik** R USA
63C2 **Irkutsk** USSR
65J4 **Irlysh** USSR
108A2 **Iron Knob** Aust
14A1 **Iron Mountain** USA
107D2 **Iron Range** Aust
14A1 **Iron River** USA

14B3	Irontown USA
10A2	Ironwood USA
10B2	Iroquois Falls Can
75B2	Iro-zaki C Japan
76A2	Irrawaddy,Mouths of the Burma
65H4	Irtysh R USSR
51B1	Irun Spain
42B2	Irvine Scot
19A3	Irving USA
79B4	Isabela Phil
32J7	Isabela I Ecuador
4H2	Isachsen Can
4H2	Isachsen,C Can
6H3	Ísafjörður Iceland
74C4	Isahaya Japan
98C2	Isangi Zaïre
47D1	Isar R Germany
47D1	Isarco R Italy
44E1	Isbister Scot
47D1	Ischgl Austria
53B2	Ischia I Italy
75B2	Ise Japan
47D2	Iseo Italy
46D1	Iserlohn Germany
53B2	Isernia Italy
75B2	Ise-wan B Japan
69E4	Ishigaki I Japan
74E2	Ishikari R Japan
74E2	Ishikari-wan B Japan
65H4	Ishim USSR
65H4	Ishim R USSR
74E3	Ishinomaki Japan
75C1	Ishioka Japan
84C1	Ishkashim Afghan
14A1	Ishpeming USA
65J4	Isil'kul USSR
99D2	Isiolo Kenya
98C2	Isiro Zaïre
92C2	Iskenderun Turk
92C2	Iskenferun Körfezi B Turk
92B1	İskilip Turk
65K4	Iskitim USSR
54B2	Iskur R Bulg
12H3	Iskut R Can/USA
23B2	Isla Mexico
34C3	Isla Bermejo I Arg
27E4	Isla Blanquilla Ven
32A2	Isla Coiba I Panama
9B4	Isla de Cedros I Mexico
29B4	Isla de Chiloé I Chile
25D2	Isla de Cozumel I Mexico
26C3	Isla de la Gonâve Cuba
26A2	Isla de la Juventud I Cuba
34D2	Isla de las Lechiguanas I Arg
3K8	Isla del Coco I Costa Rica
25D3	Isla del Maiz I Caribbean S
23B1	Isla de Lobos I Mexico
29D6	Isla de los Estados I Arg
28E2	Isla de Marajó I Brazil
105L5	Isla de Pascua I Pacific O
26A4	Isla de Providencia I Caribbean S
26A4	Isla de San Andres I Caribbean S
30G4	Isla de Santa Catarina I Brazil
33G2	Isla du Diable I French Guiana
31E2	Isla Fernando de Noronha I Brazil
29C6	Isla Grande de Tierra del Fuego I Arg/Chile
27D4	Isla la Tortuga I Ven
84C2	Islamabad Pak
24A2	Isla Magdalena I Mexico
27E4	Isla Margarita Ven
34A3	Isla Mocha Chile

17B2	Islamorada USA
10A1	Island L Can
108A2	Island Lg Aust
110B1	Islands,B of NZ
32A4	Isla Puná I Ecuador
103D6	Isla San Ambrosia I Pacific O
103D6	Isla San Felix I Pacific O
24A2	Isla Santa Margarita I Mexico
34A3	Isla Santa Maria I Chile
51C2	Islas Baleares Is Spain
96A2	Islas Canarias Is Atlantic O
51C2	Islas Columbretes Is Spain
25D3	Islas de la Bahia Is Honduras
26A4	Islas del Maíz Is Caribbean S
33E1	Islas de Margarita Is Ven
29C7	Islas Diego Ramírez Is Chile
32J7	Islas Galapagos Is Pacific O
30H6	Islas Juan Fernández Is Chile
32D1	Islas los Roques Is Ven
	Islas Malvinas = Falkland Is
105L3	Islas Revilla Gigedo Is Pacific O
29C7	Islas Wollaston Is Chile
97A3	Isla Tidra I Maur
29B5	Isla Wellington I Chile
48C2	Isle R France
104B5	Isle Amsterdam I Indian O
43D4	Isle of Wight I Eng
10B2	Isle Royale I USA
104B5	Isle St Paul I Indian O
104A6	Îsles Crozet I Indian O
105J4	Îsles de la Société Is Pacific O
105K5	Îsles Gambier I Pacific O
101D2	Isles Glorieuses Is Madag
104B6	Îsles Kerguelen Is Indian O
105K4	Îsles Marquises Is Pacific O
105J4	Îsles Tuamotu Is Pacific O
105J5	Îsles Tubai Is Pacific O
22B1	Isleton USA
92B3	Ismâ'ilîya Egypt
101D3	Isoanala Madag
101C2	Isoka Zambia
53B3	Isola Egadi I Italy
52B2	Isola Ponziane I Italy
53B3	Isole Lipari Is Italy
52C2	Isoles Tremiti Is Italy
75B1	Isosaki Japan
92B2	Isparta Turk
94B2	Israel Republic, S W Asia
51C2	Isser R Alg
48C2	Issoire France
49C2	Issoudun France
92A1	İstanbul Turk
55B3	Istiáia Greece
25C3	Istmo de Tehuantepec Isthmus Mexico
17B2	Istokpoga,L USA
52B1	Istra Pen Yugos
35B1	Itaberai Brazil
35C1	Itabira Brazil
35C2	Itabirito Brazil
31D4	Itabuna Brazil
33F4	Itacoatiara Brazil
32B2	Itagui Colombia

33F4	Itaituba Brazil
30G4	Itajaí Brazil
35B2	Itajuba Brazil
52B2	Italy Repubic, Europe
35D1	Itamaraju Brazil
35C1	Itamarandiba Brazil
35C1	Itambacuri Brazil
35C1	Itambé Mt Brazil
86C1	Itānagar India
35C1	Itanhaém Brazil
35C1	Itanhém Brazil
35C1	Itanhém R Brazil
35C1	Itaobím Brazil
35B2	Itapecerica Brazil
35C2	Itaperuna Brazil
31C5	Itapetinga Brazil
35B2	Itapetininga Brazil
35B2	Itapeva Brazil
31D2	Itapipoca Brazil
35B1	Itapuranga Brazil
30E4	Itaqui Brazil
35C1	Itarantim Brazil
35C1	Itararé Brazil
35B2	Itararé R Brazil
35C2	Itaúna Brazil
33E6	Iténez R Brazil/Bol
15C2	Ithaca USA
98C2	Itimbiri R Zaïre
35C1	Itinga Brazil
6E3	Itivdleg Greenland
75B2	Ito Japan
74D3	Itoigawa Japan
33E6	Itonomas R Bol
35B2	Itu Brazil
35B1	Itumbiara Brazil
35A1	Iturama Brazil
30C3	Iturbe Arg
35B1	Iturutaba Brazil
56B2	Itzehoe Germany
65K4	Iurga USSR
58D2	Ivacevichi USSR
35A2	Ivai R Brazil
38K5	Ivalo Fin
54A2	Ivangrad Yugos
108B2	Ivanhoe Aust
64D5	Ivano USSR
59C3	Ivano-Frankovsk USSR
61F2	Ivanovo USSR
65H3	Ivdel' USSR
98B2	Ivindo R Gabon
101D3	Ivohibe Madag
101D2	Ivongo Soanierana Madag
97B4	Ivory Coast Republic, Africa
52A1	Ivrea Italy
6C3	Ivujivik Can
74E3	Iwaki Japan
74C4	Iwakuni Japan
74E2	Iwanai Japan
97C4	Iwo Nig
69G4	Iwo Jima I Japan
23B1	Ixmiquilpa Mexico
23A2	Ixtapa Mexico
23A1	Ixtlán Mexico
75A2	Iyo Japan
75A2	Iyo-nada B Japan
65G4	Izhevsk USSR
64G3	Izhma USSR
91C5	Izkī Oman
60C4	Izmail USSR
92A2	İzmir Turk
55C3	İzmir Körfezi B Turk
92A1	İzmit Turk
92A1	İznik Turk
55C2	İznik Golü L Turk
94C2	Izra' Syria
23B2	Izúcar de Matamoros Mexico
75B2	Izumi-sano Japan
75A1	Izumo Japan
74D4	Izu-shotō Is Japan

94C2	Jabal al 'Arab Syria
95A2	Jabal as Sawdā Mts Libya
91B5	Jabal az Ẓannah UAE
94C1	Jabal Halīmah Mt Leb/Syria
83B3	Jabalpur India
59B2	Jablonec nad Nisou Czech
31D3	Jaboatão Brazil
35B2	Jaboticabal Brazil
51B1	Jaca Spain
23B1	Jacala Mexico
33F5	Jacareacanga Brazil
35B2	Jacarei Brazil
30F3	Jacarezinho Brazil
29C2	Jáchal Arg
35C1	Jacinto Brazil
13F2	Jackfish L Can
109C1	Jackson Aust
22B1	Jackson California, USA
14B2	Jackson Michigan, USA
19B3	Jackson Mississippi, USA
18C2	Jackson Missouri, USA
14B3	Jackson Ohio, USA
11B3	Jackson Tennessee, USA
111B2	Jackson,C NZ
111A2	Jackson Head Pt NZ
19B3	Jacksonville Arkansas, USA
17B1	Jacksonville Florida, USA
18B2	Jacksonville Illinois, USA
17C1	Jacksonville N Carolina, USA
19A3	Jacksonville Texas, USA
17B1	Jacksonville Beach USA
26C3	Jacmel Haiti
84B3	Jacobabad Pak
31C4	Jacobina Brazil
23A2	Jacona Mexico
	Jadotville = Likasi
32B5	Jaén Peru
50B2	Jaén Spain
	Jaffa = Tel Aviv Yafo
108A3	Jaffa,C Aust
87B3	Jaffna Sri Lanka
86B2	Jagannathganj Ghat Bang
87C1	Jagdalpur India
91C4	Jagin R Iran
87B1	Jagtial India
29F2	Jaguarão R Brazil
35B2	Jaguarialva Brazil
91B4	Jahrom Iran
85D5	Jāina India
72A2	Jainca China
85D3	Jaipur India
85C3	Jaisalmer India
90C2	Jajarm Iran
52C2	Jajce Yugos
78B4	Jakarta Indon
6E3	Jakobshavn Greenland
38J6	Jakobstad Fin
23B2	Jalaca Mexico
84B2	Jalai-Kut Afghan
23B2	Jalapa Mexico
35A2	Jales Brazil
86B1	Jaleswar Nepal
85D4	Jalgaon India
97D4	Jalingo Nig
51B1	Jalón R Spain
95B2	Jalo Oasis Libya
85C3	Jālor India
23A1	Jalostotitlan Mexico
86B1	Jalpāiguri India
23B1	Jalpan Mexico
24A2	Jama Ecuador
26B3	Jamaica I Caribbean S
26B3	Jamaica Chan Caribbean S

J

95B1	Jabal al Akhdar Mts Libya

86B2 Jamalpur Bang
78A3 Jambi Indon
85C4 Jambussar India
7B4 James B Can
5J5 Jameston USA
108A2 Jamestown Aust
8D2 Jamestown N Dakota, USA
15C2 Jamestown New York, USA
16D2 Jamestown Rhode Island, USA
23B2 Jamiltepec Mexico
87B1 Jamkhandi India
84C2 Jammu India
84D2 Jammu and Kashmir State, India
85B4 Jamnagar India
84C3 Jampur Pak
38K6 Jämsä Fin
86B2 Jamshedpur India
86B1 Janakpur Nepal
35C1 Janaúba Brazil
90B3 Jandaq Iran
109D1 Jandowae Aust
1B1 Jan Mayen I Norwegian S
35C1 Januária Brazil
85D4 Jaora India
51 Japan Empire, E Asia
74C3 Japan,S of S E Asia
104F2 Japan Trench Pacific O
32D4 Japurá R Brazil
93C2 Jarábulus Syria
35B1 Jaraguá Brazil
50B1 Jarama R Spain
94B2 Jarash Jordan
30E3 Jardim Brazil
51B2 Jardin R Spain
26B2 Jardines de la Reina Is Cuba
Jargalant = Hovd
33G3 Jari R Brazil
86C1 Jaria Jhānjail Bang
46C2 Jarny France
58B2 Jarocin Pol
59C2 Jaroslaw Pol
38G6 Järpen Sweden
72B2 Jartai China
85C4 Jasdan India
97C4 Jasikan Ghana
91C4 Jāsk Iran
59C3 Jaslo Pol
29D6 Jason Is Falkland Is
18B2 Jasper Arkansas, USA
13D2 Jasper Can
17B1 Jasper Florida, USA
14A3 Jasper Indiana, USA
19B3 Jasper Texas, USA
13D2 Jasper Nat Pk Can
58B2 Jastrowie Pol
35A1 Jatai Brazil
51B2 Játiva Spain
31B2 Jatobá Brazil
35B2 Jau Brazil
32B6 Jauja Peru
86A1 Jaunpur India
Java = Jawa
87B2 Javadi Hills India
Javari = Yavari
70B4 Java S Indon
106A2 Java Trench Indon
78B4 Jawa I Indon
71F4 Jayapura Indon
94C2 Jayrūd Syria
96B2 Jbel Ouarkziz Mts Mor
96B1 Jbel Sarhro Mt Mor
19B4 Jeanerette USA
97C4 Jebba Nig
93D2 Jebel 'Abd al 'Azīz Mt Syria
95B3 Jebel Abyad Sudan
91C5 Jebel Akhdar Mt Oman
92C4 Jebel al Lawz Mt S Arabia

94B2 Jebel ash Shaykh Mt Syria
95C2 Jebel Asoteriba Mt Sudan
94B3 Jebel Ed Dabab Mt Jordan
94B3 Jebel el Ata'ita Mt Jordan
92C3 Jebel esh Sharqi Mts Leb/Syria
94C3 Jebel Ithrīyat Mt Jordan
91C5 Jebel Ja'lan Mt Oman
94B2 Jebel Liban Mts Leb
94C2 Jebel Ma'lūlā Mt Syria
98C1 Jebel Marra Mt Sudan
94C3 Jebel Mudeisisat Mt Jordan
95C2 Jebel Oda Mt Sudan
94B3 Jebel Qasr ed Deir Mt Jordan
94B2 Jebel Um ed Daraj Mt Jordan
95B2 Jebel Uweinat Mt Sudan
42C2 Jedburgh Scot
Jedda = Jiddah
59C2 Jedrzejów Pol
19B3 Jefferson Texas, USA
11A3 Jefferson City USA
8B3 Jefferson,Mt USA
14A3 Jeffersonville USA
60C2 Jekabpils USSR
59B2 Jelena Gora Pol
60B2 Jelgava USSR
78C4 Jember Indon
57C2 Jena Germany
78B2 Jenaja I Indon
47D1 Jenbach Austria
94B2 Jenin Israel
19B3 Jennings USA
59B2 Jenseniky Upland Czech
6F3 Jensen Nunatakker Mt Greenland
6B3 Jens Munk I Can
108B3 Jeparit Aust
31D4 Jequié Brazil
35C1 Jequital R Brazil
35C1 Jequitinhonha Brazil
31C5 Jequitinhonha R Brazil
50A2 Jerez de la Frontera Spain
50A2 Jerez de los Caballeros Spain
94B3 Jericho Israel
108C3 Jerilderie Aust
48B2 Jersey I UK
10C2 Jersey City USA
15C2 Jersey Shore USA
18B2 Jerseyville USA
92C3 Jerusalem Israel
109D3 Jervis B Aust
13C2 Jervis Inlet Sd Can
52B1 Jesenice Yugos
86B2 Jessore Bang
11B3 Jesup USA
34C2 Jesus Maria Arg
16D2 Jewett City USA
54A2 Jezerce Mt Alb
58C2 Jezioro Mamry L Pol
58C2 Jezioro Śniardwy L Pol
94B2 Jezzine Leb
85C4 Jhābua India
85D4 Jhālāwār India
84C2 Jhang Maghiana Pak
85D3 Jhānsi India
86A2 Jhārsuguda India
84C2 Jhelum Pak
84C2 Jhelum R Pak
11C3 J H Kerr L USA
84D3 Jhunjhunūn India
69F2 Jiamusi China
73C4 Ji'an Jiangxi, China

74B2 Ji'an Jilin, China
73D4 Jiande China
73B4 Jiang'an China
73D4 Jiangbiancun China
73A5 Jiangcheng China
73B3 Jiang Jiang R China
73C5 Jiangmen China
72D3 Jiangsu Province, China
73C4 Jiangxi Province, China
73A3 Jiangyou China
72D1 Jianping China
73A5 Jianshui China
73D4 Jian Xi R China
73D4 Jianyang China
72E2 Jiaonan China
72E2 Jiao Xian China
72E2 Jiaozhou Wan B China
72C2 Jiaozuo China
73E3 Jiaxiang China
68B3 Jiayuguan China
81B3 Jiddah S Arabia
72D3 Jieshou China
72C2 Jiexiu China
72A3 Jigzhi China
59B3 Jihlava Czech
99E2 Jilib Somalia
69E2 Jilin China
51B1 Jiloca R Spain
9C4 Jiménez Coahuila, Mexico
99D2 Jimma Eth
72D2 Jinan China
84D3 Jind India
72B2 Jingbian China
73D4 Jingdezhen China
76C1 Jinghong China
73C3 Jingmen China
72B2 Jingning China
73B4 Jing Xiang China
73D4 Jinhua China
72C1 Jining Nei Monggol, China
72D2 Jining Shandong, China
99D2 Jinja Uganda
76C1 Jinping China
73A4 Jinsha Jiang R China
73C4 Jinshi China
72E1 Jinxi China
72E2 Jin Xian China
72E1 Jinzhou China
33E5 Jiparaná R Brazil
32A4 Jipijapa Ecuador
23A2 Jiquilpan Mexico
91C4 Jīroft Iran
73B4 Jishou China
92C2 Jisr ash Shughūr Syria
54B2 Jiu R Rom
73D4 Jiujiang China
73A4 Jiulong China
73D4 Jiulcng Jiang R China
69F2 Jixi China
94B3 Jiza Jordan
81C4 Jīzan S Arabia
97A3 Joal Sen
35C1 João Monlevade Brazil
31E3 João Pessoa Brazil
35B1 João Pirheiro Brazil
84B2 Jocoli Arg
85C3 Jodhpur India
38K6 Joensuu Fin
46C2 Joeuf France
13D2 Joffre,Mt Can
86B1 Jogbani India
87A2 Jog Falls India
101G1 Johannesburg S Africa
21B2 Johannesburg USA
6C2 Johan Pen Can
12D1 John R USA
20C2 John Day USA
20B1 John Day R USA
44C2 John o'Groats Scot

18A2 John Redmond Res USA
11B3 Johnson City Tennessee, USA
17B1 Johnston USA
27N2 Johnston Pt St Vincent
15C2 Johnstown Pennsylvania, USA
77C5 Johor Bharu Malay
49C2 Joigny France
30G4 Joinville Brazil
61H3 Jok R USSR
38H5 Jokkmokk Sweden
93E2 Jolfa Iran
10B2 Joliet USA
7C5 Joliette Can
79B4 Jolo Phil
79B4 Jolo I Phil
82D2 Joma Mt China
58C1 Jonava USSR
72A3 Jonê China
11A3 Jonesboro Arkansas, USA
19B3 Jonesboro Louisiana, USA
6B2 Jones Sd Can
58C1 Joniškis USSR
39G7 Jönköping Sweden
11A3 Joplin USA
92C3 Jordan Kingdom, S W Asia
94B2 Jordan R Israel
20C2 Jordan Valley USA
86C1 Jorhāt India
38J5 Jörn Sweden
78C3 Jorong Indon
39F7 Jørpeland Nor
79B3 Jose Pañganiban Phil
106B2 Joseph Bonaparte G Aust
64B3 Jotunheimen Mt Nor
94B2 Jouai'ya Leb
94B2 Jounié Leb
86C1 Jowal India
99E2 Jowhar Somalia
12H2 Joy,Mt Can
5F5 Juan de Fuca,Str of Can/USA
101D2 Juan de Nova I Mozam Chan
34D3 Juárez Arg
31C3 Juàzeiro Brazil
31D3 Juazeiro do Norte Brazil
99D2 Juba Sudan
99E2 Juba R Somalia
94B1 Jubail Leb
93D3 Jubbah S Arabia
96A2 Juby,C Mor
51B2 Jucar R Spain
23B2 Juchatengo Mexico
23A1 Juchipila R Mexico
23A1 Juchitlan Mexico
57C3 Judenburg Austria
30B2 Juilaca Peru
73C4 Juiling Shan Hills China
31C6 Juiz de Fora Brazil
30C3 Jujuy State, Arg
30C2 Juli Peru
33F3 Julianatop Mt Surinam
6F3 Julianehåb Greenland
46D1 Jülich Germany
84D2 Jullundur India
86A1 Jumla Nepal
94B3 Jum Suwwāna Mt Jordan
85C4 Jūnāgadh India
72D2 Junan China
9D3 Junction City USA
31B6 Jundiaí Brazil
4E4 Juneau USA
107D4 Junee Aust
22C2 June Lake USA
52A1 Jungfrau Mt Switz
16A2 Juniata R USA

29D2 Junín Arg
73A4 Junlian China
31B6 Juquiá Brazil
99C2 Jur R Sudan
42B2 Jura I Scot
49D2 Jura Mts France
44B3 Jura,Sound of Chan
 Scot
94B3 Jurf ed Darāwīsh
 Jordan
60B2 Jūrmala USSR
32D4 Juruá R Brazil
33F6 Juruena R Brazil
94C1 Jūsīyah Syria
34B2 Justo Daract Arg
32D4 Jutaí R Brazil
25D3 Juticalpa Honduras
 Jutland = Jylland
90C3 Jüymand Iran
56B1 Jylland Pen Den
38K6 Jyväskyla Fin

K

82B2 K2 Mt China/India
90C2 Kaakhka USSR
101H1 Kaapmuiden S Africa
71D4 Kabaena I Indon
97A4 Kabala Sierra Leone
99D3 Kabale Rwanda
98C3 Kabalo Zaïre
98C3 Kabambare Zaïre
99D2 Kabarole Uganda
98C3 Kabinda Zaïre
90A3 Kabir Kuh Mts Iran
100B2 Kabompo Zambia
100B2 Kabompo R Zambia
98C3 Kabongo Zaïre
84B2 Kabul Afghan
85B4 Kachchh,G of India
61J2 Kachkanar USSR
63C2 Kachug USSR
76B3 Kadan Burma
78D3 Kadapongan I Indon
85C4 Kadi India
108A2 Kadina Aust
92B2 Kadınhanı Turk
87B2 Kadiri India
60E4 Kadiyevka USSR
100B2 Kadoma Zim
99C1 Kadugli Sudan
97C3 Kaduna Nig
97C3 Kaduna R Nig
87B2 Kadūr India
97A3 Kaédi Maur
21C4 Kaena Pt Hawaiian Is
74B3 Kaesŏng N Korea
97C4 Kafanchan Nig
97A3 Kaffrine Sen
94C1 Kafrūn Bashūr Syria
100B2 Kafue Zambia
100B2 Kafue R Zambia
100D2 Kafue Nat Pk Zambia
74D3 Kaga Japan
65H6 Kagan USSR
93D1 Kağizman Turk
74C4 Kagoshima Japan
90C2 Kāhak Iran
99D3 Kahama Tanz
84B3 Kahan Pak
78C3 Kahayan R Indon
98B3 Kahemba Zaïre
46E1 Kahler Asten Mt
 Germany
91C4 Kahnūj Iran
18B1 Kahoka USA
21C4 Kahoolawe I Hawaiian
 Is
92C2 Kahramanmaraş Turk
21C4 Kahuku Pt Hawaiian Is
111B2 Kaiapoi NZ
33F2 Kaieteur Fall Guyana
72C3 Kaifeng China
110B1 Kaikohe NZ
111B2 Kaikoura NZ
111B2 Kaikoura Pen NZ
111B2 Kaikoura Range Mts NZ

73B4 Kaili China
21C4 Kailua Hawaiian Is
71E4 Kaimana Indon
75B2 Kainan Japan
97C3 Kainji Res Nig
110B1 Kaipara Harbour R
 NZ
73C5 Kaiping China
96D1 Kairouan Tunisia
22C2 Kaiser Peak Mt USA
57B3 Kaiserslautern
 Germany
74B2 Kaishantun China
58D2 Kaisiadorys USSR
110B1 Kaitaia NZ
111A3 Kaitangata NZ
84D3 Kaithal India
21C4 Kaiwi Chan Hawaiian
 Is
73B3 Kai Xian China
73A5 Kaiyuan Liaoning,
 China
74A2 Kaiyuan Yunnan,
 China
12C2 Kaiyuh Mts USA
38K6 Kajaani Fin
84B2 Kajaki Afghan
99D3 Kajiado Kenya
84B2 Kajrān Afghan
99D1 Kaka Sudan
99D2 Kakamega Kenya
75A2 Kake Japan
12H3 Kake USA
12D3 Kakhonak USA
65E5 Kakhovskoye
 Vodokhranilishche
 Res USSR
91B4 Kākī Iran
87C1 Kākināda India
75A2 Kakogawa Japan
4D2 Kaktovik USA
75C1 Kakuda Japan
55B3 Kalabáka Greece
78D1 Kalabakan Malay
100B2 Kalabo Zambia
61F3 Kalach USSR
61F4 Kalach-na-Donu USSR
86C2 Kaladan R Burma
21C4 Ka Lae C Hawaiian Is
100B3 Kalahari Desert
 Botswana
38J6 Kalajoki Fin
63D2 Kalakan USSR
70A3 Kalakepen Indon
84C1 Kalam Pak
55B3 Kalámai Greece
10B2 Kalamazoo USA
84B3 Kalat Pak
92B1 Kalecik Turk
78D3 Kalembau I Indon
99C3 Kalémié Zaïre
38L5 Kalevala USSR
86C2 Kalewa Burma
12D2 Kalgin I USA
106B4 Kalgoorlie Aust
78B4 Kalianda Indon
79B3 Kalibo Phil
98C3 Kalima Zaïre
78C3 Kalimantan Province,
 Indon
55C3 Kálimnos I Greece
86B1 Kālimpang India
60E2 Kalinin USSR
60B3 Kaliningrad USSR
60C3 Kalinkovichi USSR
8B2 Kalispell USA
58B2 Kalisz Pol
99D3 Kaliua Tanz
38J5 Kalix R Sweden
100A3 Kalkfeld Namibia
100A3 Kalkrand Namibia
108A1 Kallakoopah R Aust
38K6 Kallávesi L Fin
55C3 Kallonis Kólpos B
 Greece
39H7 Kalmar Sweden
61G4 Kalmykskaya ASSR
 Republic, USSR

100B2 Kalomo Zambia
18B1 Kalona USA
13B2 Kalone Peak Mt Can
87A2 Kalpeni I India
85D3 Kālpi India
53A3 Kalsat Khasba Tunisia
12B2 Kalskag USA
12C2 Kaltag USA
60E3 Kaluga USSR
59C3 Kalush USSR
87B2 Kalyandurg India
60E2 Kalyazin USSR
61H1 Kama R USSR
74E3 Kamaishi Japan
84C2 Kamalia Pak
110C1 Kamanawa Mts NZ
100A2 Kamanjab Namibia
84D2 Kamat Mt India
87B3 Kamban India
61H2 Kambarka USSR
97A4 Kambia Sierra Leone
59D3 Kamenets Podolskiy
 USSR
61F3 Kamenka USSR
65K4 Kamen-na-Obi USSR
61K2 Kamensk-Ural'skiy
 USSR
5H3 Kamilukuak L Can
98C3 Kamina Zaïre
7A3 Kaminak L Can
75C1 Kaminoyama Japan
5F4 Kamloops Can
93E1 Kamo USSR
75C1 Kamogawa Japan
99D2 Kampala Uganda
77C5 Kampar Malay
78A2 Kampar R Indon
56B2 Kampen Neth
76B2 Kamphaeng Phet Thai
77C3 Kampot Camb
 Kampuchea =
 Cambodia
91D4 Kamsaptar Iran
61J2 Kamskoye
 Vodokhranilishche
 Res USSR
85D4 Kāmthi India
61G3 Kamyshin USSR
61K2 Kamyshlov USSR
7C4 Kanaaupscow R Can
98C3 Kananga Zaïre
61G2 Kanash USSR
75B1 Kanayama Japan
74D3 Kanazawa Japan
4C3 Kanbisha USA
87B2 Kānchipuram India
84B2 Kandahar Afghan
64E3 Kandalaksha USSR
38L5 Kandalakshskaya
 Guba B USSR
97C3 Kandi Benin
109C2 Kandos Aust
87C3 Kandy Sri Lanka
15C2 Kane USA
6C1 Kane Basin B Can
98B1 Kanem Desert Region
 Chad
97B3 Kangaba Mali
92C2 Kangal Turk
6E3 Kangâmiut Greenland
91B4 Kangan Iran
77C4 Kangar Malay
106C4 Kangaroo I Aust
6E3 Kanga'tsiaq
 Greenland
90A3 Kangavar Iran
72C1 Kangbao China
82C3 Kangchenjunga Mt
 Nepal
73A4 Kangding China
6G3 Kangerdlugssuaq B
 Greenland
6G3 Kangerdlugssvatsaiq
 B Greenland
99D2 Kangetet Kenya
74B2 Kanggye N Korea
7D4 Kangiqsualujjuaq Can

6C3 Kangiqsujuaq Can
7C3 Kangirsuk Can
74B3 Kangnüng S Korea
98B2 Kango Gabon
68B4 Kangto Mt China
72B3 Kang Xian China
77D4 Kanh Hung Viet
98C3 Kaniama Zaïre
87B1 Kani Giri India
64F3 Kanin Nos Pt USSR
39J6 Kankaanpää Fin
14A2 Kankakee USA
14A2 Kankakee R USA
97B3 Kankan Guinea
86A2 Kānker India
87B3 Kanniyākuman India
97C3 Kano Nig
74C4 Kanoya Japan
86A1 Kānpur India
9D3 Kansas State, USA
18A2 Kansas R USA
10A3 Kansas City USA
73D5 Kanshi China
63B2 Kansk USSR
97C3 Kantchari Burkina
86B2 Kanthi India
12D2 Kantishna USA
12D2 Kantishna R USA
100B3 Kanye Botswana
68D4 Kao-hsiung Taiwan
100A2 Kaoka Veld Plain
 Namibia
97A3 Kaolack Sen
100B2 Kaoma Zambia
21C4 Kapaau Hawaiian Is
98C3 Kapanga Zaïre
6F3 Kap Cort Adelaer C
 Greenland
6H3 Kap Dalton C
 Greenland
39H7 Kapellskär Sweden
6F3 Kap Farvel C
 Greenland
6G3 Kap Gustav Holm C
 Greenland
100B2 Kapiri Zambia
78C2 Kapit Malay
19B3 Kaplan USA
57C3 Kaplice Czech
77B4 Kapoe Thai
99C3 Kapona Zaïre
52C1 Kaposvár Hung
6C2 Kap Parry C Can
6H3 Kap Ravn C
 Greenland
78B3 Kapuas R Indon
108A2 Kapunda Aust
84D2 Kapurthala India
7B5 Kapuskasing Can
109D2 Kaputar Mt Aust
93E2 Kapydzhik Mt USSR
6D2 Kap York C
 Greenland
92B1 Karabük Turk
55C2 Karacabey Turk
85B4 Karachi Pak
87A1 Karād India
60E5 Kara Daglari Mt Turk
54C5 Karadeniz Boğazi Sd
 Turk
68D1 Karaftit USSR
65J5 Karaganda USSR
65J5 Karagayly USSR
87B2 Kāraikāl India
90B2 Karaj Iran
92C3 Karak Jordan
65G5 Kara Kalpakskaya
 A.S.S.R. Republic,
 USSR
84D1 Karakax He R China
71D3 Karakelong I Indon
84D1 Karakoram Mts India
84D1 Karakoram P India/
 China
97A3 Karakoro R Maur/Sen
65G6 Karakumy Desert
 USSR
94B3 Karama Jordan

92B2 **Karaman** Turk
65K5 **Karamay** China
111B2 **Karamea** NZ
111B2 **Karamea Bight** *B* NZ
85D4 **Kāranja** India
92B2 **Karapınar** Turk
64H2 **Kara S** USSR
100A3 **Karasburg** Namibia
38K5 **Karasjok** Nor
65J4 **Karasuk** USSR
92C2 **Karataş** Turk
65H5 **Kara Tau** *Mts* USSR
76B3 **Karathuri** Burma
74B4 **Karatsu** Japan
91B4 **Karāz** Iran
93D3 **Karbalā'** Iraq
59C3 **Karcag** Hung
55B3 **Kardhítsa** Greece
64E3 **Karel'skaya ASSR**
   Republic, USSR
38J5 **Karesvando** Sweden
96B2 **Karet** *Desert Region*
   Maur
65K4 **Kargasok** USSR
97D3 **Kari** Nig
100B2 **Kariba** Zim
100B2 **Kariba** *L* Zim/Zambia
100B2 **Kariba Dam** Zim/
   Zambia
95C3 **Karima** Sudan
78B3 **Karimata** *I* Indon
86C2 **Karimganj** Bang
87B1 **Karimnagar** India
99E1 **Karin** Somalia
39J6 **Karis** Fin
99C3 **Karishimbe** *Mt* Zaïre
55B3 **Káristos** Greece
87A2 **Kārkal** India
71F4 **Karkar** *I* PNG
90A3 **Karkheh** *R* Iran
60D4 **Karkinitskiy Zaliv** *B*
   USSR
63B3 **Karlik Shan** *Mt* China
58B2 **Karlino** Pol
52C2 **Karlobag** Yugos
52C1 **Karlovac** Yugos
54B2 **Karlovo** Bulg
57C2 **Karlovy Vary** Czech
39G7 **Karlshamn** Sweden
39G7 **Karlskoga** Sweden
39H7 **Karlskrona** Sweden
57B3 **Karlsruhe** Germany
39G7 **Karlstad** Sweden
12D3 **Karluk** USA
86C2 **Karnafuli Res** Bang
84D3 **Karnal** India
87A1 **Karnataka** State, India
54C2 **Karnobat** Bulg
100B2 **Karoi** Zim
99D3 **Karonga** Malawi
95C3 **Karora** Sudan
78D3 **Karossa** Indon
55C3 **Kárpathos** *I* Greece
6E2 **Karrats Fjord**
   Greenland
93D1 **Kars** Turk
65H4 **Karsakpay** USSR
58D1 **Kārsava** USSR
80E2 **Karshi** USSR
38J6 **Karstula** Fin
94B1 **Kartaba** Leb
54C2 **Kartal** Turk
61K3 **Kartaly** USSR
90A3 **Kārūn** *R* Iran
86A1 **Karwa** India
87A2 **Kārwār** India
68D1 **Karymskoye** USSR
98B3 **Kasai** *R* Zaïre
100B2 **Kasaji** Zaïre
101C2 **Kasama** Zambia
99D3 **Kasanga** Tanz
87A2 **Kāsaragod** India
5H3 **Kasba L** Can
100B2 **Kasempa** Zambia
100B2 **Kasenga** Zaïre
99D2 **Kasese** Uganda
90B3 **Kāshān** Iran
12C2 **Kashegelok** USA

82B2 **Kashi** China
84D3 **Kāshipur** India
74D3 **Kashiwazaki** Japan
90C2 **Kashmar** Iran
66D3 **Kashmir** State, India
61F3 **Kasimov** USSR
18C2 **Kaskaskia** *R* USA
38J6 **Kaskinen** Fin
61K2 **Kasli** USSR
5G5 **Kaslo** Can
98C3 **Kasonga** Zaïre
98B3 **Kasongo-Lunda** Zaïre
55C3 **Kásos** *I* Greece
61G4 **Kaspiyskiy** USSR
95C3 **Kassala** Sudan
56B2 **Kassel** Germany
96C1 **Kasserine** Tunisia
100A2 **Kassinga** Angola
92B1 **Kastamonou** Turk
55B3 **Kastélli** Greece
92A2 **Kastellorizon** *I* Greece
55B2 **Kastoria** Greece
55C3 **Kástron** Greece
74D3 **Kasugai** Japan
75A1 **Kasumi** Japan
101C2 **Kasungu** Malawi
84C2 **Kasur** Pak
100B2 **Kataba** Zambia
98C3 **Katako-kombe** Zaïre
4D3 **Katalla** USA
63G2 **Katangli** USSR
106A4 **Katanning** Aust
55B2 **Katerini** Greece
5E4 **Kates Needle** *Mt* Can/
   USA
82D3 **Katha** Burma
106C2 **Katherine** Aust
85C4 **Kāthiāwār** *Pen* India
86B1 **Kathmandu** Nepal
84D2 **Kathua** India
86B1 **Katihār** India
100B2 **Katima Mulilo**
   Namibia
4C4 **Katmai,Mt** USA
12D3 **Katmai Nat Mon** USA
86A2 **Katni** India
109D2 **Katoomba** Aust
59B2 **Katowice** Pol
39H7 **Katrineholm** Sweden
97C3 **Katsina** Nig
97C4 **Katsina Ala** Nig
75C1 **Katsuta** Japan
75C1 **Katsuura** Japan
75B1 **Katsuy** Japan
65H6 **Kattakurgan** USSR
39G7 **Kattegat** *Str* Den/
   Sweden
21C4 **Kauai** *I* Hawaiian Is
21C4 **Kauai Chan** Hawaiian
   Is
21C4 **Kaulakahi Chan**
   Hawaiian Is
21C4 **Kaunakaki** Hawaiian Is
60B3 **Kaunas** USSR
97C3 **Kaura Namoda** Nig
38J5 **Kautokeino** Nor
55B2 **Kavadarci** Yugos
55A2 **Kavajë** Alb
87B2 **Kavali** India
55B2 **Kaválla** Greece
85B4 **Kāvda** India
75B1 **Kawagoe** Japan
75B1 **Kawaguchi** Japan
110B1 **Kawakawa** NZ
99C3 **Kawambwa** Zambia
86A2 **Kawardha** India
15C2 **Kawartha Lakes** Can
74D3 **Kawasaki** Japan
110C1 **Kawerau** NZ
110B1 **Kawhia** NZ
97B3 **Kaya** Burkina
12F3 **Kayak I** USA
78D2 **Kayan** *R* Indon
87B3 **Kāyankulam** India
97A3 **Kayes** Mali
92C2 **Kayseri** Turk
1B8 **Kazach'ye** USSR
93E1 **Kazakh** USSR

65G5 **Kazakhskaya SSR**
   Republic, USSR
61G2 **Kazan'** USSR
54C2 **Kazanlŭk** Bulg
69G4 **Kazan Retto** *Is* Japan
91B4 **Kāzerūn** Iran
61H1 **Kazhim** USSR
93E1 **Kazi Magomed** USSR
59C3 **Kazincbarcika** Hung
55B3 **Kéa** *I* Greece
21C4 **Kealaikahiki Chan**
   Hawaiian Is
8D2 **Kearney** USA
93C2 **Keban Baraji** *Res* Turk
97A3 **Kébémer** Sen
96C1 **Kebili** Tunisia
94C1 **Kebīr** *R* Leb/Syria
38H5 **Kebrekaise** *Mt*
   Sweden
59B3 **Kecskemét** Hung
58C1 **Kedainiai** USSR
97A3 **Kédougou** Sen
12J2 **Keele** *R* Can
12H2 **Keele Pk** *Mt* Can
21B2 **Keeler** USA
15D2 **Keene** New
   Hampshire, USA
100A3 **Keetmanshoop**
   Namibia
18C1 **Keewanee** USA
6A3 **Keewatin** *Region* Can
55B3 **Kefallinía** *I* Greece
94B2 **Kefar Sava** Israel
97C4 **Keffi** Nig
38A2 **Keflavik** Iceland
5G4 **Keg River** Can
76B1 **Kehsi Mansam** Burma
108B3 **Keith** Aust
44C3 **Keith** Scot
4F3 **Keith Arm** *B* Can
6D3 **Kekertuk** Can
85D3 **Kekri** India
77C5 **Kelang** Malay
77C4 **Kelantan** *R* Malay
84B1 **Kelif** USSR
92C1 **Kelkit** *R* Turk
98B3 **Kellé** Congo
4F2 **Kellet,C** Can
20C1 **Kellogg** USA
64D3 **Kelloselka** Fin
45C2 **Kells** Irish Rep
42B2 **Kells Range** *Hills* Scot
58C1 **Kelme** USSR
5G5 **Kelowna** Can
5F4 **Kelsey Bay** Can
42C2 **Kelso** Scot
20B1 **Kelso** USA
64E3 **Kem'** USSR
38L6 **Kem'** *R* USSR
97B3 **Ke Macina** Mali
13B2 **Kemano** Can
65K4 **Kemerovo** USSR
38J5 **Kemi** Fin
38K5 **Kemi** *R* Fin
38K5 **Kemijärvi** Fin
46C1 **Kempen** Region, Belg
26B2 **Kemps Bay**
   The Bahamas
109D2 **Kempsey** Aust
57C3 **Kempten** Germany
12D2 **Kenai** USA
12D3 **Kenai Mts** USA
12D2 **Kenai Pen** USA
99D2 **Kenamuke Swamp**
   Sudan
42C2 **Kendal** Eng
109D2 **Kendall** Aust
71D4 **Kendari** Indon
78C3 **Kendawangan** Indon
86B2 **Kendrāpāra** India
20C1 **Kendrick** USA
97A4 **Kenema** Sierra Leone
98B3 **Kenge** Zaïre
76B1 **Kengtung** Burma
100B3 **Kenhardt** S Africa
97A3 **Kéniéba** Mali
96B1 **Kénitra** Mor
45B3 **Kenmare** Irish Rep

45B3 **Kenmare** *R* Irish Rep
19B4 **Kenner** USA
18C2 **Kennett** USA
16B3 **Kennett Square** USA
20C1 **Kennewick** USA
5F4 **Kenny Dam** Can
7A5 **Kenora** Can
10B2 **Kenosha** USA
43E4 **Kent** County, Eng
20B1 **Kent** Washington, USA
14A2 **Kentland** USA
14B2 **Kenton** USA
4H3 **Kent Pen** Can
11B3 **Kentucky** State, USA
11B3 **Kentucky L** USA
19B3 **Kentwood** Louisiana,
   USA
14A2 **Kentwood** Michigan,
   USA
99D2 **Kenya** Republic, Africa
99D3 **Kenya,Mt** Kenya
18B1 **Keokuk** USA
86A2 **Keonchi** India
86B2 **Keonjhargarh** India
71E4 **Kepaluan Tanimbar**
   Arch Indon
6H3 **Keplavik** Iceland
59B2 **Kepno** Pol
78B2 **Kepulauan Anambas**
   Arch Indon
71E4 **Kepulauan Aru** *Arch*
   Indon
78B2 **Kepulauan Badas** *Is*
   Indon
71E4 **Kepulauan Banda** *Arch*
   Indon
71D4 **Kepulauan Banggai** *I*
   Indon
78B2 **Kepulauan Bunguran**
   Seletan *Arch* Indon
71E4 **Kepulauan Kai** *Arch*
   Indon
71D4 **Kepulauan Leti** *I* Indon
78A3 **Kepulauan Lingga** *Is*
   Indon
70A4 **Kepulauan Mentawi**
   Arch Indon
78A2 **Kepulauan Riau** *Arch*
   Indon
78D4 **Kepulauan Sabalana**
   Arch Indon
71D3 **Kepulauan Sangihe**
   Arch Indon
71D4 **Kepulauan Sula** *I*
   Indon
71D3 **Kepulauan Talaud**
   Arch Indon
78B2 **Kepulauan Tambelan**
   Is Indon
71E4 **Kepulauan Tanimbar** *I*
   Indon
71D4 **Kepulauan Togian** *I*
   Indon
71D4 **Kepulauan Tukambesi**
   Is Indon
87B2 **Kerala** State, India
108B3 **Kerang** Aust
39K6 **Kerava** Fin
60E4 **Kerch'** USSR
71F4 **Kerema** PNG
20C1 **Keremeps** Can
95C3 **Keren** Eth
104B6 **Kerguelen Ridge**
   Indian O
99D3 **Kericho** Kenya
70B4 **Kerinci** *Mt* Indon
99D2 **Kerio** *R* Kenya
80E2 **Kerki** USSR
55A3 **Kérkira** Greece
55A3 **Kérkira** *I* Greece
91C3 **Kerman** Iran
22B2 **Kerman** USA
90A3 **Kermānshāh** Iran
21B2 **Kern** *R* USA
13F2 **Kerrobert** Can
45B2 **Kerry** County, Irish Rep
17B1 **Kershaw** USA
78B3 **Kertamulia** Indon

63D3 **Kerulen** *R* Mongolia
96B2 **Kerzaz** Alg
55C2 **Keşan** Turk
74E3 **Kesennuma** Japan
38L5 **Kestenga** USSR
42C2 **Keswick** Eng
65K4 **Ket** *R* USSR
97C4 **Kéta** Ghana
78C3 **Ketapang** Indon
5E4 **Ketchikan** USA
97C3 **Ketia** Niger
85B4 **Keti Bandar** Pak
58C2 **Ketrzyn** Pol
43D3 **Kettering** Eng
14B3 **Kettering** USA
20C1 **Kettle** *R* Can
20C1 **Kettle River Range**
  Mts USA
7C3 **Kettlestone B** Can
90C3 **Kevir-i Namak** *Salt
  Flat* Iran
14A2 **Kewaunee** USA
14B1 **Key Harbour** Can
17B2 **Key Largo** USA
11B4 **Key West** USA
63C2 **Kezhma** USSR
54A1 **K'félegháza** Hung
12B2 **Kgun L** USA
94C2 **Khabab** Syria
62H3 **Khabarovsk** USSR
85B3 **Khairpur** Pak
85B3 **Khairpur** Region, Pak
100B3 **Khakhea** Botswana
55C3 **Khálki** *I* Greece
55B2 **Khalkidhíki** *Pen*
  Greece
55B3 **Khalkis** Greece
61G2 **Khalturin** USSR
85C4 **Khambhät,G of** India
85D4 **Khämgaon** India
76C2 **Kham Keut** Laos
87C1 **Khammam** India
90A2 **Khamseh** *Mts* Iran
76C2 **Khan** *R* Laos
84B1 **Khanabad** Afghan
93E3 **Khänaqin** Iraq
85D4 **Khandwa** India
84C2 **Khanewal** Pak
94C3 **Khan ez Zabib** Jordan
77D4 **Khanh Hung** Viet
55B3 **Khaniá** Greece
84C3 **Khanpur** Pak
65H3 **Khanty-Mansiysk**
  USSR
94B3 **Khan Yunis** Egypt
84D1 **Khapalu** India
68C2 **Khapcheranga** USSR
61G4 **Kharabali** USSR
86B2 **Kharagpur** India
91C4 **Khärän** Iran
84B3 **Kharan** Pak
90B3 **Kharänaq** Iran
91B4 **Khärg** *Is* Iran
95C2 **Khârga Oasis** Egypt
85D4 **Khargon** India
60E4 **Khar'kov** USSR
54C2 **Kharmanli** Bulg
61F2 **Kharovsk** USSR
95C3 **Khartoum** Sudan
95C3 **Khartoum North**
  Sudan
74C2 **Khasan** USSR
95C3 **Khashm el Girba**
  Sudan
86C1 **Khasi-Jaïntia Hills**
  India
54C2 **Khaskovo** Bulg
1B9 **Khatanga** USSR
76B3 **Khawsa** Burma
76C2 **Khe Bo** Viet
85C4 **Khed Brahma** India
51C2 **Khemis** Alg
51D2 **Kherrata** Alg
60D4 **Kherson** USSR
63D2 **Khilok** USSR
55C3 **Khíos** Greece
55C3 **Khíos** *I* Greece
60C4 **Khmel'nitskiy** USSR

59C3 **Khodorov** USSR
84B1 **Kholm** Afghan
76D3 **Khong** Laos
91B4 **Khonj** Iran
69F2 **Khor** USSR
91A3 **Khoramshahr** Iran
91B5 **Khōr Duwayhin** *B*
  UAE
84C1 **Khorog** USSR
90A3 **Khorramābad** Iran
90C3 **Khosf** Iran
84B2 **Khost** Pak
60C4 **Khotin** USSR
12C2 **Khotol** *Mt* USA
60C3 **Khoyniku** USSR
63F2 **Khrebet Dzhugdzhur**
  Mts USSR
90C2 **Khrebet Kopet Dag**
64H3 **Khrebet Pay-khoy** *Mts*
  USSR
82C1 **Khrebet Tarbagatay**
  Mts USSR
63E2 **Khrebet Tukuringra**
  Mts USSR
86B2 **Khulna** Bang
84D1 **Khunjerab** *P* China/
  India
90B3 **Khunsar** Iran
91A4 **Khurays** S Arabia
86B2 **Khurda** India
84D3 **Khurja** India
84C2 **Khushab** Pak
94B2 **Khushnīyah** Syria
59C3 **Khust** USSR
99C1 **Khuwei** Sudan
85B3 **Khuzdar** Pak
90D3 **Khvāf** Iran
61G3 **Khvalynsk** USSR
90C3 **Khvor** Iran
91B4 **Khvormüj** Iran
93D2 **Khvoy** Iran
84C1 **Khwaja Muhammad**
  Mts Afghan
84C2 **Khyber P** Afghan/Pak
99C3 **Kiambi** Zaïre
19A3 **Kiamichi** *R* USA
12B1 **Kiana** USA
98B3 **Kibangou** Congo
99D3 **Kibaya** Tanz
98C3 **Kibombo** Zaïre
99D3 **Kibondo** Tanz
99D3 **Kibungu** Rwanda
55B2 **Kičevo** Yugos
5G4 **Kicking Horse P** Can
97C3 **Kidal** Mali
43C3 **Kidderminster** Eng
97A3 **Kidira** Sen
110C1 **Kidnappers,C** NZ
56C2 **Kiel** Germany
59C2 **Kielce** Pol
56C2 **Kieler Bucht** *B*
  Germany
  Kiev = Kiyev
80E2 **Kiffa** Maur
97A3 **Kiffa** Maur
89H8 **Kigali** Rwanda
12A2 **Kigluaik Mts** USA
99C3 **Kigoma** Tanz
75B2 **Kii-sanchi** *Mts* Japan
74C4 **Kii-suido** *B* Japan
54B1 **Kikinda** Yugos
55B3 **Kikládhes** *Is* Greece
71F4 **Kikori** PNG
98B3 **Kikwit** Zaïre
21C4 **Kilauea Crater** *Mt*
  Hawaiian Is
4C3 **Kilbuck Mts** USA
74B2 **Kilchu** N Korea
109D1 **Kilcoy** Aust
45C2 **Kildare County,**
  Irish Rep
45C2 **Kildare** Irish Rep
19B3 **Kilgore** USA
99D3 **Kilifi** Kenya
99D3 **Kilimanjaro** *Mt* Tanz
99D3 **Kilindoni** Tanz
92C2 **Kilis** Turk

45B2 **Kilkee** Irish Rep
45C2 **Kilkenny County,**
  Irish Rep
45C2 **Kilkenny** Irish Rep
45B2 **Kilkieran B** Irish Rep
55B2 **Kilkis** Greece
45B1 **Killala B** Irish Rep
45B2 **Killaloe** Irish Rep
109D1 **Killarney** Aust
41B3 **Killarney** Irish Rep
19A3 **Killeen** USA
12D1 **Killik** *R* USA
44B3 **Killin** Scot
55B3 **Killíni** *Mt* Greece
45B1 **Killybegs** Irish Rep
42B2 **Kilmarnock** Scot
61H2 **Kil'mez** USSR
99D3 **Kilosa** Tanz
41B3 **Kilrush** Irish Rep
99C3 **Kilwa** Zaïre
99D3 **Kilwa Kisiwani** Tanz
99D3 **Kilwa Kivinje** Tanz
108A2 **Kimba** Aust
12F2 **Kimball,Mt** USA
13D3 **Kimberley** USA
101F1 **Kimberley** S Africa
106B2 **Kimberley Plat** Aust
74B2 **Kimch'aek** N Korea
74B3 **Kimch'ŏn** S Korea
55B3 **Kími** Greece
60E2 **Kimry** USSR
70C3 **Kinabalu** *Mt* Malay
78D1 **Kinabatangan** *R*
  Malay
14B2 **Kincardine** Can
13B1 **Kincolith** Can
19B3 **Kinder** USA
13F2 **Kindersley** Can
97A3 **Kindia** Guinea
98C3 **Kindu** Zaïre
61H3 **Kinel'** USSR
61F2 **Kineshma** USSR
109D1 **Kingaroy** Aust
21A2 **King City** USA
5F4 **Kingcome Inlet** Can
7C4 **King George Is** Can
107D4 **King I** Aust
13B2 **King I** Can
106B2 **King Leopold Range**
  Mts Aust
9B3 **Kingman** USA
98C3 **Kingombe** Zaïre
108A2 **Kingoonya** Aust
22C2 **Kingsburg** USA
21B2 **Kings Canyon Nat Pk**
  USA
108A3 **Kingscote** Aust
106B2 **King Sd** Aust
14A1 **Kingsford** USA
17B1 **Kingsland** USA
43E3 **King's Lynn** Eng
16C2 **Kings Park** USA
8B2 **Kings Peak** *Mt* USA
107C4 **Kingston** Aust
7C5 **Kingston** Can
25E3 **Kingston** Jamaica
15D2 **Kingston** New York,
  USA
111A3 **Kingston** NZ
27E4 **Kingstown** St Vincent
9D4 **Kingsville** USA
44B3 **Kingussie** Scot
4J3 **King William I** Can
100B4 **King William's Town**
  S Africa
98B3 **Kinkala** Congo
39G7 **Kinna** Sweden
44D3 **Kinnairds Head** *Pt*
  Scot
75B1 **Kinomoto** Japan
44C3 **Kinross** Scot
45B3 **Kinsale** Irish Rep
98B3 **Kinshasa** Zaïre
78D3 **Kintap** Indon
42B2 **Kintyre** *Pen* Scot
13D1 **Kinuso** Can
99D2 **Kinyeti** *Mt* Sudan
55B3 **Kiparissía** Greece

55B3 **Kiparissiakós Kólpos**
  G Greece
15C1 **Kipawa,L** Can
99D3 **Kipili** Tanz
12B3 **Kipnuk** USA
45C2 **Kippure** *Mt* Irish Rep
100B2 **Kipushi** Zaïre
63C2 **Kirensk** USSR
65J5 **Kirgizskaya SSR**
  Republic, USSR
82B1 **Kirgizskiy Khrebet** *Mts*
  USSR
98B3 **Kiri** Zaïre
105G4 **Kiribati** *Is* Pacific O
92B2 **Kırıkkale** Turk
60D2 **Kirishi** USSR
85B3 **Kirithar Range** *Mts*
  Pak
55C3 **Kirkağaç** Turk
90A2 **Kirk Bulāg Dāgh** *Mt*
  Iran
42C2 **Kirkby** Eng
44C3 **Kirkcaldy** Scot
42B2 **Kirkcudbright** Scot
38K5 **Kirkenes** Nor
7B5 **Kirkland Lake** Can
112A **Kirkpatrick,Mt** Ant
10A2 **Kirksville** USA
93D2 **Kirkük** Iraq
44C2 **Kirkwall** Scot
18B2 **Kirkwood** USA
60D3 **Kirov** USSR
61G2 **Kirov** USSR
93D1 **Kirovakan** USSR
61J2 **Kirovgrad** USSR
60D4 **Kirovograd** USSR
61H2 **Kirs** USSR
92B2 **Kirşehir** Turk
56C2 **Kiruna** Sweden
75B1 **Kiryū** Japan
98C2 **Kisangani** Zaïre
75B1 **Kisarazu** Japan
86B1 **Kishanganj** India
85C3 **Kishangarh** India
60C4 **Kishinev** USSR
75B2 **Kishiwada** Japan
99D3 **Kisii** Kenya
99D3 **Kisiju** Tanz
59B3 **Kiskunhalas** Hung
65F5 **Kislovodsk** USSR
99E3 **Kismaayo** Somalia
75B1 **Kiso-sammyaku** *Mts*
  Japan
97A4 **Kissidougou** Guinea
17B2 **Kissimmee,L** USA
99D3 **Kisumu** Kenya
59C3 **Kisvárda** Hung
97B3 **Kita** Mali
65H6 **Kitab** USSR
75C1 **Kitakata** Japan
74C4 **Kita-Kyūshū** Japan
99D2 **Kitale** Kenya
69G4 **Kitalo** *I* Japan
74E2 **Kitami** Japan
7B5 **Kitchener** Can
99D2 **Kitgum** Uganda
55B3 **Kíthira** *I* Greece
55B3 **Kíthnos** *I* Greece
94A1 **Kiti,C** Cyprus
4H3 **Kitikmeot** *Region* Can
5F4 **Kitimat** Can
38K5 **Kitnen** *R* Fin
75A2 **Kitsuki** Japan
15C2 **Kittanning** USA
38J5 **Kittilä** Fin
99D3 **Kitunda** Tanz
13B1 **Kitwanga** Can
100B2 **Kitwe** Zambia
57C3 **Kitzbühel** Austria
47E1 **Kitzbühler Alpen** *Mts*
  Austria
57C3 **Kitzingen** Germany
98C3 **Kiumbi** Zaïre
12B1 **Kivalina** USA
59D2 **Kivercy** USSR
99C3 **Kivu,L** Zaïre/Rwanda
4B3 **Kiwalik** USA
60D3 **Kiyev** USSR

61J2 **Kizel** USSR
92C2 **Kizil** *R* Turk
80D2 **Kizyl-Arvat** USSR
90B2 **Kizyl-Atrek** USSR
57C2 **Kladno** Czech
57C3 **Klagenfurt** Austria
60B2 **Klaipēda** USSR
8A2 **Klamath** USA
20B2 **Klamath** *R* USA
8A2 **Klamath Falls** USA
20B2 **Klamath Mts** USA
57C3 **Klatovy** Czech
12H3 **Klawak** USA
94B1 **Kleiat** Leb
101G1 **Klerksdorp** S Africa
60E2 **Klin** USSR
58B1 **Klintehamn** Sweden
60D3 **Klintsy** USSR
52C2 **Ključ** Yugos
59B2 **Kłodzko** Pol
12G2 **Klondike** *R* Can/USA
4D3 **Klondike Plat** Can/USA
59B3 **Klosterneuburg** Austria
12G2 **Kluane** *R* Can
12G2 **Kluane L** Can
12G2 **Kluane Nat Pk** Can
59B2 **Kluczbork** Pol
12G3 **Klukwan** USA
12E2 **Klutina L** USA
12E2 **Knight I** USA
43C3 **Knighton** Wales
52C2 **Knin** Yugos
106A4 **Knob,C** Aust
46B1 **Knokke-Heist** Belg
112C9 **Knox Coast** Ant
11B3 **Knoxville** Tennessee, USA
6H3 **Knud Ramsussens Land** *Region* Greenland
78B3 **Koba** Indon
6F3 **Kobbermirebugt** Greenland
74D4 **Kobe** Japan
56C1 **København** Den
57B2 **Koblenz** Germany
60B3 **Kobrin** USSR
71E4 **Kobroör** I Indon
12C1 **Kobuk** *R* USA
54B2 **Kočani** Yugos
76C3 **Ko Chang** I Thai
86B1 **Koch Bihar** India
47D1 **Kochel** Germany
6C3 **Koch I** Can
74C4 **Kōchi** Japan
12D3 **Kodiak** USA
12D3 **Kodiak I** USA
87B2 **Kodikkarai** India
99D2 **Kodok** Sudan
100A3 **Koes** Namibia
101G1 **Koffiefontein** S Africa
97B4 **Koforidua** Ghana
74D3 **Kōfu** Japan
75B1 **Koga** Japan
39G7 **Køge** Den
84C2 **Kohat** Pak
84B2 **Koh-i-Baba** *Mts* Afghan
84B1 **Koh-i-Hisar** *Mts* Afghan
84B2 **Koh-i-Khurd** *Mt* Afghan
86C1 **Kohīma** India
84B1 **Koh-i-Mazar** *Mt* Afghan
84B3 **Kohlu** Pak
60C2 **Kohtla Järve** USSR
75B1 **Koide** Japan
12F2 **Koidern** Can
77A4 **Koihoa** *Is* Nicobar Is
74B4 **Kōje-do** I S Korea
65H4 **Kokchetav** USSR
39J6 **Kokemaki** *L* Fin
38J6 **Kokkola** Fin
107D1 **Kokoda** PNG
14A2 **Kokomo** USA

71E4 **Kokonau** Indon
65K5 **Kokpekty** USSR
7D4 **Koksoak** *R* Can
100B4 **Kokstad** S Africa
76C3 **Ko Kut** I Thai
38L5 **Kola** USSR
71D4 **Kolaka** Indon
77B4 **Ko Lanta** I Thai
87B2 **Kolār** India
87B2 **Kolār Gold Fields** India
97A3 **Kolda** Sen
39F7 **Kolding** Den
87A1 **Kolhāpur** India
12C3 **Koligk** USA
59B2 **Kolin** Czech
57B2 **Köln** Germany
58B2 **Kolo** Pol
58B2 **Kolobrzeg** Pol
97B3 **Kolokani** Mali
60E2 **Kolomna** USSR
60C4 **Kolomyya** USSR
65K4 **Kolpashevo** USSR
68A2 **Kolpekty** USSR
55C3 **Kólpos Merabéllou** *B* Greece
55B2 **Kólpos Singitikós** *G* Greece
55B2 **Kólpos Strimonikós** *G* Greece
55B2 **Kólpos Toronaíos** *G* . Greece
38L5 **Kol'skiy Poluostrov** *Pen* USSR
38G6 **Kolvereid** Nor
100B2 **Kolwezi** Zaïre
1C7 **Kolyma** *R* USSR
54B2 **Kom** *Mt* Bulg/Yugos
99D2 **Koma** Eth
97D3 **Komaduga Gana** *R* Nig
59B3 **Komárno** Czech
101H1 **Komati** *R* S Africa
74D3 **Komatsu** Japan
75A2 **Komatsushima** Japan
64G3 **Komi A.S.S.R.** *Republic*, USSR
70C4 **Komodo** I Indon
71E4 **Komoran** I Indon
75B1 **Komoro** Japan
55C2 **Komotiní** Greece
76D3 **Kompong Cham** Camb
76C3 **Kompong Chhnang** *Mts* Camb
77C3 **Kompong Som** Camb
76C3 **Kompong Thom** Camb
76D3 **Kompong Trabek** Camb
63F2 **Komsomol'sk na Amure** USSR
65H4 **Konda** *R* USSR
99D3 **Kondoa** Tanz
87B1 **Kondukūr** India
6G3 **Kong Christian IX Land** *Region* Greenland
6F3 **Kong Frederik VI Kyst** *Mts* Greenland
64C2 **Kong Karls Land** *Is* Barents S
78D2 **Kongkemul** *Mt* Indon
98C3 **Kongolo** Zaïre
39F7 **Kongsberg** Den
39G6 **Kongsvinger** Nor
Königsberg = Kaliningrad
58B2 **Konin** Pol
54A2 **Konjic** Yugos
61F1 **Konosha** USSR
75B1 **Konosu** Japan
60D3 **Konotop** USSR
63B2 **Konsk** USSR
59C2 **Końskie** Pol
49D2 **Konstanz** Germany
97C3 **Kontagora** Nig
76D3 **Kontum** Viet
92B2 **Konya** Turk
13D3 **Kootenay** *R* Can
85C5 **Kopargaon** India
6J3 **Kópasker** Iceland
38A2 **Kópavogur** Iceland

52B1 **Koper** Yugos
80D2 **Kopet Dag** *Mts* Iran/USSR
61K2 **Kopeysk** USSR
77C4 **Ko Phangan** I Thai
77B4 **Ko Phuket** I Thai
39H7 **Köping** Sweden
87B1 **Koppal** India
52C1 **Koprivnica** Yugos
85B4 **Korangi** Pak
87C1 **Koraput** India
86A2 **Korba** India
57B2 **Korbach** Germany
4B3 **Korbuk** *R* USA
55B2 **Korçë** Alb
52C2 **Korčula** I Yugos
72E2 **Korea B** China/Korea
74B4 **Korea Str** S Korea/Japan
59D2 **Korec** USSR
92B1 **Körglu Tepesi** *Mt* Turk
97B4 **Korhogo** Ivory Coast
85B4 **Kori Creek** India
55B3 **Korinthiakós Kólpos** *G* Greece
55B3 **Kórinthos** Greece
74E3 **Kōriyama** Japan
61K3 **Korkino** USSR
92B2 **Korkuteli** Turk
82C1 **Korla** China
52C2 **Kornat** I Yugos
60D5 **Köroğlu Tepesi** *Mt* Turk
99D3 **Korogwe** Tanz
108B3 **Koroit** Aust
71E3 **Koror** Palau Is, Pacific O
59C3 **Körös** *R* Hung
60C3 **Korosten** USSR
95A3 **Koro Toro** Chad
12B3 **Korovin** I USA
69G2 **Korsakov** USSR
39G7 **Korsør** Den
46B1 **Kortrijk** Belg
55C3 **Kós** I Greece
77C4 **Ko Samui** I Thai
58B2 **Koscierzyna** Pol
107D4 **Kosciusko** *Mt* Aust
12H3 **Kosciusko I** USA
74B4 **Koshikijima-retto** I Japan
59C3 **Košice** Czech
74B3 **Kosong** N Korea
97B4 **Kossou** *L* Ivory Coast
101G1 **Koster** S Africa
99D1 **Kosti** Sudan
59D2 **Kostopol'** USSR
61F2 **Kostroma** USSR
56C2 **Kostrzyn** Pol
39H8 **Koszalin** Pol
85D3 **Kota** India
78A4 **Kotaagung** Indon
78C3 **Kotabaharu** Indon
78D3 **Kotabaru** Indon
77C4 **Kota Bharu** Malay
78A3 **Kotabum** Indon
84C2 **Kot Addu** Pak
78D1 **Kota Kinabulu** Malay
87C1 **Kotapad** India
61G2 **Kotel'nich** USSR
61F4 **Kotel'nikovo** USSR
39K6 **Kotka** Fin
64F3 **Kotlas** USSR
12B2 **Kotlik** USA
54A2 **Kotor** Yugos
60C4 **Kotovsk** USSR
85B3 **Kotri** Pak
87C1 **Kottagūdem** India
87B3 **Kottayam** India
98C2 **Kotto** *R* CAR
87B2 **Kottūru** India
12B1 **Kotzebue** USA
4B3 **Kotzebue Sd** USA
97C3 **Kouande** Benin
98C2 **Kouango** CAR
97B3 **Koudougou** Burkina
98B3 **Koulamoutou** Gabon

97B3 **Koulikoro** Mali
97B3 **Koupéla** Burkina
33G2 **Kourou** French Guiana
97B3 **Kouroussa** Guinea
98B1 **Kousséri** Cam
39K6 **Kouvola** Fin
60B3 **Kovel** USSR
Kovno = Kaunas
61F2 **Kovrov** USSR
61F3 **Kovylkino** USSR
60E1 **Kovzha** *R* USSR
77C4 **Ko Way** I Thai
73C5 **Kowloon** Hong Kong
84B2 **Kowt-e-Ashrow** Afghan
92A2 **Köyceğğiz** Turk
38L5 **Koydor** USSR
87A1 **Koyna Res** India
12B2 **Koyuk** USA
12B1 **Koyuk** *R* USA
12C2 **Koyukuk** USA
12C1 **Koyukuk** *R* USA
92C2 **Kozan** Turk
55B2 **Kozani** Greece
Kozhikode = Calicut
61G2 **Koz'modemyansk** USSR
61F2 **Koztroma** USSR
75B2 **Kōzu-shima** I Japan
39F7 **Kragerø** Nor
54B2 **Kragujevac** Yugos
77B3 **Kra,Isthmus of** Burma/Malay
Krakatau = Rakata
94C1 **Krak des Chevaliers** *Hist Site* Syria
59B2 **Kraków** Pol
54B2 **Kraljevo** Yugos
60E4 **Kramatorsk** USSR
38H6 **Kramfors** Sweden
52B1 **Kranj** Yugos
61F4 **Krapotkin** USSR
61G1 **Krasavino** USSR
61J2 **Krashnokamsk** USSR
64G2 **Krasino** USSR
59C2 **Kraśnik** Pol
61G3 **Krasnoarmeysk** USSR
60E5 **Krasnodar** USSR
61K2 **Krasnotur'insk** USSR
61J2 **Krasnoufimsk** USSR
61J3 **Krasnousol'-skiy** USSR
65G3 **Krasnovishersk** USSR
65G5 **Krasnovodsk** USSR
63B2 **Krasnoyarsk** USSR
59C2 **Krasnystaw** Pol
61G3 **Krasnyy Kut** USSR
60E4 **Krasnyy Luch** USSR
61G4 **Krasnyy Yar** USSR
76D3 **Kratie** Camb
6E2 **Kraulshavn** Greenland
56B2 **Krefeld** Germany
60D4 **Kremenchug** USSR
60D4 **Kremenchugskoye Vodokhranilische** *Res* USSR
59D2 **Kremenets** USSR
98A2 **Kribi** Cam
60D3 **Krichev** USSR
47E1 **Krimml** Austria
87B1 **Krishna** *R* India
87B2 **Krishnagiri** India
86B2 **Krishnangar** India
39F7 **Kristiansand** Nor
39G7 **Kristianstad** Sweden
64B3 **Kristiansund** Nor
39G7 **Kristinehamn** Sweden
38J6 **Kristiinankaupunki** Fin
55B3 **Kríti** I Greece
60D4 **Krivoy Rog** USSR
52B1 **Krk** I Yugos
6G3 **Kronpris Frederik Bjerge** *Mts* Greenland
39K7 **Kronshtadt** USSR
101G1 **Kroonstad** S Africa
65F5 **Kropotkin** USSR
101G1 **Krugersdorp** S Africa

78A4 **Krui** Indon
55A2 **Kruje** Alb
58D2 **Krupki** USSR
12B1 **Krusenstern,C** USA
54B2 **Kruševac** Yugos
39K7 **Krustpils** USSR
12G3 **Kruzof I** USA
65E5 **Krym** *Pen* USSR
60D5 **Krym** *R* USSR
60E5 **Krymsk** USSR
58B2 **Krzyz** Pol
96C1 **Ksar El Boukhari** Alg
96B1 **Ksar el Kebir** Mor
70A3 **Kuala** Indon
77C5 **Kuala Dungun** Malay
77C4 **Kuala Kerai** Malay
77C5 **Kuala Kubu Baharu**
      Malay
77C5 **Kuala Lipis** Malay
77C5 **Kuala Lumpur** Malay
77C4 **Kuala Trengganu**
      Malay
78D1 **Kuamut** Malay
74A2 **Kuandian** China
77C5 **Kuantan** Malay
93E1 **Kuba** USSR
71F4 **Kubar** PNG
78C2 **Kuching** Malay
70C3 **Kudat** Malay
78C4 **Kudus** Indon
61H2 **Kudymkar** USSR
57C3 **Kufstein** Austria
90C3 **Kuh Duren** *Upland*
      Iran
91C4 **Kūh e Bazmān** *Mt*
      Iran
90B3 **Kūh-e Dinar** *Mt* Iran
90C2 **Kūh-e-Hazār Masjed**
      Mts Iran
91C4 **Kūh-e Jebāl Barez** *Mts*
      Iran
90B3 **Kūh-e Karkas** *Mts*
      Iran
91C4 **Kuh-e Laleh Zar** *Mt*
      Iran
90A2 **Kūh-e Sahand** *Mt* Iran
91D4 **Kuh e Taftān** *Mt* Iran
90A2 **Kūhhaye Sabalan** *Mts*
      Iran
90A3 **Kūhhā-ye Zāgros** *Mts*
      Iran
38K6 **Kuhmo** Fin
90B3 **Kūhpāyeh** Iran
90C3 **Kūhpāyeh** *Mt* Iran
91C4 **Kūh ye Bashākerd** *Mts*
      Iran
90A2 **Kūh ye Sabalan** *Mt*
      Iran
100A3 **Kuibis** Namibia
4B4 **Kuigillingok** USA
12H3 **Kuiu I** USA
74E2 **Kuji** Japan
75A2 **Kuju-san** *Mt* Japan
12C3 **Kukaklek L** USA
54B2 **Kukës** Alb
77C5 **Kukup** Malay
91C4 **Kūl** *R* Iran
55C3 **Kula** Turk
61J4 **Kulakshi** USSR
99D2 **Kulal,Mt** Kenya
55B2 **Kulata** Bulg
60B2 **Kuldīga** USSR
61H4 **Kul'sary** USSR
84D2 **Kulu** India
92B2 **Kulu** Turk
65J4 **Kulunda** USSR
108B2 **Kulwin** Aust
61G5 **Kuma** *R* USSR
75B1 **Kumagaya** Japan
78C3 **Kumai** Indon
74C4 **Kumamoto** Japan
75B2 **Kumano** Japan
54B2 **Kumanovo** Yugos
63E2 **Kumara** China
97B4 **Kumasi** Ghana
98A2 **Kumba** Cam
87B2 **Kumbakonam** India
61J3 **Kumertau** USSR

74B3 **Kūmhwa** S Korea
39H7 **Kumla** Sweden
87A2 **Kumta** India
82C1 **Kūmüx** China
84C2 **Kunar** *R* Afghan
39K7 **Kunda** USSR
85C4 **Kundla** India
84B1 **Kunduz** Afghan
89F9 **Kunene** *R* Angola
39G7 **Kungsbacka** Sweden
61J2 **Kungur** USSR
76B1 **Kunhing** Burma
82B2 **Kunlun Shan** *Mts*
      China
73A4 **Kunming** China
74B3 **Kunsan** S Korea
38K6 **Kuopio** Fin
52C1 **Kupa** *R* Yugos
106B2 **Kupang** Indon
107D2 **Kupiano** PNG
12H3 **Kupreanof I** USA
60E4 **Kupyansk** USSR
82C1 **Kuqa** China
75B1 **Kurabe** Japan
74C4 **Kurashiki** Japan
75A1 **Kurayoshi** Japan
54C2 **Kŭrdzhali** Bulg
74C4 **Kure** Japan
60B2 **Kuressaare** USSR
63A1 **Kureyka** *R* USSR
65H4 **Kurgan** USSR
88K6 **Kuria Muria Is** Oman
38J6 **Kurikka** Fin
      Kuril Is = Kuril'skiye
      Ostrova
69H2 **Kuril'skiye Ostrova**
      USSR
87B1 **Kurnool** India
75C1 **Kuroiso** Japan
111B2 **Kurow** NZ
109D2 **Kurri Kurri** Aust
60E3 **Kursk** USSR
58C1 **Kurskiy Zaliv** *Lg*
      USSR
68A2 **Kuruktag** *R* China
100B3 **Kurunam** S Africa
74C4 **Kurume** Japan
87C3 **Kurunegala** Sri Lanka
65K5 **Kurunktag** *R* China
61J2 **Kusa** USSR
55C3 **Kuşadasi Körfezi** *B*
      Turk
55C2 **Kus Golü** *L* Turk
74D4 **Kushimoto** Japan
74E2 **Kushiro** Japan
86B2 **Kushtia** Bang
61H3 **Kushum** *R* USSR
80E2 **Kushra** Afgan
65G4 **Kushva** USSR
12B2 **Kuskokwim** *R* USA
12B3 **Kuskokwim B** USA
12C2 **Kuskokwim Mts** USA
86A1 **Kusma** Nepal
74E2 **Kussharo-ko** *L* Japan
65H4 **Kustanay** USSR
92A2 **Kütahya** Turk
78D3 **Kutai** *R* Indon
59B3 **Kutná Hora** Czech
58B2 **Kutno** Pol
98B3 **Kutu** Zaïre
86C2 **Kutubdia I** Bang
98C1 **Kutum** Sudan
7D4 **Kuujjuaq** Can
38K5 **Kuusamo** Fin
61J3 **Kuvandyk** USSR
93E4 **Kuwait** Kuwait
80C3 **Kuwait** Sheikdom,
      S W Asia
75B1 **Kuwana** Japan
65G4 **Kuybyshev** USSR
65J4 **Kuybyshev** USSR
61G3 **Kuybyshevskoye**
      Vodokhranilishche
      Res USSR
63C2 **Kuytun** USSR
60E5 **Kuzey Anadolu Daglari**
      Mts Turk
61G3 **Kuznetsk** USSR

38J4 **Kvaenangen** *Sd* Nor
12C3 **Kvichak** USA
12C3 **Kvichak** *R* USA
12C3 **Kvichak B** USA
38G5 **Kvigtind** *Mt* Nor
38H5 **Kvikkjokk** Sweden
99D3 **Kwale** Kenya
74B3 **Kwangju** S Korea
98B3 **Kwango** *R* Zaïre
100B2 **Kwekwe** Zim
12B2 **Kwethluk** USA
12B2 **Kwethluk** *R* USA
58B2 **Kwidzyn** Pol
71E4 **Kwoka** *Mt* Indon
108C3 **Kyabram** Aust
76B2 **Kyaikkami** Burma
76B2 **Kyaikto** Burma
68C1 **Kyakhta** USSR
108A2 **Kyancutta** Aust
76B1 **Kyaukme** Burma
76B1 **Kyauk-padaung**
      Burma
76A2 **Kyaukpyu** Burma
40B2 **Kyle of Lochalsh** Scot
46D1 **Kyll** *R* Germany
108B3 **Kyneton** Aust
99D2 **Kyoga** *L* Uganda
109D1 **Kyogle** Aust
74B3 **Kyŏngju** S Korea
74D3 **Kyoto** Japan
65H4 **Kyshtym** USSR
74C4 **Kyūshū** *I* Japan
104E3 **Kyushu-Palau Ridge**
      Pacific O
54B2 **Kyustendil** Bulg
68B1 **Kyzyl** USSR
65H5 **Kyzylkum** *Desert*
      USSR
65H5 **Kzyl Orda** USSR

L

99E2 **Laas Caanood**
      Somalia
46E1 **Laasphe** Germany
99E1 **Laas Qoray** Somalia
33E1 **La Asunción** Ven
96A2 **Laâyoune** Mor
23A1 **La Barca** Mexico
97A3 **Labé** Guinea
59B2 **Labe** *R* Czech
15D1 **Labelle** Can
17B2 **La Belle** USA
12G2 **Laberge,L** Can
78D1 **Labi** Brunei
13E2 **la Biche,L** Can
61F5 **Labinsk** USSR
94C1 **Laboué** Leb
34C2 **Laboulaye** Arg
7D4 **Labrador** *Region* Can
7D4 **Labrador City** Can
7E4 **Labrador S** Greenland/
      Can
33E5 **Lábrea** Brazil
78D1 **Labuan** *I* Malay
78B4 **Labuhan** Indon
76A2 **Labutta** Burma
65H3 **Labytnangi** USSR
46B2 **La Capelle** France
34C2 **La Carlota** Arg
79B3 **La Carlota** Phil
12J1 **Lac Belot** *L* Can
7C4 **Lac Bienville** *L* Can
83B4 **Laccadive Is** India
47B2 **Lac d'Annecy** *L*
      France
4G3 **Lac de Gras** *L* Can
47B1 **Lac de Joux** *L* Switz
47B1 **Lac de Neuchâtel** *L*
      Switz
23A2 **Lac de Patzcuaro** *L*
      Mexico
23A2 **Lac de Sayula** *L*
      Mexico
4F3 **Lac des Bois** *L* Can
47A2 **Lac du Bourget** *L*
      France

25D3 **La Ceiba** Honduras
108A3 **Lacepede B** Aust
48C2 **La Châtre** France
47B1 **La-Chaux-de-Fonds**
      Switz
94B3 **Lachish** *Hist Site*
      Israel
107D4 **Lachlan** *R* Aust
32B2 **La Chorrera** Panama
15D1 **Lachute** Can
7D4 **Lac Joseph** *L* Can
15C2 **Lackawanna** USA
5G4 **Lac la Biche** Can
4G3 **Lac la Martre** *L* Can
5H4 **Lac la Ronge** *L* Can
7C4 **Lac L'eau Claire** Can
52A1 **Lac Léman** *L* Switz/
      France
10C1 **Lac Manouane** *L* Can
15D1 **Lac Megantic** Can
7C4 **Lac Mistassini** *L* Can
13E2 **Lacombe** Can
15D2 **Laconia** USA
50A1 **La Coruña** Spain
10A2 **La Crosse** USA
9C3 **La Cruces** USA
7A4 **Lac Seul** *L* Can
18B2 **La Cygne** USA
84D2 **Ladākh Range** India
85C3 **Lādnūn** India
73B5 **Ladong** China
60D1 **Ladozhskoye Ozero** *L*
      USSR
6B2 **Lady Ann Str** Can
109C4 **Lady Barron** Aust
101G1 **Ladybrand** S Africa
13C3 **Ladysmith** Can
101G1 **Ladysmith** S Africa
71F4 **Lae** PNG
76C3 **Laem Ngop** Thai
56C1 **Laesø** *I* Den
10B2 **Lafayette** Indiana,
      USA
11A3 **Lafayette** Louisiana,
      USA
46B2 **La Fère** France
46B2 **La-Ferté-sous-Jouarre**
      France
97C4 **Lafia** Nig
97C4 **Lafiagi** Nig
48B2 **La Flèche** France
96C1 **La Galite** *I* Tunisia
56C1 **Lagan** *R* Sweden
31D4 **Lagarto** Brazil
96C1 **Laghouat** Alg
35C2 **Lagoa de Araruama**
      Brazil
29F2 **Lagoa dos Patos** *Lg*
      Brazil
35C2 **Lagoa Feia** Brazil
32B4 **Lago Agrio** Ecuador
35C1 **Lagoa Juparanã** *L*
      Brazil
29D2 **Lagoa mar Chiguita** *L*
      Arg
29F2 **Lagoa Mirim** *L* Brazil/
      Urug
29B6 **Lago Argentino** *L* Arg
29B5 **Lago Buenos Aries** *L*
29B5 **Lago Cochrane** *L* Arg/
      Chile
29C5 **Lago Colhué Huapi** *L*
      Arg
24B2 **Lago de Chapala** *L*
      Mexico
32A2 **Lago de Chiriqui** *L*
      Panama
23A2 **Lago de Cuitzeo** *L*
      Mexico
29B3 **Lago de la Laja** *L*
      Chile
53A2 **Lago del Coghinas** *L*
      Sardegna
32C2 **Lago de Maracaibo** *L*
      Ven
25D3 **Lago de Nicaragua** *L*
      Nic

32A1 **Lago de Perlas** *L* Nic	38J6 **Lahia** Fin	50A1 **Lamego** Port	30C2 **La Paz** Bol
52B2 **Lago di Bolsena** *L* Italy	90B2 **Lāhijān** Iran	47B2 **La Meije** *Mt* France	24A2 **La Paz** Mexico
	46D1 **Lahn** *R* Germany	32B6 **La Merced** Peru	69G2 **La Perouse** *Str* Japan/
52B2 **Lago di Bracciano** *L* Italy	46D1 **Lahnstein** Germany	21B3 **La Mesa** USA	USSR
	84C2 **Lahore** Pak	55B3 **Lamía** Greece	23A1 **La Piedad** Mexico
52A1 **Lago di Como** *L* Italy	39K6 **Lahti** Fin	42C2 **Lammermuir Hills**	20B2 **La Pine** USA
47D2 **Lago d'Idro** *L* Italy	23A2 **La Huerta** Mexico	Scot	19B3 **Laplace** USA
52B1 **Lago di Garda** *L* Italy	98B2 **Lai** Chad	39G7 **Lammhult** Sweden	23A2 **La Placita** Mexico
47C2 **Lago di Lecco** *L* Italy	73B5 **Laibin** China	79B3 **Lamon B** Phil	29E2 **La Plata** Arg
47C2 **Lago di Lugano** *L* Italy	76C1 **Lai Chau** Viet	18B1 **Lamoni** USA	13F1 **La Plonge,L** Can
47D2 **Lago d'Iseo** *L* Italy	100B4 **Laingsburg** S Africa	71F3 **Lamotrek** *I* Pacific O	14A2 **La Porte** USA
47C2 **Lago d'Orta** *L* Italy	44B2 **Lairg** Scot	43B3 **Lampeter** Wales	39K6 **Lappeenranta** Fin
29B5 **Lago General Carrera** *L* Chile	78A3 **Lais** Indon	99E3 **Lamu** Kenya	38H5 **Lappland** *Region*
	79C4 **Lais** Phil	47D1 **Lana** Italy	Sweden/Fin
52A1 **Lago Maggiore** *L* Italy	72E2 **Laiyang** China	21C4 **Lanai** *I* Hawaiian Is	34C3 **Laprida** Arg
29C5 **Lago Musters** *L* Arg	72D2 **Laizhou Wan** *B* China	21C4 **Lanai City** Hawaiian Is	1B8 **Laptev S** USSR
48B3 **Lagon** France	34A3 **Laja** *R* Chile	42C2 **Lanark** Scot	38J6 **Lapua** Fin
29B4 **Lago Nahuel Haupi** *L* Arg	30F4 **Lajes** Brazil	76B3 **Lanbi** *I* Burma	79B3 **Lapu-Lapu** Phil
	22D4 **La Jolla** USA	76C1 **Lancang** *R* China	9B4 **La Purisima** Mexico
29B5 **Lago O'Higgins** *L* Chile	9C3 **La Junta** USA	42C3 **Lancashire** County, Eng	95B2 **Laqiya Arba'in** *Well* Sudan
53A2 **Lago Omodeo** *L* Sardegna	109C2 **Lake Cargelligo** Aust		30C3 **La Quiaca** Arg
	11A3 **Lake Charles** USA	21B3 **Lancaster** California, USA	52B2 **L'Aquila** Italy
30C2 **Lago Poopó** *L* Bol	17B1 **Lake City** Florida, USA		91B4 **Lār** Iran
29B4 **Lago Ranco** *L* Chile	17C1 **Lake City** S Carolina, USA	42C2 **Lancaster** Eng	96B1 **Larache** Mor
32D6 **Lago Rogaguado** *L* Bol		18B1 **Lancaster** Mississippi, USA	8C2 **Laramie** USA
	42C2 **Lake District** Region, Eng		8C2 **Laramie Range** *Mts* USA
97C4 **Lagos** Nig	22D4 **Lake Elsinore** USA	15D2 **Lancaster** New Hampshire, USA	
50A2 **Lagos** Port	106C3 **Lake Eyre Basin** Aust	14B3 **Lancaster** Ohio, USA	50B2 **Larca** Spain
29B5 **Lago San Martin** *L* Arg/Chile	15C2 **Lakefield** Can	10C3 **Lancaster** Pennsylvania, USA	9D4 **Laredo** USA
	6D3 **Lake Harbour** Can		91B4 **Larestan** Region, Iran
24B2 **Lagos de Moreno** Mexico	22C3 **Lake Hughes** USA	17B1 **Lancaster** S Carolina, USA	Largeau = Faya
	16B2 **Lakehurst** USA		47B2 **L'Argentière** France
30C2 **Lago Titicaca** Bol/Peru	19A4 **Lake Jackson** USA	6B2 **Lancaster Sd** Can	17B2 **Largo** USA
29B5 **Lago Viedma** *L* Arg	13E2 **Lake la Biche** Can	78B3 **Landak** *R* Indon	42B2 **Largs** Scot
8B2 **La Grande** USA	17B2 **Lakeland** USA	46E2 **Landau** Germany	90A2 **Lāri** Iran
7C4 **La Grande Rivière** *R* Can	7A5 **Lake of the Woods** Can	57C3 **Landeck** Austria	30C4 **La Rioja** Arg
		8C2 **Lander** USA	30C4 **La Rioja** State, Arg
106B2 **Lagrange** Aust	20B1 **Lake Oswego** USA	34C2 **Landeta** Arg	55B3 **Lárisa** Greece
11B3 **La Grange** Georgia, USA	21A2 **Lakeport** USA	57C3 **Landsberg** Germany	85B3 **Larkana** Pak
	19B3 **Lake Providence** USA	4F2 **Lands End** *C* Can	92B3 **Larnaca** Cyprus
14A3 **La Grange** Kentucky, USA	111B2 **Lake Pukaki** NZ	43B4 **Land's End** *Pt* Eng	94A1 **Larnaca B** Cyprus
	109C3 **Lakes Entrance** Aust	57C3 **Landshut** Germany	45D1 **Larne** N Ire
19A4 **La Grange** Texas, USA	22C2 **Lakeshore** USA	39G7 **Làndskrona** Sweden	50A1 **La Robla** Spain
33E2 **La Gran Sabana** *Mts* Ven	108B1 **Lake Stewart** Aust	17A1 **Lanett** USA	46C1 **La Roche-en-Ardenne** Belg
	15C1 **Lake Traverse** Can	56B2 **Langenhagen** Germany	
47B2 **La Grave** France	8A2 **Lakeview** USA		48B2 **La Rochelle** France
48B3 **Lagronño** Spain	20B1 **Lakeview Mt** Can	47B1 **Langenthal** Switz	47B1 **La Roche-sur-Foron** France
34A3 **Laguna Aluminé** *L* Arg	19B3 **Lake Village** USA	42C2 **Langholm** Scot	
	17B2 **Lake Wales** USA	38A2 **Langjökull** *Mts* Iceland	48B2 **La Roche-sur-Yon** France
21B3 **Laguna Beach** USA	22C4 **Lakewood** California, USA	77B4 **Langkawi** *I* Malay	51B2 **La Roda** Spain
34C3 **Laguna Colorada Grande** *L* Arg	16B2 **Lakewood** New Jersey, USA	13C3 **Langley** Can	27D3 **La Romana** Dom Rep
		108C1 **Langlo** *R* Aust	5H4 **La Ronge** Can
79B3 **Laguna de Bay** *Lg* Phil	14B2 **Lakewood** Ohio, USA	47B1 **Langnau** Switz	5H4 **La Ronge,L** Can
	17B2 **Lake Worth** USA	49D2 **Langres** France	39F7 **Larvik** Nor
25D3 **Laguna de Caratasca** *Lg* Honduras	86A1 **Lakhīmpur** India	70A3 **Langsa** Indon	65J3 **Lar'yak** USSR
	85B4 **Lakhpat** India	68C2 **Lang Shan** *Mts* China	50B2 **La Sagra** *Mt* Spain
25D4 **Laguna de Chiriqui** *L* Panama	84C2 **Lakki** Pak	76D1 **Lang Son** Viet	15D1 **La Salle** Can
	55B3 **Lakonikós Kólpos** *G* Greece	48C3 **Languedoc** Region, France	18C1 **La Salle** USA
25D3 **Laguna de Managua** *L* Nic			7C5 **La Sarre** Can
	97B4 **Lakota** Ivory Coast	29B3 **Lanin** *Mt* Arg	34C1 **Las Avispas** Arg
25D3 **Laguna de Nicaragua** *L* Nic	38K4 **Laksefjord** *Inlet* Nor	79B4 **Lanoa,L** Phil	34A2 **Las Cabras** Chile
	38K4 **Lakselv** Nor	16B2 **Lansdale** USA	5G4 **Lascombe** Can
26A4 **Laguna de Perlas** *Lg* Nic	34C2 **La Laguna** Arg	7B4 **Lansdowne House** Can	9C3 **Las Cruces** USA
	32A4 **La Libertad** Ecuador		26C3 **La Selle** *Mt* Haiti
23B1 **Laguna de Pueblo Viejo** *L* Mexico	34A2 **La Ligua** Chile	16B2 **Lansford** USA	72B2 **Lasengmia** China
	50A2 **La Linea** Spain	10B2 **Lansing** USA	30B4 **La Serena** Chile
24C2 **Laguna de Tamiahua** *Lg* Mexico	85D4 **Lalitpur** India	47B2 **Lanslebourg** France	29E3 **Las Flores** Arg
	5H4 **La Loche** Can	96A2 **Lanzarote** *I* Canary Is	76B1 **Lashio** Burma
25C3 **Laguna de Términos** *Lg* Mexico	13F1 **la Loche,L** Can	72A2 **Lanzhou** China	53C3 **La Sila** *Mts* Italy
	46C1 **La Louvière** Belg	47B2 **Lanzo Torinese** Italy	90B2 **Lāsjerd** Iran
23A1 **Laguna de Yuriria** *L* Mexico	26A4 **La Luz** Nic	79B2 **Laoag** Phil	34A3 **Las Lajas** Chile
	7C5 **La Malbaie** Can	76C1 **Lao Cai** Viet	50A2 **Las Marismas** *Marshland* Spain
23B1 **Laguna le Altamira** Mexico	23B2 **La Malinche** *Mt* Mexico	72D1 **Laoha He** *R* China	
		45C2 **Laois** County, Irish Rep	96A2 **Las Palmas de Gran Canaria** Canary Is
24C2 **Laguna Madre** *Lg* Mexico	50B2 **La Mancha** Region, Spain	46B2 **Laon** France	
		32B6 **La Oroya** Peru	52A2 **La Spezia** Italy
34C2 **Laguna Mar Chiquita** *L* Arg	9C3 **Lamar** Colorado, USA	76C2 **Laos** Republic, S E Asia	29C4 **Las Plumas** Arg
	18B2 **Lamar** Missouri, USA		34C2 **Las Rosas** Arg
29B4 **Laguna Nahuel Huapi** *L* Arg	19A4 **La Marque** USA	49C2 **Lapalisse** France	20B2 **Lassen Peak** *Mt* USA
	98B3 **Lambaréné** Gabon	32B2 **La Palma** Panama	20B2 **Lassen Volcanic Nat Pk** USA
34C2 **Laguna Paiva** Arg	32A5 **Lambayeque** Peru	96A2 **La Palma** *I* Canary Is	
29B4 **Laguna Ranco** Chile	112B10 **Lambert Gl** Ant	34B3 **La Pampa** State, Arg	23B2 **Las Tinaja** Mexico
9C4 **Laguna Seca** Mexico	16B2 **Lambertville** USA	33E2 **La Paragua** Ven	98B3 **Lastoursville** Gabon
23B1 **Laguna Tortugas** *L* Mexico	4F2 **Lamblon,C** Can	29E2 **La Paz** Arg	52C2 **Lastovo** *I* Yugos
	47C2 **Lambro** *R* Italy	34B2 **La Paz** Arg	24B2 **Las Tres Marias** *Is* Mexico
70C3 **Lahad Datu** Malay	76C2 **Lam Chi** *R* Thai		
78A3 **Lahat** Indon			

34C2 **Las Varillas** Arg
9C3 **Las Vegas** USA
Latakia = Al
Lādhiqīyah
53B2 **Latina** Italy
34B2 **La Toma** Arg
32D1 **La Tortuga** *I* Ven
79B2 **La Trinidad** Phil
109C4 **Latrobe** Aust
94B3 **Latrun** Israel
7C5 **La Tuque** Can
87B1 **Lātūr** India
60B2 **Latviyskaya SSR**
Republic, USSR
107D5 **Launceston** Aust
43B4 **Launceston** Eng
29B4 **La Unión** Chile
25D3 **La Union** El Salvador
23A2 **La Union** Mexico
32B5 **La Unión** Peru
107D2 **Laura** Aust
15C3 **Laurel** Delaware, USA
16A3 **Laurel** Maryland, USA
11B3 **Laurel** Mississippi,
USA
17B1 **Laurens** USA
17C1 **Laurinburg** USA
52A1 **Lausanne** Switz
78D3 **Laut** *I* Indon
29B5 **Lautaro** *Mt* Chile
46D2 **Lauterecken** Germany
15D1 **Laval** Can
48B2 **Laval** France
22B2 **Laveaga Peak** *Mt*
USA
47C2 **Laveno** Italy
31B6 **Lavras** Brazil
4A3 **Lavrentiya** USSR
101H1 **Lavumisa** Swaziland
78D1 **Lawas** Malay
76B1 **Lawksawk** Burma
18A2 **Lawrence** Kansas,
USA
15D2 **Lawrence**
Massachusetts, USA
111A3 **Lawrence** NZ
14A3 **Lawrenceville** Illinois,
USA
9D3 **Lawton** USA
91A5 **Layla** S Arabia
99D2 **Laylo** Sudan
23A2 **Lázaro Cárdenas**
Mexico
99E1 **Laz Daua** Somalia
79B4 **Lazi** Phil
8C2 **Lead** USA
13F2 **Leader** Can
18A2 **Leavenworth** USA
58B2 **Leba** Pol
18B2 **Lebanon** Missouri,
USA
20B2 **Lebanon** Oregon, USA
15C2 **Lebanon**
Pennsylvania, USA
92C3 **Lebanon** Republic,
S W Asia
101C3 **Lebombo** *Mts*
Mozam/S Africa/
Swaziland
58B2 **Lebork** Pol
47A2 **Le Bourg-d'Oisans**
France
47B1 **Le Brassus** Switz
29B3 **Lebu** Chile
47B1 **Le Buet** *Mt* France
46B1 **Le Cateau** France
55A2 **Lecce** Italy
52A1 **Lecco** Italy
47D1 **Lech** *R* Austria
47D1 **Lechtaler Alpen** *Mts*
Austria
49C2 **Le Creusot** France
43C3 **Ledbury** Eng
13E2 **Leduc** Can
16C1 **Lee** USA
45B3 **Lee** *R* Irish Rep
41C3 **Leeds** Eng
43C3 **Leek** Eng

56B2 **Leer** Germany
17B2 **Leesburg** Florida, USA
16A3 **Leesburg** Virginia,
USA
19B3 **Leesville** USA
109C2 **Leeton** Aust
56B2 **Leeuwarden** Neth
106A4 **Leeuwin,C** Aust
22C2 **Lee Vining** USA
27E3 **Leeward Is**
Caribbean S
94A1 **Lefkara** Cyprus
79B3 **Legazpi** Phil
47D2 **Legnago** Italy
59B2 **Legnica** Pol
33F2 **Leguan Inlet** Guyana
32C4 **Leguizamo** Colombia
84D2 **Leh** India
48C2 **Le Havre** France
16B2 **Lehigh** *R* USA
16B2 **Lehighton** USA
84C2 **Leiah** Pak
59B3 **Leibnitz** Austria
43D3 **Leicester** County, Eng
43D3 **Leicester** Eng
107C2 **Leichhardt** *R* Aust
56A2 **Leiden** Neth
46B1 **Leie** *R* Belg
106C4 **Leigh Creek** Aust
43D4 **Leighton Buzzard** Eng
56B2 **Leine** *R* Germany
45C2 **Leinster** Region,
Irish Rep
57C2 **Leipzig** Germany
50A2 **Leiria** Port
39F7 **Leirvik** Nor
45B1 **Leitrim** County,
Irish Rep
73C4 **Leiyang** China
73B5 **Leizhou Bandao** *Pen*
China
73C5 **Leizhou Wan** *B* China
56A2 **Lek** *R* Neth
96C1 **Le Kef** Tunisia
99D2 **Lekemti** Eth
19B3 **Leland** USA
54A2 **Lelija** *Mt* Yugos
47B1 **Le Locle** France
48C2 **Le Mans** France
6D3 **Lemicux Is** Can
8C2 **Lemmon** USA
21B2 **Lemoore** USA
49C2 **Lempdes** France
86C2 **Lemro** *R* Burma
52C2 **Le Murge** Region, Italy
63C2 **Lena** *R* USSR
38L6 **Lendery** USSR
73C4 **Lengshujiang** China
82A1 **Leninabad** USSR
65F5 **Leninakan** USSR
60D2 **Leningrad** USSR
112B7 **Leningradskaya** *Base*
Ant
61H3 **Leninogorsk** Tatar
ASSR, USSR
68A1 **Leninogorsk** USSR
65K4 **Leninsk-Kuznetskiy**
USSR
69F2 **Leninskoye** USSR
65F6 **Lenkoran'** USSR
46E1 **Lenne** *R* Germany
16C1 **Lennox** USA
46B1 **Lens** France
63D1 **Lensk** USSR
53B3 **Lentini** Italy
76B3 **Lenya** *R* Burma
52B1 **Leoben** Austria
43C3 **Leominster** Eng
16D1 **Leominster** USA
24B2 **Leon** Mexico
25D3 **León** Nic
50A1 **Leon** Region, Spain
50A1 **León** Spain
100A3 **Leonardville** Namibia
106B3 **Leonora** Aust
35C2 **Leopoldina** Brazil
Léopoldville =
Kinshasa

60C3 **Lepel** USSR
73D4 **Leping** China
49C2 **Le Puy** France
98B2 **Léré** Chad
101G1 **Leribe** Lesotho
47C2 **Lerici** Italy
51C1 **Lérida** Spain
23A1 **Lerma** *R* Mexico
47D1 **Lermoos** Austria
55C3 **Léros** *I* Greece
44E1 **Lerwick** Scot
46A2 **Les Andelys** France
26C3 **Les Cayes** Haiti
47B2 **Les Ecrins** *Mt* France
73A4 **Leshan** China
54B2 **Leskovac** Yugos
48B3 **Les Landes** Region,
France
101G1 **Leslie** S Africa
61H2 **Lesnoy** USSR
63B2 **Lesosibirsk** USSR
101G1 **Lesotho** Kingdom,
S Africa
69F2 **Lesozavodsk** USSR
48B2 **Les Sables-d'Olonne**
France
112A **Lesser Antarctica**
Region, Ant
27D4 **Lesser Antilles** *Is*
Caribbean S
13E1 **Lesser Slave L** Can
55C3 **Lésvos** *I* Greece
58B2 **Leszno** Pol
86C2 **Letha Range** *Mts*
Burma
5G5 **Lethbridge** Can
33F3 **Lethem** Guyana
59D3 **Letichev** USSR
63D2 **Let Oktyobr'ya** USSR
78B2 **Letong** Indon
46A1 **Le Touquet-Paris-Plage**
France
76B2 **Letpadan** Burma
48C1 **Le Tréport** France
47B1 **Leuk** Switz
57A2 **Leuven** Belg
55B3 **Levádhia** Greece
38G6 **Levanger** Nor
47B2 **Levanna** *Mt* Italy
71D5 **Lévêque,C** Aust
46D1 **Leverkusen** Germany
59B3 **Levice** Czech
47D1 **Levico** Italy
110C2 **Levin** NZ
7C5 **Lévis** Can
15D2 **Levittown** USA
55B3 **Lévka Óri** *Mt* Greece
55B3 **Levkás** Greece
55B3 **Levkás** *I* Greece
106B2 **Lévque,C** Aust
54C2 **Levski** Bulg
43E4 **Lewes** Eng
40B2 **Lewis** *I* Scot
16A2 **Lewisburg** USA
111B2 **Lewis P** NZ
8B2 **Lewis Range** *Mts*
USA
8B2 **Lewiston** Idaho, USA
10C2 **Lewiston** Maine, USA
8C2 **Lewistown** Montana,
USA
15C2 **Lewistown**
Pennsylvania, USA
19B3 **Lewisville** USA
11B3 **Lexington** Kentucky,
USA
18B2 **Lexington** Missouri,
USA
15C3 **Lexington Park** USA
79C3 **Leyte G** Phil
54A2 **Lezhe** Alb
82D3 **Lhasa** China
86B1 **Lhazê** China
70A3 **Lhokseumawe** Indon
86C1 **Lhozhag** China
68B4 **Lhunze** China
Liancourt Rocks =
Tok-do

79C4 **Lianga** Phil
72B3 **Liangdang** China
73C5 **Lianjiang** China
73C5 **Lianping** China
73C5 **Lian Xian** China
72D3 **Lianyungang** China
72E1 **Liaoding Bandao** *Pen*
China
72E1 **Liaodong Wan** *B*
China
72E1 **Liao He** *R* China
72E1 **Liaoning** Province,
China
72E1 **Liaoyang** China
72E1 **Liaoyuan** China
74B2 **Liaozhong** China
4F3 **Liard** *R* Can
4F4 **Liard River** Can
46C2 **Liart** France
98B2 **Libenge** Zaïre
9C3 **Liberal** USA
57C2 **Liberec** Czech
97A4 **Liberia** Republic,
Africa
18B2 **Liberty** Missouri, USA
15D2 **Liberty** New York,
USA
19B3 **Liberty** Texas, USA
48B3 **Libourne** France
23B2 **Libres** Mexico
98A2 **Libreville** Gabon
95A2 **Libya** Republic, Africa
95B2 **Libyan Desert** Libya
95B1 **Libyan Plat** Egypt
53B3 **Licata** Italy
43D3 **Lichfield** Eng
101C2 **Lichinga** Mozam
101G1 **Lichtenburg** S Africa
14B3 **Licking** *R* USA
22B2 **Lick Observatory** USA
60C3 **Lida** USSR
39G7 **Lidköping** Sweden
53B2 **Lido di Ostia** Italy
52A1 **Liechtenstein**
Principality, Europe
57B2 **Liège** Belg
58C1 **Lielupe** *R* USSR
98C2 **Lienart** Zaïre
57C3 **Lienz** Austria
60B2 **Liepāja** USSR
46C1 **Lier** Belg
47B1 **Liestal** Switz
15C1 **Liévre** *R* Can
57C3 **Liezen** Austria
45C2 **Liffey** *R* Irish Rep
45C1 **Lifford** Irish Rep
107F3 **Lifu** *I* Nouvelle
Calédonie
109C1 **Lightning Ridge** Aust
46C2 **Ligny-en-Barrois**
France
101C2 **Ligonha** *R* Mozam
47C2 **Liguria** Region, Italy
52A2 **Ligurian S** Italy
21C4 **Lihue** Hawaiian Is
100B2 **Likasi** Zaïre
49C1 **Lille** France
39G6 **Lillehammer** Nor
46B1 **Lillers** France
39G7 **Lillestøm** Nor
13C2 **Lillooet** Can
13C2 **Lillooet** *R* Can
101C2 **Lilongwe** Malawi
79B4 **Liloy** Phil
54A2 **Lim** *R* Yugos
32B6 **Lima** Peru
50A1 **Lima** Spain
10B2 **Lima** USA
92B3 **Limassol** Cyprus
45C1 **Limavady** N Ire
34B3 **Limay** *R* Arg
34B3 **Limay Mahuida** Arg
98A2 **Limbe** Cam
101C2 **Limbe** Malawi
57B2 **Limburg** W Gem
31B6 **Limeira** Brazil
45B2 **Limerick** County,
Irish Rep

56B1 **Limfjorden** *L* Den
106C2 **Limmen Bight** *B* Aust
55C3 **Limnos** *I* Greece
31D3 **Limoeiro** Brazil
48C2 **Limoges** France
25D4 **Limón** Costa Rica
8C3 **Limon** USA
48C2 **Limousin** Region, France
79A3 **Linapacan Str** Phil
29B3 **Linares** Chile
9D4 **Linares** Mexico
50B2 **Linares** Spain
68B4 **Lincang** China
29D2 **Lincoln** Arg
18A1 **Lincoln** California, USA
42D3 **Lincoln** County, Eng
42D3 **Lincoln** Eng
18C1 **Lincoln** Illinois, USA
8D2 **Lincoln** Nebraska, USA
15D2 **Lincoln** New Hampshire, USA
111B2 **Lincoln** NZ
80A **Lincoln** *S* Greenland
20B2 **Lincoln City** USA
14B2 **Lincoln Park** USA
52A2 **L'Incudina** *Mt* Corse
57B3 **Lindau** Germany
33F2 **Linden** Guyana
39F7 **Lindesnes** *C* Nor
99D3 **Lindi** Tanz
98C2 **Lindi** *R* Zaïre
101G1 **Lindley** S Africa
55C3 **Lindos** Greece
15C2 **Lindsay** Can
105J3 **Line Is** Pacific O
72C2 **Linfen** China
76D2 **Lingao** China
79B2 **Lingayen** Phil
56B2 **Lingen** Germany
73C4 **Lingling** China
73B5 **Lingshan** China
72C2 **Lingshi** China
97A3 **Linguère** Sen
73E4 **Linhai** Rhejiang, China
31D5 **Linhares** Brazil
72B1 **Linhe** China
74B2 **Linjiang** China
39H7 **Linköping** Sweden
72D2 **Linqing** China
35B2 **Lins** Brazil
72A2 **Lintao** China
47C1 **Linthal** Switz
68D2 **Linxi** China
72A2 **Linxia** China
57C3 **Linz** Austria
79B3 **Lipa** Phil
53B3 **Lipari** *I* Italy
61E3 **Lipetsk** USSR
54B1 **Lipova** Rom
56B2 **Lippe** *R* Germany
46E1 **Lippstadt** Germany
99D2 **Lira** Uganda
98B3 **Liranga** Congo
98C2 **Lisala** Zaïre
50A2 **Lisboa** Port
Lisbon = Lisboa
45C1 **Lisburn** N Ire
45B2 **Liscannor B** Irish Rep
73D4 **Lishui** China
73C4 **Li Shui** *R* China
60E4 **Lisichansk** USSR
48C2 **Lisieux** France
46B2 **L'Isle-Adam** France
47B1 **L'Isle-sur-le-Doubs** France
107E3 **Lismore** Aust
45B2 **Listowel** Irish Rep
73B5 **Litang** China
94B2 **Litani** *R* Leb
33G3 **Litani** *R* Suriname
18C2 **Litchfield** USA
107E4 **Lithgow** Aust
16A2 **Lititz** USA
69F2 **Litovko** USSR

60B2 **Litovskaya SSR** Republic, USSR
19A3 **Little** *R* USA
11C4 **Little Abaco** *I* The Bahamas
110C1 **Little Barrier I** NZ
13E2 **Little Bow** *R* Can
25D3 **Little Cayman** *I* Caribbean S
16B3 **Little Egg Harbor** *B* USA
26C2 **Little Inagua** *I* Caribbean S
77A4 **Little Nicobar** *I* Nicobar Is
11A3 **Little Rock** USA
22D3 **Littlerock** USA
13D2 **Little Smoky** Can
13D2 **Little Smoky** *R* Can
16A3 **Littlestown** USA
15D2 **Littleton** New Hampshire, USA
74B2 **Liuhe** China
73B5 **Liuzhou** China
55B3 **Livanátais** Greece
58D1 **Līvāni** USSR
12E1 **Livengood** USA
17B1 **Live Oak** USA
21A2 **Livermore** USA
7D5 **Liverpool** Can
42C3 **Liverpool** Eng
4E2 **Liverpool B** Can
42C3 **Liverpool B** Eng
6C2 **Liverpool,C** Can
109D2 **Liverpool Range** *Mts* Aust
8B2 **Livingston** Montana, USA
19B3 **Livingston** Texas, USA
44C4 **Livingston** UK
Livingstone = Maramba
19A3 **Livingston,L** USA
52C2 **Livno** Yugos
60E3 **Livny** USSR
14B2 **Livonia** USA
52B2 **Livorno** Italy
99D3 **Liwale** Tanz
52B1 **Ljubljana** Yugos
38G6 **Ljungan** *R* Sweden
39G7 **Ljungby** Sweden
39H6 **Ljusdal** Sweden
38H6 **Ljusnan** *R* Sweden
43C4 **Llandeilo** Wales
43C4 **Llandovery** Wales
43C3 **Llandrindod Wells** Wales
42C3 **Llandudno** Wales
43B4 **Llanelli** Wales
43C3 **Llangollen** Wales
9C3 **Llano Estacado** *Plat* USA
Z4D2 **Llanos** Region, Colombia/Ven
30D2 **Llanos de Chiquitos** Region, Bol
50A2 **Llerena** Spain
43B3 **Lleyn** *Pen* Wales
63C2 **Llimsk** USSR
63C2 **Llin** USSR
89E7 **Llorin** Nig
5H4 **Lloydminster** Can
30C3 **Llullaillaco** *Mt* Arg/Chile
30C3 **Loa** *R* Chile
49C2 **Loan** France
98B3 **Loange** *R* Zaïre
100B3 **Lobatse** Botswana
98B2 **Lobaye** *R* CAR
34D3 **Loberia** Arg
100A2 **Lobito** Angola
34D3 **Lobos** Arg
47B2 **Locano** Italy
47C1 **Locarno** Switz
44B3 **Loch Awe** *L* Scot
44A3 **Lochboisdale** Scot

44A3 **Loch Bracadale** *Inlet* Scot
44B3 **Loch Broom** *Estuary* Scot
42B2 **Loch Doon** *L* Scot
44B3 **Loch Earn** *L* Scot
44B2 **Loch Eriboll** *Inlet* Scot
44B3 **Loch Ericht** *L* Scot
48C2 **Loches** France
44B3 **Loch Etive** *Inlet* Scot
44B3 **Loch Ewe** *Inlet* Scot
44B3 **Loch Fyne** *Inlet* Scot
44B3 **Loch Hourn** *Inlet* Scot
44B2 **Lochinver** Scot
44B3 **Loch Katrine** *L* Scot
44C3 **Loch Leven** *L* Scot
44B3 **Loch Linnhe** *Inlet* Scot
44B3 **Loch Lochy** *L* Scot
44B3 **Loch Lomond** *L* Scot
44B3 **Loch Long** *Inlet* Scot
44A3 **Lochmaddy** Scot
44B3 **Loch Maree** *L* Scot
44B3 **Loch Morar** *L* Scot
44C3 **Lochnagar** *Mt* Scot
44B3 **Loch Ness** *L* Scot
44B3 **Loch Rannoch** *L* Scot
44A2 **Loch Roag** *Inlet* Scot
44B3 **Loch Sheil** *L* Scot
44B2 **Loch Shin** *L* Scot
44A3 **Loch Snizort** *Inlet* Scot
44B3 **Loch Sunart** *Inlet* Scot
44B3 **Loch Tay** *L* Scot
44B3 **Loch Torridon** *Inlet* Scot
108A2 **Lock** Aust
42C2 **Lockerbie** Scot
15C2 **Lock Haven** USA
15C2 **Lockport** USA
76D3 **Loc Ninh** Viet
53C3 **Locri** Italy
94B3 **Lod** Israel
108B3 **Loddon** *R* Aust
60D1 **Lodeynoye Pole** USSR
84C3 **Lodhran** Pak
52A1 **Lodi** Italy
21A2 **Lodi** USA
98C3 **Lodja** Zaïre
47B1 **Lods** France
99D2 **Lodwar** Kenya
58B2 **Łódź** Pol
38G5 **Lofoten** *Is* Nor
8B2 **Logan** Utah, USA
4D3 **Logan,Mt** Can
14A2 **Logansport** Indiana, USA
19B3 **Logansport** Louisiana, USA
50B1 **Logroño** Spain
86A2 **Lohārdaga** India
39J6 **Lohja** Fin
76B2 **Loikaw** Burma
39J6 **Loimaa** Fin
48C2 **Loir** *R* France
49C2 **Loire** *R* France
32B4 **Loja** Ecuador
50B2 **Loja** Spain
38K5 **Lokan Tekojärvi** *Res* Fin
46B1 **Lokeren** Belg
99D2 **Lokitaung** Kenya
58D1 **Loknya** USSR
98C3 **Lokolo** *R* Zaïre
98C3 **Lokoro** *R* Zaïre
6D3 **Loks Land** *I* Can
56C2 **Lolland** *I* Den
54B2 **Lom** Bulg
98C3 **Lomami** *R* Zaïre
97A4 **Loma Mts** Sierra Leone/Guinea
47C2 **Lombardia** Region, Italy
71D4 **Lomblen** *I* Indon
78D4 **Lombok** *I* Indon
97C4 **Lomé** Togo
98C3 **Lomela** Zaïre

98C3 **Lomela** *R* Zaïre
60C2 **Lomonosov** USSR
47B1 **Lomont** Region, France
21A3 **Lompoc** USA
58C2 **Łomza** Pol
87A1 **Lonāvale** India
29B3 **Loncoche** Chile
7B5 **London** Can
43D4 **London** Eng
45C1 **Londonderry** County, N Ire
45C1 **Londonderry** N Ire
29B7 **Londonderry** *I* Chile
106B2 **Londonderry,C** Aust
30C4 **Londres** Arg
30F3 **Londrina** Brazil
21B2 **Lone Pine** USA
11C4 **Long** *I* The Bahamas
71F4 **Long** *I* PNG
78C2 **Long Akah** Malay
47E1 **Longarone** Italy
34A3 **Longavi** *Mt* Chile
27H2 **Long B** Jamaica
17C1 **Long B** USA
9B3 **Long Beach** California, USA
15D2 **Long Beach** New York, USA
15D2 **Long Branch** USA
73D5 **Longchuan** China
20C2 **Long Creek** USA
109C4 **Longford** Aust
45C2 **Longford** County, Irish Rep
45C2 **Longford** Irish Rep
44D3 **Long Forties** *Region* N Sea
72D1 **Longhua** China
7C4 **Long I** Can
10C2 **Long I** USA
16C2 **Long Island Sd** USA
7B4 **Longlac** Can
73B5 **Longlin** China
8C2 **Longmont** USA
78D2 **Longnawan** Indon
29B3 **Longquimay** Chile
107D3 **Longreach** Aust
72A2 **Longshou Shan** *Upland* China
42C2 **Longtown** Eng
15D1 **Longueuil** Can
34A3 **Longuimay** Chile
46C2 **Longuyon** France
11A3 **Longview** Texas, USA
8A2 **Longview** Washington, USA
46C2 **Longwy** France
72A3 **Longxi** China
77D3 **Long Xuyen** Viet
73D4 **Longyan** China
73B5 **Longzhou** China
47D2 **Lonigo** Italy
49D2 **Lons-le-Saunier** France
11C3 **Lookout,C** USA
99D3 **Loolmalasin** *Mt* Tanz
13D1 **Loon** *R* Can
45B2 **Loop Hd** *C* Irish Rep
76C3 **Lop Buri** Thai
98A3 **Lopez** *C* Gabon
68B2 **Lop Nur** *L* China
50A2 **Lora del Rio** Spain
10B2 **Lorain** USA
84B2 **Loralai** Pak
90B3 **Lordegān** Iran
107E4 **Lord Howe** *I* Aust
105G5 **Lord Howe Rise** Pacific O
6A3 **Lord Mayor B** Can
9C3 **Lordsburg** USA
35B2 **Lorena** Brazil
47E2 **Loreo** Italy
23A1 **Loreto** Mexico
48B2 **Lorient** France
108B3 **Lorne** Aust
57B3 **Lörrach** Germany

49D2 Lorraine Region France
9C3 Los Alamos USA
34A2 Los Andes Chile
29B3 Los Angeles Chile
9B3 Los Angeles USA
21A2 Los Banos USA
34B2 Los Cerrillos Arg
21A2 Los Gatos USA
52B2 Lošinj I Yugos
29B3 Los Lagos Chile
24B2 Los Mochis Mexico
22B3 Los Olivos USA
34A3 Los Sauces Chile
44C3 Lossiemouth Scot
27E4 Los Testigos Is Ven
29B2 Los Vilos Chile
48C3 Lot R France
34A3 Lota Chile
42C2 Lothian Region, Scot
99D2 Lotikipi Plain Sudan/Kenya
98C3 Loto Zaïre
47B1 Lötschberg Tunnel Switz
38K5 Lotta R Fin/USSR
48B2 Loudéac France
97A3 Louga Sen
41B3 Lough Allen L Irish Rep
45C2 Lough Boderg L Irish Rep
43D3 Loughborough Eng
45C2 Lough Bowna L Irish Rep
45C1 Lough Carlingford L N Ire
41B3 Lough Conn L Irish Rep
41B3 Lough Corrib L Irish Rep
41B3 Lough Derg L Irish Rep
45C2 Lough Derravaragh L Irish Rep
4H2 Loughead I Can
45C2 Lough Ennell L Irish Rep
41B3 Lough Erne L N Ire
40B2 Lough Foyle Estuary N Ire/Irish Rep
40B3 Lough Neagh L N Ire
45C1 Lough Oughter L Irish Rep
45B2 Loughrea Irish Rep
45C2 Lough Ree L Irish Rep
45C2 Lough Sheelin L Irish Rep
42B2 Lough Strangford L Irish Rep
45C1 Lough Swilly Estuary Irish Rep
14B3 Louisa USA
70C3 Louisa Reef I S E Asia
12E2 Louise,L USA
107E2 Louisiade Arch Solomon Is
11A3 Louisiana State, USA
17B1 Louisville Georgia, USA
11B3 Louisville Kentucky, USA
38L5 Loukhi USSR
48B3 Lourdes France
108C2 Louth Aust
45C2 Louth County, Irish Rep
42D3 Louth Eng
Louvain = Leuven
48C2 Louviers France
60D2 Lovat R USSR
54B2 Lovech Bulg
21B1 Lovelock USA
52B1 Lóvere Italy
9C3 Lovington USA
38L5 Lovozero USSR
6B3 Low,C Can
10C2 Lowell Massachusetts, USA

20B2 Lowell Oregon, USA
16D1 Lowell USA
111B2 Lower Hutt NZ
7C4 Lower Seal,L Can
43E3 Lowestoft Eng
58B2 Łowicz Pol
108B2 Loxton Aust
5F4 Loyd George,Mt Can
54A2 Loznica Yugos
23A2 Loz Reyes Mexico
65H3 Lozva R USSR
100B2 Luacano Angola
98C3 Luachimo Angola
98C3 Lualaba R Zaïre
100B2 Luampa Zambia
100B2 Luân Angola
73D3 Lu'an China
98B3 Luanda Angola
100A2 Luando R Angola
100B2 Luanginga R Angola
76C1 Luang Namtha Laos
76C2 Luang Prabang Laos
98B3 Luangue R Angola
100C2 Luangwa R Zambia
72D1 Luan He R China
72D1 Luanping China
100B2 Luanshya Zambia
100B2 Luapula R Zaïre
50A1 Luarca Spain
98B3 Lubalo Angola
58D2 L'uban USSR
79B3 Lubang Is Phil
100A2 Lubango Angola
9C3 Lubbock USA
56C2 Lübeck Germany
98C3 Lubefu Zaïre
98C3 Lubefu R Zaïre
99C3 Lubero Zaïre
98C3 Lubilash R Zaïre
59C2 Lublin Pol
60D3 Lubny USSR
78C2 Lubok Antu Malay
98C3 Lubudi Zaïre
98C3 Lubudi R Zaïre
78A3 Lubuklinggau Indon
100B2 Lubumbashi Zaïre
98C3 Lubutu Zaïre
79B3 Lucban Phil
52B2 Lucca Italy
42B2 Luce B Scot
19C3 Lucedale USA
79B3 Lucena Phil
59B3 Lucenec Czech
Lucerne = Luzern
73C5 Luchuan China
56C2 Luckenwalde Germany
101F1 Luckhoff S Africa
86A1 Lucknow India
100B2 Lucusse Angola
72E2 Lüda China
46D1 Lüdenscheid Germany
100A3 Lüderitz Namibia
84D2 Ludhiana India
14A2 Ludington USA
43C3 Ludlow Eng
54C2 Ludogorie Upland Bulg
17B1 Ludowici USA
54B1 Luduş Rom
39H6 Ludvika Sweden
57B3 Ludwigsburg Germany
57B3 Ludwigshafen Germany
56C2 Ludwigslust Germany
98C3 Luebo Zaïre
98C3 Luema R Zaïre
98C3 Luembe R Angola
100A2 Luena Angola
100B2 Luene R Angola
72B3 Lüeyang China
73D5 Lufeng China
11A3 Lufkin USA
60C2 Luga USSR
60C2 Luga R USSR
52A1 Lugano Switz
60E4 Lugansk USSR

101C2 Lugela Mozam
101C2 Lugenda R Mozam
50A1 Lugo Spain
54B1 Lugoj Rom
72A3 Luhuo China
98B3 Lui R Angola
100B2 Luiana Angola
100B2 Luiana R Angola
Luichow Peninsula = Leizhou Bandao
47C2 Luino Italy
98B2 Luionga R Zaïre
72B2 Luipan Shan Upland China
100B2 Luishia Zaïre
68B4 Luixi China
98C3 Luiza Zaïre
34B2 Luján Arg
34D2 Luján Arg
73D3 Lujiang China
98B3 Lukenie R Zaïre
64E4 Luki USSR
98B3 Lukolela Zaïre
58C2 Luków Pol
98C3 Lukuga R Zaïre
100B2 Lukulu Zambia
38J5 Lule R Sweden
38J5 Luleå Sweden
54C2 Lüleburgaz Turk
72C2 Lüliang Shan Mts China
19A4 Luling USA
98C2 Lulonga R Zaïre
Luluabourg = Kananga
100B2 Lumbala Angola
11C3 Lumberton USA
78D1 Lumbis Indon
86C1 Lumding India
100B2 Lumeje Angola
111A3 Lumsden NZ
39G7 Lund Sweden
101C2 Lundazi Zambia
100C3 Lundi R Zim
43B4 Lundy I Eng
56C2 Lüneburg Germany
46D2 Lunéville France
100B2 Lunga R Zambia
86C2 Lunglei India
100A2 Lungue Bungo R Angola
58D2 Luninec USSR
98B3 Luobomo Congo
73B5 Luocheng China
73C5 Luoding China
72C3 Luohe China
72C3 Luo He R Henan, China
72B2 Luo He R Shaanxi, China
73C4 Luoxiao Shan Hills China
72C3 Luoyang China
98B3 Luozi Zaïre
100B2 Lupane Zim
101C2 Lupilichi Mozam
Lu Qu = Tao He
30E4 Luque Par
45C1 Lurgan N Ire
101C2 Lurio R Mozam
90A3 Luristan Region, Iran
100B2 Lusaka Zambia
98C3 Lusambo Zaïre
55A2 Lushnjë Alb
99D3 Lushoto Tanz
68B4 Lushun China
72E2 Lüshun China
43D4 Luton Eng
60C3 Lutsk USSR
99E2 Luuq Somalia
99C3 Luvua R Zaïre
99D3 Luwegu R Tanz
100C2 Luwingu Zambia
71D4 Luwuk Indon
46D2 Luxembourg Grand Duchy, N W Europe
49D2 Luxembourg Lux
73A5 Luxi China
95C2 Luxor Egypt

61G1 Luza USSR
61G1 Luza R USSR
52A1 Luzern Switz
73B5 Luzhai China
73B4 Luzhi China
73B4 Luzhou China
35B1 Luziânia Brazil
79B2 Luzon I Phil
79B1 Luzon Str Phil
59C3 L'vov USSR
44C2 Lybster Scot
38H6 Lycksele Sweden
100B3 Lydenburg S Africa
8B3 Lyell,Mt USA
16A2 Lykens USA
43C4 Lyme B Eng
43C4 Lyme Regis Eng
11C3 Lynchburg USA
108A2 Lyndhurst Aust
15D2 Lynn USA
12G3 Lynn Canal Sd USA
17A1 Lynn Haven USA
5H4 Lynn Lake Can
5H3 Lynx L Can
49C2 Lyon France
12G3 Lyon Canal Sd USA
17B1 Lyons Georgia, USA
106A3 Lyons R Aust
47B2 Lys R Italy
61J2 Lys'va USSR
111B2 Lyttelton NZ
13C2 Lytton Can
22A1 Lytton USA
58D2 Lyubeshov USSR
60E2 Lyublino USSR

M

76C1 Ma R Viet
94B2 Ma'agan Jordan
94B2 Ma'alot Tarshiha Israel
92C5 Ma'an Jordan
73D3 Ma'anshan China
92C2 Ma'arrat an Nu'mān Syria
46C1 Maas R Neth
46C1 Maaseik Belg
79B3 Maasin Phil
57B2 Maastricht Belg
101C3 Mabalane Mozam
33F2 Mabaruma Guyana
42E3 Mablethorpe Eng
101C3 Mabote Mozam
58C2 Mabrita USSR
35C2 Macaé Brazil
58D2 M'adel USSR
9D3 McAlester USA
9D4 McAllen USA
101C2 Macaloge Mozam
33G3 Macapá Brazil
35C1 Macarani Brazil
32B4 Macas Ecuador
31D3 Macaú Brazil
73C5 Macau Dependency, China
13C2 McBride Can
12F2 McCarthy USA
13A2 McCauley I Can
42C3 Macclesfield Eng
6B1 McClintock B Can
4H2 McClintock Chan Can
16A2 McClure USA
22B2 McClure,L USA
4G2 McClure Str Can
19B3 McComb USA
8C2 McCook USA
6C2 Macculloch,C Can
13C1 McCusker,Mt Can
4F4 McDame Can
20C2 McDermitt USA
13E2 Macdonald R Can
106C3 Macdonnell Ranges Mts Aust
50A1 Macedo de Cavaleiros Port
31D3 Maceió Brazil

97B4 **Macenta** Guinea
52B2 **Macerata** Italy
108A2 **Macfarlane,L** Aust
19B3 **McGehee** USA
45B3 **MacGillycuddys Reeks** *Mts* Irish Rep
4C3 **McGrath** USA
35B2 **Machado** Brazil
101C3 **Machaíla** Mozam
99D3 **Machakos** Kenya
32B4 **Machala** Ecuador
101C3 **Machaze** Mozam
87B1 **Mācherla** India
94B2 **Machgharab** Leb
87C1 **Machilipatnam** India
32C1 **Machiques** Ven
32C6 **Machu-Picchu** *Hist Site* Peru
101C3 **Macia** Mozam
109C1 **MacIntyre** *R* Aust
107D3 **Mackay** Aust
106B3 **Mackay,L** Aust
14C2 **McKeesport** USA
13C1 **Mackenzie** Can
4F3 **Mackenzie** *R* Can
4E3 **Mackenzie B** Can
4G2 **Mackenzie King I** Can
4E3 **Mackenzie Mts** Can
14B1 **Mackinac,Str of** USA
14B1 **Mackinaw City** USA
12D2 **McKinley,Mt** USA
19A3 **McKinney** USA
6C2 **Mackinson Inlet** *B* Can
109D2 **Macksville** Aust
20B2 **Mclaoughlin,Mt** USA
109D1 **Maclean** Aust
100B4 **Maclear** S Africa
5G4 **McLennan** Can
13D2 **McLeod** *R* Can
4G3 **McLeod B** Can
106A3 **McLeod,L** Aust
13C1 **McLeod Lake** Can
4E3 **Macmillan** *R* Can
12H2 **Macmillan P** Can
20B1 **McMinnville** Oregon, USA
112B7 **McMurdo** *Base* Ant
13D2 **McNaughton L** Can
18B1 **Macomb** USA
53A2 **Macomer** Sardegna
101C2 **Macomia** Mozam
49C2 **Mâcon** France
11B3 **Macon** Georgia, USA
18B2 **Macon** Missouri, USA
100B2 **Macondo** Angola
18A2 **McPherson** USA
104F6 **Macquarie** *Is* Aust
109C2 **Macquarie** *R* Aust
109C4 **Macquarie Harbour** *B* Aust
109D2 **Macquarie,L** Aust
17B1 **McRae** USA
112B11 **Mac. Robertson Land** *Region*, Ant
45B3 **Macroom** Irish Rep
4G3 **McTavish Arm** *B* Can
108A1 **Macumba** *R* Aust
47C2 **Macunaga** Italy
4F3 **McVicar Arm** *B* Can
94B3 **Mādabā** Jordan
95A3 **Madadi** *Well* Chad
89J10 **Madagascar** *I* Indian O
95A2 **Madama** Niger
71F4 **Madang** PNG
97C3 **Madaoua** Niger
86C2 **Madaripur** Bang
90B2 **Madau** USSR
15C1 **Madawaska** *R* Can
96A1 **Madeira** *I* Atlantic O
33E5 **Madeira** *R* Brazil
24B2 **Madera** Mexico
21A2 **Madera** USA
87A1 **Madgaon** India
86B1 **Madhubani** India
86A2 **Madhya Pradesh** *State*, India

87B2 **Madikeri** India
98B3 **Madimba** Zaïre
98B3 **Madingo Kayes** Congo
98B3 **Madingou** Congo
10B3 **Madison** Indiana, USA
10B2 **Madison** Wisconsin, USA
18C2 **Madisonville** Kentucky, USA
19A3 **Madisonville** Texas, USA
78C4 **Madiun** Indon
99D2 **Mado Gashi** Kenya
47D1 **Madonna di Campiglio** Italy
87C2 **Madras** India
20B2 **Madras** USA
29A6 **Madre de Dios** *I* Chile
32D6 **Madre de Dios** *R* Bol
50B1 **Madrid** Spain
50B2 **Madridejos** Spain
78C4 **Madura** *I* Indon
87B3 **Madurai** India
75B1 **Maebashi** Japan
76B3 **Mae Khlong** *R* Thai
77B4 **Mae Nam Lunang** *R* Thai
76C2 **Mae Nam Mun** *R* Thai
76B2 **Mae Nam Ping** *R* Thai
101D2 **Maevatanana** Madag
101G1 **Mafeteng** Lesotho
109C3 **Maffra** Aust
99D3 **Mafia** *I* Tanz
101G1 **Mafikeng** S Africa
30G4 **Mafra** Brazil
92C3 **Mafraq** Jordan
32C2 **Magangué** Colombia
34D3 **Magdalena** Arg
24A1 **Magdalena** Mexico
26C4 **Magdalena** *R* Colombia
78D1 **Magdalena,Mt** Malay
7D5 **Magdalen Is** Can
56C2 **Magdeburg** Germany
31C6 **Magé** Brazil
78C4 **Magelang** Indon
47C1 **Maggia** *R* Switz
92B4 **Maghâgha** Egypt
45C1 **Magherafelt** N Ire
55A2 **Maglie** Italy
61J3 **Magnitogorsk** USSR
19B3 **Magnolia** USA
101C2 **Magoé** Mozam
15D1 **Magog** Can
23B1 **Magosal** Mexico
13E2 **Magrath** Can
7A3 **Maguse River** Can
76B1 **Magwe** Burma
90A2 **Mahābād** Iran
86B1 **Mahabharat Range** *Mts* Nepal
87A1 **Mahād** India
85D4 **Mahadeo Hills** India
101D2 **Mahajanga** Madag
100B3 **Mahalapye** Botswana
86A2 **Mahānadi** *R* India
101D2 **Mahanoro** Madag
16A2 **Mahanoy City** USA
87A1 **Maharashtra** *State*, India
86A2 **Māhāsamund** India
76C2 **Maha Sarakham** Thai
101D2 **Mahavavy** *R* Madag
87B1 **Mahbūbnagar** India
96D1 **Mahdia** Tunisia
87B2 **Mahe** India
85D4 **Mahekar** India
101D2 **Mahéli** *I* Comoros
86A2 **Mahendragarh** India
99D3 **Mahenge** Tanz
85C4 **Mahesāna** India
110C1 **Mahia Pen** NZ
85D3 **Mahoba** India
51C2 **Mahón** Spain
12J1 **Mahony L** Can
96D1 **Mahrés** Tunisia
85C4 **Mahuva** India
32C1 **Maicao** Colombia

47B1 **Maîche** France
43E4 **Maidstone** Eng
98B1 **Maiduguri** Nig
86A2 **Maihar** India
86C2 **Maijdi** Bang
76B3 **Mail Kyun** *I* Burma
84A1 **Maimana** Afghan
14B1 **Main Chan** Can
98B3 **Mai-Ndombe** *L* Zaïre
10D2 **Maine** State, USA
48B2 **Maine** *Region* France
44C2 **Mainland** *I* Scot
85D3 **Mainpuri** India
46A2 **Maintenon** France
101D2 **Maintirano** Madag
57B2 **Mainz** Germany
97A4 **Maio** *I* Cape Verde
29C2 **Maipó** *Mt* Arg/Chile
34D3 **Maipú** Arg
32D1 **Maiquetía** Ven
47B2 **Maira** *R* Italy
86C1 **Mairābāri** India
86C2 **Maiskhal I** Bang
107E4 **Maitland** New South Wales, Aust
108A2 **Maitland** S Australia, Aust
74D3 **Maizuru** Japan
70C4 **Majene** Indon
30B2 **Majes** *R* Peru
99D2 **Maji** Eth
72D2 **Majia He** *R* China
Majunga = Mahajanga
99D1 **Makale** Eth
70C4 **Makale** Indon
86B1 **Makalu** *Mt* China/ Nepal
98B2 **Makanza** Zaïre
52C2 **Makarska** Yugos
61F2 **Makaryev** USSR
Makassar = Ujung Pandang
78D3 **Makassar Str** Indon
61H4 **Makat** USSR
97A4 **Makeni** Sierra Leone
60E4 **Makeyevka** USSR
100B3 **Makgadikgadi** *Salt Pan* Botswana
61G5 **Makhachkala** USSR
99D3 **Makindu** Kenya
88H5 **Makkah** S Arabia
7E4 **Makkovik** Can
59C3 **Makó** Hung
98B2 **Makokou** Gabon
110C1 **Makorako,Mt** NZ
98B2 **Makoua** Congo
85C3 **Makrāna** India
85A3 **Makran Coast Range** *Mts* Pak
96C1 **Makthar** Tunisia
93D2 **Mākū** Iran
98C3 **Makumbi** Zaïre
74C4 **Makurazaki** Japan
97C4 **Makurdi** Nig
79B4 **Malabang** Phil
87A2 **Malabar Coast** India
89E7 **Malabo** Bioko
77C5 **Malacca,Str of** S E Asia
32C2 **Málaga** Colombia
50B2 **Málaga** Spain
101D3 **Malaimbandy** Madag
107F1 **Malaita** *I* Solomon Is
99D2 **Malakal** Sudan
84C2 **Malakand** Pak
78C4 **Malang** Indon
98B3 **Malange** Angola
97C3 **Malanville** Benin
39H7 **Mälaren** *L* Sweden
34B3 **Malargüe** Arg
12F3 **Malaspina GI** USA
93C2 **Malatya** Turk
101C2 **Malawi** *Republic*, Africa
Malawi,L = Nyasa,L
79C4 **Malaybalay** Phil
90A3 **Malāyer** Iran

70B3 **Malaysia** *Federation*, S E Asia
93D2 **Malazgirt** Turk
58B2 **Malbork** Pol
56C2 **Malchin** Germany
18C2 **Malden** USA
83B5 **Maldives Is** Indian O
104B4 **Maldives Ridge** Indian O
29F2 **Maldonado** Urug
47D1 **Male** Italy
85C4 **Malegaon** India
59B3 **Malé Karpaty** *Upland* Czech
101C2 **Malema** Mozam
84B2 **Mālestān** Afghan
61J3 **Maleuz** USSR
38H5 **Malgomaj** *L* Sweden
95B3 **Malha** *Well* Sudan
20C2 **Malheur L** USA
97B3 **Mali** Republic, Africa
78D1 **Malinau** Indon
99E3 **Malindi** Kenya
Malines = Mechelen
40B2 **Malin Head** *Pt* Irish Rep
86A2 **Malkala Range** *Mts* India
85D4 **Malkāpur** India
55C2 **Malkara** Turk
54C2 **Malko Tŭrnovo** Bulg
44B3 **Mallaig** Scot
95C2 **Mallawi** Egypt
47D1 **Málles Venosta** Italy
51C2 **Mallorca** *I* Spain
45B2 **Mallow** Irish Rep
38G6 **Malm** Nor
38J5 **Malmberget** Sweden
46D1 **Malmédy** Germany
43C4 **Malmesbury** Eng
100A4 **Malmesbury** S Africa
39G7 **Malmö** Sweden
61G2 **Malmyzh** USSR
79B3 **Malolos** Phil
15D2 **Malone** USA
101G1 **Maloti Mts** Lesotho
38F6 **Måloy** Nor
28A2 **Malpelo** *I* Colombia
34A2 **Malpo** *R* Chile
85D3 **Mālpura** India
8C2 **Malta** Montana, USA
53B3 **Malta** *Chan* Malta/ Italy
53B3 **Malta** *I* Medit S
100A3 **Maltahöhe** Namibia
42D2 **Malton** Eng
39G6 **Malung** Sweden
87A1 **Mālvan** India
19B3 **Malvern** USA
85D4 **Malwa Plat** India
65F5 **Malyy Kavkaz** *Mts* USSR
61G4 **Malyy Uzen'** *R* USSR
63D2 **Mama** USSR
61H2 **Mamadysh** USSR
99C2 **Mambasa** Zaïre
71E4 **Mamberamo** *R* Indon
98B2 **Mambéré** *R* CAR
98A2 **Mamfé** Cam
33D6 **Mamoré** *R* Bol
97A3 **Mamou** Guinea
101D2 **Mampikony** Madag
97B4 **Mampong** Ghana
94B3 **Mamshit** *Hist Site* Israel
100B3 **Mamuno** Botswana
97B4 **Man** Ivory Coast
21C4 **Mana** Hawaiian Is
101D3 **Manabo** Madag
33E4 **Manacapuru** Brazil
51C2 **Manacor** Spain
71D3 **Manado** Indon
25D3 **Managua** Nic
101D3 **Manakara** Madag
101D2 **Mananara** Madag
101D3 **Mananjary** Madag
111A3 **Manapouri** NZ
111A3 **Manapouri,L** NZ

86C1 **Manas** Bhutan
82C1 **Manas** China
65K5 **Manas Hu** *L* China
86A1 **Manaslu** *Mt* Nepal
16B2 **Manasquan** USA
33F4 **Manaus** Brazil
92B2 **Manavgat** Turk
93C2 **Manbij** Syria
42B2 **Man,Calf of** *I* Eng
87B1 **Mancheral** India
15D2 **Manchester** Connecticut, USA
42C3 **Manchester** Eng
10C2 **Manchester** New Hampshire, USA
16A2 **Manchester** Pennsylvania, USA
69E2 **Manchuria** Hist Region, China
91B4 **Mand** *R* Iran
101C2 **Manda** Tanz
35A2 **Mandaguari** Brazil
39F7 **Mandal** Nor
76B1 **Mandalay** Burma
68C2 **Mandalgovī** Mongolia
72A1 **Mandal Ovoo** Mongolia
8C2 **Mandan** USA
14A2 **Mandelona** USA
99E2 **Mandera** Eth
26B3 **Mandeville** Jamaica
101C2 **Mandimba** Mozam
86A2 **Mandla** India
101D2 **Mandritsara** Madag
85D4 **Mandsaur** India
53C2 **Manduria** Italy
85B4 **Māndvi** India
87B2 **Mandya** India
58D2 **Manevichi** USSR
42D3 **Manfield** Eng
53C2 **Manfredonia** Italy
98B1 **Manga** *Desert Region* Niger
110C1 **Mangakino** NZ
54C2 **Mangalia** Rom
98B1 **Mangalmé** Chad
87A2 **Mangalore** India
78B3 **Manggar** Indon
68B3 **Mangnia** China
101C2 **Mangoche** Malawi
101D3 **Mangoky** *R* Madag
71D4 **Mangole** *I* Indon
85B4 **Māngral** India
63E2 **Mangui** China
8D3 **Manhattan** USA
31C6 **Manhuacu** Brazil
101D2 **Mania** *R* Madag
101C2 **Manica** Mozam
7D5 **Manicouagan** *R* Can
7D4 **Manicouagan Res** Can
91A4 **Manifah** S Arabia
79B3 **Manila** Phil
109D2 **Manilla** Aust
97B3 **Maninian** Ivory Coast
86C2 **Manipur** State, India
86C2 **Manipur** *R* Burma
92A2 **Manisa** Turk
41C3 **Man,Isle of** Irish S
14A2 **Manistee** USA
14A2 **Manistee** *R* USA
14A1 **Manistique** USA
5H4 **Manitoba** Province, Can
5J4 **Manitoba,L** Can
13F2 **Manito L** Can
14A1 **Manitou Is** USA
7B5 **Manitoulin** *I* Can
14A2 **Manitowoc** USA
15C1 **Maniwaki** Can
32B2 **Manizales** Colombia
101D3 **Manja** Madag
106A4 **Manjimup** Aust
87B1 **Mānjra** India
10A2 **Mankato** USA
97B4 **Mankono** Ivory Coast
12D2 **Manley Hot Springs** USA
110B1 **Manly** NZ

85C4 **Manmād** India
78A3 **Manna** Indon
108A2 **Mannahill** Aust
87B3 **Mannar** Sri Lanka
87B3 **Mannār,G of** India
87B2 **Mannārgudi** India
57B3 **Mannheim** Germany
13D1 **Manning** Can
17B1 **Manning** USA
108A2 **Mannum** Aust
97A4 **Mano** Sierra Leone
71E4 **Manokwari** Indon
98C3 **Manono** Zaïre
76B3 **Manoron** Burma
75B1 **Mano-wan** *B* Japan
74B2 **Manp'o** N Korea
84D3 **Mānsa** India
100B2 **Mansa** Zambia
6B3 **Mansel I** Can
19B2 **Mansfield** Arkansas, USA
108C3 **Mansfield** Aust
19B3 **Mansfield** Louisiana, USA
16D1 **Mansfield** Massachusetts, USA
10B2 **Mansfield** Ohio, USA
15C2 **Mansfield** Pennsylvania, USA
71E2 **Mansyu Deep** Pacific O
32A4 **Manta** Ecuador
79A4 **Mantalingajan,Mt** Phil
32B6 **Mantaro** *R* Peru
22B2 **Manteca** USA
48C2 **Mantes** France
52B1 **Mantova** Italy
38J6 **Mantta** Fin
61F2 **Manturovo** USSR
35A2 **Manuel Ribas** Brazil
79B4 **Manukan** Phil
110B1 **Manukau** NZ
71F4 **Manus** *I* Pacific O
50B2 **Manzanares** Spain
25E2 **Manzanillo** Cuba
24B3 **Manzanillo** Mexico
63D3 **Manzhouli** USSR
94C3 **Manzil** Jordan
101C3 **Manzini** Swaziland
98B1 **Mao** Chad
72A2 **Maomao Shan** *Mt* China
73C5 **Maoming** China
101C3 **Mapai** Mozam
71E3 **Mapia** *Is* Pacific O
5H5 **Maple Creek** Can
101H1 **Maputo** Mozam
101H1 **Maputo** *R* Mozam
Ma Qu = Huange He
72A3 **Maqu** China
86B1 **Maquan He** *R* China
98B3 **Maquela do Zombo** Angola
29C4 **Maquinchao** Arg
31B3 **Marabá** Brazil
32C1 **Maracaibo** Ven
32D1 **Maracay** Ven
95A2 **Marādah** Libya
97C3 **Maradi** Niger
90A2 **Marāgheh** Iran
99D2 **Maralal** Kenya
107F1 **Maramasike** *I* Solomon Is
100B2 **Maramba** Zambia
90A2 **Marand** Iran
31B2 **Maranhōa** State, Brazil
109C1 **Maranoa** *R* Aust
32B4 **Marañón** *R* Peru
7B5 **Marathon** Can
17B2 **Marathon** Florida, USA
78D2 **Maratua** *I* Indon
23A2 **Maravatio** Mexico
79B4 **Marawi** Phil
34B2 **Marayes** Arg
50B2 **Marbella** Spain
106A3 **Marble Bar** Aust
100B3 **Marblehall** S Africa

16D1 **Marblehead** USA
57B2 **Marburg** Germany
57B2 **Marche** Belg
50A2 **Marchean** Spain
46C1 **Marche-en-Famenne** Belg
32J7 **Marchena** *I* Ecuador
17B2 **Marco** USA
34C2 **Marcos Juárez** Arg
12E2 **Marcus Baker,Mt** USA
15D2 **Marcy,Mt** USA
84C2 **Mardan** Pak
29E3 **Mar del Plata** Arg
93D2 **Mardin** Turk
99D1 **Mareb** *R* Eth
16B1 **Margaretville** USA
43E4 **Margate** Eng
54B1 **Marghita** Rom
109C4 **Maria I** Aust
104F3 **Mariana** *Is* Pacific O
13E1 **Mariana Lake** Can
104F3 **Marianas Trench** Pacific O
86C1 **Mariāni** India
19B3 **Marianna** Arkansas, USA
17A1 **Marianna** Florida, USA
7G4 **Maria Van Diemen,C** NZ
59B3 **Mariazell** Austria
52C1 **Maribor** Yugos
99C2 **Maridi** Sudan
112B5 **Marie Byrd Land** Region, Ant
27E3 **Marie Galante** *I* Caribbean S
39H6 **Mariehamn** Fin
46C1 **Mariembourg** Belg
33G2 **Marienburg** Surinam
100A3 **Mariental** Namibia
39G7 **Mariestad** Sweden
17B1 **Marietta** Georgia, USA
14B3 **Marietta** Ohio, USA
19A3 **Marietta** Oklahoma, USA
27Q2 **Marigot** Dominica
60B3 **Marijampole** USSR
31B6 **Marilia** Brazil
98B3 **Marimba** Angola
79B3 **Marinduque** *I* Phil
10B2 **Marinette** USA
30F3 **Maringá** Brazil
98C2 **Maringa** *R* Zaïre
18B2 **Marion** Arkansas, USA
18C2 **Marion** Illinois, USA
10B2 **Marion** Indiana, USA
10B2 **Marion** Ohio, USA
17C1 **Marion** S Carolina, USA
11B3 **Marion,L** USA
107E2 **Marion Reef** Aust
21B2 **Mariposa** USA
22B2 **Mariposa** *R* USA
22B2 **Mariposa Res** USA
60C5 **Marista** *R* Bulg
60E4 **Mariupol'** USSR
61G2 **Mariyskaya ASSR** Republic, USSR
94B2 **Marjayoun** Leb
58D2 **Marjina Gorki** USSR
94B3 **Marka** Jordan
99E2 **Marka** Somalia
56C1 **Markaryd** Sweden
43C3 **Market Drayton** Eng
43D3 **Market Harborough** Eng
112A2 **Markham,Mt** Ant
22C1 **Markleeville** USA
16D1 **Marlboro** Massachusetts, USA
107D3 **Marlborough** Aust
46B2 **Marle** France
19A3 **Marlin** USA
48C2 **Marmande** France
55C2 **Marmara Adi** *I* Turk
92A1 **Marmara,S of** Turk

55C3 **Marmaris** Turk
14B3 **Marmet** USA
52B1 **Marmolada** *Mt* Italy
12D3 **Marmot B** USA
47A1 **Marnay** France
46B2 **Marne** Department, France
46B2 **Marne** *R* France
98B2 **Maro** Chad
101D2 **Maroantsetra** Madag
101C2 **Marondera** Zim
33G3 **Maroni** *R* French Guiana
109D1 **Maroochydore** Aust
98B1 **Maroua** Cam
101D2 **Marovoay** Madag
11B4 **Marquesas Keys** *Is* USA
10B2 **Marquette** USA
46A1 **Marquise** France
109C2 **Marra** *R* Aust
101H1 **Marracuene** Mozam
96B1 **Marrakech** Mor
106C3 **Marree** Aust
19B4 **Marrero** USA
101C2 **Marromeu** Mozam
101C2 **Marrupa** Mozam
95C2 **Marsa Alam** Egypt
99D2 **Marsabit** Kenya
53B3 **Marsala** Italy
49D3 **Marseille** France
12B2 **Marshall** Alaska, USA
14A3 **Marshall** Illinois, USA
14B2 **Marshall** Michigan, USA
18B2 **Marshall** Missouri, ·USA
11A3 **Marshall** Texas, USA
105G3 **Marshall Is** Pacific O
18B2 **Marshfield** Missouri, USA
26B1 **Marsh Harbour** The Bahamas
19B4 **Marsh I** USA
12H2 **Marsh L** Can
76B2 **Martaban,G of** Burma
78A3 **Martapura** Indon
78C3 **Martapura** Indon
15D2 **Martha's Vineyard** *I* USA
49D2 **Martigny** Switz
59B3 **Martin** Czech
111C2 **Martinborough** NZ
34B3 **Martín de Loyola** Arg
23B1 **Martínez de la Torre** Mexico
27E4 **Martinique** *I* Caribbean S
17A1 **Martin,L** USA
15C3 **Martinsburg** USA
14B2 **Martins Ferry** USA
103G6 **Martin Vaz** *I* Atlantic O
49D3 **Martiques** France
110C2 **Marton** NZ
50B2 **Martos** Spain
78D1 **Marudi** Malay
84B2 **Maruf** Afghan
75A2 **Marugame** Japan
85C3 **Mārwār** India
65H6 **Mary** USSR
107E3 **Maryborough** Queensland, Aust
108B3 **Maryborough** Victoria, Aust
5F4 **Mary Henry,Mt** Can
10C3 **Maryland** State, USA
42C2 **Maryport** Eng
21A2 **Marysville** California, USA
18A2 **Marysville** Kansas, USA
20B1 **Marysville** Washington, USA
10A2 **Maryville** Iowa, USA
18B1 **Maryville** Missouri, USA
95A2 **Marzuq** Libya

Masada = Mezada
94B2 **Mas'adah** Syria
99D3 **Masai Steppe** *Upland* Tanz
99D3 **Masaka** Uganda
93E2 **Masally** USSR
74B3 **Masan** S Korea
101C2 **Masasi** Tanz
25D3 **Masaya** Nic
79B3 **Masbate** Phil
79B3 **Masbate** *I* Phil
96C1 **Mascara** Alg
23A1 **Mascota** Mexico
35D1 **Mascote** Brazil
101G1 **Maseru** Lesotho
66C3 **Mashad** Iran
84B2 **Mashaki** Afghan
90C2 **Mashhad** Iran
98B3 **Masi-Manimba** Zaïre
99D2 **Masindi** Uganda
99C3 **Masisi** Zaïre
90A3 **Masjed Soleyman** Iran
101E2 **Masoala** *C* Madag
10A2 **Mason City** USA
91C5 **Masqat** Oman
52B2 **Massa** Italy
10C2 **Massachusetts** State, USA
15D2 **Massachusetts B** USA
98B1 **Massakori** Chad
101C3 **Massangena** Mozam
95C3 **Massawa** Eth
15D2 **Massena** USA
98B1 **Massénya** Chad
14B1 **Massey** Can
49C2 **Massif Central** *Mts* France
98B2 **Massif de l'Adamaoua** *Mts* Cam
26C3 **Massif de la Hotte** *Mts* Haiti
101D3 **Massif de l'Isalo** *Upland* Madag
98C2 **Massif des Bongo** *Upland* CAR
49D2 **Massif du Pelvoux** *Mts* France
101D2 **Massif du Tsaratanana** *Mt* Madag
14B2 **Massillon** USA
97B3 **Massina** Region, Mali
101C3 **Massinga** Mozam
101C3 **Massingir** Mozam
61H4 **Masteksay** USSR
111C2 **Masterton** NZ
74C4 **Masuda** Japan
92C2 **Ma**ṣ**yāf** Syria
98B3 **Matadi** Zaïre
25D3 **Matagalpa** Nic
7C4 **Matagami** Can
9D4 **Matagorda B** USA
110C1 **Matakana** I NZ
100A2 **Matala** Angola
87C3 **Matale** Sri Lanka
97A3 **Matam** Sen
97C3 **Matameye** Niger
24C2 **Matamoros** Mexico
95B2 **Ma'tan as Sarra** *Well* Libya
7D5 **Matane** Can
25D2 **Matanzas** Cuba
34A2 **Mataquito** *R* Chile
87C3 **Matara** Sri Lanka
106A1 **Mataram** Indon
30B2 **Matarani** Peru
51C1 **Mataró** Spain
111A3 **Mataura** NZ
24B2 **Matehuala** Mexico
27L1 **Matelot** Trinidad
53C2 **Matera** Italy
59C3 **Mátészalka** Hung
85D3 **Mathura** India
79C4 **Mati** Phil
78D3 **Matisiri** *I* Indon
43D3 **Matlock** Eng
33F6 **Mato Grosso** Brazil
33F6 **Mato Grosso** State, Brazil

30E2 **Mato Grosso do Sul** State, Brazil
101H1 **Matola** Mozam
91C5 **Matrah** Oman
92A3 **Matrûh** Egypt
74C3 **Matsue** Japan
74E2 **Matsumae** Japan
74D3 **Matsumoto** Japan
74D4 **Matsusaka** Japan
74C4 **Matsuyama** Japan
7B5 **Mattagami** *R* Can
15C1 **Mattawa** Can
52A1 **Matterhorn** *Mt* Italy/ Switz
26C2 **Matthew Town** The Bahamas
16C2 **Mattituck** USA
18C2 **Mattoon** USA
84B2 **Matun** Afghan
27L1 **Matura B** Trinidad
33E2 **Maturin** Ven
86A1 **Mau** India
101C2 **Maúa** Mozam
49C1 **Maubeuge** France
108B2 **Maude** Aust
103J8 **Maud Seamount** Atlantic O
21C4 **Maui** *I* Hawaiian Is
34A3 **Maule** *R* Chile
14B2 **Maumee** USA
14B2 **Maumee** *R* USA
100B2 **Maun** Botswana
21C4 **Mauna Kea** *Mt* Hawaiian Is
21C4 **Mauna Loa** *Mt* Hawaiian Is
4F3 **Maunoir** *L* Can
4F3 **Maunoir,L** Can
48C2 **Mauriac** France
96A2 **Mauritania** Republic, Africa
100B2 **Mavinga** Angola
86C2 **Mawlaik** Burma
112C10 **Mawson** *Base* Ant
78B3 **Maya** *I* Indon
63F2 **Maya** *R* USSR
93D2 **Mayādin** Syria
11C4 **Mayaguana** *I* The Bahamas
27D3 **Mayagüez** Puerto Rico
97C3 **Mayahi** Niger
98B3 **Mayama** Congo
90C2 **Mayamey** Iran
42B2 **Maybole** Scot
10C3 **May,C** USA
109C4 **Maydena** Aust
46D1 **Mayen** Germany
48B2 **Mayenne** France
13D2 **Mayerthorpe** Can
18C2 **Mayfield** USA
61E5 **Maykop** USSR
65H6 **Maymaneh** Afghan
76B1 **Maymyo** Burma
4E3 **Mayo** Can
45B2 **Mayo** County, Irish Rep
16A3 **Mayo** USA
45B1 **Mayo,Mts of** Irish Rep
79B3 **Mayon** *Mt* Phil
51C2 **Mayor** *Mt* Spain
34C3 **Mayor Buratovich** Arg
110C1 **Mayor I** NZ
30D2 **Mayor P Lagerenza** Par
101D2 **Mayotte** *I* Indian O
27H2 **May Pen** Jamaica
16B3 **May Point,C** USA
47D1 **Mayrhofen** Austria
16B3 **Mays Landing** USA
14B3 **Maysville** USA
98B3 **Mayumba** Gabon
100B2 **Mazabuka** Zambia
84D1 **Mazar** China
94B3 **Mazār** Jordan
53B3 **Mazara del Vallo** Italy
84B1 **Mazar-i-Sharif** Afghan
24B2 **Mazatlán** Mexico
60B2 **Mazeikiai** USSR

94B3 **Mazra** Jordan
101C3 **Mbabane** Swaziland
98B2 **Mbaïki** CAR
99D3 **Mbala** Zambia
100B3 **Mbalabala** Zim
99D2 **Mbale** Uganda
98B2 **Mbalmayo** Cam
98B2 **Mbam** *R* Cam
101C2 **Mbamba Bay** Tanz
98B2 **Mbandaka** Zaïre
98B3 **Mbanza Congo** Angola
98B3 **Mbanza-Ngungu** Zaïre
99D3 **Mbarara** Uganda
98C2 **M'Bari** *R* CAR
98B2 **Mbènza** Congo
98B2 **Mbére** *R* Cam
99D3 **Mbeya** Tanz
98B3 **Mbinda** Congo
97A3 **Mbout** Maur
98C3 **Mbuji-Mayi** Zaïre
99D3 **Mbulu** Tanz
96B2 **Mcherrah** Region, Alg
101C2 **Mchinji** Malawi
76D3 **Mdrak** Viet
9B3 **Mead,L** USA
5H4 **Meadow Lake** Can
14B2 **Meadville** USA
7E4 **Mealy Mts** Can
109C1 **Meandarra** Aust
5G4 **Meander River** Can
45C2 **Meath** County, Irish Rep
49C2 **Meaux** France
16C1 **Mechanicville** USA
56A2 **Mechelen** Belg
96B1 **Mecheria** Alg
56C2 **Mecklenburg- Vorpommern** State Germany
56C2 **Mecklenburger Bucht** *B* Germany
101C2 **Meconta** Mozam
101C2 **Mecuburi** Mozam
101D2 **Mecufi** Mozam
101C2 **Mecula** Mozam
70A3 **Medan** Indon
34C3 **Medanos** Arg
34D2 **Médanos** Arg
32B2 **Medellin** Colombia
96D1 **Medenine** Tunisia
8A2 **Medford** USA
54C2 **Medgidia** Rom
34B2 **Media Agua** Arg
54B1 **Medias** Rom
20C1 **Medical Lake** USA
13E2 **Medicine Hat** Can
35C1 **Medina** Brazil
80B3 **Medina** S Arabia
50B1 **Medinaceli** Spain
50B1 **Medina del Campo** Spain
50A1 **Medina de Rio Seco** Spain
86B2 **Medinīpur** India
88E4 **Mediterranean S** Europe
13F2 **Medley** Can
61J3 **Mednogorsk** USSR
86D1 **Mêdog** China
98B2 **Medouneu** Gabon
61F3 **Medvedista** *R* USSR
64E3 **Medvezh'yegorsk** USSR
106A3 **Meekatharra** Aust
84D3 **Meerut** India
99D2 **Mega** Eth
55B3 **Megalópolis** Greece
55B3 **Mégara** Greece
86C1 **Meghālaya** State, India
86C2 **Meghna** *R* Bang
94B2 **Megiddo** *Hist Site* Israel
91B4 **Mehran** *R* Iran
90B3 **Mehriz** Iran
35B1 **Meia Ponte** *R* Brazil
98B2 **Meiganga** Cam

76B1 **Meiktila** Burma
47C1 **Meiringen** Switz
73A4 **Meishan** China
57C2 **Meissen** Germany
73D5 **Mei Xian** China
73D5 **Meizhou** China
30B3 **Mejillones** Chile
98B2 **Mekambo** Gabon
96B1 **Meknès** Mor
76D3 **Mekong** *R* Camb
97C3 **Mekrou** *R* Benin
77C5 **Melaka** Malay
104F4 **Melanesia** *Region* Pacific O
78C3 **Melawi** *R* Indon
107D4 **Melbourne** Aust
11B4 **Melbourne** USA
9C4 **Melchor Mu**ź**guiz** Mexico
98B1 **Melfi** Chad
5H4 **Melfort** Can
96B1 **Melilla** N W Africa
29B4 **Melimoyu** *Mt* Chile
34C2 **Melincué** Arg
34A2 **Melipilla** Chile
60E4 **Melitopol'** USSR
6D2 **Meliville Bugt** *B* Greenland
101H1 **Melmoth** S Africa
34C2 **Melo** Arg
29F2 **Melo** Urug
22B2 **Melones Res** USA
12D1 **Melozitna** *R* USA
47C1 **Mels** Switz
43D3 **Melton Mowbray** Eng
49C2 **Melun** France
5H4 **Melville** Can
27O2 **Melville,C** Dominica
4F3 **Melville Hills** *Mts* Can
106C2 **Melville I** Aust
4G2 **Melville I** Can
7E4 **Melville,L** Can
6B3 **Melville Pen** Can
45B1 **Melvin,L** Irish Rep
101D2 **Memba** Mozam
106A1 **Memboro** Indon
57C2 **Memmingen** Germany
78B2 **Mempawan** Indon
11B3 **Memphis** Tennessee, USA
19B3 **Mena** USA
43B3 **Menai Str** Wales
97C3 **Ménaka** Mali
14A2 **Menasha** USA
78C3 **Mendawai** *R* Indon
49C3 **Mende** France
99D2 **Mendebo** *Mts* Eth
43C4 **Mendip Hills** *Upland* Eng
20B2 **Mendocino,C** USA
105J2 **Mendocino Seascarp** Pacific O
22B2 **Mendota** California, USA
29C2 **Mendoza** Arg
29C3 **Mendoza** State, Arg
55C3 **Menemen** Turk
46B1 **Menen** Belg
72D3 **Mengcheng** China
78B3 **Menggala** Indon
76B1 **Menghai** China
73A5 **Mengla** China
76B1 **Menglian** China
73A5 **Mengzi** China
107D4 **Menindee** Aust
108B2 **Menindee L** Aust
108A3 **Meningie** Aust
14A1 **Menominee** USA
14A2 **Menomonee Falls** USA
100A2 **Menongue** Angola
51C1 **Menorca** *I* Spain
12F2 **Mentasta Mts** USA
78B3 **Mentok** Indon
14B2 **Mentor** USA
46B2 **Ménu** France
72A2 **Menyuan** China
61H2 **Menzelinsk** USSR

56B2 **Meppen** Germany	24C3 **México** Mexico
78D2 **Merah** Indon	23A2 **México** State, Mexico
18B2 **Meramec** R USA	18B2 **Mexico** USA
52B1 **Merano** Italy	24C2 **Mexico,G of**
71F4 **Merauke** Indon	Cent America
8A3 **Merced** USA	94B3 **Mezada** Hist Site
22B2 **Merced** R USA	Israel
29B2 **Mercedario** Mt Chile	23B2 **Mezcala** Mexico
29C2 **Mercedes** Arg	64F3 **Mezen'** USSR
29E2 **Mercedes** Buenos Aires,	64G3 **Mezhdusharskiy** I
Arg	USSR
30E4 **Mercedes** Corrientes,	85D4 **Mhow** India
Arg	23B2 **Miahuatlán** Mexico
29E2 **Mercedes** Urug	11B4 **Miami** Florida, USA
110C1 **Mercury B** NZ	18B2 **Miami** Oklahoma,
110C1 **Mercury Is** NZ	USA
4F2 **Mercy B** Can	11B4 **Miami Beach** USA
6D3 **Mercy,C** Can	90A2 **Miandowāb** Iran
99E2 **Meregh** Somalia	101D2 **Miandrivazo** Madag
76B3 **Mergui** Burma	90A2 **Miāneh** Iran
76B3 **Mergui Arch** Burma	84C2 **Mianwali** Pak
25D2 **Mérida** Mexico	73A3 **Mianyang** China
50A2 **Mérida** Spain	73C3 **Mianyang** China
32C2 **Mérida** Ven	73A3 **Mianzhu** China
11B3 **Meridian** USA	72E2 **Miaodao Qundao** Arch
109C3 **Merimbula** Aust	China
108B2 **Meringur** Aust	73B4 **Miao Ling** Upland
95C3 **Merowe** Sudan	China
106A4 **Merredin** Aust	61K3 **Miass** USSR
42B2 **Merrick** Mt Scot	59C3 **Michalovce** Czech
14A2 **Merrillville** USA	27D3 **Miches** Dom Rep
13C2 **Merritt** Can	10B2 **Michigan** State, USA
17B2 **Merritt Island** USA	14A2 **Michigan City** USA
109D2 **Merriwa** Aust	10B2 **Michigan,L** USA
99E1 **Mersa Fatma** Eth	7B5 **Michipicoten I** Can
51B2 **Mers el Kebir** Alg	23A2 **Michoacan** State,
42C3 **Mersey** R Eng	Mexico
42C3 **Merseyside** County, Eng	65F4 **Michunnsk** USSR
92B2 **Mersin** Turk	54C2 **Michurin** Bulg
77C5 **Mersing** Malay	61F3 **Michurinsk** USSR
85C3 **Merta** India	104F3 **Micronesia** Region
43C4 **Merthyr Tydfil** Wales	Pacific O
50A2 **Mertola** Port	78B2 **Midai** I Indon
99D3 **Meru** Mt Tanz	102F4 **Mid Atlantic Ridge**
60E5 **Merzifon** Turk	Atlantic O
46D2 **Merzig** Germany	46B1 **Middelburg** Neth
9B3 **Mesa** USA	20B2 **Middle Alkali L** USA
46E1 **Meschede** Germany	16D2 **Middleboro** USA
93D1 **Mescit Dağ** Mt Turk	100B4 **Middleburg** Cape
12C3 **Meshik** USA	Province, S Africa
99C2 **Meshra Er Req** Sudan	16A2 **Middleburg**
47C1 **Mesocco** Switz	Pennsylvania, USA
55B3 **Mesolóngion** Greece	101G1 **Middleburg** Transvaal,
19A3 **Mesquite** Texas, USA	S Africa
101C2 **Messalo** R Mozam	16B1 **Middleburgh** USA
53C3 **Messina** Italy	15D2 **Middlebury** USA
100B3 **Messina** S Africa	11B3 **Middlesboro** USA
55B3 **Messini** Greece	42D2 **Middlesbrough** Eng
55B3 **Messiniakós Kólpos** G	16C2 **Middletown**
Greece	Connecticut, USA
54B2 **Mesta** R Bulg	16B3 **Middletown**
52B1 **Mestre** Italy	Delaware, USA
32C3 **Meta** R Colombia	15D2 **Middletown** New
60D2 **Meta** R USSR	York, USA
32D2 **Meta** R Ven	14B3 **Middletown** Ohio,
6C3 **Meta Incognito Pen** Can	USA
19B4 **Metairie** USA	16A2 **Middletown**
20C1 **Metaline Falls** USA	Pennsylvania, USA
30D4 **Metán** Arg	96B1 **Midelt** Mor
101C2 **Metangula** Mozam	43C4 **Mid Glamorgan**
53C2 **Metaponto** Italy	County, Wales
44C3 **Methil** Scot	104B4 **Mid Indian Basin**
16D1 **Methuen** USA	Indian O
111B2 **Methven** NZ	104B4 **Mid Indian Ridge**
12H3 **Metlakatla** USA	Indian O
18C2 **Metropolis** USA	7C5 **Midland** Can
87B2 **Mettūr** India	14B2 **Midland** Michigan,
49D2 **Metz** France	USA
70A3 **Meulaboh** Indon	9C3 **Midland** Texas, USA
46A2 **Meulan** France	101D3 **Midongy Atsimo**
46C2 **Meuse** Department,	Madag
France	105G2 **Mid Pacific Mts**
49D2 **Meuse** R France	Pacific O
19A3 **Mexia** USA	20C2 **Midvale** USA
24A1 **Mexicali** Mexico	105H2 **Midway Is** Pacific O
24B2 **Mexico** Federal	18A2 **Midwest City** USA
Republic,	93D2 **Midyat** Turk
Cent America	54B2 **Midžor** Mt Yugos

59B2 **Mielec** Pol	12D2 **Minchumina,L** USA
54C1 **Miercurea-Ciuc** Rom	47D2 **Mincio** R Italy
50A1 **Mieres** Spain	79B4 **Mindanao** I Phil
16A2 **Mifflintown** USA	19B3 **Minden** Louisiana,
75A2 **Mihara** Japan	USA
72D1 **Mijun Shuiku** Res	56B2 **Minden** Germany
China	108B2 **Mindona L** Aust
65F4 **Mikhayiovka** USSR	79B3 **Mindoro** I Phil
54B2 **Mikhaylovgrad** Bulg	79B3 **Mindoro Str** Phil
61F3 **Mikhaylovka** USSR	45C3 **Mine Hd** C Irish Rep
65J4 **Mikhaylovskiy** USSR	43C4 **Minehead** Eng
38K6 **Mikkeli** Fin	30F2 **Mineiros** Brazil
55C3 **Mikonos** I Greece	19A3 **Mineola** USA
59B3 **Mikulov** Czech	23B1 **Mineral de Monte**
99D3 **Mikumi** Tanz	Mexico
74D3 **Mikuni-sammyaku**	16A2 **Minersville** USA
Mts Japan	108B2 **Mingary** Aust
75B2 **Mikura-jima** I Japan	72A2 **Minhe** China
32B4 **Milagro** Ecuador	87A3 **Minicoy** I India
Milan = Milano	73D4 **Min Jiang** R Fujian,
51C2 **Milana** Alg	China
101C2 **Milange** Mozam	73A4 **Min Jiang** R Sichuan,
52A1 **Milano** Italy	China
92A2 **Milas** Turk	22C2 **Minkler** USA
107D4 **Mildura** Aust	108A2 **Minlaton** Aust
73A5 **Mile** China	72A2 **Minle** China
93D3 **Mileh Tharthār** L Iraq	97C4 **Minna** Nig
107E3 **Miles** Aust	10A2 **Minneapolis** USA
8C2 **Miles City** USA	5J4 **Minnedosa** Can
16C2 **Milford** Connecticut,	10A2 **Minnesota** State, USA
USA	50A1 **Miño** R Spain
15C3 **Milford** Delaware,	8C2 **Minot** USA
USA	72A2 **Minqin** China
15D2 **Milford**	72A3 **Min Shan** Upland
Massachusetts, USA	China
18A1 **Milford** Nebraska,	60C3 **Minsk** USSR
USA	58C2 **Minsk Mazowiecki** Pol
16B2 **Milford** Pennsylvania,	12E2 **Minto** USA
USA	4G2 **Minto Inlet** B Can
43B4 **Milford Haven** Wales	7C4 **Minto,L** Can
43B4 **Milford Haven** Sd	63B2 **Minusinsk** USSR
Wales	72A3 **Min Xian** China
18A2 **Milford L** USA	7E5 **Miquelon** Can
111A2 **Milford Sd** NZ	22D3 **Mirage L** USA
13E2 **Milk River** Can	87A1 **Miraj** India
49C3 **Millau** France	29E3 **Miramar** Arg
16C2 **Millbrook** USA	84B2 **Miram Shah** Pak
17B1 **Milledgeville** USA	50B1 **Miranda de Ebro**
12F2 **Miller,Mt** USA	Spain
61F4 **Millerovo** USSR	47D2 **Mirandola** Italy
16A2 **Millersburg** USA	84B2 **Mir Bachchen Kūt**
108A1 **Millers Creek** Aust	Afghan
16C1 **Millers Falls** USA	78D1 **Miri** Malay
16C2 **Millerton** USA	96A3 **Mirik,C** Maur
22C2 **Millerton L** USA	63A1 **Mirnoye** USSR
108B3 **Millicent** Aust	63D1 **Mirnyy** USSR
109D1 **Millmerran** Aust	112C9 **Mirnyy** Base Ant
45B2 **Milltown Malbay**	84C2 **Mirpur** Pak
Irish Rep	85B3 **Mirpur Khas** Pak
22A2 **Mill Valley** USA	55B3 **Mirtoan S** Greece
15D3 **Millville** USA	74B3 **Miryang** S Korea
6H2 **Milne Land** I	86A1 **Mirzāpur** India
Greenland	23B2 **Misantla** Mexico
21C4 **Milolii** Hawaiian Is	84C1 **Misgar** Pak
55B3 **Milos** I Greece	14A2 **Mishawaka** USA
107D3 **Milparinka** Aust	12B1 **Misheguk Mt** USA
16A2 **Milroy** USA	75A2 **Mi-shima** I Japan
111A3 **Milton** NZ	107E2 **Misima** I Solomon Is
16A2 **Milton** Pennsylvania,	30F4 **Misiones** State, Arg
USA	59C3 **Miskolc** Hung
10B2 **Milwaukee** USA	94C2 **Mismīyah** Syria
51C2 **Mina** R Alg	71E4 **Misoöl** I Indon
93E4 **Mīnā' al Ahmadī**	95A1 **Misrātah** Libya
Kuwait	7B5 **Missinaibi** R Can
91C4 **Mīnāb** Iran	20B1 **Mission City** Can
74C4 **Minamata** Japan	15C2 **Mississauga** Can
78A2 **Minas** Indon	11A3 **Mississippi** State, USA
29E2 **Minas** Urug	11A3 **Mississippi** R USA
31B5 **Minas Gerais** State,	19C3 **Mississippi Delta** USA
Brazil	8B2 **Missoula** USA
35C1 **Minas Novas** Brazil	96B1 **Missour** Mor
25C3 **Minatitlan** Mexico	11A3 **Missouri** State, USA
76A1 **Minbu** Burma	10A2 **Missouri** R USA
76A1 **Minbya** Burma	10C1 **Mistassini,L** Can
34A2 **Mincha** Chile	30B2 **Misti** Mt Peru
44A3 **Minch,Little** Sd Scot	109C1 **Mitchell** Aust
44A2 **Minch,North** Sd Scot	8D2 **Mitchell** USA
40B2 **Minch,The** Sd Scot	107D2 **Mitchell** R Aust

11B3 **Mitchell,Mt** USA
45B2 **Mitchelstown**
Irish Rep
84C3 **Mithankot** Pak
55C3 **Mitilíni** Greece
23B2 **Mitla** Mexico
32C3 **Mitu** Colombia
99C3 **Mitumbar** *Mts* Zaïre
98C3 **Mitwaba** Zaïre
98B2 **Mitzic** Gabon
75B1 **Miura** Japan
72C3 **Mi Xian** China
69F3 **Miyake** / Japan
75B2 **Miyake-jima** / Japan
69E4 **Miyako** / Japan
74C4 **Miyakonojò** Japan
74C4 **Miyazaki** Japan
75B1 **Miyazu** Japan
74C4 **Miyoshi** Japan
72D1 **Miyun** China
99D2 **Mizan Teferi** Eth
95A1 **Mizdah** Libya
45B3 **Mizen Hd** *C* Irish Rep
54C1 **Mizil** Rom
86C2 **Mizo Hills** India
86C2 **Mizoram** Union
Territory, India
94B3 **Mizpe Ramon** Israel
112B11 **Mizuho** *Base* Ant
74E3 **Mizusawa** Japan
39H7 **Mjolby** Sweden
100B2 **Mkushi** Zambia
101H1 **Mkuzi** S Africa
57C2 **Mladá Boleslav** Czech
58C2 **Mława** Pol
52C2 **Mljet** / Yugos
100B3 **Mmabatho** S Africa
84D2 **Mnadi** India
97A4 **Moa** *R* Sierra Leone
94B3 **Moab** Region, Jordan
9C3 **Moab** USA
98B3 **Moanda** Congo
98B3 **Moanda** Gabon
99C3 **Moba** Zaïre
75C1 **Mobara** Japan
98C2 **Mobaye** CAR
98C2 **Mobayi** Zaïre
10A3 **Moberly** USA
11B3 **Mobile** USA
11B3 **Mobile B** USA
8C2 **Mobridge** USA
101D2 **Moçambique** Mozam
76C1 **Moc Chau** Viet
100B3 **Mochudi** Botswana
101D2 **Mocimboa da Praia**
Mozam
32B3 **Mocoa** Colombia
35B2 **Mococa** Brazil
34D2 **Mocoreta** *R* Arg
23B1 **Moctezuma** *R* Mexico
101C2 **Mocuba** Mozam
47B2 **Modane** France
101G1 **Modder** *R* S Africa
52B2 **Modena** Italy
46D2 **Moder** *R* France
8A3 **Modesto** USA
22B2 **Modesto Res** USA
53B3 **Modica** Italy
59B3 **Mödling** Austria
107D4 **Moe** Aust
47C1 **Moesa** *R* Switz
42C2 **Moffat** Scot
84D2 **Moga** India
35B2 **Mogi das Cruzes**
Brazil
60C3 **Mogilev** USSR
60C4 **Mogilev Podolskiy**
USSR
35B2 **Mogi-Mirim** Brazil
101D2 **Mogincual** Mozam
47E2 **Mogliano** Italy
34B2 **Mogna** Arg
68D1 **Mogocha** USSR
65K4 **Mogochin** USSR
50A2 **Moguer** Spain
110C1 **Mohaka** *R* NZ
86C2 **Mohanganj** Bang
15D2 **Mohawk** *R* USA

99D3 **Mohoro** Tanz
65J5 **Mointy** USSR
38G5 **Mo i Rana** Nor
48C3 **Moissac** France
21B2 **Mojave** USA
22D3 **Mojave** *R* USA
9B3 **Mojave Desert** USA
78C4 **Mojokerto** Indon
86B1 **Mokama** India
110B1 **Mokau** *R* NZ
22B1 **Mokelumne Aqueduct**
USA
22B1 **Mokelumne Hill** USA
22B1 **Mokelumne North**
Fork *R* USA
101G1 **Mokhotlong** Lesotho
96D1 **Moknine** Tunisia
86C1 **Mokokchùng** India
98B1 **Mokolo** Cam
74B4 **Mokp'o** S Korea
61F3 **Moksha** *R* USSR
23B1 **Molango** Mexico
55B3 **Moláoi** Greece
60C4 **Moldavskaya SSR**
Republic, USSR
38F6 **Molde** Nor
54B1 **Moldoveanu** *Mt* Rom
100B3 **Molepolole** Botswana
53C2 **Molfetta** Italy
34A3 **Molina** Chile
30B2 **Mollendo** Peru
60C3 **Molodechno** USSR
112C11 **Molodezhnaya** *Base*
Ant
21C4 **Molokai** / Hawaiian Is
61G2 **Moloma** *R* USSR
109C2 **Molong** Aust
100B3 **Molopo** *R* Botswana
98B2 **Molounddu** Cam
8D1 **Molson L** Can
71D4 **Molucca** *S* Indon
71D4 **Moluccas** *Is* Indon
101C2 **Moma** Mozam
31C3 **Mombaca** Brazil
99D3 **Mombasa** Kenya
98C2 **Mompono** Zaïre
56C2 **Mon** / Den
44A3 **Monach** *Is* Scot
49D3 **Monaco**
Principality, Europe
44B3 **Monadhliath** *Mts*
Scot
45C1 **Monaghan** County,
Irish Rep
45C1 **Monaghan** Irish Rep
27D3 **Mona Pass**
Caribbean S
13B2 **Monarch Mt** Can
5G4 **Monashee Mts** Can
41B3 **Monastereven**
Irish Rep
47B2 **Moncalieri** Italy
31B2 **Monção** Brazil
38L5 **Monchegorsk** USSR
56B2 **Mönchen-gladbach**
Germany
24B2 **Monclova** Mexico
7D5 **Moncton** Can
9C4 **Monctova** Mexico
50A1 **Mondego** *R* Port
52A2 **Mondovi** Italy
27H1 **Moneague** Jamaica
14C2 **Monessen** USA
18B2 **Monett** USA
52B1 **Monfalcone** Italy
50A1 **Monforte de Lemos**
Spain
98C2 **Monga** Zaïre
98C2 **Mongala** *R* Zaïre
99D2 **Mongalla** Sudan
76D1 **Mong Cai** Viet
98B1 **Mongo** Chad
68B2 **Mongolia** Republic,
Asia
100B2 **Mongu** Zambia
63D3 **Mönhhaan** Mongolia
21B2 **Monitor Range** *Mts*
USA

98C3 **Monkoto** Zaïre
43C4 **Monmouth** Eng
18B1 **Monmouth** USA
13C2 **Monmouth,Mt** Can
97C4 **Mono** *R* Togo
21B2 **Mono L** USA
53C2 **Monopoli** Italy
51B1 **Monreal del Campo**
Spain
19B3 **Monroe** Louisiana,
USA
14B2 **Monroe** Michigan,
USA
20B1 **Monroe** Washington,
USA
18B2 **Monroe City** USA
97A4 **Monrovia** Lib
20D3 **Monrovia** USA
56A2 **Mons** Belg
47D2 **Monselice** Italy
16C1 **Monson** USA
58B1 **Mönsterås** Sweden
101D2 **Montagne d'Ambre**
Mt Madag
96C1 **Montagnes des Ouled**
Naïl *Mts* Alg
12E3 **Montague I** USA
49C3 **Mont Aigoual** *Mt*
France
48B2 **Montaigu** France
53C3 **Montallo** *Mt* Italy
8B2 **Montana** State, USA
50A1 **Montañas de León**
Mts Spain
49C2 **Montargis** France
48C3 **Montauban** France
15D2 **Montauk** USA
15D2 **Montauk Pt** USA
49D2 **Montbéliard** France
52A1 **Mont Blanc** *Mt*
France/Italy
49C2 **Montceau les Mines**
France
51C1 **Montceny** *Mt* Spain
49D3 **Mont Cinto** *Mt* Corse
46C2 **Montcornet** France
48B3 **Mont-de-Marsin**
France
48C2 **Montdidier** France
30D2 **Monteagudo** Bol
33G4 **Monte Alegre** Brazil
52B2 **Monte Amiata** *Mt*
Italy
47D2 **Monte Baldo** *Mt* Italy
15C1 **Montebello** Can
106A3 **Monte Bello Is** Aust
47E2 **Montebelluna** Italy
49D3 **Monte Carlo** Monaco
35B1 **Monte Carmelo** Brazil
34D2 **Monte Caseros** Arg
52B2 **Monte Cimone** *Mt*
Italy
52A2 **Monte Cinto** *Mt*
Corse
34B2 **Monte Coman** Arg
52B2 **Monte Corno** *Mt* Italy
27C3 **Montecristi** Dom Rep
52B2 **Montecristo** / Italy
23A1 **Monte Escobedo**
Mexico
53C2 **Monte Gargano** *Mt*
Italy
26B3 **Montego Bay** Jamaica
47D2 **Monte Grappa** *Mt*
Italy
47C2 **Monte Lesima** *Mt*
Italy
49C3 **Montélimar** France
53B2 **Monte Miletto** *Mt*
Italy
50A2 **Montemo-o-Novo** Port
24C2 **Montemorelos** Mexico
26B5 **Montená** Colombia
54A2 **Montenegro** Region,
Yugos
35D1 **Monte Pascoal** *Mt*
Brazil
34A2 **Monte Patria** Chile

53C3 **Monte Pollino** *Mt* Italy
101C2 **Montepuez** Mozam
8A3 **Monterey** California,
USA
15C3 **Monterey** Virginia,
USA
8A3 **Monterey B** USA
32B2 **Montería** Colombia
30D2 **Montero** Bol
47B2 **Monte Rosa** *Mt* Italy/
Switz
24B2 **Monterrey** Mexico
31C5 **Montes Claros** Brazil
50B2 **Montes de Toledo** *Mts*
Spain
29E2 **Montevideo** Urug
52A2 **Monte Viso** *Mt* Italy
27P2 **Mont Gimie** *Mt* St
Lucia
11B3 **Montgomery**
Alabama, USA
96C2 **Mont Gréboun** Niger
46C2 **Montherme** France
47B1 **Monthey** Switz
19B3 **Monticello** Arkansas,
USA
16B2 **Monticello** New York,
USA
9C3 **Monticello** Utah, USA
53A2 **Monti del**
Gennargentu *Mt*
Sardegna
47D2 **Monti Lessini** *Mts*
Italy
53B3 **Monti Nebrodi** *Mts*
Italy
7C5 **Mont-Laurier** Can
48C2 **Montluçon** France
7C5 **Montmagny** Can
46C2 **Montmédy** France
49C3 **Mont Mézenc** *Mt*
France
46B2 **Montmirail** France
50B2 **Montoro** Spain
49D3 **Mont Pelat** *Mt* France
14B2 **Montpelier** Ohio, USA
10C2 **Montpelier** Vermont,
USA
49C3 **Montpellier** France
7C5 **Montréal** Can
48C1 **Montreuil** France
52A1 **Montreux** Switz
47B1 **Mont Risoux** *Mt*
France
8C3 **Montrose** Colorado,
USA
40C2 **Montrose** Scot
48B2 **Mont-St-Michel**
France
96B1 **Monts des Ksour** *Mts*
Alg
51C3 **Monts des Ouled Neil**
Mts Alg
51C2 **Monts du Hodna** *Mts*
Alg
27E3 **Montserrat** /
Caribbean S
12B1 **Monument Mt** USA
9B3 **Monument V** USA
98C2 **Monveda** Zaïre
76B1 **Monywa** Burma
52A1 **Monza** Italy
100B2 **Monze** Zambia
101H1 **Mooi** *R* S Africa
101G1 **Mooi River** S Africa
108B1 **Moomba** Aust
109D2 **Moonbi Range** *Mts*
Aust
108B1 **Moonda L** Aust
109D1 **Moonie** Aust
109C1 **Moonie** *R* Aust
108A2 **Moonta** Aust
106A4 **Moora** Aust
106A3 **Moore,L** Aust
42C2 **Moorfoot Hills** Scot
8D2 **Moorhead** USA
22C3 **Moorpark** USA
7B4 **Moose** *R* Can

5H4 **Moose Jaw** Can
5H4 **Moosomin** Can
7B4 **Moosonee** Can
16D2 **Moosup** USA
101C2 **Mopeia** Mozam
97B3 **Mopti** Mali
30B2 **Moquegua** Peru
39G6 **Mora** Sweden
31D3 **Morada** Brazil
84D3 **Morādābād** India
35B1 **Morada Nova de Minas** L Brazil
101C2 **Morafenobe** Madag
101D2 **Moramanga** Madag
27J2 **Morant Bay** Jamaica
27J2 **Morant Pt** Jamaica
87B3 **Moratuwa** Sri Lanka
59B3 **Morava** R Austria/ Czech
54B2 **Morava** R Yugos
90C2 **Moraveh Tappeh** Iran
40C2 **Moray Firth** Estuary Scot
47C1 **Morbegno** Italy
85C4 **Morbi** India
93D2 **Mor Daǧ** Mt Turk
5J5 **Morden** Can
61F3 **Mordovskaya ASSR** Republic, USSR
42C2 **Morecambe** Eng
42C2 **Morecambe B** Eng
107D3 **Moree** Aust
14B3 **Morehead** USA
47C1 **Mörel** Switz
24B3 **Morelia** Mexico
23B2 **Morelos** State, Mexico
85D3 **Morena** India
5E4 **Moresby I** Can
109D1 **Moreton I** Aust
46B2 **Moreuil** France
47B1 **Morez** France
19B4 **Morgan City** USA
22B2 **Morgan Hill** USA
14C3 **Morgantown** USA
101G1 **Morgenzon** S Africa
47B1 **Morges** Switz
46D2 **Morhange** France
74E2 **Mori** Japan
27K1 **Moriatio** Tobago
13B2 **Morice L** Can
13E2 **Morinville** Can
74E3 **Morioka** Japan
109D2 **Morisset** Aust
63D1 **Morkoka** R USSR
48B2 **Morlaix** France
27Q2 **Morne Diablotin** Mt Dominica
106C2 **Mornington** I Aust
85B3 **Moro** Pak
96B2 **Morocco** Kingdom, Africa
79B4 **Moro G** Phil
99D3 **Morogoro** Tanz
23A1 **Moroleon** Mexico
101D3 **Morombe** Madag
26B2 **Morón** Cuba
101D3 **Morondava** Madag
50A2 **Moron de la Frontera** Spain
101D2 **Moroni** Comoros
71D3 **Morotai** I Indon
99D2 **Moroto** Uganda
61F4 **Morozovsk** USSR
42D2 **Morpeth** Eng
19B2 **Morrilton** USA
35B1 **Morrinhos** Brazil
110C1 **Morrinsville** NZ
16B2 **Morristown** New Jersey, USA
15C2 **Morristown** New York, USA
16B2 **Morrisville** Pennsylvania, USA
21A2 **Morro Bay** USA
23A2 **Morro de Papanoa** Mexico
23A2 **Morro de Petatlán** Mexico

101C2 **Morrumbala** Mozam
101C3 **Morrumbene** Mozam
61F3 **Morshansk** USSR
47C2 **Mortara** Italy
34C2 **Morteros** Arg
33G6 **Mortes** R Mato Grosso, Brazil
35C2 **Mortes** R Minas Gerais, Brazil
108B3 **Mortlake** Aust
27L1 **Moruga** Trinidad
109D3 **Moruya** Aust
109C1 **Morven** Aust
44B3 **Morvern** Pen Scot
109C3 **Morwell** Aust
76B3 **Moscos Is** Burma
Moscow = Moskva
20C1 **Moscow** Idaho, USA
56B2 **Mosel** R Germany
46D2 **Moselle** Department, France
46D2 **Moselle** R France
20C1 **Moses Lake** USA
111B3 **Mosgiel** NZ
99D3 **Moshi** Tanz
38G5 **Mosjøen** Nor
63G2 **Moskal'vo** USSR
64E4 **Moskva** USSR
35C1 **Mosquito** R Brazil
39G7 **Moss** Nor
98B3 **Mossaka** Congo
100B4 **Mossel Bay** S Africa
98B3 **Mossendjo** Congo
108B2 **Mossgiel** Aust
31D3 **Mossoró** Brazil
57C2 **Most** Czech
96C1 **Mostaganem** Alg
54A2 **Mostar** Yugos
58C2 **Mosty** USSR
93D2 **Mosul** Iraq
39H7 **Motala** Sweden
42C2 **Motherwell** Scot
86A1 **Motihāri** India
51B2 **Motilla del Palancar** Spain
50B2 **Motril** Spain
111B2 **Motueka** NZ
111B2 **Motueka** R NZ
47B1 **Moudon** Switz
98B3 **Mouila** Gabon
108B2 **Moulamein** Aust
4G2 **Mould Bay** Can
49C2 **Moulins** France
76B2 **Moulmein** Burma
96B1 **Moulouya** R Mor
17B1 **Moultrie** USA
17C1 **Moultrie,L** USA
18C2 **Mound City** Illinois, USA
18A1 **Mound City** Missouri, USA
98B2 **Moundou** Chad
14B3 **Moundsville** USA
12J1 **Mountain** R Can
17A1 **Mountain Brook** USA
18B2 **Mountain Grove** USA
18B2 **Mountain Home** Arkansas, USA
22A2 **Mountain View** USA
12B2 **Mountain Village** USA
16A3 **Mount Airy** Maryland, USA
16A2 **Mount Carmel** USA
108A1 **Mount Dutton** Aust
108A2 **Mount Eba** Aust
108B3 **Mount Gambier** Aust
16B3 **Mount Holly** USA
16A2 **Mount Holly Springs** USA
108A2 **Mount Hope** Aust
106C3 **Mount Isa** Aust
108A2 **Mount Lofty Range** Mts Aust
12D2 **Mount McKinley Nat Pk** USA
106A3 **Mount Magnet** Aust
108B2 **Mount Manara** Aust
107E3 **Mount Morgan** Aust

19B3 **Mount Pleasant** Texas, USA
20B1 **Mount Rainier Nat Pk** USA
43B4 **Mounts B** Eng
20B2 **Mount Shasta** USA
11B3 **Mount Vernon** Illinois, USA
19A3 **Mount Vernon** Kentucky, USA
20B1 **Mount Vernon** Washington, USA
45C1 **Mourne Mts** N Ire
98B1 **Moussoro** Chad
86B2 **Mouths of the Ganga** India/Bang
85B4 **Mouths of the Indus** Pak
77D4 **Mouths of the Mekong** Viet
97C4 **Mouths of the Niger** Nig
47B1 **Moutier** Switz
47B2 **Moûtiers** France
96C2 **Mouydir** Mts Alg
98B3 **Mouyondzi** Congo
46C2 **Mouzon** France
59B3 **M'óvár** Hung
23A1 **Moyahua** Mexico
99D2 **Moyale** Kenya
97A4 **Moyamba** Sierra Leone
96B1 **Moyen Atlas** Mts Mor
100B4 **Moyeni** Lesotho
99D2 **Moyo** Uganda
32B5 **Moyobamba** Peru
84D1 **Moyu** China
101C3 **Mozambique** Republic, Africa
101C3 **Mozambique Chan** Mozam/Madag
61H2 **Mozhga** USSR
60C3 **Mozyr** USSR
99D3 **Mpanda** Tanz
101C2 **Mpika** Zambia
99D3 **Mporokosa** Zambia
100B2 **Mposhi** Zambia
99D3 **Mpulungu** Zambia
99D3 **Mpwapwa** Tanz
96C1 **M'Sila** Alg
60E3 **Mtsensk** USSR
101H1 **Mtubatuba** S Africa
101D2 **Mtwara** Tanz
76C2 **Muang Chainat** Thai
76C2 **Muang Chiang Rai** Thai
76C2 **Muang Kalasin** Thai
76C2 **Muang Khon Kaen** Thai
76B2 **Muang Lampang** Thai
76B2 **Muang Lamphun** Thai
76C2 **Muang Loei** Thai
76C2 **Muang Lom Sak** Thai
76C2 **Muang Nakhon Phanom** Thai
76B2 **Muang Nakhon Sawan** Thai
76C2 **Muang Nan** Thai
76C2 **Muang Phayao** Thai
76C2 **Muang Phetchabun** Thai
76C2 **Muang Phichit** Thai
76C2 **Muang Phitsanulok** Thai
76C2 **Muang Phrae** Thai
76C2 **Muang Roi Et** Thai
76C2 **Muang Sakon Nakhon** Thai
76C3 **Muang Samut Prakan** Thai
76C2 **Muang Uthai Thani** Thai
76C2 **Muang Yasothon** Thai
77C5 **Muar** Malay
78C2 **Muara** Brunei
70B4 **Muara** Indon
78A3 **Muaralakitan** Indon
78A3 **Muaratebo** Indon

78C3 **Muaratewah** Indon
78A3 **Muarenim** Indon
76A2 **Muaungmaya** Burma
99D2 **Mubende** Uganda
100C2 **Muchinga** Mts Zambia
44A3 **Muck** I Scot
109C1 **Muckadilla** Aust
35D1 **Mucuri** Brazil
35C1 **Mucuri** R Brazil
100B2 **Mucusso** Angola
69E2 **Mudanjiang** China
109C2 **Mudgee** Aust
76B2 **Mudon** Burma
101C2 **Mueda** Mozam
107F3 **Mueo** Nouvelle Calédonie
100B2 **Mufulira** Zambia
73C4 **Mufu Shan** Hills China
Mugadishu=Muqdisho
61J4 **Mugadzhary** Mts USSR
93C4 **Mughayra** S Arabia
92A2 **Muǧla** Turk
65G5 **Mugodzhary** Mts USSR
73A3 **Muguaping** China
93D3 **Muhaywir** Iraq
57C3 **Mühldorf** Germany
57C2 **Muhlhausen** Germany
38K6 **Muhos** Fin
77C4 **Mui Bai Bung** C Camb
45C2 **Muine Bheag** Irish Rep
100B2 **Mujimbeji** Zambia
59C3 **Mukachevo** USSR
78C2 **Mukah** Malay
69G4 **Muko-jima** I Japan
86A1 **Muktinath** Nepal
84B2 **Mukur** Afghan
18B2 **Mulberry** USA
12C2 **Mulchatna** R USA
34A3 **Mulchén** Chile
56C2 **Mulde** R Germany
71F5 **Mulgrave I** Aust
50B2 **Mulhacén** Mt Spain
46D1 **Mülheim** Germany
49D2 **Mulhouse** France
73A4 **Muli** China
44B3 **Mull** I Scot
87C3 **Mullaitvu** Sri Lanka
109C2 **Mullaley** Aust
106A3 **Mullewa** Aust
16B3 **Mullica** R USA
45C2 **Mullingar** Irish Rep
42B2 **Mull of Kintyre** Pt Scot
45C1 **Mull of Oa** C Scot
109D1 **Mullumbimby** Aust
100B2 **Mulobezi** Zambia
84C2 **Multan** Pak
100B2 **Mumbwa** Zambia
61G4 **Mumra** USSR
71D4 **Muna** I Indon
57C3 **München** Germany
14A2 **Muncie** USA
15C2 **Muncy** USA
56B2 **Münden** Germany
109D1 **Mundubbera** Aust
109C1 **Mungallala** Aust
109C1 **Mungallala** R Aust
99C2 **Mungbere** Zaïre
86A2 **Mungeli** India
86B1 **Munger** India
109C1 **Mungindi** Aust
Munich = München
14A1 **Munising** USA
29B6 **Muñoz Gomero,Pen** Chile
45B2 **Munster** Region, Irish Rep
47C1 **Münster** Switz
56B2 **Münster** Germany
54B1 **Muntii Apuseni** Mts Rom
54B1 **Muntii Călimanilor** Mts Rom

54B1 **Muntii Carpaţii Meridionali** *Mts* Rom	55C2 **Mustafa-Kemalpasa** Turk	19B3 **Nacogdoches** USA	101C2 **Nametil** Mozam
54B1 **Muntii Rodnei** *Mts* Rom	86A1 **Mustang** Nepal	76A3 **Nacondam** *I* Indian O	74B4 **Namhae-do** *I* S Korea
54B1 **Muntii Zarandului** *Mts* Rom	109D2 **Muswellbrook** Aust	24B1 **Nacozari** Mexico	100A2 **Namib Desert** Namibia
93C2 **Munzur Silsilesi** *Mts* Turk	95B2 **Mut** Egypt	85C4 **Nadiād** India	100A2 **Namibe** Angola
64D3 **Muomio** Fin	101C2 **Mutarara** Mozam	50B2 **Nador** Mor	100A3 **Namibia** Dependency, Africa
76C1 **Muong Khoua** Laos	101C2 **Mutare** Zim	90B3 **Nadüshan** Iran	82D3 **Namjagbarwa Feng** *Mt* China
76D3 **Muong Man** Viet	101C2 **Mutoko** Zim	59C3 **Nadvornaya** USSR	71D4 **Namlea** Indon
76D2 **Muong Nong** Laos	101D2 **Mutsamudu** Comoros	56C1 **Naestved** Den	109C2 **Namoi** *R* Aust
76C1 **Muong Ou Neua** Laos	100B2 **Mutshatsha** Zaïre	95B2 **Nafoora** Libya	13D1 **Nampa** Can
76C1 **Muong Sai** Laos	74E2 **Mutsu** Japan	75A2 **Nagahama** Japan	20C2 **Nampa** USA
76C2 **Muong Sen** Viet	74E2 **Mutsu-wan** *B* Japan	82D3 **Naga Hills** Burma	97B3 **Nampala** Mali
76C1 **Muong Sing** Laos	45B2 **Mutton** *I* Irish Rep	75B1 **Nagai** Japan	76C2 **Nam Phong** Thai
76C1 **Muong Son** Laos	72B2 **Mu Us Shamo** *Desert* China	86C1 **Nāgāland** State, India	74B3 **Namp'o** N Korea
38J5 **Muonio** Fin	98B3 **Muxima** Angola	74D3 **Nagano** Japan	101C2 **Nampula** Mozam
38J5 **Muonio** *R* Sweden/Fin	63D2 **Muya** USSR	74D3 **Nagaoka** Japan	38G6 **Namsos** Nor
99E2 **Muqdisho** Somalia	38L6 **Muyezerskiy** USSR	87B2 **Nāgappattinam** India	76B1 **Namton** Burma
52B1 **Mur** *R* Austria	99D3 **Muyinga** Burundi	85C4 **Nagar Parkar** Pak	86D2 **Namtu** Burma
74D3 **Murakami** Japan	98C3 **Muyumba** Zaïre	74B4 **Nagasaki** Japan	13B2 **Namu** Can
29B5 **Murallón** *Mt* Arg/Chile	82A1 **Muyun Kum** *Desert* USSR	75B2 **Nagashima** Japan	101C2 **Namuno** Mozam
61G2 **Murashi** USSR	84C2 **Muzaffarābad** Pak	75A2 **Nagato** Japan	46C1 **Namur** Belg
93D2 **Murat** *R* Turk	84C2 **Muzaffargarh** Pak	85C3 **Nāgaur** India	100A2 **Namutoni** Namibia
53A3 **Muravera** Sardegna	84D3 **Muzaffarnagar** India	87B3 **Nāgercoil** India	74B3 **Namwŏn** S Korea
75C1 **Murayama** Japan	86B1 **Muzaffarpur** India	85B3 **Nagha Kalat** Pak	13C3 **Nanaimo** Can
90B3 **Murcheh Khvort** Iran	64H3 **Muzhi** USSR	84D3 **Nagina** India	74B2 **Nanam** N Korea
111B2 **Murchison** NZ	82C2 **Muztag** *Mt* China	74D3 **Nagoya** Japan	109D1 **Nanango** Aust
106A3 **Murchison** *R* Aust	82B2 **Muztagata** *Mt* China	85D4 **Nāgpur** India	74D3 **Nanao** Japan
51B2 **Murcia** Region, Spain	100C2 **Mvuma** Zim	82D2 **Nagqu** China	75B1 **Nanatsu-jima** *I* Japan
51B2 **Murcia** Spain	99D3 **Mwanza** Tanz	59B3 **Nagykanizsa** Hung	73B3 **Nanbu** China
54B1 **Mureş** *R* Rom	98C3 **Mwanza** Zaïre	59B3 **Nagykörös** Hung	73D4 **Nanchang** China
46E2 **Murg** *R* Germany	98C3 **Mweka** Zaïre	69E4 **Naha** Japan	73B3 **Nanchong** China
65H6 **Murgab** *R* USSR	98C3 **Mwene Ditu** Zaïre	8A2 **Nahaimo** Can	49D2 **Nancy** France
84B2 **Murgha Kibzai** Pak	100C3 **Mwenezi** Zim	84D2 **Nāhan** India	87B1 **Nānded** India
109D1 **Murgon** Aust	99C3 **Mwenga** Zaïre	4F3 **Nahanni Butte** Can	109D2 **Nandewar Range** *Mts* Aust
86B2 **Muri** India	99C3 **Mweru** *L* Zambia	94B2 **Nahariya** Israel	85C4 **Nandurbar** India
35C2 **Muriaé** Brazil	100B2 **Mwinilunga** Zambia	90A3 **Nahāvand** Iran	87B1 **Nandyāl** India
98C3 **Muriege** Angola	83D4 **Myanaung** Burma	46D2 **Nahe** *R* Germany	98B2 **Nanga Eboko** Cam
64E3 **Murmansk** USSR	59B3 **M'yaróvar** Hung	72D2 **Nahpu** China	84C1 **Nanga Parbat** *Mt* Pak
61F2 **Murom** USSR	86D2 **Myingyan** Burma	72E1 **Naimen Qi** China	78C3 **Nangapinoh** Indon
74E2 **Muroran** Japan	76B1 **Myingyao** Burma	7D4 **Nain** Can	78C3 **Nangatayap** Indon
50A1 **Muros** Spain	76B3 **Myinmoletkat** *Mt* Burma	90B3 **Nā'in** Iran	74B2 **Nangnim Sanmaek** *Mts* N Korea
74C4 **Muroto** Japan	82D3 **Myitkyina** Burma	84D3 **Naini Tai** India	86C1 **Nang Xian** China
75A2 **Muroto-zaki** *C* Japan	76B3 **Myitta** Burma	44C3 **Nairn** Scot	67F3 **Nangzhou** China
20C2 **Murphy** Idaho, USA	86C2 **Mymensingh** Bang	99D3 **Nairobi** Kenya	87B2 **Nanjangūd** India
22B1 **Murphys** USA	69F3 **Myojin** *I* Japan	90B3 **Najafābād** Iran	72D3 **Nanjing** China
18C2 **Murray** Kentucky, USA	39F6 **Myrdal** Nor	74C2 **Najin** N Korea	**Nanking** = **Nanjing**
108B2 **Murray** *R* Aust	38B2 **Myrdalsjökur** *Mts* Iceland	75A2 **Nakama** Japan	75A2 **Nankoku** Japan
13C2 **Murray** *R* Can	17C1 **Myrtle Beach** USA	74E3 **Nakaminato** Japan	73C4 **Nan Ling** Region, China
108A3 **Murray Bridge** Aust	20B2 **Myrtle Creek** USA	75A2 **Nakamura** Japan	76D1 **Nanliu** *R* China
71F4 **Murray,L** PNG	39G7 **Mysen** Nor	75B1 **Nakano** Japan	73B5 **Nanning** China
17B1 **Murray,L** USA	56C2 **Mysiloborz** Pol	75A1 **Nakano-shima** *I* Japan	6F3 **Nanortalik** Greenland
105J2 **Murray Seacarp** Pacific O	64F3 **Mys Kanin Nos** *C* USSR	74C4 **Nakatsu** Japan	73A5 **Nanpan Jiang** *R* China
108B2 **Murrumbidgee** *R* Aust	59B3 **Myślenice** Pol	75B1 **Nakatsu-gawa** Japan	86A1 **Nānpāra** India
109C2 **Murrumburrah** Aust	69H1 **Mys Lopatka** *C* USSR	95C3 **Nakfa** Eth	73D4 **Nanping** China
109D2 **Murrurundi** Aust	87B2 **Mysore** India	93E2 **Nakhichevan** USSR	6A1 **Nansen Sd** Can
47B1 **Murten** Switz	60D5 **Mys Sarych** *C* USSR	92B4 **Nakhl** Egypt	99D3 **Nansio** Tanz
108B3 **Murtoa** Aust	16D2 **Mystic** USA	74C2 **Nakhodka** USSR	48B2 **Nantes** France
110C1 **Murupara** NZ	61H5 **Mys Tyub-Karagan** *Pt* USSR	76C3 **Nakhon Pathom** Thai	13E2 **Nanton** Can
86A2 **Murwära** India	63G2 **Mys Yelizavety** *C* USSR	76C3 **Nakhon Ratchasima** Thai	72E3 **Nantong** China
109D1 **Murwillimbah** Aust	64H2 **Mys Zhelaniya** *C* USSR	77C4 **Nakhon Si Thammarat** Thai	10C2 **Nantucket** *I* USA
93D2 **Muş** Turk	77D3 **My Tho** Viet	12H3 **Nakina** Can	35C1 **Nanuque** Brazil
54B2 **Musala** *Mt* Bulg	20B2 **Mytle Point** USA	7B4 **Nakina** Ontario, Can	72C3 **Nanyang** China
74B2 **Musan** N Korea	101C2 **Mzimba** Malawi	12C3 **Naknek** USA	72D2 **Nanyang Hu** *L* China
91C4 **Musandam** *Pen* Oman	101C2 **Mzuzú** Malawi	12C3 **Naknek L** USA	99D2 **Nanyuki** Kenya
Muscat = **Masqat**		4C4 **Nakrek** USA	74D3 **Naoetsu** Japan
91C5 **Muscat** Region, Oman		39G8 **Nakskov** Den	85B4 **Naokot** Pak
106C3 **Musgrave Range** *Mts* Aust	**N**	99D3 **Nakuru** Kenya	22A1 **Napa** USA
98B3 **Mushie** Zaïre	21C4 **Naalehu** Hawaiian Is	13D2 **Nakusp** Can	12B2 **Napaiskak** USA
14A2 **Muskegon** USA	39J6 **Naantali** Fin	61F5 **Nal'chik** USSR	15C2 **Napanee** Can
14A2 **Muskegon** *R* USA	45C2 **Naas** Irish Rep	87B1 **Nalgonda** India	65K4 **Napas** USSR
18A2 **Muskogee** USA	75B2 **Nabari** Japan	87B1 **Nallamala Range** *Mts* India	6E3 **Napassoq** Greenland
15C2 **Muskoka,L** Can	61H2 **Naberezhnyye Chelny** USSR	95A1 **Nālūt** Libya	76D2 **Nape** Laos
95C3 **Musmar** Sudan	12F2 **Nabesna** *R* USA	101H1 **Namaacha** Mozam	110C1 **Napier** NZ
99D3 **Musoma** Tanz	96D1 **Nabeul** Tunisia	65G6 **Namak** *L* Iran	**Naples** = **Napoli**
8C2 **Musselshell** *R* USA	94B2 **Nablus** Israel	90C3 **Namakzar-e Shadad** *Salt Flat* Iran	17B2 **Naples** Florida, USA
100A2 **Mussende** Angola	101D2 **Nacala** Mozam	65J5 **Namangan** USSR	19B3 **Naples** Texas, USA
48C2 **Mussidan** France	20B1 **Naches** USA	101C2 **Namapa** Mozam	73B5 **Napo** China
	101C2 **Nachingwea** Tanz	100A4 **Namaqualand** Region, S Africa	32C4 **Napo** *R* Peru/Ecuador
		109D1 **Nambour** Aust	53B2 **Napoli** Italy
		109D2 **Nambucca Heads** Aust	90A2 **Naqadeh** Iran
		77D4 **Nam Can** Viet	92C4 **Naqb Ishtar** Jordan
		82D2 **Nam Co** *L* China	75B2 **Nara** Japan
		76D1 **Nam Dinh** Viet	

97B3 **Nara** Mali	19A3 **Navasota** USA	43D3 **Nene** *R* Eng	16B2 **New Brunswick** USA
107D4 **Naracoorte** Aust	19A3 **Navasota** *R* USA	69E2 **Nenjiang** China	16B2 **Newburgh** USA
23B1 **Naranjos** Mexico	50A1 **Navia** *R* Spain	18A2 **Neodesha** USA	43D4 **Newbury** Eng
87C1 **Narasaräopet** India	34A2 **Navidad** Chile	18B2 **Neosho** USA	16D1 **Newburyport** USA
77C4 **Narathiwat** Thai	85C4 **Navlakhi** India	63C2 **Nepa** USSR	16C2 **New Canaan** USA
86C2 **Narayanganj** Bang	60D3 **Navlya** USSR	82C3 **Nepal** Kingdom, Asia	109D2 **Newcastle** Aust
87B1 **Nārāyenpet** India	24B3 **Navojoa** Mexico	86A1 **Nepalganj** Nepal	14A3 **New Castle** Indiana, USA
49C3 **Narbonne** France	55B3 **Návpaktos** Greece	45B1 **Nephin** *Mt* Irish Rep	42B2 **Newcastle** N Ire
84D2 **Narendranagar** India	55B3 **Návplion** Greece	94B3 **Neqarot** *R* Israel	14B2 **New Castle** Pennsylvania, USA
6C2 **Nares Str** Can	85C4 **Navsāri** India	34A3 **Nequén** State, Arg	101G1 **Newcastle** S Africa
58C2 **Narew** *R* Pol	94C2 **Nawá** Syria	68D1 **Nerchinsk** USSR	8C2 **Newcastle** Wyoming, USA
75C1 **Narita** Japan	86B2 **Nawāda** India	52C2 **Neretva** *R* Yugos	42D2 **Newcastle upon Tyne** Eng
85C4 **Narmada** *R* India	84B2 **Nawah** Afghan	71F2 **Nero Deep** Pacific O	106C2 **Newcastle Waters** Aust
84D3 **Nārnaul** India	85B3 **Nawrabshah** Pak	38C1 **Neskaupstaður** Iceland	45B2 **Newcastle West** Irish Rep
64H3 **Narodnaya** *Mt* USSR	73B4 **Naxi** China	46B2 **Nesle** France	84D3 **New Delhi** India
60E2 **Naro Fominsk** USSR	55C3 **Náxos** *I* Greece	7E5 **Nesleyville** Can	109D2 **New England Range** Mts Aust
99D3 **Narok** Kenya	23A1 **Nayar** Mexico	55B2 **Néstos** *R* Greece	12B3 **Newenham,C** USA
84C2 **Narowal** Pak	90C3 **Nay Band** Iran	94B2 **Netanya** Israel	43D4 **New Forest,The** Eng
107D4 **Narrabri** Aust	91B4 **Nāy Band** Iran	16B2 **Netcong** USA	7D4 **Newfoundland** Province, Can
109C1 **Narran** *L* Aust	74E2 **Nayoro** Japan	56B2 **Netherlands** Kingdom, Europe	7E5 **Newfoundland** *I* Can
109C1 **Narran** *R* Aust	94B2 **Nazareth** Israel	3M7 **Netherlands Antilles** Is Caribbean S	102F2 **Newfoundland Basin** Atlantic O
109C2 **Narrandera** Aust	48B2 **Nazay** France	86C2 **Netrakona** Bang	18B2 **New Franklin** USA
106A4 **Narrogin** Aust	32C6 **Nazca** Peru	6C3 **Nettilling L** Can	42B2 **New Galloway** Scot
109C2 **Narromine** Aust	92A2 **Nazilli** Turk	56C2 **Neubrandenburg** Germany	107E1 **New Georgia** *I* Solomon Is
85D4 **Narsimhapur** India	63B2 **Nazimovo** USSR	47B1 **Neuchâtel** Switz	7D5 **New Glasgow** Can
87C1 **Narsīpatnam** India	13C2 **Nazko** *R* Can	46C2 **Neufchâteau** Belg	71F4 **New Guinea** SE Asia
6F3 **Narssalik** Greenland	91C5 **Nazwa** Oman	48C2 **Neufchâtel** France	12D3 **Newhalen** USA
6F3 **Narssaq** Greenland	65J4 **Nazyvayevsk** USSR	46A2 **Neufchâtel-en-Bray** France	22C3 **Newhall** USA
6F3 **Narssarssuaq** Greenland	98B3 **Ndalatando** Angola	56B2 **Neumünster** Germany	10C2 **New Hampshire** State, USA
75C1 **Narugo** Japan	98C2 **Ndélé** CAR	52C1 **Neunkirchen** Austria	101H1 **New Hanover** S Africa
75A2 **Naruto** Japan	98B1 **Ndjamena** Chad	46D2 **Neunkirchen** Germany	43E4 **Newhaven** Eng
60C2 **Narva** USSR	98B3 **Ndjolé** Gabon	34B3 **Neuquén** Arg	15D2 **New Haven** USA
38H5 **Narvik** Nor	100B2 **Ndola** Zambia	29B4 **Neuquén** State, Arg	13B1 **New Hazelton** Can
84D3 **Narwāna** India	109C1 **Neabul** Aust	34B3 **Neuquén** *R* Arg	19B3 **New Iberia** USA
64G3 **Nar'yan Mar** USSR	108A1 **Neales** *R* Aust	56C2 **Neuruppin** Germany	10C2 **New Jersey** State, USA
108B1 **Narylico** Aust	55B3 **Neápolis** Greece	46D1 **Neuss** Germany	7C5 **New Liskeard** Can
65J5 **Naryn** USSR	43C4 **Neath** Wales	46E2 **Neustadt** Germany	16C2 **New London** USA
97C4 **Nasarawa** Nig	109C1 **Nebine** *R* Aust	56C2 **Neustadt** Germany	106A3 **Newman** Aust
103D5 **Nasca Ridge** Pacific O	65G6 **Nebit Dag** USSR	56C2 **Neustrelitz** Germany	22B2 **Newman** USA
16D1 **Nashua** USA	8C2 **Nebraska** State, USA	46D1 **Neuwied** Germany	43E3 **Newmarket** Eng
19B3 **Nashville** Arkansas, USA	18A1 **Nebraska City** USA	8B3 **Nevada** State, USA	45B2 **Newmarket** Irish Rep
11B3 **Nashville** Tennessee, USA	13C2 **Nechako** *R* Can	18B2 **Nevada** USA	15C3 **New Market** USA
54A1 **Našice** Yugos	19A3 **Neches** *R* USA	34A3 **Nevada de Chillán** Mts Arg/Chile	9C3 **New Mexico** State, USA
85D4 **Nāsik** India	34D3 **Necochea** Arg	23A2 **Nevada de Collima** Mexico	16C2 **New Milford** Connecticut, USA
99D2 **Nasir** Sudan	86C1 **Nêdong** China	23B2 **Nevada de Toluca** Mt Mexico	17B1 **Newnan** USA
13B1 **Nass** *R* Can	9B3 **Needles** USA	94B3 **Nevatim** Israel	109C4 **New Norfolk** Aust
26B1 **Nassau** The Bahamas	14A2 **Neenah** USA	60C2 **Nevel** USSR	11A3 **New Orleans** USA
16C1 **Nassau** USA	5J4 **Neepawa** Can	49C2 **Nevers** France	16B2 **New Paltz** USA
95C2 **Nasser,L** Egypt	46C1 **Neerpelt** Belg	109C2 **Nevertire** Aust	14B2 **New Philadelphia** USA
39G7 **Nässjö** Sweden	63C2 **Neftelensk** USSR	27E3 **Nevis** *I* Caribbean S	110B1 **New Plymouth** NZ
7C4 **Nastapoka Is** Can	99D2 **Negelli** Eth	58D2 **Nevis** *R* USSR	18B2 **Newport** Arkansas, USA
100B3 **Nata** Botswana	94B3 **Negev** *Desert* Israel	92B2 **Nevşehir** Turk	43D4 **Newport** Eng
31D3 **Natal** Brazil	60B4 **Negolu** *Mt* Rom	61K2 **Nev'yansk** USSR	14B3 **Newport** Kentucky, USA
70A3 **Natal** Indon	87B3 **Negombo** Sri Lanka	101C2 **Newala** Tanz	20B2 **Newport** Oregon, USA
101H1 **Natal** Province, S Africa	76A2 **Negrais,C** Burma	14A3 **New Albany** Indiana, USA	16A2 **Newport** Pennsylvania, USA
90B3 **Natanz** Iran	32A4 **Negritos** Peru	19C3 **New Albany** Mississippi, USA	15D2 **Newport** Rhode Island, USA
7D4 **Natashquan** Can	33E4 **Negro** *R* Amazonas, Brazil	33F2 **New Amsterdam** Guyana	15D2 **Newport** Vermont, USA
7D4 **Natashquan** *R* Can	29C4 **Negro** *R* Arg	109C1 **New Angledool** Aust	43C4 **Newport** Wales
19B3 **Natchez** USA	34D2 **Negro** *R* Urug	15C3 **Newark** Delaware, USA	20C1 **Newport** Washington, USA
19B3 **Natchitoches** USA	79B4 **Negros** *I* Phil	10C2 **Newark** New Jersey, USA	22D4 **Newport Beach** USA
108C3 **Nathalia** Aust	54C2 **Negru Voda** Rom	14B2 **Newark** Ohio, USA	11C3 **Newport News** USA
6H2 **Nathorsts Land** Region Greenland	90D3 **Nehbāndan** Iran	43D3 **Newark-upon-Trent** Eng	26B1 **New Providence** *I* Caribbean S
13C1 **Nation** *R* Can	73B4 **Neijiang** China	15D2 **New Bedford** USA	43B4 **Newquay** Eng
21B3 **National City** USA	72B1 **Nei Monggol** Autonomous Region, China	13B2 **New Bella Bella** Can	6C3 **New Quebec Crater** Can
75C1 **Natori** Japan	32B3 **Neiva** Colombia	20B1 **Newberg** USA	
58D2 **Natovl'a** USSR	99D2 **Nejo** Eth	11C3 **New Bern** USA	
99D3 **Natron** *L* Tanz	60D2 **Nelidovo** USSR	17B1 **Newberry** USA	
106A4 **Naturaliste,C** Aust	87B2 **Nellore** India	26B2 **New Bight** The Bahamas	
47D1 **Nauders** Austria	69F2 **Nel'ma** USSR	14B3 **New Boston** USA	
56C2 **Nauen** Germany	13D3 **Nelson** Can	9D4 **New Braunfels** USA	
16C2 **Naugatuck** USA	111B2 **Nelson** NZ	16C2 **New Britain** USA	
57C2 **Naumburg** Germany	7A4 **Nelson** *R* Can	7D5 **New Brunswick** Province, Can	
94B3 **Naur** Jordan	108B3 **Nelson,C** Aust		
105G4 **Nauru** *I* Pacific O	12B2 **Nelson I** USA		
63C2 **Naushki** USSR	97B3 **Néma** Maur		
23B1 **Nautla** Mexico	72A1 **Nemagt Uul** *Mt* Mongolia		
9C3 **Navajo Res** USA	58C1 **Neman** *R* USSR		
50A2 **Navalmoral de la Mata** Spain	54C1 **Nemira** *Mt* Rom		
29C7 **Navarino** *I* Chile	74F2 **Nemuro** Japan		
51B1 **Navarra** Province, Spain	63E3 **Nen** *R* China		
34D3 **Navarro** Arg	41B3 **Nenagh** Irish Rep		
	12E2 **Nenana** USA		
	12E2 **Nenana** *R* USA		

45C2 **New Ross** Irish Rep
45C1 **Newry** N Ire
New Siberian Is =
   Novosibirskye
   Ostrova
17B2 **New Smyrna Beach**
   USA
107D4 **New South Wales**
   State, Aust
12C3 **New Stuyahok** USA
18A2 **Newton** Kansas, USA
16D1 **Newton**
   Massachusetts, USA
19C3 **Newton** Mississippi,
   USA
16B2 **Newton** New York,
   USA
43C4 **Newton Abbot** Eng
45C1 **Newton Stewart** N Ire
42B2 **Newton Stewart** Scot
43C3 **Newtown** Wales
42B2 **Newtownards** N Ire
16A2 **Newville** USA
5F5 **New Westminster**
   Can
10C2 **New York** State, USA
10C2 **New York** USA
110 **New Zealand**
   Dominion, SW
   Pacific O
105G6 **New Zealand Plat**
   Pacific O
61F2 **Neya** USSR
91B4 **Neyriz** Iran
90C2 **Neyshābūr** Iran
98B3 **Nezeto** Angola
60D3 **Nezhin** USSR
98B3 **Ngabé** Congo
100B3 **Ngami** L Botswana
110C1 **Ngaruawahia** NZ
110C1 **Ngaruroro** R NZ
110C1 **Ngauruhoe,Mt** NZ
98B3 **Ngo** Congo
76D2 **Ngoc Linh** Mt Viet
98B2 **Ngoko** R Cam
68B3 **Ngoring Hu** L China
99D3 **Ngorongoro Crater**
   Tanz
98B3 **N'Gounié** R Gabon
98B1 **Nguigmi** Niger
71E3 **Ngulu** I Pacific O
97D3 **Nguru** Nig
76D3 **Nha Trang** Viet
108B3 **Nhill** Aust
101H1 **Nhlangano** Swaziland
76D2 **Nhommarath** Laos
106C2 **Nhulunbuy** Aust
97B3 **Niafounké** Mali
14A1 **Niagara** USA
15C2 **Niagara Falls** Can
15C2 **Niagara Falls** USA
70C3 **Niah** Malay
97B4 **Niakaramandougou**
   Ivory Coast
97C3 **Niamey** Niger
99C2 **Niangara** Zaïre
98C2 **Nia Nia** Zaïre
70A3 **Nias** I Indon
25D3 **Nicaragua** Republic,
   Cent America
53C3 **Nicastro** Italy
49D3 **Nice** France
26B1 **Nicholl's Town**
   The Bahamas
83D5 **Nicobar Is** Indian O
92B2 **Nicosia** Cyprus
25D3 **Nicoya,Pen de**
   Costa Rica
58C2 **Nidzica** Pol
46D2 **Niederbronn** France
56B2 **Niedersachsen** State,
   Germany
99C3 **Niemba** Zaïre
56B2 **Nienburg** Germany
46D1 **Niers** R Germany
97B4 **Niete,Mt** Lib
33F2 **Nieuw Amsterdam**
   Surinam

33F2 **Nieuw Nickerie**
   Surinam
46B1 **Nieuwpoort** Belg
92B2 **Niğde** Turk
97C3 **Niger** Republic, Africa
97C4 **Niger** R Nig
97C4 **Nigeria** Federal
   Republic, Africa
55B2 **Nigríta** Greece
75C1 **Nihommatsu** Japan
74D3 **Niigata** Japan
74C4 **Niihama** Japan
75B2 **Nii-jima** I Japan
75A2 **Niimi** Japan
74D3 **Niitsu** Japan
94B3 **Nijil** Jordan
56B2 **Nijmegen** Neth
64E3 **Nikel'** USSR
97C3 **Nikki** Benin
74D3 **Nikko** Japan
60D4 **Nikolayev** USSR
61G4 **Nikolayevsk** USSR
63G2 **Nikolayevsk-na-Amure**
   USSR
61G2 **Nikol'sk** RSFSR, USSR
61G3 **Nikol'sk** USSR
60D4 **Nikopol** USSR
92C1 **Niksar** Turk
91D4 **Nīkshahr** Iran
54A2 **Nikšić** Yugos
71D4 **Nila** I Indon
80B3 **Nile** R N E Africa
14A2 **Niles** USA
87B2 **Nilgiri Hills** India
85C4 **Nimach** India
49C3 **Nîmes** France
109C3 **Nimmitabel** Aust
99D2 **Nimule** Sudan
83B5 **Nine Degree Chan**
   Indian O
104C4 **Ninety-East Ridge**
   Indian O
109C3 **Ninety Mile Beach**
   Aust
73D4 **Ningde** China
73D4 **Ningdu** China
68B3 **Ningjing Shan** Mts
   China
76D1 **Ningming** China
73A4 **Ningnan** China
72B2 **Ningxia** Province,
   China
72B2 **Ning Xian** China
73B5 **Ninh Binh** Vietnam
107D1 **Ninigo Is** PNG
12D2 **Ninilchik** USA
8D2 **Niobrara** R USA
98B3 **Nioki** Zaïre
97B3 **Nioro du Sahel** Mali
48B2 **Niort** France
5H4 **Nipawin** Can
7B5 **Nipigon** Can
7B5 **Nipigon,L** Can
7B5 **Nipissing** R Can
14B1 **Nipissing,L** Can
87B1 **Nirmal** India
86B1 **Nirmāli** India
54B2 **Niš** Yugos
81C4 **Nisāb** Yemen
69F4 **Nishino-shima** I
   Japan
75A1 **Nishino-shima** I
   Japan
75A2 **Nishiwaki** Japan
12G2 **Nisling** R Can
12H2 **Nisutlin** R Can
7C4 **Nitchequon** Can
31C6 **Niterói** Brazil
42C2 **Nith** R Scot
59B3 **Nitra** Czech
14B3 **Nitro** USA
78C2 **Niut** Mt Malay
46C1 **Nivelles** Belg
49C2 **Nivernais** Region,
   France
38L5 **Nivskiy** USSR
87B1 **Nizāmābād** India
94B3 **Nizana** Hist Site Israel

61J2 **Nizhniye Sergi** USSR
61F3 **Nizhniy Lomov** USSR
65G4 **Nizhniy Tagil** USSR
63B1 **Nizhnyaya Tunguska**
   R USSR
93C2 **Nizip** Turk
60D4 **Nizmennost** USSR
100B2 **Njoko** R Zambia
99D3 **Njombe** Tanz
98B2 **Nkambé** Cam
101C2 **Nkhata Bay** Malawi
98B2 **Nkongsamba** Cam
97C3 **N'Konni** Niger
86C2 **Noakhali** Bang
12B1 **Noatak** USA
12C1 **Noatak** R USA
74C4 **Nobeoka** Japan
47D1 **Noce** R Italy
23A1 **Nochistlán** Mexico
23B2 **Nochixtlán** Mexico
19A3 **Nocona** USA
24A1 **Nogales** Sonora,
   Mexico
9B3 **Nogales** USA
23B2 **Nogales** Veracruz,
   Mexico
47D2 **Nogara** Italy
75A2 **Nogata** Japan
60E2 **Noginsk** USSR
34D2 **Nogoyá** Arg
34D2 **Nogoyá** R Arg
84C3 **Nohar** India
75B2 **Nojima-zaki** C Japan
98B2 **Nola** CAR
61G2 **Nolinsk** USSR
16D2 **Nomans Land** I USA
12A2 **Nome** USA
46D2 **Nomeny** France
72B1 **Nomgon** Mongolia
5H3 **Nonachol L** Can
76C2 **Nong Khai** Thai
101H1 **Nongoma** S Africa
12B1 **Noorvik** USA
13B3 **Nootka Sd** Can
98B3 **Noqui** Angola
7C5 **Noranda** Can
46B1 **Nord** Department,
   France
64D2 **Nordaustlandet** I
   Barents S
13D2 **Nordegg** Can
38F6 **Nordfjord** Inlet Nor
39F8 **Nordfriesische** Is
   Germany
56C2 **Nordhausen** Germany
56B2 **Nordrhein Westfalen**
   State, Germany
38J4 **Nordkapp** C Nor
6E3 **Nordre** Greenland
38H5 **Nord Stronfjället** Mt
   Sweden
1B9 **Nordvik** USSR
45C2 **Nore** R Irish Rep
43E3 **Norfolk** County, Eng
8D2 **Norfolk** Nebraska,
   USA
11C3 **Norfolk** Virginia, USA
107F3 **Norfolk I** Aust
18B2 **Norfolk L** USA
105G5 **Norfolk Ridge**
   Pacific O
1C10 **Noril'sk** USSR
18C1 **Normal** USA
19A2 **Norman** USA
48B2 **Normandie** Region,
   France
107D2 **Normanton** Aust
12J1 **Norman Wells** Can
4B3 **Norne** USA
15C2 **Norristown** USA
39H7 **Norrköping** Sweden
39H6 **Norrsundet** Sweden
39H7 **Norrtälje** Sweden
106B4 **Norseman** Aust
63F2 **Norsk** USSR
102J2 **North** S N W Europe
42D2 **Northallerton** Eng
106A4 **Northam** Aust

102E3 **North American Basin**
   Atlantic O
106A3 **Northampton** Aust
43D3 **Northampton** County,
   Eng
43D3 **Northampton** Eng
15D2 **Northampton** USA
4G3 **North Arm** B Can
17B1 **North Augusta** USA
6D4 **North Aulatsivik** I Can
13F2 **North Battleford** Can
7C5 **North Bay** Can
20B2 **North Bend** USA
44C3 **North Berwick** Scot
7D5 **North,C** Can
7G4 **North C** NZ
11B3 **North Carolina** State,
   USA
20B1 **North Cascade Nat Pk**
   USA
14B1 **North Chan** Can
42B2 **North Chan** Ire/Scot
8C2 **North Dakota** State,
   USA
43E4 **North Downs** Eng
14C2 **North East** USA
102H2 **North East Atlantic**
   Basin Atlantic O
4B3 **Northeast C** USA
40B3 **Northern Ireland** UK
27L1 **Northern Range** Mts
   Trinidad
106C2 **Northern Territory**
   Aust
44C3 **North Esk** R Scot
16C1 **Northfield**
   Massachusetts, USA
12D2 **North Fork** R USA
110B1 **North I** NZ
74B3 **North Korea** Republic,
   S E Asia
North Land =
   Severnaya Zemlya
19B3 **North Little Rock** USA
1B4 **North Magnetic Pole**
   Can
17B2 **North Miami** USA
17B2 **North Miami Beach**
   USA
8C2 **North Platte** USA
8C2 **North Platte** R USA
27R3 **North Pt** Barbados
14B1 **North Pt** USA
40B2 **North Rona** I Scot
44C2 **North Ronaldsay** I
   Scot
13F2 **North Saskatchewan**
   R Can
40D2 **North Sea**
   N W Europe
4D3 **North Slope** Region
   USA
109D1 **North Stradbroke** I
   Aust
110B1 **North Taranaki Bight**
   B NZ
9C3 **North Truchas Peak**
   Mt USA
44A3 **North Uist** I Scot
42C2 **Northumberland**
   County, Eng
107E3 **Northumberland Is**
   Aust
7D5 **Northumberland Str**
   Can
20B1 **North Vancouver** Can
43E3 **North Walsham** Eng
12F2 **Northway** USA
106A3 **North West C** Aust
84C2 **North West Frontier**
   Province, Pak
7D4 **North West River** Can
4F3 **North West Territories**
   Can
42D2 **North York Moors Nat**
   Pk Eng
12B2 **Norton B** USA
12B2 **Norton Sd** USA

112B1 Norvegia,C Ant
16C2 Norwalk Connecticut, USA
14B2 Norwalk Ohio, USA
39F6 Norway Kingdom, Europe
5J4 Norway House Can
6A2 Norwegian B Can
102H1 Norwegian Basin Norcwegian S
64A3 Norwegian S N W Europe
16C2 Norwich Connecticut, USA
43E3 Norwich Eng
16D1 Norwood Massachusetts, USA
14B3 Norwood Ohio, USA
54C2 Nos Emine C Bulg
74D2 Noshiro Japan
54C2 Nos Kaliakra C Bulg
44E1 Noss I Scot
91D4 Nosträbäd Iran
101D2 Nosy Barren I Madag
101D2 Nosy Bé I Madag
101E2 Nosy Boraha I Madag
101D3 Nosy Varika Madag
58B2 Notéc R Pol
5G4 Notikeuin Can
53C3 Noto Italy
39F7 Notodden Nor
75B1 Noto-hantö Pen Japan
7E5 Notre Dams B Can
43D3 Nottingham County, Eng
43D3 Nottingham I Can
6C3 Nottingham I Can
6C3 Nottingham Island Can
96A2 Nouadhibou Maur
97A3 Nouakchott Maur
107F3 Nouméa Nouvelle Calédonie
97B3 Nouna Burkina
107F3 Nouvelle Calédonie I S W Pacific O
98B3 Nova Caipemba Angola
100B2 Nova Chaves Angola
35A2 Nova Esparança Brazil
35C2 Nova Friburgo Brazil
100A2 Nova Gaia Angola
35B2 Nova Granada Brazil
35B2 Nova Horizonte Brazil
35C1 Nova Lima Brazil Nova Lisboa = Huambo
35A2 Nova Londrina Brazil
101C3 Nova Mambone Mozam
47C2 Novara Italy
7D5 Nova Scotia Province, Can
22A1 Novato USA
35C1 Nova Venécia Brazil
60D4 Novaya Kakhovka USSR
64G2 Novaya Zemlya I Barents S
54C2 Nova Zagora Bulg
31C2 Nove Russas Brazil
54A1 Nové Zámky Czech
60D2 Novgorod USSR
47C2 Novi Ligure Italy
54C2 Novi Pazar Bulg
54B2 Novi Pazar Yugos
54A1 Novi Sad Yugos
61J3 Novoalekseyevka USSR
61F3 Novoanninskiy USSR
61E4 Novocherkassk USSR
60C3 Novograd Volynskiy USSR
58D2 Novogrudok USSR
30F4 Novo Hamburgo Brazil
65H5 Novokazalinsk USSR

65K4 Novokuznetsk USSR
112B12 Novolazarevskaya Base Ant
52C1 Novo Mesto Yugos
60E3 Novomoskovsk USSR
60E5 Novorossiysk USSR
65K4 Novosibirsk USSR
1B8 Novosibirskiye Ostrova I USSR
61J3 Novotroitsk USSR
61G3 Novo Uzensk USSR
59C2 Novovolynsk USSR
61G2 Novo Vyatsk USSR
60D3 Novozybkov USSR
64J3 Novvy Port USSR
58C2 Novy Dwór Mazowiecki Pol
61K2 Novvy Lyalya USSR
64J3 Novvy Port USSR
61H5 Novvy Uzem USSR
58B2 Nowa Sól Pol
18A2 Nowata USA
86C1 Nowgong India
12D2 Nowitna R USA
109D2 Nowra Aust
90B2 Now Shahr Iran
84C2 Nowshera Pak
59C3 Nowy Sącz Pol
12H3 Noyes I USA
46B2 Noyon France
97B4 Nsawam Ghana
99D1 Nuba Mts Sudan
81B3 Nubian Desert Sudan
34A3 Nuble R Chile
9D4 Nueces R USA
5J3 Nueltin L Can
26A2 Nueva Gerona Cuba
34A3 Nueva Imperial Chile
9C4 Nueva Laredo Mexico
34D2 Nueva Palmira Urug
24B2 Nueva Rosita Mexico
26B2 Nuevitas Cuba
24B1 Nuevo Casas Grandes Mexico
24C2 Nuevo Laredo Mexico
99E2 Nugaal Region, Somalia
6E2 Nûgâtsiaq Greenland
6E2 Nugssuag Pen Greenland
6E2 Nûgussaq I Greenland
108A2 Nukey Bluff Mt Aust
93D3 Nukhayb Iraq
65G5 Nukus USSR
12C2 Nulato USA
106B4 Nullarbor Plain Aust
97D4 Numan Nig
75B1 Numata Japan
98C2 Numatinna R Sudan
74D3 Numazu Japan
71E4 Numfoor I Indon
108C3 Numurkah Aust
12B2 Nunapitchuk USA
84D2 Nunkun Mt India
53A2 Nuoro Sardegna
91B3 Nurābād Iran
47C2 Nure R Italy
108A2 Nuriootpa Aust
84C1 Nuristan Upland Afghan
61H3 Nurlat USSR
38K6 Nurmes Fin
57C3 Nürnberg Germany
108C2 Nurri,Mt Aust
93D2 Nusaybin Turk
12C3 Nushagak R USA
12C3 Nushagak B USA
12C3 Nushagak Pen USA
84B3 Nushki Pak
7D4 Nutak Can
12F2 Nutzotin Mts USA
86A1 Nuwakot Nepal
87C3 Nuwara-Eliya Sri Lanka
6C3 Nuyukjuak Can
16C2 Nyack USA
99D2 Nyahururu Kenya

108B3 Nyah West Aust
4C3 Nyai USA
68B3 Nyainqentanglha Shan Mts China
99D3 Nyakabindi Tanz
98C1 Nyala Sudan
86B1 Nyalam China
98C2 Nyamlell Sudan
100C3 Nyanda Zim
64F3 Nyandoma USSR
98B3 Nyanga R Gabon
101C2 Nyasa L Malawi/ Mozam
76B2 Nyaunglebin Burma
61J2 Nyazepetrovsk USSR
39G7 Nyborg Den
39H7 Nybro Sweden
64J3 Nyda USSR
6D1 Nyeboes Land Region Can
99D3 Nyeri Kenya
101C2 Nyimba Zambia
82D3 Nyingchi China
59C3 Nyíregyháza Hung
99D2 Nyiru,Mt Kenya
38J6 Nykarleby Fin
39F7 Nykøbing Den
39G8 Nykøbing Den
39H7 Nyköping Sweden
100B3 Nylstroom S Africa
109C2 Nymagee Aust
39H7 Nynäshamn Sweden
109C2 Nyngan Aust
47B1 Nyon Switz
98B2 Nyong R Cam
49D3 Nyons France
59B2 Nysa Pol
20C2 Nyssa USA
63D1 Nyurba USSR
99D3 Nzega Tanz
97B4 Nzérékore Guinea

O

6F3 Oaggsimiut Greenland
8C2 Oahe Res USA
21C4 Oahu I Hawaiian Is
108B2 Oakbank Aust
22B2 Oakdale USA
109D1 Oakey Aust
21A2 Oakland California, USA
20B2 Oakland Oregon, USA
14A3 Oakland City USA
14A2 Oak Lawn USA
22B2 Oakley California, USA
20B2 Oakridge USA
14C2 Oakville Can
111B3 Oamaru NZ
112B7 Oates Land Region, Ant
109C4 Oatlands Aust
23B2 Oaxaca Mexico
23B2 Oaxaca State, Mexico
65J3 Ob' R USSR
75B1 Obama Japan
111A3 Oban NZ
44B3 Oban Scot
75C1 Obanazawa Japan
47D1 Oberammergau Germany
46D1 Oberhausen Germany
47D1 Oberstdorf Germany
71D4 Obi I Indon
33F4 Obidos Brazil
74E2 Obihiro Japan
98C2 Obo CAR
99E1 Obock Djibouti
58B2 Oborniki Pol
60E3 Oboyan USSR
20B2 O'Brien USA
61H3 Obshchiy Syrt Mts USSR
64J3 Obskava Guba B USSR

97B4 Obuasi Ghana
17B2 Ocala USA
32C2 Ocana Colombia
50B2 Ocaño Spain
12G3 Ocean C USA
15C3 Ocean City Maryland, USA
16B3 Ocean City New Jersey, USA
5F4 Ocean Falls Can
22D4 Oceanside USA
19C3 Ocean Springs USA
61H2 Ocher USSR
44C3 Ochil Hills Scot
17B1 Ochlockonee R USA
27H1 Ocho Rios Jamaica
17B1 Ocmulgee R USA
17B1 Oconee R USA
14A2 Oconto USA
23A1 Ocotlán Jalisco, Mexico
23B2 Ocotlán Oaxaca, Mexico
97B4 Oda Ghana
75A1 Oda Japan
38B2 Ódáðahraun Region, Iceland
74E2 Odate Japan
74D3 Odawara Japan
39F6 Odda Nor
50A2 Odemira Port
55C3 Odemiş Turk
101G1 Odendaalsrus S Africa
39G7 Odense Den
56C2 Oder R Pol/Germany
9C3 Odessa Texas, USA
60D4 Odessa USSR
20C1 Odessa Washington, USA
97B4 Odienné Ivory Coast
59B2 Odra R Pol
31C3 Oeiras Brazil
106B1 Oekusi Indon
53C2 Ofanto R Italy
94B3 Ofaqim Israel
45C2 Offaly County, Irish Rep
49D1 Offenbach Germany
49D2 Offenburg Germany
74D3 Oga Japan
99E2 Ogaden Region, Eth
74D3 Ogaki Japan
8C2 Ogallala USA
69G4 Ogasawara Gunto Is Japan
97C4 Ogbomosho Nig
8B2 Ogden Utah, USA
15C2 Ogdensburg USA
17B1 Ogeechee R USA
12G1 Ogilvie Can
4E3 Ogilvie Mts Can
17B1 Oglethorpe,Mt USA
47D2 Oglio R Italy
47B1 Ognon R France
97C4 Ogoja Nig
98A3 Ogooué R Gabon
58C1 Ogre USSR
96B2 Oguilet Khenachich Well Mali
52C1 Ogulin Yugos
111A3 Ohai NZ
110C1 Ohakune NZ
96C2 Ohanet Alg
111A2 Ohau,L NZ
10B2 Ohio State, USA
14A3 Ohio R USA
100A2 Ohopoho Namibia
57C2 Ohre R Czech
55B2 Ohrid Yugos
55B2 Ohridsko Jezero L Yugos/Alb
110B1 Ohura NZ
33G3 Oiapoque French Guiana
68B2 Oijiaojing China
14C2 Oil City USA
21B2 Oildale USA

46B2 **Oise** Department, France
49C2 **Oise** *R* France
74C4 **Ōita** Japan
22C3 **Ojai** USA
24B2 **Ojinaga** Mexico
23B2 **Ojitlán** Mexico
75B1 **Ojiya** Japan
30C4 **Ojos del Salado** *Mt* Arg
23A1 **Ojueloz** Mexico
60E3 **Oka** *R* USSR
100A3 **Okahandja** Namibia
20C1 **Okanagan Falls** Can
13D2 **Okanagan L** Can
20C1 **Okanogan** USA
20C1 **Okanogan** *R* USA
20B1 **Okanogan Range** *Mts* Can/USA
84C2 **Okara** Pak
100A2 **Okavango** *R* Angola/Namibia
100B2 **Okavango Delta** *Marsh* Botswana
74D3 **Okaya** Japan
74C4 **Okayama** Japan
75B2 **Okazaki** Japan
17B2 **Okeechobee** USA
17B2 **Okeechobee,L** USA
17B1 **Okefenokee Swamp** USA
97C4 **Okene** Nig
85B4 **Okha** India
69G1 **Okha** USSR
86B1 **Okhaldunga** Nepal
62J3 **Okhotsk,S of** USSR
69E4 **Okinawa** *I* Japan
69E4 **Okinawa gunto** *Arch* Japan
74C3 **Oki-shoto** *Is* Japan
9D3 **Oklahoma** State, USA
18A2 **Oklahoma City** USA
18A2 **Okmulgee** USA
98B3 **Okondja** Gabon
98B3 **Okoyo** Congo
97C4 **Okpara** *R* Nig
61J4 **Oktyabr'sk** USSR
61H3 **Oktyabr'skiy** Bashkirskaya, USSR
74D2 **Okushiri-tö** *I* Japan
38A2 **Olafsvik** Iceland
39H7 **Öland** *I* Sweden
108B2 **Olary** Aust
18B2 **Olathe** USA
29D3 **Olavarría** Arg
53A2 **Olbia** Sardegna
12G1 **Old Crow** Can
56B2 **Oldenburg** Niedersachsen, Germany
56C2 **Oldenburg** Schleswig-Holstein, Germany
15C2 **Old Forge** USA
42C3 **Oldham** Eng
12D3 **Old Harbor** USA
41B3 **Old Head of Kinsale** *C* Scot
16C2 **Old Lyme** USA
13E2 **Olds** Can
15C2 **Olean** USA
63E2 **Olekma** *R* USSR
63D1 **Olekminsk** USSR
38L5 **Olenegorsk** USSR
58D2 **Olevsk** USSR
69F2 **Ol'ga** USSR
100A3 **Olifants** *R* Namibia
55B2 **Ólimbos** *Mt* Greece
35B2 **Olímpia** Brazil
23B2 **Olinala** Mexico
31E3 **Olinda** Brazil
34C2 **Oliva** Arg
29C2 **Olivares** *Mt* Arg
35C2 **Oliveira** Brazil
13D3 **Oliver** Can
30C3 **Ollague** Chile
30C3 **Ollagüe** *Mt* Bol
18C2 **Olney** USA
68E1 **Olochi** USSR

39G7 **Olofstrom** Sweden
98B3 **Olombo** Congo
59B3 **Olomouc** Czech
60D1 **Olonets** USSR
79B3 **Olongapa** Phil
48B3 **Oloron Ste Marie** France
68D1 **Olovyannaya** USSR
46D1 **Olpe** Germany
58C2 **Olsztyn** Pol
47B1 **Olten** Switz
54B2 **Oltul** *R* Rom
20B1 **Olympia** USA
20B1 **Olympic Nat Pk** USA
Olympus = Ólimbos
20B1 **Olympus,Mt** USA
65J4 **Om'** *R* USSR
75B1 **Omachi** Japan
75B2 **Omae-zaki** *C* Japan
45C1 **Omagh** N Ire
18A1 **Omaha** USA
20C1 **Omak** USA
91C5 **Oman** Sultanate, Arabian Pen
91C4 **Oman,G of** UAE
98A3 **Omboué** Gabon
99D1 **Omdurman** Sudan
23B2 **Ometepec** Mexico
13B1 **Omineca** *R* Can
13B1 **Omineca Mts** Can
75B1 **Omiya** Japan
12H3 **Ommaney,C** USA
4H2 **Ommanney B** Can
99D2 **Omo** *R* Eth
65J4 **Omsk** USSR
74B4 **Omura** Japan
74C4 **Ōmuta** Japan
61H2 **Omutninsk** USSR
78D3 **Onang** Indon
14B1 **Onaping L** Can
100A2 **Oncócua** Angola
100A2 **Ondangua** Namibia
59C3 **Ondava** *R* Czech
68D2 **Öndörhaan** Molgolia
83B5 **One and Half Degree Chan** Indian O
64E3 **Onega** USSR
64E3 **Onega** *R* USSR
15C2 **Oneida L** USA
8D2 **O'Neill** USA
69H2 **Onekotan** *I* USSR
98C3 **Onema** Zaïre
15D2 **Oneonta** USA
64E3 **Onezhskoye Ozero** *L* USSR
100A2 **Ongiva** Angola
74B3 **Ongjin** N Korea
72D1 **Ongniud Qi** China
87C1 **Ongole** India
15C2 **Onieda L** USA
101D3 **Onilahy** *R* Madag
97C4 **Onitsha** Nig
68C2 **Onjüül** Mongolia
75B1 **Ono** Japan
75B2 **Ōnohara-jima** *I* Japan
74C4 **Onomichi** Japan
106A3 **Onslow** Aust
17C1 **Onslow B** USA
75B1 **Ontake-san** *Mt* Japan
22D3 **Ontario** California, USA
20C2 **Ontario** Oregon, USA
7A4 **Ontario** Province, Can
15C2 **Ontario,L** Can/USA
51B2 **Onteniente** Spain
106C3 **Oodnadatta** Aust
106C4 **Ooldea** Aust
18A2 **Oologah L** USA
46B1 **Oostende** Belg
46B1 **Oosterschelde** *Estuary* Neth
87B2 **Ootacamund** India
13B2 **Ootsa L** Can
69H1 **Opala** USSR
98C3 **Opala** Zaïre
87C3 **Opanake** Sri Lanka
61G2 **Oparino** USSR
59B3 **Opava** Czech

17A1 **Opelika** USA
19B3 **Opelousas** USA
12C2 **Ophir** USA
58D1 **Opochka** USSR
59B2 **Opole** Pol
Oporto = Porto
110C1 **Opotiki** NZ
17A1 **Opp** USA
38F6 **Oppdal** Nor
110B1 **Opunake** NZ
54B1 **Oradea** Rom
38B2 **Oraefajökull** *Mts* Iceland
85D3 **Orai** India
96B1 **Oran** Alg
30D3 **Orán** Arg
109C2 **Orange** Aust
22D4 **Orange** California, USA
49C3 **Orange** France
19B3 **Orange** Texas, USA
100A3 **Orange** *R* S Africa
17B1 **Orangeburg** USA
101G1 **Orange Free State** Province, S Africa
17B1 **Orange Park** USA
14B2 **Orangeville** Can
56C2 **Oranienburg** Germany
79C3 **Oras** Phil
54B1 **Orăstie** Rom
54B1 **Oravita** Rom
52B2 **Orbetello** Italy
109C3 **Orbost** Aust
46B1 **Orchies** France
47B2 **Orco** *R* Italy
106B2 **Ord** *R* Aust
106B2 **Ord,Mt** Aust
93C1 **Ordu** Turk
39H7 **Örebro** Sweden
8A2 **Oregon** State, USA
14B2 **Oregon** USA
20B1 **Oregon City** USA
39H6 **Oregrund** Sweden
60E2 **Orekhovo Zuyevo** USSR
60E3 **Orel** USSR
61H3 **Orenburg** USSR
34D3 **Orense** Arg
50A1 **Orense** Spain
56C1 **Oresund** *Str* Den/Sweden
111A3 **Oreti** *R* NZ
55C3 **Orhaneli** *R* Turk
68C2 **Orhon Gol** *R* Mongolia
23B2 **Oriental** Mexico
108B1 **Orientos** Aust
51B2 **Orihuela** Spain
15C2 **Orillia** Can
33E2 **Orinoco** *R* Ven
86A2 **Orissa** State, India
53A3 **Oristano** Sardegna
38K6 **Orivesi** *L* Fin
33F4 **Oriximina** Brazil
23B2 **Orizaba** Mexico
35B1 **Orizona** Brazil
44C2 **Orkney** *I* Scot
35B2 **Orlândia** Brazil
17B2 **Orlando** USA
48C2 **Orléanais** *Region* France
48C2 **Orléans** France
63B2 **Orlik** USSR
82A3 **Ormara** Pak
79B3 **Ormoc** Phil
17B2 **Ormond Beach** USA
46C2 **Ornain** *R* France
47B1 **Ornans** France
48B2 **Orne** *R* France
38H6 **Örnsköldsvik** Sweden
32C3 **Orocué** Colombia
94B3 **Oron** Israel
Orontes = 'Āşī
79B4 **Oroquieta** Phil
59C3 **Orosháza** Hung
21A2 **Oroville** California, USA

20C1 **Oroville** Washington, USA
47B1 **Orsières** Switz
65G4 **Orsk** USSR
38F6 **Ørsta** Nor
48B3 **Orthez** France
50A1 **Ortigueira** Spain
47D1 **Ortles** *Mts* Italy
27L1 **Ortoire** *R* Trinidad
93E2 **Orūmīyeh** Iran
30C2 **Oruro** Bol
61J2 **Osa** USSR
18B2 **Osage** *R* USA
75B1 **Ōsaka** Japan
25D4 **Osa,Pen de** Costa Rica
18C2 **Osceola** Arkansas, USA
18B1 **Osceola** Iowa, USA
20C2 **Osgood Mts** USA
15C2 **Oshawa** Can
75B2 **Ō-shima** *I* Japan
10B2 **Oshkosh** USA
97C4 **Oshogbo** Nig
7B5 **Oshosh** USA
98B3 **Oshwe** Zaïre
54A1 **Osijek** Yugos
65K5 **Osinniki** USSR
58D2 **Osipovichi** USSR
18B1 **Oskaloosa** USA
60A2 **Oskarshamn** Sweden
39G7 **Oslo** Nor
92C2 **Osmaniye** Turk
56B2 **Osnabrück** Germany
30F4 **Osório** Brazil
29B4 **Osorno** Chile
50B1 **Osorno** Spain
20C1 **Osoyoos** Can
13C1 **Ospika** *R* Can
107D5 **Ossa,Mt** Aust
16C2 **Ossining** USA
60D2 **Ostashkov** USSR
Ostend = Oostende
38G6 **Østerdalen** *V* Nor
38G6 **Östersund** Sweden
56B2 **Ostfriesische Inseln** *Is* Germany
39H6 **Östhammär** Sweden
53B2 **Ostia** Italy
47D2 **Ostiglia** Italy
59B3 **Ostrava** Czech
58B2 **Ostróda** Pol
58B2 **Ostroleka** Pol
60C2 **Ostrov** USSR
64J2 **Ostrov Belyy** *I* USSR
64H1 **Ostrov Greem Bell** *I* Barents S
64F3 **Ostrov Kolguyev** *I* USSR
74F2 **Ostrov Kunashir** *I* USSR
64F2 **Ostrov Mechdusharskiy** *I* Barents S
90B2 **Ostrov Ogurchinskiy** *I* USSR
64G1 **Ostrov Rudol'fa** *I* Barents S
64G2 **Ostrov Vaygach** *I* USSR
1B7 **Ostrov Vrangelya** *I* USSR
58B2 **Ostrów** Pol
59C2 **Ostrowiec** Pol
58C2 **Ostrów Mazowiecka** Pol
50A2 **Osuna** Spain
15C2 **Osweg** USA
15C2 **Oswego** USA
43C3 **Oswestry** Eng
59B2 **Oświęcim** Pol
75B1 **Ota** Japan
111B3 **Otago Pen** NZ
110C2 **Otaki** NZ
74E2 **Otaru** Japan
32B3 **Otavalo** Ecuador
100A2 **Otavi** Namibia
75C1 **Otawara** Japan
20C1 **Othello** USA

55B3 **Óthris** *Mt* Greece
16C1 **Otis** Massachusetts, USA
10C1 **Otish Mts** Can
16B2 **Otisville** USA
100A3 **Otjiwarongo** Namibia
72B2 **Otog Qi** China
110C1 **Otorohanga** NZ
55A2 **Otranto** Italy
55A2 **Otranto,Str of** *Chan* Italy/Alb
14A2 **Otsego** USA
75B1 **Otsu** Japan
39F6 **Otta** Nor
39F7 **Otta** *R* Nor
15C1 **Ottawa** Can
18A2 **Ottawa** Kansas, USA
15C1 **Ottawa** *R* Can
7B4 **Ottawa Is** Can
7B4 **Otter Rapids** Can
6B1 **Otto Fjord** Can
101G1 **Ottosdal** S Africa
18B1 **Ottumwa** USA
46D2 **Ottweiler** Germany
97C4 **Oturkpo** Nig
· 32B5 **Otusco** Peru
108B3 **Otway,C** Aust
58C2 **Otwock** Pol
47D1 **Ötz** Austria
47D1 **Otzal** Mts Austria
76C1 **Ou** *R* Laos
19B3 **Ouachita** *R* USA
19B3 **Ouachita,L** USA
19B3 **Ouachita Mts** USA
96A2 **Ouadane** Maur
98C2 **Ouadda** CAR
98C1 **Ouaddai** *Desert Region* Chad
97B3 **Ouagadougou** Burkina
97B3 **Ouahigouya** Burkina
98C2 **Ouaka** CAR
97C3 **Oualam** Niger
96C2 **Ouallen** Alg
98C2 **Ouanda Djallé** CAR
96A2 **Ouarane** Region, Maur
96C1 **Ouargla** Alg
98C2 **Ouarra** *R* CAR
96B1 **Ouarzazate** Mor
51C2 **Ouassel** *R* Alg
98B2 **Oubangui** *R* Congo
46B1 **Oudenaarde** Belg
100B4 **Oudtshoorn** S Africa
51B2 **Oued Tlêlat** Alg
96B1 **Oued Zem** Mor
98B2 **Ouesso** Congo
96B1 **Ouezzane** Mor
98B2 **Ouham** *R* Chad
97C4 **Ouidah** Benin
96B1 **Oujda** Mor
38J6 **Oulainen** Fin
38K5 **Oulu** Fin
38K6 **Oulu** *R* Fin
38K6 **Oulujärvi** *L* Fin
95B3 **Oum Chalouba** Chad
98B1 **Oum Hadjer** Chad
95B3 **Oum Haouach** *Watercourse* Chad
38K5 **Ounas** *R* Fin
95B3 **Ounianga Kébir** Chad
46D1 **Our** *R* Germany
46B2 **Ourcq** *R* France
31C3 **Ouricurí** Brazil
35B2 **Ourinhos** Brazil
35C2 **Ouro Prêto** Brazil
46C1 **Ourthe** *R* Belg
42D2 **Ouse** *R* Eng
43E3 **Ouse** *R* Eng
40B2 **Outer Hebrides** *Is* Scot
22C4 **Outer Santa Barbara** *Chan* USA
100A3 **Outjo** Namibia
38K6 **Outokumpu** Fin
108B3 **Ouyen** Aust
47C2 **Ovada** Italy
34A2 **Ovalle** Chile
100A2 **Ovamboland** Region, Namibia

61H5 **Ova Tyuleni** *Is* USSR
38J5 **Övertorneå** Sweden
50A1 **Oviedo** Spain
60C3 **Ovruch** USSR
63E2 **Ovsyanka** USSR
111A3 **Owaka** NZ
75B2 **Owase** Japan
11B3 **Owensboro** USA
21B2 **Owens L** USA
14B2 **Owen Sound** Can
107D1 **Owen Stanley Range** *Mts* PNG
97C4 **Owerri** Nig
97C4 **Owo** Nig
14B2 **Owosso** USA
20C2 **Owyhee** *R* USA
20C2 **Owyhee Mts** USA
32B6 **Oxapampa** Peru
39H7 **Oxelösund** Sweden
43D4 **Oxford** County, Eng
43D4 **Oxford** Eng
16D1 **Oxford** Massachusetts, USA
19C3 **Oxford** Mississippi, USA
45B1 **Ox Mts** Irish Rep
22C3 **Oxnard** USA
74D3 **Oyama** Japan
13E2 **Oyen** Can
98B2 **Oyem** Gabon
44B3 **Oykel** *R* Scot
39F6 **Øyre** Nor
109C4 **Oyster B** Aust
79B4 **Ozamiz** Phil
17A1 **Ozark** USA
18B2 **Ozark Plat** USA
18B2 **Ozarks,L of the** USA
59C3 **Ózd** Hung
65K5 **Ozero Alakol** *L* USSR
65J5 **Ozero Balkhash** *L* USSR
63C2 **Ozero Baykal** *L* USSR
65J4 **Ozero Chany** *L* USSR
60C2 **Ozero Chudskoye** *L* USSR
60D2 **Ozero Il'men** *L* USSR
38L5 **Ozero Imandra** *L* USSR
82B1 **Ozero Issyk Kul'** *L* USSR
69F2 **Ozero Khanka** *L* China/USSR
38L5 **Ozero Kovdozero** *L* USSR
38L5 **Ozero Kuyto** *L* USSR
38L5 **Ozero Pyaozero** *L* USSR
65H4 **Ozero Tengiz** *L* USSR
38L5 **Ozero Topozero** *L* USSR
65K5 **Ozero Zaysan** USSR
23B1 **Ozuluama** Mexico

P

100A4 **Paarl** S Africa
44A3 **Pabbay** *I* Scot
58B2 **Pabianice** Pol
86B2 **Pabna** Bang
58D2 **Pabrade** USSR
32B5 **Pacasmayo** Peru
23B1 **Pachuca** Mexico
105K6 **Pacific-Antarctic Ridge** Pacific O
22B2 **Pacific Grove** USA
78C4 **Pacitan** Indon
35C1 **Pacuí** *R* Brazil
70B4 **Padang** Indon
56B2 **Paderborn** Germany
5J3 **Padlei** Can
86C2 **Padma** *R* Bang
47D2 **Padova** Italy
9D4 **Padre I** USA
43B4 **Padstow** Eng
108B3 **Padthaway** Aust
Padua = Padova
14A3 **Paducah** Kentucky, USA

11B3 **Paducah** USA
38L5 **Padunskoye More** *L* USSR
74A3 **Paengnyŏng-do** *I* S Korea
110C1 **Paeroa** NZ
100C3 **Pafuri** Mozam
52B2 **Pag** *I* Yugos
79B4 **Pagadian** Phil
70B4 **Pagai Selatan** *I* Indon
70B4 **Pagai Utara** *I* Indon
71F2 **Pagan** *I* Pacific O
78D3 **Pagatan** Indon
55C3 **Pagondhas** Greece
110C2 **Pahiatua** NZ
21C4 **Pahoa** Hawaiian Is
17B2 **Pahokee** USA
39K6 **Päijänne** *L* Fin
21C4 **Pailola Chan** Hawaiian Is
14B2 **Painesville** USA
9B3 **Painted Desert** USA
42B2 **Paisley** Scot
32A5 **Paita** Peru
38J5 **Pajala** Sweden
80E3 **Pakistan** Republic, Asia
76C2 **Pak Lay** Laos
86D2 **Pakokku** Burma
13E2 **Pakowki L** Can
52C1 **Pakrac** Yugos
54A1 **Paks** Hung
76C2 **Pak Sane** Laos
76D2 **Pakse** Laos
99D2 **Pakwach** Uganda
98B2 **Pala** Chad
52C2 **Palagruža** *I* Yugos
46B2 **Palaiseau** France
78C3 **Palangkaraya** Indon
87B2 **Palani** India
85C4 **Palanpur** India
100B3 **Palapye** Botswana
17B2 **Palatka** USA
71E3 **Palau Is** Pacific O
76B3 **Palaw** Burma
79A4 **Palawan** *I* Phil
79A4 **Palawan Pass** Phil
87B3 **Palayankottai** India
39J7 **Paldiski** USSR
78A3 **Palembang** Indon
50B1 **Palencia** Spain
94A1 **Paleokhorio** Cyprus
53B2 **Palermo** Italy
94B3 **Palestine** Region, Israel
19A3 **Palestine** USA
86C2 **Paletwa** Burma
87B2 **Pālghāt** India
85C3 **Pāli** India
85C4 **Pālitāna** India
87B3 **Palk Str** India/Sri Lanka
61G3 **Pallasovka** USSR
38J5 **Pallastunturi** *Mt* Fin
111B2 **Palliser B** NZ
111C2 **Palliser,C** NZ
101D2 **Palma** Mozam
51C2 **Palma de Mallorca** Spain
31D3 **Palmares** Brazil
26A5 **Palmar Sur** Costa Rica
97B4 **Palmas,C** Lib
26B2 **Palma Soriano** Cuba
17B2 **Palm Bay** USA
17B2 **Palm Beach** USA
22C3 **Palmdale** USA
31D3 **Palmeira dos Indos** Brazil
12E2 **Palmer** USA
112C3 **Palmer** *Base* Ant
112C3 **Palmer Arch** Ant
112B3 **Palmer Land** *Region* Ant
111B3 **Palmerston** NZ
110C2 **Palmerston North** NZ
16B2 **Palmerton** USA
17B2 **Palmetto** USA
53C3 **Palmi** Italy

32B3 **Palmira** Colombia
107D2 **Palm Is** Aust
21B3 **Palm Springs** USA
18B2 **Palmyra** Missouri, USA
16A2 **Palmyra** Pennsylvania, USA
86B2 **Palmyras Pt** India
22A2 **Palo Alto** USA
78B2 **Paloh** Indon
99D1 **Paloich** Sudan
21B3 **Palomar Mt** USA
70D4 **Palopo** Indon
70C4 **Palu** Indon
93C2 **Palu** Turk
84D3 **Palwal** India
97C3 **Pama** Burkina
78C4 **Pamekasan** Indon
78B4 **Pameungpeuk** Indon
48C3 **Pamiers** France
82B2 **Pamir** *Mts* China
65J6 **Pamir** *R* USSR
11C3 **Pamlico Sd** USA
9C3 **Pampa** USA
34B2 **Pampa de la Salinas** *Salt pan* Arg
34B3 **Pampa de la Varita** *Plain* Arg
32C2 **Pamplona** Colombia
50B1 **Pamplona** Spain
18C2 **Pana** USA
54B2 **Panagyurishte** Bulg
87A1 **Panaji** India
32B2 **Panamá** Panama
32A2 **Panama** Republic, Cent America
26B5 **Panama Canal** Panama
17A1 **Panama City** USA
21B2 **Panamint Range** *Mts* USA
21B2 **Panamint V** USA
47D2 **Panaro** *R* Italy
79B3 **Panay** *I* Phil
54B2 **Pancevo** Yugos
79B3 **Pandan** Phil
87B1 **Pandharpur** India
108A1 **Pandie Pandie** Aust
58C1 **Panevežys** USSR
65K5 **Panfilov** USSR
76B1 **Pang** *R* Burma
99D3 **Pangani** Tanz
99D3 **Pangani** *R* Tanz
98C3 **Pangi** Zaïre
78B3 **Pangkalpinang** Indon
6D3 **Pangnirtung** Can
76B1 **Pangtara** Burma
79B4 **Pangutaran Group** *Is* Phil
84D3 **Panipat** India
84B2 **Panjao** Afghan
74B3 **P'anmunjŏm** N Korea
86A2 **Panna** India
35A2 **Panorama** Brazil
53B3 **Pantelleria** *I* Medit S
23B1 **Pantepec** Mexico
23B1 **Panuco** Mexico
23B1 **Pánuco** *R* Mexico
73A4 **Pan Xian** China
53C3 **Paola** Italy
18B2 **Paola** USA
14A3 **Paoli** USA
59B3 **Pápa** Hung
110B1 **Papakura** NZ
23B2 **Papaloapan** *R* Mexico
23B1 **Papantla** Mexico
44E1 **Papa Stour** *I* Scot
110B1 **Papatoetoe** NZ
44C2 **Papa Westray** *I* Scot
107D1 **Papua,G of** PNG
107D1 **Papua New Guinea** Republic, S E Asia
34A2 **Papudo** Chile
76B2 **Papun** Burma
33G4 **Para** State, Brazil
31B2 **Pará** *R* Brazil
106A3 **Paraburdoo** Aust

32B6 **Paracas,Pen de** Peru
35B1 **Paracatu** Brazil
35B1 **Paracatu** R Brazil
108A2 **Parachilna** Aust
84C2 **Parachinar** Pak
54B2 **Paracin** Yugos
35C1 **Pará de Minas** Brazil
21A2 **Paradise** California, USA
18B2 **Paragould** USA
33E6 **Paraguá** R Bol
33E2 **Paragua** R Ven
30E2 **Paraguai** R Brazil
30E4 **Paraguari** Par
30E3 **Paraguay** Republic, S America
30E3 **Paraguay** R Par
31D3 **Paraiba** State, Brazil
35B2 **Paraiba** R Brazil
35C2 **Paraíba do Sul** R Brazil
97C4 **Parakou** Benin
108A2 **Parakylia** Aust
87B3 **Paramakkudi** India
33F2 **Paramaribo** Surinam
69H1 **Paramushir** I USSR
30F3 **Paraná** State, Brazil
34C2 **Paraná** Urug
29E2 **Paraná** R Arg
31B4 **Paraná** R Brazil
35A2 **Paraná** R Brazil
30G4 **Paranaguá** Brazil
35A1 **Paranaiba** Brazil
35A1 **Paranaiba** R Brazil
35A2 **Paranapanema** R Brazil
35A2 **Paranavai** Brazil
79B4 **Parang** Phil
35C1 **Paraope** R Brazil
110B2 **Paraparaumu** NZ
87B1 **Parbhani** India
94B2 **Pardes Hanna** Israel
34D3 **Pardo** Arg
35D1 **Pardo** R Bahia, Brazil
35A2 **Pardo** R Mato Grosso do Sul, Brazil
35B1 **Pardo** R Minas Gerais, Brazil
35B2 **Pardo** R Sao Paulo, Brazil
59B2 **Pardubice** Czech
69F4 **Parece Vela** Reef Pacific O
10C2 **Parent** Can
70C4 **Parepare** Indon
34C3 **Parera** Arg
70B4 **Pariaman** Indon
33E1 **Paria,Pen de** Ven
48C2 **Paris** France
14B3 **Paris** Kentucky, USA
19A3 **Paris** Texas, USA
14B3 **Parkersburg** USA
109C2 **Parkes** Aust
16B3 **Parkesburg** USA
14A2 **Park Forest** USA
20B1 **Parksville** Can
87B1 **Parli** India
47D2 **Parma** Italy
14B2 **Parma** USA
31C2 **Parnaiba** Brazil
31C2 **Parnaiba** R Brazil
55B3 **Párnon Óros** Mts Greece
60B2 **Pärnu** USSR
86B1 **Paro** Bhutan
108B1 **Paroo** R Aust
108B2 **Paroo Channel** R Aust
55C3 **Páros** I Greece
47B2 **Parpaillon** Mts France
34A3 **Parral** Chile
109D2 **Parramatta** Aust
9C4 **Parras** Mexico
6B3 **Parry B** Can
4G2 **Parry Is** Can
7C5 **Parry Sd** Can
14B1 **Parry Sound** Can
57C3 **Parsberg** Germany
5F4 **Parsnip** R Can

18A2 **Parsons** Kansas, USA
14C3 **Parsons** West Virginia, USA
48B2 **Parthenay** France
53B3 **Partinico** Italy
74C2 **Partizansk** USSR
33G4 **Paru** R Brazil
101G1 **Parys** S Africa
19A4 **Pasadena** Texas, USA
22C3 **Pasadena** California, USA
78D3 **Pasangkayu** Indon
76B2 **Pasawing** Burma
19C3 **Pascagoula** USA
54C1 **Paşcani** Rom
20C1 **Pasco** USA
46B1 **Pas-de-Calais** Department, France
39G8 **Pasewalk** Germany
91C4 **Pashū'īyeh** Iran
106B4 **Pasley,C** Aust
29E2 **Paso de los Toros** Urug
29B4 **Paso Limay** Arg
21A2 **Paso Robles** USA
45B3 **Passage West** Irish Rep
16B2 **Passaic** USA
57C3 **Passau** Germany
30E4 **Passo de los Libres** Arg
47D1 **Passo di Stelvio** Mt Italy
30F4 **Passo Fundo** Brazil
35B2 **Passos** Brazil
47B2 **Passy** France
32B4 **Pastaza** R Peru
34C3 **Pasteur** Arg
5H4 **Pas,The** Can
32B3 **Pasto** Colombia
12B2 **Pastol B** USA
47D2 **Pasubio** Mt Italy
78C4 **Pasuruan** Indon
58C1 **Pasvalys** USSR
85C4 **Pātan** India
86B1 **Patan** Nepal
108B3 **Patchewollock** Aust
110B1 **Patea** NZ
111B2 **Patea** R NZ
53B3 **Paterno** Italy
16B2 **Paterson** USA
111A3 **Paterson Inlet** B NZ
84D2 **Pathankot** India
84D2 **Patiāla** India
32B6 **Pativilca** Peru
55C3 **Pátmos** I Greece
86B1 **Patna** India
93D2 **Patnos** Turk
31D3 **Pato** Brazil
35B1 **Patos de Minas** Brazil
34B2 **Patquia** Arg
55B3 **Pátrai** Greece
35B1 **Patrocinio** Brazil
99E3 **Patta** I Kenya
78D4 **Pattallasang** Indon
77C4 **Pattani** Thai
22B2 **Patterson** California, USA
19B4 **Patterson** Louisiana, USA
12H2 **Patterson,Mt** Can
22C2 **Patterson,Mt** USA
13B1 **Pattullo,Mt** Can
31D3 **Patu** Brazil
86C2 **Patuakhali** Bang
25D3 **Patuca** R Honduras
23A2 **Patzcuaro** Mexico
48B3 **Pau** France
4F3 **Paulatuk** Can
31C3 **Paulistana** Brazil
101H1 **Paulpietersburg** S Africa
19A3 **Pauls Valley** USA
76B2 **Paungde** Burma
84D2 **Pauri** India
38H5 **Pauske** Nor
35C1 **Pavão** Brazil
47C2 **Pavia** Italy

65J4 **Pavlodar** USSR
63E2 **Pavlovich** USSR
61J2 **Pavlovka** USSR
61F2 **Pavlovo** USSR
61F3 **Pavlovsk** USSR
78C3 **Pawan** R Indon
18A2 **Pawhuska** USA
16D2 **Pawtucket** USA
47B1 **Payerne** Switz
20C2 **Payette** USA
64H3 **Pay-Khoy,Khrebet** Mts USSR
7C4 **Payne,L** Can
34D2 **Paysandu** Urug
46A2 **Pays-de-Bray** Region, France
54B2 **Pazardzhik** Bulg
13D1 **Peace** R Can
17B2 **Peace** R USA
13D1 **Peace River** Can
43D3 **Peak District Nat Pk** Eng
108A1 **Peake** R Aust
109C2 **Peak Hill** Aust
71E4 **Peak Mandala** Mt Indon
42D3 **Peak,The** Mt Eng
19B3 **Pearl** R USA
21C4 **Pearl City** Hawaiian Is
21C4 **Pearl Harbor** Hawaiian Is
4H2 **Peary Chan** Can
101C2 **Pebane** Mozam
54B2 **Peć** Yugos
35C1 **Peçanha** Brazil
19B4 **Pecan Island** USA
38L5 **Pechenga** USSR
64F3 **Pechora** R USSR
64G3 **Pechorskoye More** S USSR
53C3 **Pecoraro** Mt Italy
9C3 **Pecos** USA
9C3 **Pecos** R USA
59B3 **Pécs** Hung
108A1 **Pedirka** Aust
35C1 **Pedra Azul** Brazil
35B2 **Pedregulho** Brazil
26B3 **Pedro Cays** Is Caribbean S
30C3 **Pedro de Valdivia** Chile
30E3 **Pedro Juan Caballero** Par
34C3 **Pedro Luro** Arg
23B1 **Pedro Mentova** Mexico
87C3 **Pedro,Pt** Sri Lanka
108B2 **Peebinga** Aust
42C2 **Peebles** Scot
17C1 **Pee Dee** R USA
16C2 **Peekskill** USA
42B2 **Peel** Eng
12H1 **Peel** R Can
4J2 **Peel Sd** Can
13E1 **Peerless L** Can
71E4 **Peg Arfak** Mt Indon
111B2 **Pegasus B** NZ
83D4 **Pegu** Burma
78A3 **Pegunungan Barisan** Mts Indon
78C2 **Pegunungan Iran** Mts Malay/Indon
71E4 **Pegunungan Maoke** Mts Indon
78D3 **Pegunungan Meratus** Mts Indon
78C2 **Pegunungan Muller** Mts Indon
78C3 **Pegunungan Schwanet** Mts Indon
78A3 **Pegunungan Tigapuluh** Mts Indon
76B2 **Pegu Yoma** Mts Burma

34C3 **Pehuajó** Arg
35A2 **Peixe** R Sao Paulo, Brazil
72D3 **Pei Xian** China
78B4 **Pekalongan** Indon
77C5 **Pekan** Malay
78A2 **Pekanbaru** Indon
18C1 **Pekin** USA
Peking = Beijing
77C5 **Pelabohan Kelang** Malay
78D4 **Pelau Pelau Kangean** Is Indon
78C4 **Pelau Pelau Karimunjawa** Arch Indon
78D4 **Pelau Pelau Postilyon** Is Indon
54B1 **Peleaga** Mt Rom
63D2 **Peleduy** USSR
14B2 **Pelee I** Can
71D4 **Peleng** I Indon
12G3 **Pelican** USA
69F1 **Peliny Osipenko** USSR
34C3 **Pellegrini** Arg
38J5 **Pello** Fin
12H2 **Pelly** R Can
6A3 **Pelly Bay** Can
12G2 **Pelly Crossing** Can
12H2 **Pelly Mts** Can
30F5 **Pelotas** Brazil
30F4 **Pelotas** R Brazil
47B2 **Pelvoux** Region, France
78B4 **Pemalang** Indon
78A3 **Pematang** Indon
101D2 **Pemba** Mozam
99D3 **Pemba** I Tanz
13C2 **Pemberton** Can
13D2 **Pembina** R Can
15C1 **Pembroke** Can
17B1 **Pembroke** USA
43B4 **Pembroke** Wales
34A3 **Pemuco** Chile
78D2 **Penambo Range** Mts Malay
35A2 **Penápolis** Brazil
50A2 **Peñarroya** Spain
51B1 **Penarroya** Mt Spain
50A1 **Peña Trevina** Mt Spain
98B2 **Pende** R Chad
12J3 **Pendleton,Mt** Can
20C1 **Pendleton** USA
20C1 **Pend Oreille** R USA
31D4 **Penedo** Brazil
85D5 **Penganga** R India
73D5 **P'eng-hu Lieh-tao** Is Taiwan
72E2 **Penglai** China
73B4 **Pengshui** China
71E4 **Pengunungan Maoke** Mts Indon
26C4 **Península de la Guajiri** Pen Colombia
27E4 **Península de Paria** Pen Ven
77C5 **Peninsular Malaysia** Malay
23A1 **Penjamo** Mexico
87B2 **Penner** R India
42C2 **Pennine Chain** Mts Eng
16B3 **Penns Grove** USA
10C2 **Pennsylvania** State, USA
6D3 **Penny Highlands** Mts Can
108B3 **Penola** Aust
106C4 **Penong** Aust
42C2 **Penrith** Eng
11B3 **Pensacola** USA
112A **Pensacola Mts** Ant
78D1 **Pensiangan** Malay
13D3 **Penticton** Can
44C2 **Pentland Firth** Chan Scot
42C2 **Pentland Hills** Scot

61G3 **Penza** USSR
43B4 **Penzance** Eng
10B2 **Peoria** USA
78A3 **Perabumulih** Indon
77C5 **Perak** *R* Malay
78A2 **Perawang** Indon
32B3 **Pereira** Colombia
35A2 **Pereira Barreto** Brazil
61F4 **Perelazovskiy** USSR
12D3 **Perenosa B** USA
34C2 **Pergamino** Arg
7C4 **Peribonca** *R* Can
48C2 **Périqueux** France
25E4 **Perlas Arch de** *Is* Panama
61J2 **Perm'** USSR
Pernambuco = Recife
31D3 **Pernambuco** State, Brazil
108A2 **Pernatty Lg** Aust
54B2 **Pernik** Bulg
46B2 **Péronne** France
23B2 **Perote** Mexico
49C3 **Perpignan** France
22D4 **Perris** USA
17B1 **Perry** Florida, USA
17B1 **Perry** Georgia, USA
18A2 **Perry** Oklahoma, USA
4H3 **Perry River** Can
14B2 **Perrysburg** USA
12C3 **Perryville** Alaska, USA
18C2 **Perryville** Missouri, USA
106A4 **Perth** Aust
15C2 **Perth** Can
44C3 **Perth** Scot
16B2 **Perth Amboy** USA
32C6 **Peru** Republic, S America
18C1 **Peru** USA
103E5 **Peru-Chile Trench** Pacific O
52B2 **Perugia** Italy
52C2 **Perušic** Yugos
93D2 **Pervari** Turk
61F3 **Pervomaysk** RSFSR, USSR
60D4 **Pervomaysk** Ukraine SSR, USSR
61J2 **Pervoural'sk** USSR
52B2 **Pesaro** Italy
22A2 **Pescadero** USA
Pescadores = P'eng-hu Lieh-tao
52B2 **Pescara** Italy
47D2 **Peschiera** Italy
84C2 **Peshawar** Pak
54B2 **Peshkopi** Alb
14A1 **Peshtigo** USA
60E2 **Pestovo** USSR
94B2 **Petah Tiqwa** Israel
21A2 **Petaluma** USA
46C2 **Pétange** Lux
23A2 **Petatlán** Mexico
101C2 **Petauke** Zambia
108A2 **Peterborough** Aust
15C2 **Peterborough** Can
43D3 **Peterborough** Eng
44D3 **Peterhead** Scot
6D1 **Petermann Gletscher** *Gl* Greenland
106B3 **Petermann Range** *Mts* Aust
29B3 **Peteroa** *Mt* Arg/Chile
13F1 **Peter Pond L** Can
12H3 **Petersburg** Alaska, USA
85C4 **Petlad** India
23B2 **Petlalcingo** Mexico
25D2 **Peto** Mexico
63D2 **Petomskoye Nagor'ye** *Upland* USSR
34A2 **Petorca** Chile
14B1 **Petoskey** USA
31C3 **Petrolina** Brazil
65H4 **Petropavlovsk** USSR
35C2 **Petrópolis** Brazil
64E3 **Petrovadovsk** USSR

61G3 **Petrovsk** USSR
68C1 **Petrovsk Zabaykal'skiy** USSR
64E3 **Petrozavodsk** USSR
101G1 **Petrus** S Africa
101G1 **Petrusburg** S Africa
1B7 **Pevek** USSR
46D2 **Pfälzer Wald** Region, Germany
57B3 **Pforzheim** Germany
84D2 **Phagwara** India
85C3 **Phalodi** India
46D2 **Phalsbourg** France
87A1 **Phaltan** India
77B4 **Phangnga** Thai
76C3 **Phanom Dang** *Mts* Camb
76D3 **Phan Rang** Viet
76D3 **Phan Thiet** Viet
17A1 **Phenix City** USA
76B3 **Phet Buri** Thai
76D3 **Phiafay** Laos
19C3 **Philadelphia** Mississippi, USA
16B2 **Philadelphia** Pennsylvania, USA
Philippeville = Skikda
46C1 **Philippeville** Belg
71D2 **Philippine S** Pacific O
71D2 **Philippines** Republic, S E Asia
104E3 **Philippine Trench** Pacific O
15C2 **Philipsburg** Pennsylvania, USA
12E1 **Philip Smith Mts** USA
79B2 **Phillipine S** Phil
6B1 **Phillips B** Can
16B2 **Phillipsburg** New Jersey, USA
6B2 **Philpots Pen** Can
76C3 **Phnom Penh** Camb
9B3 **Phoenix** Arizona, USA
16B2 **Phoenixville** USA
76C1 **Phong Saly** Laos
76C2 **Phu Bia** *Mt* Laos
76D3 **Phu Cuong** Viet
77B4 **Phuket** Thai
86A2 **Phulbāni** India
76C2 **Phu Miang** *Mt* Thai
76D2 **Phu Set** *Mt* Laos
76D1 **Phu Tho** Viet
77D4 **Phu Vinh** Viet
47C2 **Piacenza** Italy
109C2 **Pian** *R* Aust
52B2 **Pianosa** *I* Italy
52C2 **Pianosa** *I* Italy
58C2 **Piaseczno** Pol
54C1 **Piatra-Neamţ** Rom
31C3 **Piauí** State, Brazil
47E2 **Piave** *R* Italy
99D2 **Pibor** *R* Sudan
99D2 **Pibor Post** Sudan
46B1 **Picardie** Region, France
19C3 **Picayune** USA
47B2 **Pic de Rochebrune** *Mt* France
34A2 **Pichilemu** Chile
34C3 **Pichi Mahuida** Arg
42D2 **Pickering** Eng
7A4 **Pickle Lake** Can
96A1 **Pico** *I* Açores
47C1 **Pico Bernina** *Mt* Switz
51C1 **Pico de Anito** *Mt* Spain
24B3 **Pico del Infiernillo** *Mt* Mexico
27C3 **Pico Duarte** *Mt* Dom Rep
31C3 **Picos** Brazil
50B1 **Picos de Europa** *Mt* Spain
109D2 **Picton** Aust
111B2 **Picton** NZ
95A2 **Pic Toussidé** *Mt* Chad
35B2 **Piedade** Brazil
22C2 **Piedra** USA

24B2 **Piedras Negras** Mexico
38K6 **Pieksämäki** Fin
38K6 **Pielinen** *L* Fin
47B2 **Piemonte** Region, Italy
8C2 **Pierre** USA
59B3 **Pieštany** Czech
101H1 **Pietermaritzburg** S Africa
100B3 **Pietersburg** S Africa
101H1 **Piet Retief** S Africa
60B4 **Pietrosu** *Mt* Rom
47E1 **Pieve di Cadore** Italy
13E2 **Pigeon L** Can
18B2 **Piggott** USA
34C3 **Pigüé** Arg
7A4 **Pikangikum L** Can
8C3 **Pikes Peak** USA
100A4 **Piketberg** S Africa
6F3 **Pikintaleq** Greenland
82B2 **Pik Kommunizma** *Mt* USSR
98B2 **Pikounda** Congo
82C1 **Pik Pobedy** *Mt* China/USSR
34D3 **Pila** Arg
58B2 **Pila** Pol
30E4 **Pilar** Par
30D3 **Pilcomayo** *R* Arg/Par
84D3 **Pilibhit** India
59B2 **Pilica** *R* Pol
109C4 **Pillar,C** Aust
55B3 **Pílos** Greece
12C3 **Pilot Point** USA
12B2 **Pilot Station** USA
19C3 **Pilottown** USA
33F4 **Pimenta** Brazil
77C4 **Pinang** *I* Malay
26A2 **Pinar del Rio** Cuba
34B2 **Pinas** Arg
46C1 **Pinche** Belg
13E2 **Pincher Creek** Can
31B2 **Pindaré** *R* Brazil
55B3 **Píndhos** *Mts* Greece
19B3 **Pine Bluff** USA
106C2 **Pine Creek** Aust
22C1 **Pinecrest** USA
22C2 **Pinedale** California, USA
22C2 **Pine Flat Res** USA
64F3 **Pinega** *R* USSR
16A2 **Pine Grove** USA
17B2 **Pine Hills** USA
17B2 **Pine I** USA
19B3 **Pineland** USA
17B2 **Pinellas Park** USA
5G3 **Pine Point** Can
47B2 **Pinerolo** Italy
19B3 **Pines,L o'the** USA
19B3 **Pineville** USA
72C3 **Pingdingshan** China
73B5 **Pingguo** China
72B2 **Pingliang** China
72B2 **Pingluo** China
73D4 **Pingtan Dao** *I* China
73E5 **P'ing tung** Taiwan
72A3 **Pingwu** China
73B5 **Pingxiang** Guangxi, China
73C4 **Pingxiang** Jiangxi, China
31B2 **Pinheiro** Brazil
70A3 **Pini** *I* Açores
55B3 **Piniós** *R* Greece
106A4 **Pinjarra** Aust
13C1 **Pink Mountain** Can
108B3 **Pinnaroo** Aust
Pinos,I de, I = Isla de la Juventud
21A2 **Pinos,Pt** USA
23B2 **Pinotepa Nacional** Mexico
70C4 **Pinrang** Indon
60C3 **Pinsk** USSR
32J7 **Pinta** *I* Ecuador
61G1 **Pinyug** USSR
8B3 **Pioche** USA
52B2 **Piombino** Italy

6H3 **Piórsá** Iceland
59B2 **Piotroków Trybunalski** Pol
44E2 **Piper** *Oilfield* N Sea
21B2 **Piper Peak** *Mt* USA
10C2 **Pipmuacan Res** Can
14B2 **Piqua** USA
35B1 **Piracanjuba** Brazil
35B2 **Piracicaba** Brazil
35B2 **Piraçununga** Brazil
35B2 **Pirai do Sul** Brazil
55B3 **Piraiévs** Greece
35B2 **Pirajui** Brazil
35A1 **Piranhas** Brazil
35C1 **Pirapora** Brazil
35B1 **Pirenópolis** Brazil
35B1 **Pires do Rio** Brazil
55B3 **Pírgos** Greece
Pirineos = Pyrénées
31C2 **Piripiri** Brazil
46D2 **Pirmasens** Germany
54B2 **Pirot** Yugos
84C2 **Pir Panjāl Range** *Mts* Pak
71D4 **Piru** Indon
22C3 **Piru Creek** *R* USA
49E3 **Pisa** Italy
32B6 **Pisco** Peru
57C3 **Pisek** Czech
84B2 **Pishin** Pak
30C4 **Pissis** *Mt* Arg
49E3 **Pistoia** Italy
50B1 **Pisuerga** *R* Spain
20B2 **Pit** *R* USA
32B3 **Pitalito** Colombia
105K5 **Pitcairn** *I* Pacific O
38H5 **Pite** *R* Sweden
38J5 **Piteå** Sweden
54B2 **Piteşti** Rom
63B2 **Pit Gorodok** USSR
38L6 **Pitkyaranta** USSR
44C3 **Pitlochry** Scot
34A3 **Pitrutquén** Chile
13B2 **Pitt I** Can
22B1 **Pittsburg** California, USA
18B2 **Pittsburg** Kansas, USA
14C2 **Pittsburgh** USA
18B2 **Pittsfield** Illinois, USA
16C1 **Pittsfield** Massachusetts, USA
109D1 **Pittsworth** Aust
86A1 **Piuthan** Nepal
47D1 **Pizzo Redorta** *Mt* Italy
38B2 **Pjórsá** Iceland
32A5 **Pjura** Peru
7E5 **Placentia B** Can
22B1 **Placerville** USA
46B1 **Plaine des Flandres** *Plain* Belg/France
96C2 **Plaine du Tidikelt** *Desert Region,* Alg
9C3 **Plainview** Texas, USA
22B2 **Planada** USA
30F2 **Planalto de Mato Grosso** *Plat* Brazil
31D3 **Planalto do Borborema** *Plat* Brazil
32A1 **Planalto do Mato Grosso** *Mts* Brazil
19A3 **Plano** USA
17B2 **Plantation** USA
17B2 **Plant City** USA
50A1 **Plasencia** Spain
61K3 **Plast** USSR
69F2 **Plastun** USSR
96C2 **Plateau du Tademait** Alg
46D2 **Plateau Lorrain** *Plat* France
48C2 **Plateaux de Limousin** *Plat* France
51C2 **Plateaux du Sersou** *Plat* Alg
26C5 **Plato** Colombia
65G5 **Plato Ustyurt** *Plat*

8C2 **Platte** *R* USA
15D2 **Plattsburgh** USA
18A1 **Plattsmouth** USA
57C2 **Plauen** Germany
60E3 **Plavsk** USSR
23A2 **Playa Azul** Mexico
32A4 **Playas** Ecuador
23B2 **Playa Vicente** Mexico
50A1 **Plaza de Moro**
    Almanzor *Mt* Spain
22B2 **Pleasanton** California,
    USA
16B3 **Pleasantville** USA
14A3 **Pleasure Ridge Park**
    USA
76D3 **Pleiku** Viet
110C1 **Plenty,B of** NZ
58B2 **Pleszew** Pol
7C4 **Pletipi,L** Can
54B2 **Pleven** Bulg
54A2 **Pljevlja** Yugos
52C2 **Ploče** Yugos
58B2 **Płock** Pol
48B2 **Ploërmel** France
54C2 **Ploiești** Rom
60B3 **Płońsk** Pol
54B2 **Plovdiv** Bulg
20C1 **Plummer** USA
12C2 **Plummer,Mt** USA
100B3 **Plumtree** Zim
22B1 **Plymouth** California,
    USA
43B4 **Plymouth** Eng
14A2 **Plymouth** Indiana,
    USA
16D2 **Plymouth**
    Massachusetts, USA
15C2 **Plymouth**
    Pennsylvania, USA
43B4 **Plymouth Sd** Eng
43C3 **Plynlimon** *Mt* Wales
57C3 **Plzeň** Czech
58B2 **Pniewy** Pol
38K6 **Pnyäselkä** *L* Fin
97B3 **Pô** Burkina
47E2 **Po** *R* Italy
97C4 **Pobé** Benin
69G2 **Pobedino** USSR
8B2 **Pocatello** USA
15C3 **Pocomoke City** USA
35B2 **Pocos de Caldas** Brazil
47D2 **Po di Volano** *R* Italy
63B1 **Podkamennaya** *R*
    USSR
60E2 **Podolsk** USSR
59D3 **Podol'skaya**
    Vozvyshennost'
    Upland USSR
60D1 **Podporozh'ye** USSR
61F1 **Podyuga** USSR
100A3 **Pofadder** S Africa
74B3 **P'ohang** S Korea
112C9 **Poinsett,C** Ant
108C2 **Point** Aust
27E3 **Pointe-à-Pitre**
    Guadeloupe
48B2 **Pointe de Barfleur** *Pt*
    France
98B3 **Pointe Noire** Congo
98A2 **Pointe Pongara** *Pt*
    Gabon
108B3 **Point Fairy** Aust
27L1 **Point Fortin** Trinidad
4B3 **Point Hope** USA
4G3 **Point L** Can
12B1 **Point Lay** USA
16B2 **Point Pleasant**
    New Jersey, USA
14B3 **Point Pleasant**
    W Virginia, USA
47B2 **Point St Bernard** *Mt*
    France
48C2 **Poitiers** France
48B2 **Poitou** Region, France
46A2 **Poix** France
85C3 **Pokaran** India
109C1 **Pokataroo** Aust
63E1 **Pokrovsk** USSR

58B2 **Poland**
    Republic, Europe
92B2 **Polatli** Turk
78D3 **Polewali** Indon
47A1 **Poligny** France
55B2 **Políyiros** Greece
87B2 **Pollāchi** India
79B3 **Polollo Is** Phil
59D2 **Polonnye** USSR
58D1 **Polotsk** USSR
60D4 **Poltava** USSR
52C1 **Pölten** Austria
64F3 **Poluostrov Kanin** *Pen*
    USSR
61H5 **Poluostrov**
    Mangyshlak *Pen*
    USSR
38L5 **Poluostrov Rybachiy**
    Pen USSR
64H2 **Poluostrov Yamal** *Pen*
    USSR
38L5 **Polyarnyy** Murmansk,
    USSR
1B8 **Polyarnyy** Yakutskaya,
    USSR
105H3 **Polynesia** *Region*
    Pacific O
32B5 **Pomabamba** Peru
35C2 **Pomba** *R* Brazil
22D3 **Pomona** USA
18A2 **Pomona Res** USA
17B2 **Pompano Beach** USA
16B2 **Pompton Lakes** USA
18A2 **Ponca City** USA
27D3 **Ponce** Puerto Rico
17B2 **Ponce de Leon B** USA
87B2 **Pondicherry** India
6C2 **Pond Inlet** Can
50A1 **Ponferrade** Spain
98C2 **Pongo** *R* Sudan
101H1 **Pongola** *R* S Africa
87B2 **Ponnāni** India
86C2 **Ponnyadoung Range**
    Mts Burma
13E2 **Ponoka** Can
64F3 **Ponoy** USSR
48B2 **Pons** France
35D1 **Ponta da Baleia** *Pt*
    Brazil
96A1 **Ponta Delgada** Açores
98B3 **Ponta do Padrão** *Pt*
    Angola
35C2 **Ponta dos Búzios** *Pt*
    Brazil
30F4 **Ponta Grossa** Brazil
35B2 **Pontal** Brazil
46D2 **Pont-à-Mousson**
    France
30E3 **Ponta Pora** Brazil
49D2 **Pontarlier** France
19B3 **Pontchartrain,L** USA
52B2 **Pontedera** Italy
52A2 **Ponte Leccia** Corse
50A1 **Pontevedra** Spain
18C1 **Pontiac** Illinois, USA
14B2 **Pontiac** Michigan,
    USA
78B3 **Pontianak** Indon
48B2 **Pontivy** France
46B2 **Pontoise** France
19C3 **Pontotoc** USA
43C4 **Pontypool** Wales
43C4 **Pontypridd** Wales
43D4 **Poole** Eng
    Poona = Pune
108B2 **Pooncarie** Aust
108B2 **Poopelloe,L** *L* Aust
12C2 **Poorman** USA
32B3 **Popayán** Colombia
46B1 **Poperinge** Belg
108B2 **Popilta L** Aust
18B2 **Poplar Bluff** USA
19C3 **Poplarville** USA
107D1 **Popndetta** PNG
23B2 **Popocatepetl** *Mt*
    Mexico
98B3 **Popokabaka** Zaïre
71F4 **Popondetta** PNG

54C2 **Popovo** Bulg
85B4 **Porbandar** India
13A2 **Porcher I** Can
12F1 **Porcupine** *R* Can/USA
52B1 **Poreč** Yugos
35A2 **Porecatu** Brazil
39J6 **Pori** Fin
111B2 **Porirua** NZ
38H5 **Porjus** Sweden
69G2 **Poronaysk** USSR
47B1 **Porrentruy** Switz
38K4 **Porsangen** *Inlet* Nor
39F7 **Porsgrunn** Nor
45C1 **Portadown** N Ire
8D2 **Portage la Prairie** Can
13C3 **Port Alberni** Can
50A2 **Portalegre** Port
9C3 **Portales** USA
7C5 **Port Alfred** Can
100B4 **Port Alfred** S Africa
13B2 **Port Alice** Can
19B3 **Port Allen** USA
20B1 **Port Angeles** USA
26B3 **Port Antonio** Jamaica
45C2 **Portarlington**
    Irish Rep
19B4 **Port Arthur** USA
108A2 **Port Augusta** Aust
26C3 **Port-au-Prince** Haiti
14B2 **Port Austin** USA
108B3 **Port Campbell** Aust
86B2 **Port Canning** India
7D5 **Port Cartier** Can
111B3 **Port Chalmers** NZ
17B2 **Port Charlotte** USA
16C2 **Port Chester** USA
15C2 **Port Colborne** Can
15C2 **Port Credit** Can
109C4 **Port Davey** Aust
26C3 **Port-de-Paix** Haiti
77C5 **Port Dickson** Malay
100C4 **Port Edward** S Africa
35C1 **Porteirinha** Brazil
14B2 **Port Elgin** Can
100B4 **Port Elizabeth** S Africa
27N2 **Porter Pt** St Vincent
21B2 **Porterville** USA
107D4 **Port Fairy** Aust
98A3 **Port Gentil** Gabon
19B3 **Port Gibson** USA
12D3 **Port Graham** USA
20B1 **Port Hammond** Can
89E7 **Port Harcourt** Nig
13B2 **Port Hardy** Can
7D5 **Port Hawkesbury** Can
106A3 **Port Hedland** Aust
    Port Heiden = Meshik
43B3 **Porthmadog** Wales
7E4 **Port Hope Simpson**
    Can
22C3 **Port Hueneme** USA
14B2 **Port Huron** USA
50A2 **Portimāo** Port
109D2 **Port Jackson** *B* Aust
16C2 **Port Jefferson** USA
16B2 **Port Jervis** USA
109D2 **Port Kembla** Aust
14B2 **Portland** Indiana, USA
10C2 **Portland** Maine, USA
109C2 **Portland** New South
    Wales, Aust
20B1 **Portland** Oregon, USA
108B3 **Portland** Victoria, Aust
27H2 **Portland Bight** *B*
    Jamaica
43C4 **Portland Bill** *Pt* Eng
109C4 **Portland,C** Aust
13A1 **Portland Canal** Can/
    USA
110C1 **Portland I** NZ
27H2 **Portland Pt** Jamaica
45C2 **Port Laoise** Irish Rep
108A2 **Port Lincoln** Aust
97A4 **Port Loko** Sierra
    Leone
101E3 **Port Louis** Mauritius
108B3 **Port MacDonnell** Aust
13B2 **Port McNeill** Can

109D2 **Port Macquarie** Aust
12B3 **Port Moller** USA
107D1 **Port Moresby** PNG
100A3 **Port Nolloth** S Africa
16B3 **Port Norris** USA
89E7 **Port Novo** Benin
50A1 **Porto** Port
30F5 **Pôrto Alegre** Brazil
33F6 **Pôrto Artur** Brazil
35A2 **Pôrto 15 de Novembro**
    Brazil
30F3 **Pôrto E Cunha** Brazil
52B2 **Portoferraio** Italy
27E4 **Port of Spain** Trinidad
47D2 **Portomaggiore** Italy
97C4 **Porto Novo** Benin
20B1 **Port Orchard** USA
20B2 **Port Orford** USA
96A1 **Porto Santo** *I* Medeira
31D5 **Pôrto Seguro** Brazil
53A2 **Porto Torres**
    Sardegna
53A2 **Porto Vecchio** Corse
33E5 **Pôrto Velho** Brazil
111A3 **Port Pegasus** *B* NZ
108B3 **Port Phillip B** Aust
108A2 **Port Pirie** Aust
44A3 **Portree** Scot
20B1 **Port Renfrew** Can
27J2 **Port Royal** Jamaica
17B1 **Port Royal Sd** USA
45C1 **Portrush** N Ire
92B3 **Port Said** Egypt
17A2 **Port St Joe** USA
100B4 **Port St Johns** S Africa
7E4 **Port Saunders** Can
100C4 **Port Shepstone**
    S Africa
13A2 **Port Simpson** Can
2702 **Portsmouth** Dominica
43D4 **Portsmouth** Eng
14B3 **Portsmouth** Ohio,
    USA
11C3 **Portsmouth** Virginia,
    USA
109D2 **Port Stephens** *B* Aust
95C3 **Port Sudan** Sudan
19C3 **Port Sulphur** USA
38K5 **Porttipahdan Tekojärvi**
    Res Fin
50A2 **Portugal**
    Republic, Europe
14A2 **Port Washington** USA
77C5 **Port Weld** Malay
32D6 **Porvenir** Bol
39K6 **Porvoo** Fin
30E4 **Posadas** Arg
50A2 **Posadas** Spain
47D1 **Poschiavo** Switz
6B2 **Posheim Pen** Can
90C3 **Posht-e Badam** Iran
71D4 **Poso** Indon
58D1 **Postavy** USSR
14B2 **Post Clinton** USA
7C4 **Poste-de-la-Baleine**
    Can
100B3 **Postmasburg** S Africa
52B1 **Postojna** Yugos
74C2 **Pos'yet** USSR
101G1 **Potchetstroom**
    S Africa
19B2 **Poteau** USA
53C2 **Potenza** Italy
100B3 **Potgietersrus** S Africa
97D3 **Potiskum** Nig
20C1 **Potlatch** USA
15C3 **Potomac** *R* USA
30C2 **Potosi** Bol
30C4 **Potrerillos** Chile
56C2 **Potsdam** Germany
16B2 **Pottstown** USA
16A2 **Pottsville** USA
16C2 **Poughkeepsie** USA
35B2 **Pouso Alegre** Brazil
110C1 **Poverty B** NZ
61F3 **Povorino** USSR
7C4 **Povungnituk** Can
8C2 **Powder** *R* USA

Powell Creek

106C2 **Powell Creek** Aust
9B3 **Powell,L** USA
13C3 **Powell River** Can
8C2 **Power** R USA
43C3 **Powys** County, Wales
73D4 **Poyang Hu** L China
92B2 **Pozantı** Turk
23B1 **Poza Rica** Mexico
58B2 **Poznań** Pol
30E3 **Pozo Colorado** Par
53B2 **Pozzuoli** Italy
97B4 **Pra** R Ghana
76C3 **Prachin Buri** Thai
76B3 **Prachuap Khiri Khan** Thai
59B2 **Praděd** Mt Czech
49C3 **Pradelles** France
35D1 **Prado** Italy
Prague = Praha
57C2 **Praha** Czech
97A4 **Praia** Cape Verde
33E5 **Prainha** Brazil
18B2 **Prairie Village** USA
76C3 **Prakhon Chai** Thai
35B1 **Prata** Brazil
35B1 **Prata** R Brazil
Prates = Dongsha Qundao
49E3 **Prato** Italy
16B1 **Prattsville** USA
17A1 **Prattville** USA
48B1 **Prawle Pt** Eng
78D4 **Praya** Indon
47D1 **Predazzo** Italy
63B2 **Predivinsk** USSR
58C2 **Pregolyu** R USSR
76D3 **Prek Kak** Camb
56C2 **Prenzlau** Germany
76A3 **Preparis** I Burma
76A2 **Preparis North Chan** Burma
59B3 **Přerov** Czech
23A2 **Presa del Infiernillo** Mexico
9B3 **Prescott** Arizona, USA
19B3 **Prescott** Arkansas, USA
15C2 **Prescott** Can
30D4 **Presidencia Roque Sáenz Peña** Arg
35A2 **Presidente Epitácio** Brazil
112C2 **Presidente Frei** Base Ant
23B2 **Presidente Miguél Aleman** L Mexico
35A2 **Presidente Prudente** Brazil
30F3 **Presidenté Vargas** Brazil
35A2 **Presidente Venceslau** Brazil
59C3 **Prešov** Czech
55B2 **Prespansko Jezero** L Yugos
10D2 **Presque Isle** USA
42C3 **Preston** Eng
8B2 **Preston** Idaho, USA
18B2 **Preston** Missouri, USA
42B2 **Prestwick** Scot
31B6 **Prêto** Brazil
35B1 **Prêto** R Brazil
101G1 **Pretoria** S Africa
55B3 **Préveza** Greece
76D3 **Prey Veng** Camb
8B3 **Price** USA
13B2 **Price** I Can
60D4 **Prichernomorskaya Nizmennost'** Lowland USSR
27M2 **Prickly Pt** Grenada
58C1 **Priekule** USSR
100B3 **Prieska** S Africa
20C1 **Priest L** USA
20C1 **Priest River** USA

61G4 **Prikaspiyskaya Nizmennost'** Region USSR
55B2 **Prilep** Yugos
60D3 **Priluki** USSR
34C2 **Primero** R Arg
39K6 **Primorsk** USSR
60E4 **Primorsko-Akhtarsk** USSR
13F2 **Primrose L** Can
5H4 **Prince Albert** Can
4F2 **Prince Albert,C** Can
4G2 **Prince Albert Pen** Can
4G2 **Prince Albert Sd** Can
6C3 **Prince Charles I** Can
112B10 **Prince Charles Mts** Ant
7D5 **Prince Edward I** Can
13C2 **Prince George** Can
4H2 **Prince Gustaf Adolp** S Can
5E4 **Prince of Wales** I USA
71F5 **Prince of Wales I** Aust
4H2 **Prince of Wales I** Can
4G2 **Prince of Wales Str** Can
4F2 **Prince Patrick I** Can
6A2 **Prince Regent Inlet** Str Can
13A2 **Prince Rupert** Can
107D2 **Princess Charlotte B** Aust
13B2 **Princess Royal I** Can
27L1 **Princes Town** Trinidad
13C3 **Princeton** Can
18C2 **Princeton** Kentucky, USA
18B1 **Princeton** Missouri, USA
16B2 **Princeton** New Jersey, USA
4D3 **Prince William** USA
12E2 **Prince William Sd** USA
97C4 **Principe** I W Africa
20B2 **Prineville** USA
12E1 **Pringle,Mt** USA
6F3 **Prins Christian Sund** Sd Greenland
112B12 **Prinsesse Astrid Kyst** Region, Ant
112B12 **Prinsesse Ragnhild Kyst** Region, Ant
64B2 **Prins Karls Forland** I Barents S
25D3 **Prinzapolca** Nic
58D2 **Pripyat'** R USSR
54B2 **Priština** Yugos
56C2 **Pritzwalk** Germany
61F3 **Privolzhskaya Vozvyshennost'** Upland USSR
54B2 **Prizren** Yugos
78C4 **Probolinggo** Indon
5G5 **Procatello** USA
87B2 **Proddatür** India
25D2 **Progreso** Mexico
20B2 **Project City** USA
61F5 **Prokhladnyy** USSR
65K4 **Prokop'yevsk** USSR
61F4 **Proletarskaya** USSR
64G2 **Proliv Karskiye Vorota** Str USSR
83D4 **Prome** Burma
31D4 **Propriá** Brazil
20B2 **Prospect** Oregon, USA
107D3 **Prosperine** Aust
59B3 **Prostějov** Czech
6E2 **Prøven** Greenland
49D3 **Provence** Region, France
16D2 **Providence** USA
15D2 **Provincetown** USA

49C2 **Provins** France
8B2 **Provo** USA
13E2 **Provost** Can
4D2 **Prudhoe Bay** USA
6D2 **Prudhoe Land** Greenland
58C2 **Pruszkow** Pol
60C4 **Prutul** R USSR
58C2 **Pruzhany** USSR
18A2 **Pryor** USA
59C3 **Przemys'l** Pol
55C3 **Psará** I Greece
60C2 **Pskov** USSR
58D2 **Ptich** R USSR
55B2 **Ptolemaïs** Greece
32C5 **Pucallpa** Peru
73D4 **Pucheng** China
34A3 **Pucón** Chile
38K5 **Pudasjärvi** Fin
87B2 **Pudukkottai** India
23B2 **Puebla** Mexico
23B2 **Puebla** State, Mexico
50A1 **Puebla de Sanabria** Spain
50A1 **Puebla de Trives** Spain
9C2 **Pueblo** USA
34B3 **Puelches** Arg
34B3 **Puelén** Arg
23A2 **Puenta Ixbapa** Mexico
34B2 **Puente del Inca** Arg
32A5 **Puerta Aguja** Peru
30B2 **Puerta Coles** Peru
34B2 **Puerta de los Llanos** Arg
31D3 **Puerta do Calcanhar** Pt Brazil
32C1 **Puerta Gallinas** Colombia
23B2 **Puerta Maldonado** Pt Mexico
32A2 **Puerta Mariato** Panama
29C5 **Puerta Médanosa** Pt Arg
23A2 **Puerta Mongrove** Mexico
25E4 **Puerta San Blas** Pt Panama
23A2 **Puerta San Telmo** Mexico
29B5 **Puerto Aisén** Chile
25D4 **Puerto Armuelles** Panama
33F6 **Puerto Artur** Brazil
32B3 **Puerto Asis** Colombia
32D2 **Puerto Ayacucho** Ven
25D3 **Puerto Barrios** Guatemala
32C2 **Puerto Berrio** Colombia
32D1 **Puerto Cabello** Ven
25D3 **Puerto Cabezas** Nic
32D2 **Puerto Carreño** Colombia
25D4 **Puerto Cortes** Costa Rica
25D3 **Puerto Cortés** Honduras
96A2 **Puerto del Rosario** Canary Is
30F3 **Puerto E Cunha** Brazil
32C1 **Puerto Fijo** Ven
31B3 **Puerto Franco** Brazil
32D6 **Puerto Heath** Bol
25D2 **Puerto Juarez** Mexico
33E1 **Puerto la Cruz** Ven
50B2 **Puertollano** Spain
27C4 **Puerto Lopez** Colombia
29D4 **Puerto Madryn** Arg
32D6 **Puerto Maldonado** Peru
23B2 **Puerto Marquéz** Mexico
29B4 **Puerto Montt** Chile
30E3 **Puerto Murtinho** Brazil

29B6 **Puerto Natales** Chile
24A1 **Puerto Peñasco** Mexico
29D4 **Puerto Pirámides** Arg
27C3 **Puerto Plata** Dom Rep
79A4 **Puerto Princesa** Phil
32B3 **Puerto Rico** Colombia
27D3 **Puerto Rico** I Caribbean S
27D3 **Puerto Rico Trench** Caribbean S
23A2 **Puerto San Juan de Lima** Mexico
33G4 **Puerto Santanga** Brazil
30E2 **Puerto Suárez** Bol
24B2 **Puerto Vallarta** Mexico
29B4 **Puerto Varas** Chile
30D2 **Puerto Villarroel** Bol
61G3 **Pugachev** USSR
84C3 **Pugal** India
51C1 **Puigcerdá** Spain
111B2 **Pukaki,L** L NZ
74B2 **Pukch'ŏng** N Korea
110B1 **Pukekobe** NZ
111B2 **Puketeraki Range** Mts NZ
52B2 **Pula** Yugos
15C2 **Pulaski** New York, USA
71E4 **Pulau Kolepom** I Indon
70A4 **Pulau Pulau Batu** Is Indon
58C2 **Pulawy** Pol
87C2 **Pulicat,L** India
84B1 **Pul-i-Khumri** Afghan
87B3 **Puliyangudi** India
20C1 **Pullman** USA
71E3 **Pulo Anna Merir** I Pacific O
79B2 **Pulog,Mt** Phil
38L5 **Pulozero** USSR
58C2 **Pultusk** Pol
30C4 **Puna de Atacama** Arg
86B1 **Punakha** Bhutan
84C2 **Punch** Pak
87A1 **Pune** India
23A2 **Punéper** Mexico
98C3 **Punia** Zaïre
34A2 **Punitaqui** Chile
84C2 **Punjab** Province, Pak
84D2 **Punjab** State, India
30B2 **Puno** Peru
24A2 **Punta Abreojos** Pt Mexico
53C3 **Punta Alice** Pt Italy
34C3 **Punta Alta** Arg
29B6 **Punta Arenas** Chile
24A2 **Punta Baja** Pt Mexico
34A2 **Punta Curaumilla** Pt Chile
100A2 **Punta da Marca** Pt Angola
101C3 **Punta de Barra Falsa** Pt Mozam
29F2 **Punta del Este** Urug
24A2 **Punta Eugenia** Pt Mexico
25D3 **Punta Gorda** Belize
17B2 **Punta Gorda** USA
34A3 **Punta Lavapié** Pt Chile
34A2 **Punta Lengua de Vaca** Pt Chile
53B2 **Punta Licosa** Pt Italy
34A1 **Punta Poroto** Pt Chile
9B4 **Punta San Antonia** Pt Mexico
34A2 **Punta Topocalma** Chile
73C4 **Puqi** China
64J3 **Pur** R USSR
19A2 **Purcell** USA
12C1 **Purcell Mt** USA
13D2 **Purcell Mts** Can
34A3 **Purén** Chile

86B2 **Puri** India
87B1 **Pūrna** India
86B1 **Pūrnia** India
76C3 **Pursat** Camb
23A1 **Puruandro** Mexico
33E4 **Purus** *R* Brazil
19C3 **Purvis** USA
78B4 **Purwokerto** Indon
78C4 **Purworejo** Indon
85D5 **Pusad** India
74B3 **Pusan** S Korea
60D2 **Pushkin** USSR
58D1 **Pustochka** USSR
82D3 **Puta** Burma
34A2 **Putaendo** Chile
110C1 **Putaruru** NZ
73D4 **Putian** China
16D2 **Putnam** USA
87B3 **Puttalam** Sri Lanka
56C2 **Puttgarden** Germany
32B4 **Putumayo** *R* Ecuador
78C2 **Putussibau** Indon
38K6 **Puulavesl** *L* Fin
20B1 **Puyallup** USA
49C2 **Puy de Sancy** *Mt*
France
111A3 **Puysegur Pt** NZ
99C3 **Pweto** Zaïre
43B3 **Pwllheli** Wales
76B2 **Pyapon** Burma
61F5 **Pyatigorsk** USSR
74B3 **P'yŏngyang** N Korea
108B3 **Pyramid Hill** Aust
21B1 **Pyramid L** USA
111A2 **Pyramid,Mt** NZ
48B3 **Pyrénées** *Mts* France
58D1 **Pytalovo** USSR
76B2 **Pyu** Burma

Q

94B2 **Qabatiya** Israel
94C3 **Qā'el Hafīra** *Mud Flats*
Jordan
94C3 **Qa'el Jinz** *Mud Flats*
Jordan
68B3 **Qaidam Pendi** *Salt*
Flat China
94C2 **Qa Khanna** *Salt Marsh*
Jordan
99D1 **Qala'en Nahl** Sudan
84B2 **Qalat** Afghan
94C1 **Qal'at al Hisn** Syria
81C3 **Qal'at Bīshah**
S Arabia
93E3 **Qal'at Sālih** Iraq
68B3 **Qamdo** China
99E2 **Qardho** Somalia
95B2 **Qara** Egypt
90A3 **Qare Shīrin** Iran
91A4 **Qaryat al Ulyā**
S Arabia
94C3 **Qasr el Kharana**
Jordan
91D4 **Qasr-e-Qand** Iran
95B2 **Qasr Farafra** Egypt
94C2 **Qatana** Syria
91B4 **Qatar** Emirate,
Arabian Pen
94C3 **Qatrāna** Jordan
95B2 **Qattāra Depression**
Egypt
90C3 **Qāyen** Iran
90A2 **Qazvīn** Iran
95C2 **Qena** Egypt
90A2 **Qeydār** Iran
91B4 **Qeys** *I* Iran
94B3 **Qeziot** Israel
73B5 **Qian Jiang** *R* China
72E1 **Qian Shan** *Upland*
China
72E3 **Qidong** China
73B4 **Qijiang** China
84B2 **Qila Saifullah** Pak
72A2 **Qilian** China
68B3 **Qilian Shan** China
72B3 **Qin'an** China

72E2 **Qingdao** China
72A2 **Qinghai** Province,
China
68B3 **Qinghai Hu** *L* China
72D3 **Qingjiang** Jiangsu,
China
73D4 **Qingjiang** Jiangxi,
China
72B3 **Qing Jiang** *R* China
72C2 **Qingshuihe** China
72B2 **Qingshui He** *R* China
72B2 **Qingtonxia** China
72B2 **Qingyang** China
74B2 **Qingyuan** Liaoning,
China
73D4 **Qingyuan** Zhejiang,
China
82C2 **Qing Zang** *Upland*
China
72D2 **Qinhuangdao** China
72B3 **Qin Ling** *Mts* China
73B5 **Qinzhou** China
76E2 **Qionghai** China
73A3 **Qionglai Shan** *Upland*
China
76D1 **Qiongzhou Haixia** *Str*
China
69E2 **Qiqihar** China
94B2 **Qiryat Ata** Israel
94B3 **Qiryat Gat** Israel
94B2 **Qiryat Shemona** Israel
94B2 **Qiryat Yam** Israel
94B2 **Qishon** *R* Israel
63A3 **Qitai** China
73C4 **Qiyang** China
72B1 **Qog Qi** China
90B2 **Qolleh-ye Damavand**
Mt Iran
90B3 **Qom** Iran
90B3 **Qomisheh** Iran
Qomolangma Feng =
Everest,Mt
94C1 **Qornet es Saouda** *Mt*
Leb
6E3 **Qôrnoq** Greenland
90A2 **Qorveh** Iran
91C4 **Qotābad** Iran
16C1 **Quabbin Res** USA
16B2 **Quakertown** USA
77C3 **Quam Phu Quoc** *I* Viet
76D2 **Quang Ngai** Viet
76D2 **Quang Tri** Viet
77D4 **Quan Long** Viet
73D5 **Quanzhou** Fujian,
China
73C4 **Quanzhou** Guangxi,
China
5H4 **Qu' Appelle** *R* Can
91C5 **Quarayyāt** Oman
13B2 **Quatsino Sd** Can
90C2 **Quchan** Iran
109C3 **Queanbeyan** Aust
15D1 **Québec** Can
7C4 **Quebec** Province, Can
35B1 **Quebra-Anzol** *R* Brazil
34D2 **Quebracho** Urug
30F4 **Quedas do Iguaçu**
Brazil/Arg
16A3 **Queen Anne** USA
13B2 **Queen Bess,Mt** Can
5E4 **Queen Charlotte** *Is*
Can
13B2 **Queen Charlotte Sd**
Can
13B2 **Queen Charlotte Str**
Can
4H1 **Queen Elizabeth Is**
Can
112B9 **Queen Mary Land**
Region, Ant
4H3 **Queen Maud G** Can
112A **Queen Maud Mts** Ant
16C2 **Queens** Borough, New
York, USA
108B3 **Queenscliff** Aust
107D3 **Queensland** State,
Aust
109C4 **Queenstown** Aust

111A3 **Queenstown** NZ
100B4 **Queenstown** S Africa
16A3 **Queenstown** USA
98B3 **Quela** Angola
101C2 **Quelimane** Mozam
34C3 **Quemuquemú** Arg
13C2 **Quensel L** Can
34D3 **Quequén** Arg
34D3 **Quequén** *R* Arg
23A1 **Querétaro** Mexico
23A1 **Queretaro** State,
Mexico
13C2 **Quesnel** Can
84B2 **Quetta** Pak
25C3 **Quezaltenango**
Guatemala
79B3 **Quezon City** Phil
100A2 **Quibala** Angola
98B3 **Quibaxe** Angola
32B2 **Quibdó** Colombia
48B2 **Quiberon** France
98B3 **Quicama Nat Pk**
Angola
73A4 **Quijing** China
34A2 **Quilima** Chile
34C2 **Quilino** Arg
32C6 **Quillabamba** Peru
30C2 **Quillacollo** Bol
48C3 **Quillan** France
5H4 **Quill L** Can
5H4 **Quill Lakes** Can
34A2 **Quillota** Chile
87B3 **Quilon** India
108B1 **Quilpie** Aust
34A2 **Quilpué** Chile
98B3 **Quimbele** Angola
48B2 **Quimper** France
48B2 **Quimperlé** France
21A2 **Quincy** California,
USA
10A3 **Quincy** Illinois, USA
16D1 **Quincy**
Massachusetts, USA
34B2 **Quines** Arg
12B3 **Quinhagak** USA
76D3 **Qui Nhon** Viet
50B2 **Quintanar de la Orden**
Spain
34A2 **Quintero** Chile
34C2 **Quinto** *R* Arg
34A3 **Quirihue** Chile
100A2 **Quirima** Angola
109D2 **Quirindi** Aust
101D2 **Quissanga** Mozam
101C3 **Quissico** Mozam
32B4 **Quito** Ecuador
31D2 **Quixadá** Brazil
108A2 **Quorn** Aust
95C2 **Quseir** Egypt
6E3 **Qutdligssat** Greenland
Quthing = Moyeni
73B3 **Qu Xian** Sichuan,
China
73D4 **Qu Xian** Zhejiang,
China
76D2 **Quynh Luu** Viet
72C2 **Quzhou** China
86C1 **Qüzü** China

R

38J6 **Raahe** Fin
44A3 **Raasay** *I* Scot
44A3 **Raasay,Sound of** *Chan*
Scot
52B2 **Rab** *I* Yugos
78D4 **Raba** Indon
59B3 **Rába** *R* Hung
96B1 **Rabat** Mor
94B3 **Rabba** Jordan
80B3 **Rabigh** S Arabia
47B2 **Racconigi** Italy
7E5 **Race,C** Can
94B2 **Rachaya** Leb
57C3 **Rachel** *Mt* Germany
76D3 **Rach Gia** Viet
14A2 **Racine** USA

59D3 **Rădăuţi** Rom
85C4 **Radhanpur** India
27L1 **Radix,Pt** Trinidad
58C2 **Radom** Pol
59B2 **Radomsko** Pol
58C1 **Radviliškis** USSR
4G3 **Rae** Can
86A1 **Rāe Bareli** India
6B3 **Rae Isthmus** Can
4G3 **Rae L** Can
110C1 **Raetihi** NZ
34C2 **Rafaela** Arg
94B3 **Rafah** Egypt
98C2 **Rafai** CAR
93D3 **Rafhā Al Jumaymah**
S Arabia
91C3 **Rafsanjān** Iran
98C2 **Raga** Sudan
27R3 **Ragged Pt** Barbados
95A2 **Raguba** Libya
53B3 **Ragusa** Italy
99D1 **Rahad** *R* Sudan
84C3 **Rahimyar Khan** Pak
90B3 **Rāhjerd** Iran
34D2 **Raíces** Arg
87B1 **Rāichur** India
86A2 **Raigarh** India
108B3 **Rainbow** Aust
17A1 **Rainbow City** USA
20B1 **Rainier** USA
20B1 **Rainier,Mt** USA
10A2 **Rainy L** Can
12D2 **Rainy P** USA
10A2 **Rainy River** Can
86A2 **Raipur** India
87C1 **Rājahmundry** India
78C2 **Rajang** *R* Malay
84C3 **Rajanpur** Pak
87B3 **Rājapālaiyam** India
85C3 **Rājasthan** State, India
84D3 **Rājgarh** India
85D4 **Rājgarh** State, India
85C4 **Rājkot** India
86B2 **Rājmahāl Hills** India
86A2 **Raj Nāndgaon** India
85C4 **Rājpipla** India
86B2 **Rajshahi** Bang
85D4 **Rajur** India
111B2 **Rakaia** *R* NZ
78B4 **Rakata** *I* Indon
82C3 **Raka Zangbo** *R* China
59C3 **Rakhov** USSR
100B3 **Rakops** Botswana
58D2 **Rakov** USSR
11C3 **Raleigh** USA
7A5 **Ralny L** Can
94B2 **Rama** Israel
94B3 **Ramallah** Israel
87B3 **Rāmanāthapuram**
India
69G3 **Ramapo Deep**
Pacific O
94B2 **Ramat Gan** Israel
46A2 **Rambouillet** France
86B2 **Rāmgarh** Bihar, India
85C3 **Rāmgarh** Rajasthan,
India
90A3 **Rāmhormoz** Iran
94B3 **Ramla** Israel
91C5 **Ramlat Al Wahibah**
Region, Oman
21B3 **Ramona** USA
84D3 **Rāmpur** India
85D4 **Rāmpura** India
90B2 **Rāmsar** Iran
42B2 **Ramsey** Eng
16B2 **Ramsey** USA
43B4 **Ramsey I** Wales
43E4 **Ramsgate** Eng
94C2 **Ramtha** Jordan
71F4 **Ramu** *R* PNG
34A2 **Rancagua** Chile
86B2 **Rānchi** India
86A2 **Rānchi Plat** India
39G7 **Randers** Den
101G1 **Randfontein** S Africa
15D2 **Randolph** Vermont,
USA

111B3 Ranfurly NZ
86C2 Rangamati Bang
111B2 Rangiora NZ
110C1 Rangitaiki *R* NZ
111B2 Rangitate *R* NZ
110C1 Rangitikei *R* NZ
76B2 Rangoon Burma
86B1 Rangpur India
87B2 Rānibennur India
8A2 Ranier,Mt *Mt* USA
86B2 Rānīganj India
109C2 Rankins Springs Aust
6A3 Ranklin Inlet Can
85B4 Rann of Kachchh
    Flood Area India
77B4 Ranong Thai
70A3 Rantauparapat Indon
18C1 Rantoul USA
49D3 Rapallo Italy
34A2 Rapel *R* Chile
6D3 Raper,C Can
8C2 Rapid City USA
14A1 Rapid River USA
15C3 Rappahannock *R* USA
47C1 Rapperswil Switz
16B2 Raritan B USA
95C2 Ras Abu Shagara *C*
    Sudan
93D2 Ra's al 'Ayn Syria
91C5 Ra's al Hadd *C* Oman
91C4 Ras al Kaimah UAE
91C4 Ras-al-Kuh *C* Iran
81D4 Ra's al Madrakah *C*
    Oman
91A4 Ra's az Zawr *C*
    S Arabia
95C2 Rås Bânas *C* Egypt
94A3 Ras Burûn *C* Egypt
99D1 Ras Dashan *Mt* Eth
90A3 Ra's-e-Barkan *Pt* Iran
92A3 Râs el Kenâyis *Pt*
    Egypt
81D4 Ra's Fartak *C* Yemen
95C2 Râs Ghârib Egypt
99D1 Rashad Sudan
94B3 Rashâdîya Jordan
92B3 Rashîd Egypt
90A2 Rasht Iran
91C5 Ra's Jibish *C* Oman
99E1 Ras Khanzira *C*
    Somalia
84B3 Ras Koh *Mt* Pak
95C2 Râs Muhammad *C*
    Egypt
96A2 Ras Nouadhibou *C*
    Maur
69H2 Rasshua *I* USSR
61F3 Rasskazovo USSR
91A4 Ra's Tanāqib *C*
    S Arabia
91B4 Ra's Tannūrah
    S Arabia
57B3 Rastatt Germany
    Ras Uarc = Cabo Tres
    Forcas
99F1 Ras Xaafuun *C*
    Somalia
84C3 Ratangarh India
76B3 Rat Buri Thai
85D3 Rath India
56C2 Rathenow Germany
45B2 Rathkeale Irish Rep
45C1 Rathlin *I* N Ire
45B2 Ráth Luirc Irish Rep
85D4 Ratlām India
87A1 Ratnāgiri India
87C3 Ratnapura Sri Lanka
58C2 Ratno USSR
47D1 Rattenberg Austria
39H6 Rättvik Sweden
12H3 Ratz,Mt Can
34D3 Rauch Arg
110C1 Raukumara Range
    Mts NZ
35C2 Raul Soares Brazil
39J6 Rauma Fin
86A2 Raurkela India
90A3 Ravānsar Iran

90C3 Rāvar Iran
59C2 Rava Russkaya USSR
16C1 Ravena USA
52B2 Ravenna Italy
57B3 Ravensburg Germany
107D2 Ravenshoe Aust
84C2 Ravi *R* Pak
84C2 Rawalpindi Pak
58B2 Rawicz Pol
106B4 Rawlinna Aust
8C2 Rawlins USA
93D2 Rawndiz Iraq
29C4 Rawson Arg
78C3 Raya *Mt* Indon
87B2 Rāyadurg India
94C2 Rayak Leb
7E5 Ray,C Can
91C4 Rāyen Iran
22C2 Raymond California,
    USA
20B1 Raymond
    Washington, USA
109D2 Raymond Terrace
    Aust
12D1 Ray Mts USA
23B1 Rayon Mexico
90A2 Razan Iran
54C2 Razgrad Bulg
54C2 Razim *L* Rom
43D4 Reading Eng
16B2 Reading USA
4G3 Read Island Can
16C1 Readsboro USA
34B2 Real de Padre Arg
34C3 Realicó Arg
95B2 Rebiana *Well* Libya
95B2 Rebiana Sand Sea
    Libya
38L6 Reboly USSR
106B4 Recherche,Arch of the
    Is Aust
31E3 Recife Brazil
107F2 Récifs D'Entrecasteaux
    Nouvelle Calédonie
46D1 Recklinghausen
    Germany
30E4 Reconquista Arg
19B3 Red *R* USA
77C4 Redang *I* Malay
16B2 Red Bank New Jersey,
    USA
21A1 Red Bluff USA
42D2 Redcar Eng
13E2 Redcliff Can
109D1 Redcliffe Aust
108B2 Red Cliffs Aust
13E2 Red Deer Can
13E2 Red Deer *R* Can
20B2 Redding USA
10A2 Red L USA
7A4 Red Lake Can
22D3 Redlands USA
16A3 Red Lion USA
20B2 Redmond USA
18A1 Red Oak USA
48B2 Redon France
22C4 Redondo Beach USA
12D2 Redoubt V USA
73B5 Red River Delta
    Vietnam
80B3 Red Sea Africa/
    Arabian Pen
13E2 Redwater Can
22A2 Redwood City USA
14A2 Reed City USA
22C2 Reedley USA
20B2 Reedsport USA
111B2 Reefton NZ
93C2 Refahiye Turk
35D1 Regência Brazil
57C3 Regensburg Germany
96C2 Reggane Alg
53C3 Reggio di Calabria
    Italy
47D2 Reggio Nell'Emilia
    Italy
54B1 Reghin Rom
5H4 Regina Can

100A3 Rehoboth Namibia
15C3 Rehoboth Beach USA
94B3 Rehovot Israel
32D1 Reicito Ven
43D4 Reigate Eng
46C2 Reims France
5H4 Reindeer *R* Can
50B1 Reinosa Spain
16A3 Reisterstown USA
101G1 Reitz S Africa
4H3 Reliance Can
108A2 Remarkable,Mt Aust
78C4 Rembang Indon
91C4 Remeshk Iran
46D1 Remscheid Germany
18C2 Rend,L USA
56B2 Rendsburg Germany
15C1 Renfrew Can
78A3 Rengat Indon
34A2 Rengo Chile
59D3 Reni USSR
99D1 Renk Sudan
6H2 Renland *Pen*
    Greenland
108B2 Renmark Aust
107F2 Rennell *I* Solomon Is
48B2 Rennes France
21B2 Reno USA
47D2 Reno *R* Italy
15C2 Renovo USA
16C1 Rensselaer USA
20B1 Renton USA
70D4 Reo Indon
35B2 Reprêsa de Furnas
    Dam Brazil
35B1 Reprêsa Três Marias
    Dam Brazil
20C1 Republic USA
41B3 Republic of Ireland
    NW Europe
6B3 Repulse Bay Can
15C1 Réservoir Baskatong
    Res Can
7C5 Réservoire Cabonga
    Res Can
7C5 Réservoire Gouin *Res*
    Can
10D1 Réservoire
    Manicouagan *Res*
    Can
90B2 Reshteh-ye Alborz
    Mts Iran
72A2 Reshui China
30E4 Resistencia Arg
54B1 Resita Rom
6A2 Resolute Can
111A3 Resolution I NZ
6D3 Resolution Island Can
101H1 Ressano Garcia
    Mozam
34B2 Retamito Arg
46C2 Rethel France
55B3 Réthimnon Greece
89K10 Reunion *I* Indian O
51C1 Reus Spain
47C1 Reuss *R* Switz
47D1 Reutte Austria
61K3 Revda USSR
13D2 Revelstoke Can
24A3 Revillagigedo *Is*
    Mexico
12H3 Revillagigedo I USA
46C2 Revin France
94B3 Revivim Israel
86A2 Rewa India
84D3 Rewari India
8B2 Rexburg USA
38A2 Reykjavik Iceland
24C2 Reynosa Mexico
48B2 Rezé France
58D1 Rezekne USSR
61K2 Rezh USSR
47C1 Rhätikon *Mts* Austria/
    Switz
94B1 Rhazīr Republic, Leb
56B2 Rhein *R* W Europe
56B2 Rheine Germany
47B1 Rheinfielden Switz

49D2 Rheinland Pfalz
    Region, Germany
47C1 Rheinwaldhorn *Mt*
    Switz
    Rhine = Rhein
16C2 Rhinebeck USA
10B2 Rhinelander USA
47C2 Rho Italy
15D2 Rhode Island State,
    USA
16D2 Rhode Island Sd USA
    Rhodes = Ródhos
49C3 Rhône *R* France
43C3 Rhyl Wales
31D4 Riachão do Jacuipe
    Brazil
50A1 Ria de Arosa *B* Spain
50A1 Ria de Betanzos *B*
    Spain
50A1 Ria de Corcubion *B*
    Spain
50A1 Ria de Lage *B* Spain
50A1 Ria de Sta Marta *B*
    Spain
50A1 Ria de Vigo *B* Spain
84C2 Riāsi Pak
50A1 Ribadeo Spain
35A2 Ribas do Rio Pardo
    Brazil
101C2 Ribauè Mozam
42C3 Ribble *R* Eng
35B2 Ribeira Brazil
35B2 Ribeirão Prêto Brazil
32D6 Riberalta Bol
15C2 Rice L Can
10A2 Rice Lake USA
101H1 Richard's Bay S Africa
19A3 Richardson USA
12G1 Richardson Mts Can
8B3 Richfield USA
20C1 Richland USA
22A2 Richmond California,
    USA
101H1 Richmond Natal,
    S Africa
109D2 Richmond New South
    Wales, Aust
111B2 Richmond NZ
107D3 Richmond
    Queensland, Aust
10C3 Richmond Virginia,
    USA
111B2 Richmond Range *Mts*
    NZ
15C2 Rideau,L Can
17B1 Ridgeland USA
15C2 Ridgway USA
27D4 Riecito Ven
47D1 Rienza *R* Italy
57C2 Riesa Germany
29B6 Riesco *I* Chile
101F1 Riet *R* S Africa
52B2 Rieti Italy
50B2 Rif *Mts* Mor
58C1 Riga USSR
60B2 Riga,G of USSR
91C4 Rīgān Iran
20C1 Riggins USA
7E4 Rigolet Can
39J6 Riihimaki Fin
52B1 Rijeka Yugos
13E2 Rimbey Can
39H7 Rimbo Sweden
52B2 Rimini Italy
54C1 Rîmnicu Sârat Rom
54B1 Rîmnicu Vilcea Rom
10D2 Rimouski Can
23A1 Rincón de Romos
    Mexico
39F7 Ringkøbing Den
98A2 Rio Benito Eq Guinea
32D5 Rio Branco Brazil
24B1 Rio Bravo del Norte *R*
    Mexico/USA
32C1 Riochacha Colombia
35B2 Rio Claro Brazil
27L1 Rio Claro Trinidad
34C3 Rio Colorado Arg

34C2 **Rio Cuarto** Arg
31D4 **Rio de Jacuipe** Brazil
35C2 **Rio de Janeiro** Brazil
35C2 **Rio de Janeiro** State, Brazil
29E3 **Rio de la Plata** *Est* Arg/Urug
29C6 **Rio Gallegos** Arg
29C6 **Rio Grande** Arg
30F5 **Rio Grande** Brazil
26A4 **Rio Grande** Nic
25D3 **Rio Grande** *R* Nic
24B2 **Rio Grande** *R* Mexico/USA
23A1 **Rio Grande de Santiago** Mexico
31D3 **Rio Grande do Norte** State, Brazil
30F4 **Rio Grande do Sul** State, Brazil
103G6 **Rio Grande Rise** Atlantic O
26C4 **Riohacha** Colombia
49C2 **Riom** France
32B4 **Riombamba** Ecuador
30C2 **Rio Mulatos** Bol
29C3 **Rio Negro** State, Arg
30F4 **Rio Pardo** Brazil
34C2 **Rio Tercero** Arg
33E6 **Rio Theodore Roosevelt** *R* Brazil
29B6 **Rio Turbio** Arg
35A1 **Rio Verde** Brazil
23A1 **Rio Verde** Mexico
14B3 **Ripley** Ohio, USA
14B3 **Ripley** West Virginia, USA
42D2 **Ripon** Eng
22B2 **Ripon** USA
94B3 **Rishon le Zion** Israel
16A3 **Rising Sun** USA
39F7 **Risør** Nor
6E2 **Ritenberk** Greenland
22C2 **Ritter,Mt** USA
20C1 **Ritzville** USA
34B2 **Rivadavia** Arg
34A1 **Rivadavia** Chile
34C3 **Rivadavia Gonzalez Moreno** Arg
47D2 **Riva de Garda** Italy
34C3 **Rivera** Arg
29E2 **Rivera** Urug
22B2 **Riverbank** USA
97B4 **River Cess** Lib
16C2 **Riverhead** USA
108B3 **Riverina** Aust
111A3 **Riversdale** NZ
22D4 **Riverside** USA
13B2 **Rivers Inlet** Can
111A3 **Riverton** NZ
8C2 **Riverton** USA
17B2 **Riviera Beach** USA
7C4 **Rivière aux Feuilles** *R* Can
7D4 **Rivière de la Baleine** *R* Can
7D4 **Rivière du Petit Mècatina** *R* Can
46C2 **Rivigny-sur-Ornain** France
93D1 **Rize** Turk
72D2 **Rizhao** China
Rizhskiy Zaliv = Riga,G of
39F7 **Rjukan** Nor
6B2 **Roanes Pen** Can
49C2 **Roanne** France
17A1 **Roanoke** Alabama, USA
11C3 **Roanoke** Virginia, USA
11C3 **Roanoke** *R* USA
45B3 **Roaringwater B** Irish Rep
38J6 **Robertsforz** Sweden
19B2 **Robert S Kerr Res** USA
97A4 **Robertsport** Lib

7C5 **Roberval** Can
30H6 **Robinson Crusoe** *I* Chile
108B2 **Robinvale** Aust
13D2 **Robson,Mt** Can
24A3 **Roca Partida** *I* Mexico
103G5 **Rocas** *I* Atlantic O
31E2 **Rocas** *I* Brazil
29F2 **Rocha** Urug
42C3 **Rochdale** Eng
48B2 **Rochefort** France
5G3 **Rocher River** Can
108B3 **Rochester** Aust
7C5 **Rochester** Can
43E4 **Rochester** Eng
10A2 **Rochester** Minnesota, USA
15D2 **Rochester** New Hampshire, USA
10C2 **Rochester** New York, USA
10B2 **Rockford** USA
11B3 **Rock Hill** USA
10A2 **Rock Island** USA
108B3 **Rocklands Res** Aust
17B2 **Rockledge** USA
8C2 **Rock Springs** Wyoming, USA
110B2 **Rocks Pt** NZ
109C3 **Rock,The** Aust
16C2 **Rockville** Connecticut, USA
14A3 **Rockville** Indiana, USA
16A3 **Rockville** Maryland, USA
14B1 **Rocky Island L** Can
13E2 **Rocky Mountain House** Can
8B1 **Rocky Mts** Can/USA
12B2 **Rocky Pt** USA
56C2 **Rødbyhavn** Den
34B2 **Rodeo** Arg
49C3 **Rodez** France
55C3 **Ródhos** Greece
55C3 **Ródhos** *I* Greece
52C2 **Rodi Garganico** Italy
54B2 **Rodopi Planina** *Mts* Bulg
106A3 **Roebourne** Aust
46C1 **Roermond** Neth
46B1 **Roeselare** Belg
6B3 **Roes Welcome Sd** Can
18B2 **Rogers** USA
14B1 **Rogers City** USA
20B2 **Rogue** *R* USA
85B3 **Rohn** Pak
84D3 **Rohtak** India
58C1 **Roja** USSR
35A2 **Rolândia** Brazil
18B2 **Rolla** USA
109C1 **Roma** Aust
52B2 **Roma** Italy
47C2 **Romagnano** Italy
17C1 **Romain,C** USA
54C1 **Roman** Rom
103H5 **Romanche Gap** Atlantic O
71D4 **Romang** *I* Indon
60B4 **Romania** Republic, E Europe
17B2 **Romano,C** USA
49D2 **Romans sur Isère** France
79B3 **Romblon** Phil
Rome = Roma
17A1 **Rome** Georgia, USA
15C2 **Rome** New York, USA
49C2 **Romilly-sur-Seine** France
15C3 **Romney** USA
60D3 **Romny** USSR
56B1 **Rømø** *I* Den
47B1 **Romont** Switz
48C2 **Romoratin** France
50A2 **Ronda** Spain
33E6 **Rondônia** Brazil
24F6 **Rondônia** State, Brazil

30F2 **Rondonópolis** Brazil
73B4 **Rong'an** China
73B4 **Rongchang** China
72E2 **Rongcheng** China
73B4 **Rongjiang** China
73B4 **Rong Jiang** *R* China
76A1 **Rongklang Range** *Mts* Burma
39G7 **Rønne** Den
39H7 **Ronneby** Sweden
112B2 **Ronne Ice Shelf** Ant
46B1 **Ronse** Belg
46A1 **Ronthieu** Region, France
9C3 **Roof Butte** *Mt* USA
84D3 **Roorkee** India
46C1 **Roosendaal** Neth
112B6 **Roosevelt I** Ant
106C2 **Roper** *R* Aust
33E3 **Roraima** State, Brazil
33E2 **Roraime** *Mt* Ven
38G6 **Røros** Nor
47C1 **Rorschach** Switz
38G6 **Rørvik** Nor
27Q2 **Rosalie** Dominica
22C3 **Rosamond L** USA
34C2 **Rosario** Arg
31C2 **Rosário** Brazil
34D2 **Rosario del Tala** Arg
48B2 **Roscoff** France
45B2 **Roscommon** County, Irish Rep
41B3 **Roscommon** Irish Rep
45C2 **Roscrea** Irish Rep
27E3 **Roseau** Dominica
109C4 **Rosebery** Aust
20B2 **Roseburg** USA
19A4 **Rosenberg** USA
57C3 **Rosenheim** Germany
13F2 **Rosetown** Can
54B2 **Roşiori de Vede** Rom
39G7 **Roskilde** Den
60D3 **Roslavl'** USSR
61E2 **Roslyatino** USSR
111B2 **Ross** NZ
12H2 **Ross** *R* Can
40B3 **Rossan** *Pt* Irish Rep
53C3 **Rossano** Italy
19C3 **Ross Barnet Res** USA
15C1 **Rosseau L** *L* Can
107E2 **Rossel** *I* Solomon Is
112A **Ross Ice Shelf** Ant
60D2 **Rossiyskaya S.F.S.R.** Republic, USSR
20B1 **Ross L** USA
13D3 **Rossland** Can
45C2 **Rosslare** Irish Rep
111C2 **Ross,Mt** Maur
97A3 **Rosso** Maur
43C4 **Ross-on-Wye** Eng
60E4 **Rossosh** USSR
4E3 **Ross River** Can
112B6 **Ross S** Ant
91B4 **Rostāq** Iran
56C2 **Rostock** Germany
Rostov = Rostov-na-Donu
61E4 **Rostov-na-Donu** USSR
17B1 **Roswell** Georgia, USA
9C3 **Roswell** New Mexico, USA
71F2 **Rota** Pacific O
56B2 **Rotenburg** Niedersachsen, Germany
46E1 **Rothaar-Geb** *Region* Germany
112C3 **Rothera** *Base* Ant
42D3 **Rotherham** Eng
42B2 **Rothesay** Scot
71D5 **Roti** *I* Indon
108C2 **Roto** Aust
111B2 **Rotoiti,L** NZ
111B2 **Rotorua,L** NZ
110C1 **Rotorua** NZ
110C1 **Rotorua,L** NZ
56A2 **Rotterdam** Neth

46B1 **Roubaix** France
48C2 **Rouen** France
42E3 **Rough** *Oilfield* N Sea
Roulers = Roeselare
101E3 **Round I** Mauritius
109D2 **Round Mt** Aust
8C2 **Roundup** USA
44C2 **Rousay** *I* Scot
48C3 **Roussillon** Region, France
10C2 **Rouyn** Can
38K5 **Rovaniemi** Fin
47D2 **Rovereto** Italy
47D2 **Rovigo** Italy
52B1 **Rovinj** Yugos
59D2 **Rovno** USSR
90A2 **Row'ān** Iran
109C1 **Rowena** Aust
6C3 **Rowley I** Can
106A2 **Rowley Shoals** Aust
79A3 **Roxas** Palawan, Phil
79B3 **Roxas** Panay, Phil
111A3 **Roxburgh** NZ
45C2 **Royal Canal** Irish Rep
43D3 **Royal Leamington Spa** Eng
14B2 **Royal Oak** USA
43E4 **Royal Tunbridge Wells** Eng
48B2 **Royan** France
46B2 **Roye** France
43D3 **Royston** Eng
59C3 **Rožňava** Czech
46B2 **Rozoy** France
61F3 **Rtishchevo** USSR
99D3 **Ruaha Nat Pk** Tanz
110C1 **Ruahine Range** *Mts* NZ
110C1 **Ruapehu,Mt** NZ
65D3 **Rub al Khālī** *Desert* S Arabia
44A3 **Rubha Hunish** Scot
35A2 **Rubinéia** Brazil
65K4 **Rubtsoysk** USSR
12C2 **Ruby** USA
91C4 **Rudan** Iran
90A2 **Rūdbār** Iran
69F2 **Rudnaya Pristan'** USSR
54B2 **Rudoka Planina** *Mt* Yugos
72E3 **Rudong** China
14B1 **Rudyard** USA
46A1 **Rue** France
48C2 **Ruffec** France
99D3 **Rufiji** *R* Tanz
34C2 **Rufino** Arg
97A3 **Rufisque** Sen
100B2 **Rufunsa** Zambia
43D3 **Rugby** Eng
39G8 **Rügen** *I* Germany
56B2 **Ruhr** *R* Germany
73D4 **Ruijin** China
54B2 **Rujen** *Mt* Bulg/Yugos
99D3 **Rukwa** *L* Tanz
44A3 **Rum** *I* Scot
54A1 **Ruma** Yugos
91A4 **Rumāh** S Arabia
98C2 **Rumbek** Sudan
26C2 **Rum Cay** *I* Caribbean S
47A2 **Rumilly** France
106C2 **Rum Jungle** Aust
101C2 **Rumphi** Malawi
111B2 **Runanga** NZ
110C1 **Runaway,C** NZ
100A2 **Rundu** Namibia
99D3 **Rungwa** Tanz
99D3 **Rungwa** *R* Tanz
99D3 **Rungwe** *Mt* Tanz
82C2 **Ruoqiang** China
68C2 **Ruo Shui** *R* China
54C1 **Rupea** Rom
7C4 **Rupert** *R* Can
46D1 **Rur** *R* Germany
32D6 **Rurrenabaque** Bol
101C2 **Rusape** Zim
54C2 **Ruse** Bulg

18B1 **Rushville** Illinois, USA
108B3 **Rushworth** Aust
19A3 **Rusk** USA
17B2 **Ruskin** USA
110B1 **Russell** NZ
18B2 **Russellville** Arkansas, USA
18C2 **Russellville** Kentucky, USA
21A2 **Russian** *R* USA
60B3 **Russian Socialist Federated Soviet Rep** USSR
93E1 **Rustavi** USSR
101G1 **Rustenburg** S Africa
19B3 **Ruston** USA
99C3 **Rutana** Burundi
46E1 **Rüthen** Germany
23B2 **Rutla** Mexico
15D2 **Rutland** USA
84D2 **Rutog** China
Ruvu = Pangani
101D2 **Ruvuma** *R* Tanz/Mozam
99D2 **Ruwenzori Range** *Mts* Uganda/Zaïre
101C2 **Ruya** *R* Zim
59B3 **Ružomberok** Czech
99C3 **Rwanda** Republic, Africa
60E3 **Ryazan'** USSR
61F3 **Ryazhsk** USSR
60E2 **Rybinsk** USSR
60E2 **Rybinskoye Vodokhranilishche** *Res* USSR
13D1 **Rycroft** Can
43D4 **Ryde** Eng
43E4 **Rye** Eng
20C2 **Rye Patch Res** USA
60D3 **Ryl'sk** USSR
61G4 **Ryn Peskt** *Desert* USSR
74D3 **Ryōtsu** Japan
59D3 **Ryskany** USSR
69E4 **Ryūkyū Retto** *Arch* Japan
59C2 **Rzeszów** Pol
60D2 **Rzhev** USSR

S

91B3 **Sa'ādatābād** Iran
56C2 **Saale** *R* Germany
47B1 **Saanen** Switz
46D2 **Saar** *R* Germany
46D2 **Saarbrücken** Germany
46D2 **Saarburg** Germany
39J7 **Saaremaa** *I* USSR
46D2 **Saarland** State, Germany
46D2 **Saarlouis** Germany
34C3 **Saavedra** Arg
54A2 **Šabac** Yugos
51C1 **Sabadell** Spain
75B1 **Sabae** Japan
78D1 **Sabah** State, Malay
26C4 **Sabanalarga** Colombia
70A3 **Sabang** Indon
87C1 **Sabari** *R* India
94B2 **Sabastiya** Israel
30C2 **Sabaya** Bol
93C3 **Sab'Bi'ār** Syria
94C2 **Sabhā** Jordan
95A2 **Sabhā** Libya
101C3 **Sabi** *R* Zim
24B2 **Sabinas** Mexico
24B2 **Sabinas Hidalgo** Mexico
19A3 **Sabine** *R* USA
19B4 **Sabine L** USA
91B5 **Sabkhat Maṭṭi** *Salt Marsh* UAE
94A3 **Sabkhet El Bardawîl** *Lg* Egypt
79B3 **Sablayan** Phil

7D5 **Sable,C** Can
17B2 **Sable,C** USA
7D5 **Sable I** Can
90C2 **Sabzevār** Iran
20C1 **Sacajawea Peak** USA
10A1 **Sachigo** *R* Can
57C2 **Sachsen** State, Germany
56C2 **Sachsen-Anhalt** State, Germany
4F2 **Sachs Harbour** Can
47B1 **Säckingen** Germany
22B1 **Sacramento** USA
22B1 **Sacramento** *R* USA
21A1 **Sacramento** *V* USA
9C3 **Sacramento Mts** USA
81C4 **Sa'dah** Yemen
54B2 **Sadanski** Bulg
82D3 **Sadiya** India
50A2 **Sado** *R* Port
74D3 **Sado-shima** *I* Japan
85C3 **Sādri** India
Safad = Zefat
84A2 **Safed Koh** *Mts* Afghan
39G7 **Saffle** Sweden
92C3 **Safi** Jordan
96B1 **Safi** Mor
90D3 **Safidabeh** Iran
94C1 **Ṣāfītā** Syria
93E3 **Safwān** Iraq
75A2 **Saga** Japan
76B1 **Sagaing** Burma
75B2 **Sagami-nada** *B* Japan
85D4 **Sāgar** India
16C2 **Sag Harbor** USA
14B2 **Saginaw** USA
14B2 **Saginaw B** USA
26B2 **Sagua de Tánamo** Cuba
26B2 **Sagua la Grande** Cuba
7C5 **Saguenay** *R* Can
51B2 **Sagunto** Spain
94C3 **Sahāb** Jordan
50A1 **Sahagún** Spain
96C2 **Sahara** *Desert* N Africa
84D3 **Saharanpur** India
84C2 **Sahiwal** Pak
93D3 **Ṣahrā al Hijārah** *Desert Region* Iraq
23A1 **Sahuayo** Mexico
107D1 **Saibai I** Aust
96C1 **Saïda** Alg
94B2 **Säida** Leb
91C4 **Sa'īdabad** Iran
51B2 **Saidia** Mor
86B1 **Saidpur** India
84C2 **Saidu** Pak
75A1 **Saigō** Japan
76D3 **Saigon** Viet
86C2 **Saiha** India
68D2 **Saihan Tal** China
75A2 **Saijo** Japan
74C4 **Saiki** Japan
42C2 **St Abb's Head** *Pt* Scot
43D4 **St Albans** Eng
15D2 **St Albans** Vermont, USA
14B3 **St Albans** West Virginia, USA
43C4 **St Albans Head** *C* Eng
13E2 **St Albert** Can
46B1 **St Amand-les-Eaux** France
48C2 **St Amand-Mont Rond** France
101D2 **St André** *C* Madag
17A2 **St Andrew B** USA
44C3 **St Andrews** Scot
17B1 **St Andrew Sd** USA
27H1 **St Ann's Bay** Jamaica
7E4 **St Anthony** Can
108B3 **St Arnaud** Aust
17B2 **St Augustine** USA
43B4 **St Austell** Eng
46D2 **St-Avold** France
42C2 **St Bees Head** *Pt* Eng

47B2 **St-Bonnet** France
43B4 **St Brides B** Wales
48B2 **St-Brieuc** France
15C2 **St Catharines** Can
27M2 **St Catherine,Mt** Grenada
17B1 **St Catherines I** USA
43D4 **St Catherines Pt** Eng
49C2 **St Chamond** France
18B2 **St Charles** MIssouri, USA
14B2 **St Clair** USA
14B2 **St Clair,L** Can/USA
14B2 **St Clair Shores** USA
49D2 **St Claud** France
10A2 **St Cloud** USA
47B1 **Ste Croix** Switz
27E3 **St Croix** *I* Caribbean S
43B4 **St Davids Head** *Pt* Wales
46B2 **St Denis** France
101E3 **St Denis** Réunion
46C2 **St Dizier** France
12F2 **St Elias,Mt** USA
12G2 **St Elias Mts** Can
48B2 **Saintes** France
49C2 **St Étienne** France
18B2 **St Francis** *R* USA
100B4 **St Francis,C** S Africa
47C1 **St Gallen** Switz
48C3 **St-Gaudens** France
109C1 **St George** Aust
17B1 **St George** South Carolina, USA
9B3 **St George** Utah, USA
17B2 **St George I** Florida, USA
20B2 **St George,Pt** USA
15D1 **St-Georges** Can
27E4 **St George's** Grenada
45C3 **St George's Chan** Irish Rep/Wales
46A2 **St Germain-en-Laye** France
47B2 **St-Gervais** France
47C1 **St Gotthard** *P* Switz
43B4 **St Govans Head** *Pt* Wales
22A1 **St Helena** USA
103H5 **St Helena** *I* Atlantic O
100A4 **St Helena B** S Africa
17B1 **St Helena Sd** USA
109C4 **St Helens** Aust
42C3 **St Helens** Eng
20B1 **St Helens** USA
20B1 **St Helens,Mt** USA
48B2 **St Helier** Jersey
47B1 **St Hippolyte** France
46C1 **St-Hubert** Belg
7C5 **St-Hyacinthe** Can
14B1 **St Ignace** USA
43B4 **St Ives** Eng
18B2 **St James** Missouri, USA
5E4 **St James,C** Can
15D1 **St Jean** Can
48B2 **St Jean-d'Angely** France
47B2 **St-Jean-de-Maurienne** France
10C2 **St Jean,L** Can
15D1 **St-Jérôme** Can
20C1 **St Joe** *R* USA
7D5 **Saint John** Can
7E5 **St John's** Can
14B2 **St Johns** Michigan, USA
17B2 **St Johns** *R* USA
15D2 **St Johnsbury** USA
15D1 **St-Joseph** Can
19B3 **St Joseph** Louisiana, USA
14A2 **St Joseph** Michigan, USA
18B2 **St Joseph** Missouri, USA
27L1 **St Joseph** Trinidad

14B2 **St Joseph** *R* USA
14B1 **St Joseph I** Can
7A4 **St Joseph,L** Can
47B1 **St Julien** France
48C2 **St-Junien** France
46B2 **St-Just-en-Chaussée** France
4B2 **St Kilda** *I* Scot
27E3 **St Kitts** *I* Caribbean S
47A1 **St-Laurent** France
7D5 **St Lawrence** *R* Can
7D5 **Saint Lawrence,G of** Can
4A3 **St Lawrence I** USA
15C2 **St Lawrence Seaway** Can/USA
48B2 **St Lô** France
97A3 **St Louis** Sen
11A3 **St Louis** USA
27E4 **St Lucia** *I* Caribbean S
101H1 **St Lucia,L** S Africa
44E1 **St Magnus** *B* Scot
48B2 **St Malo** France
101D3 **Ste Marie** *C* Madag
20C1 **St Maries** USA
27E3 **St Martin** *I* Caribbean S
108A2 **St Mary Peak** *Mt* Aust
109C4 **St Marys** Aust
15C2 **St Marys** USA
17B1 **St Marys** *R* USA
46C2 **Ste-Menehould** France
12B2 **St Michael** USA
16A3 **St Michaels** USA
47B2 **St-Michel** France
46C2 **St-Mihiel** France
47C1 **St Moritz** Switz
48B2 **St-Nazaire** France
46C1 **St-Niklaas** Belg
46B1 **St-Omer** France
13E2 **St Paul** Can
10A2 **St Paul** Minnesota, USA
97A4 **St Paul** *R* Lib
17B2 **St Petersburg** USA
7E5 **St Pierre** Can
15D1 **St Pierre,L** Can
46B1 **St-Pol-Sur-Ternoise** France
59B3 **St Pölten** Austria
46B2 **St Quentin** France
49D3 **St Raphaël** France
101D2 **St Sébastien** *C* Madag
17B1 **St Simons I** USA
17B1 **St Stephen** USA
14B2 **St Thomas** Can
49D3 **St-Tropez** France
46C1 **St Truiden** Belg
46A1 **St-Valéry-sur-Somme** France
101D3 **St Vincent** *C* Madag
27E4 **St Vincent** *I* Caribbean S
108A2 **St Vincent,G** Aust
46D1 **St-Vith** Germany
46D2 **St Wendel** Germany
71F2 **Saipan** *I* Pacific O
84B2 **Saiydabad** Afghan
30C2 **Sajama** *Mt* Bol
74D4 **Sakai** Japan
75A2 **Sakaidi** Japan
75A1 **Sakaiminato** Japan
93D4 **Sakākah** S Arabia
10C1 **Sakami,L** Can
100B2 **Sakania** Zaïre
101D3 **Sakaraha** Madag
60D5 **Sakarya** *R* Turk
58C1 **Sakasleja** USSR
74D3 **Sakata** Japan
97C4 **Saketél** Benin
69G1 **Sakhalin** *I* USSR
69E4 **Sakishima gunto** *Is* Japan
97A4 **Sal** *I* Cape Verde
61F4 **Sal** *R* USSR

39H7 **Sala** Sweden
34D3 **Saladillo** Arg
34C2 **Saladillo** R Arg
34D3 **Salado** R
   Buenos Aires, Arg
34B3 **Salado** R Mendoza/
   San Luis, Arg
30D4 **Salado** R Sante Fe,
   Arg
97B4 **Salaga** Ghana
76C3 **Sala Hintoun** Camb
98B1 **Salal** Chad
81D4 **Salālah** Oman
34A2 **Salamanca** Chile
23A1 **Salamanca** Mexico
50A1 **Salamanca** Spain
15C2 **Salamanca** USA
98B2 **Salamat** R Chad
71F4 **Salamaua** PNG
15C2 **Salamonica** USA
78D1 **Salang** Indon
38H5 **Salangen** Nor
30C3 **Salar de Arizaro** Arg
30C3 **Salar de Atacama**
   Salt Pan Chile
30C2 **Salar de Coipasa**
   Salt Pan Bol
30C3 **Salar de Uyuni**
   Salt Pan Bol
47C2 **Salasomaggiore** Italy
61J3 **Salavat** USSR
70D4 **Salayar** Indon
105L5 **Sala y Gomez** I
   Pacific O
34C3 **Salazar** Arg
48C2 **Salbris** France
12E2 **Salcha** R USA
100A4 **Saldanha** S Africa
94C2 **Saldhad** Syria
34C3 **Saldungaray** Arg
58C1 **Saldus** USSR
109C3 **Sale** Aust
18C2 **Salem** Illinois, USA
87B2 **Salem** India
16D1 **Salem** Massachusetts,
   USA
16B3 **Salem** New Jersey,
   USA
20B2 **Salem** Oregon, USA
78C4 **Salembu Besar** I
   Indon
39G6 **Salen** Sweden
53B2 **Salerno** Italy
42C3 **Salford** Eng
54A1 **Salgót** Hung
59B3 **Salgótarjan** Hung
31D3 **Salgueiro** Brazil
55C3 **Salihli** Turk
101C2 **Salima** Malawi
39K6 **Salimaa** L Fin
18A2 **Salina** Kansas, USA
53B3 **Salina** I Italy
23B2 **Salina Cruz** Mexico
30C3 **Salina de Arizoto** Arg
34B3 **Salina Grande**
   Salt Pan Arg
34B2 **Salina La Antigua**
   Salt Pan Arg
35C1 **Salinas** Brazil
22B2 **Salinas** USA
22B2 **Salinas** R USA
34B3 **Salinas de Llancaneb**
   Salt Pan Arg
34B2 **Salinas Grandes** Salt
   Pan Arg
19B3 **Saline** R Arkansas,
   USA
27M2 **Salines,Pt** Grenada
31B2 **Salinópolis** Brazil
47A1 **Salins** France
   Salisbury = Harare
43D4 **Salisbury** Eng
15C3 **Salisbury** Maryland,
   USA
6C3 **Salisbury I** Can
43D4 **Salisbury Plain** Eng
38K5 **Salla** Fin
47B2 **Sallanches** France

18B2 **Sallisaw** USA
6C3 **Salluit** Can
86A1 **Sallyana** Nepal
93D2 **Salmas** Iran
38L6 **Salmi** USSR
20C1 **Salmo** Can
8B2 **Salmon** USA
13D2 **Salmon Arm** Can
8B2 **Salmon River Mts**
   USA
39J6 **Salo** Fin
47D2 **Salò** Italy
49D3 **Salon-de-Provence**
   France
   Salonica =
   Thessaloníki
54B1 **Salonta** Rom
38K6 **Salpausselka** Region,
   Fin
34B2 **Salsacate** Arg
61F4 **Sal'sk** USSR
94B2 **Salt** Jordan
30C3 **Salta** Arg
30C3 **Salta** State, Arg
24B2 **Saltillo** Mexico
8B2 **Salt Lake City** USA
34C2 **Salto** Arg
34D2 **Salto** Urug
32C3 **Salto Angostura**
   Waterfall Colombia
35D1 **Salto da Divisa** Brazil
33E2 **Salto del Angel**
   Waterfall Ven
30E3 **Salto del Guaira**
   Waterfall Brazil
32C4 **Salto Grande**
   Waterfall Colombia
84C2 **Salt Range** Mts Pak
27H2 **Salt River** Jamaica
17B1 **Saluda** USA
47B2 **Saluzzo** Italy
31D4 **Salvador** Brazil
19B4 **Salvador,L** USA
23A1 **Salvatierra** Mexico
91B5 **Salwah** Qatar
76B1 **Salween** R Burma
93E2 **Sal'yany** USSR
57C3 **Salzburg** Austria
56C2 **Salzgitter** Germany
56C2 **Salzwedel** Germany
68B1 **Samagaltay** USSR
79B4 **Samales Group** Is Phil
27D3 **Samaná** Dom Rep
92C2 **Samandaği** Turk
84B1 **Samangan** Afghan
79C3 **Samar** I Phil
107E2 **Samarai** PNG
78D3 **Samarinda** Indon
80E2 **Samarkand** USSR
93D3 **Sāmarrā'** Iraq
79B3 **Samar S** Phil
86A2 **Sambalpur** India
78B2 **Sambas** Indon
101E2 **Sambava** Madag
84D3 **Sambhal** India
78D3 **Samboja** Indon
59C3 **Sambor** USSR
46B1 **Sambre** R France
74B3 **Samch'ŏk** S Korea
99D3 **Same** Tanz
47C1 **Samedan** Switz
46A1 **Samer** France
100B2 **Samfya** Zambia
76B1 **Samka** Burma
76C1 **Sam Neua** Laos
55C3 **Sámos** I Greece
55C2 **Samothráki** I Greece
34C2 **Sampacho** Arg
78D3 **Sampaga** Indon
78C3 **Sampit** Indon
78C3 **Sampit** R Indon
19B3 **Sam Rayburn Res**
   USA
76C3 **Samrong** Camb
56C1 **Samsø** I Den
92C1 **Samsun** Turk
97B3 **San** Mali
76D3 **San** R Camb

59C2 **San** R Pol
81C4 **Şan'ā'** Yemen
98B2 **Sanaga** R Cam
29C2 **San Agustín** Arg
79C4 **San Agustin,C** Phil
90A2 **Sanandaj** Iran
22B1 **San Andreas** USA
25C3 **San Andrés Tuxtla**
   Mexico
9C3 **San Angelo** USA
53A3 **San Antioco** Sardegna
53A3 **San Antioco** I Medit S
34A2 **San Antonio** Chile
9C3 **San Antonio** New
   Mexico, USA
79B2 **San Antonio** Phil
9D4 **San Antonio** R Texas,
   USA
51C2 **San Antonio Abad**
   Spain
25D2 **San Antonio,C** Cuba
26A2 **San Antonio de los**
   Banos Cuba
22D3 **San Antonio,Mt** USA
29C4 **San Antonio Oeste**
   Arg
34D3 **San Augustin** Arg
34B2 **San Augustin de Valle**
   Féril Arg
85D4 **Sanawad** India
23A1 **San Bartolo** Mexico
24A3 **San Benedicto** I
   Mexico
22B2 **San Benito** R USA
22B2 **San Benito Mt** USA
22D3 **San Bernardino** USA
34A2 **San Bernardo** Chile
17A2 **San Blas,C** USA
34A3 **San Carlos** Chile
32A1 **San Carlos** Nic
79B2 **San Carlos** Phil
29B4 **San Carlos de**
   Bariloche Arg
69E4 **San-chung** Taiwan
61G2 **Sanchursk** USSR
34A3 **San Clemente** Chile
22D4 **San Clemente** USA
21B3 **San Clemente I** USA
34C2 **San Cristóbal** Arg
25C3 **San Cristóbal** Mexico
32C2 **San Cristóbal** Ven
32J7 **San Cristóbal** I
   Ecuador
107F2 **San Cristobal** I
   Solomon Is
25E2 **Sancti Spíritus** Cuba
78C3 **Sandai** Indon
70C3 **Sandakan** Malay
44C2 **Sanday** I Scot
9C3 **Sanderson** USA
13F1 **Sandfly L** Can
21B3 **San Diego** USA
92B2 **Sandikli** Turk
86A1 **Sandīla** India
39F7 **Sandnes** Nor
38G5 **Sandnessjøen** Nor
98C3 **Sandoa** Zaïre
59C2 **Sandomierz** Pol
38D3 **Sandoy** Føroyar
20C1 **Sandpoint** USA
49D2 **Sandrio** Italy
18A2 **Sand Springs** USA
106A3 **Sandstone** Aust
73C4 **Sandu** China
14B2 **Sandusky** USA
39H6 **Sandviken** Sweden
7A4 **Sandy L** Can
34C2 **San Elcano** Arg
9B3 **San Felipe** Baja Cal,
   Mexico
34A2 **San Felipe** Chile
23A1 **San Felipe**
   Guanajuato, Mexico
27D4 **San Felipe** Ven
51C1 **San Feliu de Guixols**
   Spain
28A5 **San Felix** I Pacific O
34A2 **San Fernando** Chile

79B2 **San Fernando** Phil
79B2 **San Fernando** Phil
50A2 **San Fernando** Spain
27E4 **San Fernando**
   Trinidad
22C3 **San Fernando** USA
32D2 **San Fernando** Ven
17B2 **Sanford** Florida, USA
12F2 **Sanford,Mt** USA
34C2 **San Francisco** Arg
27C3 **San Francisco** Dom
   Rep
22A2 **San Francisco** USA
22A2 **San Francisco B** USA
24B2 **San Francisco del Oro**
   Mexico
23A1 **San Francisco del**
   Rincon Mexico
22D3 **San Gabriel Mts** USA
85C5 **Sangamner** India
18C2 **Sangamon** R USA
71F2 **Sangan** I Pacific O
87B1 **Sangāreddi** India
78D4 **Sangeang** I Indon
22C2 **Sanger** USA
72C2 **Sanggan He** R China
78C2 **Sanggau** Indon
98B2 **Sangha** R Congo
85B3 **Sanghar** Pak
76B3 **Sangkhla Buri** Thai
78D2 **Sangkulirang** Indon
87A1 **Sāngli** India
98B2 **Sangmélima** Cam
9B3 **San Gorgonio Mt** USA
9C3 **Sangre de Cristo** Mts
   USA
34C2 **San Gregorio** Arg
22A2 **San Gregorio** USA
84D2 **Sangrūr** India
30E4 **San Ignacio** Arg
79B3 **San Isidro** Phil
32B2 **San Jacinto** Colombia
21B3 **San Jacinto Peak** Mt
   USA
34A3 **San Javier** Chile
34D2 **San Javier** Sante Fe,
   Arg
74D3 **Sanjō** I Japan
31C6 **São João del Rei**
   Brazil
22B2 **San Joaquin** R USA
22B2 **San Joaquin Valley**
   USA
32A1 **San José** Costa Rica
25C3 **San José** Guatemala
79B2 **San Jose** Luzon, Phil
79B3 **San Jose** Mindoro,
   Phil
22B2 **San Jose** USA
9B4 **San José** I Mexico
30D2 **San José de Chiquitos**
   Bol
34D2 **San José de Feliciano**
   Arg
34B2 **San José de Jachal**
   Arg
34C2 **San José de la**
   Dormida Arg
31B6 **San José do Rio Prêto**
   Brazil
24B2 **San José del Cabo**
   Mexico
34B2 **San Juan** Arg
27D3 **San Juan** Puerto Rico
34B2 **San Juan** State, Arg
27L1 **San Juan** Trinidad
32D2 **San Juan** Ven
26B2 **San Juan** Mt Cuba
8C3 **San Juan** Mts USA
34B2 **San Juan** R Arg
23B2 **San Juan** R Mexico
25D3 **San Juan** R Nic/
   Costa Rica
23B2 **San Juan Bautista**
   Mexico
30E4 **San Juan Bautista** Par
22B2 **San Juan Bautista**
   USA

25D3 San Juan del Norte Nic
27D4 San Juan de los Cayos Ven
23A1 San Juan de loz Lagoz Mexico
23A1 San Juan del Rio Mexico
25D3 San Juan del Sur Nic
20B1 San Juan Is USA
23B2 San Juan Tepozcolula Mexico
29C5 San Julián Arg
34C2 San Justo Arg
98C3 Sankuru R Zaïre
22A2 San Leandro USA
32B3 San Lorenzo Ecuador
34C2 San Lorenzo Arg
22B2 San Lucas USA
34B2 San Luis Arg
34B2 San Luis State, Arg
23A1 San Luis de la Paz Mexico
21A2 San Luis Obispo USA
23A1 San Luis Potosi Mexico
22B2 San Luis Res USA
53A3 Sanluri Sardegna
33D2 San Maigualida Mts Ven
34D3 San Manuel Arg
34A2 San Marcos Chile
23B2 San Marcos Mexico
52B2 San Marino Republic, Europe
34B2 San Martin Mendoza, Arg
112C3 San Martin Base Ant
47D1 San Martino di Castroza Italy
23B2 San Martin Tuxmelucan Mexico
22A2 San Mateo USA
30E2 San Matias Bol
72C3 Sanmenxia China
25D3 San Miguel El Salvador
22B3 San Miguel I USA
23A1 San Miguel del Allende Mexico
34D3 San Miguel del Monte Arg
30C4 San Miguel de Tucumán Arg
73D4 Sanming China
9B3 San Nicolas I USA
34C2 San Nicolás de los Arroyos Arg
101G1 Sannieshof S Africa
97B4 Sanniquellie Lib
59C3 Sanok Pol
26B5 San Onofore Colombia
22D4 San Onofre USA
79B3 San Pablo Phil
22A1 San Pablo B USA
34D2 San Pedro Buenos Aires, Arg
97B4 San Pédro Ivory Coast
30D3 San Pedro Jujuy, Arg
30E3 San Pedro Par
22C4 San Pedro Chan USA
9C4 San Pedro de los Colonias Mexico
25D3 San Pedro Sula Honduras
53A3 San Pietro I Medit S
24A1 San Quintin Mexico
34B2 San Rafael Arg
22A2 San Rafael USA
22C3 San Rafael Mts USA
49D3 San Remo Italy
34D2 San Salvador Arg
26C2 San Salvador I Caribbean S
32J7 San Salvador I Ecuador

30C3 San Salvador de Jujuy Arg
51B1 San Sebastian Spain
53C2 San Severo Italy
30C2 Santa Ana Bol
25C3 Santa Ana Guatemala
22D4 Santa Ana USA
22D4 Santa Ana Mts USA
34A3 Santa Bárbara Chile
24B2 Santa Barbara Mexico
22C3 Santa Barbara USA
22C4 Santa Barbara I USA
22B3 Santa Barbara Chan USA
22C3 Santa Barbara Res USA
22C4 Santa Catalina I USA
22C4 Santa Catalina,G of USA
30F4 Santa Catarina State, Brazil
26B2 Santa Clara Cuba
22B2 Santa Clara USA
22C3 Santa Clara R USA
29C6 Santa Cruz Arg
30D2 Santa Cruz Bol
34A2 Santa Cruz Chile
79B3 Santa Cruz Phil
29B5 Santa Cruz State, Arg
22A2 Santa Cruz USA
22C4 Santa Cruz I USA
35D1 Santa Cruz Cabrália Brazil
22C3 Santa Cruz Chan USA
96A2 Santa Cruz de la Palma Canary Is
26B2 Santa Cruz del Sur Cuba
96A2 Santa Cruz de Tenerife Canary Is
100B2 Santa Cruz do Cuando Angola
35B2 Santa Cruz do Rio Pardo Brazil
22A2 Santa Cruz Mts USA
34D2 Santa Elena Arg
33E3 Santa Elena Ven
34C2 Santa Fe Arg
34C2 Santa Fe State, Arg
9C3 Santa Fe USA
35A1 Santa Helena de Goiás Brazil
73B3 Santai China
29B6 Santa Inés I Chile
34B3 Santa Isabel La Pampa, Arg
34C2 Santa Isabel Sante Fe, Arg
107E1 Santa Isabel I Solomon Is
21A2 Santa Lucia Ra USA
21A2 Santa Lucia Range Mts USA
97A4 Santa Luzia I Cape Verde
9B4 Santa Margarita I Mexico
22D4 Santa Margarita R USA
30F4 Santa Maria Brazil
26C4 Santa Maria Colombia
21A3 Santa Maria USA
96A1 Santa Maria I Açores
23B1 Santa Maria R Queretaro, Mexico
23A1 Santa Maria del Rio Mexico
32C1 Santa Marta Colombia
22C3 Santa Monica USA
22C4 Santa Monica B USA
29E2 Santana do Livramento Brazil
32B3 Santander Colombia
50B1 Santander Spain
51C2 Santañy Spain
22C3 Santa Paula USA
31C2 Santa Quitéria Brazil
33G4 Santarem Brazil

50A2 Santarém Port
22A1 Santa Rosa California, USA
25D3 Santa Rosa Honduras
34C3 Santa Rosa La Pampa, Arg
34B2 Santa Rosa Mendoza, Arg
34B2 Santa Rosa San Luis, Arg
22B3 Santa Rosa I USA
24A2 Santa Rosalía Mexico
20C2 Santa Rosa Range Mts
31D3 Santa Talhada Brazil
35C1 Santa Teresa Brazil
53A2 Santa Teresa di Gallura Sardegna
22B3 Santa Ynez R USA
22B3 Santa Ynez Mts USA
17C1 Santee R USA
47C2 Santhia Italy
34A2 Santiago Chile
27C3 Santiago Dom Rep
32A2 Santiago Panama
79B2 Santiago Phil
32B4 Santiago R Peru
50A1 Santiago de Compostela Spain
26B2 Santiago de Cuba Cuba
30D4 Santiago del Estero Arg
30D4 Santiago del Estero State, Arg
22D4 Santiago Peak Mt USA
31C5 Santo State, Brazil
35A2 Santo Anastatácio Brazil
30F4 Santo Angelo Brazil
97A4 Santo Antão I Cape Verde
35A2 Santo Antonio da Platina Brazil
27D3 Santo Domingo Dom Rep
35B2 Santos Brazil
35C2 Santos Dumont Brazil
30E4 Santo Tomé Arg
29B5 San Valentin Mt Chile
34A2 San Vicente Chile
98B3 Sanza Pomba Angola
30E4 São Borja Brazil
35B2 São Carlos Brazil
33G5 São Félix Mato Grosso, Brazil
35C2 São Fidélis Brazil
35C1 São Francisco Brazil
31D3 São Francisco R Brazil
30G4 São Francisco do Sul Brazil
35B1 São Gotardo Brazil
99D3 Sao Hill Tanz
35C2 São João da Barra Brazil
35B2 São João da Boa Vista Brazil
35C1 São João da Ponte Brazil
35C2 São João del Rei Brazil
35B2 São Joaquim da Barra Brazil
96A1 São Jorge I Açores
35B2 São José do Rio Prêto Brazil
35B2 São José dos Campos Brazil
31C2 São Luis Brazil
35B1 São Marcos R Brazil
35C1 São Maria do Suaçui Brazil
35D1 São Mateus Brazil
35C1 São Mateus R Brazil
96A1 São Miguel I Açores
49C2 Saône R France

97A4 São Nicolau I Cape Verde
35B2 São Paulo Brazil
35A2 São Paulo State, Brazil
31C3 São Raimundo Nonato Brazil
35B1 São Romão Brazil
35B2 São Sebastia do Paraiso Brazil
35A1 São Simão Goias, Brazil
35B2 São Simão Sao Paulo, Brazil
97A4 São Tiago I Cape Verde
97C4 São Tomé I W Africa
97C4 São Tomé and Principe Republic, W Africa
96B2 Saoura Watercourse Alg
35B2 São Vicente Brazil
97A4 São Vincente I Cape Verde
55C2 Sápai Greece
78D4 Sape Indon
97C4 Sapele Nig
74E2 Sapporo Japan
53C2 Sapri Italy
18A2 Sapulpa USA
90A2 Saqqez Iran
10C2 Saquenay R Can
90A2 Saräb Iran
54C1 Sarata USSR
54A2 Sarajevo Yugos
90D2 Sarakhs Iran
61J3 Saraktash USSR
63A2 Sarala USSR
15D2 Saranac L USA
15D2 Saranac Lake USA
55B3 Sarandë Alb
79C4 Sarangani Is Phil
61G3 Saransk USSR
61H2 Sarapul USSR
17B2 Sarasota USA
15D2 Saratoga Springs USA
78C2 Saratok Malay
61G3 Saratov USSR
61G3 Saratovskoye Vodokhranilishche Res USSR
67F4 Sarawak State, Malay
92A2 Saraykoy Turk
90C3 Sarbisheh Iran
47D1 Sarca R Italy
95A2 Sardalas Libya
90A2 Sar Dasht Iran
52A2 Sardegna I Medit S
Sardinia = Sardegna
38H5 Sarektjåkkå Mt Sweden
84C2 Sargodha Pak
98B2 Sarh Chad
90B2 Sārī Iran
94B2 Sarida R Isreal
93D1 Sarikamiş Turk
107D3 Sarina Aust
47B1 Sarine R Switz
84B1 Sar-i-Pul Afghan
95B2 Sarir Libya
95A2 Sarir Tibesti Desert Libya
74B3 Sariwŏn N Korea
48B2 Sark I UK
92C2 Sarkišla Turk
71E4 Sarmi Indon
29C5 Sarmiento Arg
39G6 Särna Sweden
47C1 Sarnen Switz
14B2 Sarnia Can
58D2 Sarny USSR
6E2 Saroaq Greenland
84B2 Sarobi Afghan
78A3 Sarolangun Indon
55B3 Saronikós Kólpos G Greece
47C2 Saronno Italy
55C2 Saros Körfezi B Turk
39G7 Sarpsborg Nor

46D2 **Sarralbe** France
46D2 **Sarrebourg** France
46D2 **Sarreguemines** France
46D2 **Sarre-Union** France
51B1 **Sarrion** Spain
85B3 **Sartanahu** Pak
53A2 **Sartène** Corse
48B2 **Sarthe** R France
61H4 **Sarykamys** USSR
65H5 **Sarysu** R USSR
86A2 **Sasarām** India
74B4 **Sasebo** Japan
5H4 **Saskatchewan** Province, Can
5H4 **Saskatchewan** R Can
13F2 **Saskatoon** Can
101G1 **Sasolburg** S Africa
61F3 **Sasovo** USSR
97B4 **Sassandra** Ivory Coast
97B4 **Sassandra** R Ivory Coast
53A2 **Sassari** Sardegna
56C2 **Sassnitz** Germany
47D2 **Sassuolo** Italy
34C2 **Sastre** Arg
87A1 **Sātāra** India
4G2 **Satellite B** Can
78D4 **Satengar** Is Indon
39H6 **Säter** Sweden
17B1 **Satilla** R USA
61J2 **Satka** USSR
84D2 **Satluj** R India
86A2 **Satna** India
85C4 **Sātpura Range** Mts India
54B1 **Satu Mare** Rom
34D2 **Sauce** Arg
39F7 **Sauda** Nor
80C3 **Saudi Arabia** Kingdom, Arabian Pen
46D2 **Sauer** R Germany/Lux
46D1 **Sauerland** Region, Germany
38B1 **Sauðárkrókur** Iceland
14A2 **Saugatuck** USA
16C1 **Saugerties** USA
13B2 **Saugstad,Mt** Can
7B5 **Sault Sainte Marie** Can
14B1 **Sault Ste Marie** Can
14B1 **Sault Ste Marie** USA
71E4 **Saumlaki** Indon
48B2 **Saumur** France
98C3 **Saurimo** Angola
27M2 **Sauteurs** Grenada
54A2 **Sava** R Yugos
97C4 **Savalou** Benin
17B1 **Savannah** Georgia, USA
17B1 **Savannah** R USA
76C2 **Savannakhet** Laos
26B3 **Savanna la Mar** Jamaica
7A4 **Savant Lake** Can
76D2 **Savarane** Laos
97C4 **Savé** Benin
101C3 **Save** R Mozam
90B3 **Sāveh** Iran
46D2 **Saverne** France
47B2 **Savigliano** Italy
46B2 **Savigny** France
49D2 **Savoie** Region France
49D3 **Savona** Italy
38K6 **Savonlinna** Fin
4A3 **Savoonga** USA
38K5 **Savukoski** Fin
71D4 **Savu S** Indon
76A1 **Saw** Burma
85D3 **Sawai Mādhopur** India
78A2 **Sawang** Indon
76B2 **Sawankhalok** Thai
75C1 **Sawara** Japan
95A2 **Sawknah** Libya
12E1 **Sawtooth Mt** USA
106B2 **Sawu** I Indon
97C3 **Say** Niger

84B1 **Sayghan** Afghan
72B1 **Sayhandulaan** Mongolia
91B5 **Sayhūt** Yemen
61G4 **Saykhin** USSR
68D2 **Saynshand** Mongolia
61H5 **Say-Utes** USSR
16C2 **Sayville** USA
13B2 **Sayward** Can
57C3 **Sázava** R Czech
51C2 **Sbisseb** R Alg
42C2 **Scafell Pike** Mt Eng
44E1 **Scalloway** Scot
44C2 **Scapa Flow** Sd Scot
15C2 **Scarborough** Can
42D2 **Scarborough** Eng
27E4 **Scarborough** Tobago
44A2 **Scarp** I Scot
45B2 **Scarriff** Irish Rep
52A1 **Schaffhausen** Switz
57C3 **Scharding** Austria
46D1 **Scharteberg** Mt Germany
7D4 **Schefferville** Can
46B1 **Schelde** R Belg
10C2 **Schenectady** USA
47D2 **Schio** Italy
46D1 **Schleiden** Germany
56B2 **Schleswig** Germany
56B2 **Schleswig Holstein** State, Germany
16B1 **Schoharie** USA
71F4 **Schouten** Is PNG
7B5 **Schreiber** Can
21B2 **Schurz** USA
16A2 **Schuykill Haven** USA
16B2 **Schuylkill** R USA
57B3 **Schwabische Alb** Upland Germany
57B3 **Schwarzwald** Upland Germany
12C1 **Schwatka Mts** USA
47D1 **Schwaz** Austria
57C2 **Schweinfurt** Germany
101G1 **Schweizer Reneke** S Africa
56C2 **Schwerin** Germany
47C1 **Schwyz** Switz
53B3 **Sciacca** Italy
14B3 **Scioto** R USA
109D2 **Scone** Aust
6H2 **Scoresby Sd** Greenland
103F7 **Scotia Ridge** Atlantic O
103F7 **Scotia S** Atlantic O
44B3 **Scotland** Country, UK
112B7 **Scott** Base Ant
13B2 **Scott,C** Can
9C2 **Scott City** USA
112C6 **Scott I** Ant
6C2 **Scott Inlet** B Can
20B2 **Scott,Mt** USA
106B2 **Scott Reef** Timor S
8C2 **Scottsbluff** USA
17A1 **Scottsboro** USA
109C4 **Scottsdale** Aust
10C2 **Scranton** USA
47D1 **Scuol** Switz
    Scutari = Shkodër
5J4 **Seal** R Can
108B3 **Sea Lake** Aust
18B2 **Searcy** USA
22B2 **Seaside** California, USA
20B1 **Seaside** Oregon, USA
16B3 **Seaside Park** USA
20B1 **Seattle** USA
22A1 **Sebastopol** USA
58D1 **Sebez** USSR
17B2 **Sebring** USA
111A3 **Secretary I** NZ
18B2 **Sedalia** USA
46C2 **Sedan** France
111B2 **Seddonville** NZ
94B3 **Sede Boqer** Israel
94B3 **Sederot** Israel
97A3 **Sédhiou** Sen

94B3 **Sedom** Israel
100A3 **Seeheim** Namibia
111B2 **Sefton,Mt** NZ
77C5 **Segamat** Malay
51B2 **Segorbe** Spain
97B3 **Ségou** Mali
    Segovia = Coco
50B1 **Segovia** Spain
51C1 **Segre** R Spain
97B4 **Séguéla** Ivory Coast
96A2 **Seguia el Hamra** Watercourse Mor
34C2 **Segundo** R Arg
78D2 **Seguntur** Indon
50B2 **Segura** R Spain
85B3 **Sehwan** Pak
46D2 **Seille** R France
38J6 **Seinäjoki** Fin
48C2 **Seine** R France
46B2 **Seine-et-Marne** Department, France
99D3 **Sekenke** Tanz
20B1 **Selah** USA
71E4 **Selaru** I Indon
78D4 **Selat Alas** Str Indon
78B3 **Selat Bangka** Str Indon
78A3 **Selat Berhala** B Indon
71E4 **Selat Dampier** Str Indon
78B3 **Selat Gaspar** Str Indon
78D4 **Selat Lombok** Str Indon
78D4 **Selat Sape** Str Indon
78A4 **Selat Sunda** Str Indon
71D4 **Selat Wetar** Chan Indon
12B1 **Selawik** USA
12C1 **Selawik** L USA
12B1 **Selawik L** USA
42D3 **Selby** Eng
55C3 **Selçuk** Turk
12D3 **Seldovia** USA
100B3 **Selebi Pikwe** Botswana
6H3 **Selfoss** Iceland
95B2 **Selima Oasis** Sudan
5J4 **Selkirk** Can
42C2 **Selkirk** Scot
13D2 **Selkirk Mts** Can
22C2 **Selma** California, USA
50B2 **Selouane** Mor
12H2 **Selous,Mt** Can
78B3 **Selta Karimata** Str Indon
32C5 **Selvas** Region, Brazil
107D3 **Selwyn** Aust
4E3 **Selwyn Mts** Can
78C4 **Semarang** Indon
61E2 **Semenov** USSR
12C3 **Semidi Is** USA
60E3 **Semiluki** USSR
19A2 **Seminole** Oklahoma, USA
17B1 **Seminole,L** USA
65K4 **Semipalatinsk** USSR
79B3 **Semirara Is** Phil
90B3 **Semirom** Iran
78C2 **Semitau** Indon
90B2 **Semnān** Iran
46C2 **Semois** R Belg
23B2 **Sempoala** Hist Site, Mexico
32D5 **Sena Madureira** Brazil
100B2 **Senanga** Zambia
19C3 **Senatobia** USA
74E3 **Sendai** Honshū, Japan
74C4 **Sendai** Kyūshū, Japan
85D4 **Sendwha** India
15C2 **Seneca Falls** USA
97A3 **Senegal** Republic, Africa
97A3 **Sénégal** R Maur Sen
101G1 **Senekal** S Africa
31D4 **Senhor do Bonfim** Brazil
52B2 **Senigallia** Italy

52C2 **Senj** Yugos
69E4 **Senkaku Gunto** Is Japan
46B2 **Senlis** France
99D1 **Sennar** Sudan
7C5 **Senneterre** Can
49C2 **Sens** France
54A1 **Senta** Yugos
98C3 **Sentery** Zaïre
13C2 **Sentinel Peak** Mt Can
85D4 **Seoni** India
    Seoul = Soul
110B2 **Separation Pt** NZ
76D2 **Sepone** Laos
7D4 **Sept-Iles** Can
95A2 **Séquédine** Niger
21B2 **Sequoia** Nat Pk, USA
71D4 **Seram** I Indon
78B4 **Serang** Indon
78B2 **Serasan** I Indon
54A2 **Serbia** Region, Yugos
61F3 **Serdobsk** USSR
77C5 **Seremban** Malay
99D3 **Serengeti Nat Pk** Tanz
100C2 **Serenje** Zambia
59D3 **Seret** R USSR
61G2 **Sergach** USSR
65H3 **Sergino** USSR
31D4 **Sergipe** State, Brazil
78C2 **Seria** Brunei
78C2 **Serian** Malay
55B3 **Sérifos** I Greece
47C2 **Serio** R Italy
95B2 **Serir Calanscio** Desert Libya
46C2 **Sermaize-les-Bains** France
71D4 **Sermata** I Indon
61H3 **Sernovodsk** USSR
65H4 **Serov** USSR
100B3 **Serowe** Botswana
50A2 **Serpa** Port
60E3 **Serpukhov** USSR
35B2 **Serra da Canastra** Mts Brazil
50A1 **Serra da Estrela** Mts Port
35B2 **Serra da Mantiqueira** Mts Brazil
35A1 **Serra da Mombuca** Brazil
35C1 **Serra do Cabral** Mt Brazil
33F5 **Serra do Cachimbo** Mts Brazil
35A1 **Serra do Caiapó** Mts Brazil
35A2 **Serra do Cantu** Mts Brazil
35C2 **Serra do Caparaó** Mts Brazil
31C5 **Serra do Chifre** Brazil
35C1 **Serra do Espinhaço** Mts Brazil
35B2 **Serra do Mar** Mts Brazil
35A2 **Serra do Mirante** Mts Brazil
33G3 **Serra do Navio** Brazil
35B2 **Serra do Paranapiacaba** Mts Brazil
33F6 **Serra dos Caiabis** Mts Brazil
35A2 **Serra dos Dourados** Mts Brazil
33E6 **Serra dos Parecis** Mts Brazil
35B1 **Serra dos Pilões** Mts Brazil
35A1 **Serra Dourada** Mts Brazil
33F6 **Serra Formosa** Mts Brazil
55B2 **Sérrai** Greece
25D3 **Serrana Bank** Is Caribbean S

51B1 **Serrana de Cuenca**
Mts Spain
35A1 **Serranópolis** Brazil
33E3 **Serra Pacaraima** *Mts*
Brazil/Ven
33E3 **Serra Parima** *Mts*
Brazil
33G3 **Serra Tumucumaque**
Brazil
46B2 **Serre** *R* France
34B2 **Serrezuela** Arg
31D4 **Serrinha** Brazil
6G3 **Serrmilik** Greenland
35C1 **Serro** Brazil
35A2 **Sertanópolis** Brazil
72A3 **Sêrtar** China
78C3 **Seruyan** *R* Indon
100A2 **Sesfontein** Namibia
100B2 **Sesheke** Zambia
47B2 **Sestriere** Italy
74D2 **Setana** Japan
49C3 **Sète** France
35C1 **Sete Lagoas** Brazil
96C1 **Sétif** Alg
75B1 **Seto** Japan
75A2 **Seto Naikai** *S* Japan
96B1 **Settat** Mor
42C2 **Settle** Eng
5G4 **Settler** Can
50A2 **Sêtúbal** Port
93E1 **Sevan,Oz** *L* USSR
60D5 **Sevastopol'** USSR
7B4 **Severn** *R* Can
43C3 **Severn** *R* Eng
1B9 **Severnaya Zemlya** *I*
USSR
63C2 **Severo-Baykalskoye**
Nagorye *Mts* USSR
60E4 **Severo Donets** USSR
64E3 **Severodvinsk** USSR
64H3 **Severo Sos'va** *R*
USSR
8B3 **Sevier** *R* USA
8B3 **Sevier L** USA
50A2 **Sevilla** Spain
Seville = Sevilla
54C2 **Sevlievo** Bulg
97A4 **Sewa** *R* Sierra Leone
12E2 **Seward** Alaska, USA
18A1 **Seward** Nebraska,
USA
12A1 **Seward Pen** USA
13D1 **Sexsmith** Can
89K8 **Seychelles** *Is* Indian O
38C1 **Seyðisfjörður** Iceland
92C2 **Seyhan** Turk
60E3 **Seym** *R* USSR
108C3 **Seymour** Aust
16C2 **Seymour** Connecticut,
USA
14A3 **Seymour** Indiana,
USA
46B2 **Sézanne** France
96D1 **Sfax** Tunisia
54C1 **Sfinto Gheorghe** Rom
56A2 **'s-Gravenhage** Neth
72B3 **Shaanxi** Province,
China
98C3 **Shabunda** Zaïre
82B2 **Shache** China
112C9 **Shackleton Ice Shelf**
Ant
85B3 **Shadadkot** Pak
91B3 **Shādhām** *R* Iran
43C4 **Shaftesbury** Eng
29G8 **Shag Rocks** *Is*
South Georgia
90A3 **Shāhābād** Iran
94C2 **Shahbā** Syria
91C3 **Shahdap** Iran
86A2 **Shahdol** India
90A2 **Shāhīn Dezh** Iran
90C3 **Shāh Kūh** Iran
91C3 **Shahr-e Bābak** Iran
Shahresa = Qomisheh
90B3 **Shahr Kord** Iran
87B1 **Shājābād** India
84D3 **Shājahānpur** India

85D4 **Shājāpur** India
61F4 **Shakhty** USSR
61G2 **Shakhun'ya** USSR
97C4 **Shaki** Nig
12B2 **Shaktoolik** USA
61J2 **Shamary** USSR
99D2 **Shambe** Sudan
16A2 **Shamokin** USA
16B1 **Shandaken** USA
72D2 **Shandong** Province,
China
73C5 **Shangchuan Dao** *I*
China
72C1 **Shangdu** China
73E3 **Shanghai** China
72C3 **Shangnan** China
100B2 **Shangombo** Zambia
73D4 **Shangra** China
73B5 **Shangsi** China
72C1 **Shang Xian** China
41B3 **Shannon** *R* Irish Rep
72D3 **Shanqiu** China
74B2 **Shansonggang** China
63F2 **Shantarskiye Ostrova**
I USSR
73D5 **Shantou** China
72C2 **Shanxi** Province,
China
72D3 **Shan Xian** China
73C5 **Shaoguan** China
73E4 **Shaoxing** China
73C4 **Shaoyang** China
44C2 **Shapinsay** *I* Scot
94C2 **Shaqqā** Syria
90C2 **Sharifābād** Iran
91C4 **Sharjah** UAE
106A3 **Shark B** Aust
90C2 **Sharlauk** USSR
94B2 **Sharon,Plain of** Israel
61G2 **Sharya** USSR
99D2 **Shashamanna** Eth
73C3 **Shashi** China
20B2 **Shasta L** USA
20B2 **Shasta,Mt** USA
93E3 **Shaṭṭ al Gharrat** *R*
Iraq
94B3 **Shaubak** Jordan
13F3 **Shaunavon** Can
22C2 **Shaver L** USA
16B2 **Shawangunk Mt** USA
15D1 **Shawinigan** Can
19A2 **Shawnee** Oklahoma,
USA
73D4 **Sha Xian** China
106B3 **Shay Gap** Aust
94C2 **Shaykh Miskīn** Syria
99E1 **Shaykh 'Uthmān**
Yemen
60E3 **Shchigry** USSR
60D3 **Shchors** USSR
65J4 **Shchuchinsk** USSR
14A2 **Sheboygan** USA
98B2 **Shebshi** *Mts* Nig
12F1 **Sheenjek** *R* USA
45C1 **Sheep Haven** *Estuary*
Irish Rep
43E4 **Sheerness** Eng
94B2 **Shefar'am** Israel
42D3 **Sheffield** Eng
84C2 **Shekhupura** Pak
13B1 **Shelagyote Peak** *Mt*
Can
16C1 **Shelburne Falls** USA
14A2 **Shelby** Michigan, USA
8B2 **Shelby** Montana, USA
14A3 **Shelbyville** Indiana,
USA
12H2 **Sheldon,Mt** Can
12D3 **Shelikof Str** USA
109D2 **Shellharbour** Aust
111A3 **Shelter Pt** NZ
20B1 **Shelton** USA
93E1 **Shemakha** USSR
18A1 **Shenandoah** USA
15C3 **Shenandoah** *R* USA
15C3 **Shenandoah Nat Pk**
USA
97C4 **Shendam** Nig

95C2 **Shendi** Sudan
72C2 **Shenmu** China
72E1 **Shenyang** China
73C5 **Shenzhen** China
85D3 **Sheopur** India
59D2 **Shepetovka** USSR
108C3 **Shepparton** Aust
6B2 **Sherard,C** Can
43C4 **Sherborne** Eng
97A4 **Sherbro I** Sierra
Leone
15D1 **Sherbrooke** Can
85C3 **Shergarh** India
19B3 **Sheridan** Arkansas,
USA
8C2 **Sheridan** Wyoming,
USA
19A3 **Sherman** USA
56B2 **s-Hertogenbosh** Neth
12H3 **Sheslay** Can
40C1 **Shetland** *Is* Scot
61H5 **Shevchenko** USSR
91B4 **Sheyk Sho'eyb** *I* Iran
69H2 **Shiashkotan** *I* USSR
84B1 **Shibarghan** Afghan
74D3 **Shibata** Japan
99E2 **Shibeli** *R* Eth
95C1 **Shibin el Kom** Egypt
75B1 **Shibukawa** Japan
72C2 **Shijiazhuang** China
84B3 **Shikarpur** Pak
67G3 **Shikoku** *I* Japan
75A2 **Shikoku-sanchi** *Mts*
Japan
86B1 **Shiliguri** India
68D1 **Shilka** USSR
68D1 **Shilka** *R* USSR
16B2 **Shillington** USA
86C1 **Shillong** India
61F3 **Shilovo** USSR
75A2 **Shimabara** Japan
75B2 **Shimada** Japan
69E1 **Shimanovsk** USSR
74D3 **Shimizu** Japan
75B2 **Shimoda** Japan
87B2 **Shimoga** India
74C4 **Shimonoseki** Japan
75B1 **Shimura** Japan
91C5 **Shinaș** Oman
74D4 **Shingū** Japan
75C1 **Shinjō** Japan
74D3 **Shinminato** Japan
94C1 **Shinshār** Syria
99D3 **Shinyanga** Tanz
74E3 **Shiogama** Japan
75B2 **Shiono-misaki** *C*
Japan
73A5 **Shiping** China
16A2 **Shippensburg** USA
72B3 **Shiquan** China
75C1 **Shirakawa** Japan
75B1 **Shirane-san** *Mt* Japan
75B1 **Shirani-san** *Mt* Japan
91B4 **Shiraz** Iran
90B3 **Shir Kūh** Iran
75B1 **Shirotori** Japan
90C2 **Shirvān** Iran
12A1 **Shishmaref** USA
12A1 **Shishmaref Inlet** USA
4B3 **Shishmaret** USA
72B2 **Shitanjing** China
14A3 **Shively** USA
85D3 **Shivpuri** India
94B3 **Shivta** *Hist Site* Israel
101C2 **Shiwa Ngandu**
Zambia
72C3 **Shiyan** China
72B2 **Shizuishan** China
75B1 **Shizuoka** Japan
54A2 **Shkodër** Alb
109D2 **Shoalhaven** *R* Aust
75A2 **Shobara** Japan
87B2 **Shoranūr** India
87B1 **Shorāpur** India
21B2 **Shoshone Mts** USA
60D3 **Shostka** USSR
19B3 **Shreveport** USA
43C3 **Shrewsbury** Eng

43C3 **Shropshire** County,
Eng
72E1 **Shuangliao** China
69F2 **Shuangyashan** China
61J4 **Shubar kuduk** USSR
72D2 **Shu He** *R* China
73A4 **Shuicheng** China
84C3 **Shujaabad** Pak
85D4 **Shujālpur** India
68B2 **Shule He** China
54C2 **Shumen** Bulg
61G2 **Shumerlya** USSR
73D4 **Shuncheng** China
12C1 **Shungnak** USA
72C2 **Shuo Xian** China
91C4 **Shūr Gaz** Iran
100B2 **Shurugwi** Zim
13D2 **Shuswap L** Can
61F2 **Shuya** USSR
12D3 **Shuyak I** USA
82D3 **Shwebo** Burma
76B2 **Shwegyin** Burma
84A2 **Siah Koh** *Mts*
Afghan
84C2 **Sialkot** Pak
Sian = Xi'an
79C4 **Siarao** *I* Phil
79B4 **Siaton** Phil
58C1 **Šiauliai** USSR
65G4 **Sibay** USSR
101H1 **Sibayi L** *S* Africa
52C2 **Šibenik** Yugos
70A4 **Siberut** *I* Indon
84B3 **Sibi** Pak
68C1 **Sibirskoye** USSR
98B3 **Sibiti** Congo
99D3 **Sibiti** *R* Tanz
54B1 **Sibiu** Rom
70A3 **Sibolga** Indon
86C1 **Sibsāgār** India
78C2 **Sibu** Malay
79B4 **Sibuguay B** Phil
98B2 **Sibut** CAR
79B3 **Sibuyan** *I* Phil
79B3 **Sibuyan S** Phil
73A3 **Sichuan** Province,
China
53B3 **Sicilia** *I* Medit S
53B3 **Sicilian Chan** Italy/
Tunisia
Sicily = Sicilia
32C6 **Sicuani** Peru
85C4 **Siddhapur** India
87B1 **Siddipet** India
86A2 **Sidhi** India
95B1 **Sidi Barrani** Egypt
96B1 **Sidi Bel Abbès** Alg
44C3 **Sidlaw Hills** Scot
112B5 **Sidley,Mt** Ant
20B1 **Sidney** Can
8C2 **Sidney** Nebraska, USA
15C2 **Sidney** New York,
USA
14B2 **Sidney** Ohio, USA
17B1 **Sidney Lanier,L** USA
Sidon = Säida
58C2 **Siedlce** Pol
46D1 **Sieg** *R* Germany
46D1 **Siegburg** Germany
46D1 **Siegen** Germany
76C3 **Siem Reap** Camb
52B2 **Siena** Italy
58B2 **Sierpc** Pol
23B2 **Sierra Andrés Tuxtla**
Mexico
34B3 **Sierra Auca Mahuida**
Mts Arg
9C3 **Sierra Blanca** USA
51B1 **Sierra de Albarracin**
Mts Spain
50B2 **Sierra de Alcaraz** *Mts*
Spain
34B2 **Sierra de Cordoba** *Mts*
Arg
50A1 **Sierra de Gredos** *Mts*
Spain
50A2 **Sierra de Guadalupe**
Mts Spain

Soan-kundo

50B1 **Sierra de Guadarrama** *Mts* Spain
51B1 **Sierra de Guara** *Mts* Spain
51B1 **Sierra de Gudar** *Mts* Spain
23B2 **Sierra de Juárez** Mexico
34C3 **Sierra de la Ventana** *Mts* Arg
51C1 **Sierra del Codi** *Mts* Spain
34B2 **Sierra del Morro** *Mt* Arg
34B3 **Sierra del Nevado** *Mts* Arg
24B2 **Sierra de los Alamitos** *Mts* Mexico
50B2 **Sierra de los Filabres** Spain
23A1 **Sierra de los Huicholes** Mexico
23B2 **Sierra de Miahuatlán** Mexico
23A1 **Sierra de Morones** *Mts* Mexico
50A2 **Sierra de Ronda** *Mts* Spain
34B2 **Sierra de San Luis** *Mts* Arg
50B2 **Sierra de Segura** *Mts* Spain
50B1 **Sierra de Urbion** *Mts* Spain
34B2 **Sierra de Uspallata** *Mts* Arg
34B2 **Sierra de Valle Fértil** *Mts* Arg
23B2 **Sierra de Zongolica** Mexico
34C2 **Sierra Grande** *Mts* Arg
97A4 **Sierra Leone** Republic, Africa
97A4 **Sierra Leone,C** Sierra Leone
79B2 **Sierra Madre** *Mts* Phil
23A2 **Sierra Madre del Sur** *Mts* Mexico
24B2 **Sierra Madre Occidental** *Mts* Mexico
24C2 **Sierra Madre Oriental** *Mts* Mexico
34B2 **Sierra Malanzan** *Mts* Arg
9C4 **Sierra Mojada** Mexico
50A2 **Sierra Morena** *Mts* Spain
50B2 **Sierra Nevada** *Mts* Spain
21A2 **Sierra Nevada** *Mts* USA
32C1 **Sierra Nevada de Santa Marta** *Mts* Colombia
34B2 **Sierra Pié de Palo** *Mts* Arg
47B1 **Sierre** Switz
55B3 **Sífnos** *I* Greece
59C3 **Sighet** Rom
54B1 **Sighisoara** Rom
38B1 **Siglufjörður** Iceland
50B1 **Sigüenza** Spain
97B3 **Siguiri** Guinea
85E4 **Sihora** India
93D2 **Siirt** Turk
68B3 **Sikai Hu** *L* China
85D3 **Sīkar** India
84B2 **Sikaram** *Mt* Afghan
97B3 **Sikasso** Mali
18C2 **Sikeston** USA
55C3 **Síkinos** *I* Greece
55B3 **Sikionía** Greece
86B1 **Sikkim** State, India
50A1 **Sil** *R* Spain
47D1 **Silandro** Italy
23A1 **Silao** Mexico
79B3 **Silay** Phil
86C2 **Silchar** India
96C2 **Silet** Alg
86A1 **Silgarhi** Nepal
92B2 **Silifke** Turk
82C2 **Siling Co** *L* China
54C2 **Silistra** Bulg
39F7 **Silkeborg** Den
47E1 **Sillian** Austria
18B2 **Siloam Springs** USA
19B3 **Silsbee** USA
95A3 **Siltou** *Well* Chad
58C1 **Šilute** USSR
93D2 **Silvan** Turk
35B1 **Silvania** Brazil
85C4 **Silvassa** India
21B2 **Silver City** Nevada, USA
9C3 **Silver City** New Mexico, USA
20B2 **Silver Lake** USA
16A3 **Silver Spring** USA
13B2 **Silverthrone Mt** Can
108B2 **Silverton** Aust
47C1 **Silvretta** *Mts* Austria/ Switz
78C2 **Simanggang** Malay
76C1 **Simao** China
90A3 **Simareh** *R* Iran
55C3 **Simav** Turk
55C3 **Simav** *R* Turk
15C2 **Simcoe,L** Can
70A3 **Simeulue** *I* Indon
60D5 **Simferopol'** USSR
55C3 **Sími** *I* Greece
84D2 **Simla** India
46D1 **Simmern** Germany
13B2 **Simoon Sound** Can
49D2 **Simplon** *Mt* Switz
47C1 **Simplon** *P* Switz
4C2 **Simpson,C** USA
106C3 **Simpson Desert** Aust
6B3 **Simpson Pen** Can
39G7 **Simrishamn** Sweden
69H2 **Simushir** *I* USSR
99E2 **Sinadogo** Somalia
92B4 **Sinai** *Pen* Egypt
32B2 **Sincelejo** Colombia
17B1 **Sinclair,L** USA
85D3 **Sind** *R* India
85B3 **Sindh** Region, Pak
55C3 **Sindirği** Turk
86B2 **Sindri** India
50A2 **Sines** Port
99D1 **Singa** Sudan
77C5 **Singapore** Republic, S E Asia
77C5 **Singapore,Str of** S E Asia
78D4 **Singaraja** Indon
99D3 **Singida** Tanz
78B2 **Singkawang** Indon
109D2 **Singleton** Aust
78A3 **Singtep** *I* Indon
76B1 **Singu** Burma
53A2 **Siniscola** Sardgena
93D2 **Sinjär** Iraq
84B2 **Sinkai Hills** *Mts* Afghan
95C3 **Sinkat** Sudan
82C1 **Sinkiang** Autonomous Region, China
33G2 **Sinnamary** French Guiana
92C1 **Sinop** Turk
54B1 **Sintana** Rom
78C2 **Sintang** Indon
50A2 **Sintra** Port
32B2 **Sinú** *R* Colombia
74A2 **Sinŭiju** N Korea
59B3 **Siofok** Hung
47B1 **Sion** Switz
8D2 **Sioux City** USA
8D2 **Sioux Falls** USA
10A2 **Sioux Lookout** Can
79B4 **Sipalay** Phil
27L1 **Siparia** Trinidad
69E2 **Siping** China
112B3 **Siple** *Base* Ant
112B5 **Siple I** Ant
79B3 **Sipocot** Phil
70A4 **Sipora** Indon
79B4 **Siquijor** *I* Phil
87B2 **Sira** India
53C3 **Siracusa** Italy
86B2 **Sirajganj** Bang
13C2 **Sir Alexander,Mt** Can
91B5 **Sir Banī Yās** *I* UAE
106C2 **Sir Edward Pellew Group** *Is* Aust
54C1 **Siret** *R* Rom
12J2 **Sir James McBrien,Mt** Can
87B2 **Sir Kālahasti** India
13D2 **Sir Laurier,Mt** Can
93D2 **Şirnak** Turk
85C4 **Sirohi** India
87B1 **Sironcha** India
85D4 **Sironj** India
55B3 **Síros** *I* Greece
91B4 **Sirri** *I* Iran
84D3 **Sirsa** India
13D2 **Sir Sandford,Mt** Can
87A2 **Sirsi** India
95A1 **Sirt** Libya
95A1 **Sirte Desert** Libya
95A1 **Sirte,G of** Libya
52C1 **Sisak** Yugos
76C2 **Sisaket** Thai
76C3 **Sisophon** Camb
46B2 **Sissonne** France
90D3 **Sistan** Region, Iran/ Afghan
49D3 **Sisteron** France
63B2 **Sistig Khem** USSR
86A1 **Sītāpur** India
55C3 **Sitía** Greece
4E4 **Sitka** USA
12D3 **Sitkalidak I** USA
12D3 **Sitkinak** *I* USA
76B2 **Sittang** *R* Burma
46C1 **Sittard** Neth
86C2 **Sittwe** Burma
78C4 **Situbondo** Indon
92C2 **Sivas** Turk
93C2 **Siverek** Turk
92B2 **Sivrihisar** Turk
95B2 **Siwa** Egypt
84D2 **Siwalik Range** *Mts* India
86A1 **Siwalik Range** *Mts* Nepal
72D3 **Siyang** China
56C1 **Sjaelland** *I* Den
39G7 **Skagen** Den
39F7 **Skagerrak** *Str* Nor/ Den
20B1 **Skagit** *R* USA
20B1 **Skagit Mt** Can
4E4 **Skagway** USA
39G7 **Skara** Sweden
59C2 **Skarzysko-Kamienna** Pol
5F4 **Skeena** *R* Can
13B1 **Skeena Mts** Can
4D3 **Skeenjek** *R* USA
42E3 **Skegness** Eng
38H5 **Skellefte** *R* Sweden
38J6 **Skellefteå** Sweden
55B3 **Skíathos** *I* Greece
45B3 **Skibbereen** Irish Rep
5E4 **Skidegate** Can
58C2 **Skiemiewice** Pol
39F7 **Skien** Nor
96C1 **Skikda** Alg
74C4 **Skikoku** *I* Japan
42D3 **Skipton** Eng
55B3 **Skíros** *I* Greece
39F7 **Skive** Den
56B1 **Skjern** Den
6F3 **Skjoldungen** Greenland
14A2 **Skokie** USA
55B3 **Skópelos** *I* Greece
54B2 **Skopje** Yugos
39G7 **Skövde** Sweden
63E2 **Skovorodino** USSR
4C3 **Skwentna** USA
58B2 **Skwierzyna** Pol
40B2 **Skye** *I* Scot
39G7 **Slagelse** Den
45C2 **Slaney** *R* Irish Rep
54B2 **Slatina** Rom
78C4 **Slaung** Indon
5G3 **Slave** *R* Can
13E1 **Slave Lake** Can
65J4 **Slavgorod** Rossiyskaya, USSR
59D2 **Slavuta** USSR
60E4 **Slavyansk** USSR
44B3 **Sleat,Sound of** *Chan* Scot
12C2 **Sleetmute** USA
19C3 **Slidell** USA
16B2 **Slide Mt** USA
45C2 **Slieve Bloom** *Mts* Irish Rep
45B1 **Sligo** County, Irish Rep
41B3 **Sligo** Irish Rep
41B3 **Sligo** *B* Irish Rep
54C2 **Sliven** Bulg
54C2 **Slobozia** Rom
13D3 **Slocan** Can
58D2 **Slonim** USSR
43D4 **Slough** Eng
22B2 **Slough** *R* USA
59B3 **Slovensko** Region, Czech
56C2 **Slubice** Pol
59D2 **Sluch'** *R* USSR
68C1 **Sludyanka** USSR
58B2 **Słupsk** Pol
58D2 **Slutsk** USSR
58D2 **Slutsk** *R* USSR
41A3 **Slyne Head** *Pt* Irish Rep
63C2 **Slyudyanka** USSR
7D4 **Smallwood Res** Can
54B2 **Smederevo** Yugos
54B2 **Smederevska Palanka** Yugos
60D4 **Smela** USSR
15C2 **Smethport** USA
13E1 **Smith** Can
4F3 **Smith Arm** *B* Can
13B2 **Smithers** Can
7C3 **Smith I** Can
13B2 **Smith Sd** Can
15C2 **Smiths Falls** Can
109C4 **Smithton** Aust
13D1 **Smoky** *R* Can
109D2 **Smoky C** Aust
13E2 **Smoky Lake** Can
38F6 **Smøla** *I* Nor
60D3 **Smolensk** USSR
55B2 **Smólikas** *Mt* Greece
54B2 **Smolyan** Bulg
58D2 **Smorgon'** USSR
16B3 **Smyrna** Delaware, USA
17B1 **Smyrna** Georgia, USA
42B2 **Snaefell** *Mt* Eng
38B2 **Snafell** *Mt* Iceland
8B2 **Snake** *R* USA
8B2 **Snake River Canyon** USA
56B2 **Sneek** Neth
45B3 **Sneem** Irish Rep
22B2 **Snelling** USA
59B2 **Snĕžka** *Mt* Pol/Czech
38F6 **Snøhetta** *Mt* Nor
20B1 **Snohomish** USA
20B1 **Snoqualmie P** USA
76D3 **Snoul** Camb
43B3 **Snowdon** *Mt* Wales
43B3 **Snowdonia Nat Pk** Wales
4G3 **Snowdrift** Can
5H4 **Snow Lake** Can
108A2 **Snowtown** Aust
109C3 **Snowy Mts** Aust
9C3 **Snyder** USA
74B4 **Soan-kundo** *I* S Korea

99D2 **Sobat** *R* Sudan
31C2 **Sobral** Brazil
58C2 **Sochaczew** Pol
61E5 **Sochi** USSR
9C3 **Socorro** USA
24A3 **Socorro** *I* Mexico
34A2 **Socos** Chile
81D4 **Socotra** *I* Yemen
38K5 **Sodankylä** Fin
99D2 **Soddo** Eth
39H6 **Soderhamn** Sweden
39H7 **Södertälje** Sweden
99C1 **Sodiri** Sudan
46E1 **Soest** Germany
101C2 **Sofala** Mozam
Sofia = Sofiya
54B2 **Sofiya** Bulg
69G4 **Sofu Gan** *I* Japan
32C2 **Sogamoso** Colombia
39F6 **Sognefjorden** *Inlet* Nor
82D2 **Sog Xian** China
95C2 **Sohâg** Egypt
84D3 **Sohīpat** India
46B1 **Soignies** Belg
46B2 **Soissons** France
85C3 **Sojat** India
74A3 **Sŏjosŏn-man** *B* N Korea
92A2 **Söke** Turk
97C4 **Sokodé** Togo
61E2 **Sokol** USSR
58C2 **Sokołka** Pol
97B3 **Sokolo** Mali
6H3 **Søkongens Øy** *I* Greenland
99D1 **Sokota** Eth
97C3 **Sokoto** Nig
97C3 **Sokoto** *R* Nig
111A3 **Solander I** NZ
79B2 **Solano** Phil
87B1 **Solapur** India
47D1 **Solbad Hall** Austria
47D1 **Sölden** Austria
12D2 **Soldotna** USA
26C4 **Soledad** Colombia
43D4 **Solent** *Sd* Eng
46B1 **Solesmes** France
58D2 **Soligorsk** USSR
61J2 **Solikamsk** USSR
32C4 **Solimões** *R* Peru
46D1 **Solingen** Germany
65G4 **Sol'Itesk** USSR
38H6 **Sollefteå** Sweden
61H3 **Sol'lletsk** USSR
70B4 **Solok** Indon
105G4 **Solomon** *Is* Pacific O
47B1 **Solothurn** Switz
39F8 **Soltau** Germany
22B3 **Solvang** USA
42C2 **Solway Firth** *Estuary* Eng/Scot
100B2 **Solwezi** Zambia
75C1 **Sōma** Japan
55C3 **Soma** Turk
81C5 **Somalia** Republic, E Africa
54A1 **Sombor** Yugos
107D2 **Somerset** Aust
43C4 **Somerset** County, Eng
16D2 **Somerset** Massachusetts, USA
15C2 **Somerset** Pennsylvania, USA
100B4 **Somerset East** S Africa
6A2 **Somerset I** Can
16B3 **Somers Point** USA
16B2 **Somerville** USA
19A3 **Somerville Res** USA
54B1 **Somes** *R* Rom
46B2 **Somme** Department, France
46B2 **Somme** *R* France
46C2 **Sommesous** France
86A2 **Son** *R* India
74A3 **Sŏnch'ŏn** N Korea
39F8 **Sønderborg** Den

6E3 **Søndre Strømfjord** Greenland
47C1 **Sondrio** Italy
76D3 **Song Ba** *R* Viet
76D3 **Song Cau** Viet
101C2 **Songea** Tanz
73E3 **Songjiang** China
77C4 **Songkhla** Thai
74B3 **Songnim** N Korea
77C5 **Sông Pahang** *R* Malay
72A3 **Songpan** China
72C1 **Sonid Youqi** China
76C1 **Son La** Viet
85B3 **Sonmiani** Pak
85B3 **Sonmiani Bay** Pak
22A1 **Sonoma** USA
22B2 **Sonora** California, USA
24A2 **Sonora** *R* Mexico
9B3 **Sonoran Desert** USA
22C1 **Sonora P** USA
25D3 **Sonsonate** El Salvador
71E3 **Sonsorol** *I* Pacific O
10B2 **Soo Canals** Can/USA
13C3 **Sooke** Can
58B2 **Sopot** Pol
59B3 **Sopron** Hung
22B2 **Soquel** USA
53B2 **Sora** Italy
94B3 **Sored** *R* Israel
15D1 **Sorel** Can
109C4 **Sorell** Aust
92C2 **Sorgun** Turk
50B1 **Soria** Spain
38J5 **Sørkjosen** Nor
64C2 **Sørksop** *I* Barents S
61H4 **Sor Mertvyy Kultuk** *Plain* USSR
35B2 **Sorocaba** Brazil
61H3 **Sorochinsk** USSR
71F3 **Soroi** *I* Pacific O
60C4 **Sorok** USSR
71E4 **Sorong** Indon
71E4 **Sorong** Province, Indon
99D2 **Soroti** Uganda
38J4 **Sørøya** *I* Nor
53B2 **Sorrento** Italy
38K5 **Sorsatunturi** *Mt* Fin
38H5 **Sorsele** Sweden
79B3 **Sorsogon** Phil
38L6 **Sortavala** USSR
74B3 **Sŏsan** S Korea
59B2 **Sosnowiec** Pol
65H4 **Sos'va** USSR
64H4 **Sos'va** *R* USSR
98B2 **Souanké** Congo
97B4 **Soubré** Ivory Coast
16B2 **Souderton** USA
27P2 **Soufrière** St Lucia
27N2 **Soufrière** *V* St Vincent
48C3 **Souillac** France
96C1 **Souk Ahras** Alg
74B3 **Soul** S Korea
51C2 **Soummam** *R* Alg
Sour = Tyr
101G1 **Sources,Mt aux** Lesotho
31D3 **Sousa** Brazil
96D1 **Sousse** Tunisia
100B4 **South Africa** Republic, Africa
16B2 **South Amboy** USA
14B2 **Southampton** Can
43D4 **Southampton** Eng
16C2 **Southampton** USA
6B3 **Southampton I** Can
28F6 **South Atlantic O**
7D4 **South Aulatsivik I** Can
106C3 **South Australia** State, Aust
104E5 **South Australian Basin** Indian O
19C3 **Southaven** USA
17B2 **South Bay** USA
14B1 **South Baymouth** Can

14A2 **South Bend** Indiana, USA
20B1 **South Bend** Washington, USA
16D1 **Southbridge** USA
South Cape = Ka Lae
11B3 **South Carolina** State, USA
70C2 **South China S** S E Asia
8C2 **South Dakota** State, USA
16C1 **South Deerfield** USA
43D4 **South Downs** Eng
109C4 **South East C** Aust
111A2 **Southen Alps** *Mts* NZ
5H4 **Southend** Can
43E4 **Southend-on-Sea** Eng
111A2 **Southern Alps** *Mts* NZ
106A4 **Southern Cross** Aust
5J4 **Southern Indian L** Can
27H2 **Southfield** Jamaica
105G5 **South Fiji Basin** Pacific O
12D2 **South Fork** *R* Alaska, USA
22B1 **South Fork** *R* California, USA
28F8 **South Georgia** *I* S Atlantic O
43C4 **South Glamorgan** County, Wales
14A2 **South Haven** USA
5J3 **South Henik L** Can
104F3 **South Honshu Ridge** Pacific O
111A2 **South I** NZ
16C2 **Southington** USA
74B3 **South Korea** Republic, S E Asia
21A2 **South Lake Tahoe** USA
112C8 **South Magnetic Pole** Ant
17B2 **South Miami** USA
16A3 **South Mt** USA
4F3 **South Nahanni** *R* Can
26G1 **South Negril Pt** Jamaica
103F8 **South Orkney** *Is* Atlantic O
8C2 **South Platte** *R* USA
80E **South Pole** Ant
42C3 **Southport** Eng
27R3 **South Pt** Barbados
16B2 **South River** USA
44C2 **South Ronaldsay** *I* Scot
103G7 **South Sandwich Trench** Atlantic O
22A2 **South San Francisco** USA
5H4 **South Saskatchewan** *R* Can
42D2 **South Shields** Eng
110B1 **South Taranaki Bight** *B* NZ
44A3 **South Uist** *I* Scot
South West Africa = Namibia
107D5 **South West C** Aust
105J5 **South West Pacific Basin** Pacific O
103D5 **South West Peru Ridge** Pacific O
43D3 **South Yorkshire** County, Eng
58C1 **Sovetsk** RSFSR, USSR
61G2 **Sovetsk** RSFSR, USSR
98B3 **Soyo Congo** Angola
60D3 **Sozh** *R* USSR
46C1 **Spa** Belg
50A1 **Spain** Kingdom
Spalato = Split
43D3 **Spalding** Eng
14B1 **Spanish** *R* Can

26B3 **Spanish Town** Jamaica
21B2 **Sparks** USA
11B3 **Spartanburg** USA
55B3 **Spartí** Greece
69F2 **Spassk Dal'niy** USSR
27R3 **Speightstown** Barbados
12E2 **Spenard** USA
14A3 **Spencer** Indiana, USA
8D2 **Spencer** Iowa, USA
6A3 **Spencer Bay** Can
108A3 **Spencer,C** Aust
108A2 **Spencer G** Aust
6C3 **Spencer I** Can
111B2 **Spenser Mts** NZ
45C1 **Sperrin** *Mts* N Ire
44C3 **Spey** *R* Scot
57B3 **Speyer** Germany
27K1 **Speyside** Tobago
47B1 **Spiez** Switz
12F1 **Spike Mt** USA
20C1 **Spirit Lake** USA
5G4 **Spirit River** Can
Spitsbergen = Svalbard
57C3 **Spittal** Austria
38F6 **Spjelkavik** Nor
52C2 **Split** Yugos
47C1 **Splügen** Switz
20C1 **Spokane** USA
55C3 **Sporádhes** *Is* Greece
20C2 **Spray** USA
56C2 **Spree** *R* Germany
100A3 **Springbok** S Africa
18B2 **Springdale** USA
10B3 **Springfield** Illinois, USA
10C2 **Springfield** Massachusetts, USA
18B2 **Springfield** Missouri, USA
14B3 **Springfield** Ohio, USA
20B2 **Springfield** Oregon, USA
15D2 **Springfield** Vermont, USA
100B4 **Springfontein** S Africa
101G1 **Springs** S Africa
41D3 **Spurn Head** *Pt* Eng
13C3 **Squamish** Can
60E3 **Sredne-Russkaya Vozvyshennost** *Upland* USSR
63B1 **Sredne Sibirskoye Ploskogorve** *Tableland* USSR
61J2 **Sredniy Ural** *Mts* USSR
76D3 **Srepok** *R* Camb
68D1 **Sretensk** USSR
76C3 **Sre Umbell** Camb
83C5 **Sri Lanka** Republic, S Asia
84C2 **Srīnagar** Pak
87A1 **Srīvardhan** India
58B2 **Sroda** Pol
30H6 **Sta Clara** *I* Chile
32J7 **Sta Cruz** *I* Ecuador
56B2 **Stade** Germany
44A3 **Staffa** *I* Scot
43C3 **Stafford** County, Eng
43C3 **Stafford** Eng
16C2 **Stafford Springs** USA
Stalingrad = Volgograd
6A1 **Stallworthy,C** Can
59C2 **Stalowa Wola** Pol
32J7 **Sta Maria** *I* Ecuador
16C2 **Stamford** Connecticut, USA
16B1 **Stamford** New York, USA
100A3 **Stampriet** Namibia
101G1 **Standerton** S Africa
14B2 **Standish** USA
101H1 **Stanger** S Africa
22B2 **Stanislaus** *R* USA

54B2 **Stanke Dimitrov** Bulg
109C4 **Stanley** Aust
29E6 **Stanley** Falkland Is
87B2 **Stanley Res** India
Stanleyville =
Kisangani
25D3 **Stann Creek** Belize
63E2 **Stanovoy Khrebet** Mts
USSR
47C1 **Stans** Switz
109D1 **Stanthorpe** Aust
59C2 **Starachowice** Pol
54B2 **Stara Planiná** Mts
Bulg
60D2 **Staraya Russa** USSR
54C2 **Stara Zagora** Bulg
58B2 **Stargard** Pol
19C3 **Starkville** USA
57C3 **Starnberg** Germany
58B2 **Starogard Gdanski** Pol
59D3 **Starokonstantinov**
USSR
43C4 **Start Pt** Eng
60E3 **Staryy Oskol** USSR
15C2 **State College** USA
16B2 **Staten I** USA
17B1 **Statesboro** USA
15C3 **Staunton** USA
39F7 **Stavanger** Nor
46C1 **Stavelot** Belg
61F4 **Stavropol'** USSR
108B3 **Stawell** Aust
58B2 **Stawno** Pol
20B2 **Stayton** USA
12B2 **Stebbins** USA
12F2 **Steele,Mt** Can
16A2 **Steelton** USA
20C2 **Steens Mt** USA
6E2 **Steenstrups Gletscher**
Gl Greenland
4H2 **Stegi** Swaziland
101H1 **Stegi** Swaziland
47D1 **Steinach** Austria
8D2 **Steinback** Can
38G6 **Steinkjer** Nor
13C2 **Stein Mt** Can
23B2 **Stemaco** Mexico
46C2 **Stenay** France
56C2 **Stendal** Germany
110B2 **Stephens,C** NZ
108B2 **Stephens Creek** Aust
14A1 **Stephenson** USA
12H3 **Stephens Pass** USA
7E5 **Stephenville** Can
100B4 **Sterkstroom** S Africa
8C2 **Sterling** Colorado,
USA
14B2 **Sterling Heights** USA
61J3 **Sterlitamak** USSR
13E2 **Stettler** Can
14B2 **Steubenville** USA
4D3 **Stevens Village** USA
13B1 **Stewart** Can
21B2 **Stewart** USA
12G2 **Stewart** R Can
12G2 **Stewart Crossing** Can
111A3 **Stewart I** NZ
107F1 **Stewart Is** Solomon Is
4E3 **Stewart River** Can
16A3 **Stewartstown** USA
101G1 **Steyn** S Africa
57C3 **Steyr** Austria
12G3 **Stika** USA
12H3 **Stikine** R Can
12H3 **Stikine Ranges** Mts
Can
18A2 **Stillwater** Oklahoma,
USA
21B2 **Stillwater Range** Mts
USA
108A2 **Stirling** Aust
44C3 **Stirling** Scot
16C1 **Stockbridge** USA
59B3 **Stockerau** Austria
39H7 **Stockholm** Sweden
42C3 **Stockport** Eng
22B2 **Stockton** California,
USA

42D2 **Stockton** Eng
18B2 **Stockton L** USA
43C3 **Stoke-on-Trent** Eng
38A2 **Stokkseyri** Iceland
38G5 **Stokmarknes** Nor
39K8 **Stolbtsy** USSR
58D2 **Stolin** USSR
16B3 **Stone Harbor** USA
44C3 **Stonehaven** Scot
19A3 **Stonewall** USA
12D2 **Stony** R USA
38H5 **Storavan** L Sweden
38G6 **Støren** Nor
109C4 **Storm B** Aust
44A2 **Stornoway** Scot
59D3 **Storozhinets** USSR
16C2 **Storrs** USA
38G6 **Storsjon** L Sweden
38H5 **Storuman** Sweden
16D1 **Stoughton** USA
43E3 **Stowmarket** Eng
45C1 **Strablane** N Ire
109C4 **Strahan** Aust
56C2 **Stralsund** Germany
38F6 **Stranda** Nor
39H7 **Strängnäs** Sweden
42B2 **Stranraer** Scot
49D2 **Strasbourg** France
15C3 **Strasburg** USA
14B2 **Stratford** Can
16C2 **Stratford** Connecticut,
USA
110B1 **Stratford** NZ
43D3 **Stratford-on-Avon**
Eng
108A3 **Strathalbyn** Aust
42B2 **Strathclyde** Region,
Scot
13E2 **Strathmore** Can
18C1 **Streator** USA
47C2 **Stresa** Italy
53C3 **Stretto de Messina** Str
Italy/Sicily
38D3 **Streymoy** Føroyar
53C3 **Stroboli** I Italy
6E3 **Strømfjord** Greenland
44C2 **Stromness** Scot
18A1 **Stromsburg** USA
38H6 **Stromsund** Sweden
38G6 **Ströms Vattudal** L
Sweden
44C2 **Stronsay** I Scot
43C4 **Stroud** Eng
16B2 **Stroudsburg** USA
54B2 **Struma** R Bulg
43B3 **Strumble Head** Pt
Wales
55B2 **Strumica** Yugos
59C3 **Stryy** USSR
59C3 **Stryy** R USSR
108B1 **Strzelecki Creek** R
Aust
17B2 **Stuart** Florida, USA
13C2 **Stuart** R Can
12B2 **Stuart I** USA
13C2 **Stuart L** Can
47D1 **Stubaier Alpen** Mts
Austria
60C3 **Stuch** R USSR
76D3 **Stung Sen** Camb
76D3 **Stung Treng** Camb
52A2 **Stura** R Italy
112C7 **Sturge I** Ant
14A2 **Sturgeon Bay** USA
14C1 **Sturgeon Falls** Can
18C2 **Sturgis** Kentucky,
USA
14A2 **Sturgis** Michigan,
USA
106B2 **Sturt Creek** R Aust
108B1 **Sturt Desert** Aust
100B4 **Stuttemeim** S Africa
19B3 **Stuttgart** USA
57B3 **Stuttgart** Germany
38A1 **Stykkishólmur** Iceland
59D2 **Styr** R USSR
35C1 **Suaçuí Grande** R
Brazil

81B4 **Suakin** Sudan
73E5 **Su-ao** Taiwan
34C2 **Suardi** Arg
78B2 **Subi** I Indon
54A1 **Subotica** Yugos
60C4 **Suceava** Rom
45B2 **Suck** R Irish Rep
30C2 **Sucre** Bol
35A1 **Sucuriú** R Brazil
98C1 **Sudan** Republic,
Africa
14B1 **Sudbury** Can
43E3 **Sudbury** Eng
99C2 **Sudd** Swamp Sudan
33F2 **Suddie** Guyana
98C2 **Sue** R Sudan
4H2 **Suerdrup Is** Can
92B4 **Suez** Egypt
92B3 **Suez Canal** Egypt
92B4 **Suez,G of** Egypt
16B2 **Suffern** USA
43E3 **Suffolk** County, Eng
109D2 **Sugarloaf Pt** Aust
91C5 **Suhār** Oman
68C1 **Sühbaatar** Mongolia
84B3 **Sui** Pak
72C2 **Suide** China
69E2 **Suihua** China
73B3 **Suining** China
46C2 **Suippes** France
41B3 **Suir** R Irish Rep
73C3 **Sui Xian** China
72E1 **Suizhong** China
85C3 **Sujāngarth** India
78B4 **Sukabumi** Indon
78C4 **Sukadana** Borneo,
Indon
78B4 **Sukadana** Sumatra,
Indon
74E3 **Sukagawa** Japan
78C3 **Sukaraya** Indon
60E3 **Sukhinichi Shchekino**
USSR
61F2 **Sukhona** R USSR
61F5 **Sukhumi** USSR
6E3 **Sukkertoppen**
Greenland
6E3 **Sukkertoppen** L
Greenland
38L6 **Sukkozero** USSR
85B3 **Sukkur** Pak
87C1 **Sukma** India
100A3 **Sukses** Namibia
75A2 **Sukumo** Japan
13C1 **Sukunka** R Can
60E3 **Sula** R USSR
84B3 **Sulaiman Range** Mts
Pak
70C4 **Sulawesi** I Indon
93E3 **Sulaymānīyah** Iraq
54C1 **Sulina** Rom
38H5 **Sulitjelma** Nor
32A4 **Sullana** Peru
18B2 **Sullivan** USA
13B2 **Sullivan Bay** Can
13E2 **Sullivan L** Can
52B2 **Sulmona** Italy
19B3 **Sulphur** Louisiana,
USA
19A3 **Sulphur** Oklahoma,
USA
19A3 **Sulphur Springs** USA
86A1 **Sultānpur** India
79B4 **Sulu Arch** Phil
70C3 **Sulu S** Philip
30D4 **Sumampa** Arg
70B4 **Sumatera** I Indon
70C4 **Sumba** I Indon
78D4 **Sumbawa** I Indon
78D4 **Sumbawa Besar**
Indon
99D3 **Sumbawanga** Tanz
100A2 **Sumbe** Angola
44E2 **Sumburgh Head** Pt
Scot
78C4 **Sumenep** Indon
69G3 **Sumisu** I Japan
13D3 **Summerland** Can

5F4 **Summit Lake** Can
21B2 **Summit Mt** USA
111B2 **Sumner,L** NZ
75A2 **Sumoto** Japan
17B1 **Sumter** USA
60D3 **Sumy** USSR
16A2 **Sunbury** USA
34C2 **Sunchales** Arg
74B3 **Sunch'ŏn** N Korea
74B4 **Sunch'ŏn** S Korea
86A2 **Sundargarh** India
86B2 **Sunderbans** Swamp
India
42D2 **Sunderland** Eng
13E2 **Sundre** Can
15C1 **Sundridge** Can
38H6 **Sundsvall** Sweden
38D3 **Suduroy** Føroyar
78D3 **Sungaianyar** Indon
78A3 **Sungaisalak** Indon
20C1 **Sunnyside** USA
21A2 **Sunnyvale** USA
63D1 **Suntar** USSR
97B4 **Sunyani** Ghana
75A2 **Suō-nada** B Japan
38K6 **Suonejoki** Fin
86B1 **Supaul** India
18A1 **Superior** Nebraska,
USA
10A2 **Superior** Wisconsin,
USA
10B2 **Superior,L** Can/USA
76C3 **Suphan Buri** Thai
93D2 **Süphan Dağ** Turk
71E4 **Supiori** I Indon
93E3 **Suq ash Suyukh** Iraq
72D3 **Suqian** China
Suqutra = Socotra
91C5 **Sür** Oman
78C4 **Surabaya** Indon
75B2 **Suraga-wan** B Japan
78C4 **Surakarta** Indon
61G3 **Surar** R USSR
109C1 **Surat** Aust
85C4 **Sürat** India
84C3 **Süratgarh** India
77B4 **Surat Thani** Thai
85C4 **Surendranagar** India
16B3 **Surf City** USA
64J3 **Surgut** USSR
87B1 **Suriäpet** India
49D2 **Sürich** Switz
79C4 **Surigao** Phil
76C3 **Surin** Thai
33F3 **Surinam** Republic,
S America
43D4 **Surrey** County, Eng
47C1 **Sursee** Switz
38A2 **Surtsey** I Iceland
78A3 **Surulangan** Indon
47B2 **Susa** Italy
75A2 **Susa** Japan
75A2 **Susaki** Japan
21A1 **Susanville** USA
47D1 **Süsch** Switz
12E2 **Susitna** R USA
16A3 **Susquehanna** R USA
16B2 **Sussex** USA
43D4 **Sussex West** Eng
13B1 **Sustut Peak** Mt Can
100B4 **Sutherland** S Africa
84C2 **Sutlej** R Pak
21A2 **Sutter Creek** USA
14B3 **Sutton** USA
12C3 **Sutwik I** USA
74D3 **Suwa** Japan
58C2 **Suwałki** Pol
17B2 **Suwannee** R USA
94B2 **Suweilih** Jordan
74B3 **Suwŏn** S Korea
72D3 **Su Xian** China
75B1 **Suzaka** Japan
73E3 **Suzhou** China
74D3 **Suzu** Japan
75B2 **Suzuka** Japan
75B1 **Suzu-misaki** C Japan
64C2 **Svalbard** Is Barents S
59C3 **Svalyava** USSR

38G5 **Svartisen** Mt Nor
76D3 **Svay Rieng** Camb
38G6 **Sveg** Sweden
39G7 **Svendborg** Den
65H4 **Sverdlovsk** USSR
6A1 **Sverdrup Chan** Can
69F2 **Svetlaya** USSR
58C2 **Svetlogorsk** USSR
39K6 **Svetogorsk** USSR
54B2 **Svetozarevo** Yugos
54C2 **Svilengrad** Bulg
58D2 **Svir'** USSR
59B3 **Svitavy** Czech
69E1 **Svobodnyy** USSR
38G5 **Svolvaer** Nor
107E3 **Swain Reefs** Aust
17B1 **Swainsboro** USA
100A3 **Swakopmund**
  Namibia
42D2 **Swale** R Eng
70C3 **Swallow Reef** /
  S E Asia
87B2 **Swämihalli** India
25D3 **Swan** / Honduras
43D4 **Swanage** Eng
108B3 **Swan Hill** Aust
13D2 **Swan Hills** Can
13D2 **Swan Hills** Mts Can
26A3 **Swan I** Caribbean S
5H4 **Swan River** Can
43C4 **Swansea** Wales
43C4 **Swansea B** Wales
101G1 **Swartruggens**
  S Africa
  Swatow = Shantou
101H1 **Swaziland** Kingdom,
  S Africa
39G7 **Sweden** Kingdom,
  N Europe
20B2 **Sweet Home** USA
9C3 **Sweetwater** USA
100B4 **Swellendam** S Africa
59B2 **Świdnica** Pol
58B2 **Świdwin** Pol
58B2 **Świebodzin** Pol
58B2 **Świecie** Pol
5H4 **Swift Current** Can
43D4 **Swindon** Eng
45B2 **Swinford** Irish Rep
56C2 **Świnoujście** Pol
49D2 **Switzerland** Federal
  Republic, Europe
45C2 **Swords** Irish Rep
109D2 **Sydney** Aust
7D5 **Sydney** Can
64G3 **Syktyvkar** USSR
17A1 **Sylacauga** USA
38G6 **Sylarna** Mt Sweden
86C2 **Sylhet** Bang
56B1 **Sylt** / Germany
14B2 **Sylvania** USA
112C11 **Syowa** Base Ant
  Syracuse = Siracusa
15C2 **Syracuse** USA
65H5 **Syrdal'ya** R USSR
93C2 **Syria** Republic, S W
  Asia
61J2 **Sysert'** USSR
61G3 **Syzran'** USSR
56C2 **Szczecin** Pol
58B2 **Szczecinek** Pol
58C2 **Szczytno** Pol
59C3 **Szeged** Hung
59B3 **Székesfehérvár** Hung
59B3 **Szekszard** Hung
59B3 **Szolnok** Hung
59B3 **Szombathely** Hung
58B2 **Szprotawa** Pol

T

90C3 **Tabas** Iran
23A1 **Tabasco** Mexico
32D4 **Tabatinga** Brazil
96B2 **Tabelbala** Alg
76C3 **Tabeng** Camb
13E2 **Taber** Can

79B3 **Tablas** / Phil
100A4 **Table Mt** S Africa
12F1 **Table Mt** USA
18B2 **Table Rock Res** USA
78B3 **Taboali** Indon
57C3 **Tábor** Czech
99D3 **Tabora** Tanz
97B4 **Tabou** Ivory Coast
90A2 **Tabrīz** Iran
92C4 **Tabūk** S Arabia
23A2 **Tacámbaro** Mexico
82C1 **Tacheng** China
79C3 **Tacloban** Phil
30B2 **Tacna** Peru
8A2 **Tacoma** USA
99E1 **Tadjoura** Djibouti
87B2 **Tādpatri** India
65H6 **Tadzhen** USSR
82A2 **Tadzhikskaya SSR**
  Republic, USSR
74B3 **Taebaek Sanmaek**
  Mts S Korea
74B3 **Taegu** S Korea
74B4 **Taehŭksan** / S Korea
74B3 **Taejŏn** S Korea
51B1 **Tafalla** Spain
96C2 **Tafasaset**
  Watercourse Alg
43C4 **Taff** R Wales
94B3 **Tafila** Jordan
97A3 **Tagant** Region, Maur
79B4 **Tagbilaran** Phil
96B2 **Taguenout Hagguerete**
  Well Maur
107E2 **Tagula** / Solomon Is
79C4 **Tagum** Phil
  Tagus = Tejo
96C2 **Tahat** Mt Alg
105J4 **Tahiti** / Pacific O
18A2 **Tahlequah** USA
21A2 **Tahoe City** USA
21A2 **Tahoe,L** USA
97C3 **Tahoua** Niger
71D3 **Tahuna** Indon
72D2 **Tai'an** China
72B3 **Taibai Shan** Mt China
72D1 **Taibus Qi** China
73E5 **T'ai-chung** Taiwan
111B3 **Taieri** R NZ
72C2 **Taihang Shan** China
110C1 **Taihape** NZ
72E3 **Tai Hu** L China
108A3 **Tailem Bend** Aust
44B3 **Tain** Scot
73E5 **T'ai-nan** Taiwan
35C1 **Taiobeiras** Brazil
73E5 **T'ai pei** Taiwan
77C5 **Taiping** Malay
75C1 **Taira** Japan
78A3 **Tais** Indon
75A1 **Taisha** Japan
29B5 **Taitao,Pen de** Chile
73E5 **T'ai-tung** Taiwan
38K5 **Taivelkoski** Fin
69E4 **Taiwan** Republic,
  China
  Taiwan Haixia =
  Formosa Str
72C2 **Taiyuan** China
72D3 **Taizhou** China
81C4 **Ta'izz** Yemen
50B1 **Tajo** R Spain
76B2 **Tak** Thai
74D3 **Takada** Japan
75A2 **Takahashi** Japan
110B2 **Takaka** NZ
74C4 **Takamatsu** Japan
74D3 **Takaoka** Japan
110B1 **Takapuna** NZ
74D3 **Takasaki** Japan
75B1 **Takayama** Japan
74D3 **Takefu** Japan
76C3 **Takeo** Camb
75A2 **Takeo** Japan
  Take-shima = Tok-do
90A2 **Takestān** Iran
75A2 **Taketa** Japan
70A3 **Takingeun** Indon

4G3 **Takjvak L** Can
99D1 **Takkaze** R Eth
13B1 **Takla L** Can
13B1 **Takla Landing** Can
12B2 **Takslesluk L** USA
12H2 **Taku Arm** R Can
23A1 **Tala** Mexico
59B3 **Talabanya** Hung
84C2 **Talagang** Pak
34A2 **Talagante** Chile
87B3 **Talaimannar** Sri Lanka
97C3 **Talak** Desert Region,
  Niger
78A3 **Talangbetutu** Indon
32A4 **Talara** Peru
50B2 **Talavera de la Reina**
  Spain
34A3 **Talca** Chile
34A3 **Talcahuano** Chile
86B2 **Tālcher** India
82B1 **Taldy Kurgan** USSR
71D4 **Taliabu** Indon
84B1 **Taligan** Afghan
99D2 **Tali Post** Sudan
78D4 **Taliwang** Indon
12D2 **Talkeetna** USA
12E2 **Talkeetna Mts** USA
17A1 **Talladega** USA
93D2 **Tall 'Afar** Iraq
17B1 **Tallahassee** USA
94C1 **Tall Bīsah** Syria
60B2 **Tallinn** USSR
92C3 **Tall Kalakh** Syria
19B3 **Tallulah** USA
60D4 **Tal'noye** USSR
58C2 **Talpaki** USSR
30B4 **Taltal** Chile
109C1 **Talwood** Aust
78D1 **Tamabo Range** Mts
  Malay
97B4 **Tamale** Ghana
96C2 **Tamanrasset** Alg
96C2 **Tamanrasset**
  Watercourse Alg
16B2 **Tamaqua** USA
  Tamatave =
  Toamasina
23A2 **Tamazula** Jalisco,
  Mexico
23B2 **Tamazulapán** Mexico
23B1 **Tamazunchale** Mexico
97A3 **Tambacounda** Sen
61F3 **Tambov** USSR
50A1 **Tambre** R Spain
98C2 **Tambura** Sudan
97A3 **Tamchaket** Maur
50A1 **Tamega** R Port
23B1 **Tamiahua** Mexico
87B2 **Tamil Nādu**
  State, India
54B1 **Tamis** R Rom
76D2 **Tam Ky** Viet
17B2 **Tampa** USA
17B2 **Tampa B** USA
39J6 **Tampere** Fin
23B1 **Tampico** Mexico
68D2 **Tamsagbulag**
  Mongolia
86C2 **Tamu** Burma
23B1 **Tamuis** Mexico
109D2 **Tamworth** Aust
43D3 **Tamworth** Eng
38K4 **Tana** Nor
99D1 **Tana** L Eth
99E3 **Tana** R Kenya
38K5 **Tana** R Nor/Fin
75B2 **Tanabe** Japan
38K4 **Tanafjord** Inlet Nor
78D3 **Tanahgrogot** Indon
71E4 **Tanahmerah** Indon
12D1 **Tanana** USA
12E2 **Tanana** R USA
  Tananarive =
  Antananarivo
47C2 **Tanaro** R Italy
74B2 **Tanch'ŏn** N Korea
99E1 **Tandaho** Eth
34D3 **Tandil** Arg

78B2 **Tandjong Datu** Pt
  Indon
71E4 **Tandjung d'Urville** C
  Indon
78D3 **Tandjung Layar** C
  Indon
78B3 **Tandjung Lumut** C
  Indon
78D2 **Tandjung Mangkalihet**
  C Indon
78C3 **Tandjung Sambar** C
  Indon
78C2 **Tandjung Sirik** C
  Malay
71E4 **Tandjung Vals** C
  Indon
85B3 **Tando Adam** Pak
85B3 **Tando Muhammad**
  Khan Pak
108B2 **Tandou L** Aust
87B1 **Tāndūr** India
110C1 **Taneatua** NZ
76B2 **Tanen Range** Mts
  Burma/Thai
96B2 **Tanezrouft** Desert
  Region Alg
91C4 **Tang** Iran
99D3 **Tanga** Tanz
60E4 **Tanganrog** USSR
99C3 **Tanganyika,L** Tanz/
  Zaire
96B1 **Tanger** Mor
82C2 **Tanggula Shan** Mts
  China
  Tangier = Tanger
78A2 **Tangjungpinang**
  Indon
82C2 **Tangra Yumco** L
  China
72D2 **Tangshan** China
79B4 **Tangub** Phil
63C2 **Tanguy** USSR
79B4 **Tanjay** Phil
78C4 **Tanjong Bugel** C
  Indon
78B4 **Tanjong Cangkuang** C
  Indon
78C3 **Tanjong Puting** C
  Indon
78C3 **Tanjong Selatan** C
  Indon
78D3 **Tanjung** Indon
70A3 **Tanjungbalai** Indon
78A3 **Tanjung Jabung** Pt
  Indon
78B3 **Tanjungpandan** Indon
78B4 **Tanjung Priok** Indon
78D2 **Tanjungredeb** Indon
78D2 **Tanjungselor** Indon
84C2 **Tank** Pak
68B1 **Tannu Ola** Mts USSR
97B4 **Tano** R Ghana
97C3 **Tanout** Niger
23B1 **Tanquián** Mexico
73E4 **Tan-shui** Taiwan
86A1 **Tansing** Nepal
95C1 **Tanta** Egypt
96A2 **Tan-Tan** Mor
4B3 **Tanunak** USA
99D3 **Tanzania** Republic,
  Africa
72A3 **Tao He** R China
101D3 **Taolañaro** Madag
72B2 **Taole** China
96B1 **Taourirt** Mor
60C2 **Tapa** USSR
25C3 **Tapachula** Mexico
33F4 **Tapajós** R Brazil
34C3 **Tapalquén** Arg
70B4 **Tapan** Indon
111A3 **Tapanui** NZ
32D5 **Tapauá** R Brazil
85D4 **Tapi** R India
86B1 **Taplejung** Nepal
111B2 **Tapuaeniku** Mt NZ
35B2 **Tapuaritinga** Brazil
79B4 **Tapul Group** Is Phil
33E4 **Tapurucuara** Brazil

109D1 **Tara** Aust	13C2 **Tatla Lake** Can	21B3 **Tehachapi Mts** USA	11B3 **Tennessee** State, USA
65J4 **Tara** USSR	59B3 **Tatry** *Mts* Pol/Czech	21B2 **Tehachapi P** USA	18C2 **Tennessee** *R* USA
65J4 **Tara** *R* USSR	75A2 **Tatsuno** Japan	4J3 **Tehek L** Can	34A2 **Teno** Chile
54A2 **Tara** *R* Yugos	85B4 **Tatta** Pak	90B2 **Tehrān** Iran	78D1 **Tenom** Malay
97D4 **Taraba** *R* Nig	35B2 **Tatuí** Brazil	23B2 **Tehuacán** Mexico	25C3 **Tenosique** Mexico
30D2 **Tarabuco** Bol	93D2 **Tatvan** Turk	23B2 **Tehuantepec** Mexico	109D1 **Tenterfield** Aust
Tarābulus = Tripoli	31C3 **Tauá** Brazil	23B2 **Tehuitzingo** Mexico	17B2 **Ten Thousand Is** USA
50B1 **Taracón** Spain	35B2 **Taubaté** Brazil	43B3 **Teifi** *R* Wales	23A1 **Teocaltiche** Mexico
110C1 **Taradale** NZ	110C1 **Taumarunui** NZ	50A2 **Tejo** *R* Port	35C1 **Teófilo Otôni** Brazil
78D2 **Tarakan** Indon	101F1 **Taung** S Africa	23A2 **Tejupilco** Mexico	23B2 **Teotihiucan** Hist Site,
44A3 **Taransay** *I* Scot	76B2 **Taungdwingyi** Burma	111B2 **Tekapo,L** NZ	Mexico
53C2 **Taranto** Italy	76B1 **Taung-gyi** Burma	82B1 **Tekeli** USSR	23B2 **Teotitlan** Mexico
32B5 **Tarapoto** Peru	76A2 **Taungup** Burma	92A1 **Tekirdağ** Turk	23A1 **Tepatitlan** Mexico
49C2 **Tarare** France	84C2 **Taunsa** Pak	55C2 **Tekir Dağlari** *Mts*	24B2 **Tepehuanes** Mexico
110C2 **Tararua Range** *Mts*	43C4 **Taunton** Eng	Turk	23B2 **Tepeji** Mexico
NZ	16D2 **Taunton** USA	86C2 **Teknaf** Bang	23A1 **Tepic** Mexico
96C2 **Tarat** Alg	46E1 **Taunus** Region,	110C1 **Te Kuiti** NZ	57C2 **Teplice** Czech
110C1 **Tarawera** NZ	Germany	25D3 **Tela** Honduras	110C1 **Te Puke** NZ
51B1 **Tarazona** Spain	110C1 **Taupo** NZ	94B2 **Tel Aviv Yafo** Israel	23A1 **Tequila** Mexico
44C3 **Tarbat Ness** *Pen* Scot	110C1 **Taupo,L** NZ	34B3 **Telén** Arg	23B2 **Tequistepec** Mexico
84C2 **Tarbela Res** Pak	58C1 **Taurage** USSR	21B2 **Telescope Peak** *Mt*	51C1 **Ter** *R* Spain
42B2 **Tarbert** Strathclyde,	110C1 **Tauranga** NZ	USA	97C3 **Téra** Niger
Scot	110C1 **Tauranga Harbour** *B*	33F5 **Teles Pires** *R* Brazil	75B1 **Teradomari** Japan
44A3 **Tarbert** Western Isles,	NZ	47D1 **Telfs** Austria	52B2 **Teramo** Italy
Scot	110B1 **Tauroa Pt** NZ	63A2 **Teli** USSR	96A1 **Terceira** *I* Açores
48C3 **Tarbes** France	7A3 **Tavani** Can	94B3 **Tell el Meise** *Mt*	59D3 **Tereboviya** USSR
106C4 **Tarcoola** Aust	7A3 **Tavani** Can	Jordan	31C3 **Teresina** Brazil
109C2 **Tarcoon** Aust	65H4 **Tavda** *R* USSR	12A1 **Teller** USA	35C2 **Teresópolis** Brazil
109D2 **Taree** Aust	43B4 **Tavistock** Eng	87B2 **Tellicherry** India	92C1 **Terme** Turk
96A2 **Tarfaya** Mor	76B3 **Tavoy** Burma	77C5 **Telok Anson** Malay	80E2 **Termez** USSR
95A1 **Tarhūnah** Libya	76B3 **Tavoy Pt** Burma	78D2 **Tělok Darvel** Malay	52B2 **Termoli** Italy
91B5 **Tarīf** UAE	92A2 **Tavsanli** Turk	71E4 **Tělok Flamingo** *B*	71D3 **Ternate** Indon
30D3 **Tarija** Bol	111B2 **Tawa** NZ	Indon	52B2 **Terni** Italy
87B2 **Tarikere** India	19A3 **Tawakoni,L** USA	78C3 **Tělok Kumai** *B* Indon	59D3 **Ternopol** USSR
81C4 **Tarīm** Yemen	14B2 **Tawas City** USA	78B4 **Tělok Pelabuanratu** *B*	13B2 **Terrace** Can
99D3 **Tarime** Tanz	70C3 **Tawau** Malay	Indon	53B2 **Terracina** Italy
82C1 **Tarim He** *R* China	98C1 **Taweisha** Sudan	78D4 **Tělok Saleh** *B* Indon	100B3 **Terrafirma** S Africa
82C2 **Tarim Pendi** *Basin*	79B4 **Tawitawi** *I* Phil	78C3 **Tělok Sampit** *B* Indon	112C8 **Terre Adélie** Region,
China	79B4 **Tawitawi Group** *Is*	78B3 **Tělok Sukadona** *B*	Ant
84B2 **Tarin Kut** Afghan	Phil	Indon	19B4 **Terre Bonne B** USA
18A1 **Tarkio** USA	23B2 **Taxco** Mexico	23B2 **Teloloapán** Mexico	14A3 **Terre Haute** USA
79B2 **Tarlac** Phil	23B2 **Taxcoco** Mexico	64G3 **Tel'pos-iz** *Mt* USSR	19A3 **Terrell** USA
32B6 **Tarma** Peru	44C3 **Tay** *R* Scot	58C1 **Telšiai** USSR	56B2 **Terschelling** *I* Neth
49C3 **Tarn** *R* France	78C3 **Tayan** Indon	78C3 **Telukbatang** Indon	51D1 **Teruel** Spain
59C2 **Tarnobrzeg** Pol	12B1 **Taylor** Alaska, USA	71E4 **Teluk Berau** *B* Indon	4C2 **Teshekpuk** USA
59C3 **Tarnów** Pol	13C1 **Taylor** Can	78B4 **Telukbetung** Indon	4C2 **Teshekpuk L** USA
107D3 **Taroom** Aust	14B2 **Taylor** Michigan, USA	70D4 **Teluk Bone** *B* Indon	74E2 **Teshio** *R* Japan
51C1 **Tarragona** Spain	19A3 **Taylor** Texas, USA	71E4 **Teluk Cendrawasih** *B*	68B2 **Tesiyn Gol** *Mts*
109C4 **Tarraleah** Aust	18C2 **Taylorville** USA	Indon	Mongolia
51C1 **Tarrasa** Spain	80B3 **Tayma'** S Arabia	78D3 **Teluk Mandar** *B*	12H2 **Teslin** Can
16C2 **Tarrytown** USA	63B1 **Taymura** *R* USSR	Indon	12H3 **Teslin** *R* Can
92B2 **Tarsus** Turk	76D3 **Tay Ninh** Viet	71D4 **Teluk Tolo** *B* Indon	12H3 **Teslin L** Can
44D2 **Tartan** *Oilfield* N Sea	63B2 **Tayshet** USSR	70D3 **Teluk Tomini** *B* Indon	63B3 **Teslyn Gol** *R*
47D2 **Tartaro** *R* Italy	68B2 **Tayshir** Mongolia	71D3 **Teluk Weda** *B* Indon	Mongolia
60C2 **Tartu** USSR	44C3 **Tayside** Region, Scot	14B1 **Temagami,L** Can	96C2 **Tessalit** Mali
92C3 **Tartūs** Syria	79A3 **Taytay** Phil	23B2 **Temascal** Mexico	97C3 **Tessaoua** Niger
35C1 **Tarumirim** Brazil	90D3 **Tayyebāt** Iran	78A3 **Tembesi** *R* Indon	101C2 **Tete** Mozam
70A3 **Tarutung** Indon	96B1 **Taza** Mor	78A3 **Tembilahan** Indon	23A2 **Tetela** Mexico
52B1 **Tarvisio** Italy	95B2 **Tazerbo** Region, Libya	27E5 **Temblador** Ven	96B1 **Tetouan** Mor
80D1 **Tashauz** USSR	12E2 **Tazlina L** USA	77C5 **Temerloh** Malay	61G2 **Tetyushi** USSR
86C1 **Tashigang** Bhutan	64J3 **Tazovskiy** USSR	65G5 **Temir** USSR	30D3 **Teuco** *R* Arg
82A1 **Tashkent** USSR	65F5 **Tbilisi** USSR	65J4 **Temirtau** USSR	23A1 **Teúl de Gonzalez**
65K4 **Tashtagol** USSR	98B3 **Tchibanga** Gabon	15C1 **Temiscaming** Can	**Ortega** Mexico
63A2 **Tashtyp** USSR	95A2 **Tchigai,Plat du** Niger	109C2 **Temora** Aust	71D4 **Teun** *I* Indon
78B4 **Tasikmalaya** Indon	97C3 **Tchin Tabaradene**	9B3 **Tempe** USA	52B2 **Tevere** *R* Italy
94B2 **Tasil** Syria	Niger	19A3 **Temple** USA	42C2 **Teviot** *R* Scot
6E2 **Tasiussaq** Greenland	98B2 **Tcholliré** Cam	45C2 **Templemore** Irish Rep	65J4 **Tevriz** USSR
95A3 **Tasker** *Well* Niger	58B2 **Tczew** Pol	23B1 **Tempoal** Mexico	111A3 **Te Waewae B** NZ
110B2 **Tasman B** NZ	111A3 **Te Anau** NZ	34A3 **Temuco** Chile	78C3 **Tewah** Indon
107D5 **Tasmania** *I* Aust	111A3 **Te Anau,L** NZ	111B2 **Temuka** NZ	109D1 **Tewantin** Aust
111B2 **Tasman Mts** NZ	110C1 **Te Aroha** NZ	32B4 **Tena** Ecuador	72A3 **Têwo** China
109C4 **Tasman Pen** Aust	110C1 **Te Awamutu** NZ	87C1 **Tenāli** India	19B3 **Texarkana** USA
107E4 **Tasman S** NZ/Aust	96C1 **Tebessa** Alg	23B2 **Tenancingo** Mexico	19B3 **Texarkana,L** USA
92C1 **Taşova** Turk	23A2 **Teboman** Mexico	76B3 **Tenasserim** Burma	109D1 **Texas** Aust
96C2 **Tassili du Hoggar**	23A2 **Tecailtlān** Mexico	43B4 **Tenby** Wales	9C3 **Texas** State, USA
Desert Region, Alg	21B3 **Tecate** Mexico	83D5 **Ten Degree Chan**	19B4 **Texas City** USA
96C2 **Tassili N'jjer** *Desert*	61K2 **Techa** *R* USSR	Indian O	56A2 **Texel** *I* Neth
Region, Alg	23A1 **Tecolotlán** Mexico	98B1 **Ténéré** *Desert Region*	19A3 **Texoma,L** USA
96B2 **Tata** Mor	23A2 **Tecpan** Mexico	Niger	101G1 **Teyateyaneng**
96D1 **Tataouine** Tunisia	54C1 **Tecuci** Rom	96A2 **Tenerife** *I* Canary Is	Lesotho
65J4 **Tatarsk** USSR	18A1 **Tecumseh** USA	76B1 **Teng** *R* Burma	23B2 **Teziutlán** Mexico
61G2 **Tatarskaya ASSR**	80E2 **Tedzhen** USSR	78D3 **Tenggarong** Indon	86C1 **Tezpur** India
Republic, USSR	65H6 **Tedzhen** *R* USSR	72A2 **Tengger Shamo**	76C1 **Tha** Laos
69G2 **Tatarskiy Proliv** *Str*	42D2 **Tees** *R* Eng	*Desert* China	101G1 **Thabana Ntlenyana**
USSR	33E4 **Tefé** Brazil	87B3 **Tenkāsi** India	*Mt* Lesotho
75B1 **Tateyama** Japan	78B4 **Tegal** Indon	100B2 **Tenke** Zaïre	101G1 **Thaba Putsoa** *Mt*
5G3 **Tathlina L** Can	78B4 **Tegineneng** Indon	97B3 **Tenkodogo** Burkina	Lesotho
12E2 **Tatitlek** USA	25D3 **Tegucigalpa** Honduras	106C2 **Tennant Creek** Aust	76B3 **Thagyettaw** Burma

76D1 **Thai Binh** Viet
76C2 **Thailand** Kingdom, S E Asia
76C3 **Thailand,G of** Thai
76D1 **Thai Nguyen** Viet
76C2 **Thakhek** Laos
84C2 **Thal** Pak
77C4 **Thale Luang** *L* Thai
109C1 **Thallon** Aust
110C1 **Thames** NZ
43E4 **Thames** *R* Eng
76D2 **Thanh Hoah** Viet
87B2 **Thanjavur** India
85C3 **Thar Desert** India
108B1 **Thargomindah** Aust
55B2 **Thásos** *I* Greece
76B2 **Thaton** Burma
76B2 **Thayetmyo** Burma
5F5 **The Dalles** USA
91B4 **The Gulf** S W Asia
4H3 **Thelon** *R* Can
107E3 **Theodore** Aust
9B3 **Theodore Roosevelt L** USA
55B2 **Thermaïkós Kólpos** *G* Greece
8C2 **Thermopolis** USA
4F2 **Thesiger B** Can
14B1 **Thessalon** Can
55B2 **Thessaloníki** Greece
43E3 **Thetford** Eng
15D1 **Thetford Mines** Can
101G1 **Theunissen** S Africa
19B4 **Thibodaux** USA
5J4 **Thicket Portage** Can
8D2 **Thief River Falls** USA
20B2 **Thielsen,Mt** USA
49C2 **Thiers** France
97A3 **Thiès** Sen
99D3 **Thika** Kenya
86B1 **Thimphu** Bhutan
49D2 **Thionville** France
55C3 **Thíra** *I* Greece
42D2 **Thirsk** Eng
39F7 **Thisted** Den
55B3 **Thívai** Greece
48C2 **Thiviers** France
17B1 **Thomaston** Georgia, USA
45C2 **Thomastown** Irish Rep
17B1 **Thomasville** Georgia, USA
6A2 **Thom Bay** Can
5J4 **Thompson** Can
18B1 **Thompson** *R* USA
4G3 **Thompson Landing** Can
13C2 **Thompson R** Can
16C2 **Thompsonville** USA
17B1 **Thomson** USA
107D3 **Thomson** *R* Aust
76C3 **Thon Buri** Thai
76B2 **Thongwa** Burma
47B1 **Thonon-les-Bains** France
42C2 **Thornhill** Scot
48B2 **Thouars** France
15C2 **Thousand Is** Can/USA
13E2 **Three Hills** Can
7G4 **Three Kings Is** NZ
76B2 **Three Pagodas P** Thai
14A2 **Three Rivers** Michigan, USA
20B2 **Three Sisters** *Mt* USA
6D2 **Thule** Greenland
47B1 **Thun** Switz
10B2 **Thunder Bay** Can
47B1 **Thuner See** *L* Switz
77B4 **Thung Song** Thai
47C1 **Thur** *R* Switz
57C2 **Thüringen** State, Germany
57C2 **Thüringen Wald** *Upland* Germany
45C2 **Thurles** Irish Rep
71F5 **Thursday I** Aust
44C2 **Thurso** Scot

112B4 **Thurston I** Ant
47C1 **Thusis** Switz
108B1 **Thylungra** Aust
73B5 **Tiandong** China
73B5 **Tian'e** China
72D2 **Tianjin** China
73B5 **Tianlin** China
82C1 **Tiän Shan** *Mts* C Asia
72B3 **Tianshui** China
72A2 **Tianzhu** China
96C1 **Tiaret** Alg
35A2 **Tibagi** *R* Brazil
94B2 **Tiberias** Israel
94B2 **Tiberias,L** Israel
    Tiber,R = Tevere,R
95A2 **Tibesti** *Mountain Region* Chad
82C2 **Tibet** Autonomous Region, China
108B1 **Tibooburra** Aust
86A1 **Tibrikot** Nepal
24A2 **Tiburón** *I* Mexico
97B3 **Tichitt** Maur
96A2 **Tichla** Mor
47C2 **Ticino** *R* Italy/Switz
15D2 **Ticonderoga** USA
25D2 **Ticul** Mexico
97A3 **Tidjikja** Maur
47C1 **Tiefencastel** Switz
74A2 **Tieling** China
46B1 **Tielt** Belg
46C1 **Tienen** Belg
65J5 **Tien Shan** *Mts* China/USSR
72D2 **Tientsin** China
39H6 **Tierp** Sweden
23B2 **Tierra Blanca** Mexico
23B2 **Tierra Colorada** Mexico
29C6 **Tierra del Fuego** Territory, Arg
28C8 **Tierra del Fuego** *I* Arg/Chile
35B2 **Tietê** Brazil
35A2 **Tiete** *R* Brazil
14B2 **Tiffin** USA
17B1 **Tifton** USA
32B4 **Tigre** *R* Peru
33E2 **Tigre** *R* Ven
93E3 **Tigris** *R* Iraq
23B1 **Tihuatlán** Mexico
21B3 **Tijuana** Mexico
85D4 **Tikamgarh** India
60D2 **Tikhin** USSR
61F4 **Tikhoretsk** USSR
93D3 **Tikrīt** Iraq
1B8 **Tiksi** USSR
46C1 **Tilburg** Neth
43E4 **Tilbury** Eng
30C3 **Tilcara** Arg
108B1 **Tilcha** Aust
76A1 **Tilin** Burma
97C3 **Tillabéri** Niger
20B1 **Tillamook** USA
97C3 **Tília** Niger
55C3 **Tílos** *I* Greece
108B2 **Tilpa** Aust
32B3 **Tiluá** Colombia
64G3 **Timanskiy Kryazh** *Mts* USSR
111B2 **Timaru** NZ
60E4 **Timashevsk** USSR
55B3 **Timbákion** Greece
19B4 **Timbalier B** USA
97B3 **Timbédra** Maur
    Timbuktu = Tombouctou
97B3 **Timétrine Monts** *Mts* Mali
97C3 **Timia** Niger
96C2 **Timimoun** Alg
54B1 **Timişoara** Rom
10B2 **Timmins** Can
106B1 **Timor** *I* Indon
106B2 **Timor S** Aust/Indon
34C3 **Timrå** Swe
79C4 **Tinaca Pt** Phil
27D5 **Tinaco** Ven

87B2 **Tindivanam** India
96B2 **Tindouf** Alg
96B2 **Tinfouchy** Alg
96C2 **Tin Fouye** Alg
6F3 **Tingmiarmiut** Greenland
32B5 **Tingo Maria** Peru
97B3 **Tingrela** Ivory Coast
86B1 **Tingri** China
71F2 **Tinian** Pacific O
30C4 **Tinogasta** Arg
55C3 **Tínos** *I* Greece
43B4 **Tintagel Head** *Pt* Eng
96C2 **Tin Tarabine** *Watercourse* Alg
108B3 **Tintinara** Aust
96C2 **Tin Zaouaten** Alg
22C2 **Tioga P** USA
77C5 **Tioman** *I* Malay
47D1 **Tione** Italy
45C2 **Tipperary** County, Irish Rep
41B3 **Tipperary** Irish Rep
18B2 **Tipton** Missouri, USA
87B2 **Tiptūr** India
23A2 **Tiquicheo** Mexico
55A2 **Tiranë** Alb
47D1 **Tirano** Italy
60C4 **Tiraspol** USSR
87B2 **Tirchchirãppalli** India
55C3 **Tire** Turk
93C1 **Tirebolu** Turk
44A3 **Tiree** *I* Scot
54C2 **Tîrgovişte** Rom
54B1 **Tîrgu Jiu** Rom
54B1 **Tîrgu Mureş** Rom
84C1 **Tirich Mir** *Mt* Pak
96A2 **Tiris** Region, Mor
61J3 **Tirlyanskiy** USSR
54B1 **Tîrnăveni** Rom
55B3 **Tírnavos** Greece
85D4 **Tirodi** India
47D1 **Tirol** Province, Austria
53A2 **Tirso** *R* Sardegna
87B3 **Tiruchchendür** India
87B3 **Tirunelveli** India
87B2 **Tirupati** India
87B2 **Tiruppur** India
87B2 **Tiruppattür** India
87B2 **Tiruvannamalai** India
19A3 **Tishomingo** USA
94C2 **Tisīyah** Syria
59C3 **Tisza** *R* Hung
86A2 **Titlagarh** India
54A2 **Titograd** Yugos
54B2 **Titova Mitrovica** Yugos
54A2 **Titovo Užice** Yugos
52C1 **Titovo Velenje** Yugos
54B2 **Titov Veles** Yugos
98C2 **Titule** Zaïre
17B2 **Titusville** USA
43C4 **Tiverton** Eng
52B2 **Tivoli** Italy
23B2 **Tixtla** Mexico
99E2 **Tiyeglow** Somalia
23B2 **Tizayuca** Mexico
25D2 **Tizimin** Mexico
96C1 **Tizi Ouzou** Alg
96B2 **Tiznit** Mor
23A1 **Tizpan el Alto** Mexico
23B2 **Tlacolula** Mexico
23B2 **Tlacotalpan** Mexico
23A2 **Tlalchana** Mexico
23B2 **Tlalnepantla** Mexico
23B2 **Tlalpan** Mexico
23A1 **Tlaltenango** Mexico
23B2 **Tlancualpicán** Mexico
23B2 **Tlapa** Mexico
23B2 **Tlapacoyan** Mexico
23A1 **Tlaquepaque** Mexico
23B2 **Tlaxcala** Mexico
23B2 **Tlaxcala** State, Mexico
23B2 **Tlaxiaco** Mexico
96B1 **Tlemcen** Alg
101D2 **Toamasina** Madag
34C3 **Toay** Arg
75B2 **Toba** Japan

84B2 **Toba and Kakar Ranges** *Mts* Pak
27E4 **Tobago** *I* Caribbean S
13C2 **Toba Inlet** *Sd* Can
65H4 **Tobal** *R* USSR
71D3 **Tobelo** Indon
14B1 **Tobermory** Can
44A3 **Tobermory** Scot
71E3 **Tobi** *I* Pacific O
21B1 **Tobin,Mt** USA
65H4 **Tobol** *R* USSR
70D4 **Toboli** Indon
65H4 **Tobol'sk** USSR
    Tobruk = Tubruq
31B2 **Tocantins** *R* Brazil
17B1 **Toccoa** USA
47C1 **Toce** *R* Italy
30B3 **Tocopilla** Chile
30C3 **Tocorpuri** *Mt* Chile
32D1 **Tocuyo** *R* Ven
85D3 **Toda** India
47C1 **Tödi** *Mt* Switz
75A1 **Todong** S Korea
9B4 **Todos Santos** Mexico
13E2 **Tofield** Can
13B3 **Tofino** Can
12B3 **Togiak** USA
12B3 **Togiak B** USA
97C4 **Togo** Republic, Africa
72C1 **Togtoh** China
12F2 **Tok** USA
74E2 **Tokachi** *R* Japan
75B1 **Tokamachi** Japan
95C3 **Tokar** Sudan
69E4 **Tokara Retto** *Arch* Japan
92C1 **Tokat** Turk
74B3 **Tökchök-kundo** *Arch* S Korea
75A1 **Tok-do** *I* S Korea
82B1 **Tokmak** USSR
110C1 **Tokomaru Bay** NZ
12H3 **Toku** *R* Can/USA
78C3 **Tokung** Indon
69E4 **Tokuno** *I* Japan
74C4 **Tokushima** Japan
75A2 **Tokuyama** Japan
74D3 **Tökyö** Japan
110C1 **Tolaga Bay** NZ
30F3 **Toledo** Brazil
50B2 **Toledo** Spain
14B2 **Toledo** USA
19B3 **Toledo Bend Res** USA
101D3 **Toliara** Madag
23B1 **Toliman** Mexico
32B3 **Tolina** *Mt* Colombia
51B1 **Tolosa** Spain
29B3 **Toltén** Chile
23B2 **Toluca** Mexico
61G3 **Tol'yatti** USSR
74E2 **Tomakomai** Japan
78D1 **Tomani** Malay
58C2 **Tomaszów Mazowiecka** Pol
11B3 **Tombigbee** *R* USA
98B3 **Tomboco** Angola
35C2 **Tombos** Brazil
97B3 **Tombouctou** Mali
100A2 **Tombua** Angola
34A3 **Tomé** Chile
50B2 **Tomelloso** Spain
50A2 **Tomer** Port
106B3 **Tomkinson Range** *Mts* Aust
63E2 **Tommot** USSR
55B2 **Tomorrit** *Mt* Alb
65K4 **Tomsk** USSR
16B3 **Toms River** USA
25C3 **Tonalá** Mexico
20C1 **Tonasket** USA
15C2 **Tonawanda** USA
105H4 **Tonga** *Is* Pacific O
101H1 **Tongaat** S Africa
73D3 **Tongcheng** China
72B2 **Tongchuan** China
72A2 **Tongde** China
46C1 **Tongeren** Belg
76E2 **Tonggu Jiao** *I* China

73A5 **Tonghai** China
74B2 **Tonghua** China
74B3 **Tongjosŏn-man** N Korea
76D1 **Tongkin,G of** China/ Viet
72E1 **Tonglia** China
73D3 **Tongling** China
108B2 **Tongo** Aust
34A2 **Tongoy** Chile
73B4 **Tongren** Guizhou, China
72A2 **Tongren** Qinghai, China
86C1 **Tongsa** Bhutan
76B1 **Tongta** Burma
68B3 **Tongtian He** *R* China
44B2 **Tongue** Scot
72D2 **Tong Xian** China
72B2 **Tongxin** China
73B4 **Tongzi** China
63B3 **Tonhil** Mongolia
9C4 **Tonich** Mexico
99C2 **Tonj** Sudan
85D3 **Tonk** India
18A2 **Tonkawa** USA
76C3 **Tonle Sap** *L* Camb
21B2 **Tonopah** USA
12E2 **Tonsina** USA
8B2 **Tooele** USA
109D1 **Toogoolawah** Aust
108B1 **Toompine** Aust
109D1 **Toowoomba** Aust
22C1 **Topaz L** USA
18A2 **Topeka** USA
9C4 **Topolobampo** Mexico
20B1 **Toppenish** USA
55C3 **Torbali** Turk
90C2 **Torbat-e-Heydarīyeh** Iran
90D2 **Torbat-e Jām** Iran
43C4 **Torbay** Eng
12D2 **Torbert,Mt** USA
50A1 **Tordesillas** Spain
56C2 **Torgau** Germany
46B1 **Torhout** Belg
99D2 **Tori** Eth
69G3 **Tori** *I* Japan
47B2 **Torino** Italy
99D2 **Torit** Sudan
35A1 **Torixoreu** Brazil
50A1 **Tormes** *R* Spain
13E2 **Tornado Mt** Can
38J5 **Torne** *L* Sweden
38H5 **Torneträsk** Sweden
7D4 **Torngat** *Mts* Can
38J5 **Tornio** Fin
34C3 **Tornquist** Arg
15C2 **Toronto** Can
60D2 **Toropets** USSR
99D2 **Tororo** Uganda
92B2 **Toros Dağlari** *Mts* Turk
22C4 **Torrance** USA
50A2 **Torrão** Port
51C1 **Torreblanca** Spain
53B2 **Torre del Greco** Italy
50B1 **Torrelavega** Spain
50B2 **Torremolinos** Spain
108A2 **Torrens,L** Aust
24B2 **Torreón** Mexico
47B2 **Torre Pellice** Italy
107D2 **Torres Str** Aust
50A2 **Torres Vedras** Port
16C2 **Torrington** Connecticut, USA
8C2 **Torrington** Wyoming, USA
9C4 **Torrón** Mexico
38D3 **Tórshavn** Føroyar
47C2 **Tortona** Italy
51C1 **Tortosa** Spain
90C2 **Torūd** Iran
58B2 **Toruń** Pol
40B2 **Tory** *I* Irish Rep
60D2 **Torzhok** USSR
75A2 **Tosa** Japan
74C4 **Tosa-shimizu** Japan

74C4 **Tosa-wan** *B* Japan
75B2 **To-shima** *I* Japan
39L7 **Tosno** USSR
60D2 **Tosno** USSR
75A2 **Tosu** Japan
92B1 **Tosya** Turk
61F1 **Tot'ma** USSR
43C4 **Totnes** Eng
33F2 **Totness** Surinam
23B2 **Totolapan** Mexico
51B2 **Totona** Spain
109C2 **Tottenham** Aust
74C3 **Tottori** Japan
97B4 **Touba** Ivory Coast
97A3 **Touba** Sen
96B1 **Toubkal** *Mt* Mor
97B3 **Tougan** Burkina
96C1 **Touggourt** Alg
97A3 **Tougué** Guinea
46C2 **Toul** France
49D3 **Toulon** France
48C3 **Toulouse** France
97B4 **Toumodi** Ivory Coast
76B2 **Toungoo** Burma
46B1 **Tourcoing** France
96A2 **Tourine** Maur
46B1 **Tournai** Belg
48C2 **Tours** France
74E2 **Towada** Japan
74E2 **Towada-ko** *L* Japan
15C2 **Towanda** USA
107D2 **Townsville** Aust
16A3 **Towson** USA
43C4 **Towy** *R* Wales
74D3 **Toyama** Japan
75B1 **Toyama-wan** *B* Japan
75B2 **Toyohashi** Japan
75B2 **Toyonaka** Japan
75A1 **Toyooka** Japan
74D3 **Toyota** Japan
96C1 **Tozeur** Tunisia
46D2 **Traben-Trarbach** Germany
93C1 **Trabzon** Turk
22B2 **Tracy** California, USA
34A3 **Traiguén** Chile
13D3 **Trail** Can
41B3 **Tralee** Irish Rep
45B2 **Tralee B** Irish Rep
45C2 **Tramore** Irish Rep
39G7 **Tranås** Sweden
77B4 **Trang** Thai
71E4 **Trangan** *I* Indon
109C2 **Trangie** Aust
12E2 **Transalaskan Pipeline** USA
100B3 **Transvaal** Province, S Africa
Transylvanian Alps = Muntii Carpaţii Meridionali
53B3 **Trapani** Italy
109C3 **Traralgon** Aust
97A3 **Trarza** Region, Maur
76C3 **Trat** Thai
108B2 **Traveller's** *L* Aust
56C2 **Travemünde** Germany
14A2 **Traverse City** USA
12C1 **Traverse Peak** *Mt* USA
111B2 **Travers,Mt** NZ
47C2 **Trebbia** *R* Italy
59B3 **Třebíč** Czech
54A2 **Trebinje** Yugos
57C3 **Trebon** Czech
29F2 **Treinta y Tres** Urug
29C4 **Trelew** Arg
39G7 **Trelleborg** Sweden
43B3 **Tremadog B** Wales
15D1 **Tremblant,Mt** Can
13C2 **Trembleur L** Can
16A2 **Tremont** USA
59B3 **Trenčín** Czech
34C3 **Trenque Lauquén** Arg
43D3 **Trent** *R* Eng
47D1 **Trentino** Region, Italy
47D1 **Trento** Italy
15C2 **Trenton** Can

18B1 **Trenton** Missouri, USA
16B2 **Trenton** New Jersey, USA
7E5 **Trepassey** Can
34C3 **Tres Arroyos** Arg
35B2 **Tres Corações** Brazil
30F3 **Três Lagoas** Brazil
34C3 **Tres Lomas** Arg
22B2 **Tres Pinos** USA
35C2 **Três Rios** Brazil
47C2 **Treviglio** Italy
47E2 **Treviso** Italy
47C2 **Trezzo** Italy
87B2 **Trichūr** India
108C2 **Trida** Aust
46D2 **Trier** Germany
52B1 **Trieste** Italy
45C2 **Trim** Irish Rep
87C3 **Trincomalee** Sri Lanka
33E6 **Trinidad** Bol
29E2 **Trinidad** Urug
9C3 **Trinidad** USA
34C3 **Trinidad** *I* Arg
27E4 **Trinidad** *I* Caribbean S
103G6 **Trindade** *I* Atlantic O
27E4 **Trinidad & Tobago** Republic, Caribbean S
19A3 **Trinity** USA
9D3 **Trinity** *R* USA
7E5 **Trinity B** Can
12D3 **Trinity Is** USA
17A1 **Trion** USA
94B1 **Tripoli** Leb
95A1 **Tripoli** Libya
55B3 **Tripolis** Greece
86C2 **Tripura** State, India
103H6 **Tristan da Cunha** *Is* Atlantic O
87B3 **Trivandrum** India
59B3 **Trnava** Czech
107E1 **Trobriand Is** PNG
15D1 **Trois-Riviéres** Can
65H4 **Troitsk** USSR
39G7 **Trollhättan** Sweden
38F6 **Trollheimen** *Mt* Nor
89K9 **Tromelin** *I* Indian O
38H5 **Tromsø** Nor
38G6 **Trondheim** Nor
38G6 **Trondheimfjord** *Inlet* Nor
42B2 **Troon** Scot
102J3 **Tropic of Cancer**
103J6 **Tropic of Capricorn**
96B2 **Troudenni** Mali
7A4 **Trout L** Ontario, Can
17A1 **Troy** Alabama, USA
16C1 **Troy** New York, USA
14B2 **Troy** Ohio, USA
54B2 **Troyan** Bulg
49C2 **Troyes** France
91B5 **Trucial Coast** Region, UAE
21A2 **Truckee** *R* USA
25D3 **Trujillo** Honduras
32B5 **Trujillo** Peru
50A2 **Trujillo** Spain
32C2 **Trujillo** Ven
109C2 **Trundle** Aust
7D5 **Truro** Can
43B4 **Truro** Eng
71E3 **Trust Territories of the Pacific Is** Pacific O
68B2 **Tsagaan Nuur** *L* Mongolia
68B1 **Tsagan-Tologoy** USSR
101D2 **Tsaratanana** Madag
100B3 **Tsau** Botswana
99D3 **Tsavo** Kenya
99D3 **Tsavo Nat Pk** Kenya
65J4 **Tselinograd** USSR
100A3 **Tses** Namibia
68B2 **Tsetserleg** Mongolia
68C2 **Tsetserleg** Mongolia
97C4 **Tsévié** Togo
100B3 **Tshabong** Botswana

100B3 **Tshane** Botswana
98B3 **Tshela** Zaïre
98C3 **Tshibala** Zaïre
98C3 **Tshikapa** Zaïre
98C3 **Tshuapa** *R* Zaïre
101D3 **Tsihombe** Madag
61F4 **Tsimlyanskoye Vodokhranilishche** *Res* USSR
Tsinan = Jinan
Tsingtao = Qingdao
101D2 **Tsiroanomandidy** Madag
13B2 **Tsitsutl Peak** *Mt* Can
58D2 **Tsna** *R* USSR
72B1 **Tsogt Ovoo** Mongolia
75B2 **Tsu** Japan
75B1 **Tsubata** Japan
74E3 **Tsuchiura** Japan
74E2 **Tsugaru-kaikyō** *Str* Japan
100A2 **Tsumeb** Namibia
100A3 **Tsumis** Namibia
75B1 **Tsunugi** Japan
74D3 **Tsuruga** Japan
74D3 **Tsuruoka** Japan
75B1 **Tsushima** Japan
74B4 **Tsushima** *I* Japan
74C3 **Tsuyama** Japan
50A1 **Tua** *R* Port
45B2 **Tuam** Irish Rep
60E5 **Tuapse** USSR
111A3 **Tuatapere** NZ
30G4 **Tubarão** Brazil
94B2 **Tubas** Israel
79A4 **Tubbataha Reefs** *Is* Phil
57B3 **Tübingen** Germany
95B1 **Tubruq** Libya
16B3 **Tuckerton** USA
9B3 **Tucson** USA
30C4 **Tucumán** State, Arg
34B2 **Tucunuco** Arg
33E2 **Tucupita** Ven
51B1 **Tudela** Spain
93C3 **Tudmur** Syria
101H1 **Tugela** *R* S Africa
109D2 **Tuggerah** *L* Aust
12D3 **Tugidak** *I* USA
79B2 **Tuguegarao** Phil
63F2 **Tugur** USSR
72D2 **Tuhai He** *R* China
4E3 **Tuktoyaktuk** USA
58C1 **Tukums** USSR
99D3 **Tukuyu** Tanz
84B1 **Tukzar** Afghan
60E3 **Tula** USSR
23B1 **Tulancingo** Mexico
78A3 **Tulangbawang** *R* Indon
32B3 **Tulcán** Colombia
60C5 **Tulcea** Rom
100B3 **Tuli** Zim
94B2 **Tulkarm** Israel
48C2 **Tulle** France
19B3 **Tullos** USA
45C2 **Tullow** Irish Rep
18A2 **Tulsa** USA
93C3 **Tulūl ash Shāmīyah** *Desert Region* Syria/ S Arabia
63C2 **Tulun** USSR
78C4 **Tulungagung** Indon
32B3 **Tumaco** Colombia
109C3 **Tumbarumba** Aust
32A4 **Tumbes** Ecuador
108A2 **Tumby Bay** Aust
74B2 **Tumen** China
87B2 **Tumkūr** India
77C4 **Tumpat** Malay
85D4 **Tumsar** India
97B3 **Tumu** Ghana
109C3 **Tumut** Aust
109C3 **Tumut** *R* Aust
27L1 **Tunapuna** Trinidad
93C2 **Tunceli** Turk
99D3 **Tunduma** Zambia
101C2 **Tunduru** Tanz

54C2 **Tundzha** R Bulg
87B1 **Tungabhadra** R India
68D4 **Tung-Chiang** Taiwan
38B2 **Tungnafellsjökull** Mts Iceland
12J2 **Tungsten** Can
63B1 **Tunguska** R USSR
87C1 **Tuni** India
96D1 **Tunis** Tunisia
88E4 **Tunisia** Republic, N Africa
32C2 **Tunja** Colombia
12B2 **Tuntutuliak** USA
12B2 **Tununak** USA
34B2 **Tunuyán** Arg
34B2 **Tunuyán** R Arg
73D4 **Tunxi** China
22C2 **Tuolumne Meadows** USA
35A2 **Tupã** Brazil
35B1 **Tupaciguara** Brazil
19C3 **Tupelo** USA
30C3 **Tupiza** Bol
15D2 **Tupper Lake** USA
34B2 **Tupungato** Arg
29C2 **Tupungato** Mt Arg
86C1 **Tura** India
63C1 **Tura** USSR
61K2 **Tura** R USSR
90C2 **Turãn** Iran
63B2 **Turan** USSR
93C3 **Turayf** S Arabia
80E3 **Turbat** Pak
32B2 **Turbo** Colombia
54B1 **Turda** Rom
63A3 **Turfan Depression** China
65H4 **Turgay** USSR
63B3 **Turgen Uul** Mt Mongolia
54C2 **Turgovishte** Bulg
92A2 **Turgutlu** Turk
92C1 **Turhal** Turk
39K7 **Türi** USSR
51B2 **Turia** R Spain
Turin = Torino
61K2 **Turinsk** USSR
69F2 **Turiy Rog** USSR
99D2 **Turkana,L** Kenya/Eth
80E1 **Turkestan** Region, C Asia
82A1 **Turkestan** USSR
92C2 **Turkey** Republic, W Asia
80D1 **Turkmenskaya SSR** Republic, USSR
90B2 **Turkmenskiy Zaliv** B USSR
27C2 **Turks Is** Caribbean S
39J6 **Turku** Fin
99D2 **Turkwel** R Kenya
22B2 **Turlock** USA
22B2 **Turlock L** USA
110C2 **Turnagain,C** NZ
25D3 **Turneffe I** Belize
16C1 **Turners Falls** USA
46C1 **Turnhout** Belg
13F1 **Turnor L** Can
54B2 **Turnu Măgurele** Rom
63A3 **Turpan** China
26B2 **Turquino** Mt Cuba
80E1 **Turtkul'** USSR
18A2 **Turtle Creek Res** USA
13F2 **Turtle L** Can
63A1 **Turukhansk** USSR
68C1 **Turuntayevo** USSR
35A1 **Turvo** R Goias, Brazil
35B2 **Turvo** R São Paulo, Brazil
58C2 **Tur'ya** R USSR
19C3 **Tuscaloosa** USA
18C2 **Tuscola** USA
90C3 **Tusharik** Iran
87B3 **Tuticorin** India
54C2 **Tutrakan** Bulg
57B3 **Tuttlingen** Germany
68C2 **Tuul Gol** R Mongolia
105G4 **Tuvalu** Is Pacific O

63B2 **Tuvinskaya** Republic, USSR
23A2 **Tuxpan** Jalisco, Mexico
24B2 **Tuxpan** Nayarit, Mexico
23B1 **Tuxpan** Veracruz, Mexico
23B2 **Tuxtepec** Mexico
25C3 **Tuxtla Gutiérrez** Mexico
50A1 **Túy** Spain
76D3 **Tuy Hoa** Viet
92B2 **Tuz Gölü** Salt L Turk
93D3 **Tuz Khurmãtũ** Iraq
54A2 **Tuzla** Yugos
42C2 **Tweed** R Eng/Scot
109D1 **Tweed Heads** Aust
42C2 **Tweedsmuir Hills** Scot
7E5 **Twillingate** Can
8B2 **Twin Falls** USA
111B2 **Twins,The** Mt NZ
14A2 **Two Rivers** USA
63E2 **Tygda** USSR
19A3 **Tyler** USA
65K3 **Tym** R USSR
69G1 **Tymovskoye** USSR
42D2 **Tyne** R Eng
42D2 **Tyne and Wear** County, Eng
42D2 **Tynemouth** Eng
38G6 **Tynset** Nor
12D3 **Tyonek** USA
94B2 **Tyr** Leb
Tyre = Tyr
45C1 **Tyrone** County, N Ire
108B3 **Tyrrell,L** Aust
53B2 **Tyrrhenian S** Italy
65H4 **Tyumen'** USSR
43B3 **Tywyn** Wales
55B3 **Tzoumérka** Mt Greece

U

99E2 **Uarsciek** Somalia
35C2 **Ubá** Brazil
35C1 **Ubaí** Brazil
98B2 **Ubangi** R CAR
47B2 **Ubaye** R France
75A2 **Ube** Japan
50B2 **Ubeda** Spain
6E2 **Ubekendt Ejland** I Greenland
35B1 **Uberaba** Brazil
35B1 **Uberlândia** Brazil
76C2 **Ubon Ratchathani** Thai
58D2 **Ubort** R USSR
98C3 **Ubundi** Zaïre
32C5 **Ucayali** R Peru
84C3 **Uch** Pak
74E2 **Uchiura-wan** B Japan
63F2 **Uchur** R USSR
85C4 **Udaipur** India
86B1 **Udaipur Garhi** Nepal
34D3 **Udaquiola** Arg
39G7 **Uddevalla** Sweden
38H5 **Uddjaur** L Sweden
87B1 **Udgir** India
84D2 **Udhampur** India
61H2 **Udmurtskaya ASSR** Republic, USSR
76C2 **Udon Thani** Thai
63F2 **Udskaya Guba** B USSR
87A2 **Udupi** India
75B1 **Ueda** Japan
99C2 **Uele** R Zaïre
56C2 **Uelzen** Germany
98C2 **Uere** R Zaïre
61J3 **Ufa** USSR
61J2 **Ufa** R USSR
100A3 **Ugab** R Namibia
99D3 **Ugaila** R Tanz
12D3 **Ugak B** USA
99D2 **Uganda** Republic, Africa
12C3 **Ugashik B** USA
12C3 **Ugashik L** USA

47B2 **Ugine** France
69G2 **Uglegorsk** USSR
60E2 **Uglich** USSR
60E3 **Ugra** R USSR
44A3 **Uig** Scot
98B3 **Uige** Angola
61H4 **Uil** USSR
8B2 **Uinta Mts** USA
100B4 **Uitenhage** S Africa
59C3 **Ujfehértó** Hung
75B2 **Uji** Japan
99C3 **Ujiji** Tanz
30C3 **Ujina** Chile
85D4 **Ujjain** India
70C4 **Ujung Pandang** Indon
99D3 **Ukerewe** I Tanz
86C1 **Ukhrul** India
21A2 **Ukiah** California, USA
20C1 **Ukiah** Oregon, USA
58C1 **Ukmerge** USSR
60C4 **Ukrainskaya** Republic, USSR
68C2 **Ulaanbaatar** Mongolia
68B2 **Ulaangom** Mongolia
72C1 **Ulaan Uul** Mongolia
82C1 **Ulangar Hu** L China
68C1 **Ulan Ude** USSR
68B3 **Ulan Ul Hu** L China
34B2 **Ulapes** Arg
74B3 **Ulchin** S Korea
54A2 **Ulcinj** Yugos
68D2 **Uldz** Mongolia
68B2 **Uliastay** Mongolia
58D1 **Ulla** USSR
109D3 **Ulladulla** Aust
44B3 **Ullapool** Scot
38H5 **Ullsfjorden** Inlet Nor
42C2 **Ullswater** L Eng
74C3 **Ullung-do** I S Korea
57C3 **Ulm** Germany
108A1 **Uloowaranie,L** Aust
74B3 **Ulsan** S Korea
45C1 **Ulster** Region, N Ire
65K5 **Ulungur He** R China
65K5 **Ulungur Hu** L China
44A3 **Ulva** I Scot
42C2 **Ulverston** Eng
109C4 **Ulverstone** Aust
63G2 **Ulya** R USSR
61G3 **Ul'yanovsk** USSR
60D4 **Uman** USSR
6E2 **Umanak** Greenland
86A2 **Umaria** India
85B3 **Umarkot** Pak
108A1 **Umaroona,L** Aust
20C1 **Umatilla** USA
38L5 **Umba** USSR
99D3 **Umba** R Tanz
38H6 **Ume** R Sweden
38J6 **Umea** Sweden
101H1 **Umfolozi** R S Africa
4C3 **Umiat** USA
91C4 **Umm al Qaiwain** UAE
91C5 **Umm as Samīm** Salt Marsh Oman
99C1 **Umm Bell** Sudan
99D1 **Umm Hagar** Eth
98C1 **Umm Keddada** Sudan
99D1 **Umm Ruwaba** Sudan
91B5 **Umm Sa'id** Qatar
100B2 **Umnaiti** R Zim
20B2 **Umpqua** R USA
85D4 **Umred** India
100B4 **Umtata** S Africa
35A2 **Umuarama** Brazil
52C1 **Una** R Yugos
35B1 **Unai** Brazil
12B2 **Unalakleet** USA
80C3 **Unayzah** S Arabia
16C2 **Uncasville** USA
101G1 **Underberg** S Africa
60D3 **Unecha** USSR
94B3 **Uneisa** Jordan
7D4 **Ungava B** Can
30F4 **União de Vitória** Brazil
34B3 **Unión** Arg
18B2 **Union** Missouri, USA
17B1 **Union** S Carolina, USA

14C2 **Union City** Pennsylvania, USA
62C3 **Union of Soviet Socialist Reps** Asia
17A1 **Union Springs** USA
15C3 **Uniontown** USA
91B5 **United Arab Emirates** Arabian Pen
36C3 **United Kingdom** Kingdom, W Europe
2H4 **United States of America**
6B1 **United States Range** Mts Can
13F2 **Unity** Can
20C2 **Unity** USA
46D1 **Unna** Germany
86A1 **Unnão** India
44E1 **Unst** I Scot
13A1 **Unuk** R USA
92C1 **Únye** Turk
61F2 **Unzha** R USSR
33E2 **Upata** Ven
98C3 **Upemba Nat Pk** Zaïre
6E2 **Upernavik** Greenland
22D3 **Upland** USA
100B3 **Uplington** S Africa
14B2 **Upper Arlington** USA
13D2 **Upper Arrow L** Can
111C2 **Upper Hutt** NZ
20B2 **Upper Klamath L** USA
20B2 **Upper L** USA
45C1 **Upper Lough Erne** L N Ire
27L1 **Upper Manzanilla** Trinidad
7C4 **Upper Seal,L** Can
39H7 **Uppsala** Sweden
72B1 **Urad Qianqi** China
91A4 **Urairah** S Arabia
61H3 **Ural** R USSR
109D2 **Uralla** Aust
61H3 **Ural'sk** USSR
65G4 **Uralskiy Khrebet** Mts USSR
5H4 **Uranium City** Can
75B1 **Urawa** Japan
18C1 **Urbana** Illinois, USA
14B2 **Urbana** Ohio, USA
52B2 **Urbino** Italy
42C2 **Ure** R Eng
61G2 **Uren'** USSR
93C2 **Urfa** Turk
80E1 **Urgench** USSR
84B2 **Urgun** Afghan
55C3 **Urla** Turk
54B2 **Uroševac** Yugos
31B4 **Uruaçu** Brazil
23A2 **Uruapan** Mexico
35B1 **Urucuia** R Brazil
30E4 **Uruguaiana** Brazil
29E2 **Uruguay** Republic, S America
29E2 **Uruguay** R Urug
82C1 **Ürümqi** China
69H2 **Urup** I USSR
84B2 **Uruzgan** Afghan
61F3 **Uryupinsk** USSR
61H2 **Urzhum** USSR
54C2 **Urziceni** Rom
82C1 **Usa** China
75A2 **Usa** Japan
64G3 **Usa** R USSR
92A2 **Uşak** Turk
100A3 **Usakos** Namibia
99D3 **Ushashi** Tanz
65J5 **Ush Tobe** USSR
29C6 **Ushuaia** Arg
63E2 **Ushumun** USSR
43C4 **Usk** R Wales
92A1 **Üsküdar** Turk
63C1 **Usolye Sibirskoye** USSR
34B2 **Uspallata** Arg
69F2 **Ussuriysk** USSR
47C1 **Uster** Switz
53B3 **Ustica** I Italy
57C2 **Ústi nad Labem** Czech

65J4	**Ust'Ishim** USSR
58B2	**Ustka** Pol
65K5	**Ust'-Kamenogorsk** USSR
63B2	**Ust Karabula** USSR
61J2	**Ust'Katav** USSR
63C2	**Ust'-Kut** USSR
61E4	**Ust Labinsk** USSR
63F1	**Ust'Maya** USSR
1C8	**Ust'Nera** USSR
63E2	**Ust'Nyukzha** USSR
63C2	**Ust'Ordynskiy** USSR
64G3	**Ust'Tsil'ma** USSR
63F2	**Ust'Umal'ta** USSR
75A2	**Usuki** Japan
25C3	**Usumacinta** R Guatemala/Mexico
101H1	**Usutu** R Swaziland
8B3	**Utah** State, USA
8B2	**Utah L** USA
58D1	**Utena** USSR
85B3	**Uthal** Pak
10C2	**Utica** USA
51B2	**Utiel** Spain
13D1	**Utikuma L** Can
56B2	**Utrecht** Neth
101H1	**Utrecht** S Africa
50A2	**Utrera** Spain
38K5	**Utsjoki** Fin
74D3	**Utsunomiya** Japan
76C2	**Uttaradit** Thai
86A1	**Uttar Pradesh** State, India
65H4	**Uval** USSR
107F3	**Uvéa** I Nouvelle Calédonie
99D3	**Uvinza** Tanz
99C3	**Uvira** Zaïre
6E2	**Uvkusigssat** Greenland
39J6	**Uvsikaupunki** Fin
68B1	**Uvs Nuur** L China
74C4	**Uwajima** Japan
72B2	**Uxin Qi** China
63B2	**Uyar** USSR
30C3	**Uyuni** Bol
80E1	**Uzbekskaya S.S.R.** Republic, USSR
48C2	**Uzerche** France
59C3	**Uzhgorod** USSR
60E3	**Uzlovaya** USSR
92A1	**Uzunköprü** Turk

V

101F1	**Vaal** R S Africa
101G1	**Vaal Dam** Res S Africa
100B3	**Vaalwater** S Africa
38J6	**Vaasa** Fin
59B3	**Vác** Hung
30F4	**Vacaria** Brazil
35C1	**Vacaria** R Minas Gerais, Brazil
21A2	**Vacaville** USA
85C4	**Vadodara** India
38K4	**Vadsø** Nor
47C1	**Vaduz** Leichtenstein
38D3	**Vágar** Føroyar
29E3	**Va Gesell** Arg
59B3	**Váh** R Czech
87B2	**Vaigai** R India
65K3	**Vakh** R USSR
60B4	**Vâlcea** Rom
29C4	**Valcheta** Arg
47D2	**Valdagno** Italy
60D2	**Valday** USSR
60D2	**Valdayskaya Vozvyshennost'** Upland USSR
32D2	**Val de la Pascua** Ven
50B2	**Valdepeñas** Spain
12E2	**Valdez** USA
29B3	**Valdivia** Chile
46B2	**Val d'Oise** Department France
17B1	**Valdosta** USA

20C2	**Vale** USA
13D2	**Valemount** Can
31D4	**Valença** Bahia, Brazil
35C2	**Valença** Rio de Janeiro, Brazil
49C3	**Valence** France
51B2	**Valencia** Region, Spain
51B2	**Valencia** Spain
32D1	**Valencia** Ven
45A3	**Valencia** I Irish Rep
50A2	**Valencia de Alcantara** Spain
46B1	**Valenciennes** France
47C2	**Valenza** Italy
32C2	**Valera** Ven
39K7	**Valga** USSR
64E4	**Valikiyo** USSR
54A2	**Valjevo** Yugos
39J6	**Valkeakoski** Fin
25D2	**Valladolid** Mexico
50B1	**Valladolid** Spain
47B2	**Valle d'Aosta** Region, Italy
27D5	**Valle de la Pascua** Ven
23A1	**Valle de Santiago** Mexico
47B2	**Valle d'Isére** France
32C1	**Valledupar** Colombia
97C3	**Vallée de l'Azaouak** V Niger
97C3	**Vallée Tilemis** V Mali
30D2	**Valle Grande** Bol
22A1	**Vallejo** USA
30B4	**Vallenar** Chile
53B3	**Valletta** Malta
8D2	**Valley City** USA
20B2	**Valley Falls** USA
15D1	**Valleyfield** Can
13D1	**Valleyview** Can
47E2	**Valli di Comacchio** Lg Italy
51C1	**Valls** Spain
58D1	**Valmiera** USSR
35A2	**Valparaiso** Brazil
34A2	**Valparaiso** Chile
23A1	**Valparaiso** Mexico
17A1	**Valparaiso** USA
101G1	**Vals** R S Africa
85C4	**Valsåd** India
60E3	**Valuyki** USSR
50A2	**Valverde del Camino** Spain
38J6	**Vammala** Fin
93D2	**Van** Turk
63C1	**Vanavara** USSR
18B2	**Van Buren** Arkansas, USA
13C3	**Vancouver** Can
20B1	**Vancouver** USA
5F5	**Vancouver I** Can
12G2	**Vancouver,Mt** Can
18C2	**Vandalia** Illinois, USA
14B3	**Vandalia** Ohio, USA
13C2	**Vanderhoof** Can
106C2	**Van Diemen G** Aust
39G7	**Vänern** L Sweden
39G7	**Vänersborg** Sweden
101D3	**Vangaindrano** Madag
93D2	**Van Gölü** Salt L Turk
76C2	**Vang Vieng** Laos
9C3	**Van Horn** USA
15C1	**Vanier** Can
1C6	**Vankarem** USSR
38H6	**Vännäs** Sweden
48B2	**Vannes** France
47B2	**Vanoise** Mts France
100A4	**Vanrhynsdorp** S Africa
6B3	**Vansittart I** Can
105G4	**Vanuatu** Is Pacific O
14B2	**Van Wert** USA
47C2	**Varallo** Italy
90B2	**Varāmīn** Iran
86A1	**Vārānasi** India
38K4	**Varangerfjord** Inlet Nor
38K4	**Varangerhalvøya** Pen Nor
52C1	**Varazdin** Yugos

39G7	**Varberg** Sweden
39F7	**Varde** Den
38L4	**Vardø** Nor
58C2	**Varéna** USSR
47C2	**Varenna** Italy
47C2	**Varese** Italy
35B2	**Varginha** Brazil
38K6	**Varkaus** Fin
54C2	**Varna** Bulg
39G7	**Värnamo** Sweden
17B1	**Varnville** USA
35C1	**Várzea da Palma** Brazil
47C2	**Varzi** Italy
50B1	**Vascongadas** Region, Spain
60D3	**Vasil'kov** USSR
14B2	**Vassar** USA
39H7	**Västerås** Sweden
39H7	**Västervik** Sweden
52B2	**Vasto** Italy
65J4	**Vasyugan** R USSR
38B2	**Vatnajökull** Mts Iceland
38A1	**Vatneyri** Iceland
54C1	**Vatra Dornei** Rom
39G7	**Vättern** L Sweden
9C3	**Vaughn** USA
32C3	**Vaupés** R Colombia
13E2	**Vauxhall** Can
87C3	**Vavunija** Sri Lanka
39G7	**Växjö** Sweden
64G2	**Vaygach, Ostrov** I USSR
34C2	**Vedia** Arg
38G5	**Vega** I Nor
13E2	**Vegreville** Can
50A2	**Vejer de la Frontera** Spain
39F7	**Vejle** Den
52C2	**Velebit** Mts Yugos
35C1	**Velhas** R Brazil
39K7	**Velikaya** R USSR
60D2	**Velikiye Luki** USSR
61G1	**Velikiy Ustyug** USSR
54C2	**Veliko Tŭrnovo** Bulg
97A3	**Vélingara** Sen
87B2	**Vellore** India
61F1	**Vel'sk** USSR
87B3	**Vembanad L** India
34C2	**Venado Tuerto** Arg
35B2	**Vençeslau Braz** Brazil
49C2	**Vendôme** France
12E1	**Venetie** USA
47D2	**Veneto** Region, Italy
47E2	**Venezia** Italy
32D2	**Venezuela** Republic, S America
87A1	**Vengurla** India
12C3	**Veniaminof** V USA
	Venice = Venezia
87B2	**Venkatagiri** India
56B2	**Venlo** Neth
58C1	**Venta** R USSR
101G1	**Ventersburg** S Africa
58C1	**Ventspils** USSR
32D3	**Ventuari** R Ven
22C3	**Ventura** USA
60D1	**Vepsovskaya Vozvyshennost'** Upland USSR
30D4	**Vera** Arg
51B2	**Vera** Spain
23B2	**Veracruz** Mexico
23B1	**Veracruz** State, Mexico
85C4	**Verāval** India
47C2	**Verbania** Italy
47C2	**Vercelli** Italy
35A1	**Verde** R Goias, Brazil
23A1	**Verde** R Jalisco, Mexico
35A1	**Verde** R Mato Grosso do Sul, Brazil
23B2	**Verde** R Oaxaca, Mexico
	Verde,C = Cap Vert
35C1	**Verde Grande** R Brazil

34C3	**Verde,Pen** Arg
49D3	**Verdon** R France
46C2	**Verdun** France
101G1	**Vereeniging** S Africa
61H2	**Vereshchagino** USSR
97A3	**Verga,C** Guinea
34D3	**Vergara** Arg
50A1	**Verin** Spain
98C3	**Verissimo Sarmento** Angola
63D2	**Verkh Angara** R USSR
61J3	**Verkhneural'sk** USSR
63E1	**Verkhnevilyuysk** USSR
1C8	**Verkhoyansk** USSR
35A1	**Vermelho** R Brazil
13E2	**Vermilion** Can
10C2	**Vermont** State, USA
22B2	**Vernalis** USA
13D2	**Vernon** Can
46A2	**Vernon** France
9D3	**Vernon** USA
17B2	**Vero Beach** USA
54B2	**Veroia** Greece
47D2	**Verolanuova** Italy
47D2	**Verona** Italy
46B2	**Versailles** France
101H1	**Verulam** S Africa
46C1	**Verviers** Belg
46B2	**Vervins** France
46C2	**Vesle** R France
49D2	**Vesoul** France
38G5	**Vesterålen** Is Nor
38G5	**Vestfjorden** Inlet Nor
38A2	**Vestmannaeyjar** Iceland
53B2	**Vesuvio** Mt Italy
59B3	**Veszprém** Hung
39H7	**Vetlanda** Sweden
61F2	**Vetluga** R USSR
46B1	**Veurne** Belg
47B1	**Vevey** Switz
46A2	**Vexin** Region, France
47A2	**Veynes** France
50A1	**Viana do Castelo** Port
49E3	**Viareggio** Italy
39F7	**Viborg** Den
53C3	**Vibo Valentia** Italy
112C2	**Vice-commodoro Marambio** Base Ant
52B1	**Vicenza** Italy
51C1	**Vich** Spain
32D3	**Vichada** R Colombia
61F2	**Vichuga** USSR
49C2	**Vichy** France
19B3	**Vicksburg** USA
35C2	**Vicosa** Brazil
106C4	**Victor Harbour** Aust
34C2	**Victoria** Arg
13C3	**Victoria** Can
34A3	**Victoria** Chile
73C5	**Victoria** Hong Kong
78D1	**Victoria** Malay
108B3	**Victoria** State, Aust
9D4	**Victoria** USA
106C2	**Victoria** R Aust
107D4	**Victoria** State Aust
26B2	**Victoria de las Tunas** Cuba
100B2	**Victoria Falls** Zambia/Zim
4G2	**Victoria I** Can
108B2	**Victoria,L** Aust
99D3	**Victoria,L** C Africa
112B2	**Victoria Land** Region, Ant
86C2	**Victoria,Mt** Burma
99D2	**Victoria Nile** R Uganda
111B2	**Victoria Range** Mts NZ
106C2	**Victoria River Downs** Aust
4H3	**Victoria Str** Can
15D1	**Victoriaville** Can
100B4	**Victoria West** S Africa
34B3	**Victorica** Arg

21B3 **Victorville** USA
34A2 **Vicuña** Chile
34C2 **Vicuña Mackenna** Arg
17B1 **Vidalia** USA
54C2 **Videle** Rom
54B2 **Vidin** Bulg
85D4 **Vidisha** India
58D1 **Vidzy** USSR
29D4 **Viedma** Arg
26A4 **Viéjo** Costa Rica
51C1 **Viella** Spain
Vienna = Wien
18C2 **Vienna** Illinois, USA
14B3 **Vienna** W Virginia, USA
49C2 **Vienne** France
48C2 **Vienne** R France
76C2 **Vientiane** Laos
47C1 **Vierwaldstätter See** L Switz
48C2 **Vierzon** France
53C2 **Vieste** Italy
70B2 **Vietnam** Republic, S E Asia
76D1 **Vietri** Viet
27P2 **Vieux Fort** St Lucia
79B2 **Vigan** Phil
47C2 **Vigevano** Italy
48B3 **Vignemale** Mt France
50A1 **Vigo** Spain
87C1 **Vijayawāda** India
55A2 **Vijosë** R Alb
38B2 **Vik** Iceland
54B2 **Vikhren** Mt Bulg
13E2 **Viking** Can
38G6 **Vikna** I Nor
101C2 **Vila da Maganja** Mozam
101C2 **Vila Machado** Mozam
101C3 **Vilanculos** Mozam
50A1 **Vila Real** Port
101C2 **Vila Vasco da Gama** Mozam
35C2 **Vila Velha** Brazil
58D2 **Vileyka** USSR
38H6 **Vilhelmina** Sweden
33E6 **Vilhena** Brazil
60C2 **Viljandi** USSR
101G1 **Viljoenskroon** S Africa
59D3 **Vilkovo** USSR
9C3 **Villa Ahumada** Mexico
34B2 **Villa Atuel** Arg
50A1 **Villaba** Spain
23A2 **Villa Carranza** Mexico
52B1 **Villach** Austria
34B2 **Villa Colon** Arg
34C2 **Villa Constitución** Arg
34C1 **Villa de Maria** Arg
23A1 **Villa de Reyes** Mexico
34B2 **Villa Dolores** Arg
47D2 **Villafranca di Verona** Italy
34C2 **Villa General Mitre** Arg
34B2 **Villa General Roca** Arg
34D2 **Villaguay** Arg
25C3 **Villahermosa** Mexico
23A1 **Villa Hidalgo** Mexico
34C2 **Villa Huidobro** Arg
34C3 **Villa Iris** Arg
34C2 **Villa Maria** Arg
30D3 **Villa Montes** Bol
23A1 **Villanueva** Mexico
50A1 **Villa Nova de Gaia** Port
50A2 **Villanueva de la Serena** Spain
51C1 **Villanueva-y-Geltrú** Spain
34B3 **Villa Regina** Arg
51B2 **Villarreal** Spain
29B3 **Villarrica** Chile
30E4 **Villarrica** Par
50B2 **Villarrobledo** Spain
34D2 **Villa San José** Arg
34C2 **Villa Valeria** Arg
32C3 **Villavicencio** Colombia

49C2 **Villefranche** France
7C5 **Ville-Marie** Can
51B2 **Villena** Spain
46B2 **Villeneuve-St-Georges** France
48C3 **Villeneuve-sur-Lot** France
19B3 **Ville Platte** USA
46B2 **Villers-Cotterêts** France
49C2 **Villeurbanne** France
101G1 **Villiers** S Africa
87B2 **Villupuram** India
58D2 **Vilnius** USSR
63D1 **Vilyuy** USSR
63E1 **Vilyuysk** USSR
34A2 **Viña del Mar** Chile
51C1 **Vinaroz** Spain
14A3 **Vincennes** USA
38H5 **Vindel** R Sweden
85D4 **Vindhya Range** Mts India
16B3 **Vineland** USA
16D2 **Vineyard Haven** USA
76D2 **Vinh** Viet
76D3 **Vinh Cam Ranh** B Viet
77D4 **Vinh Loi** Viet
77D3 **Vinh Long** Viet
18A2 **Vinita** USA
54A1 **Vinkovci** Yugos
60C4 **Vinnitsa** USSR
112B3 **Vinson Massif** Upland Ant
100A3 **Vioolsdrift** S Africa
47D1 **Vipiteno** Italy
79B3 **Virac** Phil
87B2 **Virddhāchalam** India
100A2 **Virei** Angola
35C1 **Virgem da Lapa** Brazil
101G1 **Virginia** S Africa
10C3 **Virginia** State, USA
10A2 **Virginia** USA
21B2 **Virginia City** USA
27E3 **Virgin Is** Caribbean S
52C1 **Virovitica** Yugos
46C2 **Virton** Belg
87B3 **Virudunagar** India
52C2 **Vis** I Yugos
21B2 **Visalia** USA
79B3 **Visayan S** Phil
39H7 **Visby** Sweden
4H2 **Viscount Melville Sd** Can
54A2 **Višegrad** Yugos
50A1 **Viseu** Port
83C4 **Vishākhapatnam** India
47B1 **Visp** Switz
21B3 **Vista** USA
Vistula = Wisla
57C3 **Vitavia** R Czech
87A1 **Vite** India
60D2 **Vitebsk** USSR
52B2 **Viterbo** Italy
50A1 **Vitigudino** Spain
63D2 **Vitim** R USSR
50B1 **Vitora** Spain
31C6 **Vitória** Brazil
31C4 **Vitória da Conquista** Brazil
48B2 **Vitré** France
46C2 **Vitry-le-Francois** France
38J5 **Vittangi** Sweden
53B3 **Vittoria** Italy
47E2 **Vittorio Veneto** Italy
69H2 **Vityaz Depth** Pacific O
50A1 **Vivero** Spain
63B1 **Vivi** R USSR
34D3 **Vivorata** Arg
63C2 **Vizhne-Angarsk** USSR
83C4 **Vizianagaram** India
54B1 **Vladeasa** Mt Rom
61F5 **Vladikavkaz** USSR
65F4 **Vladimir** USSR
59C2 **Vladimir Volynskiy** USSR
74C2 **Vladivostok** USSR
56A2 **Vlieland** I Neth

46B1 **Vlissingen** Neth
55A2 **Vlorë** Alb
57C3 **Vöcklabruck** Austria
76D3 **Voeune Sai** Camb
47C2 **Voghera** Italy
101D2 **Vohibinany** Madag
101E2 **Vohimarina** Madag
99D3 **Voi** Kenya
97B4 **Voinjama** Lib
49D2 **Voiron** France
26A5 **Volcán Baru** Mt Panama
23B2 **Volcán Citlaltepetl** Mt Mexico
30C3 **Volcán Lullaillaco** Mt Chile
34A3 **Volcáno Copahue** Mt Chile
34A3 **Volcáno Domuyo** Mt Arg
Volcano Is = Kazan Retto
29B3 **Volcáno Lanin** Mt Arg
30C3 **Volcán Ollagüe** Mt Chile
34A3 **Volcáno Llaima** Mt Chile
34B2 **Volcáno Maipo** Mt Arg
34A3 **Volcáno Peteroa** Mt Chile
34B3 **Volcáno Tromen** V Arg
23A2 **Volcán Paracutin** Mt Mexico
32B3 **Volcán Puraće** Mt Colombia
34A2 **Volcán Tinguiririca** Mt Arg/Chile
61J2 **Volchansk** USSR
61G4 **Volga** R USSR
61F4 **Volgodonsk** USSR
61F4 **Volgograd** USSR
61G3 **Volgogradskoye Vodokhranilishche** Res USSR
60D2 **Volkhov** USSR
60D2 **Volkhov** R USSR
58C2 **Volkovysk** USSR
101G1 **Volksrust** S Africa
61F2 **Vologda** USSR
48B2 **Volognes** France
55B3 **Vólos** Greece
61G3 **Vol'sk** USSR
22B2 **Volta** USA
97B3 **Volta Blanche** R Burkina
97B4 **Volta,L** Ghana
97B3 **Volta Noire** R Burkina
35C2 **Volta Redonda** Brazil
97B3 **Volta Rouge** R Burkina
60C3 **Volynskiy** USSR
61F4 **Volzhskiy** USSR
12D2 **Von Frank Mt** USA
6J3 **Vopnafjörður** Iceland
47C1 **Voralberg** Province, Austria
47C1 **Vorder Rhein** R Switz
56C1 **Vordingborg** Den
64H3 **Vorkuta** USSR
39G6 **Vorma** R Nor
60E3 **Voronezh** USSR
38M5 **Voron'ya** R USSR
39K7 **Voru** USSR
49D2 **Vosges** Mt France
68B1 **Voshnyy Saytocan** Mts USSR
39F6 **Voss** Nor
63B2 **Vostochnyy Sayan** Mts USSR
112B9 **Vostok** Base Ant
61H2 **Votkinsk** USSR
46C2 **Vouziers** France
60D4 **Voznesensk** USSR
54B2 **Vranje** Yugos
54B2 **Vratsa** Bulg
54A1 **Vrbas** Yugos

52C2 **Vrbas** R Yugos
52B1 **Vrbovsko** Yugos
101G1 **Vrede** S Africa
33F2 **Vreed en Hoop** Guyana
54B1 **Vršac** Yugos
52C2 **Vrtoče** Yugos
100B3 **Vryburg** S Africa
101H1 **Vryheid** S Africa
54A1 **Vukovar** Yugos
13E2 **Vulcan** Can
53B3 **Vulcano** I Italy
77D3 **Vung Tau** Viet
38J5 **Vuollerim** Sweden
38L6 **Vyartsilya** USSR
61H2 **Vyatka** R USSR
69F2 **Vyazemskiy** USSR
60D2 **Vyaz'ma** USSR
61F2 **Vyazniki** USSR
60C1 **Vyborg** USSR
64G3 **Vym'** R USSR
43C3 **Vyrnwy** R Wales
60D2 **Vyshiy Volochek** USSR
59B3 **Vyškov** Czech
60E1 **Vytegra** USSR

W

97B3 **Wa** Ghana
13E1 **Wabasca** Can
5G4 **Wabasca** R Can
13E1 **Wabasca L** Can
14A2 **Wabash** USA
14A3 **Wabash** R USA
5J4 **Wabowden** Can
7D4 **Wabush** Can
17B2 **Waccasassa B** USA
16D1 **Wachusett Res** USA
19A3 **Waco** USA
85B3 **Wad** Pak
95A2 **Waddān** Libya
5F4 **Waddington,Mt** Can
93E4 **Wadi al Bātin** Watercourse Iraq
93D3 **Wadi al Ghudāf** Watercourse Iraq
94C2 **Wadi al Harīr** V Syria
93D3 **Wadi al Mirah** Watercourse Iraq/ S Arabia
93D3 **Wadi al Ubayyid** Watercourse Iraq
93D3 **Wadi Ar'ar** Watercourse S Arabia
91A5 **Wadi as Hsabā'** Watercourse S Arabia
92C3 **Wadi as Sirhān** V Jordan/S Arabia
94C2 **Wadi az Zaydi** V Syria
94C3 **Wadi edh Dhab'i** V Jordan
94A3 **Wadi el 'Arish** V Egypt
94C3 **Wadi el Ghadaf** V Jordan
94B3 **Wadi el Hasa** V Jordan
94C3 **Wadi el Janab** V Jordan
94B3 **Wadi el Jeib** V Israel/ Jordan
95B3 **Wadi el Milk** Watercourse Sudan
92A3 **Wadi el Natrun** Watercourse Egypt
94B3 **Wadi es Sir** Jordan
94B3 **Wadi Fidan** V Jordan
94B3 **Wadi Hareidin** V Egypt
93D3 **Wadi Hawrān** R Iraq
95B3 **Wadi Howa** Watercourse Sudan
98C1 **Wadi Ibra** Watercourse Sudan

94C2 **Wadi Luhfi**
   Watercourse Jordan
94B3 **Wadi Mujib** *V* Jordan
94B3 **Wadi Qītaiya** *V* Egypt
80B3 **Wadi Sha'it**
   Watercourse Egypt
99D1 **Wad Medani** Sudan
93E4 **Wafra** Kuwait
6B3 **Wager B** Can
6A3 **Wager Bay** Can
109C3 **Wagga Wagga** Aust
106A4 **Wagin** Aust
95A2 **Waha** Libya
21C4 **Wahaiwa** Hawaiian Is
18A1 **Wahoo** USA
8D2 **Wahpeton** USA
87A1 **Wai** India
111B2 **Waiau** NZ
111A3 **Waiau** *R* NZ
111B2 **Waiau** *R* NZ
71E3 **Waigeo** *I* Indon
110C1 **Waihi** NZ
110C1 **Waikaremoana,L** NZ
110C1 **Waikato** *R* NZ
108A2 **Waikerie** Aust
111B3 **Waikouaiti** NZ
21C4 **Wailuku** Hawaiian Is
111B2 **Waimakariri** *R* NZ
111B2 **Waimate** NZ
21C4 **Waimea** Hawaiian Is
106B1 **Waingapu** Indon
13E2 **Wainwright** Can
4B2 **Wainwright** USA
111B2 **Waipara** NZ
110C2 **Waipukurau** NZ
111C2 **Wairarapa,L** NZ
111B2 **Wairau** *R* NZ
110C1 **Wairoa** NZ
110C1 **Wairoa** *R* NZ
111B2 **Waitaki** *R* NZ
110B1 **Waitara** NZ
110C1 **Waitomo** NZ
110B1 **Waiuku** NZ
75B1 **Wajima** Japan
99E2 **Wajir** Kenya
75B1 **Wakasa-wan** *B*
   Japan
111A3 **Wakatipu,L** NZ
74D4 **Wakayama** Japan
42D3 **Wakefield** Eng
27H1 **Wakefield** Jamaica
16D2 **Wakefield** Rhode
   Island, USA
76B2 **Wakema** Burma
69G2 **Wakkanai** Japan
108B3 **Wakool** *R* Aust
59B2 **Wałbrzych** Pol
109D2 **Walcha** Aust
58B2 **Wałcz** Pol
46D1 **Waldbröl** Germany
16B2 **Walden** USA
99D1 **Waldia** Eth
43C3 **Wales** Country, UK
12A1 **Wales** USA
6B3 **Wales I** Can
109C2 **Walgett** Aust
112B4 **Walgreen Coast**
   Region, Ant
99C3 **Walikale** Zaïre
21B2 **Walker** *L* USA
14B2 **Walkerton** Can
8B2 **Wallace** USA
108A2 **Wallaroo** Aust
109C3 **Walla Walla** Aust
20C1 **Walla Walla** USA
16C2 **Wallingford** USA
105H4 **Wallis and Futuna** *Is*
   Pacific O
20C1 **Wallowa** USA
20C1 **Wallowa Mts** *Mts*
   USA
109C1 **Wallumbilla** Aust
18B2 **Walnut Ridge** USA
110C1 **Walouru** NZ
43D3 **Walsall** Eng
9C3 **Walsenburg** USA
9C3 **Walsenburgh** USA
17B1 **Walterboro** USA

17A1 **Walter F George Res**
   USA
16D1 **Waltham** USA
100A3 **Walvis Bay** S Africa
103J6 **Walvis Ridge**
   Atlantic O
97C4 **Wamba** Nig
98B3 **Wamba** *R* Zaïre
18A2 **Wamego** USA
84B2 **Wana** Pak
108B1 **Wanaaring** Aust
111A2 **Wanaka** NZ
111A2 **Wanaka,L** NZ
14B1 **Wanapitei L** Can
109C1 **Wandoan** Aust
108B3 **Wanganella** Aust
110C1 **Wanganui** NZ
110C1 **Wanganui** *R* NZ
109C3 **Wangaratta** Aust
99E2 **Wanle Weyne** Somalia
76E2 **Wanning** China
87B1 **Wanparti** India
73B3 **Wanxian** China
73B3 **Wanyuan** China
13D2 **Wapiti** *R* Can
18B2 **Wappapello,L** USA
16C2 **Wappingers Falls** USA
87B1 **Warangal** India
109C4 **Waratah** Aust
108C3 **Waratah B** Aust
108C3 **Warburton** Aust
108A1 **Warburton** *R* Aust
109C1 **Ward** *R* Aust
101G1 **Warden** S Africa
99E2 **Warder** Eth
85D4 **Wardha** India
111A3 **Ward,Mt** NZ
5F4 **Ware** Can
16C1 **Ware** USA
16D2 **Wareham** USA
109D1 **Warialda** Aust
76C2 **Warin Chamrap** Thai
100B3 **Warmbad** S Africa
16B2 **Warminster** USA
21B2 **Warm Springs** USA
56C2 **Warnemünde**
   Germany
20B2 **Warner Mts** USA
17B1 **Warner Robins** USA
108B3 **Warracknabeal** Aust
108A1 **Warrandirinna,L** Aust
107D3 **Warrego** *R* Aust
19B3 **Warren** Arkansas,
   USA
109C2 **Warren** Aust
16D2 **Warren**
   Massachusetts, USA
14B2 **Warren** Ohio, USA
15C2 **Warren** Pennsylvania,
   USA
45C1 **Warrenpoint** N Ire
18B2 **Warrensburg** USA
101F1 **Warrenton** S Africa
15C3 **Warrenton** USA
97C4 **Warri** Nig
108A1 **Warrina** Aust
42C3 **Warrington** Eng
108B3 **Warrnambool** Aust
   Warsaw = Warszawa
58C2 **Warszawa** Pol
59B2 **Warta** *R* Pol
109D1 **Warwick** Aust
43D3 **Warwick** County, Eng
43D3 **Warwick** Eng
16B2 **Warwick** New York,
   USA
16D2 **Warwick** Rhode
   Island, USA
8B3 **Wasatch Range** *Mts*
   USA
101H1 **Wasbank** S Africa
21B2 **Wasco** USA
4H2 **Washburn L** Can
85D4 **Wāshīm** India
10C3 **Washington** District of
   Columbia, USA
17B1 **Washington** Georgia,
   USA

14A3 **Washington** Indiana,
   USA
18B2 **Washington** Missouri,
   USA
16B2 **Washington** New
   Jersey, USA
14B2 **Washington**
   Pennsylvania, USA
8A2 **Washington** State,
   USA
14B3 **Washington Court**
   House USA
6D1 **Washington Land** Can
15D2 **Washington,Mt** USA
43E3 **Wash,The** Eng
85A3 **Washuk** Pak
12E2 **Wasilla** USA
26A4 **Waspán** Nic
70D4 **Watampone** Indon
16C2 **Waterbury** USA
45C2 **Waterford** County,
   Irish Rep
41B3 **Waterford** Irish Rep
45C2 **Waterford Harbour**
   Irish Rep
46C1 **Waterloo** Belg
10A2 **Waterloo** USA
15C2 **Watertown** New York,
   USA
101H1 **Waterval-Boven**
   S Africa
10D2 **Waterville** Maine, USA
16C1 **Watervliet** USA
5G4 **Waterways** Can
43D4 **Watford** Eng
15C2 **Watkins Glen** USA
8C1 **Watrous** Can
99C2 **Watsa** Zaïre
12J2 **Watson Lake** Can
22B2 **Watsonville** USA
71F4 **Wau** PNG
99C2 **Wau** Sudan
7B5 **Waua** Can
109D2 **Wauchope** Aust
17B2 **Wauchula** USA
14A2 **Waukegan** USA
10B2 **Wausau** USA
14A2 **Wauwatosa** USA
106C2 **Wave Hill** Aust
43E3 **Waveney** *R* Eng
14B3 **Waverly** Ohio, USA
46C1 **Wavre** Belg
10B2 **Wawa** Can
95A2 **Wāw Al Kabīr** Libya
95A2 **Wāw an Nāmūs** *Well*
   Libya
22C2 **Wawona** USA
19A3 **Waxahachie** USA
17B1 **Waycross** USA
17B1 **Waynesboro** Georgia,
   USA
19C3 **Waynesboro**
   Mississippi, USA
16A3 **Waynesboro**
   Pennsylvania, USA
15C3 **Waynesboro** Virginia,
   USA
18B2 **Waynesville** Missouri,
   USA
84B2 **Wazi Khwa** Afghan
43E4 **Weald,The** *Upland*
   Eng
42C2 **Wear** *R* Eng
19A3 **Weatherford** Texas,
   USA
20B2 **Weaverville** USA
14B1 **Webbwood** Can
16D1 **Webster** USA
18B2 **Webster Groves** USA
29D6 **Weddell I** Falkland Is
112C2 **Weddell S** Ant
13C2 **Wedge Mt** Can
20B2 **Weed** USA
101H1 **Weenen** S Africa
109C2 **Wee Waa** Aust
72D1 **Weichang** China
57C3 **Weiden** Germany
72D2 **Weifang** China

72E2 **Weihai** China
72C3 **Wei He** *R* Henan,
   China
72C2 **Wei He** *R* Shaanxi,
   China
109C1 **Weilmoringle** Aust
73A4 **Weining** China
107D2 **Weipa** Aust
14B2 **Weirton** USA
20C2 **Weiser** USA
72D3 **Weishan Hu** *L* China
57C2 **Weissenfels**
   Germany
17A1 **Weiss L** USA
101G1 **Welkom** S Africa
15C2 **Welland** Can
43D3 **Welland** *R* Eng
106C2 **Wellesley Is** Aust
12G2 **Wellesley L** Can
43D3 **Wellingborough** Eng
109C2 **Wellington** Aust
18A2 **Wellington** Kansas,
   USA
111B2 **Wellington** NZ
6A2 **Wellington Chan** Can
13C2 **Wells** Can
43C4 **Wells** Eng
110B1 **Wellsford** NZ
106B3 **Wells,L** Aust
57C3 **Wels** Austria
43C3 **Welshpool** Wales
13D1 **Wembley** Can
7C4 **Wemindji** Can
20B1 **Wenatchee** USA
20C1 **Wenatchee** *R* USA
97B4 **Wenchi** Ghana
72E2 **Wenden** China
73E4 **Wenling** China
32J7 **Wenman** *I* Ecuador
73A5 **Wenshan** China
107D4 **Wenthaggi** Aust
108B2 **Wentworth** Aust
72A3 **Wen Xian** China
73E4 **Wenzhou** China
73C4 **Wenzhou** China
101G1 **Wepener** S Africa
12G1 **Wernecke Mts** Can
57C2 **Werra** *R* Germany
109D2 **Werris Creek** Aust
56B2 **Wesel** Germany
56B2 **Weser** *R* Germany
106C2 **Wessel Is** Aust
14A2 **West Allis** USA
104C4 **West Australian Basin**
   Indian O
104C5 **West Australian Ridge**
   Indian O
19C3 **West B** USA
86B2 **West Bengal** State,
   India
43D3 **West Bromwich** Eng
16B3 **West Chester** USA
46D1 **Westerburg** Germany
56B2 **Westerland** Germany
16D2 **Westerly** USA
106A3 **Western Australia**
   State, Aust
87A1 **Western Ghats** *Mts*
   India
44A3 **Western Isles** Scot
96A2 **Western Sahara**
   Region, Mor
105H4 **Western Samoa** *Is*
   Pacific O
46B1 **Westerschelde**
   Estuary Neth
46D1 **Westerwald** Region,
   Germany
49D1 **Westfalen** Region,
   Germany
29D6 **West Falkland** *I*
   Falkland Is
16C1 **Westfield**
   Massachusetts, USA
15C2 **Westfield** New York,
   USA
18C2 **West Frankfort** USA
109C1 **Westgate** Aust

43C4 **West Glamorgan**
  County, Wales
102E3 **West Indies** *Is*
  Caribbean S
13E2 **Westlock** Can
14B2 **West Lorne** Can
45C2 **Westmeath** County,
  Irish Rep
18B2 **West Memphis** USA
43D3 **West Midlands**
  County, Eng
43D4 **Westminster** Eng
16A3 **Westminster**
  Maryland, USA
17B1 **Westminster**
  S Carolina, USA
100B3 **West Nicholson** Zim
78D1 **Weston** Malay
14B3 **Weston** USA
43C4 **Weston-super-Mare**
  Eng
17B2 **West Palm Beach** USA
18B2 **West Plains** USA
22B1 **West Point** California,
  USA
19C3 **West Point**
  Mississippi, USA
16C2 **West Point** New York,
  USA
12F2 **West Point** *Mt* USA
45B2 **Westport** Irish Rep
111B2 **Westport** NZ
40C2 **Westray** *I* Scot
13C2 **West Road** *R* Can
42E3 **West Side** *Oilfield*
  N Sea
11B3 **West Virginia** State,
  USA
22C1 **West Walker** *R* USA
109C2 **West Wyalong** Aust
42D3 **West Yorkshire**
  County, Eng
71D4 **Wetar** *I* Indon
13E2 **Wetaskiwin** Can
99D3 **Wete** Tanz
46E1 **Wetzlar** Germany
Wevok = Cape
  Lisburne
71F4 **Wewak** PNG
19A2 **Wewoka** USA
45C2 **Wexford** County,
  Irish Rep
45C2 **Wexford** Irish Rep
5H5 **Weyburn** Can
43C4 **Weymouth** Eng
16D1 **Weymouth** USA
110C1 **Whakatane** NZ
110C1 **Whakatane** *R* NZ
44E1 **Whalsay** *I* Scot
110B1 **Whangarei** NZ
42D3 **Wharfe** *R* Eng
19A4 **Wharton** USA
111B2 **Whataroa** NZ
16A3 **Wheaton** Maryland,
  USA
8B3 **Wheeler Peak** *Mt*
  Nevada, USA
9C3 **Wheeler Peak** *Mt*
  New Mexico, USA
14B2 **Wheeling** USA
13C3 **Whistler** Can
15C2 **Whitby** Can
42D2 **Whitby** Eng
18B2 **White** *R* Arkansas,
  USA
12F2 **White** *R* Can
14A3 **White** *R* Indiana, USA
8C2 **White** *R* S Dakota,
  USA
7E4 **White B** Can
108B2 **White Cliffs** Aust
40C2 **White Coomb** *Mt*
  Scot
13D2 **Whitecourt** Can
14A1 **Whitefish Pt** USA
7D4 **Whitegull L** Can
15D2 **Whitehall** New York,
  USA

16B2 **Whitehall**
  Pennsylvania, USA
42C2 **Whitehaven** Eng
12G2 **Whitehorse** Can
110C1 **White I** NZ
19B4 **White L** USA
109C4 **Whitemark** Aust
21B2 **White Mountain Peak**
  Mt USA
12E1 **White Mts** Alaska,
  USA
15D2 **White Mts**
  New Hampshire,
  USA
99D1 **White Nile** *R* Sudan
16C2 **White Plains** USA
7B5 **White River** Can
15D2 **White River Junction**
  USA
White S = Beloye More
13B2 **Whitesail L** Can
20B1 **White Salmon** USA
17C1 **Whiteville** USA
97B4 **White Volta** *R* Ghana
42B2 **Whithorn** Scot
17B1 **Whitmire** USA
21B2 **Whitney,Mt** USA
12E2 **Whittier** Alaska, USA
22C4 **Whittier** California,
  USA
5H3 **Wholdia L** Can
108A2 **Whyalla** Aust
14B2 **Wiarton** Can
18A2 **Wichita** USA
9D3 **Wichita Falls** USA
44C2 **Wick** Scot
45C2 **Wicklow** County,
  Irish Rep
45C2 **Wicklow** Irish Rep
45C2 **Wicklow** *Mts*
  Irish Rep
109C1 **Widgeegoara** *R* Aust
46D1 **Wied** *R* Germany
59B2 **Wielun** Pol
59B3 **Wien** Austria
59B3 **Wiener Neustadt**
  Austria
58C2 **Wieprz** *R* Pol
46E1 **Wiesbaden** Germany
42C3 **Wigan** Eng
19C3 **Wiggins** USA
42B2 **Wigtown** Scot
42B2 **Wigtown B** Scot
47C1 **Wil** Switz
20C1 **Wilbur** USA
108B2 **Wilcannia** Aust
21B2 **Wildcat Peak** *Mt* USA
47B1 **Wildhorn** *Mt* Switz
13E2 **Wild Horse** Can
47D1 **Wildspitze** *Mt* Austria
17B2 **Wildwood** Florida,
  USA
16B3 **Wildwood** New
  Jersey, USA
101G1 **Wilge** *R* S Africa
56B2 **Wilhelmshaven**
  Germany
15C2 **Wilkes-Barre** USA
112B8 **Wilkes Land** Ant
13F2 **Wilkie** Can
20B2 **Willamette** *R* USA
108B2 **Willandra** *R* Aust
20B1 **Willapa B** USA
9C3 **Willcox** USA
27D4 **Willemstad** Curaçao
108A1 **William Creek** Aust
108B3 **William,Mt** Aust
21A2 **Williams** California,
  USA
13C2 **Williams Lake** Can
15C2 **Williamsport** USA
16C1 **Williamstown**
  Massachusetts, USA
14B3 **Williamstown**
  W Virginia, USA
16C2 **Willimantic** USA
16B2 **Willingboro** USA
13D2 **Willingdon,Mt** Can

107E2 **Willis Group** *Is* Aust
17B2 **Williston** Florida, USA
100B4 **Williston** S Africa
13C1 **Williston L** Can
8D2 **Willmar** USA
108A3 **Willoughby,C** Aust
13C2 **Willow** *R* Can
20B2 **Willow Ranch** USA
21A2 **Willows** USA
18B2 **Willow Springs** USA
108A2 **Wilmington** Aust
16B3 **Wilmington** Delaware,
  USA
17C1 **Wilmington** N
  Carolina, USA
7A5 **Wilnona** USA
11C3 **Wilson** USA
108B1 **Wilson** *R* Aust
6B3 **Wilson,C** Can
22C3 **Wilson,Mt** California,
  USA
20B1 **Wilson,Mt** Oregon,
  USA
109C3 **Wilsons Promontory**
  Pen Aust
43D4 **Wiltshire** County, Eng
46C2 **Wiltz** Lux
106B3 **Wiluna** Aust
14A2 **Winamac** USA
101G1 **Winburg** S Africa
16C1 **Winchendon** USA
15C1 **Winchester** Can
43D4 **Winchester** Eng
16C1 **Winchester** New
  Hampshire, USA
15C3 **Winchester** Virginia,
  USA
42C2 **Windermere** Eng
100A3 **Windhoek** Namibia
107D3 **Windorah** Aust
8C2 **Wind River Range** *Mts*
  USA
109D2 **Windsor** Aust
16C2 **Windsor** Connecticut,
  USA
43D4 **Windsor** Eng
7D5 **Windsor** Nova Scotia,
  Can
14B2 **Windsor** Ontario, Can
15D1 **Windsor** Quebec, Can
17B1 **Windsor Forest** USA
16C2 **Windsor Locks** USA
27E4 **Windward Is**
  Caribbean S
26C3 **Windward Pass**
  Caribbean S
13E1 **Winefred L** Can
18A2 **Winfield** Kansas, USA
109D2 **Wingham** Aust
34C3 **Winifreda** Arg
7B4 **Winisk** *R* Can
7B4 **Winisk L** Can
76B2 **Winkana** Burma
20B1 **Winlock** USA
97B4 **Winneba** Ghana
14A2 **Winnebago,L** USA
20C2 **Winnemucca** USA
19B3 **Winnfield** USA
5J4 **Winnipeg** Can
5J4 **Winnipeg,L** Can
5J4 **Winnipegosis** Can
4J4 **Winnipegosis,L** Can
15D2 **Winnipesaukee,L** USA
10A2 **Winona** Minnesota,
  USA
19C3 **Winona** Mississippi,
  USA
15D2 **Winooski** USA
9B3 **Winslow** USA
16C2 **Winsted** USA
11B3 **Winston-Salem** USA
46E1 **Winterberg** Germany
17B2 **Winter Garden** USA
17B2 **Winter Park** USA
22B1 **Winters** USA
47C1 **Winterthur** Switz
107D3 **Winton** Aust
111A3 **Winton** NZ

43E3 **Wisbech** Eng
10B2 **Wisconsin** State, USA
7B5 **Wisconsin Rapids**
  USA
12D1 **Wiseman** USA
58B2 **Wisla** *R* Pol
56C2 **Wismar** Germany
33F2 **Witagron** Surinam
101G1 **Witbank** S Africa
9D3 **Witchita Falls** USA
43D3 **Witham** *R* Eng
42E3 **Withernsea** Eng
43D4 **Witney** Eng
46D1 **Witten** Germany
56C2 **Wittenberg** Germany
106A3 **Wittenoom** Aust
46D1 **Wittlich** Germany
58B2 **Wladyslawowo** Pol
58B2 **Włoclawek** Pol
58C2 **Włodawa** Pol
109C3 **Wodonga** Aust
47C1 **Wohlen** Switz
71E4 **Wokam** Indon
43D4 **Woking** Eng
71F3 **Woleai** *I* Pacific O
20B2 **Wolf Creek** USA
8C2 **Wolf Point** USA
57C3 **Wolfsberg** Austria
56C2 **Wolfsburg** Germany
5H4 **Wollaston L** Can
5H4 **Wollaston Lake** Can
4G3 **Wollaston Pen** Can
109D2 **Wollongong** Aust
101G1 **Wolmaransstad**
  S Africa
59B2 **Wolow** Pol
108B3 **Wolseley** Aust
43C3 **Wolverhampton** Eng
16A2 **Womelsdorf** USA
109D1 **Wondai** Aust
74B3 **Wŏnju** S Korea
108B2 **Wonominta** *R* Aust
13C1 **Wonowon** Can
74B3 **Wŏnsan** N Korea
108C3 **Wonthaggi** Aust
108A2 **Woocalla** Aust
16B3 **Woodbine** USA
15C3 **Woodbridge** USA
5G4 **Wood Buffalo Nat Pk**
  Can
109D1 **Woodburn** Aust
20B1 **Woodburn** Aust
16B3 **Woodbury** USA
12F1 **Woodchopper** USA
21A2 **Woodland** California,
  USA
20B1 **Woodland**
  Washington, USA
107E1 **Woodlark** *I* PNG
106C4 **Woodmera** Aust
106C3 **Woodroffe,Mt** Aust
14B2 **Woodstock** Ontario,
  Can
16B3 **Woodstown** USA
110C2 **Woodville** NZ
19B3 **Woodville** USA
108A2 **Woomera** Aust
15D2 **Woonsocket** USA
14B2 **Wooster** USA
43C3 **Worcester** Eng
100A4 **Worcester** S Africa
16D1 **Worcester** USA
47E1 **Wörgl** Austria
42C2 **Workington** Eng
8C2 **Worland** USA
46E2 **Worms** Germany
43B4 **Worms Head** *Pt*
  Wales
43D4 **Worthing** Eng
8D2 **Worthington** USA
71D4 **Wowoni** *I* Indon
12H3 **Wrangell** USA
12H3 **Wrangell I** USA
12F2 **Wrangell Mts** USA
40B2 **Wrath,C** Scot
43C3 **Wrexham** Wales
17B1 **Wrightsville** USA
22D3 **Wrightwood** USA

4F3 **Wrigley** Can
59B2 **Wrocław** Pol
58B2 **Wrzésnia** Pol
69E2 **Wuchang** China
76E1 **Wuchuan** China
72E2 **Wuda** China
72C2 **Wuding He** R China
72A3 **Wudu** China
73C4 **Wugang** China
72B2 **Wuhai** China
73C3 **Wuhan** China
73D3 **Wuhu** China
73D5 **Wuhua** China
84D2 **Wüjang** China
72B1 **Wujia He** R China
73B4 **Wu Jiang** R China
97C4 **Wukari** Nig
73B4 **Wuling Shan** Mts China
97D4 **Wum** Cam
73A4 **Wumeng Shan** Upland China
46D1 **Wuppertal** Germany
72B2 **Wuqi** China
72D2 **Wuqing** China
57B3 **Würzburg** Germany
57C2 **Wurzen** Germany
72C2 **Wutai Shan** Mt China
71F4 **Wuvulu** I Pacific O
72A2 **Wuwei** China
73E3 **Wuxi** China
73E3 **Wuxing** China
72C2 **Wuyang** China
73D4 **Wuyi Shan** Mts China
72B1 **Wuyuan** China
76D2 **Wuzhi Shan** Mts China
72B2 **Wuzhong** China
73C5 **Wuzhou** China
14B2 **Wyandotte** USA
109C1 **Wyandra** Aust
43C4 **Wye** R Eng
43C4 **Wylye** R Eng
43E3 **Wymondham** Eng
106B2 **Wyndham** Aust
18B2 **Wynne** USA
4G2 **Wynniatt B** Can
109C4 **Wynyard** Aust
8C2 **Wyoming** State, USA
14A2 **Wyoming** USA
109D2 **Wyong** Aust

X

84D1 **Xaidulla** China
72D1 **Xai Moron He** R China
101C3 **Xai Xai** Mozam
23B2 **Xaltinguis** Mexico
100A2 **Xangongo** Angola
46D1 **Xanten** Germany
55B2 **Xánthi** Greece
100B3 **Xau,L** Botswana
14B3 **Xenia** USA
68B4 **Xiaguan** China
72A2 **Xiahe** China
73D5 **Xiamen** China
72B3 **Xi'an** China
73B4 **Xianfeng** China
73C3 **Xiangfan** China
73C4 **Xiang Jiang** R China
73C4 **Xiangtan** Province, China
73C4 **Xianning** China
72B3 **Xianyang** China
73C4 **Xiao Shui** R China
73D4 **Xiapu** China
73A4 **Xichang** China
23B1 **Xicotepec** Mexico
76C2 **Xieng Khouang** Laos
73B4 **Xifeng** China
86B1 **Xigazê** China
72A1 **Xi He** R China
72B2 **Xiji** China
73C5 **Xi Jiang** R China
72E1 **Xiliao He** R China
73B5 **Xilin** China

23B1 **Xilitla** Mexico
73D4 **Xinfeng** China
72C1 **Xinghe** China
73D5 **Xingning** China
73B4 **Xingren** China
72C2 **Xingtai** China
33G4 **Xingu** R Brazil
68B2 **Xingxingxia** China
73A4 **Xingyi** China
72A2 **Xining** China
72E2 **Xinjin** Liaoning, China
73A3 **Xinjin** Sichuan, China
72D2 **Xinwen** China
72C2 **Xin Xian** China
72C2 **Xinxiang** China
73C3 **Xinyang** China
73C5 **Xinyi** Guangdong, China
72D3 **Xinyi** Jiangsu, China
72D1 **Xi Ujimqin Qi** China
74A2 **Xiuyan** China
23B2 **Xochimilco** Mexico
73D3 **Xuancheng** China
73B3 **Xuanhan** China
72D1 **Xuanhua** China
73A4 **Xuanwei** China
72C3 **Xuchang** China
99E2 **Xuddur** Somalia
72A2 **Xunhua** China
73C5 **Xun Jiang** R China
69E2 **Xunke** China
73D5 **Xunwu** China
73C4 **Xupu** China
76E1 **Xuwen** China
73B4 **Xuyong** China
72D3 **Xuzhou** China

Y

73A4 **Ya'an** China
108B3 **Yaapeet** Aust
98B2 **Yabassi** Cam
68C1 **Yablonovyy Khrebet** Mts USSR
94C2 **Yabrūd** Syria
20B2 **Yachats** USA
30D3 **Yacuiba** Bol
87B1 **Yādgīr** India
95A1 **Yafran** Libya
23A1 **Yahualica** Mexico
98C2 **Yahuma** Zaïre
75B1 **Yaita** Japan
75B2 **Yaizu** Japan
73A4 **Yajiang** China
20B1 **Yakima** USA
20B1 **Yakima** R USA
97B3 **Yako** Burkina
98C2 **Yakoma** Zaïre
74E2 **Yakumo** Japan
12G3 **Yakutat** USA
12G3 **Yakutat B** USA
63E1 **Yakutsk** USSR
77C4 **Yala** Thai
23B2 **Yalalag** Mexico
98C2 **Yaloké** CAR
109C3 **Yallourn** Aust
68B3 **Yalong** R China
73A4 **Yalong Jiang** R China
54C2 **Yalova** Turk
60D5 **Yalta** USSR
74B2 **Yalu Jiang** R China
74D3 **Yamagata** Japan
74C4 **Yamaguchi** Japan
68D1 **Yamarovka** USSR
109D1 **Yamba** New S Wales, Aust
108B2 **Yamba** S Australia, Aust
99C2 **Yambio** Sudan
54C2 **Yambol** Bulg
71E4 **Yam Kinneret = Tiberias,L**
108B1 **Yamma Yamma,L** Aust
97B4 **Yamoussoukro** Ivory Coast

85D3 **Yamuna** R India
86C1 **Yamzho Yumco** L China
63F1 **Yana** R USSR
108B3 **Yanac** Aust
75A2 **Yanagawa** Japan
87C1 **Yanam** India
72B2 **Yan'an** China
80B3 **Yanbu'al Bahr** S Arabia
108B2 **Yancannia** Aust
72E3 **Yancheng** China
72B2 **Yanchi** China
108B1 **Yandama** R Aust
98C2 **Yangambi** Zaïre
72C1 **Yang He** R China
73C5 **Yangjiang** China
72C2 **Yangquan** China
73C5 **Yangshan** China
73C3 **Yangtze Gorges** China
72E3 **Yangtze,Mouths of the** China
72D3 **Yangzhou** China
73B4 **Yanhe** China
74B2 **Yanji** China
108C3 **Yanko** R Aust
8D2 **Yankton** USA
68A2 **Yanqi** China
72D1 **Yan Shan** Hills
108B1 **Yantabulla** Aust
72E2 **Yantai** China
72D2 **Yanzhou** China
98B2 **Yaoundé** Cam
71E4 **Yapen** I Indon
71E3 **Yap Is** Pacific O
24B2 **Yaqui** R Mexico
61G2 **Yaransk** USSR
32C3 **Yari** R Colombia
74D3 **Yariga-dake** Mt Japan
82B2 **Yarkant He** R China
86C1 **Yarlung Zangbo Jiang** R China
7D5 **Yarmouth** Can
94B2 **Yarmūk** R Syrla/Jordan
61E2 **Yaroslavl'** USSR
94B2 **Yarqon** R Israel
109C3 **Yarram** Aust
109D1 **Yarraman** Aust
109C3 **Yarrawonga** Aust
60D2 **Yartsevo** USSR
63B1 **Yartsevo** USSR
32B2 **Yarumal** Colombia
97C3 **Yashi** Nig
97C4 **Yashikera** Nig
61F4 **Yashkul'** USSR
84C1 **Yasin** Pak
59C3 **Yasinya** USSR
109C2 **Yass** Aust
109C2 **Yass** R Aust
75A1 **Yasugi** Japan
18A2 **Yates Center** USA
98C2 **Yatolema** Zaïre
74C4 **Yatsushiro** Japan
94B3 **Yatta** Israel
32C4 **Yavari** Peru
85D4 **Yavatmāl** India
74C4 **Yawatahama** Japan
76D2 **Ya Xian** China
90B3 **Yazd** Iran
90B3 **Yazd-e Khvāst** Iran
19B3 **Yazoo** R USA
19B3 **Yazoo City** USA
76B2 **Ye** Burma
59D3 **Yedintsy** USSR
108A2 **Yeelanna** Aust
60E3 **Yefremov** USSR
61F4 **Yegorlyk** R USSR
99D2 **Yei** Sudan
60E3 **Yelets** USSR
44E1 **Yell** I Scot
87C1 **Yellandu** India
Yellow = Huang He
8B1 **Yellowhead P** Can
4G3 **Yellowknife** Can
5G4 **Yellowmead P** Can
109C2 **Yellow Mt** Aust
69E3 **Yellow Sea** China/Korea

8C2 **Yellowstone** R USA
8B2 **Yellowstone L** USA
6B1 **Yelverton B** Can
97C3 **Yelwa** Nig
81C4 **Yemen** Republic, Arabian Pen
76C1 **Yen Bai** Viet
97B4 **Yendi** Ghana
76B1 **Yengan** Burma
63B2 **Yeniseysk** USSR
63B1 **Yeniseyskiy Kryazh** Ridge USSR
64J2 **Yeniseyskiy Zal** B USSR
12D2 **Yentna** R USA
43C4 **Yeo** R Eng
109C2 **Yeoval** Aust
43C4 **Yeovil** Eng
63C1 **Yerbogachen** USSR
65F5 **Yerevan** USSR
21B2 **Yerington** USA
21B3 **Yermo** USA
63E2 **Yerofey** USSR
69E1 **Yerofey-Pavlovich** USSR
94B3 **Yeroham** Israel
61G3 **Yershov** USSR
Yerushalayim = Jerusalem
92C1 **Yeşil** R Turk
94B2 **Yesud Hama'ala** Israel
109D1 **Yetman** Aust
96B2 **Yetti** Maur
93E1 **Yevlakh** USSR
60D4 **Yevpatoriya** USSR
72E2 **Ye Xian** China
60E4 **Yeysk** USSR
55B2 **Yiannitsá** Greece
73A4 **Yibin** China
73C3 **Yichang** China
69E2 **Yichun** China
72B2 **Yijun** China
54C2 **Yildiz Dağlari** Upland Turk
92C2 **Yıldızeli** Turk
73A5 **Yiliang** China
72B2 **Yinchuan** China
72D3 **Ying He** R China
72E1 **Yingkou** China
73D3 **Yingshan** Hubei, China
72B3 **Yingshan** Sichuan, China
73D4 **Yingtan** China
82C1 **Yining** China
72B1 **Yin Shan** Upland China
99D2 **Yirga Alem** Eth
99D2 **Yirol** Sudan
63D3 **Yirshi** China
73B5 **Yishan** China
72D2 **Yishui** China
55B3 **Yíthion** Greece
38J6 **Yivieska** Fin
73C4 **Yiyang** China
38K5 **Yli-Kitka** L Fin
38J5 **Ylilornio** Sweden
19A4 **Yoakum** USA
23B2 **Yogope** Mexico
78C4 **Yogyakarta** Indon
13D2 **Yoho Nat Pk** Can
98B2 **Yokadouma** Cam
75B2 **Yokkaichi** Japan
75B1 **Yokohama** Japan
75B1 **Yokosuka** Japan
74C3 **Yonago** Japan
74E3 **Yonezawa** Japan
73D4 **Yong'an** China
72A2 **Yongchang** China
74B3 **Yŏngch'on** S Korea
73B4 **Yongchuan** China
72A2 **Yongdeng** China
73D5 **Yongding** China
72D2 **Yongding He** R China
74B3 **Yŏngdŏk** S Korea
74B3 **Yŏnghŭng** N Korea

74B3 **Yongju** S Korea
72B2 **Yongning** China
16C2 **Yonkers** USA
49C2 **Yonne** R France
42D3 **York** Eng
18A1 **York** Nebraska, USA
16A3 **York** Pennsylvania, USA
107D2 **York,C** Aust
108A2 **Yorke Pen** Aust
108A3 **Yorketown** Aust
7A4 **York Factory** Can
41C3 **Yorkshire Moors** Moorland Eng
42D2 **Yorkshire Wolds** Upland Eng
5H4 **Yorkton** Can
22B2 **Yosemite L** USA
22C1 **Yosemite Nat Pk** USA
75A2 **Yoshii** R Japan
75A2 **Yoshino** R Japan
61G2 **Yoshkar Ola** USSR
74B4 **Yŏsu** S Korea
41B3 **Youghal** Irish Rep
45C3 **Youghal Harb** Irish Rep
73B5 **You Jiang** R China
109C2 **Young** Aust
34D2 **Young** Urug
111A2 **Young Range** Mts NZ
13E2 **Youngstown** Can
14B2 **Youngstown** Ohio, USA
22A1 **Yountville** USA
73B4 **Youyang** China
92B2 **Yozgat** Turk
20B2 **Yreka** USA
39G7 **Ystad** Sweden
43C3 **Ystwyth** R Wales
44C3 **Ythan** R Scot
73C4 **Yuan Jiang** R Hunan, China
73A5 **Yuan Jiang** R Yunnan, China
73A4 **Yuanmu** China
72C2 **Yuanping** China
21A2 **Yuba City** USA
74E2 **Yūbari** Japan
25D3 **Yucatan** Pen Mexico
25D2 **Yucatan Chan** Mexico/ Cuba
72C2 **Yuci** China
63F2 **Yudoma** R USSR
73D4 **Yudu** China
73A4 **Yuexi** China
73C4 **Yueyang** China
54A2 **Yugoslavia** Federal Republic, Europe
73B5 **Yu Jiang** R China
12C2 **Yukon** R Can/USA
4E3 **Yukon Territory** Can
76E1 **Yulin** Guangdong, China
73C5 **Yulin** Guangxi, China
72B2 **Yulin** Shaanxi, China
9B3 **Yuma** USA
68B3 **Yumen** China
72D2 **Yunan** China
34A3 **Yungay** Chile
73C5 **Yunkai Dashan** Hills China
108A2 **Yunta** Aust
72C3 **Yunxi** China
72C3 **Yun Xian** China
73B3 **Yunyang** China
32B5 **Yurimaguas** Peru
73E5 **Yu Shan** Mt Taiwan
38L6 **Yushkozero** USSR
82D2 **Yushu** Tibet, China
73A5 **Yuxi** China
74F2 **Yuzhno-Kuril'sk** USSR
69G2 **Yuzhno-Sakhalinsk** USSR
61J3 **Yuzh Ural** Mts USSR

46A2 **Yvelines** Department, France
47B1 **Yverdon** Switz

Z

56A2 **Zaandam** Neth
63C2 **Zabakalskiy** USSR
93D2 **Zāb al Babir** R Iraq
93D2 **Zāb as Saghīr** R Iraq
68D2 **Zabaykal'sk** USSR
59B3 **Zabreh** Czech
59B2 **Zabrze** Pol
23A2 **Zacapu** Mexico
24B2 **Zacatecas** Mexico
23B2 **Zacatepec** Morelos, Mexico
23B2 **Zacatepec** Oaxaca, Mexico
23B2 **Zacatlan** Mexico
23A1 **Zacoalco** Mexico
23B1 **Zacualtipan** Mexico
52C2 **Zadar** Yugos
76B3 **Zadetkyi** I Burma
50A2 **Zafra** Spain
95C1 **Zagazig** Egypt
96B1 **Zagora** Mor
60E2 **Zagorsk** USSR
52C1 **Zagreb** Yugos
91D4 **Zāhedān** Iran
94B2 **Zahle** Leb
51C2 **Zahrez Chergui** Marshland Alg
61H2 **Zainsk** USSR
98C3 **Zaïre** Republic, Africa
98B3 **Zaïre** R Zaïre/Congo
54B2 **Zaječar** Yugos
68C1 **Zakamensk** USSR
93D2 **Zakho** Iraq
55B3 **Zákinthos** I Greece
59B3 **Zakopane** Pol
59B3 **Zalaegerszeg** Hung
54B1 **Zalău** Rom
56C2 **Zalew Szczeciński** Lg Pol
98C1 **Zalingei** Sudan
63F2 **Zaliv Akademii** B USSR
65G5 **Zaliv Kara-Bogaz Gol** B USSR
74C2 **Zaliv Petra Velikogo** B USSR
69G2 **Zaliv Turpeniya** B USSR
89H9 **Zambesi** R Mozam
100B2 **Zambezi** Zambia
100B2 **Zambezi** R Zambia
100B2 **Zambia** Republic, Africa
79B4 **Zamboanga** Phil
79B4 **Zamboanga Pen** Phil
58C2 **Zambrów** Pol
32B4 **Zamora** Ecuador
23A2 **Zamora** Mexico
50A1 **Zamora** Spain
59C2 **Zamość** Pol
72A3 **Zamtang** China
98B3 **Zanaga** Congo
50B2 **Záncara** R Spain
84D2 **Zanda** China
14B3 **Zanesville** USA
84D2 **Zangla** India
90A2 **Zanjān** Iran
34B2 **Zanjitas** Arg
34B2 **Zanjon** R Arg
99D3 **Zanzibar** Tanz
99D3 **Zanzibar** I Tanz
96C2 **Zaouallallaz** Alg
72D3 **Zaozhuang** China
93D2 **Zap** R Turk
39K7 **Zapadnaja Dvina** R USSR
58C1 **Zapadno Dvina** R USSR
65H3 **Zapadno-Sibirskaya Nizmennost'** Lowland USSR

63B2 **Zapadnyy Sayan** Mts USSR
34A3 **Zapala** Arg
60E4 **Zaporozh'ye** USSR
93C2 **Zara** Turk
23A1 **Zaragoza** Mexico
50B1 **Zaragoza** Spain
90B2 **Zarand** Iran
90C3 **Zarand** Iran
80C2 **Zaranj** Afghan
33D2 **Zarara** Ven
58D1 **Zarasai** USSR
34D2 **Zárate** Arg
90B3 **Zard Kuh** Mt Iran
12H3 **Zarembo I** USA
84B2 **Zarghun Shahr** Afghan
84B2 **Zargun** Mt Pak
97C3 **Zaria** Nig
92C3 **Zarqa** Jordan
94B2 **Zarqa** R Jordan
32B4 **Zaruma** Ecuador
58B2 **Zary** Pol
96D1 **Zarzis** Tunisia
84D2 **Zāsar** Mts India
84D2 **Zāskār** R India
94C2 **Zatara** R Jordan
Zatoka Gdańska = Gdańsk,G of
69E1 **Zavitinsk** USSR
59B2 **Zawiercie** Pol
95A2 **Zawilah** Libya
63C2 **Zayarsk** USSR
65K5 **Zaysan** USSR
82C1 **Zaysan** USSR
82D3 **Zayü** China
68B4 **Zayü** Mt China
58B2 **Zduńska Wola** Pol
46B1 **Zeebrugge** Belg
94B3 **Zeelim** Israel
101G1 **Zeerust** S Africa
94B2 **Zefat** Israel
97C3 **Zegueren** Watercourse Mali
99E1 **Zeila** Somalia
57C2 **Zeitz** Germany
72A2 **Zekog** China
61G2 **Zelenodol'sk** USSR
39K6 **Zelenogorsk** USSR
47D1 **Zell** Austria
95A2 **Zelten** Libya
98C2 **Zemio** CAR
64F1 **Zemlya Aleksandry** I Barents S
64F2 **Zemlya Frantsa Iosifa** Is Barents S
64F1 **Zemlya Georga** I Barents S
64H1 **Zemlya Vil'cheka** I Barents S
73B4 **Zenning** China
47B1 **Zermatt** Switz
63E2 **Zeya** USSR
63E2 **Zeya** Res USSR
50A1 **Zêzere** R Port
94B1 **Zghorta** Leb
58B2 **Zgierz** Pol
72D1 **Zhangjiakou** China
73D4 **Zhangping** China
72D2 **Zhangwei He** R China
72E1 **Zhangwu** China
72A2 **Zhanye** China
73D5 **Zhangzhou** China
73C5 **Zhanjiang** China
73A4 **Zhanyi** China
73C5 **Zhaoqing** China
73A4 **Zhaotong** China
72D2 **Zhaoyang Hu** L China
61J4 **Zharkamys** USSR
63E1 **Zhatay** USSR
73D4 **Zhejiang** Province, China
67F3 **Zhengou** China
72C3 **Zhengzhou** China
72D3 **Zhenjiang** China
73A4 **Zhenxiong** China
73B4 **Zhenyuan** China
61F3 **Zherdevka** USSR

73C3 **Zhicheng** China
68C1 **Zhigalovo** USSR
73B4 **Zhijin** China
58D2 **Zhitkovichi** USSR
60C3 **Zhitomir** USSR
60D3 **Zhlobin** USSR
60C4 **Zhmerinka** USSR
84B2 **Zhob** Pak
58D2 **Zhodino** USSR
72B2 **Zhongning** China
73C5 **Zhongshan** China
72B2 **Zhongwei** China
68B4 **Zhougdian** China
73E3 **Zhoushan Quandao** Arch China
72E2 **Zhuanghe** China
72A3 **Zhugqu** China
73C3 **Zhushan** China
73C4 **Zhuzhou** China
72D2 **Zibo** China
106C3 **Ziel,Mt** Aust
58B2 **Zielona Gora** Pol
76A1 **Zigaing** Burma
73A4 **Zigong** China
97A3 **Ziguinchor** Sen
23A2 **Zihuatanejo** Mexico
94B2 **Zikhron Ya'aqov** Israel
59B3 **Žilina** Czech
47D1 **Ziller** R Austria
47D1 **Zillertaler Alpen** Mts Austria
58D1 **Zilupe** USSR
63C2 **Zima** USSR
23B1 **Zimapan** Mexico
23B2 **Zimatlan** Mexico
100B2 **Zimbabwe** Republic, Africa
94B3 **Zin** R Israel
23B2 **Zinacatepec** Mexico
23A2 **Zinapécuaro** Mexico
97C3 **Zinder** Niger
73C4 **Zi Shui** China
23A2 **Zitácuaro** Mexico
57C2 **Zittau** Germany
72D2 **Ziya He** R China
72A3 **Ziyang** China
61J2 **Zlatoust** USSR
59B3 **Zlin** Czech
65K4 **Zmeinogorsk** USSR
58B2 **Znin** Pol
59B3 **Znoimo** Czech
100B3 **Zoekmekaar** S Africa
47B1 **Zofinger** Switz
72A3 **Zoigê** China
59D3 **Zolochev** USSR
101C2 **Zomba** Malawi
98B2 **Zongo** Zaïre
92B1 **Zonguldak** Turk
97B4 **Zorzor** Lib
96A2 **Zouerate** Maur
54B1 **Zrenjanin** Yugos
47C1 **Zug** Switz
47D1 **Zugspitze** Mt Germany
50A2 **Zújar** R Spain
100C2 **Zumbo** Mozam
23B2 **Zumpango** Mexico
97C4 **Zungeru** Nig
73B4 **Zunyi** China
76D1 **Zuo** R China
73B5 **Zuo Jiang** R China
47C1 **Zürich** Switz
47C1 **Zürichsee** L Switz
95A1 **Zuwārah** Libya
61H2 **Zuyevka** USSR
100B4 **Zvishavane** Zim
59B3 **Zvolen** Czech
54A2 **Zvornik** Yugos
97B4 **Zwedru** Lib
46D2 **Zweibrücken** Germany
47B1 **Zweisimmen** Switz
57C2 **Zwickau** Germany
56B2 **Zwolle** Neth
58C2 **Zyrardów** Pol
65K5 **Zyryanovsk** USSR
59B3 **Żywiec** Pol
94A1 **Zyyi** Cyprus